ENGLISH / THAI

อังกฤษ / ไทย

OXFORD PICTURE DICTIONARY

SECOND EDITION

OPD

Jayme Adelson-Goldstein

Norma Shapiro

Translation reviewed by Wilawan Gawichai

OXFORD
UNIVERSITY PRESS

198 Madison Avenue
New York, NY 10016 USA

Great Clarendon Street, Oxford OX2 6DP UK

Oxford University Press is a department of the University of Oxford.
It furthers the University's objective of excellence in research, scholarship,
and education by publishing worldwide in

Oxford New York

Auckland Cape Town Dar es Salaam Hong Kong Karachi
Kuala Lumpur Madrid Melbourne Mexico City Nairobi
New Delhi Shanghai Taipei Toronto

With offices in

Argentina Austria Brazil Chile Czech Republic France Greece
Guatemala Hungary Italy Japan Poland Portugal Singapore
South Korea Switzerland Thailand Turkey Ukraine Vietnam

OXFORD and OXFORD ENGLISH are registered trademarks of
Oxford University Press.

© Oxford University Press 2009

Library of Congress Cataloging-in-Publication Data

Adelson-Goldstein, Jayme.
    The Oxford picture dictionary. Monolingual /
Jayme Adelson-Goldstein and Norma Shapiro.– 2nd ed.
        p. cm.
    Includes index.
    ISBN-13: 978-0-19-474018-0
    1. Picture dictionaries, English. 2. English
language–Textbooks for foreign speakers.
I. Shapiro, Norma. II. Title.
PE1629.S52 2008
423'.1–dc22

                            2007041017

Database right Oxford University Press (maker)

Executive Publishing Manager: Stephanie Karras
Managing Editor: Sharon Sargent
Development Editors: Glenn Mathes II, Bruce Myint, Katie La Storia
Associate Development Editors: Olga Christopoulos, Hannah Ryu, Meredith Stoll
Design Manager: Maj-Britt Hagsted
Project Manager: Allison Harm
Senior Designers: Stacy Merlin, Michael Steinhofer
Designer: Jaclyn Smith
Senior Production Artist: Julie Armstrong
Production Layout Artist: Colleen Ho
Cover Design: Stacy Merlin
Senior Image Editor: Justine Eun
Image Editors: Robin Fadool, Fran Newman, Jenny Vainisi
Manufacturing Manager: Shanta Persaud
Manufacturing Controller: Eve Wong
Translated by: Techno-Graphics & Translations, Inc.

ISBN: 978 0 19 474018 0

Printed in Hong Kong

10 9 8 7 6 5 4 3 2 1

The OPD team thanks the following artists for their storyboarding and sketches:
Cecilia Aranovich, Chris Brandt, Giacomo Ghiazza, Gary Goldstein, Gordan Kljucec,
Vincent Lucido, and Glenn Urieta

Illustrations by: Lori Anzalone: 13, 70-71, 76-77; Joe "Fearless" Arenella/Will Sumpter:
178; Argosy Publishing: 66-67 (call-outs), 98-99, 108-109, 112-113 (call-outs), 152, 178,
193, 194-195, 196, 197, 205; Barbara Bastian: 4, 15, 17, 20-21, 162 (map), 198, 216-217
(map), 220-221; Philip Batini/AA Reps: 50; Thomas Bayley/Sparks Literary Agency:
158-159; Sally Bensusen: 211, 214; Annie Bissett: 112; Peter Bollinger/Shannon
Associates: 14-15; Higgens Bond/Anita Grien: 226; Molly Borman-Pullman: 116, 117;
Jim Fanning/Ravenhill Represents: 80-81; Mike Gardner: 10, 12, 17, 22, 132, 114-115,
142-143, 174, 219, 228-229; Garth Glazier/AA Reps: 106, 118-119; Dennis Godfrey/
Mike Wepplo: 204; Steve Graham: 124-125, 224; Graphic Map & Chart Co.: 200-201,
202-203; Julia Green/Mendola Art: 225; Glenn Gustafson: 9, 27, 48, 76, 100, 101,
117, 132, 133, 136, 155, 161, 179, 196; Barbara Harmon: 212-213, 215; Ben Hasler/
NB Illustration: 94-95, 101, 148-149, 172, 182, 186-187; Betsy Hayes: 134, 138-139;
Matthew Holmes: 75; Stewart Holmes/Illustration Ltd.: 192; Janos Jantner/Beehive
Illustration: 5, 13, 82-83, 122-123, 130-131, 146-147, 164-165, 184, 185; Ken Joudrey/
Munro Campagna: 52, 68-69, 177, 208-209; Bob Kaganich/Deborah Wolfe: 10, 40-41,
121; Steve Karp: 230, 231; Mike Kasun/Munro Campagna: 218; Graham Kennedy:
27; Marcel Laverdet/AA Reps: 23; Jeffrey Lindberg: 33, 42-43, 92-93, 133, 160-161,
170-171, 176; Dennis Lyall/Artworks: 198; Chris Lyons:/Lindgren & Smith: 173, 191;
Alan Male/Artworks: 210, 211; Jeff Mangiat/Mendola Art: 53, 54, 55, 56, 57, 58, 59,
66-67; Adrian Mateescu/The Studio: 188-189, 232-233; Karen Minot: 28-29; Paul
Mirocha/The Wiley Group: 194, 216-217; Peter Miserendino/P.T. Pie Illustrations:
198; Lee Montgomery/Illustration Ltd.: 4; Roger Motzkus: 229; Laurie O'Keefe: 111,
216-217; Daniel O'Leary/Illustration Ltd.: 8-9, 26, 34-35, 78, 135, 136-137, 238; Vilma
Ortiz-Dillon: 16, 20-21, 60, 98-99, 100, 211; Terry Pazcko: 46-47, 144-145, 152, 180,
227; David Preiss/Munro Campagna: 5; Pronk & Associates: 192-193; Tony Randazzo/
AA Reps: 156, 234-235; Mike Renwick/Creative Eye: 126-127; Mark Riedy/Scott Hull
Associates: 48-49, 79, 140, 153; Jon Rogers/AA Reps: 112; Jeff Sanson/Schumann &
Co.: 84-85, 240-241; David Schweitzer/Munro Campagna: 162-163; Ben Shannon/
Magnet Reps: 11, 64-65, 90, 91, 96, 97, 166-167, 168-169, 179, 239; Reed Sprunger/
Jae Wagoner Artists Rep.: 18-19, 232-233; Studio Liddell/AA Reps: 27; Angelo Tillary:
108-109; Ralph Voltz/Deborah Wolfe: 50-51, 128-129, 141, 154, 175, 236-237;
Jeff Wack/Mendola Art: 24, 25, 86-87, 102-103, 134-135, 231; Brad Walker: 104-105,
150-151, 157, 206-207; Wendy Wassink: 110-111; John White/The Neis Group: 199;
Eric Wilkerson: 32, 138; Simon Williams/Illustration Ltd.: 2-3, 6-7, 30-31, 36, 38-39,
44-45, 72-73; Lee Woodgate/Eye Candy Illustration: 222-223; Andy Zito: 62-23; Craig
Zuckerman: 14, 88-89, 112-113, 120-121, 194-195.

Chapter icons designed by Von Glitschka/Scott Hull Associates

Cover Art by CUBE/Illustration Ltd (hummingbird, branch); Paul Mirocha/The Wiley
Group (cherry); Mark Riedy/Scott Hull Associates (stamp); 9 Surf Studios (lettering).

Studio photography for Oxford University Press done by Dennis Kitchen Studio: 37,
61, 72, 73, 74, 75, 95, 96, 100, 180, 181, 183, 226.

Stock Photography: Age FotoStock: 238 (flute; clarinet; bassoon; saxophone; violin; cello;
bass; guitar; trombone; trumpet; xylophone; harmonica); Comstock, 61 (window);
Morales, 221 (bat); Franco Pizzochero, 98 (cashmere); Thinkstock, 61 (sink); Alamy:
Corbis, 61 (table); Gary Crabbe, 220 (park ranger); The Associated Press: 198 (strike;
soldiers in trench); Joe Rosenthal, 198 (Iwo Jima); Neil Armstrong, 198 (Buzz Aldrin
on Moon); CORBIS: Philip Gould, 198 (Civil War); Photo Library, 220 (Yosemite Falls);
Danita Delimont: Greg Johnston, 220 (snorkeling); Jamie & Judy Wild, 220 (El Capitan);
Getty Images: 198 (Martin Luther King, Jr.); Amana Images, 61 (soapy plates), The
Granger Collection: 198 (Jazz Age); The Image Works: Kelly Spranger, 220 (sea turtle);
Inmagine: 238 (oboe; tuba; French horn; piano; drums; tambourine; accordion);
istockphoto: 61 (oven), 98 (silk), 99 (suede; lace; velvet); Jupiter Images: 61 (tiles); 98
(wool); 99 (corduroy); Foodpix, 98 (linen); Rob Melnychuk/Brand X Pictures, 61 (glass
shower door); Jupiter Unlimited: 220 (seagulls); 238 (electric keyboard); Comstock, 99
(denim); Mary Evans Picture Library: 198 (women in factory); NPS Photo: Peter Jones,
221 (Carlsbad Cavern entrance; tour; cavern; spelunker); OceanwideImages.com:
Gary Bell, 220 (coral); Photo Edit, Inc: David Young-Wolff, 220 (trail); Picture History:
198 (Hiram Rhodes); Robertstock: 198 (Great Depression); Punchstock: 98 (t-shirt),
Robert Glusic, 31 (Monument Valley); Roland Corporation: 238 (organ); SuperStock: 99
(leather); 198 (Daniel Boone); Shutterstock: Marek Szumlas, 94 (watch); United States
Mint: 126; Veer: Brand X Pictures, 220 (deer); Photodisc, 220 (black bear); Yankee Fleet,
Inc.: 220 (Fort Jefferson; Yankee Freedom Ferry).

This second edition of
the Oxford Picture Dictionary
is lovingly dedicated to
the memory of Norma Shapiro.

Her ideas, her pictures, and
her stories continue to teach,
inspire, and delight.

Acknowledgments

The publisher and authors would like to acknowledge the following individuals for their invaluable feedback during the development of this program:

Dr. Macarena Aguilar, Cy-Fair College, Houston, TX

Joseph F. Anselme, Atlantic Technical Center, Coconut Creek, FL

Stacy Antonopoulos, Monterey Trail High School, Elk Grove, CA

Carol Antunano, The English Center, Miami, FL

Irma Arencibia, Thomas A. Edison School, Union City, NJ

Suzi Austin, Alexandria City Public School Adult Program, Alexandria, FL

Patricia S. Bell, Lake Technical Center, Eustis, FL

Jim Brice, San Diego Community College District, San Diego, CA

Phil Cackley, Arlington Education and Employment Program (REEP), Arlington, VA

Frieda Caldwell, Metropolitan Adult Education Program, San Jose, CA

Sandra Cancel, Robert Waters School, Union City, NJ

Anne Marie Caney, Chula Vista Adult School, Chula Vista, CA

Patricia Castro, Harvest English Institute, Newark, NJ

Paohui Lola Chen, Milpitas Adult School, Milpitas, CA

Lori Cisneros, Atlantic Vo-Tech, Ft. Lauderdale, FL

Joyce Clapp, Hayward Adult School, Hayward, CA

Stacy Clark, Arlington Education and Employment Program (REEP), Arlington, VA

Nancy B. Crowell, Southside Programs for Adults in Continuing Education, Prince George, VA

Doroti da Cunha, Hialeah-Miami Lakes Adult Education Center, Miami, FL

Paula Da Silva-Michelin, La Guardia Community College, Long Island City, NY

Cynthia L. Davies, Humble I.S.D., Humble, TX

Christopher Davis, Overfelt Adult Center, San Jose, CA

Beverly De Nicola, Capistrano Unified School District, San Juan Capistrano, CA

Beatriz Diaz, Miami-Dade County Public Schools, Miami, FL

Druci J. Diaz, Hillsborough County Public Schools, Tampa, FL

Marion Donahue, San Dieguito Adult School, Encinitas, CA

Nick Doorn, International Education Services, South Lyon, MI

Mercedes Douglass, Seminole Community College, Sanford, FL

Jenny Elliott, Montgomery College, Rockville, MD

Paige Endo, Mt. Diablo Adult Education, Concord, CA

Megan Ernst, Glendale Community College, Glendale, CA

Elizabeth Escobar, Robert Waters School, Union City, NJ

Joanne Everett, Dave Thomas Education Center, Pompano Beach, FL

Jennifer Fadden, Arlington Education and Employment Program (REEP), Arlington, VA

Judy Farron, Fort Myers Language Center, Fort Myers, FL

Sharyl Ferguson, Montwood High School, El Paso, TX

Dr. Monica Fishkin, University of Central Florida, Orlando, FL

Nancy Frampton, Reedley College, Reedley, CA

Lynn A. Freeland, San Dieguito Union High School District, Encinitas, CA

Cathy Gample, San Leandro Adult School, San Leandro, CA

Hillary Gardner, Center for Immigrant Education and Training, Long Island City, NY

Martha C. Giffen, Alhambra Unified School District, Alhambra, CA

Jill Gluck, Hollywood Community Adult School, Los Angeles, CA

Carolyn Grimaldi, LaGuardia Community College, Long Island City, NY

William Gruenholz, USD Adult School, Concord, CA

Sandra G. Gutierrez, Hialeah-Miami Lakes Adult Education Center, Miami, FL

Conte Gúzman-Hoffman, Triton College, River Grove, IL

Amanda Harllee, Palmetto High School, Palmetto, FL

Mercedes Hearn, Tampa Bay Technical Center, Tampa, FL

Robert Hearst, Truman College, Chicago, IL

Patty Heiser, University of Washington, Seattle, WA

Joyce Hettiger, Metropolitan Education District, San Jose, CA

Karen Hirsimaki, Napa Valley Adult School, Napa, CA

Marvina Hooper, Lake Technical Center, Eustis, FL

Katie Hurter, North Harris College, Houston, TX

Nuchamon James, Miami Dade College, Miami, FL

Linda Jennings, Montgomery College, Rockville, MD

Bonnie Boyd Johnson, Chapman Education Center, Garden Grove, CA

Fayne B. Johnson, Broward County Public Schools, Fort Lauderdale, FL

Stavroula Katseyeanis, Robert Waters School, Union City, NJ

Dale Keith, Broadbase Consulting, Inc. at Kidworks USA, Miami, FL

Blanche Kellawon, Bronx Community College, Bronx, NY

Mary Kernel, Migrant Education Regional Office, Northwest Educational Service District, Anacortes, WA

Karen Kipke, Antioch High School Freshman Academy, Antioch, TN

Jody Kirkwood, ABC Adult School, Cerritos, CA

Matthew Kogan, Evans Community Adult School, Los Angeles, CA

Ineza Kuceba, Renton Technical College, Renton, WA

John Kuntz, California State University, San Bernadino, San Bernadino, CA

Claudia Kupiec, DePaul University, Chicago, IL

E.C. Land, Southside Programs for Adult Continuing Education, Prince George, VA

Betty Lau, Franklin High School, Seattle, WA

Patt Lemonie, Thomas A. Edison School, Union City, NJ

Lia Lerner, Burbank Adult School, Burbank, CA

Krystyna Lett, Metropolitan Education District, San Jose, CA

Renata Lima, TALK International School of Languages, Fort Lauderdale, FL

Luz M. Lopez, Sweetwater Union High School District, Chula Vista, CA

Osmara Lopez, Bronx Community College, Bronx, NY

Heather Lozano, North Lake College, Irving, TX

Betty Lynch, Arlington Education and Employment Program (REEP), Arlington, VA

Meera Madan, REID Park Elementary School, Charlotte, NC

Ivanna Mann Thrower, Charlotte Mecklenburg Schools, Charlotte, NC

Michael R. Mason, Loma Vista Adult Center, Concord, CA

Holley Mayville, Charlotte Mecklenburg Schools, Charlotte, NC

Margaret McCabe, United Methodist Cooperative Ministries, Clearwater, FL

Todd McDonald, Hillsborough Adult Education, Tampa, FL

Nancy A. McKeand, ESL Consultant, St. Benedict, LA

Rebecca L. McLain, Gaston College, Dallas, NC

John M. Mendoza, Redlands Adult School, Redlands, CA

Bet Messmer, Santa Clara Adult Education Center, Santa Clara, CA

Christina Morales, BEGIN Managed Programs, New York, NY

Lisa Munoz, Metropolitan Education District, San Jose, CA

Mary Murphy-Clagett, Sweetwater Union High School District, Chula Vista, CA

Jonetta Myles, Rockdale County High School, Conyers, GA

Marwan Nabi, Troy High School, Fullerton, CA

Dr. Christine L. Nelsen, Salvation Army Community Center, Tampa, FL

Michael W. Newman, Arlington Education and Employment Program (REEP), Arlington, VA

Rehana Nusrat, Huntington Beach Adult School, Huntington Beach, CA

Cindy Oakley-Paulik, Embry-Riddle Aeronautical University, Daytona Beach, FL

Acknowledgments

Janet Ochi-Fontanott, Sweetwater Union High School District, Chula Vista, CA

Lorraine Pedretti, Metropolitan Education District, San Jose, CA

Isabel Pena, BE/ESL Programs, Garland, TX

Margaret Perry, Everett Public Schools, Everett, WA

Dale Pesmen, PhD, Chicago, IL

Cathleen Petersen, Chapman Education Center, Garden Grove, CA

Allison Pickering, Escondido Adult School, Escondido, CA

Ellen Quish, LaGuardia Community College, Long Island City, NY

Teresa Reen, Independence Adult Center, San Jose, CA

Kathleen Reynolds, Albany Park Community Center, Chicago, IL

Melba I. Rillen, Palmetto High School, Palmetto, FL

Lorraine Romero, Houston Community College, Houston, TX

Eric Rosenbaum, BEGIN Managed Programs, New York, NY

Blair Roy, Chapman Education Center, Garden Grove, CA

Arlene R. Schwartz, Broward Community Schools, Fort Lauderdale, FL

Geraldyne Blake Scott, Truman College, Chicago, IL

Sharada Sekar, Antioch High School Freshman Academy, Antioch, TN

Dr. Cheryl J. Serrano, Lynn University, Boca Raton, FL

Janet Setzekorn, United Methodist Cooperative Ministries, Clearwater, FL

Terry Shearer, EDUCALL Learning Services, Houston, TX

Elisabeth Sklar, Township High School District 113, Highland Park, IL

Robert Stein, BEGIN Managed Programs, New York, NY

Ruth Sutton, Township High School District 113, Highland Park, IL

Alisa Takeuchi, Chapman Education Center, Garden Grove, CA

Grace Tanaka, Santa Ana College School of Continuing Education, Santa Ana, CA

Annalisa Te, Overfelt Adult Center, San Jose, CA

Don Torluemke, South Bay Adult School, Redondo Beach, CA

Maliheh Vafai, Overfelt Adult Center, San Jose, CA

Tara Vasquez, Robert Waters School, Union City, NJ

Nina Velasco, Naples Language Center, Naples, FL

Theresa Warren, East Side Adult Center, San Jose, CA

Lucie Gates Watel, Truman College, Chicago, IL

Wendy Weil, Arnold Middle School, Cypress, TX

Patricia Weist, TALK International School of Languages, Fort Lauderdale, FL

Dr. Carole Lynn Weisz, Lehman College, Bronx, NY

Desiree Wesner, Robert Waters School, Union City, NJ

David Wexler, Napa Valley Adult School, Napa, CA

Cynthia Wiseman, Borough of Manhattan Community College, New York, NY

Debbie Cullinane Wood, Lincoln Education Center, Garden Grove, CA

Banu Yaylali, Miami Dade College, Miami, FL

Hongyan Zheng, Milpitas Adult Education, Milpitas, CA

Arlene Zivitz, ESOL Teacher, Jupiter, FL

The publisher, authors, and editors would like to thank the following people for their expertise in reviewing specific content areas:

Ross Feldberg, Tufts University, Medford, MA

William J. Hall, M.D. FACP/FRSM (UK), Cumberland Foreside, ME

Jill A. Horohoe, Arizona State University, Tempe, AZ

Phoebe B. Rouse, Louisiana State University, Baton Rouge, LA

Dr. Susan Rouse, Southern Wesleyan University, Central, SC

Dr. Ira M. Sheskin, University of Miami, Coral Gables, FL

Maiko Tomizawa, D.D.S., New York, NY

The publisher would like to thank the following for their permission to reproduce copyrighted material:

p. 26: Penny, nickel, dime, quarter-dollar, half-dollar, and dollar coin images from the United States Mint.

pp. 125, 134–135: U.S. Postal Service Priority Mail Logo, Express Mail Logo, Certified Mail, Ready Pack Packaging, Letter Carrier Uniform, Postal Clerk Uniform, Automated Postal Center, Round Top Collection Mailbox, and Lady Liberty Stamp Image are trademarks and copyrighted material of the United States Postal Service and are used with permission.

p. 152: Metrocard is an MTA trademark and is used with permission.

p. 152: Metro token for L.A.'s bus and rail system used with permission.

p. 229: Little League used courtesy of Little League® Baseball and Softball.

p. 231: Frisbee®, a registered trademark of Wham-O, Inc.

Table of Contents สารบัญ

Introduction คำนำ . . . . .ix–xi

1. Everyday Language ภาษาที่ใช้ในชีวิตประจำวัน

Meeting and Greeting การพบปะและการทักทาย 2–3
Personal Information ข้อมูลส่วนตัว 4
School โรงเรียน. 5
A Classroom ห้องเรียน 6–7
Studying การเรียน 8–9
Succeeding in School การบรรลุผลสำเร็จในโรงเรียน 10
A Day at School วันหนึ่งที่โรงเรียน 11
Everyday Conversation บทสนทนาในชีวิตประจำวัน 12
Weather สภาพอากาศ. 13
The Telephone โทรศัพท์ 14–15
Numbers ตัวเลข 16
Measurements การตวงวัดต่างๆ 17
Time เวลา 18–19
The Calendar ปฏิทิน .20–21
Calendar Events รายการงานต่างๆตามปฏิทิน 22
Describing Things การบรรยายสิ่งของ 23
Colors สีต่างๆ. 24
Prepositions คำบุพบท 25
Money เงิน 26
Shopping การซื้อของ 27
Same and Different เหมือนกันและต่างกัน 28–29

2. People ผู้คน

Adults and Children ผู้ใหญ่และเด็ก 30–31
Describing People การบรรยายเกี่ยวกับผู้คน 32
Describing Hair การบรรยายลักษณะผม 33
Families ครอบครัว 34–35
Childcare and Parenting การดูแลเด็กและการเป็นผู้ปกครอง 36–37
Daily Routines กิจวัตรประจำวัน 38–39
Life Events and Documents เหตุการณ์ในชีวิตและเอกสารต่างๆ 40–41
Feelings ความรู้สึก 42–43
A Family Reunion การพบปะรวมญาติ 44–45

3. Housing บ้านเรือน

The Home บ้าน. 46–47
Finding a Home หาบ้าน 48–49
Apartments อพาร์ตเมนต์ / ห้องชุด 50–51
Different Places to Live ที่อยู่อาศัยในที่ต่างๆ. 52
A House and Yard บ้านและสนาม 53
A Kitchen ครัว 54
A Dining Area บริเวณรับประทานอาหาร 55
A Living Room ห้องนั่งเล่น 56
A Bathroom ห้องน้ำ. 57
A Bedroom ห้องนอน 58
The Kids' Bedroom ห้องนอนของเด็ก 59
Housework งานบ้าน 60
Cleaning Supplies ของใช้ในการทำความสะอาด 61
Household Problems and Repairs ปัญหาในบ้านและการซ่อมแซม . . .62–63
The Tenant Meeting การประชุมผู้เช่า 64–65

Contents สารบัญ

4. Food อาหาร

Back from the Market กลับจากตลาด 66–67
Fruit ผลไม้ 68
Vegetables ผัก 69
Meat and Poultry เนื้อสัตว์และเนื้อสัตว์ปีก 70
Seafood and Deli อาหารทะเลและอาหารรายการพิเศษ 71
A Grocery Store ร้านขายของชำ 72–73
Containers and Packaging ภาชนะบรรจุและบรรจุภัณฑ์ 74
Weights and Measurements น้ำหนักและการตวงวัด 75
Food Preparation and Safety การเตรียมอาหารและความปลอดภัย 76–77
Kitchen Utensils เครื่องทำครัว 78
Fast Food Restaurant ร้านอาหารจานด่วน .79
A Coffee Shop Menu รายการอาหารในร้านกาแฟ 80–81
A Restaurant ร้านอาหาร / ภัตตาคาร .82–83
The Farmer's Market ตลาดเกษตรกร .84–85

5. Clothing เสื้อผ้า

Everyday Clothes เสื้อผ้าที่ใช้ในชีวิตประจำวัน 86–87
Casual, Work, and Formal Clothing เสื้อผ้าแบบลำลอง แบบทำงาน และแบบ
เป็นทางการ 88–89
Seasonal Clothing เสื้อผ้าตามฤดูกาล 90
Underwear and Sleepwear ชุดชั้นในและชุดนอน 91
Workplace Clothing เสื้อผ้าชุดทำงาน .92–93
Shoes and Accessories รองเท้าและเครื่องประดับ 94–95
Describing Clothes การบรรยายเกี่ยวกับเสื้อผ้า 96–97
Making Clothes การตัดเย็บเสื้อผ้า 98–99
Making Alterations การแก้ไขดัดแปลง 100
Doing the Laundry ซักเสื้อผ้า 101
A Garage Sale ขายของใช้แล้ว 102–103

6. Health สุขภาพ

The Body ร่างกาย 104–105
Inside and Outside the Body ภายในและภายนอกร่างกาย 106–107
Personal Hygiene สุขอนามัยส่วนตัว 108–109
Symptoms and Injuries อาการและการบาดเจ็บ 110
Illnesses and Medical Conditions การเจ็บป่วยและสภาวะป่วยไข้ 111
A Pharmacy ร้านขายยา 112–113
Taking Care of Your Health การดูแลสุขภาพของคุณเอง 114–115
Medical Emergencies เหตุฉุกเฉินด้านการรักษาพยาบาล 116
First Aid การปฐมพยาบาล 117
Medical Care การดูแลรักษา 118
Dental Care การดูแลรักษาฟัน 119
Hospital โรงพยาบาล 120–121
A Health Fair งานออกร้านเกี่ยวกับสุขภาพ 122–123

7. Community ชุมชน

Downtown ในเมือง 124–125
City Streets ถนนในเมือง 126–127
An Intersection ทางแยก 128–129
A Mall ศูนย์การค้า 130–131
The Bank ธนาคาร 132
The Library ห้องสมุด 133
The Post Office ไปรษณีย์ 134–135
Department of Motor Vehicles (DMV) หน่วยงานรัฐแผนกยานยนต์ (DMV) . . 136–137
Government and Military Service รัฐบาลและราชการทหาร 138–139
Civic Rights and Responsibilities สิทธิและหน้าที่ของพลเมือง 140
The Legal System กระบวนการทางกฎหมาย 141
Crime อาชญากรรม 142
Public Safety ความปลอดภัยในที่สาธารณะ 143
Emergencies and Natural Disasters เหตุฉุกเฉินและภัยธรรมชาติ . . 144–145
Emergency Procedures ขั้นตอนปฏิบัติในเหตุฉุกเฉิน 146–147
Community Cleanup การเก็บกวาดในชุมชน 148–149

8. Transportation การขนส่ง

Basic Transportation การขนส่งขั้นพื้นฐาน 150–151
Public Transportation การขนส่งสาธารณะ 152
Prepositions of Motion คำบุพบทการเคลื่อนไหว 153
Traffic Signs เครื่องหมายจราจร 154
Directions and Maps ทิศทางและแผนที่ 155
Cars and Trucks รถยนต์และรถบรรทุก 156
Buying and Maintaining a Car การซื้อและการซ่อมบำรุงรักษารถ . . 157
Parts of a Car ชิ้นส่วนอะไหล่รถ 158–159
An Airport สนามบิน 160–161
Taking a Trip การเดินทาง 162–163

9. Work งาน

The Workplace ที่ทำงาน 164–165
Jobs and Occupations A-C งานและอาชีพ เรียงตามอักษร A-C . . 166
Jobs and Occupations C-H งานและอาชีพ เรียงตามอักษร C-H . . 167
Jobs and Occupations H-P งานและอาชีพ เรียงตามอักษร H-P . . 168
Jobs and Occupations P-W งานและอาชีพ เรียงตามอักษร P-W . . 169
Job Skills ทักษะการทำงาน 170
Office Skills ทักษะการทำงานในสำนักงาน 171
Career Planning การวางแผนงานอาชีพ 172
Job Search การหางาน 173
Interview Skills ทักษะในการสัมภาษณ์ 174
A Factory โรงงาน 175
Landscaping and Gardening การจัดสวนและการทำสวน . . 176
Farming and Ranching การทำไร่และการทำทุ่งเลี้ยงปศุสัตว์ . . 177
Construction การก่อสร้าง 178
Job Safety ความปลอดภัยในการทำงาน 179
Tools and Building Supplies เครื่องมือและวัสดุก่อสร้าง . . 180–181
An Office สำนักงาน 182–183
A Hotel โรงแรม 184
Food Service บริการด้านอาหาร 185
A Bad Day at Work วันไม่ดีในที่ทำงาน 186–187

Contents สารบัญ

10. Areas of Study สาขาวิชา

Schools and Subjects โรงเรียนและวิชาต่างๆ 188–189
English Composition การเรียงความภาษาอังกฤษ 190–191
Mathematics วิชาคำนวณ 192–193
Science วิทยาศาสตร์ 194–195
Computers คอมพิวเตอร์ 196
The Internet อินเทอร์เน็ต 197
U.S. History ประวัติศาสตร์สหรัฐอเมริกา 198
World History ประวัติศาสตร์โลก 199
North America and Central America อเมริกาเหนือและอเมริกากลาง 200–201
World Map แผนที่โลก 202–203
Geography and Habitats ภูมิศาสตร์และที่อยู่อาศัย 204
The Universe จักรวาล 205
A Graduation การสำเร็จการศึกษา 206–207

11. Plants and Animals พืชและสัตว์

Nature Center ศูนย์ธรรมชาติ 208–209
Trees and Plants ต้นไม้และพืชพันธุ์ 210
Flowers ดอกไม้ 211
Marine Life, Amphibians, and Reptiles สิ่งมีชีวิตในทะเล สัตว์ครึ่งบกครึ่งน้ำ
และสัตว์เลื้อยคลาน 212–213
Birds, Insects, and Arachnids นก แมลง และ แมง 214
Domestic Animals and Rodents สัตว์เลี้ยงและสัตว์ประเภทหนู 215
Mammals สัตว์เลี้ยงลูกด้วยนม 216–217
Energy and Conservation พลังงานและการประหยัดพลังงาน 218–219
U.S. National Parks วนอุทยานแห่งชาติในสหรัฐอเมริกา 220–221

12. Recreation การพักผ่อนหย่อนใจ

Places to Go สถานที่น่าไป 222–223
The Park and Playground สวนสาธารณะและลานเด็กเล่น 224
The Beach ชายหาด 225
Outdoor Recreation การสันทนาการภายนอก 226
Winter and Water Sports กีฬาฤดูหนาวและกีฬาทางน้ำ 227
Individual Sports กีฬาประเภทรายบุคคล 228
Team Sports กีฬาประเภททีม 229
Sports Verbs คำกริยาด้านกีฬา 230
Sports Equipment เครื่องกีฬา 231
Hobbies and Games งานอดิเรกและเกม 232–233
Electronics and Photography เครื่องไฟฟ้าและการถ่ายภาพ 234–235
Entertainment การบันเทิง 236–237
Music ดนตรี 238
Holidays วันหยุดเทศกาล 239
A Birthday Party งานวันเกิด 240–241

Verb Guide คำแนะนำเกี่ยวกับคำกริยา 242–244
How to Use the Index วิธีใช้ดัชนี 245
English Index ดัชนีอังกฤษ 246–281
Geographical Index ดัชนีทางภูมิศาสตร์ 282–284
Thai Index ดัชนีไทย 285–304
Research Bibliography รายการหนังสือศึกษาค้นคว้า 305

Teaching with the *Oxford Picture Dictionary* Program

The following general guidelines will help you prepare single and multilevel lessons using the OPD program. For step-by-step, topic-specific lesson plans, see *OPD Lesson Plans*.

1. Use Students' Needs to Identify Lesson Objectives

- Create communicative objectives based on your learners' needs assessments (*see OPD 2e Assessment Program*).
- Make sure objectives state what students will be able to do at the end of the lesson. For example: *Students will be able to respond to basic classroom commands and requests for classroom objects.* (pp. 6–7, A Classroom)
- For multilevel classes, identify a low-beginning, high-beginning, and low-intermediate objective for each topic.

2. Preview the Topic

Identify what your students already know about the topic.

- Ask general questions related to the topic.
- Have students list words they know from the topic.
- Ask questions about the picture(s) on the page.

3. Present the New Vocabulary

Research shows that it is best to present no more than 5–7 new words at a time. Here are a few presentation techniques:

- Say each new word and describe it within the context of the picture. Have volunteers act out verbs and verb sequences.
- Use Total Physical Response commands to build vocabulary comprehension.
- For long or unfamiliar word lists, introduce words by categories or select the words your students need most.
- Ask a series of questions to build comprehension and give students an opportunity to say the new words. Begin with *yes/no* questions: *Is #16 chalk?* Progress to *or* questions: *Is #16 chalk or a marker?* Finally, ask *Wh-* questions: *What can I use to write on this paper?*
- Focus on the words that students want to learn. Have them write 3–5 new words from each topic, along with meaning clues such as a drawing, translation, or sentence.

More vocabulary and **Grammar Point** sections provide additional presentation opportunities (see p. 5, School). For multilevel presentation ideas, see *OPD Lesson Plans*.

4. Check Comprehension

Make sure that students understand the target vocabulary. Here are two activities you can try:

- Say vocabulary words, and have students point to the correct items in their books. Walk around the room, checking if students are pointing to the correct pictures.
- Make true/false statements about the target vocabulary. Have students hold up two fingers for true, three for false.

5. Provide Guided and Communicative Practice

The exercise bands at the bottom of the topic pages provide a variety of guided and communicative practice opportunities and engage students' higher-level thinking.

6. Provide More Practice

OPD Second Edition offers a variety of components to facilitate vocabulary acquisition. Each of the print and electronic materials listed below offers suggestions and support for single and multilevel instruction.

OPD Lesson Plans Step-by-step multilevel lesson plans feature 3 CDs with multilevel listening, context-based pronunciation practice, and leveled reading practice. Includes multilevel teaching notes for *The OPD Reading Library*.

OPD Audio CDs or Audio Cassettes Each word in *OPD's* word list is recorded by topic.

Low-Beginning, High-Beginning, and Low-Intermediate Workbooks Guided practice for each page in *OPD* features linked visual contexts, realia, and listening practice.

Classic Classroom Activities A photocopiable resource of interactive multilevel activities, grammar practice, and communicative tasks.

The OPD Reading Library Readers include civics, academic content, and workplace themes.

Overhead Transparencies Vibrant transparencies help to focus students on the lesson.

OPD Presentation Software A multilevel interactive teaching tool using interactive whiteboard and LCD technology. Audio, animation, and video instructional support bring each dictionary topic to life.

The OPD CD-ROM An interactive learning tool featuring four-skill practice based on *OPD* topics.

Bilingual Editions *OPD* is available in numerous bilingual editions including Spanish, Chinese, Vietnamese, Arabic, Korean, and many more.

My hope is that OPD makes it easier for you to take your learners from comprehension to communication. Please share your thoughts with us as you make the book your own.

Jayme Adelson-Goldstein

Jayme Adelson-Goldstein

OPDteam.us@oup.com

Welcome to the
OPD SECOND EDITION

The second edition of the *Oxford Picture Dictionary* expands on the best aspects of the 1998 edition with:

- New artwork presenting words within meaningful, real-life contexts
- An updated word list to meet the needs of today's English language learners
- 4,000 English words and phrases, including 285 verbs
- 40 new topics with 12 intro pages and 12 story pages
- Unparalleled support for vocabulary teaching

Subtopics present the words in easy-to-learn "chunks."

Color coding and icons make it easy to navigate through *OPD*.

New art and rich contexts improve vocabulary acquisition.

Revised practice activities help students from low-beginning through low-intermediate levels.

Public Transportation

A Bus Stop

BUS 10 Northbound

Main	Elm	Oak
6:00	6:10	6:13
6:30	6:40	6:43
7:00	7:10	7:13
7:30	7:40	7:43

Transfer

1. bus route
2. fare
3. rider
4. schedule
5. transfer

A Subway Station

6. subway car
7. platform
8. turnstile
9. vending machine
10. token
11. fare card

A Train Station

12. ticket window
13. conductor
14. track
15. ticket
16. one-way trip
17. round trip

Airport Transportation

18. taxi stand
19. shuttle
20. town car
21. taxi driver
22. taxi license
23. meter

More vocabulary

hail a taxi: to raise your hand to get a taxi
miss the bus: to get to the bus stop after the bus leaves

Ask your classmates. Share the answers.

1. Is there a subway system in your city?
2. Do you ever take taxis? When?
3. Do you ever take the bus? Where?

152

x

NEW! Intro pages open each unit with key vocabulary related to the unit theme. Clear, engaging artwork promotes questions, conversations, and writing practice for all levels.

Each intro page teaches key vocabulary items within the unit theme.

Practice activities make it easy to manage multilevel classrooms.

NEW! Story pages close each unit with a lively scene for reviewing vocabulary and teaching additional language. Meanwhile, rich visual contexts recycle words from the unit.

Pre-reading questions build students' previewing and predicting skills.

High-interest readings promote literacy skills.

Post-reading questions and role-play activities support critical thinking and encourage students to use the language they have learned.

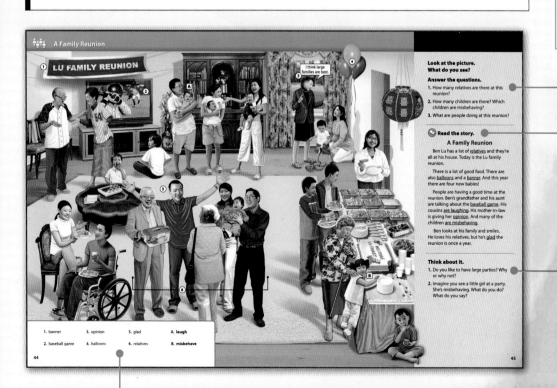

The thematic word list previews words that students will encounter in the story.

A. **Say**, "Hello."
พูดว่า "สวัสดี"

B. **Ask**, "How are you?"
ถามว่า "สบายดีไหม"

C. **Introduce** yourself.
แนะนำ ตนเอง

D. **Smile**.
ยิ้ม

E. **Hug**.
กอด

F. **Wave**.
โบกมือ

Tell your partner what to do. Take turns.

1. *Say*, "Hello."
2. *Bow.*
3. *Smile.*
4. *Shake hands.*
5. *Wave.*
6. *Say*, "Goodbye."

Dictate to your partner. Take turns.

A: *Write smile.*
B: *Is it spelled s-m-i-l-e?*
A: *Yes, that's right.*

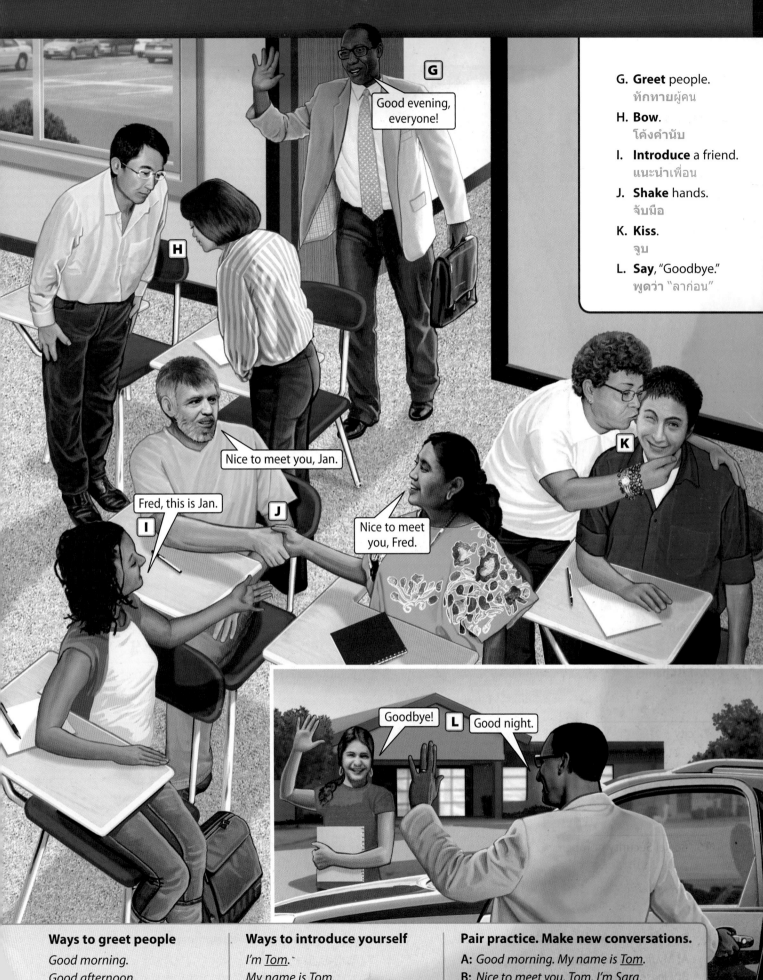

G. **Greet** people.
ทักทายผู้คน

H. **Bow**.
โค้งคำนับ

I. **Introduce** a friend.
แนะนำเพื่อน

J. **Shake** hands.
จับมือ

K. **Kiss**.
จูบ

L. **Say**, "Goodbye."
พูดว่า "ลาก่อน"

Ways to greet people

Good morning.
Good afternoon.
Good evening.

Ways to introduce yourself

I'm Tom.
My name is Tom.

Pair practice. Make new conversations.

A: *Good morning. My name is Tom.*
B: *Nice to meet you, Tom. I'm Sara.*
A: *Nice to meet you, Sara.*

3

A. Say your name.
บอกชื่อของคุณ

B. Spell your name.
สะกดชื่อของคุณ

C. Print your name.
เขียนชื่อของคุณด้วย
ตัวบรรจง

D. Sign your name.
เซ็นชื่อของคุณ

Filling Out a Form การกรอกแบบฟอร์ม

(813) 555-1234

(813) 555-8976

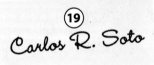

COSTA RICA
San Jose

School Registration Form แบบฟอร์มการลงทะเบียนเข้าโรงเรียน

1. name:
ชื่อ

_____

2. first name
ชื่อตัว

3. middle initial
ชื่อกลาง

4. last name
นามสกุล

5. address
ที่อยู่

6. apartment number
หมายเลขอพาร์ตเม้นต์

7. city
เมือง

8. state
วัฐ

9. ZIP code
รหัสไปรษณีย์

10. area code
รหัสโทรฯทางไกล

11. phone number
หมายเลขโทรศัพท์

12. cell phone number
หมายเลขโทรศัพท์มือถือ

13. date of birth (DOB)
วันที่เกิด (เดือน / วัน / ปี)

14. place of birth
สถานที่เกิด

15. Social Security number
หมายเลขประกันสังคม

16. sex:
เพศ

17. male
ชาย

18. female
หญิง

19. signature
ลายมือชื่อ

Pair practice. Make new conversations.

A: *My first name is Carlos.*
B: *Please spell Carlos for me.*
A: *C-a-r-l-o-s*

Ask your classmates. Share the answers.

1. Do you like your first name?
2. Is your last name from your mother? father? husband?
3. What is your middle name?

Campus วิทยาเขต / อาณาบริเวณโรงเรียน

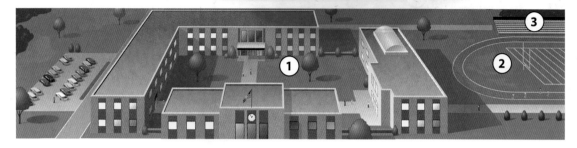

1. quad
   จัตุรัส /
   พื้นที่โล่งสี่เหลี่ยม
2. field
   สนาม
3. bleachers
   อัฒจันทร์
4. principal
   อาจารย์ใหญ่
5. assistant principal
   ผู้ช่วยอาจารย์ใหญ่
6. counselor
   อาจารย์แนะแนว
7. classroom
   ห้องเรียน
8. teacher
   ครู

Administrators ผู้บริหาร

Around Campus บริเวณโดยรอบโรงเรียน

9. restrooms
   ห้องน้ำ
10. hallway
    โถงทางเดิน
11. locker
    ตู้เก็บของ
12. main office
    สำนักงานใหญ่
13. clerk
    เสมียน / เจ้าหน้าที่ /
    พนักงาน
14. cafeteria
    โรงอาหาร
15. computer lab
    ห้องปฏิบัติการ
    คอมพิวเตอร์
16. teacher's aide
    ผู้ช่วยครู
17. library
    ห้องสมุด
18. auditorium
    ห้องประชุมใหญ่
19. gym
    โรงพลศึกษา
20. coach
    ผู้ฝึกซ้อม
21. track
    ลู่วิ่งแข่ง

More vocabulary

Students do not pay to go to a **public school**.
Students pay to go to a **private school**.
A church, mosque, or temple school is a **parochial school**.

Grammar Point: contractions of the verb *be*

He + is = He's   *He's a teacher.*
She + is = She's   *She's a counselor.*
They + are = They're *They're students.*

1. **chalkboard**
   กระดาน
2. **screen**
   จอภาพ
3. **whiteboard**
   กระดานขาว
4. **teacher / instructor**
   ครู / ผู้สอน
5. **student**
   นักเรียน / นักศึกษา
6. **LCD projector**
   จอฉายภาพเรืองแสง LCD
7. **desk**
   โต๊ะทำงาน / โต๊ะเรียน
8. **headphones**
   ชุดหูฟัง

A. **Raise** your hand.
ยกมือขึ้น

B. **Talk** to the teacher.
พูดกับครู

C. **Listen** to a CD.
ฟังซีดี

D. **Stand up**.
ยืนขึ้น

E. **Write** on the board.
เขียนบนกระดาน

F. **Sit down. / Take** a seat.
นั่งลง / หาที่นั่งลง

G. **Open** your book.
เปิดหนังสือของคุณ

H. **Close** your book.
ปิดหนังสือของคุณ

I. **Pick up** the pencil.
หยิบดินสอขึ้นมา

J. **Put down** the pencil.
วางดินสอ

9. clock นาฬิกา	**11. chair** เก้าอี้	**13. alphabet** ตัวอักษร	**15. computer** คอมพิวเตอร์
10. bookcase ชั้นวางหนังสือ	**12. map** แผนที่	**14. bulletin board** กระดานติดประกาศ	**16. overhead projector** เครื่องฉายสไลด์

17. dry erase marker ปากกาสำหรับทำเครื่องหมาย แบบลบได้เมื่อแห้ง	**21. (pencil) eraser** ยางลบ (ดินสอ)	**25. textbook** ตำรา	**29. spiral notebook** สมุดจดที่มีสันเป็นเกลียว
18. chalk ชอล์กเขียนกระดาน	**22. pen** ปากกา	**26. workbook** หนังสือแบบฝึกหัด	**30. dictionary** พจนานุกรม
19. eraser ที่ลบกระดาน	**23. pencil sharpener** เครื่องเหลาดินสอ	**27. 3-ring binder / notebook** แฟ้มเอกสาร / สมุดจด แบบเย็บสามห่วง	**31. picture dictionary** พจนานุกรมภาพ
20. pencil ดินสอ	**24. marker** ปากกาสำหรับทำเครื่องหมาย	**28. notebook paper** กระดาษ / สมุดบันทึก	

Look at the picture.
Describe the classroom.

A: There's a chalkboard.
B: There are fifteen students.

Ask your classmates. Share the answers.
1. Do you like to raise your hand in class?
2. Do you like to listen to CDs in class?
3. Do you ever talk to the teacher?

Learning New Words การเรียนรู้คำใหม่ๆ

A. Look up the word.
ค้นหาคำ / ศัพท์

B. Read the definition.
อ่านคำจำกัดความ / ความหมาย

C. Translate the word.
แปลคำ

D. Check the pronunciation.
ตรวจดูการออกเสียง

E. Copy the word.
คัดลอกคำ

F. Draw a picture.
วาดรูป

Working with Your Classmates ทำงานกับเพื่อนร่วมชั้นเรียน

G. Discuss a problem.
อภิปรายถึงปัญหา

H. Brainstorm solutions / answers.
ระดมพลังสมองหาทางออก / คำตอบ

I. Work in a group.
ทำงานเป็นกลุ่ม

J. Help a classmate.
ช่วยเหลือเพื่อนร่วมชั้นเรียน

Working with a Partner ทำงานเป็นคู่

K. Ask a question.
ถามคำถาม

L. Answer a question.
ตอบคำถาม

M. Share a book.
ใช้ / ดูหนังสือด้วยกัน

N. Dictate a sentence.
บอกประโยคให้เขียนตาม

Following Directions ทำตามคำสั่ง

O. **Fill in** the blank.
เติมในช่องว่าง

P. **Choose** the correct answer.
เลือกคำตอบที่ถูกต้อง

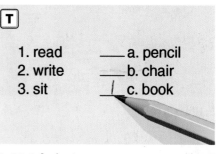

Q. **Circle** the answer.
ทำวงกลมรอบคำตอบ

R. **Cross out** the word.
ขีดฆ่าคำ

Underline the action.
1. Open the book.
2. Close the book.
3. Give me the book.

S. **Underline** the word.
ขีดเส้นใต้คำ

1. read _____ a. pencil
2. write _____ b. chair
3. sit _____ c. book

T. **Match** the items.
จับคู่คำ

Check the box next to each action.
- ☑ stand   ☑ sit
- ☐ pen   ☑ write
- ☐ paper   ☐ book

U. **Check** the correct boxes.
กาเครื่องหมายในกล่องที่ถูกต้อง

V. **Label** the picture.
ใส่ป้ายระบุภาพ

1. enp   _pen_
2. rappe _paper_
3. okob   _book_

W. **Unscramble** the words.
จัดระเบียบคำเหล่านี้

4 Close the book.
1 Pick up the book.
2 Open the book.
3 Read the book.

X. **Put** the sentences in order.
จัดประโยคเหล่านี้ให้ถูกต้อง

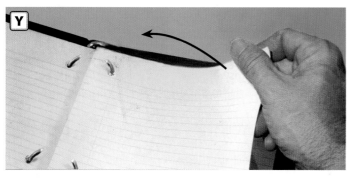

Y. **Take out** a piece of paper.
เอากระดาษออกมาแผ่นหนึ่ง

Z. **Put away** your books.
เก็บหนังสือต่างๆของคุณไว้

Ask your classmates. Share the answers.
1. Do you like to work in a group?
2. Do you ever share a book?
3. Do you like to answer questions?

Think about it. Discuss.
1. How can classmates help each other?
2. Why is it important to ask questions in class?
3. How can students check their pronunciation? Explain.

Ways to Succeed วิธีที่จะบรรลุผลสำเร็จ

A. Set goals.
ตั้งเป้าหมาย

B. Participate in class.
เข้าร่วมงานในชั้นเรียน

C. Take notes.
จดบันทึกต่างๆ

D. Study at home.
ขยันเรียนเองที่บ้าน

E. Pass a test.
สอบผ่าน

F. Ask for help.
ขอความช่วยเหลือ

G. Make progress.
ทำให้มีความคืบหน้า

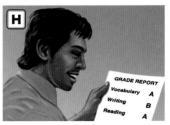

H. Get good grades.
ทำให้ได้คะแนนดี

Taking a Test ทำข้อสอบ

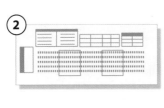

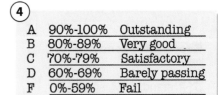

1. test booklet
สมุดข้อสอบ

2. answer sheet
แผ่นคำตอบ

3. score
คะแนน

4. grades
ระดับคะแนน

I. Clear off your desk.
เก็บของออกไปจากโต๊ะของ
คุณให้หมด

J. Work on your own.
ทำงานด้วยตนเอง

K. Bubble in the answer.
ระบายลงในวงที่คำตอบ

L. Check your work.
ตรวจดูงานของคุณ

M. Erase the mistake.
ลบข้อที่ผิด

N. Correct the mistake.
แก้ข้อที่ผิดให้ถูก

O. Hand in your test.
ส่งคืนข้อสอบของคุณ

A. **Enter** the room.
เข้าไปในห้อง

B. **Turn on** the lights.
เปิดไฟ

C. **Walk** to class.
เดินไปที่ห้องเรียน

D. **Run** to class.
วิ่งไปที่ห้องเรียน

E. **Lift / Pick up** the books.
ยก / หยิบหนังสือขึ้นมา

F. **Carry** the books.
ถือ / ขนหนังสือ

G. **Deliver** the books.
ส่งมอบหนังสือ

H. **Take** a break
หยุดพัก

I. **Eat**.
กิน

J. **Drink**.
ดื่ม

K. **Buy** a snack.
ซื้อของว่าง / ของกินเล่น

L. **Have** a conversation.
มีการสนทนา

M. **Go back** to class.
กลับไปที่ห้องเรียน

N. **Throw away** trash.
โยนขยะทิ้ง

O. **Leave** the room.
ออกไปจากห้อง

P. **Turn off** the lights.
ปิดไฟ

Grammar Point: present continuous

Use **be** + verb + *ing*
He **is** walk**ing**. They **are** enter**ing**.
Note: He is runn**ing**. They are leav**ing**.

Look at the pictures.
Describe what is happening.

A: They are <u>entering the room</u>.
B: He is <u>walking</u>.

11

A. **start** a conversation
เริ่มการสนทนา

B. **make** small talk
ทำการพูดคุยเรื่องเล็กน้อยทั่วไป

C. **compliment** someone
เอ่ยปากชมใครบางคน

D. **offer** something
หยิบยื่นเสนอบางสิ่งบางอย่าง

E. **thank** someone
ขอบคุณใครบางคน

F. **apologize**
ขอโทษ

G. **accept** an apology
ยอมรับการขอโทษ

H. **invite** someone
เชื้อเชิญใครบางคน

I. **accept** an invitation
ยอมรับการเชิญชวน

J. **decline** an invitation
ปฏิเสธการเชิญชวน

K. **agree**
เห็นด้วย

L. **disagree**
ไม่เห็นด้วย

M. **explain** something
อธิบายบางสิ่งบางอย่าง

N. **check** your understanding
ตรวจสอบความเข้าใจของคุณ

More vocabulary

request: to ask for something

accept a compliment: to thank someone for a compliment

Pair practice. Follow the directions.

1. Start a conversation with your partner.
2. Make small talk with your partner.
3. Compliment each other.

Temperature อุณหภูมิ

1. Fahrenheit
   ฟาเรนไฮท์
2. Celsius
   เซลเซียส
3. hot
   ร้อน
4. warm
   อุ่น
5. cool
   เย็น
6. cold
   หนาว
7. freezing
   เยือกแข็ง
8. degrees
   องศา

A Weather Map แผนที่แสดงสภาพอากาศ

9. sunny / clear
   มีแดด / ท้องฟ้าโปร่ง
10. cloudy
    มีเมฆมาก
11. raining
    ฝนตก
12. snowing
    หิมะตก

Weather Conditions สภาวะต่างๆของอากาศ

13. heat wave
    คลื่นความร้อน
14. smoggy
    เป็นหมอกควัน
15. humid
    ชื้น
16. thunderstorm
    พายุฝนฟ้าคะนอง
17. lightning
    ฟ้าแลบ
18. windy
    ลมแรง
19. dust storm
    พายุฝุ่น
20. foggy
    คลุ้มหมอก
21. hailstorm
    พายุลูกเห็บ
22. icy
    เป็นน้ำแข็งลื่นไถล
23. snowstorm / blizzard
    พายุหิมะ / พายุหิมะรุนแรง

Ways to talk about the weather

It's <u>sunny</u> in <u>Dallas</u>.
What's the temperature?
It's <u>108</u>. They're having <u>a heat wave</u>.

Pair practice. Make new conversations.

A: What's the weather like in <u>Chicago</u>?
B: It's <u>raining</u> and it's <u>cold</u>. It's <u>30</u> degrees.

PARTS OF A PHONE

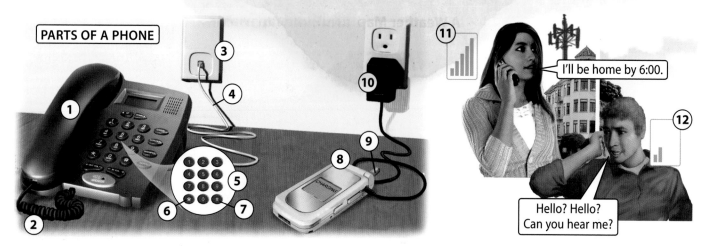

1. **receiver / handset**
หูโทรศัพท์ /
ชุดรับและโทรศัพท์

2. **cord**
สายของเครื่องโทรศัพท์

3. **phone jack**
แจ็คเสียบสายโทรศัพท์

4. **phone line**
สายโทรศัพท์

5. **key pad**
แป้นคีย์

6. **star key**
คีย์ดอกจัน

7. **pound key**
คีย์เครื่องหมายสี่เหลี่ยม

8. **cellular phone**
โทรศัพท์มือถือ

9. **antenna**
เสาอากาศ

10. **charger**
เครื่องอัดไฟ

11. **strong signal**
สัญญาณแรงดี

12. **weak signal**
สัญญาณอ่อน

13. **headset**
ชุดหูฟัง

14. **wireless headset**
ชุดหูฟังแบบไร้สาย

15. **calling card**
บัตรโทรศัพท์

16. **access number**
หมายเลขการเข้าถึง

17. **answering machine**
เครื่องตอบรับโทรศัพท์

18. **voice message**
ข้อความเสียง

19. **text message**
ข้อความตัวอักษร

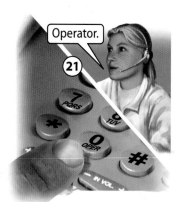

20. **Internet phone call**
การโทรศัพท์ผ่านระบบ
อินเทอร์เน็ต

21. **operator**
พนักงานรับโทรศัพท์

22. **directory assistance**
พนักงานบริการข้อมูลทาง
โทรศัพท์

23. **automated phone system**
ระบบโทรศัพท์อัตโนมัติ

24. cordless phone
โทรศัพท์ไร้สาย

25. pay phone
โทรศัพท์สาธารณะ
(หยอดเหรียญหรือใช้บัตร)

26. TDD*
ระบบโทรศัพท์สำหรับ
คนหูหนวก

27. smart phone
โทรศัพท์อัจฉริยะ

Reading a Phone Bill การอ่านใบเรียกเก็บเงินค่าโทรศัพท์

28. phone bill
ใบเรียกเก็บเงินค่าโทรศัพท์

29. area code
รหัสเขตพื้นที่โทรศัพท์

30. phone number
หมายเลขโทรศัพท์

31. local call
การโทรในท้องถิ่น

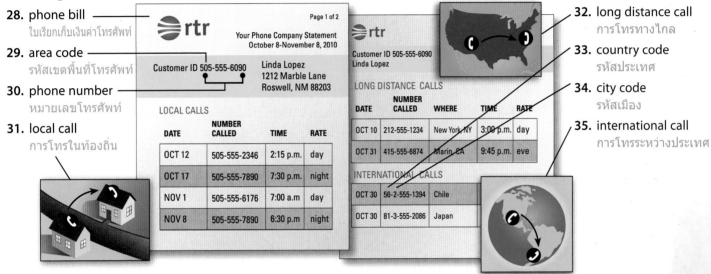

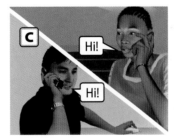

rtr

Page 1 of 2

Your Phone Company Statement
October 8-November 8, 2010

Customer ID 505-555-6090

Linda Lopez
1212 Marble Lane
Roswell, NM 88203

LOCAL CALLS

DATE	NUMBER CALLED	TIME	RATE
OCT 12	505-555-2346	2:15 p.m.	day
OCT 17	505-555-7890	7:30 p.m.	night
NOV 1	505-555-6176	7:00 a.m	day
NOV 8	505-555-7890	6:30 p.m	night

rtr

Customer ID 505-555-6090
Linda Lopez

LONG DISTANCE CALLS

DATE	NUMBER CALLED	WHERE	TIME	RATE
OCT 10	212-555-1234	New York, NY	3:00 p.m.	day
OCT 31	415-555-6874	Marin, CA	9:45 p.m.	eve

INTERNATIONAL CALLS

| OCT 30 | 56-2-555-1394 | Chile |
| OCT 30 | 81-3-555-2086 | Japan |

32. long distance call
การโทรทางไกล

33. country code
รหัสประเทศ

34. city code
รหัสเมือง

35. international call
การโทรระหว่างประเทศ

Making a Phone Call การโทรศัพท์

A. Dial the phone number.
ต่อหมายเลขโทรฯ

B. Press "send".
กด "ส่ง"

C. Talk on the phone.
พูดในโทรศัพท์

D. Hang up. / Press "end".
วางหู / กด "จบ"

Making an Emergency Call การโทรเร่งด่วนฉุกเฉิน

E. Dial 911.
ต่อ 911

F. Give your name.
แจ้งชื่อของคุณ

G. State the emergency.
แจ้งเหตุเร่งด่วนฉุกเฉินนั้น

H. Stay on the line.
ถือสายรออยู่

*telecommunication device for the deaf

SAN DIEGO
235 miles

Weight | 1.39
Price per lb. 5.99
Total | 8.33

Cardinal Numbers ตัวเลขจำนวนนับ

0	zero ศูนย์	20	twenty ยี่สิบ
1	one หนึ่ง	21	twenty-one ยี่สิบเอ็ด
2	two สอง	22	twenty-two ยี่สิบสอง
3	three สาม	23	twenty-three ยี่สิบสาม
4	four สี่	24	twenty-four ยี่สิบสี่
5	five ห้า	25	twenty-five ยี่สิบห้า
6	six หก	30	thirty สามสิบ
7	seven เจ็ด	40	forty สี่สิบ
8	eight แปด	50	fifty ห้าสิบ
9	nine เก้า	60	sixty หกสิบ
10	ten สิบ	70	seventy เจ็ดสิบ
11	eleven สิบเอ็ด	80	eighty แปดสิบ
12	twelve สิบสอง	90	ninety เก้าสิบ
13	thirteen สิบสาม	100	one hundred หนึ่งร้อย
14	fourteen สิบสี่	101	one hundred one หนึ่งร้อยหนึ่ง
15	fifteen สิบห้า	1,000	one thousand หนึ่งพัน
16	sixteen สิบหก	10,000	ten thousand หนึ่งหมื่น
17	seventeen สิบเจ็ด	100,000	one hundred thousand หนึ่งแสน
18	eighteen สิบแปด	1,000,000	one million หนึ่งล้าน
19	nineteen สิบเก้า	1,000,000,000	one billion หนึ่งพันล้าน

Ordinal Numbers เลขแสดงลำดับที่

1st	first ที่หนึ่ง	16th	sixteenth ที่สิบหก
2nd	second ที่สอง	17th	seventeenth ที่สิบเจ็ด
3rd	third ที่สาม	18th	eighteenth ที่สิบแปด
4th	fourth ที่สี่	19th	nineteenth ที่สิบเก้า
5th	fifth ที่ห้า	20th	twentieth ที่ยี่สิบ
6th	sixth ที่หก	21st	twenty-first ที่ยี่สิบเอ็ด
7th	seventh ที่เจ็ด	30th	thirtieth ที่สามสิบ
8th	eighth ที่แปด	40th	fortieth ที่สี่สิบ
9th	ninth ที่เก้า	50th	fiftieth ที่ห้าสิบ
10th	tenth ที่สิบ	60th	sixtieth ที่หกสิบ
11th	eleventh ที่สิบเอ็ด	70th	seventieth ที่เจ็ดสิบ
12th	twelfth ที่สิบสอง	80th	eightieth ที่แปดสิบ
13th	thirteenth ที่สิบสาม	90th	ninetieth ที่เก้าสิบ
14th	fourteenth ที่สิบสี่	100th	one hundredth ที่ร้อย
15th	fifteenth ที่สิบห้า	1,000th	one thousandth ที่พัน

Roman Numerals เลขโรมัน

I = 1	VII = 7	XXX = 30
II = 2	VIII = 8	XL = 40
III = 3	IX = 9	L = 50
IV = 4	X = 10	C = 100
V = 5	XV = 15	D = 500
VI = 6	XX = 20	M = 1,000

A. **divide**
แบ่ง / หาร

75% of 10 = 7.5

B. **calculate**
คำนวณ

2 inches

C. **measure**
วัด / ตวง

1 mi. = 1.6 km

D. **convert**
แปลงค่า

Fractions and Decimals เศษส่วนและทศนิยม

1. **one whole**
$1 = 1.00$
หนึ่งจำนวนเต็ม

2. **one half**
$1/2 = .5$
ครึ่งหนึ่ง

3. **one third**
$1/3 = .333$
เศษหนึ่งส่วนสาม

4. **one fourth**
$1/4 = .25$
เศษหนึ่งส่วนสี่

5. **one eighth**
$1/8 = .125$
เศษหนึ่งส่วนแปด

Percents เปอร์เซ็นต์

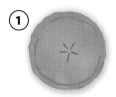

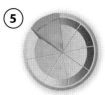

6. **calculator**
เครื่องคิดเลข

7. **decimal point**
จุดทศนิยม

8. **100 percent**
100 เปอร์เซ็นต์

9. **75 percent**
75 เปอร์เซ็นต์

10. **50 percent**
50 เปอร์เซ็นต์

11. **25 percent**
25 เปอร์เซ็นต์

12. **10 percent**
10 เปอร์เซ็นต์

Measurement การวัด

13. **ruler**
ไม้บรรทัด

14. **centimeter [cm]**
เซนติเมตร [ซม.]

15. **inch [in.]**
นิ้ว [น.]

Dimensions ขนาดสัดส่วน

16. **height**
ความสูง

17. **length**
ความยาว

18. **depth**
ความลึก

19. **width**
ความกว้าง

Equivalencies

12 inches = 1 foot

3 feet = 1 yard

1,760 yards = 1 mile

1 inch = 2.54 centimeters

1 yard = .91 meters

1 mile = 1.6 kilometers

Time เวลา

Telling Time การบอกเวลา

1. hour
ชั่วโมง

2. minutes
นาที

3. seconds
วินาที

4. a.m.
ตั้งแต่เที่ยงคืนถึง 11 นาฬิกา 59 นาที

5. p.m.
ตั้งแต่เที่ยงวันถึง 23 นาฬิกา 59 นาที

6. 1:00
one o'clock
หนึ่งนาฬิกา

7. 1:05
one-oh-five
five after one
หนึ่งนาฬิกาห้านาที
ห้านาทีหลังหนึ่งนาฬิกา

8. 1:10
one-ten
ten after one
หนึ่งนาฬิกาสิบนาที
สิบนาทีหลังหนึ่งนาฬิกา

9. 1:15
one-fifteen
a quarter after one
หนึ่งนาฬิกาสิบห้านาที
สิบห้านาทีหลังหนึ่งนาฬิกา

10. 1:20
one-twenty
twenty after one
หนึ่งนาฬิกายี่สิบนาที
ยี่สิบนาทีหลังหนึ่งนาฬิกา

11. 1:30
one-thirty
half past one
หนึ่งนาฬิกาสามสิบนาที
สามสิบนาทีหลังหนึ่งนาฬิกา

12. 1:40
one-forty
twenty to two
หนึ่งนาฬิกาสี่สิบนาที
อีกยี่สิบนาทีจะสองนาฬิกา

13. 1:45
one-forty-five
a quarter to two
หนึ่งนาฬิกาสี่สิบห้านาที
อีกสิบห้านาทีจะสองนาฬิกา

Times of Day เวลาต่างๆในหนึ่งวัน

14. sunrise
เวลาพระอาทิตย์ขึ้น

15. morning
เช้า

16. noon
เที่ยงวัน

17. afternoon
บ่าย

18. sunset
เวลาพระอาทิตย์ตก

19. evening
เย็น / ค่ำ

20. night
กลางคืน

21. midnight
เที่ยงคืน

Ways to talk about time

I wake up at 6:30 a.m.
I wake up at 6:30 in the morning.
I wake up at 6:30.

Pair practice. Make new conversations.

A: *What time do you wake up on weekdays?*
B: *At 6:30 a.m. How about you?*
A: *I wake up at 7:00.*

22. early
เร็วก่อนกำหนด

23. on time
ตรงตามกำหนดเวลา

24. late
สาย

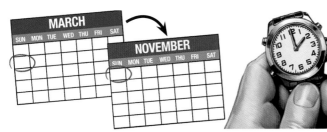

25. daylight saving time
เวลาที่ต้องปรับตามฤดูกาล

26. standard time
เวลามาตรฐาน

Time Zones เขตต่างๆของเวลา

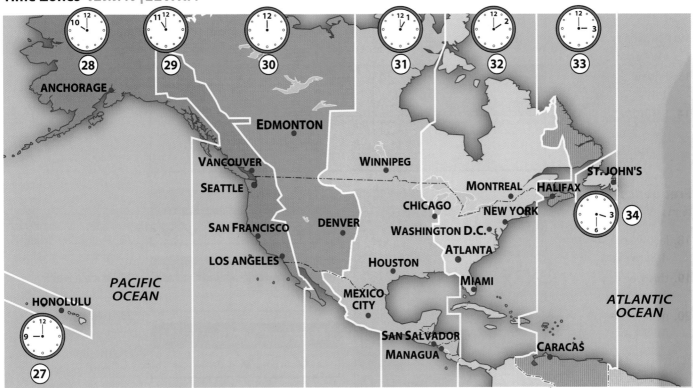

27. Hawaii-Aleutian time
เวลาในเขตฮาวาย-อลูเชิ่น

28. Alaska time
เวลาในเขตอาลาสกา

29. Pacific time
เวลาในเขตฝั่งแปซิฟิก

30. Mountain time
เวลาในเขตภูเขาค่อนทางตะวันตก

31. Central time
เวลาในเขตตอนกลาง

32. Eastern time
เวลาในเขตตะวันออก

33. Atlantic time
เวลาในเขตฝั่งแอตแลนดิก

34. Newfoundland time
เวลาในเขตนิวฟาวด์แลนด์

Ask your classmates. Share the answers.

1. When do you watch television? study? relax?
2. Do you like to stay up after midnight?
3. Do you like to wake up late on weekends?

Think about it. Discuss.

1. What is your favorite time of day? Why?
2. Do you think daylight saving time is a good idea? Why or why not?

19

1. date
   วันที่
2. day
   วัน
3. month
   เดือน
4. year
   ปี

5. today
   วันนี้
6. tomorrow
   วันพรุ่งนี้
7. yesterday
   เมื่อวาน

Days of the Week
วันต่างๆในสัปดาห์

8. Sunday
   วันอาทิตย์
9. Monday
   วันจันทร์
10. Tuesday
    วันอังคาร
11. Wednesday
    วันพุธ
12. Thursday
    วันพฤหัสบดี
13. Friday
    วันศุกร์
14. Saturday
    วันเสาร์

MAY

SUN	MON	TUE	WED	THU	FRI	SAT
1	2	3	4	5	6	7
8	9	10	11	12	13	14
15	16	17	18	19	20	21
22	23	24	25	26	27	28
29	30	31				

15. week
    สัปดาห์
16. weekdays
    วันทำงาน
17. weekend
    วันหยุดสุดสัปดาห์

Frequency
ความถี่

18. last week
    สัปดาห์ที่แล้ว
19. this week
    สัปดาห์นี้
20. next week
    สัปดาห์หน้า

MAY

SUN	MON	TUE	WED	THU	FRI	SAT
X1	X2	X3	X4	X5	X6	X7
8	9	10	11	12	13	14
15	16	17	18	19	20	21
22	23	24	25	26	27	28

SUN	MON	TUE	WED	THU	FRI	SAT
✓	✓	✓	✓	✓	✓	✓

SUN	MON	TUE	WED	THU	FRI	SAT
	✓					

SUN	MON	TUE	WED	THU	FRI	SAT
	✓		✓			

SUN	MON	TUE	WED	THU	FRI	SAT
	✓	✓		✓		

21. every day / daily
    ทุกวัน / รายวัน
22. once a week
    สัปดาห์ละครั้ง
23. twice a week
    สัปดาห์ละสองครั้ง
24. three times a week
    สัปดาห์ละสามครั้ง

Ways to say the date
Today is <u>May 10th</u>. It's the <u>tenth</u>.
Yesterday was <u>May 9th</u>.
The party is on <u>May 21st</u>.

Pair practice. Make new conversations.
A: *The <u>test</u> is on <u>Friday</u>, <u>June 14th</u>.*
B: *Did you say <u>Friday</u>, the <u>fourteenth</u>?*
A: *Yes, the <u>fourteenth</u>.*

㉕ JAN

SUN	MON	TUE	WED	THU	FRI	SAT
					1	2
3	4	5	6	7	8	9
10	11	12	13	14	15	16
17	18	19	20	21	22	23
24/31	25	26	27	28	29	30

㉖ FEB

SUN	MON	TUE	WED	THU	FRI	SAT
1	2	3	4	5	6	
7	8	9	10	11	12	13
14	15	16	17	18	19	20
21	22	23	24	25	26	27
28						

㉗ MAR

SUN	MON	TUE	WED	THU	FRI	SAT
	1	2	3	4	5	6
7	8	9	10	11	12	13
14	15	16	17	18	19	20
21	22	23	24	25	26	27
28	29	30	31			

㉘ APR

SUN	MON	TUE	WED	THU	FRI	SAT
				1	2	3
4	5	6	7	8	9	10
11	12	13	14	15	16	17
18	19	20	21	22	23	24
25	26	27	28	29	30	

㉙ MAY

SUN	MON	TUE	WED	THU	FRI	SAT
						1
2	3	4	5	6	7	8
9	10	11	12	13	14	15
16	17	18	19	20	21	22
23/30	24/31	25	26	27	28	29

㉚ JUN

SUN	MON	TUE	WED	THU	FRI	SAT
		1	2	3	4	5
6	7	8	9	10	11	12
13	14	15	16	17	18	19
20	21	22	23	24	25	26
27	28	29	30			

㉛ JUL

SUN	MON	TUE	WED	THU	FRI	SAT
				1	2	3
4	5	6	7	8	9	10
11	12	13	14	15	16	17
18	19	20	21	22	23	24
25	26	27	28	29	30	31

㉜ AUG

SUN	MON	TUE	WED	THU	FRI	SAT
1	2	3	4	5	6	7
8	9	10	11	12	13	14
15	16	17	18	19	20	21
22	23	24	25	26	27	28
29	30	31				

㉝ SEP

SUN	MON	TUE	WED	THU	FRI	SAT
			1	2	3	4
5	6	7	8	9	10	11
12	13	14	15	16	17	18
19	20	21	22	23	24	25
26	27	28	29	30		

㉞ OCT

SUN	MON	TUE	WED	THU	FRI	SAT
					1	2
3	4	5	6	7	8	9
10	11	12	13	14	15	16
17	18	19	20	21	22	23
24/31	25	26	27	28	29	30

㉟ NOV

SUN	MON	TUE	WED	THU	FRI	SAT
	1	2	3	4	5	6
7	8	9	10	11	12	13
14	15	16	17	18	19	20
21	22	23	24	25	26	27
28	29	30				

㊱ DEC

SUN	MON	TUE	WED	THU	FRI	SAT
			1	2	3	4
5	6	7	8	9	10	11
12	13	14	15	16	17	18
19	20	21	22	23	24	25
26	27	28	29	30	31	

Months of the Year
เดือนต่างๆในหนึ่งปี

25. January
มกราคม

26. February
กุมภาพันธ์

27. March
มีนาคม

28. April
เมษายน

29. May
พฤษภาคม

30. June
มิถุนายน

31. July
กรกฎาคม

32. August
สิงหาคม

33. September
กันยายน

34. October
ตุลาคม

35. November
พฤศจิกายน

36. December
ธันวาคม

Seasons
ฤดูต่างๆ

37. spring
ฤดูใบไม้ผลิ

38. summer
ฤดูร้อน

39. fall / autumn
ฤดูใบไม้ร่วง

40. winter
ฤดูหนาว

Dictate to your partner. Take turns.

A: *Write Monday.*
B: *Is it spelled M-o-n-d-a-y?*
A: *Yes, that's right.*

Ask your classmates. Share the answers.

1. What is your favorite day of the week? Why?
2. What is your busiest day of the week? Why?
3. What is your favorite season of the year? Why?

1. birthday
วันเกิด

2. wedding
แต่งงาน

3. anniversary
วันครบรอบ

4. appointment
การนัดหมาย

5. parent-teacher conference
การประชุมครู-ผู้ปกครอง

6. vacation
วันหยุดพักผ่อน

7. religious holiday
วันหยุดทางศาสนา

8. legal holiday
วันหยุดตามกฎหมาย

Legal Holidays วันหยุดตามกฎหมาย

9. New Year's Day
วันขึ้นปีใหม่

10. Martin Luther King Jr. Day
วันระลึกมาร์ติน ลูเธอร์ คิง
จูเนียร์

11. Presidents' Day
วันประธานาธิบดี

12. Memorial Day
วันระลึกทหารที่เสียชีวิตใน
สงครามต่างๆ

13. Fourth of July /
Independence Day
วันที่สี่ของเดือนกรกฎาคม /
วันระลึกเอกราชของสหรัฐฯ

14. Labor Day
วันแรงงาน

15. Columbus Day
วันระลึกโคลัมบัส

16. Veterans Day
วันทหารผ่านศึก

17. Thanksgiving
วันขอบคุณพระเจ้า

18. Christmas
วันคริสต์มาส

Pair practice. Make new conversations.

A: *When is your birthday?*
B: *It's on January 31st. How about you?*
A: *It's on December 22nd.*

Ask your classmates. Share the answers.

1. What are the legal holidays in your native country?
2. When is Labor Day in your native country?
3. When do you celebrate the New Year in your native country?

1. **little** hand
   มือเล็ก
2. **big** hand
   มือใหญ่

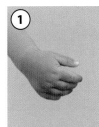
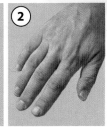

13. **heavy** box
    หีบหนัก
14. **light** box
    หีบเบา

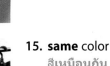

3. **fast** driver
   คนขับรถเร็ว
4. **slow** driver
   คนขับรถช้า

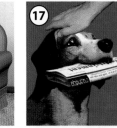

15. **same** color
    สีเหมือนกัน
16. **different** colors
    สีต่างกัน

5. **hard** chair
   เก้าอี้แข็ง
6. **soft** chair
   เก้าอี้นุ่ม

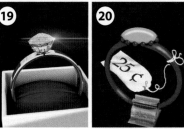

17. **good** dog
    สุนัขนิสัยดี
18. **bad** dog
    สุนัขนิสัยไม่ดี

7. **thick** book
   หนังสือหนา
8. **thin** book
   หนังสือบาง

19. **expensive** ring
    แหวนราคาแพง
20. **cheap** ring
    แหวนราคาถูก

9. **full** glass
   แก้วเต็ม
10. **empty** glass
    แก้วเปล่า

21. **beautiful** view
    ทัศนียภาพที่สวยงาม
22. **ugly** view
    ทัศนียภาพที่ไม่น่าดู

11. **noisy** children /
    loud children
    เด็กส่งเสียงรบกวน /
    เด็กส่งเสียงดัง
12. **quiet** children
    เด็กเงียบ

23. **easy** problem
    โจทย์ง่าย
24. **difficult** problem /
    hard problem
    โจทย์ยาก

$$1 + 1 = 2$$

$$x^2 - 22\tfrac{1}{2}x$$
$$=$$
$$-8\tfrac{1}{3}x^2 - 11\tfrac{2}{3}$$

Ask your classmates. Share the answers.

1. Are you a slow driver or a fast driver?
2. Do you prefer a hard bed or a soft bed?
3. Do you like loud parties or quiet parties?

Use the new words.
Look at page 150–151. Describe the things you see.

A: _The street_ is _hard_.
B: _The truck_ is _heavy_.

23

Sweaters Online

Now on Sale

Protected

Basic Colors สีหลัก

1. red
แดง

2. yellow
เหลือง

3. blue
น้ำเงิน

4. orange
ส้ม

5. green
เขียว

6. purple
ม่วง

7. pink
ชมพู

8. violet
ม่วงเข้ม

9. turquoise
เขียวไข่กา

10. dark blue
น้ำเงินเข้ม

11. light blue
ฟ้าอ่อน

12. bright blue
ฟ้าจรัส

Neutral Colors สีกลางๆ

13. black
ดำ

14. white
ขาว

15. gray
เทา

16. cream / ivory
ขาวครีม / ขาวงาช้าง

17. brown
น้ำตาล

18. beige / tan
สีเนื้อ / น้ำตาลอ่อน

Ask your classmates. Share the answers.

1. What colors are you wearing today?

2. What colors do you like?

3. Is there a color you don't like? What is it?

Use the new words. Look at pages 86–87.

Take turns naming the colors you see.

A: *His shirt is <u>blue</u>.*

B: *Her shoes are <u>white</u>.*

1. The yellow sweaters are **on the left**.
เสื้อกันหนาวสีเหลืองอยู่**ทางซ้าย**

2. The purple sweaters are **in the middle**.
เสื้อกันหนาวสีม่วงอยู่**ตรงกลาง**

3. The brown sweaters are **on the right**.
เสื้อกันหนาวสีน้ำตาลอยู่**ทางขวา**

4. The red sweaters are **above** the blue sweaters.
เสื้อกันหนาวสีแดง**อยู่บน**เสื้อกันหนาวสีฟ้า

5. The blue sweaters are **below** the red sweaters.
เสื้อกันหนาวสีฟ้า**อยู่ใต้**เสื้อกันหนาวสีแดง

6. The turquoise sweater is **in** the box.
เสื้อกันหนาวสีเขียวไข่กาอยู่**ในกล่อง**

7. The white sweater is **in front of** the black sweater.
เสื้อกันหนาวสีขาวอยู่**ข้างหน้า**เสื้อกันหนาวสีดำ

8. The black sweater is **behind** the white sweater.
เสื้อกันหนาวสีดำอยู่**ข้างหลัง**เสื้อกันหนาวสีขาว

9. The orange sweater is **on** the gray sweater.
เสื้อกันหนาวสีส้มอยู่**บน**เสื้อกันหนาวสีเทา

10. The violet sweater is **next to** the gray sweater.
เสื้อกันหนาวสีม่วงเข้มอยู่**ถัดจาก**เสื้อกันหนาวสีเทา

11. The gray sweater is **under** the orange sweater.
เสื้อกันหนาวสีเทาอยู่**ข้างใต้**เสื้อกันหนาวสีส้ม

12. The green sweater is **between** the pink sweaters.
เสื้อกันหนาวสีเขียวอยู่**ระหว่าง**เสื้อกันหนาวสีชมพู

More vocabulary

near: in the same area
far from: not near

Role play. Make new conversations.

A: *Excuse me. Where are the <u>red</u> sweaters?*
B: *They're <u>on the left</u>, <u>above</u> the <u>blue</u> sweaters.*
A: *Thanks very much.*

Coins เหรียญ

1. $.01 = 1¢
   a penny / 1 cent
   หนึ่งเพนนี / หนึ่งเซ็นต์

2. $.05 = 5¢
   a nickel / 5 cents
   หนึ่งนิคเกิล / ห้าเซ็นต์

3. $.10 = 10¢
   a dime / 10 cents
   หนึ่งไดม์ / สิบเซ็นต์

4. $.25 = 25¢
   a quarter / 25 cents
   หนึ่งควอเตอร์ / ยี่สิบห้าเซ็นต์

5. $.50 = 50¢
   a half dollar
   ครึ่งดอลลาร์

6. $1.00
   a dollar coin
   เหรียญหนึ่งดอลลาร์

Bills ธนบัตร

7. $1.00
   a dollar
   หนึ่งดอลลาร์

8. $5.00
   five dollars
   ห้าดอลลาร์

9. $10.00
   ten dollars
   สิบดอลลาร์

10. $20.00
    twenty dollars
    ยี่สิบดอลลาร์

11. $50.00
    fifty dollars
    ห้าสิบดอลลาร์

12. $100.00
    one hundred dollars
    ร้อยดอลลาร์

Do you have change for a dollar?

Yes, I do.

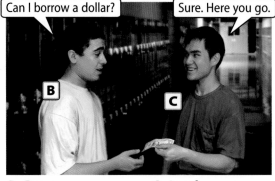

Can I borrow a dollar?

Sure. Here you go.

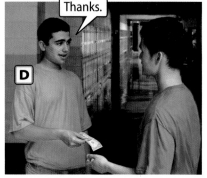

Thanks.

A. **Get** change.
แลกเงินปลีก /
แลกเงินธนบัตรเป็นเหรียญ

B. **Borrow** money.
ยืมเงิน

C. **Lend** money.
ให้ยืมเงิน

D. **Pay back** the money.
จ่ายคืนเงิน

Pair practice. Make new conversations.

A: *Do you have change for a dollar?*
B: *Sure. How about two quarters and five dimes?*
A: *Perfect!*

Think about it. Discuss.

1. Is it a good idea to lend money to a friend? Why or why not?
2. Is it better to carry a dollar or four quarters? Why?
3. Do you prefer dollar coins or dollar bills? Why?

Ways to Pay วิธีจ่ายเงิน

A. pay cash
จ่ายเงินสด

B. use a credit card
ใช้บัตรเครดิต

C. use a debit card
ใช้บัตรเดบิต [บัตรที่มีเงินไว้ล่วงหน้า]

D. write a (personal) check
เขียนเช็ค (ส่วนตัว)

E. use a gift card
ใช้บัตรกำนัล

F. cash a traveler's check
เบิกขึ้นเงินเช็คเดินทาง

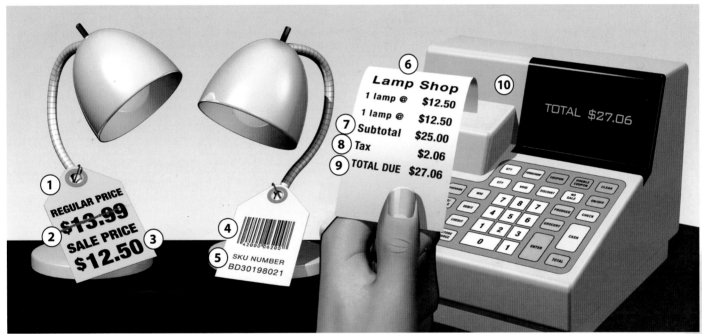

1. price tag
ป้ายราคา

2. regular price
ราคาปกติ

3. sale price
ราคาลด

4. bar code
แถบรหัส

5. SKU number
หมายเลขรหัสสินค้า
ในสต๊อค

6. receipt
ใบเสร็จรับเงิน

7. price / cost
ราคา / ค่า

8. sales tax
ภาษีการขาย

9. total
ยอดรวม

10. cash register
เครื่องรับทอนเงิน

G. buy / pay for
ซื้อ / จ่ายเงินค่าสินค้า

H. return
คืนของ / คืนเงิน

I. exchange
แลกเปลี่ยน

1. **twins**
   คู่แฝด
2. **sweater**
   เสื้อกันหนาว
3. **matching**
   เข้าคู่กัน
4. **disappointed**
   ผิดหวัง
5. **navy blue**
   สีกรมท่า
6. **happy**
   มีความสุข
A. **shop**
   หาซื้อ
B. **keep**
   เก็บไว้

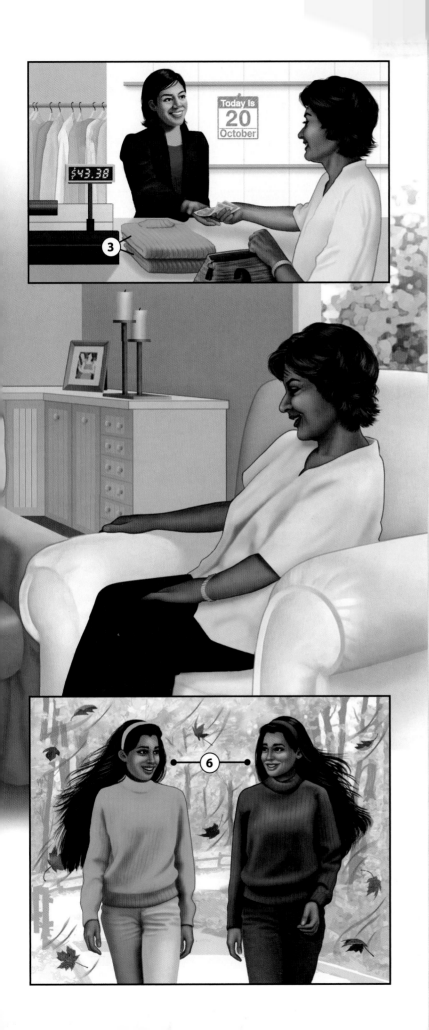

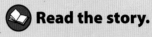

Look at the pictures.
What do you see?

Answer the questions.

1. Who is the woman shopping for?
2. Does she buy matching sweaters or different sweaters?
3. How does Anya feel about her green sweater? What does she do?
4. What does Manda do with her sweater?

Read the story.

Same and Different

Mrs. Kumar likes to <u>shop</u> for her <u>twins</u>. Today she's looking at <u>sweaters</u>. There are many different colors on sale. Mrs. Kumar chooses two <u>matching</u> green sweaters.

The next day, Manda and Anya open their gifts. Manda likes the green sweater, but Anya is <u>disappointed</u>. Mrs. Kumar understands the problem. Anya wants to be different.

Manda <u>keeps</u> her sweater. But Anya goes to the store. She exchanges her green sweater for a <u>navy blue</u> sweater. It's an easy answer to Anya's problem. Now the twins can be warm, <u>happy</u>, and different.

Think about it.

1. Do you like to shop for other people? Why or why not?
2. Imagine you are Anya. Would you keep the sweater or exchange it? Why?

29

1. man
   ผู้ชาย (คนเดียว)
2. woman
   ผู้หญิง (คนเดียว)
3. women
   ผู้หญิง (หลายคน)
4. men
   ผู้ชาย (หลายคน)
5. senior citizen
   ผู้สูงอายุ

Listen and point. Take turns.

A: *Point to a <u>woman</u>.*
B: *Point to a <u>senior citizen</u>.*
A: *Point to an <u>infant</u>.*

Dictate to your partner. Take turns.

A: *Write <u>woman</u>.*
B: *Is that spelled <u>w-o-m-a-n</u>?*
A: *Yes, that's right, <u>woman</u>.*

6. infant
ทารก

7. baby
เด็กอ่อน

8. toddler
เด็กวัยหัดเดิน

9. 6-year-old boy
เด็กชายวัย 6 ขวบ

10. 10-year-old girl
เด็กหญิงวัย 10 ขวบ

11. teenager / teen
เด็กวัยรุ่น / วัยรุ่น

Ways to talk about age

1 month – 3 months old = **infant**	13 – 19 years old = **teenager**
18 months – 3 years old = **toddler**	18+ years old = **adult**
3 years old – 12 years old = **child**	62+ years old = **senior citizen**

Pair practice. Make new conversations.

A: *How old is Sandra?*
B: *She's thirteen years old.*
A: *Wow, she's a teenager now!*

31

Age วัย

1. young
   วัยหนุ่มสาว
2. middle-aged
   วัยกลางคน
3. elderly
   วัยชรา

Height ความสูง

4. tall
   สูง
5. average height
   ความสูงโดยเฉลี่ย /
   ความสูงปานกลาง
6. short
   เตี้ย

Weight น้ำหนัก

7. heavy / fat
   ท้วม / อ้วน
8. average weight
   น้ำหนักโดยเฉลี่ย /
   น้ำหนักปานกลาง
9. thin / slender
   ผอม / บอบบาง

Disabilities ความพิการ

10. physically challenged
    มีความลำบากทางกาย
11. sight impaired / blind
    พิการทางตา / ตาบอด
12. hearing impaired / deaf
    พิการทางหู / หูหนวก

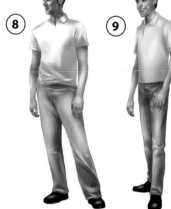

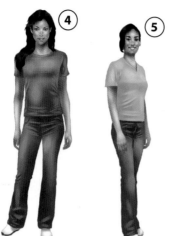

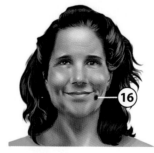

Prepositions of Motion p.153

Appearance รูปลักษณ์ภายนอก

13. attractive
    น่าดึงดูดใจ /
    หน้าตาดี
14. cute
    น่ารัก /
    น่าเอ็นดู
15. pregnant
    มีครรภ์
16. mole
    ไฝ
17. pierced ear
    เจาะต่างหู
18. tattoo
    ลายสัก

Ways to describe people

He's a heavy, young man.
She's a pregnant woman with a mole.
He's sight impaired.

Use the new words. Look at pages 2–3.
Describe the people and point. Take turns.

A: *He's a tall, thin, middle-aged man.*
B: *She's a short, average-weight young woman.*

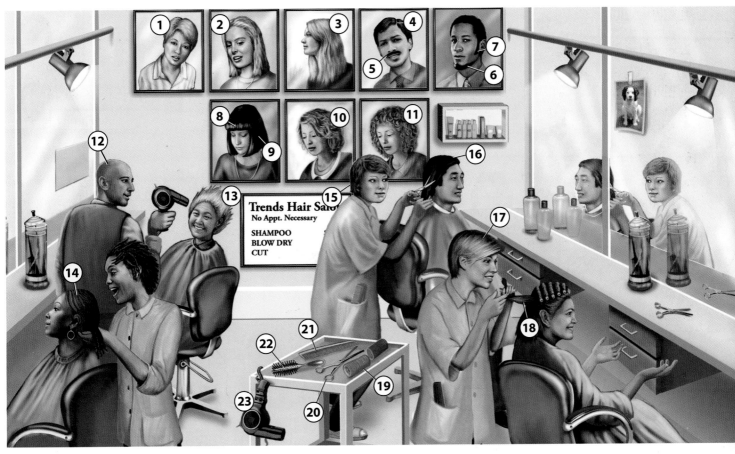

1. **short hair**
   ผมสั้น

2. **shoulder-length hair**
   ผมยาวประบ่า

3. **long hair**
   ผมยาว

4. **part**
   แสก

5. **mustache**
   หนวด

6. **beard**
   เครา

7. **sideburns**
   จอน

8. **bangs**
   หน้าม้า

9. **straight hair**
   ผมตรง

10. **wavy hair**
    ผมเป็นลอน

11. **curly hair**
    ผมหยิก

12. **bald**
    โล้น

13. **gray hair**
    ผมสีเทา / ผมหงอก

14. **corn rows**
    ถักเป็นแถว

15. **red hair**
    ผมสีแดง

16. **black hair**
    ผมสีดำ

17. **blond hair**
    ผมสีบลอนด์

18. **brown hair**
    ผมสีน้ำตาล

19. **rollers**
    โรลม้วนผม

20. **scissors**
    กรรไกร

21. **comb**
    หวี

22. **brush**
    แปรง

23. **blow dryer**
    เครื่องเป่าแห้ง

Style Hair ทรงผม

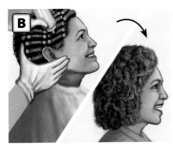

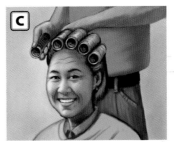

A. **cut** hair
ตัดผม

B. **perm** hair
ดัดผม

C. **set** hair
เซ็ทผม

D. **color** hair / **dye** hair
ทำสีผม / ย้อมผม

Ways to talk about hair

Describe hair in this order: length, style, and then color.
She has <u>long</u>, <u>straight</u>, <u>brown</u> *hair.*

Role play. Talk to a stylist.

A: *I need a new hairstyle.*
B: *How about* <u>short</u> *and* <u>straight</u>?
A: *Great. Do you think I should* <u>dye</u> *it?*

1. grandmother
   ย่า / ยาย
2. grandfather
   ปู่ / ตา
3. mother
   แม่
4. father
   พ่อ
5. sister
   พี่ (น้อง) สาว
6. brother
   พี่ (น้อง) ชาย
7. aunt
   ป้า
8. uncle
   ลุง
9. cousin
   ลูกพี่ลูกน้อง

Tim Lee's Family

Immediate Family

GRANDPARENTS · Min · Lu · PARENTS · Rose · Ken · Lynn · Dan · CHILDREN · Tim · Lily · Alex · Emily

10. mother-in-law
    แม่ยาย / แม่สามี
11. father-in-law
    พ่อตา / พ่อสามี
12. wife
    ภรรยา
13. husband
    สามี
14. daughter
    ลูกสาว
15. son
    ลูกชาย
16. sister-in-law
    พี่ (น้อง) สะใภ้
17. brother-in-law
    พี่ (น้อง) เขย
18. niece
    หลานสาว
19. nephew
    หลานชาย

Ana Garcia's Family

Extended Family

Eva · Sam · Ana · Tito · Marta · Carlos · Sara · Felix · Alice · Eddie

More vocabulary

Tim is Min and Lu's **grandson**.
Lily and Emily are Min and Lu's **granddaughters**.
Alex is Min's youngest **grandchild**.

Ana is Tito's **wife**.
Ana is Eva and Sam's **daughter-in-law**.
Carlos is Eva and Sam's **son-in-law**.

20. married couple
คู่ที่แต่งงานแล้ว

21. divorced couple
คู่ที่หย่ากันแล้ว

22. single mother
แม่ที่เลี้ยงลูกโดยลำพัง

23. single father
พ่อที่เลี้ยงลูกโดยลำพัง

Carol, Bruce, and Lisa

Lisa, Age 4

Lisa Green's Family

Lisa, Age 7

24. remarried
แต่งงานใหม่

25. stepfather
พ่อเลี้ยง

26. stepmother
แม่เลี้ยง

27. half sister
พี่ (น้อง) สาว
ร่วมบิดาหรือมารดา

28. half brother
พี่ (น้อง) ชาย
ร่วมบิดาหรือมารดา

29. stepsister
พี่ (น้อง) สาว
ต่างบิดามารดา

30. stepbrother
พี่ (น้อง) ชาย
ต่างบิดามารดา

Rick | Carol | Bruce | Sue

Lisa, Today

Mary | David | Kim | Bill

More vocabulary

Bruce is Carol's **former husband** or **ex-husband**.
Carol is Bruce's **former wife** or **ex-wife**.
Lisa is the **stepdaughter** of both Rick and Sue.

Look at the pictures.
Name the people.

A: *Who is Lisa's half sister?*
B: *Mary is. Who is Lisa's stepsister?*

A. hold
อุ้ม

B. nurse
ให้นมแม่

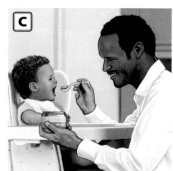

C. feed
ป้อนอาหาร

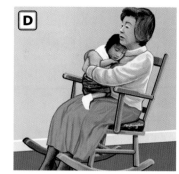

D. rock
โยก

E. undress
ถอดเสื้อผ้า

F. bathe
อาบน้ำ

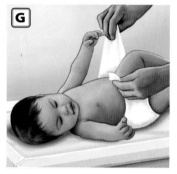

G. change a diaper
เปลี่ยนผ้าอ้อม

H. dress
ใส่เสื้อผ้า

I. comfort
ปลอบโยน

Good job!

J. praise
ชมเชย

No!

K. discipline
ฝึกฝนวินัย

L. buckle up
ใส่เข็มขัดนิรภัย

M. play with
เล่นด้วย

N. read to
อ่านให้ฟัง

O. sing a lullaby
ร้องเพลงกล่อม

P. kiss goodnight
จูบราตรีสวัสดิ์

Look at the pictures.
Describe what is happening.

A: She's <u>changing her baby's diaper</u>.
B: He's <u>kissing his son goodnight</u>.

Ask your classmates. Share the answers.

1. Do you like to take care of children?
2. Do you prefer to read to children or play with them?
3. Can you sing a lullaby? Which one?

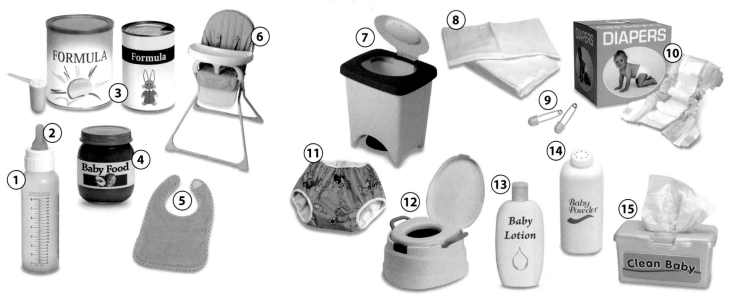

1. **bottle**
   ขวด / ขวดนม

2. **nipple**
   หัวนม

3. **formula**
   นมผงสำหรับทารก

4. **baby food**
   อาหารทารก

5. **bib**
   ผ้าปิดอกกันเปื้อน

6. **high chair**
   เก้าอี้สูงสำหรับเด็ก

7. **diaper pail**
   ถังใส่ผ้าอ้อม

8. **cloth diaper**
   ผ้าอ้อมที่ทำด้วยผ้า

9. **safety pins**
   เข็มกลัดซ่อนปลาย

10. **disposable diaper**
    ผ้าอ้อมแบบใช้แล้วทิ้ง

11. **training pants**
    กางเกงรองกันเลอะ

12. **potty seat**
    กระโถนเด็ก

13. **baby lotion**
    โลชั่นสำหรับทารก

14. **baby powder**
    แป้งสำหรับทารก

15. **wipes**
    กระดาษ / ผ้าชื้นสำหรับเช็ด

16. **baby bag**
    กระเป๋าสัมภาระของทารก

17. **baby carrier**
    ที่ใส่ทารก

18. **stroller**
    ล้อเข็นเด็ก

19. **car safety seat**
    ที่นั่งนิรภัยในรถสำหรับเด็ก

20. **carriage**
    ล้อเข็นเด็กแบบมีมุง

21. **rocking chair**
    เก้าอี้โยก

22. **nursery rhymes**
    นิทานกล่อมเด็ก

23. **teddy bear**
    ตุ๊กตาหมี

24. **pacifier**
    หัวนมหลอก

25. **teething ring**
    ห่วงให้เด็กกัดตอนฟันงอก

26. **rattle**
    ของเล่นส่งเสียงให้เด็กเพลิน

27. **night light**
    ไฟสำหรับเปิดทิ้งไว้ตอน
    กลางคืน

Dictate to your partner. Take turns.

A: *Write pacifier.*
B: *Was that pacifier, p-a-c-i-f-i-e-r?*
A: *Yes, that's right.*

Think about it. Discuss.

1. How can parents discipline toddlers? teens?
2. What are some things you can say to praise a child?
3. Why are nursery rhymes important for young children?

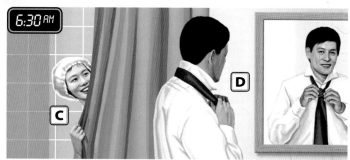

A. wake up
ตื่นนอน

B. get up
ลุกขึ้น

C. take a shower
อาบน้ำฝักบัว

D. get dressed
แต่งตัว

E. eat breakfast
รับประทานอาหารเช้า

F. make lunch
ทำอาหารกลางวัน

G. take the children to school /
drop off the kids
พาเด็กไปโรงเรียน /
ส่งเด็กลงที่โรงเรียน

H. take the bus to school
ขึ้นรถประจำทางไปโรงเรียน

I. drive to work / **go** to work
ขับรถไปทำงาน / ไปทำงาน

J. go to class
ไปที่ชั้นเรียน

K. work
ทำงาน

L. go to the grocery store
ไปที่ร้านขายของชำ

M. pick up the kids
ไปรับเด็ก

N. leave work
ออกไปจากที่ทำงาน

Grammar Point: third person singular

For *he* and *she*, add **-s** or **-es** to the verb:

He wakes up.　　　　*He watches TV.*

He gets up.　　　　*She goes to the store.*

These verbs are different (irregular):

*Be: She **is** in school at 10:00 a.m.*

*Have: He **has** dinner at 6:30 p.m.*

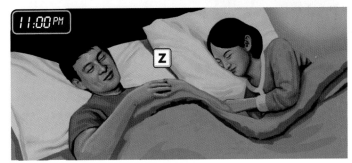

O. clean the house
ทำความสะอาดบ้าน

P. exercise
บริหารร่างกาย

Q. cook dinner / **make** dinner
หุงหาอาหารเย็น / ทำอาหารเย็น

R. come home / **get** home
มาบ้าน / ถึงบ้าน

S. have dinner / **eat** dinner
รับประทานอาหารเย็น / กินอาหารเย็น

T. do homework
ทำการบ้าน

U. relax
พักผ่อน

V. read the paper
อ่านหนังสือพิมพ์

W. check email
ตรวจดูอีเมล

X. watch TV
ดูทีวี

Y. go to bed
ไปนอน

Z. go to sleep
ไปหลับ

Pair practice. Make new conversations.

A: *When does he* <u>*go to work*</u>?
B: *He* <u>*goes to work*</u> *at* <u>*8:00 a.m.*</u> *When does she* <u>*go to class*</u>?
A: *She* <u>*goes to class*</u> *at* <u>*10:00 a.m.*</u>

Ask your classmates. Share the answers.

1. Who cooks dinner in your family?
2. Who goes to the grocery store?
3. Who goes to work?

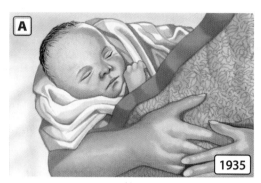

A. be born
เกิด

B. start school
เริ่มไปโรงเรียน

C. immigrate
ย้ายถิ่นฐานเข้ามา

D. graduate
เรียนจบ

E. learn to drive
หัดขับรถ

F. get a job
ได้งานทำ

G. become a citizen
ได้สัญชาติเป็นพลเมือง

H. fall in love
ตกหลุมรัก

1. birth certificate
ใบเกิด

2. Resident Alien card / green card
บัตรบุคคลต่างด้าวที่อาศัยอยู่ในสหรัฐฯ / กรีนคาร์ด

3. diploma
ปริญญา

4. driver's license
ใบขับขี่

5. Social Security card
บัตรประกันสังคม

6. Certificate of Naturalization
ใบรับรองการแปลงสัญชาติ

Grammar Point: past tense

start		immigrate	retire	
learn	+ed	graduate	die	+d
travel				

These verbs are different (irregular):

be – was	go – went	buy – bought
get – got	have – had	
become – became	fall – fell	

I. go to college
ไป / เข้าวิทยาลัย (มหาวิทยาลัย)

1956

J. get engaged
รับหมั้น

1958

7. college degree
ใบวุฒิปริญญา

K. get married
แต่งงาน

1959

L. have a baby
มีลูก

1961

8. marriage license
ทะเบียนสมรส

M. buy a home
ซื้อบ้าน

1965

N. become a grandparent
เป็นปู่ย่า / ตายาย (มีหลาน)

1986

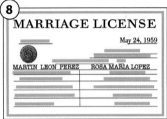

9. deed
โฉนด

O. retire
เกษียณ

2000

P. travel
เดินทาง

2005

10. passport
หนังสือเดินทาง

Q. volunteer
อาสาสมัคร

2006

R. die
ตาย

2008

11. death certificate
ใบมรณะ / ใบรับรองมรณภาพ

More vocabulary

When a husband dies, his wife becomes a **widow**.
When a wife dies, her husband becomes a **widower**.

Ask your classmates. Share the answers.

1. When did you start school?
2. When did you get your first job?
3. Do you want to travel?

1. hot
ร้อน

2. thirsty
หิวน้ำ

3. sleepy
ง่วงนอน

4. cold
หนาว

5. hungry
หิวข้าว

6. full / satisfied
อิ่ม / พอใจ

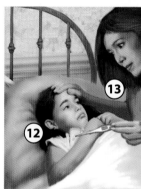

7. disgusted
รังเกียจ /
สะอิดสะเอียน

8. calm
สงบ

9. uncomfortable
อึดอัด / ไม่ค่อยสบาย

10. nervous
ประหม่า / พรั่นใจ

11. in pain
กำลังเจ็บปวด

12. sick
ป่วย

13. worried
วิตกกังวล

14. well
สบายดี

15. relieved
โล่งใจ

16. hurt
เจ็บปวดใจ / กาย

17. lonely
ว้าเหว่ / เดียวดาย

18. in love
กำลังมีความรัก

Pair practice. Make new conversations.

A: *How are you doing?*
B: *I'm <u>hungry</u>. How about you?*
A: *I'm <u>hungry</u> and <u>thirsty</u>, too!*

Use the new words.
Look at pages 40–41. Describe what each person is feeling.

A: *Martin is <u>excited</u>.*
B: *Martin's mother is <u>proud</u>.*

19. sad
เศร้า

20. homesick
คิดถึงบ้าน

21. proud
ภูมิใจ

22. excited
ตื่นเต้น

23. scared / afraid
หวาดกลัว / กลัว

24. embarrassed
อับอายขายหน้า

$$14 \, (\tan 63°) \qquad T = V_0 / g$$
$$79.00 - .40 \, (79.00)$$

$$s = 1/2 \, gt^2 + V_0 \, t + n$$
$$\sin^2 t + \cos^2 t + 1 \qquad \tan(\pi - t) = -\tan t$$

25. bored
เบื่อหน่าย

26. confused
สับสน / งุนงง

27. frustrated
คับข้องใจ

28. upset
อารมณ์เสีย

29. angry
โกรธ

30. surprised
ประหลาดใจ

31. happy
มีความสุข

32. tired
เหนื่อย

Ask your classmates. Share the answers.

1. Do you ever feel homesick?
2. What makes you feel frustrated?
3. Describe a time when you were very happy.

More vocabulary

exhausted: very tired
furious: very angry
humiliated: very embarrassed

overjoyed: very happy
starving: very hungry
terrified: very scared

1. banner
แผ่นป้าย

2. baseball game
เกมเบสบอล

3. opinion
ความเห็น

4. balloons
ลูกโป่ง

5. glad
ดีใจ

6. relatives
ญาติพี่น้อง

A. **laugh**
หัวเราะ

B. **misbehave**
ประพฤติไม่เหมาะสม

I think large families are best.

Look at the picture.
What do you see?

Answer the questions.

1. How many relatives are there at this reunion?

2. How many children are there? Which children are misbehaving?

3. What are people doing at this reunion?

Read the story.

A Family Reunion

Ben Lu has a lot of <u>relatives</u> and they're all at his house. Today is the Lu family reunion.

There is a lot of good food. There are also <u>balloons</u> and a <u>banner</u>. And this year there are four new babies!

People are having a good time at the reunion. Ben's grandfather and his aunt are talking about the <u>baseball game</u>. His cousins <u>are laughing</u>. His mother-in-law is giving her <u>opinion</u>. And many of the children <u>are misbehaving</u>.

Ben looks at his family and smiles. He loves his relatives, but he's <u>glad</u> the reunion is once a year.

Think about it.

1. Do you like to have large parties? Why or why not?

2. Imagine you see a little girl at a party. She's misbehaving. What do you do? What do you say?

45

The Home   บ้าน

1. roof
   หลังคา

2. bedroom
   ห้องนอน

3. door
   ประตู

4. bathroom
   ห้องน้ำ

5. kitchen
   ครัว

6. floor
   พื้น

7. dining area
   บริเวณรับประทานอาหาร

Listen and point. Take turns.

A: *Point to the kitchen.*
B: *Point to the living room.*
A: *Point to the basement.*

Dictate to your partner. Take turns.

A: *Write kitchen.*
B: *Was that k-i-t-c-h-e-n?*
A: *Yes, that's right, kitchen.*

8. attic
   ห้องใต้หลังคา
9. kids' bedroom
   ห้องนอนของเด็ก
10. baby's room
    ห้องของทารก
11. window
    หน้าต่าง
12. living room
    ห้องนั่งเล่น
13. basement
    ห้องใต้ถุน
14. garage
    โรงรถ

Ways to give locations

I'm home.
I'm in the kitchen.
I'm on the roof.

Pair practice. Make new conversations.

A: *Where's the man?*
B: *He's in the attic. Where's the teenager?*
A: *She's in the laundry room.*

1. Internet listing
รายการเสนอขายในอินเทอร์เน็ต

2. classified ad
โฆษณาที่จัดหมวดหมู่ทางสิ่งพิมพ์

Abbreviations

apt = apartment
bdrm = bedroom
ba = bathroom
kit = kitchen
yd = yard
util = utilities
incl = included
mo = month
furn = furnished
unfurn = unfurnished
mgr = manager
eves = evenings

3. furnished apartment
อพาร์ตเมนต์ที่มีเครื่องเรือน

4. unfurnished apartment
อพาร์ตเมนต์ที่ไม่มีเครื่องเรือน

Gas   Water   Electricity   Phone   Cable   DSL

5. utilities
สาธารณูปโภคต่างๆ (เช่น น้ำ ไฟ แก๊ส)

Renting an Apartment การเช่าอพาร์ตเมนต์

A. Call the manager.
โทรถึงผู้จัดการ

B. Ask about the features.
สอบถามเกี่ยวกับรายละเอียดต่างๆ

Are utilities included?
No, they aren't.

C. Submit an application.
ยื่นใบสมัคร

D. Sign the rental agreement.
เซ็นสัญญาข้อตกลงการเช่า

E. Pay the first and last month's rent.
จ่ายค่าเช่าของเดือนแรกและเดือนสุดท้าย

F. Move in.
ย้ายเข้า

More vocabulary

lease: a monthly or yearly rental agreement
redecorate: to change the paint and furniture in a home
move out: to pack and leave a home

Ask your classmates. Share the answers.

1. How did you find your home?
2. Do you like to paint or arrange furniture?
3. Does gas or electricity cost more for you?

Buying a House การซื้อบ้าน

G. Meet with a realtor.
พบกับตัวแทนผู้ซื้อขายบ้านและที่ดิน

H. Look at houses.
ดูบ้าน

$$$$$$

I. Make an offer.
ยื่นข้อเสนอ

Congratulations!

TOWN BANK

APPROVED

J. Get a loan.
เอาเงินกู้

K. Take ownership.
รับเอากรรมสิทธิ์

Mr. Young Chang
4445 2nd Street
Passville, CA 00543

Pay to the order of *Towne Bank* $ 2000.00

Two Thousand and 00/100 Dollars

L. Make a mortgage payment.
ทำการจ่ายเงินจำนอง

Moving In การย้ายเข้า

KITCHEN

M. Pack.
เก็บของลงหีบห่อ

N. Unpack.
รื้อของออกจากหีบห่อ

We have a new address.

PHONE ✓
DWP ✓
GAS ✓
CABLE ✓

GAS

O. Put the utilities in your name.
ใส่การใช้บริการสาธารณูปโภคต่างๆ
ในชื่อของคุณ

P. Paint.
ทาสี

Q. Arrange the furniture.
จัดเครื่องเรือน

Welcome!

R. Meet the neighbors.
พบเพื่อนบ้าน

Ways to ask about a home's features

Are <u>utilities</u> included?
Is <u>the kitchen</u> large and sunny?
Are <u>the neighbors</u> quiet?

Role play. Talk to an apartment manager.

A: *Hi. I'm calling about <u>the apartment</u>.*
B: *OK. It's <u>unfurnished</u> and rent is $<u>800</u> a month.*
A: *<u>Are utilities included</u>?*

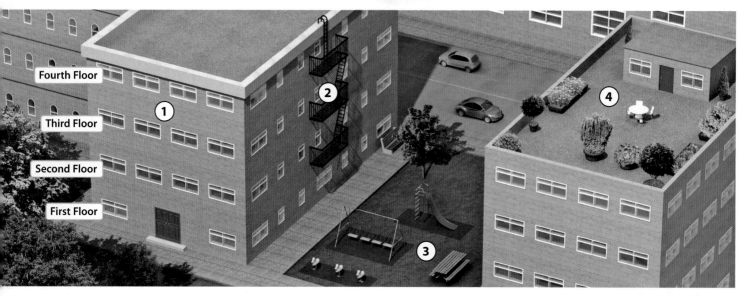

Fourth Floor

Third Floor

Second Floor

First Floor

1. **apartment building**
อาคารอพาร์ตเมนต์

2. **fire escape**
ทางหนีไฟ

3. **playground**
ลานเด็กเล่น

4. **roof garden**
สวนบนหลังคา

Entrance ทางเข้า

Apartment Available
2BD + 2BA
555-4263

5. **intercom / speaker**
ระบบสื่อสารภายในอาคาร /
ลำโพง

6. **tenant**
ผู้เช่า

7. **vacancy sign**
ป้ายประกาศห้องว่างให้เช่า

8. **manager / superintendent**
ผู้จัดการ / ผู้ดูแล

Lobby ห้องโถงรับแขก

9. **elevator**
ลิฟท์

10. **stairs / stairway**
บันได / ทางบันได

11. **mailboxes**
ตู้จดหมาย

Basement ใต้ถุนอาคาร

LAUNDRY ROOM

RECREATION ROOM

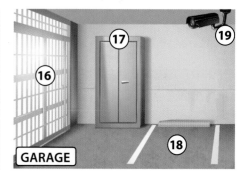

GARAGE

12. **washer**
เครื่องซักผ้า

13. **dryer**
เครื่องอบผ้า

14. **big-screen TV**
ทีวีจอใหญ่

15. **pool table**
โต๊ะบิลเลียด

16. **security gate**
ประตูเพื่อความปลอดภัย

17. **storage locker**
ตู้เก็บของ

18. **parking space**
ที่จอดรถ

19. **security camera**
กล้องถ่ายรูปเพื่อความ
ปลอดภัย

Grammar Point: *there is / there are*
singular: there is   **plural:** there are
There is a recreation room in the basement.
There are mailboxes in the lobby.

Look at the pictures.
Describe the apartment building.
A: *There's <u>a pool table</u> in the recreation room.*
B: *There are <u>parking spaces</u> in the garage.*

APARTMENT COMPLEX

20. balcony
ระเบียง / มุข

21. courtyard
ลานบ้าน

22. swimming pool
สระว่ายน้ำ

23. trash bin
ถังขยะ

24. alley
ตรอก

Hallway โถงทางเดิน

25. emergency exit
ทางออกฉุกเฉิน

26. trash chute
ช่องทิ้งขยะ

Rental Office สำนักงานเช่า

27. landlord
เจ้าของบ้านเช่า

28. lease / rental agreement
สัญญาเช่า /
ข้อตกลงการเช่า

An Apartment Entryway ทางเข้าอพาร์ตเมนต์

It's Joe.

Come up.

29. smoke detector
เครื่องตรวจจับควันไฟ

30. key
กุญแจ

31. buzzer
กริ่ง

32. peephole
ช่องมองดู

33. door chain
โซ่ประตู

34. dead-bolt lock
ล็อคแบบลั่นกลอน

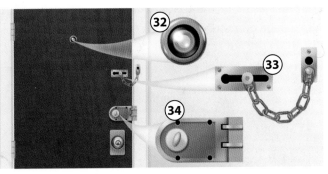

More vocabulary

upstairs: the floor(s) above you
downstairs: the floor(s) below you
fire exit: another name for emergency exit

Role play. Talk to a landlord.

A: *Is there a swimming pool in this complex?*
B: *Yes, there is. It's near the courtyard.*
A: *Is there…?*

51

1. the city / an urban area
เมือง / บริเวณตัวเมือง

2. the suburbs
ชานเมือง

3. a small town / a village
เมืองเล็ก / หมู่บ้าน

4. the country / a rural area
ชนบท

5. condominium / condo
คอนโดมิเนียม / คอนโด

6. townhouse
ทาวน์เฮ้าส์ / ห้องแถว

7. mobile home
บ้านแบบเคลื่อนย้ายได้

8. college dormitory / dorm
หอพักวิทยาลัย / หอพัก

9. farm
ฟาร์ม / ไร่

10. ranch
พื้นที่กว้างสำหรับเลี้ยงปศุสัตว์

11. senior housing
ที่อยู่อาศัยสำหรับคนชรา

12. nursing home
ที่อยู่อาศัยคนชราที่มีคนดูแล

13. shelter
ที่หลบภัย / ที่พักพิงยามยาก

More vocabulary

co-op: an apartment building owned by residents
duplex: a house divided into two homes
two-story house: a house with two floors

Think about it. Discuss.

1. What's good and bad about these places to live?
2. How are small towns different from cities?
3. How do shelters help people in need?

Front Yard and House สนามหน้าบ้านและบ้าน

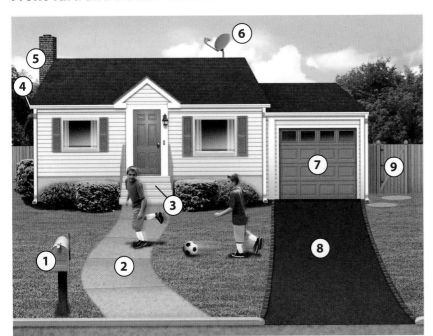

Front Porch ระเบียงหน้าบ้าน

1. **mailbox**
   ตู้จดหมาย

2. **front walk**
   ทางเดินหน้าบ้าน

3. **steps**
   ขั้นบันได

4. **gutter**
   รางน้ำ

5. **chimney**
   ปล่องไฟ

6. **satellite dish**
   จานดาวเทียม

7. **garage door**
   ประตูโรงรถ

8. **driveway**
   ทางรถเข้าออก

9. **gate**
   ประตูรั้ว

10. **storm door**
    ประตูกันพายุ

11. **front door**
    ประตูหน้า

12. **doorknob**
    ลูกบิดประตู

13. **porch light**
    ไฟหน้าบ้าน

14. **doorbell**
    กริ่งที่ประตู

15. **screen door**
    ประตูมุ้งลวด

Backyard สนามหลังบ้าน

16. **patio**
    ระเบียงหลังบ้าน

17. **grill**
    เตาปิ้งย่าง

18. **sliding glass door**
    ประตูกระจกแบบเลื่อน

19. **patio furniture**
    โต๊ะเก้าอี้สนาม

20. **flower bed**
    แปลงดอกไม้

21. **hose**
    สายยางรดน้ำ

22. **sprinkler**
    หัวฉีดรดน้ำ

23. **hammock**
    เปลญวน

24. **garbage can**
    ถังขยะ

25. **compost pile**
    กองปุ๋ยหมัก

26. **lawn**
    สนามหญ้า

27. **vegetable garden**
    สวนครัว

A. **take** a nap
   งีบหลับ

B. **garden**
   สวน

1. cabinet ตู้	**8.** dishwasher เครื่องล้างชาม	**15.** toaster oven เตาอบปิ้งขนาดเล็ก	**22.** counter เคาน์เตอร์
2. shelf ชั้น	**9.** refrigerator ตู้เย็น	**16.** pot หม้อ	**23.** drawer ลิ้นชัก
3. paper towels กระดาษเช็ดมือ	**10.** freezer ตู้แช่แข็ง	**17.** teakettle กาต้มน้ำ	**24.** pan กระทะก้นแบน
4. sink อ่างน้ำ	**11.** coffeemaker เครื่องทำกาแฟ	**18.** stove เตา	**25.** electric mixer เครื่องผสมแบบไฟฟ้า
5. dish rack ตะแกรงวางถ้วยชาม	**12.** blender เครื่องปั่นผสมอาหาร	**19.** burner หัวเผา	**26.** food processor เครื่องตัด / หั่น / เตรียมอาหาร
6. toaster เครื่องปิ้งขนมปัง	**13.** microwave เตาไมโครเวฟ	**20.** oven เตาอบ	**27.** cutting board เขียง
7. garbage disposal เครื่องย่อยขยะทิ้ง	**14.** electric can opener เครื่องเปิดกระป๋องแบบไฟฟ้า	**21.** broiler ชั้นอบอย่างในเตา	**28.** mixing bowl ชามอ่างสำหรับผสม

Ways to talk about location using *on* and *in*

Use **on** for the counter, shelf, burner, stove, and cutting board. *It's on the counter.* Use **in** for the dishwasher, oven, sink, and drawer. *Put it in the sink.*

Pair practice. Make new conversations.

A: *Please move <u>the blender</u>.*
B: *Sure. Do you want it <u>in the cabinet</u>?*
A: *No, put it <u>on the counter</u>.*

1. dish / plate
ถ้วยชาม / จาน

2. bowl
ถ้วย

3. fork
ส้อม

4. knife
มีด

5. spoon
ช้อน

6. teacup
ถ้วยชา

7. coffee mug
เหยือกกาแฟ

8. dining room chair
เก้าอี้ในห้องอาหาร

9. dining room table
โต๊ะในห้องอาหาร

10. napkin
กระดาษ / ผ้าเช็ดปาก

11. placemat
แผ่นรองจาน

12. tablecloth
ผ้าปูโต๊ะ

13. salt and pepper shakers
ที่ใส่เกลือและพริกไทย

14. sugar bowl
ถ้วยน้ำตาล

15. creamer
ถ้วยครีม

16. teapot
กาน้ำชา

17. tray
ถาด

18. light fixture
โคมไฟ

19. fan
พัดลม

20. platter
จานเสิร์ฟอาหาร

21. serving bowl
ชามใหญ่เสิร์ฟอาหาร

22. hutch
ตู้แบบมีชั้นภายในและลิ้นชัก

23. vase
แจกัน

24. buffet
ตู้เก็บเครื่องใช้ในห้องอาหาร

Ways to make requests at the table

May I have <u>the sugar bowl</u>?
Would you pass <u>the creamer,</u> please?
Could I have <u>a coffee mug</u>?

Role play. Request items at the table.

A: *What do you need?*
B: *Could I have a <u>coffee mug</u>?*
A: *Certainly. And would you...*

55

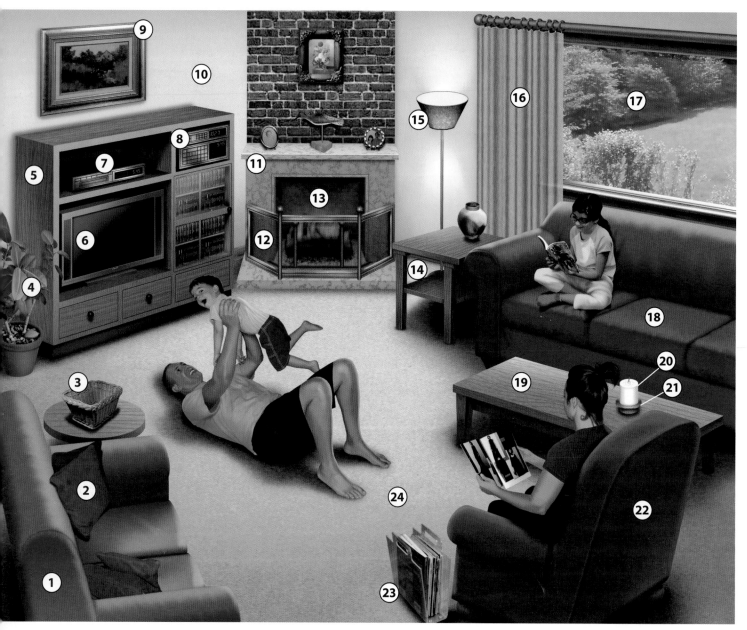

1. love seat
   เก้าอี้นวมแบบนั่งสองคน

2. throw pillow
   หมอนพิง

3. basket
   ตะกร้า

4. houseplant
   ต้นไม้ประดับภายในบ้าน

5. entertainment center
   ศูนย์รวมเครื่องบันเทิง

6. TV (television)
   ทีวี (เครื่องรับโทรทัศน์)

7. DVD player
   เครื่องเล่นดีวีดี

8. stereo system
   ระบบสเตริโอ

9. painting
   ภาพวาด

10. wall
    ฝาผนัง

11. mantle
    แท่นเหนือเตาผิง

12. fire screen
    แผงกันไฟ

13. fireplace
    เตาผิง

14. end table
    โต๊ะข้างเก้าอี้

15. floor lamp
    โคมไฟแบบตั้งพื้น

16. drapes
    ผ้าม่าน

17. window
    หน้าต่าง

18. sofa / couch
    โซฟา / เก้าอี้นวมยาว

19. coffee table
    โต๊ะรับแขก

20. candle
    เทียน

21. candle holder
    เชิงเทียน

22. armchair / easy chair
    เก้าอี้แบบมีที่วางแขน /
    เก้าอี้เอนหลัง

23. magazine holder
    ที่ใส่หนังสือพิมพ์ / นิตยสาร

24. carpet
    พรม

Use the new words.
Look at pages 44–45. Name the things in the room.

A: *There's a TV.*
B: *There's a carpet.*

More vocabulary

light bulb: the light inside a lamp
lampshade: the part of the lamp that covers the light bulb
sofa cushions: the pillows that are part of the sofa

1. **hamper**
   ที่ใส่เสื้อผ้ารอซัก

2. **bathtub**
   อ่างอาบน้ำ

3. **soap dish**
   จานใส่สบู่

4. **soap**
   สบู่

5. **rubber mat**
   แผ่นยางปูพื้นในอ่าง

6. **washcloth**
   ผ้าผืนเล็กสำหรับอาบน้ำ

7. **drain**
   รูระบายน้ำเสีย

8. **faucet**
   ก๊อกน้ำ

9. **hot water**
   น้ำร้อน

10. **cold water**
    น้ำเย็น

11. **grab bar**
    ราวจับ

12. **tile**
    กระเบื้องปูผนังหรือพื้น

13. **showerhead**
    หัวฝักบัว

14. **shower curtain**
    ม่านกันน้ำกระเซ็น

15. **towel rack**
    ราวผ้าเช็ดตัว

16. **bath towel**
    ผ้าเช็ดตัว

17. **hand towel**
    ผ้าเช็ดมือ

18. **mirror**
    กระจกเงา

19. **toilet paper**
    กระดาษชำระ

20. **toilet brush**
    แปรงขัดโถส้วม

21. **toilet**
    โถส้วม

22. **medicine cabinet**
    ตู้เก็บยา

23. **toothbrush**
    แปรงสีฟัน

24. **toothbrush holder**
    ที่ใส่แปรงสีฟัน

25. **sink**
    อ่าง

26. **wastebasket**
    ตะกร้าใส่ขยะ

27. **scale**
    ที่ชั่งน้ำหนัก

28. **bath mat**
    พรมเช็ดเท้าในห้องน้ำ

More vocabulary

stall shower: a shower without a bathtub
half bath: a bathroom with no shower or tub
linen closet: a closet for towels and sheets

Ask your classmates. Share the answers.

1. Is your toothbrush on the sink or in the medicine cabinet?
2. Do you have a bathtub or a shower?
3. Do you have a shower curtain or a shower door?

1. **dresser / bureau**
   ตู้เสื้อผ้า /
   ตู้มีลิ้นชักใส่เสื้อผ้า

2. **drawer**
   ลิ้นชัก

3. **photos**
   ภาพถ่าย

4. **picture frame**
   กรอบรูป

5. **closet**
   ห้อง /
   ตู้ในผนังสำหรับเก็บเสื้อผ้า

6. **full-length mirror**
   กระจกเงาเต็มตัว

7. **curtains**
   ผ้าม่าน

8. **mini-blinds**
   บังตาขนาดเล็ก

9. **bed**
   เตียง

10. **headboard**
    แผงหัวเตียง

11. **pillow**
    หมอน

12. **fitted sheet**
    ผ้าปูที่นอนแบบกระชับส่วน
    ล่าง

13. **flat sheet**
    ผ้าปูที่นอนส่วนบน

14. **pillowcase**
    ปลอกหมอน

15. **blanket**
    ผ้าห่ม

16. **quilt**
    ผ้านวม

17. **dust ruffle**
    ผ้าจีบฟูบังฝุ่น

18. **bed frame**
    ฐานเตียง

19. **box spring**
    แท่นสปริงรองฟูก

20. **mattress**
    ฟูก

21. **wood floor**
    พื้นไม้

22. **rug**
    พรมผืน

23. **night table / nightstand**
    โต๊ะหัวเตียง / โต๊ะข้างเตียง

24. **alarm clock**
    นาฬิกาปลุก

25. **lamp**
    โป๊ะไฟ

26. **lampshade**
    โคมโป๊ะไฟ

27. **light switch**
    สวิทช์ไฟ

28. **outlet**
    จุดเสียบปลั๊กไฟ

Look at the pictures.
Describe the bedroom.

A: *There's a lamp on the nightstand*.
B: *There's a mirror in the closet*.

Ask your classmates. Share the answers.

1. Do you prefer a hard or a soft mattress?
2. Do you prefer mini-blinds or curtains?
3. How many pillows do you like on your bed?

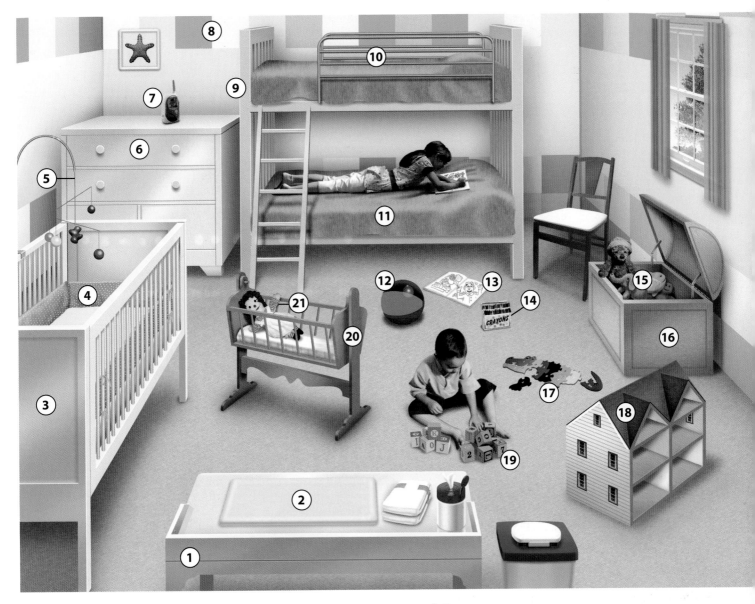

Furniture and Accessories
เฟอร์นิเจอร์และเครื่องใช้ต่างๆ

1. changing table
   โต๊ะสำหรับเปลี่ยนผ้าอ้อม

2. changing pad
   แผ่นปูรองสำหรับเปลี่ยนผ้าอ้อม

3. crib
   ที่นอนเด็ก

4. bumper pad
   แผ่นกันชน

5. mobile
   ของเล่นแบบแขวนประดับ

6. chest of drawers
   ตู้ลิ้นชัก

7. baby monitor
   เครื่องเฝ้าระวังเด็ก

8. wallpaper
   กระดาษปะแต่งฝาผนัง

9. bunk beds
   เตียงสองชั้น

10. safety rail
    ราวกันตก

11. bedspread
    ผ้าคลุมเตียง

Toys and Games
ของเล่นและเกม

12. ball
    บอล

13. coloring book
    สมุดสำหรับระบายสี

14. crayons
    สีเทียน

15. stuffed animals
    ตุ๊กตาผ้ารูปสัตว์ต่างๆ

16. toy chest
    หีบใส่ของเล่น

17. puzzle
    เกมต่อภาพ

18. dollhouse
    บ้านตุ๊กตา

19. blocks
    บล็อกของเล่น

20. cradle
    เปล

21. doll
    ตุ๊กตา

Pair practice. Make conversations.

A: *Where's the changing pad?*
B: *It's on the changing table.*

Think about it. Discuss.

1. Which toys help children learn? How?
2. Which toys are good for older and younger children?
3. What safety features does this room need? Why?

A. **dust** the furniture
ปัดฝุ่นตามเครื่องเรือน

B. **recycle** the newspapers
นำหนังสือพิมพ์ไปใช้ทำ
ประโยชน์ใหม่

C. **clean** the oven
ทำความสะอาดเตาอบ

D. **mop** the floor
เช็ดถูพื้น

E. **polish** the furniture
ขัดเงาเครื่องเรือน

F. **make** the bed
ทำที่นอน

G. **put away** the toys
เก็บของเล่นเข้าที่

H. **vacuum** the carpet
ดูดฝุ่นตามพรม

I. **wash** the windows
เช็ดล้างหน้าต่าง

J. **sweep** the floor
กวาดพื้น

K. **scrub** the sink
ขัดอ่าง

L. **empty** the trash
เทขยะทิ้ง

M. **wash** the dishes
ล้างชาม

N. **dry** the dishes
เช็ดถ้วยชามให้แห้ง

O. **wipe** the counter
เช็ดบนเคาน์เตอร์

P. **change** the sheets
เปลี่ยนผ้าปูที่นอน

Q. **take out** the garbage
เอาขยะออกไป

Pair practice. Make new conversations.

A: *Let's clean this place. First, I'll sweep the floor.*
B: *I'll mop the floor when you finish.*

Ask your classmates. Share the answers.

1. Who does the housework in your home?
2. How often do you wash the windows?
3. When should kids start to do housework?

  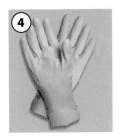   

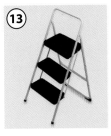     

1. feather duster
   ไม้ขนไก่ปัดฝุ่น
2. recycling bin
   ถังขยะรีไซเคิล
3. oven cleaner
   น้ำยาทำความสะอาดเตาอบ
4. rubber gloves
   ถุงมือยาง
5. steel-wool soap pads
   แผ่นใยเหล็กสำหรับขัด
6. sponge mop
   ฟองน้ำถูพื้น
7. bucket / pail
   ถังน้ำ
8. furniture polish
   น้ำยาขัดเงาเครื่องเรือน

9. rags
   ผ้าขี้ริ้ว
10. vacuum cleaner
    เครื่องดูดฝุ่น
11. vacuum cleaner attachments
    อุปกรณ์ของเครื่องดูดฝุ่น
12. vacuum cleaner bag
    ถุงฝุ่นในเครื่องดูดฝุ่น
13. stepladder
    กระไดแบบเป็นขั้น
14. glass cleaner
    น้ำยาเช็ดกระจก
15. squeegee
    แผ่นปาดเช็ดน้ำจากกระจก
16. broom
    ไม้กวาด

17. dustpan
    ภาชนะรับฝุ่นผง
18. cleanser
    น้ำยาทำความสะอาด
19. sponge
    ฟองน้ำ
20. scrub brush
    แปรงขัด
21. dishwashing liquid
    น้ำยาล้างจาน
22. dish towel
    ผ้าเช็ดจาน
23. disinfectant wipes
    แผ่นเช็ดฆ่าเชื้อโรค
24. trash bags
    ถุงขยะ

Ways to ask for something

Please hand me the squeegee.
Can you get me the broom?
I need the sponge mop.

Pair practice. Make new conversations.

A: *Please hand me the sponge mop.*
B: *Here you go. Do you need the bucket?*
A: *Yes, please. Can you get me the rubber gloves, too?*

61

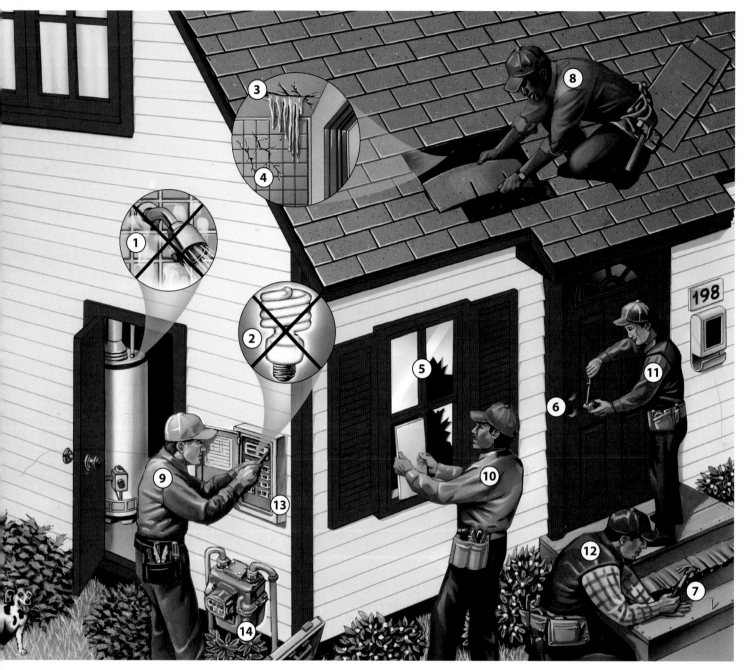

1. The water heater is **not working**.
   เครื่องทำน้ำร้อน**ไม่ทำงาน**

2. The power is **out**.
   ไฟดับ

3. The roof is **leaking**.
   หลังคารั่ว

4. The tile is **cracked**.
   กระเบื้อง**แตกร้าว**

5. The window is **broken**.
   กระจกหน้าต่าง**แตก**

6. The lock is **broken**.
   ล็อคประตูเสีย

7. The steps are **broken**.
   บันได**หัก**

8. roofer
   ช่างทำหลังคา

9. electrician
   ช่างไฟฟ้า

10. repair person
    คนงานซ่อมแซม

11. locksmith
    คนซ่อมล็อคประตู

12. carpenter
    ช่างไม้

13. fuse box
    ตู้ฟิวส์ไฟฟ้า

14. gas meter
    มิเตอร์แก๊ส

More vocabulary

fix: to repair something that is broken
pests: termites, fleas, rats, etc.
exterminate: to kill household pests

Pair practice. Make new conversations.

A: *The faucet is <u>leaking</u>.*
B: *Let's call <u>the plumber</u>. He can fix it.*

15. The furnace is **broken**.
เครื่องทำความอุ่นเสีย

16. The pipes are **frozen**.
ท่อเป็นน้ำแข็ง

17. The faucet is **dripping**.
ก๊อกน้ำไหลหยดปิดไม่สนิท

18. The sink is **overflowing**.
น้ำไหลลันอ่าง

19. The toilet is **stopped up**.
ส้วมอุดตัน

20. plumber
คนซ่อมระบบน้ำ

21. exterminator
คนกำจัดแมลง

22. termites
ปลวก

23. ants
มด

24. bedbugs
หมัดที่นอน

25. fleas
เหา

26. cockroaches / roaches
แมลงสาบใหญ่ / แมลงสาบเล็ก

27. rats
หนูตัวใหญ่

28. mice*
หนูตัวเล็ก(หลายตัว)

*Note: one mouse, two mice

Ways to ask about repairs

How much will this repair cost?
When can you begin?
How long will the repair take?

Role play. Talk to a repair person.

A: *Can you fix <u>the roof</u>?*
B: *Yes, but it will take <u>two weeks</u>.*
A: *How much will the repair cost?*

THE NEXT DAY...

LATER THAT EVENING...

1. roommates
เพื่อนร่วมห้อง

2. party
งานสังสรรค์

3. music
ดนตรี / เพลง

4. DJ
คนเปิดเพลง

5. noise
เสียง

6. irritated
ถูกรบกวน

7. rules
กฎระเบียบ

8. mess
เลอะเทอะ / รกรุงรัง

9. invitation
คำเชิญ /
การเชิญชวน

A. dance
เต้นรำ

THE NEXT SATURDAY...

Look at the pictures. What do you see?

Answer the questions.

1. What happened in apartment 2B? How many people were there?

2. How did the neighbor feel? Why?

3. What rules did they write at the tenant meeting?

4. What did the roommates do after the tenant meeting?

Read the story.

The Tenant Meeting

Sally Lopez and Tina Green are roommates. They live in apartment 2B. One night they had a big party with music and a DJ. There was a mess in the hallway. Their neighbors were very unhappy. Mr. Clark in 2A was very irritated. He hates noise!

The next day there was a tenant meeting. Everyone wanted rules about parties and loud music. The girls were very embarrassed.

After the meeting, the girls cleaned the mess in the hallway. Then they gave each neighbor an invitation to a new party. Everyone had a good time at the rec room party. Now the tenants have two new rules and a new place to dance.

Think about it.

1. What are the most important rules in an apartment building? Why?

2. Imagine you are the neighbor in 2A. What do you say to Tina and Sally?

65

Back from the Market กลับจากตลาด

1. fish
   ปลา
2. meat
   เนื้อ
3. chicken
   ไก่
4. cheese
   เนยแข็ง
5. milk
   นม
6. butter
   เนย
7. eggs
   ไข่
8. vegetables
   ผัก

Listen and point. Take turns.

A: *Point to the vegetables.*
B: *Point to the bread.*
A: *Point to the fruit.*

Pair Dictation

A: *Write vegetables.*
B: *Please spell vegetables for me.*
A: *V-e-g-e-t-a-b-l-e-s.*

9. fruit
ผลไม้

10. rice
ข้าว

11. bread
ขนมปัง

12. pasta
อาหารประเภทแป้ง

13. grocery bag
ถุงใส่ของชำ

14. shopping list
รายการจับจ่ายซื้อของ

15. coupons
คูปอง

Shopping list (14):
✓ milk
✓ bread
✓ lettuce
✓ grapes

Coupons (15):
NO EXPIRATION DATE
Save $1.00
on 2 cans of Soup

NO EXPIRATION DATE
50¢ off
any Cereal

Ways to talk about food.

Do we need <u>eggs</u>?

Do we have any <u>pasta</u>?

We have some <u>vegetables</u>, but we need <u>fruit</u>.

Role play. Talk about your shopping list.

A: *Do we need eggs?*

B: *No, we have some.*

A: *Do we have any...*

1. apples แอปเปิ้ล	**9. tangerines** ส้มเขียวหวาน	**17. blackberries** แบล็คเบอร์รี่	**25. raisins** องุ่นแห้ง / ลูกเกด
2. bananas กล้วย	**10. peaches** ท้อ	**18. watermelons** แตงโม	**26. prunes** ลูกพรุน
3. grapes องุ่น	**11. cherries** เชอร์รี่	**19. melons** แตง	**27. figs** ผลมะเดื่อ
4. pears สาลี่	**12. apricots** แอพริคอท	**20. papayas** มะละกอ	**28. dates** อินทผลัม
5. oranges ส้ม	**13. plums** พลัม	**21. mangoes** มะม่วง	**29. a bunch of bananas** กล้วยจำนวนหนึ่ง
6. grapefruit ส้มสรวง	**14. strawberries** สตรอเบอร์รี่	**22. kiwi** กีวี	**30. ripe banana** กล้วยสุก
7. lemons มะนาวเหลือง	**15. raspberries** ราสเบอร์รี่	**23. pineapples** สับปะรด	**31. unripe banana** กล้วยยังไม่สุก
8. limes มะนาว	**16. blueberries** บลูเบอร์รี่	**24. coconuts** มะพร้าว	**32. rotten banana** กล้วยเน่า

Pair practice. Make new conversations.

A: *What's your favorite fruit?*
B: *I like apples. Do you?*
A: *I prefer bananas.*

Ask your classmates. Share the answers.

1. Which fruit do you put in a fruit salad?
2. What kinds of fruit are common in your native country?
3. What kinds of fruit are in your kitchen right now?

1. lettuce
ผักกาดหอม

2. cabbage
กะหล่ำปลี

3. carrots
แครอท

4. radishes
หัวผักกาดแดง

5. beets
หัวบีท

6. tomatoes
มะเขือเทศ

7. bell peppers
พริกหยวก

8. string beans
ถั่วแขก

9. celery
ต้นขึ้นฉ่าย

10. cucumbers
แตงกวา

11. spinach
ผักปวยเล้ง

12. corn
ข้าวโพด

13. broccoli
บร็อคโคลี่

14. cauliflower
กะหล่ำดอก

15. bok choy
ผักฮ่องเต้

16. turnips
หัวเทอร์นิป / หัวบนดิน

17. potatoes
มันฝรั่ง

18. sweet potatoes
มันเทศ

19. onions
หัวหอม

20. green onions / scallions
ต้นหอม

21. peas
ถั่วลันเตา

22. artichokes
หัวอาติโชก

23. eggplants
มะเขือม่วง

24. squash
แตงประเภทฟักทอง /
น้ำเต้า

25. zucchini
แตงชูคินี

26. asparagus
หน่อไม้ฝรั่ง

27. mushrooms
เห็ด

28. parsley
ผักชีฝรั่ง

29. chili peppers
พริกชี้ฟ้า

30. garlic
กระเทียม

31. a **bag of** lettuce
ผักสลัด**ถุง**หนึ่ง

32. a **head of** lettuce
ผักสลัด**หัว**หนึ่ง

Pair practice. Make new conversations.

A: *Do you eat broccoli?*
B: *Yes. I like most vegetables, but not peppers.*
A: *Really? Well, I don't like cauliflower.*

Ask your classmates. Share the answers.

1. Which vegetables do you eat raw? cooked?
2. Which vegetables do you put in a green salad?
3. Which vegetables are in your refrigerator right now?

MEAT

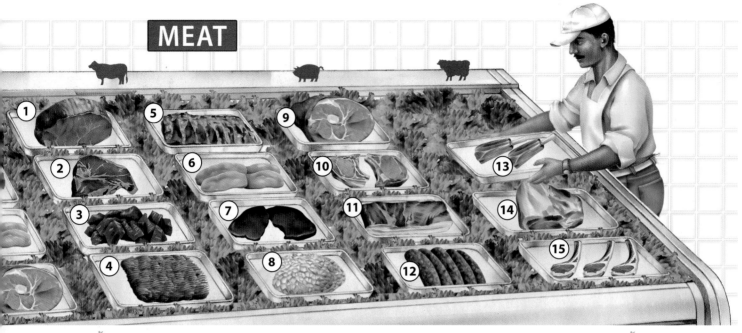

Beef เนื้อวัว

1. roast
   อบ
2. steak
   สเต็ก
3. stewing beef
   เนื้อสำหรับตุ๋น
4. ground beef
   เนื้อวัวบด

5. beef ribs
   ซี่โครงวัว
6. veal cutlets
   เนื้อลูกวัว
7. liver
   ตับ
8. tripe
   ผ้าขี้ริ้ว / เครื่องในวัว

Pork หมู

9. ham
   ขาหลังหมูส่วนบน
10. pork chops
    เนื้อแดงหมูติดมัน
11. bacon
    หมูเบคอน / หมูสามชั้น
12. sausage
    ไส้กรอก

Lamb เนื้อแกะ

13. lamb shanks
    ขาแกะส่วนล่าง
14. leg of lamb
    ขาแกะส่วนบน
15. lamb chops
    เนื้อแดงแกะติดมัน

POULTRY

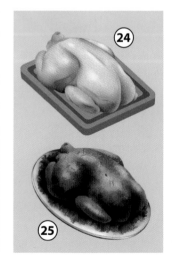

Poultry เนื้อสัตว์ปีก

16. chicken
    ไก่
17. turkey
    ไก่งวง

18. duck
    เป็ด
19. breasts
    เนื้อหน้าอก

20. wings
    ปีก
21. legs
    ขา

22. thighs
    ขาส่วนบน
23. drumsticks
    น่อง

24. **raw** chicken
    ไก่ดิบ
25. **cooked** chicken
    ไก่สุก

More vocabulary

vegetarian: a person who doesn't eat meat
boneless: meat and poultry without bones
skinless: poultry without skin

Ask your classmates. Share the answers.

1. What kind of meat do you eat most often?
2. What kind of meat do you use in soups?
3. What part of the chicken do you like the most?

SEAFOOD

Fish ปลา

1. trout
ปลาเทราต์

2. catfish
ปลาดุก

3. whole salmon
แซลมอนทั้งตัว

4. salmon steak
แซลมอนตัดแบบขวางลำตัว

5. swordfish
ปลาดาบ

6. halibut steak
ฮาลิบัทตัดแบบขวางลำตัว

7. tuna
ทูน่า

8. cod
คอด

Shellfish ประเภทหอยปู

9. crab
ปู

10. lobster
กุ้งก้ามกราม

11. shrimp
กุ้ง

12. scallops
หอยแครง

13. mussels
หอยแมลงภู่

14. oysters
หอยนางรม

15. clams
หอยกาบ

16. fresh fish
ปลาสด

17. frozen fish
ปลา**แช่แข็ง**

DELI

18. white bread
ขนมปังขาว

19. wheat bread
ขนมปังแป้งข้าวสาลีไม่ขัดสี

20. rye bread
ขนมปังแป้งไร

21. roast beef
เนื้อวัวอบ

22. corned beef
เนื้อวัวหมักปรุงรส

23. pastrami
เนื้อวัวหมักรมควัน

24. salami
ไส้กรอกชนิดหนึ่ง

25. smoked turkey
เนื้อไก่งวงรมควัน

26. American cheese
เนยแข็งอเมริกัน

27. Swiss cheese
เนยแข็งสวิส

28. cheddar cheese
เนยแข็งเชดดา

29. mozzarella cheese
เนยแข็งโมซซาเรลลา

Ways to order at the counter

I'd like some <u>roast beef</u>.
I'll have <u>a halibut steak</u> and some <u>shrimp</u>.
Could I get some <u>Swiss cheese</u>?

Pair practice. Make new conversations.

A: *What can I get for you?*
B: *I'd like some <u>roast beef</u>. How about a pound?*
A: *A pound of <u>roast beef</u> coming up!*

71

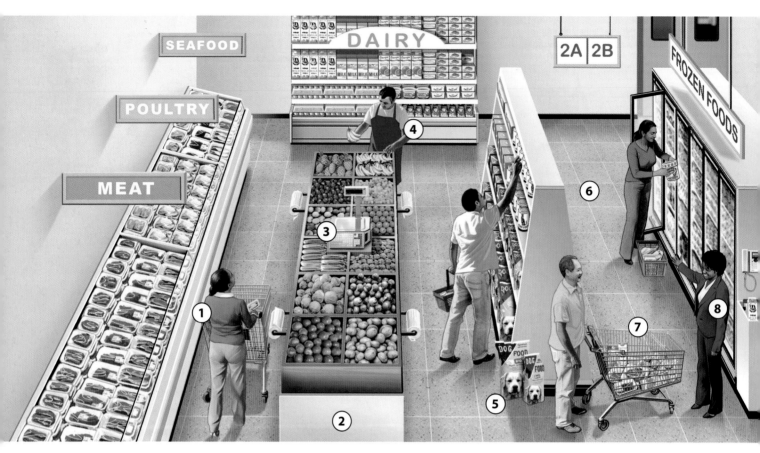

SEAFOOD

DAIRY

2A 2B

FROZEN FOODS

POULTRY

MEAT

1. customer ลูกค้า	**3.** scale ตาชั่ง / ที่ชั่งน้ำหนัก	**5.** pet food อาหารสัตว์	**7.** cart รถเข็นใส่ของ
2. produce section แผนกผักผลไม้สด	**4.** grocery clerk พนักงานในร้าน	**6.** aisle ทางเดินระหว่างชั้นวางของ	**8.** manager ผู้จัดการ

Canned Foods
อาหารกระป๋อง

17. beans
ถั่ว

18. soup
ซุป

19. tuna
ปลาทูน่า

Dairy
อาหารประเภทนมเนย

20. margarine
เนยเทียม

21. sour cream
ครีมเปรี้ยว

22. yogurt
โยเกิร์ต

Grocery Products
ผลิตภัณฑ์ของชำ

23. aluminum foil
แผ่นฟอยล์อะลูมิเนียม

24. plastic wrap
แผ่นพลาสติก

25. plastic storage bags
ถุงพลาสติกจัดเก็บอาหาร

Frozen Foods
อาหารแช่แข็ง

26. ice cream
ไอศครีม

27. frozen vegetables
ผักแช่แข็ง

28. frozen dinner
อาหารเย็นสำเร็จแช่แข็ง

Ways to ask for information in a grocery store

Excuse me, where are the carrots?

Can you please tell me where to find the dog food?

Do you have any lamb chops today?

Pair practice. Make conversations.

A: *Can you please tell me where to find the dog food?*

B: *Sure. It's in aisle 1B. Do you need anything else?*

A: *Yes, where are the carrots?*

9. shopping basket
ตะกร้าจับจ่าย

10. self-checkout
จุดจ่ายค่าสินค้าด้วยตนเอง

11. line
คิว

12. checkstand
ที่วางของรอคิดเงิน

13. cashier
พนักงานเก็บเงิน

14. bagger
พนักงานใส่ของลงถุง

15. cash register
เครื่องบันทึกจำนวนเงิน

16. bottle return
แผนกรับคืนขวด

Baking Products
ผลิตภัณฑ์ประเภท
ทำขนมปัง

29. flour
แป้ง

30. sugar
น้ำตาล

31. oil
น้ำมัน

Beverages
เครื่องดื่ม

32. apple juice
น้ำแอปเปิ้ล

33. coffee
กาแฟ

34. soda / pop
โซดา / น้ำหวาน

Snack Foods
อาหารว่าง

35. potato chips
มันฝรั่งทอดแผ่นบาง

36. nuts
ลูกนัทต่างๆ

37. candy bar
ขนมหวานชนิดแท่ง

Baked Goods
สินค้าประเภทอบ

38. cookies
คุกกี้

39. cake
เค้ก

40. bagels
ขนมปังรูปวง

Ask your classmates. Share the answers.

1. What is your favorite grocery store?
2. Do you prefer to shop alone or with friends?
3. Which foods from your country are hard to find?

Think about it. Discuss.

1. Is it better to shop every day or once a week? Why?
2. Why do grocery stores put snacks near the checkstands?
3. What's good and what's bad about small grocery stores?

Containers and Packaging ภาชนะบรรจุและบรรจุภัณฑ์

1. bottles
ขวด

2. jars
ขวดปากกว้าง

3. cans
กระป๋อง

4. cartons
กล่อง

5. containers
ภาชนะบรรจุ

6. boxes
กล่อง / หีบ

7. bags
ถุง

8. packages
หลายห่อ

9. six-packs
ชุดรวมหกชิ้น

10. loaves
ท่อน / ก้อน

11. rolls
ม้วน

12. tubes
หลอด

13. a bottle of water
น้ำหนึ่งขวด

14. a jar of jam
แยมหนึ่งขวด

15. a can of beans
ถั่วหนึ่งกระป๋อง

16. a carton of eggs
ไข่หนึ่งกล่อง

17. a container of cottage cheese
เนยแข็งคอทเทจหนึ่งภาชนะ

18. a box of cereal
ธัญพืชหนึ่งกล่อง

19. a bag of flour
แป้งหนึ่งถุง

20. a package of cookies
คุกกี้หนึ่งห่อ

21. a six-pack of soda (pop)
โซดา (น้ำหวาน) รวมกันหกกระป๋อง

22. a loaf of bread
ขนมปังหนึ่งก้อน

23. a roll of paper towels
กระดาษเช็ดมือหนึ่งม้วน

24. a tube of toothpaste
ยาสีฟันหนึ่งหลอด

Grammar Point: count and non-count

Some foods can be counted: *an apple, two apples.*
Some foods can't be counted: *some rice, some water.*
For non-count foods, count containers: *two bags of rice.*

Pair practice. Make conversations.

A: *How many boxes of cereal do we need?*
B: *We need two boxes.*

Weights and Measurements

A

A. Measure the ingredients.
ตวงเครื่องปรุง

B

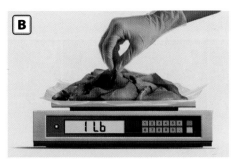

B. Weigh the food.
ชั่งน้ำหนักอาหาร

C

1 cup = 237 milliliters

C. Convert the measurements.
แปลงค่ามาตรตวงวัดต่างๆ

Liquid Measures การตวงของเหลว

①
1 fl. oz.

②
1 c.

③
1 pt.

④
1 qt.

⑤
1 gal.

Dry Measures การตวงวัดของแห้ง

⑥
1 tsp.

⑦
1 TBS.

⑧
1/4 c.

⑨
1/2 c.

⑩
1 c.

Weight น้ำหนัก

⑪

⑫

1. a fluid ounce of milk
นมหนึ่งออนซ์

2. a cup of oil
น้ำมันหนึ่งถ้วยตวง

3. a pint of frozen yogurt
โยเกิร์ตหนึ่งไพนต์ (สองถ้วยตวง)

4. a quart of milk
นมหนึ่งควอท (สี่ถ้วยตวง)

5. a gallon of water
น้ำหนึ่งแกลลอน

6. a teaspoon of salt
เกลือหนึ่งช้อนชา

7. a tablespoon of sugar
น้ำตาลหนึ่งช้อนโต๊ะ

8. a quarter cup of brown sugar
น้ำตาลแดงเศษหนึ่งส่วนสี่ถ้วยตวง

9. a half cup of raisins
องุ่นแห้งครึ่งถ้วยตวง

10. a cup of flour
แป้งหนึ่งถ้วยตวง

11. an ounce of cheese
เนยแข็งหนึ่งออนซ์

12. a pound of roast beef
เนื้อวัวอบหนึ่งปอนด์

Equivalencies

3 tsp. = 1 TBS.	2 c. = 1 pt.
2 TBS. = 1 fl. oz.	2 pt. = 1 qt.
8 fl. oz. = 1 c.	4 qt. = 1 gal.

Volume

1 fl. oz. = 30 ml
1 c. = 237 ml
1 pt. = .47 L
1 qt. = .95 L
1 gal. = 3.79 L

Weight

1 oz. = 28.35 grams (g)
1 lb. = 453.6 g
2.205 lbs. = 1 kilogram (kg)
1 lb. = 16 oz.

Food Safety ความปลอดภัยด้านอาหาร

A. **clean**
สะอาด

B. **separate**
แยกต่างหาก

C. **cook**
ทำสุก

D. **chill**
แช่เย็น

A. Clean counters!
20 SECONDS
Wash your hands!

B. Use separate cutting boards for vegetables and meat!

C. Cook to the right temperature!

D. Refrigerate leftovers quickly!

Ways to Serve Meat and Poultry วิธีต่างๆในการเสิร์ฟเนื้อและเนื้อสัตว์ปีก

1. fried chicken
ไก่ทอด

2. barbecued / grilled ribs
ซี่โครงย่าง / ย่างบาร์บิคิว

3. broiled steak
สเต็กย่างในชั้นเตาอบ

4. roasted turkey
ไก่งวงอบ

5. boiled ham
แฮมต้มสุก

6. stir-fried beef
เนื้อวัวผัด

Ways to Serve Eggs วิธีการเสิร์ฟอาหารประเภทไข่

7. scrambled eggs
ไข่กวนด้วยนมเนย

8. hardboiled eggs
ไข่ต้มแข็ง

9. poached eggs
ไข่ดาวทอดในน้ำ

10. eggs sunny-side up
ไข่ดาวสุกด้านเดียว

11. eggs over easy
ไข่ดาวสุกเล็กน้อยสองด้าน

12. omelet
ไข่เจียว

Role play. Make new conversations.

A: *How do you like your eggs?*
B: *I like them <u>scrambled</u>. And you?*
A: *I like them <u>hardboiled</u>.*

Ask your classmates. Share the answers.

1. Do you use separate cutting boards?
2. What is your favorite way to serve meat? poultry?
3. What are healthy ways of preparing meat? poultry?

Cheesy Tofu Vegetable Casserole ผักอบกับเต้าหู้เนยแข็ง

A. Preheat the oven.
เปิดเตาอบให้ร้อนก่อน

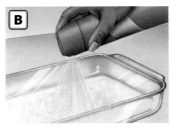

B. Grease a baking pan.
ทาน้ำมันในถาดอบ

C. Slice the tofu.
ตัดเต้าหู้เป็นแผ่น

D. Steam the broccoli.
นึ่งบร๊อคโคลี่

E. Saute the mushrooms.
ผัดเห็ด

F. Spoon sauce on top.
ตักซอสราดหน้า

G. Grate the cheese.
ขูดเนยแข็ง

H. Bake.
อบ

Easy Chicken Soup ซุปไก่แบบง่าย

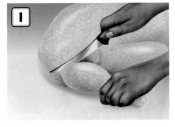

I. Cut up the chicken.
ตัดเนื้อไก่เป็นชิ้นๆ

J. Dice the celery.
หั่นต้นขึ้นฉ่ายเป็นชิ้นเล็กๆ

K. Peel the carrots.
ปอกแครอท

L. Chop the onions.
สับหัวหอม

M. Boil the chicken.
ต้มไก่

N. Add the vegetables.
เติมผัก

O. Stir.
คน

P. Simmer.
ต้มไฟอ่อน

Quick and Easy Cake เค้กแบบง่ายและรวดเร็ว

Q. Break 2 eggs into a microwave-safe bowl.
ตอกไข่ 2 ฟอง ลงในชาม
อ่างที่ใส่เตาไมโครเวฟได้

R. Mix the ingredients.
ผสมเครื่องปรุงต่างๆ

S. Beat the mixture.
ตีส่วนผสมนั้น

T. Microwave for 5 minutes.
อบในไมโครเวฟเป็นเวลา
5 นาที

1. can opener
   เครื่องเปิดกระป๋อง

2. grater
   ที่ขูด

3. steamer
   ภาชนะใช้นึ่ง

4. plastic storage container
   ภาชนะพลาสติก
   สำหรับเก็บอาหาร

5. frying pan
   กระทะสำหรับทอด

6. pot
   หม้อ

7. ladle
   ทัพพี

8. double boiler
   หม้อตุ๋น

9. wooden spoon
   ช้อนไม้

10. casserole dish
    ชามแคซเซอโรล

11. garlic press
    ที่บดกระเทียม

12. carving knife
    มีดหั่นเนื้อก้อน

13. roasting pan
    ถาดสำหรับอบหรืออย่าง

14. roasting rack
    ตะแกรงสำหรับอบหรืออย่าง

15. vegetable peeler
    มีดสำหรับปอกเปลือก

16. paring knife
    มีดปอกผลไม้

17. colander
    กระชอนล้างผัก

18. kitchen timer
    นาฬิกาตั้งเวลาในครัว

19. spatula
    พายสำหรับตักหรือป้าย

20. eggbeater
    ที่ตีไข่

21. whisk
    ที่ปั่นไข่แบบแส้

22. strainer
    กระชอน

23. tongs
    คีมคีบ

24. lid
    ฝา

25. saucepan
    กระทะก้นลึก / หม้อ

26. cake pan
    ถาดอบเค้ก

27. cookie sheet
    ถาดอบคุกกี้

28. pie pan
    ถาดอบพาย

29. pot holders
    ผ้าใช้จับของร้อน

30. rolling pin
    ไม้กลิ้งนวดแป้ง

31. mixing bowl
    ชามอ่างสำหรับผสม

Pair practice. Make new conversations.

A: *Please hand me the whisk.*

B: *Here's the whisk. Do you need anything else?*

A: *Yes, pass me the casserole dish.*

Use the new words.

Look at page 77. Name the kitchen utensils you see.

A: *Here's a grater.*

B: *This is a mixing bowl.*

1. hamburger แฮมเบอร์เกอร์	**7.** nachos นาโชส	**13.** ice-cream cone ไอศครีมใส่ในโคน	**19.** plastic utensils ช้อนส้อมมีดพลาสติก
2. french fries มันฝรั่งหั่นแท่งทอด	**8.** taco ทาโก	**14.** milkshake นมปั่น	**20.** sugar substitute น้ำตาลเทียม
3. cheeseburger ชีสเบอร์เกอร์	**9.** burrito เบอร์ริโต	**15.** donut โดนัท	**21.** ketchup ซอสมะเขือเทศ
4. onion rings หอมใหญ่ชุบแป้งทอดเป็นวง	**10.** pizza พิซซ่า	**16.** muffin มัฟฟิน	**22.** mustard มัสตาร์ด
5. chicken sandwich แซนด์วิชไก่	**11.** soda น้ำอัดลม	**17.** counterperson พนักงานที่เคาน์เตอร์	**23.** mayonnaise มายองเนส
6. hot dog ฮอทดอก	**12.** iced tea ชาเย็น	**18.** straw หลอดดูด	**24.** salad bar โต๊ะสลัด

Grammar Point: yes/no questions (*do*)

Do you like hamburgers? Yes, I do.
Do you like nachos? No, I don't.

Think about it. Discuss.

1. Do you think that fast food is bad for people? Why or why not?
2. What fast foods do you have in your country?
3. Do you have a favorite fast food restaurant? Which one?

1. **bacon**
   เบคอน

2. **sausage**
   ไส้กรอก

3. **hash browns**
   มันฝรั่งหั่นฝอยผัด

4. **toast**
   ขนมปังปิ้ง

5. **English muffin**
   ขนมปังมัฟฟินแบบอังกฤษ

6. **biscuits**
   ขนมปังแบบบิสคิด

7. **pancakes**
   แพนเค้ก

8. **waffles**
   ขนมรังผึ้ง

9. **hot cereal**
   ธัญพืชร้อน

10. **grilled cheese sandwich**
    แซนด์วิชกรอบไส้เนยแข็ง

11. **pickle**
    แตงกวาดอง

12. **club sandwich**
    แซนด์วิชบางวาง
    ซ้อนเป็นชั้น

13. **spinach salad**
    สลัดผักปวยเล้ง

14. **chef's salad**
    สลัดชนิดหนึ่ง

15. **dinner salad**
    สลัดผัก

16. **soup**
    ซุป

17. **rolls**
    ขนมปังก้อนเล็ก

18. **coleslaw**
    สลัดกะหล่ำปลี

19. **potato salad**
    สลัดมันฝรั่ง

20. **pasta salad**
    สลัดพาสต้า

21. **fruit salad**
    สลัดผลไม้

BREAKFAST SPECIAL

Served 6 a.m. to 11 a.m.

Two egg omelet with one side

HONEY

JELLY

SYRUP

LUNCH

Served 11 a.m. to 2 p.m.

All sandwiches come with soup or salad

CRACKERS

SIDE SALADS

SALAD DRESSINGS

Thousand Island

Ranch

Italian

Blue Cheese

Ways to order from a menu

I'd like a grilled cheese sandwich.

I'll have a bowl of tomato soup.

Could I get the chef's salad with ranch dressing?

Pair practice. Make conversations.

A: *I'd like a grilled cheese sandwich, please.*

B: *Anything else for you?*

A: *Yes, I'll have a bowl of tomato soup with that.*

DINNER

DESSERTS

BEVERAGES

22. roast chicken
ไก่อบ

23. mashed potatoes
มันฝรั่งบด

24. steak
สเต็ก

25. baked potato
มันฝรั่งอบ

26. spaghetti
สปาเกตตี

27. meatballs
ลูกชิ้น

28. garlic bread
ขนมปังกระเทียม

29. grilled fish
ปลาย่าง

30. rice
ข้าว

31. meatloaf
เนื้ออบดอบ

32. steamed vegetables
ผักนึ่ง

33. layer cake
เค้กชั้น

34. cheesecake
เค้กชีส

35. pie
พาย

36. mixed berries
เบอร์รี่ต่างๆผสมกัน

37. coffee
กาแฟ

38. decaf coffee
กาแฟแบบไม่มีคาเฟอีน

39. tea
ชา

40. herbal tea
ชาสมุนไพร

41. cream
ครีม

42. low-fat milk
นมไขมันต่ำ

Ask your classmates. Share the answers.

1. Do you prefer vegetable soup or chicken soup?
2. Do you prefer tea or coffee?
3. Which desserts on the menu do you like?

Role play. Order a dinner from the menu.

A: *Are you ready to order?*
B: *I think so. I'll have* the roast chicken.
A: *Would you also like…?*

1. **dining room**
   ห้องรับประทานอาหาร

2. **hostess**
   พนักงานต้อนรับหญิง

3. **high chair**
   เก้าอี้สูงสำหรับเด็ก

4. **booth**
   บริเวณจัดเป็นสัดส่วนเฉพาะ

5. **to-go box**
   กล่องใส่อาหารเพื่อนำออก

6. **patron / diner**
   ผู้รับบริการ /
   ผู้มารับประทานอาหาร

7. **menu**
   เมนู / รายการอาหาร

8. **server / waiter**
   พนักงานเสิร์ฟ /
   พนักงานเสิร์ฟชาย

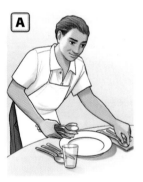   

A. **set** the table
จัดโต๊ะ

B. **seat** the customer
จัดให้ลูกค้านั่ง

C. **pour** the water
เทน้ำ

D. **order** from the menu
สั่งจากรายการอาหาร

E. **take** the order
จดรับรายการที่สั่ง

F. **serve** the meal
เสิร์ฟอาหาร

G. **clear / bus** the dishes
เก็บ / ยกกลับ ถ้วยชาม

H. **carry** the tray
ถือ/ยกถาด

I. **pay** the check
จ่ายเงินตามใบเรียกเก็บ
ค่าอาหาร

J. **leave** a tip
วางเงินทิปทิ้งไว้

More vocabulary

eat out: to go to a restaurant to eat
take out: to buy food at a restaurant and take it
home to eat

Look at the pictures.
Describe what is happening.

A: *She's seating the customer.*
B: *He's taking the order.*

9. server / waitress
พนักงานเสิร์ฟ /
พนักงานเสิร์ฟหญิง

10. dessert tray
ถาดของหวาน

11. bread basket
ตะกร้าขนมปัง

12. busser
พนักงานเก็บถ้วยชามใช้แล้ว

13. dish room
ห้องล้างชาม

14. dishwasher
เครื่องล้างชาม

15. kitchen
ครัว

16. chef
พ่อครัว

 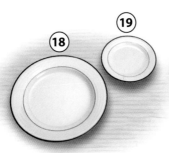  

 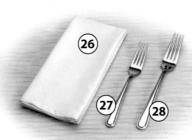  

17. place setting
การจัดวางถ้วยชาม

18. dinner plate
จานอาหารหลัก

19. bread-and-butter plate
จานขนมปังและเนย

20. salad plate
จานสลัด

21. soup bowl
ถ้วยซุป

22. water glass
แก้วน้ำ

23. wine glass
แก้วไวน์

24. cup
ถ้วยกาแฟ

25. saucer
จานรอง

26. napkin
ผ้า / กระดาษเช็ดปาก

27. salad fork
ส้อมสำหรับสลัด

28. dinner fork
ส้อมสำหรับอาหารหลัก

29. steak knife
มีดตัดสเต็ก

30. knife
มีด

31. teaspoon
ช้อนชา

32. soupspoon
ช้อนซุป

Pair practice. Make new conversations.

A: *Excuse me, this <u>spoon</u> is dirty.*

B: *I'm so sorry. I'll get you a clean <u>spoon</u> right away.*

A: *Thanks.*

Role play. Talk to a new busser.

A: *Do the <u>salad forks</u> go on <u>the left</u>?*

B: *Yes. They go <u>next to the dinner forks</u>.*

A: *What about the…?*

83

1. **live music**
   ดนตรีแสดงสด

2. **organic**
   ผักไร้สารเคมี

3. **lemonade**
   น้ำมะนาว

4. **sour**
   เปรี้ยว

5. **samples**
   ตัวอย่าง

6. **avocados**
   อะโวคาโด

7. **vendors**
   คนขาย

8. **sweets**
   ขนมหวานต่างๆ

9. **herbs**
   สมุนไพร

A. **count**
   นับ

HOT FOOD

Cara's Bakery

CHIVES DILL

PARSLEY

Look at the pictures. What do you see?

Answer the questions.

1. How many vendors are at the market today?

2. Which vegetables are organic?

3. What are the children eating?

4. What is the woman counting? Why?

Read the story.

The Farmers' Market

On Saturdays, the Novaks go to the farmers' market. They like to visit the <u>vendors</u>. Alex Novak always goes to the hot food stand for lunch. His children love to eat the fruit <u>samples</u>. Alex's father usually buys some <u>sweets</u> and <u>lemonade</u>. The lemonade is very <u>sour</u>.

Nina Novak likes to buy <u>organic</u> <u>herbs</u> and vegetables. Today, she is buying <u>avocados</u>. The market worker <u>counts</u> eight avocados. She gives Nina one more for free.

There are other things to do at the market. The Novaks like to listen to the <u>live music</u>. Sometimes they meet friends there. The farmers' market is a great place for families on a Saturday afternoon.

Think about it.

1. What's good or bad about shopping at a farmers' market?

2. Imagine you are at the farmers' market. What will you buy?

85

1. shirt
   เสื้อเชิ้ต

2. jeans
   กางเกงยีนส์

3. dress
   ชุดเสื้อกระโปรงติดกัน

4. T-shirt
   เสื้อยืดคอกลม

5. baseball cap
   หมวกแก็ป

6. socks
   ถุงเท้า

7. athletic shoes
   รองเท้ากีฬา

A. **tie**
   ผูก

BEST OF JAZZ
CONCERT

TICKETS

BEST OF JAZZ

Listen and point. Take turns.

A: *Point to the dress.*
B: *Point to the T-shirt.*
A: *Point to the baseball cap.*

Dictate to your partner. Take turns.

A: *Write dress.*
B: *Is that spelled d-r-e-s-s?*
A: *Yes. That's right.*

ONE NIGHT ONLY

DOORS OPEN AT 8:00

8. blouse
เสื้อผู้หญิง

9. handbag
กระเป๋าถือ

10. skirt
กระโปรง

11. suit
ชุดสูท

12. slacks / pants
กางเกงขายาว

13. shoes
รองเท้า

14. sweater
เสื้อกันหนาว /
เสื้อสเวตเตอร์

B. **put on**
สวม / ใส่

Ways to compliment clothes

That's a pretty <u>dress</u>!
Those are great <u>shoes</u>!
I really like your <u>baseball cap</u>!

Role play. Compliment a friend.

A: *<u>That's a pretty dress</u>! <u>Green</u> is a great color on you.*
B: *Thanks! I really like your…*

87

เสื้อผ้าแบบลำลอง แบบทำงาน
และแบบเป็นทางการ

Casual Clothes เสื้อผ้าแบบลำลอง

1. cap
   หมวกแก็ป

2. cardigan sweater
   เสื้อกันหนาวแบบเปิดด้านหน้า

3. pullover sweater
   เสื้อกันหนาวแบบสวมทางศีรษะ

4. sports shirt
   เสื้อกีฬา

5. maternity dress
   กระโปรงชุดหญิงมีครรภ์

6. overalls
   ชุดเอี๊ยม

7. knit top
   เสื้อยืด

8. capris
   กางเกงสามส่วน

9. sandals
   รองเท้าสาน

Work Clothes เสื้อผ้าชุดทำงาน

10. uniform
    เครื่องแบบ

11. business suit
    ชุดสูทนักธุรกิจ

12. tie
    เนคไท

13. briefcase
    กระเป๋าเอกสาร

More vocabulary

three piece suit: matching jacket, vest, and slacks
outfit: clothes that look nice together
in fashion / in style: clothes that are popular now

Describe the people. Take turns.

A: *She's wearing a maternity dress.*
B: *He's wearing a uniform.*

Formal Clothes เสื้อผ้าแบบเป็นทางการ

14. sports jacket / sports coat
เสื้อสูทแบบลำลอง

15. vest
เสื้อกั๊ก

16. bow tie
ไทหูกระต่าย

17. tuxedo
ชุดทักซิโด

18. evening gown
ชุดราตรี

19. clutch bag
กระเป๋าหนีบ

20. cocktail dress
ชุดคอกเทล

21. high heels
รองเท้าส้นสูง

Exercise Wear ชุดใส่ออกกำลังกาย

22. sweatshirt / hoodie
เสื้อใส่ออกกำลังกาย /
เสื้อกีฬามีส่วนคลุมศีรษะ

23. sweatpants
กางเกงใส่ออกกำลังกาย

24. tank top
เสื้อกล้าม

25. shorts
กางเกงขาสั้น

Ask your classmates. Share the answers.

1. What's your favorite outfit?

2. Do you like to wear formal clothes? Why or why not?

3. Do you prefer to exercise in shorts or sweatpants?

Think about it. Discuss.

1. What jobs require formal clothes? Uniforms?

2. What's good and bad about wearing school uniforms?

3. What is your opinion of today's popular clothing?

1. hat
หมวก

2. (over)coat
เสื้อกันหนาวตัวยาว
(คลุมถึงเข่า)

3. headband
แถบคลุมศีรษะ

4. leather jacket
เสื้อแจ๊คเก็ตหนัง

5. winter scarf
ผ้าพันคอกันหนาว

6. gloves
ถุงมือ

7. headwrap
ผ้าพันศีรษะ

8. jacket
แจ๊คเก็ต

9. parka
เสื้อกันหนาวมีหมวก
คลุมศีรษะ

10. mittens
ถุงมือแบบไม่มีนิ้ว

11. ski hat
หมวกเล่นสกี

12. leggings
กางเกงยืดแนบเนื้อ

13. earmuffs
ที่ครอบหูกันหนาว

14. down vest
เสื้อกั๊กนวมขนนก

15. ski mask
หน้ากากเล่นสกี

16. down jacket
เสื้อแจ๊คเก็ตนวมขนนก

17. umbrella
ร่ม

18. raincoat
เสื้อกันฝน

19. poncho
เสื้อแบบผ้าคลุมกันฝน

20. rain boots
รองเท้าบู๊ทกันฝน

21. trench coat
เสื้อโค๊ทกันฝน

22. swimming trunks
กางเกงขาสั้นสำหรับว่ายน้ำ

23. straw hat
หมวกฟาง

24. windbreaker
เสื้อกันลม

25. cover-up
เสื้อคลุม

26. swimsuit / bathing suit
ชุดว่ายน้ำ / ชุดอาบน้ำ

27. sunglasses
แว่นตากันแดด

Grammar Point: *should*

*It's raining. You **should** take an umbrella.*
*It's snowing. You **should** wear a scarf.*
*It's sunny. You **should** wear a straw hat.*

Pair practice. Make new conversations.

A: *It's <u>snowing</u>. You should wear <u>a scarf</u>.*
B: *Don't worry. I'm wearing my <u>parka</u>.*
A: *Good, and don't forget your <u>mittens</u>.*

Unisex Underwear
ชุดชั้นในแบบใช้ได้ทั้งหญิงชาย

1. undershirt
เสื้อรองใน

2. thermal undershirt
เสื้อรองในแบบอุ่นพิเศษ

3. long underwear
ชุดรองในแบบยาว

Men's Underwear
ชุดชั้นในของผู้ชาย

4. boxer shorts
กางเกงขาสั้นแบบนักมวย

5. briefs
กางเกงในตัวเล็ก

6. athletic supporter / jockstrap
กระจับ

Unisex Socks
ถุงเท้าหญิงชาย

7. ankle socks
ถุงเท้ายาวถึงแค่ข้อเท้า

8. crew socks
ถุงเท้ายาวถึงน่อง

9. dress socks
ถุงเท้าแบบสวยงาม

Women's Socks
ถุงเท้าหญิง

10. low-cut socks
ถุงเท้าสั้น

11. anklets
ถุงเท้ายาวถึงข้อเท้า

12. knee highs
ถุงน่องยาวถึงเข่า

Women's Underwear ชุดชั้นในของผู้หญิง

13. (bikini) panties
กางเกงในสตรี (บิกินี)

14. briefs / underpants
กางเกงในตัวเล็ก

15. body shaper / girdle
กางเกงในรัดรูป / กางเกงรัดหน้าท้อง

16. garter belt
สายยึดถุงใยบัว

17. stockings
ถุงใยบัวยาวถึงต้นขา

18. panty hose
ถุงใยบัวยาวถึงเอว

19. tights
กางเกงยึดชั้นในแบบเต็มถึงเอว

20. bra
เสื้อใน

21. camisole
เสื้อรองใน

22. full slip
ชุดรองในเต็มตัว

23. half slip
กระโปรงรองใน

Sleepwear ชุดนอน

24. pajamas
ชุดเสื้อและกางเกงนอน

25. nightgown
เสื้อนอนยาวหญิง

26. slippers
รองเท้าแตะ

27. blanket sleeper
เสื้อนอนอุ่นแบบเต็มตัว

28. nightshirt
เสื้อนอนยาวชาย

29. robe
เสื้อคลุมยาว

More vocabulary

lingerie: underwear or sleepwear for women
loungewear: very casual clothing for relaxing around the home

Ask your classmates. Share the answers.

1. What kind of socks are you wearing today?
2. What kind of sleepwear do you prefer?
3. Do you wear slippers at home?

Construction Worker

Road Worker

Automotive Painter

Food Processor

1. hard hat
หมวกแข็งใส่ทำงาน

2. work shirt
เสื้อใส่ทำงาน

3. tool belt
เข็มขัดเครื่องมือ

4. Hi-Visibility safety vest
เสื้อกั๊กที่มองเห็นได้แต่ไกล
เพื่อความปลอดภัย

5. work pants
กางเกงใส่ทำงาน

6. steel toe boots
รองเท้าบู๊ทที่มีเหล็กคลุม
ปลายเท้า

7. ventilation mask
หน้ากากระบายอากาศ

8. coveralls
เสื้อคลุมทั้งตัวสำหรับทำงาน

9. bump cap
หมวกกันชน

10. safety glasses
แว่นตานิรภัย

11. apron
ผ้ากันเปื้อน

Manager   **Salesperson**

Farmworker

Ranch Hand

12. blazer
เสื้อนอก

13. tie
เนคไท

14. polo shirt
เสื้อโปโล

15. name tag
ป้ายชื่อ

16. bandana
ผ้าคาดศีรษะ

17. work gloves
ถุงมือทำงาน

18. cowboy hat
หมวกคาวบอย

19. jeans
กางเกงยีนส์

Pair practice. Make new conversations.

A: *What do* <u>construction workers</u> *wear to work?*

B: *They wear* <u>hard hats</u> *and* <u>tool belts</u>.

A: *What do* <u>road workers</u> *wear to work?*

Use the new words.

Look at pages 166–169. Name the workplace clothing you see.

A: *He's wearing* <u>a hard hat</u>.

B: *She's wearing* <u>scrubs</u>.

Security Guard

Emergency Worker

Counterperson
Chef
Line Cook

20. security shirt
เสื้อพนักงานรักษาความ
ปลอดภัย

21. badge
เข็มกลัดเครื่องหมาย

22. security pants
กางเกงพนักงานรักษาความ
ปลอดภัย

23. helmet
หมวกนิรภัย

24. jumpsuit
ชุดเสื้อกางเกงติดกัน
สำหรับทำงาน

25. hairnet
เน็ทคลุมผม

26. smock
เสื้อคลุมทำงาน

27. disposable gloves
ถุงมือที่ใช้แล้วทิ้ง

28. chef's hat
หมวกหัวหน้าคนครัว

29. chef's jacket
เสื้อหัวหน้าคนครัว

30. waist apron
ผ้ากันเปื้อนคาดเอว

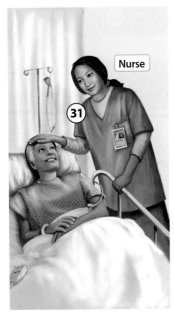

Nurse

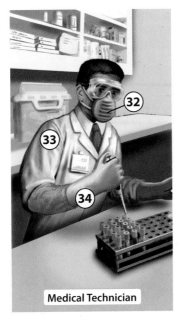

Medical Technician

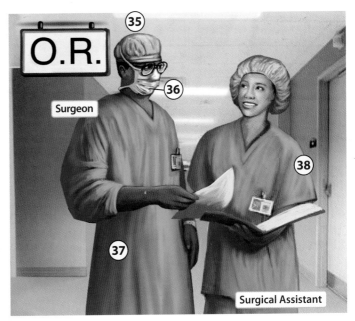

O.R.
Surgeon
Surgical Assistant

31. scrubs
เสื้อคลุมทำงานพยาบาล

32. face mask
หน้ากาก

33. lab coat
เสื้อคลุมทำงานห้องแล็บ

34. latex gloves
ถุงมือยาง

35. surgical scrub cap
หมวกศัลยกรรม (ผ่าตัด)

36. surgical mask
หน้ากากศัลยกรรม

37. surgical gown
เสื้อคลุมศัลยกรรม

38. surgical scrubs
เสื้อคลุมทำงานศัลยกรรม

Ask your classmates. Share the answers.

1. Which of these outfits would you like to wear?
2. Which of these items are in your closet?
3. Do you wear safety clothing at work? What kinds?

Think about it. Discuss.

1. What other jobs require helmets? disposable gloves?
2. Is it better to have a uniform or wear your own clothes at work? Why?

A. purchase
ซื้อ

B. wait in line
รอในคิว

1. suspenders
สายรั้งกางเกง

2. purses / handbags
กระเป๋า / กระเป๋าถือ

3. salesclerk
พนักงานขาย

4. customer
ลูกค้า

5. display case
ตู้โชว์

6. belts
เข็มขัด

13. wallet
กระเป๋าสตางค์

14. change purse / coin purse
กระเป๋าเศษสตางค์ / กระเป๋าใส่เหรียญ

15. cell phone holder
ซองใส่โทรศัพท์มือถือ

16. (wrist)watch
นาฬิกา(ข้อมือ)

17. shoulder bag
กระเป๋าสะพายไหล่

18. backpack
กระเป๋าสะพายหลัง / เป้แบกหลัง

19. tote bag
ย่าม / กระเป๋าแบบใส่ของ

20. belt buckle
หัวเข็มขัด

21. sole
พื้นรองเท้า

22. heel
ส้นรองเท้า

23. toe
นิ้วเท้า / ปลายเท้า

24. shoelaces
เชือกผูกรองเท้า

More vocabulary

gift: something you give or receive from friends or family for a special occasion
present: a gift

Grammar Point: object pronouns

My **sister** loves jewelry. I'll buy **her** a necklace.
My **dad** likes belts. I'll buy **him** a belt buckle.
My **friends** love scarves. I'll buy **them** scarves.

7. shoe department
แผนกรองเท้า

8. jewelry department
แผนกเครื่องประดับกาย

9. bracelets
กำไลข้อมือ

10. necklaces
สร้อยคอ

11. hats
หมวก

12. scarves
ผ้าพันคอ

C. **try on** shoes
ลองสวมรองเท้า

D. **assist** a customer
ช่วยเหลือลูกค้า

25. high heels
รองเท้าส้นสูง

26. pumps
รองเท้าหุ้มส้นเตี้ย

27. flats
รองเท้าส้นเตี้ย

28. boots
รองเท้าบู๊ท

29. oxfords
รองเท้าพื้นราบมีเชือกผูก

30. loafers
รองเท้าพื้นราบไม่มีเชือกผูก

31. hiking boots
รองเท้าบู๊ทสำหรับเดินเขา

32. tennis shoes
รองเท้าเทนนิส /
รองเท้ากีฬาแบบธรรมดา

33. chain
สร้อย

34. beads
ลูกปัด

35. locket
จี้ห้อยคอแบบตลับ

36. pierced earrings
ต่างหูแบบเจาะ

37. clip-on earrings
ต่างหูแบบหนีบ

38. pin
เข็มกลัด

39. string of pearls
สร้อยไข่มุก

40. ring
แหวน

Ways to talk about accessories

I need <u>a hat</u> to wear with <u>this scarf</u>.
I'd like <u>earrings</u> to go with <u>the necklace</u>.
Do you have <u>a belt</u> that would go with my <u>shoes</u>?

Role play. Talk to a salesperson.

A: *Do you have <u>boots</u> that would go with <u>this skirt</u>?*
B: *Let me see. How about <u>these brown ones</u>?*
A: *Perfect. I also need…*

Describing Clothes

การบรรยายเกี่ยวกับเสื้อผ้า

Sizes ขนาด

1. extra small
   เล็กเป็นพิเศษ

2. small
   เล็ก

3. medium
   กลาง

4. large
   ใหญ่

5. extra large
   ใหญ่เป็น
   พิเศษ

6. one-size-fits-all
   ขนาดเดียวใส่
   ได้ทุกคน

Styles แบบ

7. **crewneck** sweater
   เสื้อกันหนาว / เสื้อสเวตเตอร์**คอกลม**

8. **V-neck** sweater
   เสื้อกันหนาว**คอตัววี**

9. **turtleneck** sweater
   เสื้อกันหนาว**คอตั้ง**

10. **scoop neck** sweater
    เสื้อกันหนาว**คอกว้าง**

11. **sleeveless** shirt
    เสื้อแขนกุด

12. **short-sleeved** shirt
    เสื้อเชิ้ตแขนสั้น

13. **3/4-sleeved** shirt
    เสื้อแขนสามส่วน

14. **long-sleeved** shirt
    เสื้อแขนยาว

15. **mini**-skirt
    กระโปรงมินิ

16. **short** skirt
    กระโปรงสั้น

17. **mid-length / calf-length** skirt
    กระโปรงยาวแค่เข่า /
    กระโปรงยาวครึ่งน่อง

18. **long** skirt
    กระโปรงยาว

Patterns ลวดลาย

19. solid
    สีล้วนไม่มีลาย

20. striped
    ลายทาง

21. polka-dotted
    ลายจุด

22. plaid
    ลายแถบตาราง

23. print
    ลายพิมพ์

24. checked
    ลายตาหมากรุก

25. floral
    ลายดอก

26. paisley
    ลายเพสลี่

Ask your classmates. Share the answers.

1. Do you prefer crewneck or V-neck sweaters?
2. Do you prefer checked or striped shirts?
3. Do you prefer short-sleeved or sleeveless shirts?

Role play. Talk to a salesperson.

A: *Excuse me. I'm looking for this <u>V-neck sweater</u> in <u>large</u>.*
B: *Here's a <u>large</u>. It's on sale for $<u>19.99</u>.*
A: *Wonderful! I'll take it. I'm also looking for…*

96

Comparing Clothing การเปรียบเทียบเสื้อผ้า

27. **heavy** jacket	29. **tight** pants	31. **low** heels	33. **plain** blouse	35. **narrow** tie
แจ็คเก็ตหนา	กางเกงรัดรูป	ส้นเตี้ย	เสื้อแบบเรียบ	เนคไทแบบเส้นแคบ
28. **light** jacket	30. **loose** / **baggy** pants	32. **high** heels	34. **fancy** blouse	36. **wide** tie
แจ็คเก็ตบาง	กางเกงหลวม	ส้นสูง	เสื้อแต่งหรูหรา	เนคไทแบบเส้นกว้าง

Clothing Problems ปัญหาเกี่ยวกับเสื้อผ้า

37. It's **too small**.
ตัวเล็กเกินไป

38. It's **too big**.
ตัวใหญ่เกินไป

39. The zipper is **broken**.
ซิปเสีย

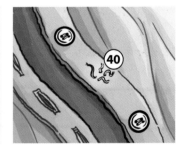

40. A button is **missing**.
กระดุมหลุดหาย

41. It's **ripped** / **torn**.
มีฉีก / ขาด

42. It's **stained**.
มีรอยเปื้อน

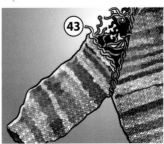

43. It's **unraveling**.
มีหลุดรุ่ย

44. It's **too expensive**.
มีราคาแพงเกินไป

More vocabulary

refund: money you get back when you return an item to the store
complaint: a statement that something is not right
customer service: the place customers go with their complaints

Role play. Return an item to a salesperson.

A: *Welcome to Shopmart. How may I help you?*
B: *This sweater is new, but it's unraveling.*
A: *I'm sorry. Would you like a refund?*

Making Clothes

การตัดเย็บเสื้อผ้า

Types of Material ชนิดของผ้า

1. cotton
ผ้าฝ้าย

2. linen
ผ้าลินิน

3. wool
ผ้าขนสัตว์

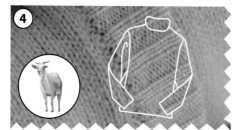

4. cashmere
ผ้าขนสัตว์ชนิดพิเศษ

5. silk
ผ้าไหม

6. leather
หนัง

A Garment Factory โรงงานตัดเย็บเสื้อผ้า

Parts of a Sewing Machine
ส่วนประกอบของจักรเย็บผ้า

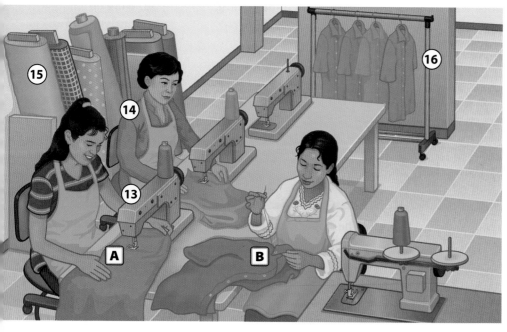

A. sew by machine
เย็บด้วยเครื่อง

B. sew by hand
เย็บด้วยมือ

13. sewing machine
จักรเย็บผ้า

14. sewing machine operator
ผู้เดินเครื่องจักรเย็บผ้า

15. bolt of fabric
ม้วนผ้า

16. rack
ราวแขวน

17. needle
เข็ม

18. needle plate
แท่นรับเข็ม

19. presser foot
เท้าเข็ม

20. feed dog / feed bar
ตัวป้อน

21. bobbin
กระสวยด้าย

More vocabulary

fashion designer: a person who makes original clothes
natural materials: cloth made from things that grow in nature
synthetic materials: cloth made by people, such as nylon

Use the new words.
Look at pages 86–87. Name the materials you see.

A: *That's* <u>*denim*</u>.
B: *That's* <u>*leather*</u>.

Types of Material ชนิดของผ้า

7. denim
ผ้าเดนิม (ผ้ายีน)

8. suede
ผ้าหนังกลับ

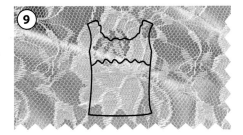

9. lace
ลูกไม้

10. velvet
กำมะหยี่

11. corduroy
ผ้าลูกฟูก

12. nylon
ผ้าไนลอน

A Fabric Store ร้านขายผ้า

Closures
ส่วนประกอบเสื้อผ้าเพื่อกระชับปิด

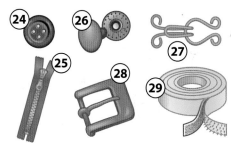

Trim ส่วนประกอบเพื่อตกแต่ง

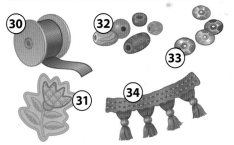

22. pattern
ต้นแบบสำหรับตัด

23. thread
ด้าย

24. button
กระดุม

25. zipper
ซิป

26. snap
กระดุมแป๊บ

27. hook and eye
ตะขอและห่วงเกี่ยว

28. buckle
หัวเข็มขัด

29. hook and loop fastener
ตะขอและห่วงรัด

30. ribbon
แถบโบว์

31. appliqué
ดอกลายสำหรับ
เย็บติด

32. beads
ลูกปัด

33. sequins
เลื่อม

34. fringe
แถบระบาย

Ask your classmates. Share the answers.

1. Can you sew?

2. What's your favorite type of material?

3. How many types of material are you wearing today?

Think about it. Discuss.

1. Do most people make or buy clothes in your country?

2. Is it better to make or buy clothes? Why?

3. Which materials are best for formal clothes?

An Alterations Shop ร้านรับซ่อมแก้ไขดัดแปลงเสื้อผ้า

1. dressmaker
   ช่างเย็บผ้า

2. dressmaker's dummy
   หุ่นสำหรับช่างเย็บผ้า

3. tailor
   ช่างตัดเสื้อผู้ชาย

4. collar
   ปกเสื้อ

5. waistband
   ขอบเอว

6. sleeve
   แขนเสื้อ

7. pocket
   กระเป๋า(เสื้อหรือกางเกง)

8. hem
   ชายกระโปรง

9. cuff
   พับชายกางเกง

Sewing Supplies เครื่องใช้ในการตัดเย็บ

10. needle
    เข็ม

11. thread
    ด้าย

12. (straight) pin
    เข็มหมุด

13. pin cushion
    หมอนปักเข็ม

14. safety pin
    เข็มกลัดซ่อนปลาย

15. thimble
    ปลอกนิ้ว

16. pair of scissors
    กรรไกร

17. tape measure
    สายวัดตัว

18. seam ripper
    เครื่องเลาะผ้า

Alterations การแก้ไขดัดแปลง

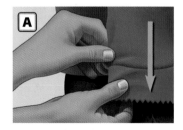

A. **Lengthen** the pants.
ทำขากางเกงให้ยาวขึ้น

B. **Shorten** the pants.
ทำขากางเกงให้สั้นลง

C. **Let out** the pants.
ขยายขนาดกางเกง

D. **Take in** the pants.
ลดขนาดกางเกง

Pair practice. Make new conversations.

A: *Would you hand me the thread?*
B: *OK. What are you going to do?*
A: *I'm going to take in these pants.*

Ask your classmates. Share the answers.

1. Is there an alterations shop near your home?
2. Do you ever go to a tailor or a dressmaker?
3. What sewing supplies do you have at home?

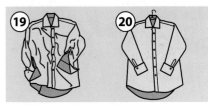

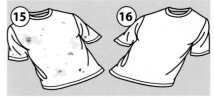

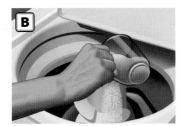

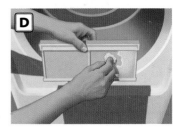

1. laundry
เสื้อผ้าที่ต้องซัก

2. laundry basket
ตะกร้าใส่เสื้อผ้าที่ต้องซัก

3. washer
เครื่องซักผ้า

4. dryer
เครื่องอบผ้า

5. dryer sheets
แผ่นสำหรับใส่ไปกับ
ผ้าเวลาอบ

6. fabric softener
น้ำยาปรับผ้านุ่ม

7. bleach
น้ำยาฟอกสี

8. laundry detergent
ผง / น้ำยาซักฟอก

9. clothesline
ราวตากผ้า

10. clothespin
แหนบหนีบผ้า

11. hanger
ไม้แขวน

12. spray starch
สเปรย์ลงแป้ง

13. iron
เตารีด

14. ironing board
โต๊ะรีดผ้า

15. **dirty** T-shirt
เสื้อยืด**สกปรก**

16. **clean** T-shirt
เสื้อยืดสะอาด

17. **wet** shirt
เสื้อ**เปียก**

18. **dry** shirt
เสื้อแห้ง

19. **wrinkled** shirt
เสื้อยับ

20. **ironed** shirt
เสื้อที่รีดแล้ว

A. Sort the laundry.
จำแนกเสื้อผ้าที่ต้องซัก

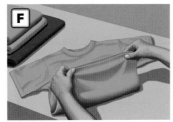

B. Add the detergent.
เติมผงซักฟอก

C. Load the washer.
ใส่เสื้อผ้าในเครื่องซัก

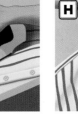

D. Clean the lint trap.
ทำความสะอาดตะแกรง
กรองใยผ้า

E. Unload the dryer.
เอาเสื้อผ้า**ออก**จากเครื่องอบ
ผ้า

F. Fold the laundry.
พับเสื้อผ้า

G. Iron the clothes.
รีดเสื้อผ้า

H. Hang up the clothes.
แขวนเสื้อผ้า

wash in cold water

no bleach

line dry

dry clean only, do not wash

Pair practice. Make new Conversations.

A: *I have to* <u>*sort the laundry*</u>. *Can you help?*
B: *Sure. Here's* <u>*the laundry basket*</u>.
A: *Thanks a lot!*

1. flyer
   ป้ายโฆษณา

2. used clothing
   เสื้อผ้าใช้แล้ว

3. sticker
   สติคเกอร์

4. folding card table
   โต๊ะเล็กแบบพับได้

5. folding chair
   เก้าอี้พับ

6. clock radio
   นาฬิกาแบบมีวิทยุ

7. VCR
   เครื่องเล่นวีซีอาร์

A. **bargain**
   ต่อรองราคา

B. **browse**
   เดินดู

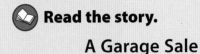

Look at the pictures.
What do you see?

Answer the questions.

1. What kind of used clothing do you see?
2. What information is on the flyer?
3. Why are the stickers different colors?
4. How much is the clock radio? the VCR?

Read the story.

A Garage Sale

Last Sunday, I had a garage sale. At 5:00 a.m., I put up flyers in my neighborhood. Next, I put price stickers on my used clothing, my VCR, and some other old things. At 7:00 a.m., I opened my folding card table and folding chair. Then I waited.

At 7:05 a.m., my first customer arrived. She asked, "How much is the sweatshirt?"

"Two dollars," I said.

She said, "It's stained. I can give you seventy-five cents." We bargained for a minute and she paid $1.00.

All day people came to browse, bargain, and buy. At 7:00 p.m., I had $85.00.

Now I know two things: Garage sales are hard work and nobody wants to buy an old clock radio!

Think about it.

1. Do you like to buy things at garage sales? Why or why not?
2. Imagine you want the VCR. How will you bargain for it?

The Body ร่างกาย

1. head
   หัว
2. hair
   ผม
3. neck
   คอ
4. chest
   หน้าอก
5. back
   หลัง
6. nose
   จมูก
7. mouth
   ปาก
8. foot
   เท้า

Listen and point. Take turns.

A: *Point to the chest.*
B: *Point to the neck.*
A: *Point to the mouth.*

Dictate to your partner. Take turns.

A: *Write hair.*
B: *Did you say hair?*
A: *That's right, h-a-i-r.*

9. leg
ขา

10. toe
นิ้วเท้า

11. eye
ตา

12. ear
หู

13. shoulder
ไหล่

14. arm
แขน

15. hand
มือ

16. finger
นิ้วมือ

Grammar Point: imperatives

*Please **touch*** your right foot.
Put your hands on your feet.
Don't put your hands on your shoulders.

Pair practice. Take turns giving commands.

A: <u>Raise</u> your <u>arms</u>.
B: <u>Touch</u> your <u>feet</u>.
A: <u>Put</u> your <u>hand</u> on your <u>shoulder</u>.

105

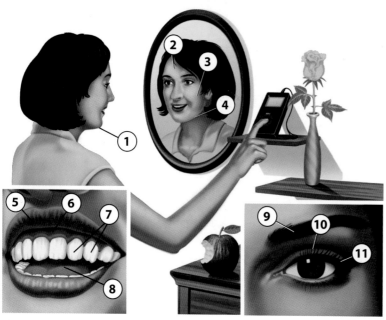

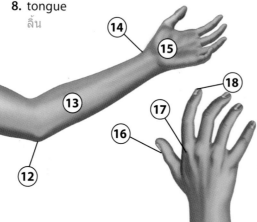

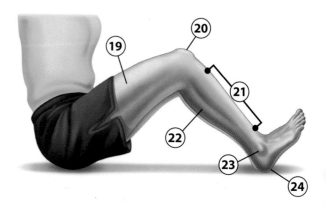

The Face
หน้า

1. chin
   คาง
2. forehead
   หน้าผาก
3. cheek
   แก้ม
4. jaw
   กราม

The Mouth
ปาก

5. lip
   ริมฝีปาก
6. gums
   เหงือก
7. teeth
   ฟัน
8. tongue
   ลิ้น

The Eye
ตา

9. eyebrow
   คิ้ว
10. eyelid
    เปลือกตา
11. eyelashes
    ขนตา

The Senses
ประสาทสัมผัส

A. see
   มองเห็น
B. hear
   ได้ยิน
C. smell
   ได้กลิ่น

D. taste
   ได้รส
E. touch
   ได้จับต้อง / สัมผัส

The Arm, Hand, and Fingers แขน มือ นิ้วมือ

12. elbow
    ศอก
13. forearm
    แขนส่วนล่าง
14. wrist
    ข้อมือ

15. palm
    ฝ่ามือ
16. thumb
    นิ้วหัวแม่มือ
17. knuckle
    ข้อนิ้วมือ
18. fingernail
    เล็บนิ้วมือ

The Leg and Foot ขาและเท้า

19. thigh
    ต้นขา
20. knee
    เข่า
21. shin
    หน้าแข้ง

22. calf
    น่อง
23. ankle
    ข้อเท้า
24. heel
    ส้นเท้า

More vocabulary

torso: the part of the body from the shoulders to the pelvis
limbs: arms and legs
toenail: the nail on your toe

Pair practice. Make new conversations.

A: *Is your <u>arm</u> OK?*
B: *Yes, but now my <u>elbow</u> hurts.*
A: *I'm sorry to hear that.*

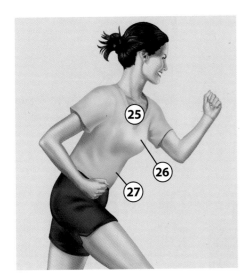

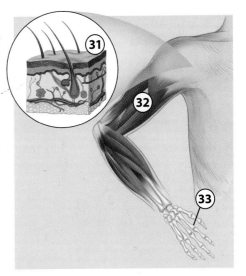

25. chest
หน้าอก

26. breast
ทรวงอก / เต้านม

27. abdomen
บริเวณท้อง

28. shoulder blade
แผงไหล่

29. lower back
หลังส่วนล่าง

30. buttocks
ก้น

31. skin
ผิวหนัง

32. muscle
กล้ามเนื้อ

33. bone
กระดูก

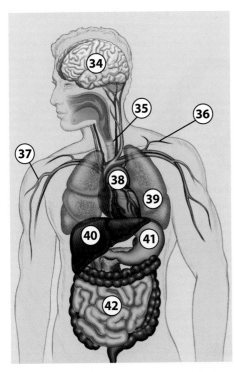

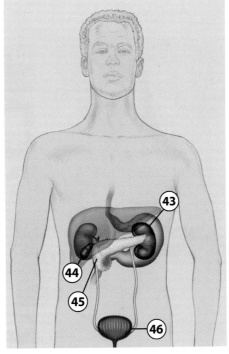

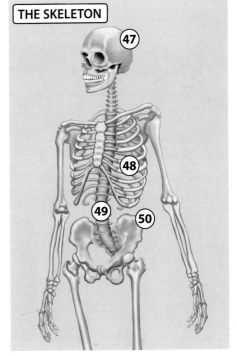

THE SKELETON

34. brain
สมอง

35. throat
ในคอ

36. artery
เส้นโลหิตแดง

37. vein
เส้นโลหิตดำ

38. heart
หัวใจ

39. lung
ปอด

40. liver
ตับ

41. stomach
กระเพาะ

42. intestines
ลำไส้

43. kidney
ไต

44. gallbladder
ถุงน้ำดี

45. pancreas
ตับอ่อน

46. bladder
กระเพาะปัสสาวะ

47. skull
กะโหลกศีรษะ

48. rib cage
กระดูกซี่โครง

49. spinal column
กระดูกสันหลัง

50. pelvis
กระดูกเชิงกราน

A. take a shower
อาบน้ำ (จากฝักบัว)

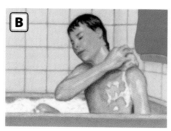

B. take a bath / **bathe**
อาบน้ำ (ในอ่าง)

C. use deodorant
ใช้ยาดับกลิ่นตัว

D. put on sunscreen
ทาครีมกันแดด

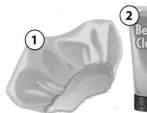

1. shower cap
   หมวกอาบน้ำ

2. shower gel
   สบู่เหลว

3. soap
   สบู่

4. bath powder
   แป้งทาตัว

5. deodorant / antiperspirant
   ยาดับกลิ่นตัว / ยากันกลิ่นเหงื่อ

6. perfume / cologne
   น้ำหอม / โคโลญ

7. sunscreen
   น้ำยากันแดด

8. sunblock
   ครีมกันแสงแดด

9. body lotion / moisturizer
   โลชั่นทาตัว /
   โลชั่นเพื่อความชุ่มชื้น

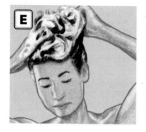
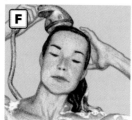

E. wash…hair
สระ…ผม

F. rinse…hair
ล้าง…(แชมพู)
ออกจากผม

G. comb…hair
หวี…ผม

H. dry…hair
เป่า…ผมให้แห้ง

I. brush…hair
แปรง…ผม

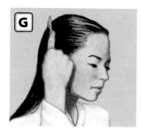
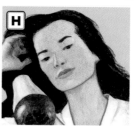

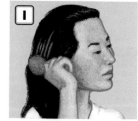

10. shampoo
    แชมพูสระผม

11. conditioner
    น้ำยาปรับเส้นผม

12. hair spray
    สเปรย์ผม

13. comb
    หวี

14. brush
    แปรง

15. pick
    หวีสับ

16. hair gel
    เจลใส่ผม

17. curling iron
    โรลไฟฟ้าม้วนผม

18. blow dryer
    เครื่องเป่าผมแห้ง

19. hair clip
    แหนบหนีบผม

20. barrette
    กิ๊บรวบผม

21. bobby pins
    กิ๊บผม

More vocabulary

unscented: a product without perfume or scent

hypoallergenic: a product that is better for people with allergies

Think about it. Discuss.

1. Which personal hygiene products should someone use before a job interview?

2. What is the right age to start wearing makeup? Why?

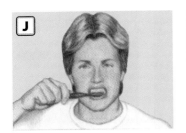

J. brush...teeth
แปรง...ฟัน

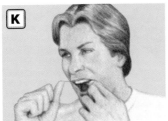

K. floss...teeth
ขัด...ฟัน (ด้วยด้ายขัดฟัน)

L. gargle
บ้วนปาก

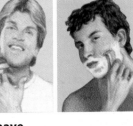

M. shave
โกน

22. toothbrush
แปรงฟัน

23. toothpaste
ยาสีฟัน

24. dental floss
ด้ายขัดฟัน

25. mouthwash
น้ำยาล้างปาก

26. electric shaver
เครื่องโกนหนวดไฟฟ้า

27. razor
มีดโกน

28. razorblade
ใบมีดโกน

29. shaving cream
ครีมโกนหนวด

30. aftershave
น้ำยาทาหลังโกน

N. cut...nails
ตัด...เล็บ

O. polish...nails
แต่ง...เล็บ

P. put on / apply
ใส่ / ทา

Q. take off / remove
เอาออก / เช็ดออก

Makeup เครื่องแต่งหน้า

31. nail clipper
เครื่องตัดเล็บ

32. emery board
ที่ฝนเล็บ

33. nail polish
สีทาเล็บ

34. eyebrow pencil
ดินสอเขียนคิ้ว

35. eye shadow
อายแชโดว์ (สีทาเปลือกตา)

36. eyeliner
ดินสอเขียนขอบตา

37. blush
สีทาแก้ม

38. lipstick
ลิปสติก

39. mascara
สีป้ายขนตา

40. foundation
ครีมรองพื้น

41. face powder
แป้งผัดหน้า

42. makeup remover
น้ำยาล้างเครื่องแต่งหน้าออก

  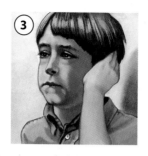  

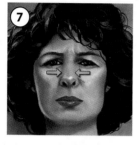 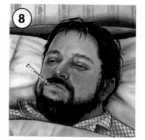  

1. headache
ปวดศีรษะ

2. toothache
ปวดฟัน

3. earache
ปวดหู

4. stomachache
ปวดท้อง

5. backache
ปวดหลัง

6. sore throat
เจ็บคอ

7. nasal congestion
คัดจมูก

8. fever / temperature
ไข้ / ตัวร้อนมีไข้

9. chills
เยือกหนาว / หนาวสั่น

10. rash
ผื่น

A. **cough**
ไอ

B. **sneeze**
จาม

C. **feel** dizzy
รู้สึกวิงเวียน

D. **feel** nauseous
รู้สึกคลื่นเหียน

E. **throw up / vomit**
อาเจียน / สำรอก

 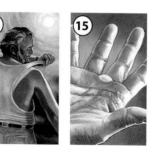  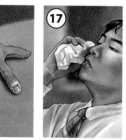

11. insect bite
แมลงกัดต่อย

12. bruise
ฟกช้ำ

13. cut
บาด

14. sunburn
ไหม้แดด

15. blister
ตุ่มพอง

16. swollen finger
นิ้วบวม

17. bloody nose
เลือดกำเดาไหล

18. sprained ankle
ข้อเท้าเคล็ด

Look at the pictures.
Describe the symptoms and injuries.

A: *He has a backache.*
B: *She has a toothache.*

Think about it. Discuss.

1. What are some common cold symptoms?

2. What do you recommend for a stomachache?

3. What is the best way to stop a bloody nose?

Common Illnesses and Childhood Diseases การเจ็บป่วยที่เป็นกันโดยทั่วไป และโรคต่างๆในวัยเด็ก

1. cold
   หวัด

2. flu
   ไข้หวัดใหญ่

3. ear infection
   หูน้ำหนวก

4. strep throat
   คออักเสบ

5. measles
   หัด

6. chicken pox
   อีสุกอีใส

7. mumps
   คางทูม

8. allergies
   ภูมิแพ้ต่างๆ

Serious Medical Conditions and Diseases โรคต่างๆและสภาวะป่วยไข้ขั้นรุนแรง

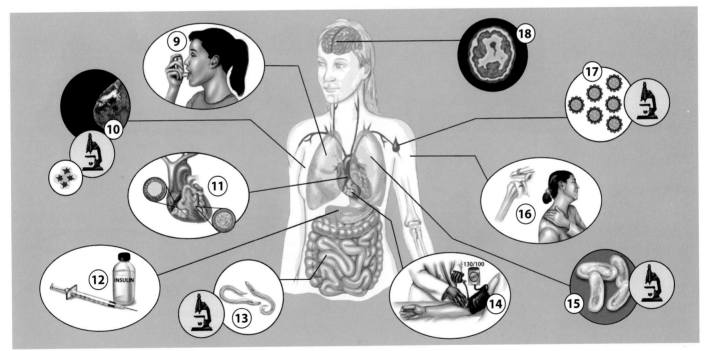

9. asthma
   หึดหอบ

10. cancer
    มะเร็ง

11. heart disease
    โรคหัวใจ

12. diabetes
    เบาหวาน

13. intestinal parasites
    พยาธิในลำไส้

14. high blood pressure / hypertension
    ความดันโลหิตสูง / ความดันสูง

15. TB (tuberculosis)
    วัณโรค (ทีบี)

16. arthritis
    ข้ออักเสบ

17. HIV (human immunodeficiency virus)
    HIV (ไวรัสที่ทำให้ภูมิคุ้มกันบกพร่อง
    นำไปสู่โรคเอดส์)

18. dementia
    โรคสมองเสื่อม

More vocabulary

AIDS (acquired immune deficiency syndrome): a medical condition that results from contracting the HIV virus

Alzheimer's disease: a disease that causes dementia

coronary disease: heart disease

infectious disease: a disease that is spread through air or water

influenza: flu

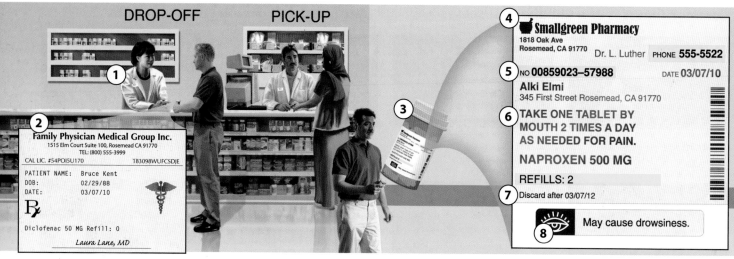

DROP-OFF   PICK-UP

Family Physician Medical Group Inc.
1515 Elm Court Suite 100, Rosemead CA 91770
TEL: (800) 555-3999
CAL LIC. #54POI5U170   183098WUFCSDJE

PATIENT NAME: Bruce Kent
DOB: 02/29/88
DATE: 03/07/10

℞

Diclofenac 50 MG Refill: 0

Laura Lane, MD

Smallgreen Pharmacy
1818 Oak Ave
Rosemead, CA 91770
Dr. L. Luther   PHONE **555-5522**

NO **00859023–57988**   DATE **03/07/10**

Alki Elmi
345 First Street Rosemead, CA 91770

**TAKE ONE TABLET BY
MOUTH 2 TIMES A DAY
AS NEEDED FOR PAIN.**

NAPROXEN 500 MG

REFILLS: 2

Discard after 03/07/12

May cause drowsiness.

1. pharmacist
   เภสัชกร

2. prescription
   ใบสั่งยาจากแพทย์

3. prescription medication
   ยาตามใบสั่งแพทย์

4. prescription label
   ป้ายใบสั่งยาจากแพทย์

5. prescription number
   หมายเลขใบสั่งยา

6. dosage
   ขนาดรับประทาน / ที่ใช้

7. expiration date
   วันหมดอายุ

8. warning label
   ฉลากคำเตือน

Medical Warnings คำเตือนทางการแพทย์

A. **Take** with food or milk.
กินพร้อมกับอาหารหรือนม

B. **Take** one hour before eating.
กินก่อนอาหารหนึ่งชั่วโมง

C. **Finish** all medication.
ใช้ยานั้นให้หมด

D. **Do not take** with dairy products.
อย่ากินพร้อมกับอาหารประเภทนมเนย

E. **Do not drive or operate** heavy machinery.
อย่าขับรถหรือทำงานกับเครื่องจักรกล

F. **Do not drink** alcohol.
อย่าดื่มเครื่องดื่มมีนเมา

More vocabulary

prescribe medication: to write a prescription
fill prescriptions: to prepare medication for patients
pick up a prescription: to get prescription medication

Role play. Talk to the pharmacist.

A: *Hi. I need to pick up a prescription for* <u>Jones</u>.
B: *Here's your medication,* <u>Mr. Jones</u>. *Take these* <u>once a day with milk or food</u>.

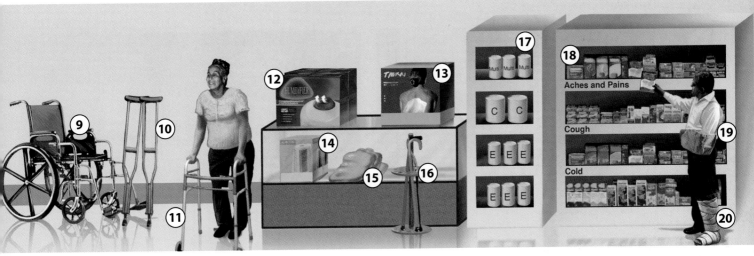

9. wheelchair
ที่นั่งล้อเข็น

10. crutches
ไม้พยุงตัว

11. walker
ที่พยุงตัวช่วยเดิน

12. humidifier
เครื่องทำความชื้น

13. heating pad
แผ่นทำความอบอุ่น

14. air purifier
เครื่องกรองอากาศ

15. hot water bottle
ถุงน้ำร้อน

16. cane
ไม้เท้า

17. vitamins
วิตามิน

18. over-the-counter medication
ยาที่ซื้อได้โดยไม่มีใบสั่งแพทย์

19. sling
ผ้าช่วยพยุง / ผ้าพันแผล

20. cast
เฝือก

Types of Medication ชนิดของยา

21. pill
ยาเม็ด

22. tablet
เม็ดแบน

23. capsule
แคปซูล

24. ointment
ยาแบบขี้ผึ้ง
(แบบทาๆ)

25. cream
ครีม

Over-the-Counter Medication ยาที่ซื้อได้โดยไม่มีใบสั่งแพทย์

26. pain reliever
ยาบรรเทาปวด

27. cold tablets
ยาเม็ดแก้หวัด

28. antacid
ยาลดกรดในกระเพาะ

29. cough syrup
ยาแก้ไอชนิดน้ำเชื่อม

30. throat lozenges
ยาอมแก้เจ็บคอ

31. eye drops
ยาหยอดตา

32. nasal spray
ยาพ่นในจมูก

33. inhaler
ที่สูดดม

Ways to talk about medication

Use *take* for pills, tablets, capsules, and cough syrup.
Use *apply* for ointments and creams.
Use *use* for drops, nasal sprays, and inhalers.

Ask your classmates. Share the answers.

1. What pharmacy do you go to?
2. Do you ever ask the pharmacist for advice?
3. Do you take any vitamins? Which ones?

Ways to Get Well วิธีที่จะหายป่วย

A. Seek medical attention.
ขอรับการตรวจรักษาจากแพทย์

B. Get bed rest.
นอนพักผ่อน

C. Drink fluids.
ดื่มน้ำ / เครื่องดื่มของเหลว

D. Take medicine.
กินยา

Ways to Stay Well วิธีที่จะมีสุขภาพดี ไม่ป่วยไข้

E. Stay fit.
ออกกำลังกายเป็นประจำ

F. Eat a healthy diet.
กินอาหารที่มีประโยชน์

G. Don't smoke.
อย่าสูบบุหรี่

H. Have regular checkups.
มีการตรวจร่างกายเป็นประจำ

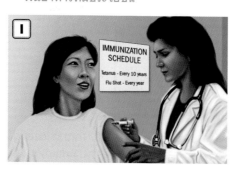

I. Get immunized.
รับการฉีดวัคซีน

J. Follow medical advice.
ปฏิบัติตามคำแนะนำของแพทย์

More vocabulary

injection: medicine in a syringe that is put into the body

immunization / vaccination: an injection that stops serious diseases

Ask your classmates. Share the answers.

1. How do you stay fit?
2. What do you do when you're sick?
3. Which two foods are a part of your healthy diet?

Types of Health Problems ประเภทของปัญหาด้านสุขภาพ

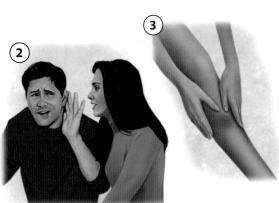

1. vision problems
ปัญหาด้านการมองเห็น

2. hearing loss
การสูญเสียความสามารถในการได้ยิน

3. pain
ความเจ็บปวด

4. stress
ตึงเครียด

5. depression
ซึมเศร้า

Help with Health Problems ความช่วยเหลือเกี่ยวกับปัญหาด้านสุขภาพ

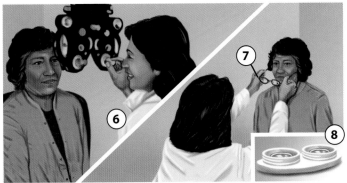

6. optometrist
ผู้เชี่ยวชาญด้านสายตา

8. contact lenses
คอนแทคเลนส์

9. audiologist
ผู้เชี่ยวชาญด้านการได้ยิน

10. hearing aid
เครื่องช่วยการได้ยิน

7. glasses
แว่นตา

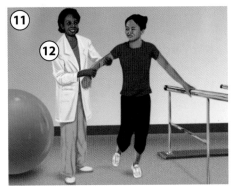

11. physical therapy
กายภาพบำบัด

13. talk therapy
การบำบัดปัญหาด้านการพูด

15. support group
กลุ่มสนับสนุน

12. physical therapist
ผู้ชำนาญด้านกายภาพบำบัด

14. therapist
ผู้ชำนาญการบำบัด

Ways to ask about health problems

Are you in pain?
Are you having vision problems?
Are you experiencing depression?

Pair practice. Make new conversations.

A: *Do you know a good optometrist?*
B: *Why? Are you having vision problems?*
A: *Yes, I might need glasses.*

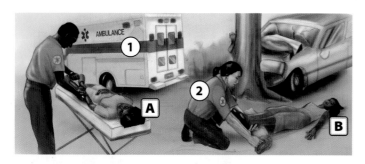

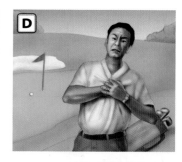

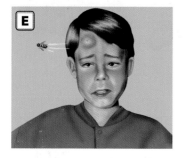

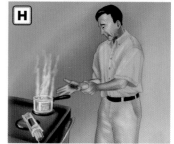

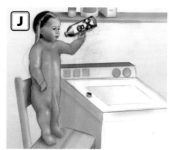

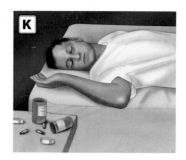

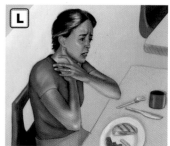

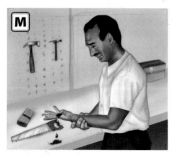

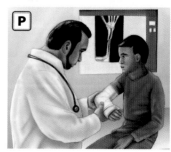

1. ambulance
รถพยาบาล

2. paramedic
แพทย์ / ผู้ช่วยแพทย์ภาคสนาม

A. be unconscious
หมดสติ

B. be in shock
มีอาการช็อค แน่นิ่ง

C. be injured / **be** hurt
ได้รับบาดเจ็บ / บาดเจ็บ

D. have a heart attack
มีอาการโรคหัวใจ

E. have an allergic reaction
มีอาการโรคภูมิแพ้

F. get an electric shock
ถูกไฟฟ้าดูด

G. get frostbite
มีอาการเนื้อเยื่อตายเนื่องจากความเย็นจัด

H. burn (your)self
ไหม้ (ตนเอง)

I. drown
จมน้ำ

J. swallow poison
กลืนสิ่งเป็นพิษ

K. overdose on drugs
กินยาเกินขนาด

L. choke
สำลัก

M. bleed
เลือดไหล

N. can't breathe
หายใจไม่ได้

O. fall
หกล้ม

P. break a bone
กระดูกหัก

Grammar Point: past tense

For past tense add –ed:
burned, drowned, swallowed,
overdosed, choked

These verbs are different (irregular):

be – was, were	bleed – bled
have – had	can't – couldn't
get – got	break – broke

First Aid การปฐมพยาบาล

1. first aid kit
ชุดปฐมพยาบาล

2. first aid manual
คู่มือการปฐมพยาบาล

3. medical emergency bracelet
สร้อยข้อมือระบุเกี่ยวกับ
ผู้ป่วยในกรณีฉุกเฉิน

Inside the Kit ภายในชุดปฐมพยาบาล

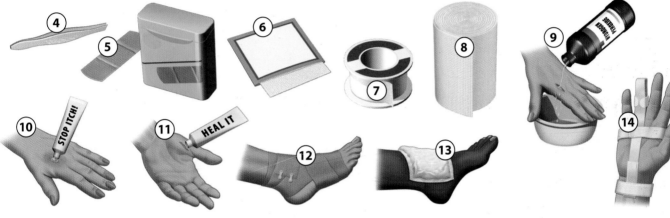

 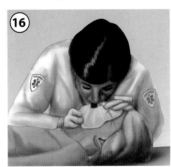 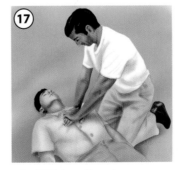 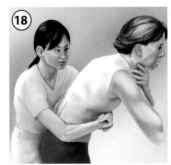

4. tweezers
คีมเล็ก

5. adhesive bandage
แผ่นปิดแผล

6. sterile pad
แผ่นฆ่าเชื้อแล้ว

7. sterile tape
เทปฆ่าเชื้อแล้ว

8. gauze
ผ้าก๊อสใช้ปิดแผล

9. hydrogen peroxide
น้ำยาล้างแผล

10. antihistamine cream
ครีมแก้อาการแพ้

11. antibacterial ointment
ยาฆ่าเชื้อแบคทีเรีย

12. elastic bandage
ผ้ายืดพันแผล

13. ice pack
ถุงน้ำแข็ง

14. splint
เครื่องดาม

First Aid Procedures ขั้นตอนการปฐมพยาบาล

15. stitches
ฝีเย็บ

16. rescue breathing
ช่วยการหายใจ

17. CPR (cardiopulmonary resuscitation)
การปั๊มช่วยให้หัวใจ
และปอดฟื้น

18. Heimlich maneuver
การช่วยคนสำลักหลอดลม
อุดตัน โดยวิธีเฮมลิค

Pair practice. Make new conversations.

A: *What do we need in the first aid kit?*
B: *We need <u>tweezers</u> and <u>gauze</u>.*
A: *I think we need <u>sterile tape</u>, too.*

Think about it. Discuss.

1. What are the three most important first aid items? Why?
2. Which first aid procedures should everyone know? Why?
3. What are some good places to keep a first aid kit?

In the Waiting Room ในห้องนั่งรอ

HEALTH FIRST
Name: Andre Zolmar
Group Number: 98765
Membership Number: 60756789

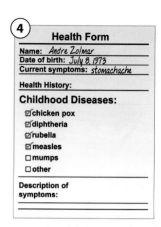

Health Form
Name: *Andre Zolmar*
Date of birth: *July 8, 1973*
Current symptoms: *stomachache*

Health History:

Childhood Diseases:
☑ chicken pox
☑ diphtheria
☑ rubella
☑ measles
☐ mumps
☐ other

Description of symptoms:

1. appointment
การนัดหมาย

2. receptionist
พนักงานต้อนรับ

3. health insurance card
บัตรประกันสุขภาพ

4. health history form
แบบฟอร์มประวัติสุขภาพ

In the Examining Room ในห้องตรวจ

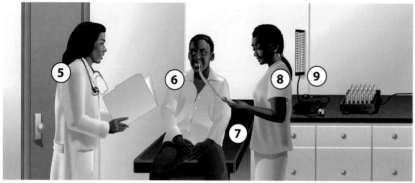

5. doctor
หมอ

6. patient
คนไข้

7. examination table
โต๊ะ / เตียงตรวจ

8. nurse
พยาบาล

9. blood pressure gauge
เครื่องวัดความดันโลหิต

10. stethoscope
อุปกรณ์ตรวจฟังเสียงหัวใจ

11. thermometer
อุปกรณ์วัดไข้

12. syringe
เข็มฉีดยา

Medical Procedures ขั้นตอนการดูแลรักษา

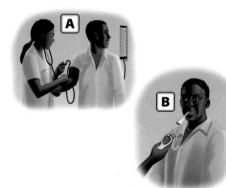

A. check…blood pressure
ตรวจวัด...ความดันโลหิต

B. take…temperature
วัด...ไข้

C. listen to…heart
ฟัง...การเต้นของหัวใจ

D. examine…eyes
ตรวจดู...ตา

E. examine…throat
ตรวจดู...คอ

F. draw…blood
เจาะเก็บ...เลือด

Grammar Point: future tense with *will* + verb

To show a future action, use *will* + verb.
The subject pronoun contraction of *will* is *-'ll*.
She **will draw** your blood. = She'**ll draw** your blood.

Role play. Talk to a medical receptionist.

A: *Will the nurse <u>examine my eyes</u>?*
B: *No, but she'll <u>draw your blood</u>.*
A: *What will the doctor do?*

Dentistry ทันตกรรม

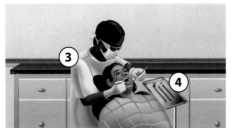

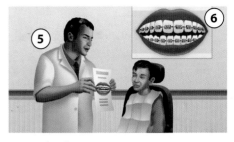

1. dentist
   ทันตแพทย์
2. dental assistant
   ผู้ช่วยงานทันตกรรม

3. dental hygienist
   ผู้ทำความสะอาดฟัน
4. dental instruments
   เครื่องมือทันตกรรม

Orthodontics ทันตกรรมจัดฟัน

5. orthodontist
   ทันตแพทย์ผู้เชี่ยวชาญการจัดฟัน
6. braces
   อุปกรณ์การดัดฟัน

Dental Problems ปัญหาเกี่ยวกับฟัน

 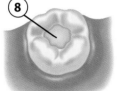  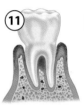

7. cavity / decay
   ฟันเป็นรู / ฟันผุ
8. filling
   การอุดฟัน

9. crown
   ครอบฟัน
10. dentures
    การขุดฟันเทียม

11. gum disease
    โรคเหงือก
12. plaque
    คราบหินปูน

An Office Visit การไปพบทันตแพทย์

A. **clean**…teeth
   ทำความสะอาด…ฟัน

B. **take** x-rays
   ถ่าย…เอ็กซ์เรย์

C. **numb** the mouth
   ฉีดยาชาในปาก

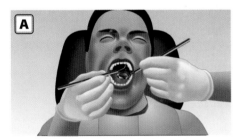

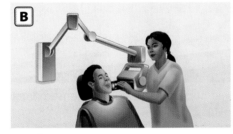

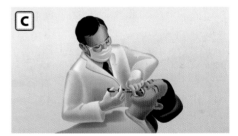

D. **drill** a tooth
   กรอฟัน

E. **fill** a cavity
   อุดฟันที่เป็นรู

F. **pull** a tooth
   ถอนฟัน

Ask your classmates. Share the answers.

1. Do you know someone with braces? Who?
2. Do dentists make you nervous? Why or why not?
3. How often do you go to the dentist?

Role play. Talk to a dentist.

A: *I think I have a cavity.*
B: *Let me take a look.*
A: *Will I need a filling?*

Medical Specialists แพทย์ผู้เชี่ยวชาญเฉพาะทาง

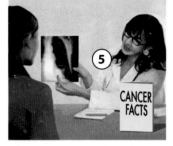

1. internist
แพทย์ผู้เชี่ยวชาญเกี่ยวกับ
อวัยวะภายใน

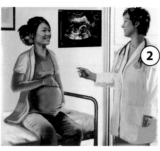

2. obstetrician
สูติแพทย์

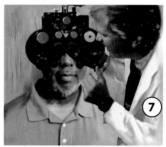

3. cardiologist
แพทย์ผู้เชี่ยวชาญด้านโรค
หัวใจ

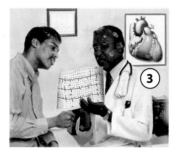

4. pediatrician
กุมารแพทย์

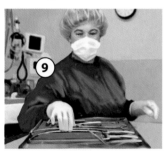

5. oncologist
ผู้เชี่ยวชาญเกี่ยวกับเนื้องอก
วิทยา

6. radiologist
ผู้เชี่ยวชาญเกี่ยวกับ
รังสีวิทยา

7. ophthalmologist
จักษุแพทย์

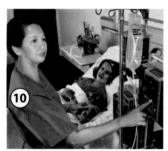

8. psychiatrist
จิตแพทย์

Nursing Staff เจ้าหน้าที่พยาบาล

9. surgical nurse
พยาบาลห้องผ่าตัด

10. registered nurse (RN)
พยาบาลที่มีวุฒิและได้ขึ้น
ทะเบียนแล้ว

11. licensed practical nurse (LPN)
พยาบาลที่มีใบอนุญาตให้
ปฏิบัติงานบางส่วน

12. certified nursing assistant (CNA)
ผู้ช่วยพยาบาลที่ได้รับ
การรับรอง

Hospital Staff เจ้าหน้าที่โรงพยาบาล

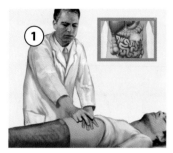

13. administrator
ผู้บริหาร

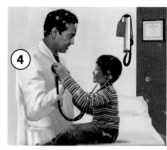

14. admissions clerk
เจ้าหน้าที่แผนกรับผู้ป่วย

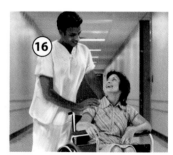

15. dietician
นักโภชนาการ

16. orderly
พนักงานทั่วไปใน
โรงพยาบาล

More vocabulary

Gynecologists examine and treat women.
Nurse practitioners can give medical exams.
Nurse midwives deliver babies.

Chiropractors move the spine to improve health.
Orthopedists treat bone and joint problems.

A Hospital Room ห้องในโรงพยาบาล

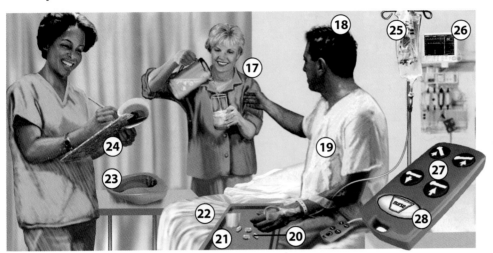

Lab ห้องแล็บ

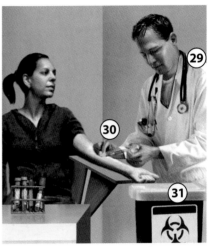

17. volunteer
อาสาสมัคร

18. patient
ผู้ป่วย

19. hospital gown
เสื้อผู้ป่วย

20. medication
ยา

21. bed table
โต๊ะข้างเตียง

22. hospital bed
เตียงผู้ป่วย

23. bed pan
กระโถนแบบนอน

24. medical chart
แผงข้อมูลการดูแลรักษา

25. IV (intravenous drip)
การให้ยาหรือน้ำเกลือแบบ
หยดเข้าเส้น

26. vital signs monitor
เครื่องเฝ้าระวังสัญญาณ
สำคัญของชีวิต

27. bed control
ตัวควบคุมปรับระดับเตียง

28. call button
ปุ่มเรียก

29. phlebotomist
ผู้ชำนาญการเจาะหลอดโลหิตดำ

30. blood work / blood test
งานเกี่ยวกับโลหิต / ตรวจสอบโลหิต

31. medical waste disposal
ที่ทิ้งขยะด้านการแพทย์

Emergency Room Entrance
ทางเข้าห้องฉุกเฉิน

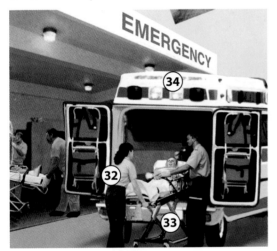

Operating Room
ห้องผ่าตัด

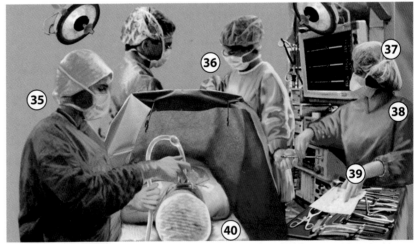

32. emergency medical technician (EMT)
เจ้าหน้าที่ห้องฉุกเฉิน

33. stretcher / gurney
เปลหาม / เตียงล้อเลื่อน

34. ambulance
รถพยาบาล

35. anesthesiologist
วิสัญญีแพทย์

36. surgeon
ศัลยแพทย์
(หมอผ่าตัด)

37. surgical cap
หมวกศัลยกรรม

38. surgical gown
เสื้อคลุมศัลยกรรม

39. surgical gloves
ถุงมือศัลยกรรม

40. operating table
โต๊ะผ่าตัด

Dictate to your partner. Take turns.

A: *Write this sentence. She's a volunteer.*
B: *She's a what?*
A: *Volunteer. That's v-o-l-u-n-t-e-e-r.*

Role play. Ask about a doctor.

A: *I need to find a good surgeon.*
B: *Dr. Jones is a great surgeon. You should call him.*
A: *I will! Please give me his number.*

1. low-cost exam
การตรวจที่เสีย
ค่าใช้จ่ายน้อย

2. acupuncture
การฝังเข็ม

3. booth
พื้นที่จัดเฉพาะเพื่อ
แสดงสินค้า

4. yoga
โยคะ

5. aerobic exercise
กายบริหารแบบ
แอโรบิค

6. demonstration
การสาธิต

7. sugar-free
ที่ปราศจากน้ำตาล

8. nutrition label
ฉลากแสดงคุณค่า
อาหาร

A. **check** ... pulse
ตรวจ...ชีพจร

B. **give** a lecture
ให้...คำแนะนำ
(สั่งสอน)

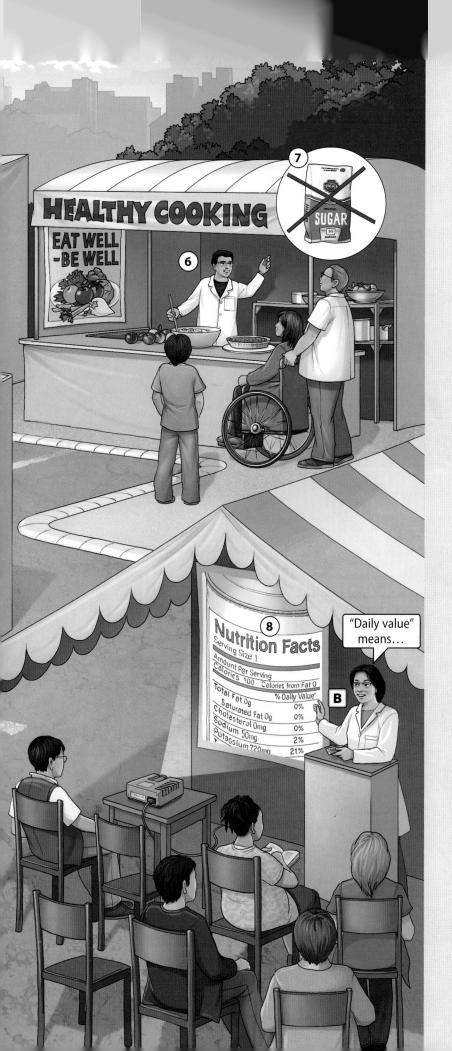

Look at the picture. What do you see?

Answer the questions.

1. How many different booths are there at the health fair?
2. What kinds of exams and treatments can you get at the fair?
3. What kinds of lectures and demonstrations are there?
4. How much is an acupuncture treatment? a medical screening?

Read the story.

A Health Fair

Once a month the Fadool Health Clinic has a health fair. You can get a low-cost medical exam at one booth. The nurses check your blood pressure and check your pulse. At another booth you can get a free eye exam. And an acupuncture treatment is only $5.00.

You can learn a lot at the fair. This month a doctor is giving a lecture on nutrition labels. There is also a demonstration on sugar-free cooking. You can learn to do aerobic exercise and yoga, too.

Do you want to get healthy and stay healthy? Then come to the Fadool Clinic Health Fair!

Think about it.

1. Which booths at this fair look interesting to you? Why?
2. Do you read nutrition labels? Why or why not?

1. parking garage
   อาคารที่จอดรถ

2. office building
   อาคารสำนักงาน

3. hotel
   โรงแรม

4. Department of
   Motor Vehicles
   หน่วยงานรัฐแผนก
   ยานยนต์

5. bank
   ธนาคาร

6. police station
   สถานีตำรวจ

7. bus station
   สถานีรถโดยสาร

8. city hall
   ศาลากลาง

Listen and point. Take turns.

A: *Point to the bank.*
B: *Point to the hotel.*
A: *Point to the restaurant.*

Dictate to your partner. Take turns.

A: *Write bank.*
B: *Is that spelled b-a-n-k?*
A: *Yes, that's right.*

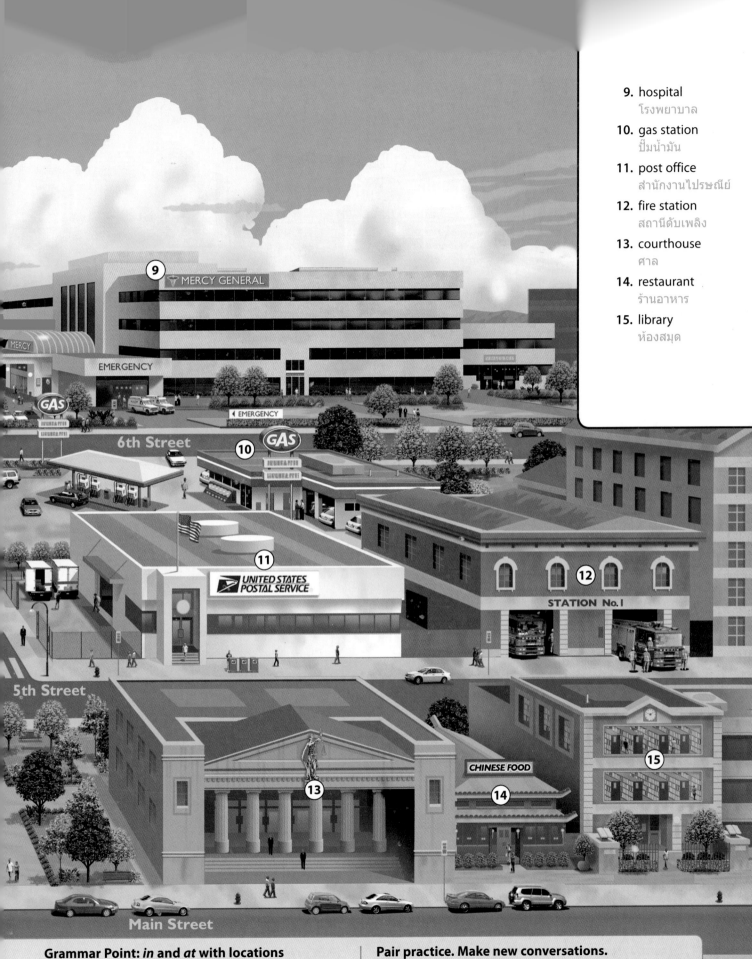

9. hospital
โรงพยาบาล

10. gas station
ปั๊มน้ำมัน

11. post office
สำนักงานไปรษณีย์

12. fire station
สถานีดับเพลิง

13. courthouse
ศาล

14. restaurant
ร้านอาหาร

15. library
ห้องสมุด

MERCY GENERAL

MERCY

EMERGENCY

◄ EMERGENCY

GAS

GAS

6th Street

UNITED STATES POSTAL SERVICE

STATION No. I

5th Street

CHINESE FOOD

Main Street

Grammar Point: *in* and *at* with locations

Use *in* when you are inside the building. *I am in (inside) the bank*. Use *at* to describe your general location. *I am at the bank*.

Pair practice. Make new conversations.

A: *I'm in the <u>bank</u>. Where are you?*
B: *I'm at the <u>bank</u>, too, but I'm outside.*
A: *OK. I'll meet you there.*

1. **stadium**
   อาคารสนามกีฬา

2. **construction site**
   พื้นที่การก่อสร้าง

3. **factory**
   โรงงาน

4. **car dealership**
   ตัวแทนขายรถยนต์

5. **mosque**
   สุเหร่า

6. **movie theater**
   โรงภาพยนตร์

7. **shopping mall**
   ศูนย์การค้า

8. **furniture store**
   ร้านขายเครื่องเรือน

9. **school**
   โรงเรียน

10. **gym**
    โรงยิม / โรงบริหารร่างกาย

11. **coffee shop**
    ร้านกาแฟ / คอฟฟี่ชอป

12. **motel**
    ที่พักแรมที่มีห้องพักพร้อมที่จอดรถ

Ways to state your destination using *to* and *to the*

Use *to* for schools, churches, and synagogues.
*I'm going **to** _school_.*
Use ***to the*** for all other locations. *I have to go **to the** _bakery_.*

Pair practice. Make new conversations.

A: *Where are you going today?*
B: *I'm going to _school_. How about you?*
A: *I have to go to the _bakery_.*

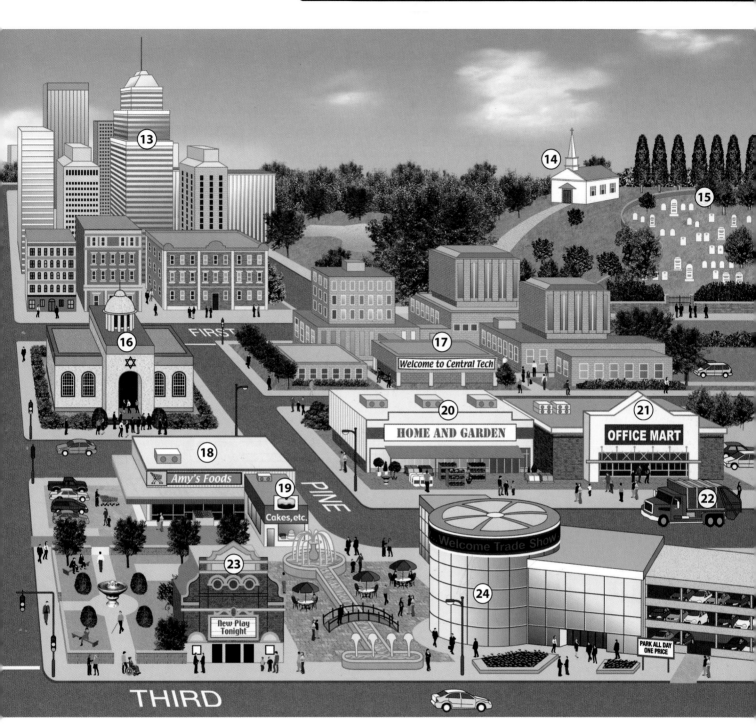

13. skyscraper / high-rise
ตึกระฟ้า / อาคารสูง

14. church
โบสถ์

15. cemetery
สุสาน

16. synagogue
สุเหร่ายิว

17. community college
วิทยาลัยชุมชน

18. supermarket
ซูเปอร์มาร์เก็ต / ร้านขายของชำ

19. bakery
ร้านขนมปัง

20. home improvement store
ร้านขายอุปกรณ์การซ่อมแซมบ้าน

21. office supply store
ร้านขายเครื่องใช้ในสำนักงาน

22. garbage truck
รถขยะ

23. theater
โรงมหรสพ

24. convention center
ศูนย์การประชุม

Ways to give locations

The mall is on 2nd Street.
The mall is on the corner of 2nd and Elm.
The mall is next to the movie theater.

Ask your classmates. Share the answers.

1. Where's your favorite coffee shop?
2. Where's your favorite supermarket?
3. Where's your favorite movie theater?

127

1. laundromat
   ร้านซักผ้าด้วยเครื่อง

2. dry cleaners
   ร้านซักแห้ง

3. convenience store
   ร้านสะดวกซื้อ

4. pharmacy
   ร้านขายยา

5. parking space
   ที่จอดรถ

6. handicapped parking
   ที่จอดรถสำหรับคนพิการ

7. corner
   มุม

8. traffic light
   ไฟสัญญาณจราจร

9. bus
   รถโดยสาร

10. fast food restaurant
    ร้านอาหารจานด่วน

11. drive-thru window
    หน้าต่างให้ขับรถผ่านไปสั่งซื้ออาหาร

12. newsstand
    ร้านหนังสือพิมพ์ข้างถนน

13. mailbox
    ตู้ไปรษณีย์ / ตู้รับจดหมาย

14. pedestrian
    คนเดินเท้า

15. crosswalk
    ทางข้าม

A. **cross** the street
   ข้ามถนน

B. **wait for** the light
   รอสัญญาณไฟ

C. **jaywalk**
   เดินข้ามถนนนอกทาง

Pair practice. Make new conversations.

A: *I have a lot of errands to do today.*
B: *Me, too. First, I'm going to* the laundromat.
A: *I'll see you there after I stop at* the copy center.

Think about it. Discuss.

1. Which businesses are good to have in a neighborhood? Why?
2. Would you like to own a small business? If yes, what kind? If no, why not?

16. bus stop ป้ายจอดรถประจำทาง	22. bike จักรยาน	28. cart ล้อเข็น
17. donut shop ร้านขายโดนัท	23. pay phone โทรศัพท์แบบหยอดเหรียญ	29. street vendor คนขายของข้างถนน
18. copy center ร้านถ่ายเอกสาร	24. sidewalk ฟุทบาท / ทางเดินข้างถนน	30. childcare center ศูนย์ดูแลเด็ก
19. barbershop ร้านตัดผมชาย	25. parking meter มิเตอร์จอดรถ	D. **ride** a bike ขี่จักรยาน
20. video store ร้านวิดีโอ	26. street sign ป้ายชื่อถนน	E. **park** the car จอดรถ
21. curb ขอบถนน	27. fire hydrant หัวฉีดดับเพลิง	F. **walk** a dog พาหมามาเดิน

More vocabulary

neighborhood: the area close to your home
do errands: to make a short trip from your home to
buy or pick up things

Ask your classmates. Share the answers.

1. What errands do you do every week?
2. What stores do you go to in your neighborhood?
3. What things can you buy from a street vendor?

1. music store
   ร้านดนตรี / เพลง

2. jewelry store
   ร้านเครื่องประดับกาย

3. nail salon
   ร้านแต่งเล็บ

4. bookstore
   ร้านหนังสือ

5. toy store
   ร้านของเล่น

6. pet store
   ร้านสัตว์เลี้ยงดูเล่น

7. card store
   ร้านขายการ์ด

8. florist
   ร้านดอกไม้

9. optician
   ร้านแว่นตา

10. shoe store
    ร้านรองเท้า

11. play area
    บริเวณเด็กเล่น

12. guest services
    แผนกบริการข้อมูลของศูนย์

More vocabulary

beauty shop: hair salon

men's store: men's clothing store

gift shop: a store that sells t-shirts, mugs, and other small gifts

Pair practice. Make new conversations.

A: *Where is the florist?*

B: *It's on the first floor, next to the optician.*

13. department store
ห้างใหญ่

14. travel agency
ตัวแทนบริการท่องเที่ยว

15. food court
ศูนย์อาหาร

16. ice cream shop
ร้านไอศครีม

17. candy store
ร้านลูกกวาด

18. hair salon
ร้านทำผม

19. maternity store
ร้านขายของสำหรับหญิงมีครรภ์

20. electronics store
ร้านขายเครื่องไฟฟ้า

21. elevator
ลิฟท์

22. cell phone kiosk
ซุ้มขายโทรศัพท์มือถือ

23. escalator
บันไดเลื่อน

24. directory
ผังแสดงชื่อและที่ตั้งร้าน

Ways to talk about plans

Let's go to the <u>card store</u>.
I have to go to the <u>card store</u>.
I want to go to the <u>card store</u>.

Role play. Talk to a friend at the mall.

A: *Let's go to the <u>card store</u>. I need to buy <u>a card</u> for <u>Maggie's birthday</u>.*
B: *OK, but can we go to the <u>shoe store</u> next?*

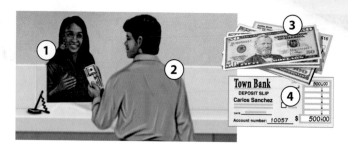

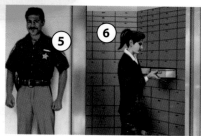

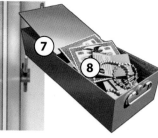

1. teller
พนักงานธนาคาร

2. customer
ลูกค้า

3. deposit
นำฝาก

4. deposit slip
ใบนำฝาก

5. security guard
เจ้าหน้าที่รักษาความปลอดภัย

6. vault
ห้องนิรภัย / ตู้เซฟ

7. safety deposit box
ตู้ฝากนิรภัย

8. valuables
สิ่งของมีค่าต่างๆ

Opening an Account การเปิดบัญชี

9. account manager
ผู้จัดการบัญชี

10. passbook
สมุดคู่ฝาก

11. savings account number
หมายเลขบัญชีฝากประจำ

12. check book
สมุดเช็ค

13. check
เช็ค

14. checking account number
หมายเลขบัญชีกระแสรายวัน

15. ATM card
บัตรเอทีเอ็ม

16. bank statement
ใบแสดงดุลบัญชี

17. balance
ดุลบัญชี / ยอดคงเหลือ

A. Cash a check.
ขึ้นเงินจากเช็ค

B. Make a deposit.
ทำการฝาก

C. Bank online.
ธนาคารทางออนไลน์

The ATM (Automated Teller Machine) เอทีเอ็ม (ATM - เครื่องรับจ่ายเงินอัตโนมัติ)

D. Insert your ATM card.
สอดบัตรเอทีเอ็มของคุณ

E. Enter your PIN.*
ใส่รหัส (PIN) ของคุณ

F. Withdraw cash.
ถอนเงินสด

G. Remove your card.
เอาบัตรของคุณออก

*PIN = personal identification number

A. get a library card
รับบัตรห้องสมุด

B. look for a book
ค้นหาหนังสือ

C. check out a book
ตรวจยืมหนังสือออก

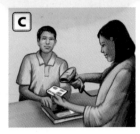

D. return a book
คืนหนังสือ

E. pay a late fine
จ่ายค่าปรับที่คืนช้า

1. **library clerk**
   เจ้าหน้าที่ห้องสมุด

2. **circulation desk**
   โต๊ะตรวจยืมและคืนหนังสือ

3. **library patron**
   สมาชิกห้องสมุด

4. **periodicals**
   วารสาร

5. **magazine**
   นิตยสาร

6. **newspaper**
   หนังสือพิมพ์

7. **headline**
   พาดหัวข่าว

8. **atlas**
   สมุดแผนที่

9. **reference librarian**
   บรรณารักษ์แผนกหนังสือ
   อ้างอิง

10. **self-checkout**
    ตรวจยืมออกด้วยตนเอง

11. **online catalog**
    รายการหนังสือทาง
    ออนไลน์

12. **picture book**
    หนังสือภาพ

13. **biography**
    ประวัติบุคคล

14. **title**
    ชื่อเรื่อง

15. **author**
    ผู้แต่ง

16. **novel**
    นวนิยาย

17. **audiobook**
    หนังสือแบบฟังเสียง

18. **videocassette**
    เทปวิดีโอ

19. **DVD**
    ดีวีดี

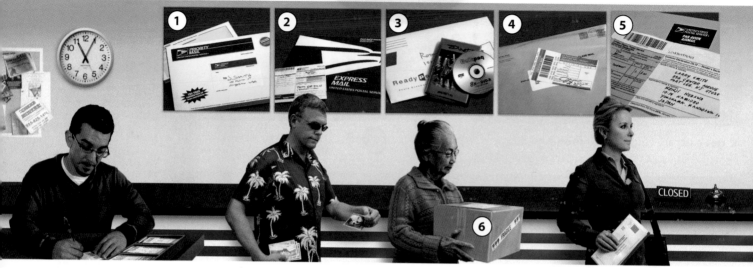

1. **Priority Mail®**
   ไปรษณีย์ด่วนไม่ประกันความรวดเร็ว

2. **Express Mail®**
   ไปรษณีย์ด่วนพิเศษแบบประกันความรวดเร็ว

3. **media mail**
   ไปรษณีย์สำหรับวัสดุสื่อ

4. **Certified Mail™**
   ไปรษณีย์ลงทะเบียน

5. **airmail**
   ไปรษณีย์ทางอากาศ

6. **ground post / parcel post**
   ไปรษณีย์ภาคพื้นดิน (ธรรมดา) / วัสดุไปรษณีย์

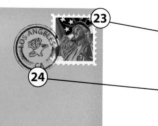

13. **letter**
    จดหมาย

14. **envelope**
    ซองจดหมาย

15. **greeting card**
    บัตรอวยพร

16. **post card**
    ไปรษณียบัตร

17. **package**
    หีบห่อ

18. **book of stamps**
    สมุดแสตมป์

19. **postal forms**
    แบบฟอร์มไปรษณีย์

20. **letter carrier**
    พนักงานส่งจดหมาย

21. **return address**
    ที่อยู่ของผู้ส่ง

22. **mailing address**
    จ่าหน้าผู้รับ

23. **stamp**
    แสตมป์

24. **postmark**
    ดราไปรษณีย์

21 Sonya Enriquez
258 Quentin Avenue
Los Angeles, CA 90068-141

22 Cindy Lin
807 Glenn Drive
Charlotte, NC 28201

Ways to talk about sending mail

This letter has to <u>get there tomorrow</u>. (**Express Mail®**)
This letter has to <u>arrive in two days</u>. (**Priority Mail®**)
This letter can go in <u>regular mail</u>. (**First Class**)

Pair practice. Make new conversations.

A: *Hi. <u>This letter has to get there tomorrow</u>.*
B: *You can send it by <u>Express Mail®</u>.*
A: *OK. I need <u>a book of stamps</u>, too.*

7. postal clerk
พนักงานไปรษณีย์

8. scale
ตาชั่ง

9. post office box (PO box)
ตู้ไปรษณีย์ (ตู้ ปณ.)

10. automated postal center (APC)
ศูนย์บริการไปรษณีย์อัตโนมัติ

11. stamp machine
เครื่องขายแสตมป์

12. mailbox
ตู้รับไปรษณีย์ / ตู้รับจดหมาย

Sending a Card การส่งการ์ด

A. Write a note in a card.
เขียนข้อความลงในการ์ด

B. Address the envelope.
เขียนที่อยู่ (จ่าหน้า) ซอง

C. Put on a stamp.
ติดแสตมป์

D. Mail the card.
ส่งการ์ดทางไปรษณีย์

E. Deliver the card.
นำส่งการ์ดไปถึง

F. Receive the card.
รับการ์ด

G. Read the card.
อ่านการ์ด

H. Write back.
เขียนตอบกลับ

More vocabulary

overnight / next day mail: Express Mail®
postage: the cost to send mail
junk mail: mail you don't want

Think about it. Discuss.

1. What kind of mail do you send overnight?
2. Do you want to be a letter carrier? Why or why not?
3. Do you get junk mail? What do you do with it?

135

Quiet Please

No Talking

BUCKLE UP / IT'S THE LAW!

CLOSED

Vehicle Registration →

Forms

Handbooks

Information

California Driver Handbook

104 105
106 107
108 109

109

1. DMV handbook
คู่มือดีเอ็มวี

2. testing area
บริเวณทดสอบ

3. DMV clerk
เจ้าหน้าที่ดีเอ็มวี

4. photo
ภาพถ่าย

5. fingerprint
ลายพิมพ์นิ้วมือ

6. vision exam
การตรวจสายตา

7. window
ช่อง / หน้าต่าง

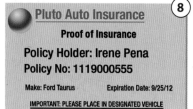

Pluto Auto Insurance
Proof of Insurance
Policy Holder: Irene Pena
Policy No: 1119000555
Make: Ford Taurus   Expiration Date: 9/25/12
IMPORTANT: PLEASE PLACE IN DESIGNATED VEHICLE

CALIFORNIA
DRIVERS LICENSE
EXPIRES 07-29-16   N57881049   CLASS
Irene Pena
1313 Balboa Blvd,
Van Nuys, CA 91064
Irene Pena
DONOR   DOB 7-29-70

AUG *California* 2012
2OPD008

8. proof of insurance
หลักฐานการประกัน

9. driver's license
ใบขับขี่

10. expiration date
วันหมดอายุ

11. driver's license number
หมายเลขใบขับขี่

12. license plate
ป้ายทะเบียนรถ

13. registration sticker / tag
สติดเกอร์การจดทะเบียน / ป้าย

More vocabulary

expire: a license is no good, or **expires**, after the expiration date
renew a license: to apply to keep a license before it expires
vanity plate: a more expensive, personal license plate

Ask your classmates. Share the answers.

1. How far is the DMV from your home?
2. Do you have a driver's license? If yes, when does it expire? If not, do you want one?

Getting Your First License การขอใบขับขี่เป็นครั้งแรก

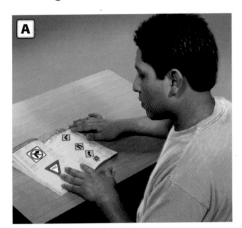

A. Study the handbook.
ศึกษาคู่มือ

B. Take a driver education course.*
เข้าเรียนวิชาการขับขี่

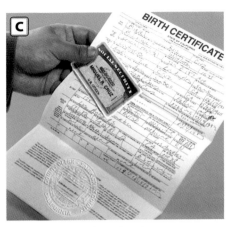

C. Show your identification.
แสดงเอกสารระบุตัวบุคคล

D. Pay the application fee.
จ่ายค่าสมัคร

E. Take a written test.
ทำแบบทดสอบ

F. Get a learner's permit.
รับใบอนุญาตสำหรับผู้กำลังหัดขับ

G. Take a driver's training course.*
เข้าฝึกหัดวิชาการขับขี่

H. Pass a driving test.
ผ่านการทดสอบการขับขี่

I. Get your license.
รับใบขับขี่

*Note: This is not required for drivers 18 and older.

Ways to request more information

What do I do next?
What's the next step?
Where do I go from here?

Role play. Talk to a DMV clerk.

A: *I want to apply for* <u>*a driver's license*</u>.
B: *Did you* <u>*study the handbook*</u>?
A: *Yes, I did.* <u>*What do I do next*</u>?

137

Federal Government รัฐบาลกลาง

Legislative Branch
ฝ่ายนิติบัญญัติ

1. U.S. Capitol
   อาคารรัฐสภา
   สหรัฐฯ
2. Congress
   สภาคองเกรส
3. House of
   Representatives
   สภาผู้แทนราษฎร
4. congressperson
   สมาชิกรัฐสภา
5. Senate
   วุฒิสภา (สภาสูง)
6. senator
   วุฒิสมาชิก

Executive Branch
ฝ่ายบริหาร

7. White House
   ทำเนียบขาว
8. president
   ประธานาธิบดี
9. .vice president
   รองประธานาธิบดี
10. Cabinet
    คณะรัฐมนตรี

Judicial Branch
ฝ่ายตุลาการ

11. Supreme Court
    ศาลสูง
12. justices
    ผู้พิพากษา
13. chief justice
    หัวหน้าผู้พิพากษา

The Military การทหาร

14. Army
    กองทัพบก
15. Navy
    กองทัพเรือ
16. Air Force
    กองทัพอากาศ
17. Marines
    นาวิกโยธิน
18. Coast Guard
    ยามฝั่ง
19. National Guard
    กองรักษาการณ์
    แห่งชาติ

State Government รัฐบาลระดับรัฐ

20. governor
ผู้ว่าการรัฐ

21. lieutenant governor
รองผู้ว่าการรัฐ

22. state capital
เมืองหลวงของรัฐ

23. Legislature
ฝ่ายนิติบัญญัติ

24. assemblyperson
สมาชิกสภาแห่งรัฐ

25. state senator
วุฒิสมาชิกของรัฐ

City Government รัฐบาลท้องถิ่น (ระดับเมือง)

26. mayor
นายกเทศมนตรี

27. city council
สภาผู้บริหาร

28. councilperson
สมาชิกสภาผู้บริหาร / สมาชิกเทศมนตรี

An Election การเลือกตั้ง

A. **run for** office
สมัครรับเลือกเข้าดำรง
ตำแหน่ง

29. political campaign
การหาเสียงสนับสนุนทาง
การเมือง

B. **debate**
การโต้วาที

30. opponent
ฝ่ายตรงกันข้าม (คู่แข่งขัน)

C. **get elected**
ได้รับเลือกตั้ง

31. election results
ผลการเลือกตั้ง

D. **serve**
เข้าปฏิบัติงาน

32. elected official
ผู้ได้รับเลือกตั้ง

More vocabulary

term: the period of time an elected official serves

political party: a group of people with the same
political goals

Think about it. Discuss.

1. Should everyone have to serve in the military? Why or
why not?

2. Would you prefer to run for city council or mayor? Why?

Responsibilities หน้าที่ความรับผิดชอบ

A. vote
ลงคะแนนเสียง

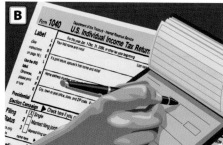

B. pay taxes
เสียภาษี

C. obey the law
เคารพกฎหมาย

D. register with Selective Service*
ขึ้นทะเบียนไว้กับหน่วยงานคัดเลือก

E. serve on a jury
ทำหน้าที่ในคณะลูกขุน

F. be informed
รับรู้ข้อมูลข่าวสาร

Citizenship Requirements ข้อกำหนดของสถานภาพการเป็นพลเมือง

G. be 18 or older
มีอายุไม่ต่ำกว่า 18 ปี

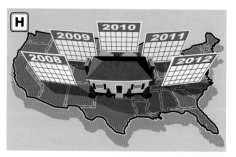

H. live in the U.S. for 5 years
อาศัยอยู่ในสหรัฐอเมริกาเป็นเวลา 5 ปี

I. take a citizenship test
ทำข้อทดสอบเพื่อการเป็นพลเมือง

Rights สิทธิ

1. peaceful assembly
การชุมนุมอย่างสันติ

2. free speech
เสรีภาพในการพูด

3. freedom of religion
เสรีภาพในการนับถือ
ศาสนา

4. freedom of the press
เสรีภาพทางสื่อสิ่งพิมพ์

5. fair trial
การพิจารณาคดีอย่าง
เป็นธรรม

*Note: All males 18 to 26 who live in the U.S. are required to register with Selective Service.

A. arrest a suspect
จับกุมผู้ต้องสงสัย

1. police officer
เจ้าหน้าที่ตำรวจ

2. handcuffs
กุญแจมือ

B. hire a lawyer / hire an attorney
ว่าจ้างนักกฎหมาย / ว่าจ้างทนาย

3. guard
เจ้าหน้าที่รักษาการณ์

4. defense attorney
ทนายฝ่ายจำเลย

Bail is set at $20,000.

C. appear in court
ปรากฏตัวในศาล

5. defendant
จำเลย

6. judge
ผู้พิพากษา

D. stand trial
เข้ารับการพิจารณาคดี

7. courtroom
ห้องพิจารณาคดี

8. jury
คณะลูกขุน

9. evidence
หลักฐาน

10. prosecuting attorney
ทนายฝ่ายดำเนินคดี / อัยการ

11. witness
พยาน

12. court reporter
ผู้ทำรายงานศาล

13. bailiff
ตำรวจศาล / เจ้าหน้าที่ออกหมายจับ

Guilty.

E. convict the defendant
พิพากษาจำเลย

14. verdict*
คำตัดสิน

7 years

F. sentence the defendant
ตัดสินลงโทษจำเลย

G. go to jail / go to prison
ไปเข้าตาราง / เข้าคุก

15. convict / prisoner
ผู้ถูกตัดสินว่าผิด / นักโทษ

H. be released
ถูกปล่อยตัว / พ้นโทษ

*Note: There are two possible verdicts, "guilty" and "not guilty."

Look at the pictures.
Describe what happened.

A: The <u>police officer</u> <u>arrested a suspect</u>.
B: He put <u>handcuffs</u> on him.

Think about it. Discuss.

1. Would you want to serve on a jury? Why or why not?
2. Look at the crimes on page 142. What sentence would you give for each crime? Why?

141

1. vandalism
   การทำลายทรัพย์สิน
2. burglary
   การลักขโมย

3. assault
   การทำร้ายร่างกาย
4. gang violence
   กลุ่มอันธพาล /
   ก่อเหตุรุนแรง

5. drunk driving
   การขับรถขณะมึนเมา
6. illegal drugs
   ยาเสพติด /
   ยาผิดกฎหมาย

7. arson
   การลอบวางเพลิง
8. shoplifting
   การขโมยของในร้าน

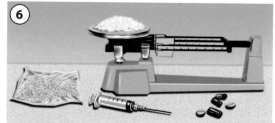

9. identity theft
   การขโมยใช้ข้อมูล
   ส่วนบุคคล
10. victim
    ผู้รับเคราะห์

11. mugging
    การทำร้ายแย่งชิงทรัพย์
12. murder
    ฆาตกรรม
13. gun
    ปืน

More vocabulary

steal: to take money or things from someone illegally
commit a crime: to do something illegal
criminal: someone who does something illegal

Think about it. Discuss.

1. Is there too much crime on TV or in the movies? Explain.
2. How can communities help stop crime?

A. **Walk** with a friend.
เดินกับเพื่อน

B. **Stay** on well-lit streets.
อยู่บนถนนที่มีแสงไฟสว่างดี

C. **Conceal** your PIN number.
ปกปิดหมายเลขรหัสประจำ
ตัวของคุณ

D. **Protect** your purse or
wallet.
ระวังกระเป๋าถือหรือ
กระเป๋าสตางค์ของคุณ

E. **Lock** your doors.
ล็อคประตูของคุณ

F. Don't **open** your door to
strangers.
อย่าเปิดประตูให้คนแปลกหน้า

G. Don't **drink** and **drive**.
อย่าขับรถในขณะมีนเมา

H. **Shop** on secure websites.
ซื้อของทางออนไลน์จาก
เว็บไซท์ที่ปลอดภัย

I. **Be** aware of your
surroundings.
ตระหนักถึงสิ่งแวดล้อมของ
คุณเสมอ

J. **Report** suspicious packages.
รายงาน หากพบเห็นหีบห่อ
น่าสงสัย

K. **Report** crimes to the
police.
รายงานอาชญากรรมต่างๆ
ต่อเจ้าหน้าที่ตำรวจ

L. **Join** a Neighborhood
Watch.
เข้าร่วมกิจกรรมเฝ้าระวังใน
ชุมชน

More vocabulary

sober: not drunk
designated drivers: sober drivers who drive
drunk people home safely

Ask your classmates. Share the answers.

1. Do you feel safe in your neighborhood?
2. Look at the pictures. Which of these things do you do?
3. What other things do you do to stay safe?

1. lost child
   เด็กหาย

2. car accident
   อุบัติเหตุทางรถ

3. airplane crash
   เครื่องบินตก

4. explosion
   เหตุระเบิด

5. earthquake
   แผ่นดินไหว

6. mudslide
   โคลนถล่ม

7. forest fire
   ไฟป่า

8. fire
   ไฟไหม้

9. firefighter
   พนักงานดับเพลิง

10. fire truck
    รถดับเพลิง

Ways to report an emergency

First, give your name. *My name is* <u>*Tim Johnson*</u>.
Then, state the emergency and give the address.
There was <u>*a car accident*</u> *at* <u>*219 Elm Street*</u>.

Role play. Call 911.

A: *911 Emergency Operator.*
B: *My name is* <u>*Lisa Diaz*</u>. *There is* <u>*a fire*</u> *at* <u>*323 Oak Street*</u>.
Please hurry!

11. drought
ภัยแล้ง

12. famine
ข้าวยากหมากแพง

13. blizzard
พายุหิมะ

14. hurricane
พายุรุนแรง

15. tornado
พายุหมุน

16. volcanic eruption
ภูเขาไฟระเบิด

17. tidal wave / tsunami
คลื่นยักษ์ / สึนามิ

18. avalanche
หิมะถล่ม

19. flood
น้ำท่วม

20. search and rescue team
คณะผู้ค้นหาและช่วยชีวิต

Ask your classmates. Share the answers.

1. Which natural disaster worries you the most?
2. Which natural disaster worries you the least?
3. Which disasters are common in your local area?

Think about it. Discuss.

1. What organizations can help you in an emergency?
2. What are some ways to prepare for natural disasters?
3. Where would you go in an emergency?

Before an Emergency ก่อนเกิดเหตุฉุกเฉิน

A. Plan for an emergency.
วางแผนการรับมือกับเหตุฉุกเฉิน

1. meeting place
สถานที่ประชุม

2. out-of-state contact
ผู้ที่ติดต่อได้ภายนอกรัฐ

3. escape route
ทางหนี

4. gas shut-off valve
วาล์วปิดแก๊ส

5. evacuation route
เส้นทางอพยพผู้คนออกไป

B. Make a disaster kit.
ทำชุดบรรเทาทุกข์

6. warm clothes
เสื้อผ้ากันหนาว

7. blankets
ผ้าห่ม

8. can opener
เครื่องเปิดกระป๋อง

9. canned food
อาหารกระป๋อง

10. packaged food
อาหารสำเร็จ

11. bottled water
น้ำดื่มบรรจุขวด

12. moist towelettes
ผ้าเย็น

13. toilet paper
กระดาษชำระ

14. flashlight
ไฟฉาย

15. batteries
แบตเตอรี่

16. matches
ไม้ขีดไฟ

17. cash and coins
เงินสดและเหรียญ

18. first aid kit
ชุดปฐมพยาบาล

19. copies of ID and credit cards
สำเนาเอกสารแสดงตัวบุคคลและบัตรเครดิต

20. copies of important papers
สำเนาเอกสารสำคัญต่างๆ

Pair practice. Make new conversations.

A: *What do we need for our disaster kit?*
B: *We need blankets and matches.*
A: *I think we also need batteries.*

Ask your classmates. Share the answers.

1. Who would you call first after an emergency?
2. Do you have escape and evacuation routes planned?
3. Are you a calm person in case of an emergency?

During an Emergency ในระหว่างเหตุฉุกเฉิน

C. Watch the weather.
ติดตามข่าวสภาพอากาศ

Hurricane Watch

D. Pay attention to warnings.
ใส่ใจดูหรือฟังคำเตือน

Hurricane Watch

E. Remain calm.
ตั้งอยู่ในความสงบ

Go to a shelter.

F. Follow directions.
ปฏิบัติตามคำสั่ง

Shelter

G. Help people with disabilities.
ช่วยเหลือผู้ที่มีความพิการ

Shelter

H. Seek shelter.
เสาะหาที่หลบภัย

I. Stay away from windows.
อยู่ให้ไกลจากหน้าต่าง

J. Take cover.
เข้าที่กำบัง

K. Evacuate the area.
อพยพออกไปจากพื้นที่

After an Emergency หลังเหตุฉุกเฉิน

We're OK.

Great.

L. Call out-of-state contacts.
โทรศัพท์ถึงผู้ที่ติดต่อได้ภายนอกรัฐ

M. Clean up debris.
เก็บกวาดสิ่งปรักหักพัง

N. Inspect utilities.
ตรวจสอบสาธารณูปโภคต่างๆ
(เช่น ไฟฟ้า แก๊ส)

Ways to say you're OK

I'm fine.
We're OK here.
Everything's under control.

Ways to say you need help

We need help.
Someone is hurt.
I'm injured. Please get help.

Role play. Prepare for an emergency.

A: *They just issued <u>a hurricane</u> warning.*
B: *OK. We need to stay calm and follow directions.*
A: *What do we need to do first?*

1. **graffiti**
การขีดเขียนเลอะ
เทอะในที่สาธารณะ

2. **litter**
ขยะเกลื่อนกลาด

3. **streetlight**
ไฟถนน

4. **hardware store**
ร้านขายอุปกรณ์
ก่อสร้าง

5. **petition**
การร้องเรียน

A. **give** a speech
กล่าวคำปราศรัย

B. **applaud**
ปรบมือ

C. **change**
เปลี่ยน

Look at the pictures.
What do you see?

Answer the questions.

1. What were the problems on Main Street?

2. What was the petition for?

3. Why did the city council applaud?

4. How did the people change the street?

 Read the story.

Community Cleanup

Marta Lopez has a donut shop on Main Street. One day she looked at her street and was very upset. She saw graffiti on her donut shop and the other stores. Litter was everywhere. All the streetlights were broken. Marta wanted to fix the lights and clean up the street.

Marta started a petition about the streetlights. Five hundred people signed it. Then she gave a speech to the city council. The council members voted to repair the streetlights. Everyone applauded. Marta was happy, but her work wasn't finished.

Next, Marta asked for volunteers to clean up Main Street. The hardware store manager gave the volunteers free paint. Marta gave them free donuts and coffee. The volunteers painted and cleaned. They changed Main Street. Now Main Street is beautiful and Marta is proud.

Think about it.

1. What are some problems in your community? How can people help?

2. Imagine you are Marta. What do you say in your speech to the city council?

1. car
   รถยนต์
2. passenger
   ผู้โดยสาร
3. taxi
   แท็กซี่
4. motorcycle
   รถมอเตอร์ไซค์
5. street
   ถนน
6. truck
   รถบรรทุก / รถกระบะ
7. train
   รถไฟ
8. (air)plane
   เครื่องบิน

Listen and point. Take turns.

A: Point to <u>the motorcycle</u>.
B: Point to <u>the truck</u>.
A: Point to <u>the train</u>.

Dictate to your partner. Take turns.

A: Write <u>motorcycle</u>.
B: Could you repeat that for me?
A: <u>Motorcycle</u>. <u>M-o-t-o-r-c-y-c-l-e</u>.

9. helicopter
เฮลิคอปเตอร์

10. airport
สนามบิน

11. subway station
สถานีรถใต้ดิน

12. subway
รถใต้ดิน

13. bus stop
ป้ายจอดรถประจำทาง

14. bus
รถประจำทาง

15. bicycle
จักรยาน

Ways to talk about using transportation

Use **take** for buses, trains, subways, taxis, planes, and helicopters. Use **drive** for cars and trucks. Use **ride** for bicycles and motorcycles.

Pair practice. Make new conversations.

A: *How do you get to school?*
B: *I take the bus. How about you?*
A: *I ride a bicycle to school.*

A Bus Stop ป้ายจอดรถประจำทาง

BUS 10 Northbound		
Main	Elm	Oak
6:00	6:10	6:13
6:30	6:40	6:43
7:00	7:10	7:13
7:30	7:40	7:43

New York City Transit
MTA **Transfer**
◄ Going your way

A Subway Station สถานีรถใต้ดิน

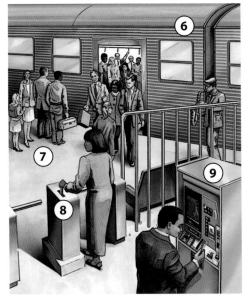

MTA RED LINE
OPENING DAY
JUNE 24, 2000
1 FARE
NORTH HOLLYWOOD

MTA
MetroCard
◄ Insert this way/This side facing you

1. bus route
   เส้นทางการเดิน
   รถประจำทาง
2. fare
   ค่าโดยสาร
3. rider
   ผู้โดยสารรถ
   ประจำทาง
4. schedule
   ตารางเวลา
5. transfer
   บัตรผ่าน /
   เปลี่ยนเส้นทาง

6. subway car
   ขบวนรถใต้ดิน
7. platform
   ชานชาลา
8. turnstile
   ช่องหมุนผ่าน
9. vending machine
   เครื่องขายอัตโนมัติ
10. token
    เหรียญแทนเงิน
11. fare card
    บัตรค่าโดยสาร

A Train Station สถานีรถไฟ

Airport Transportation การขนส่งที่สนามบิน

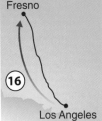

HART DAVIS/DAMON
From
DOVER, NH
To
BOSTON NRTH STA,MA
Carrier 2V   Train 684   Date 17FEB03
Accom 2V   Space/Car
BUSINESS CL
Form of Payment
AP   XXXX0456791   Ax

Fresno
Los Angeles

Fresno
Los Angeles

12. ticket window
    หน้าต่างขายตั๋ว
13. conductor
    พนักงานเดินตั๋ว
14. track
    ราง
15. ticket
    ตั๋ว
16. one-way trip
    เที่ยวเดียว
17. round trip
    ไปกลับ

18. taxi stand
    จุดแท็กซี่หยุดรอรับส่ง
19. shuttle
    รถวิ่งบริการเฉพาะที่
20. town car
    รถยนต์ในเมือง
21. taxi driver
    คนขับแท็กซี่
22. taxi license
    ใบอนุญาตแท็กซี่
23. meter
    มิเตอร์

More vocabulary

hail a taxi: to raise your hand to get a taxi
miss the bus: to get to the bus stop after the bus leaves

Ask your classmates. Share the answers.

1. Is there a subway system in your city?
2. Do you ever take taxis? When?
3. Do you ever take the bus? Where?

A. go under the bridge
ไปใต้สะพาน

B. go over the bridge
ไปบนสะพาน

C. walk up the steps
เดินขึ้นบันได

D. walk down the steps
เดินลงบันได

E. get into the taxi
ขึ้นแท็กซี่

F. get out of the taxi
ออกจากแท็กซี่

G. run across the street
วิ่งข้ามถนน

H. run around the corner
วิ่งไปตามหัวมุม

I. get on the highway
ขึ้นไปทางไฮเวย์

J. get off the highway
ออกจากไฮเวย์

K. drive through the tunnel
ขับผ่านเข้าไปในอุโมงค์

Grammar Point: *into, out of, on, off*

Use *get into* for taxis and cars.
Use *get on* for buses, trains, planes, and highways.

Use *get out of* for taxis and cars.
Use *get off* for buses, trains, planes, and highways.

1. stop
หยุด

2. do not enter / wrong way
ห้ามเข้า / ผิดทาง

3. one way
รถวิ่งทางเดียว

4. speed limit
ขีดจำกัดความเร็ว

5. U-turn OK
กลับรถได้

6. no outlet / dead end
ไม่มีทางออก / ทางตัน

7. right turn only
เลี้ยวขวาเท่านั้น

8. no left turn
ห้ามเลี้ยวซ้าย

9. yield
ให้ทาง

10. merge
ทางเชื่อม

11. no parking
ห้ามจอด

12. handicapped parking
ที่จอดสำหรับผู้พิการ

13. pedestrian crossing
ทางข้ามสำหรับคนเดินเท้า

14. railroad crossing
ทางข้ามรางรถไฟ

15. school crossing
ทางข้ามของโรงเรียน

16. road work
งานถนน

17. U.S. route / highway marker
ทางหลวงระหว่างรัฐในสหรัฐฯ /
เครื่องหมายทางหลวง

18. hospital
โรงพยาบาล

Pair practice. Make new conversations.
A: *Watch out! The sign says <u>no left turn</u>.*
B: *Sorry, I was looking at the <u>stop sign</u>.*
A: *That's OK. Just be careful!*

Ask your classmates. Share the answers.
1. How many traffic signs are on your street?
2. What's the speed limit on your street?
3. What traffic signs are the same in your native country?

Directions ทิศทาง

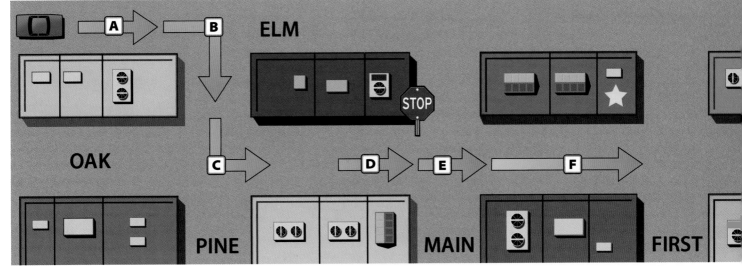

A. Go straight on Elm Street.
ตรงไปตามถนนเอล์ม

B. Turn right on Pine Street.
เลี้ยวขวาเข้าถนนไพน์

C. Turn left on Oak Street.
เลี้ยวซ้ายเข้าถนนโอ๊ค

D. Stop at the corner.
หยุดที่หัวมุมถนน

E. Go past Main Street.
ไปผ่านเลยถนนเมน

F. Go one block to First Street.
ไปหนึ่งบล็อคถึงถนนเฟิร์ส

Maps แผนที่

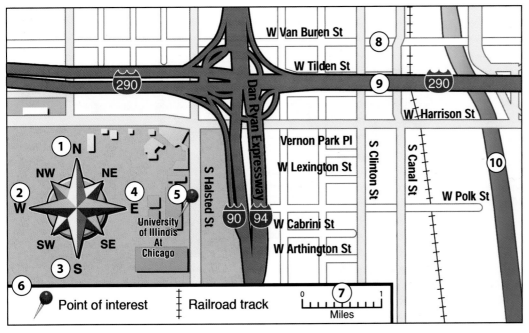

1. north
เหนือ

3. south
ใต้

5. symbol
สัญลักษณ์

8. street
ถนน

11. GPS (global positioning system)
ระบบการหาตำแหน่งบนพื้นโลก

2. west
ตะวันตก

4. east
ตะวันออก

6. key
หมายสำคัญ

9. highway
ไฮเวย์ / ทางหลวง

12. Internet map
แผนที่ทางอินเทอร์เน็ต

7. scale
สเกล / สัดส่วนการย่อขนาด

10. river
แม่น้ำ

Role play. Ask for directions.

A: *I'm lost. I need to get to <u>Elm and Pine</u>.*
B: *Go <u>straight on Oak</u> and <u>make a right on Pine</u>.*
A: *Thanks so much.*

Ask your classmates. Share the answers.

1. How often do you use Internet maps? GPS? paper maps?
2. What was the last map you used? Why?

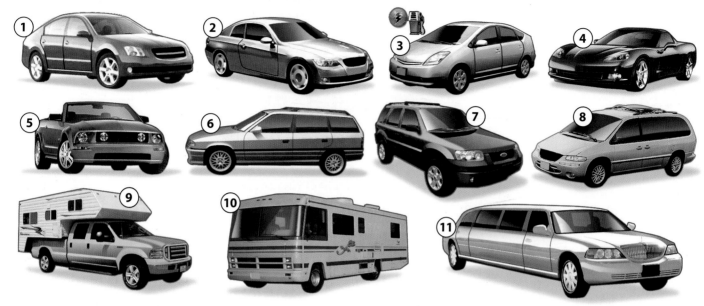

1. 4-door car / sedan
รถยนต์สี่ประตู / รถเก๋ง

2. 2-door car / coupe
รถยนต์สองประตู / คูเป้

3. hybrid
รถยนต์พลังงานน้ำมันและไฟฟ้า

4. sports car
รถยนต์สปอร์ต

5. convertible
รถเปิดประทุน

6. station wagon
รถตู้

7. SUV (sport–utility vehicle)
รถยนต์แบบใช้งานการกีฬา (เอสยูวี)

8. minivan
รถตู้ขนาดเล็ก

9. camper
รถนอนค้างแรม

10. RV (recreational vehicle)
รถเพื่อการพักผ่อนหย่อนใจ (อาร์วี)

11. limousine / limo
รถรับแขกพิเศษ / รถลิโม

12. pickup truck
รถบรรทุกเล็ก

13. cargo van
รถตู้ขนของ

14. tow truck
รถบรรทุกสำหรับลากจูง

15. tractor trailer / semi
รถบรรทุกลากพ่วง

16. cab
บริเวณห้องคนขับ

17. trailer
ส่วนลากพ่วง

18. moving van
รถขนย้าย

19. dump truck
รถเทขยะ

20. tank truck
รถถังบรรจุของเหลว

21. school bus
รถโรงเรียน

Pair practice. Make new conversations.

A: *I have a new car!*
B: *Did you get a hybrid?*
A: *Yes, but I really wanted a sports car.*

More vocabulary

make: the name of the company that makes the car
model: the style of the car

Buying a Used Car การซื้อรถมือสอง

'04 Compact. Only $3,000.

'05 Sedan. Must sell. Great deal!

How many miles does it have?

FOR SALE

It's in good condition.

A. Look at car ads.
หาดูโฆษณารถ

B. Ask the seller about the car.
ถามคนขายเกี่ยวกับรถ

C. Take the car to a mechanic.
นำรถไปให้ช่างดู

It's $2,500.

I can give you $2,000.

D. Negotiate a price.
ต่อรองราคา

E. Get the title from the seller.
รับใบทะเบียนเจ้าของรถจากผู้ขาย

F. Register the car.
ขึ้นทะเบียนรถ

Taking Care of Your Car การดูแลรถของคุณ

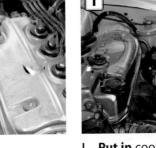

G. Fill the tank with gas.
เติมน้ำมันรถ

H. Check the oil.
ตรวจดูน้ำมันเครื่อง

I. Put in coolant.
ใส่น้ำยาทำความเย็น

J. Go for a smog check.*
นำรถไปตรวจปริมาณไอเสีย

K. Replace the windshield wipers.
เปลี่ยนแผงยางที่ปัดน้ำฝนหน้ารถ

L. Fill the tires with air.
เติมลมรถ

*smog check = emissions test

Ways to request service

Please check the oil.
Could you fill the tank?
Put in coolant, please.

Think about it. Discuss.

1. What's good and bad about a used car?
2. Do you like to negotiate car prices? Why?
3. Do you know any good mechanics? Why are they good?

At the Dealer
ที่ตัวแทนจำหน่าย

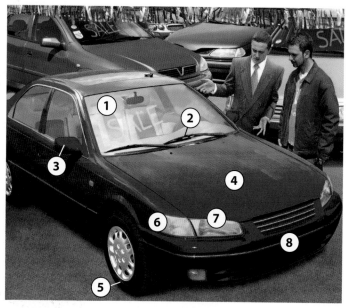

At the Mechanic
ที่อู่รถ

1. windshield
กระจกหน้ารถ

2. windshield wipers
ที่ปัดน้ำฝน

3. sideview mirror
กระจกเงามองด้านข้าง

4. hood
กระโปรงหน้ารถ

5. tire
ยางรถ

6. turn signal
ไฟเลี้ยว

7. headlight
ไฟหน้ารถ

8. bumper
กันชน

9. hubcap / wheel cover
ฝาครอบล้อรถ

10. gas tank
ถังน้ำมัน

11. trunk
กระโปรงหลังรถ /
ที่เก็บของหลังรถ

12. license plate
ป้ายทะเบียน

13. tail light
ไฟท้ายรถ

14. brake light
ไฟเบรค

15. tail pipe
ท่อไอเสีย

16. muffler
ท่อเก็บเสียง

Under the Hood
ภายใต้กระโปรงหน้ารถ

Inside the Trunk
ภายในกระโปรงหลังรถ

17. fuel injection system
ระบบฉีดจ่ายเชื้อเพลิง

18. engine
เครื่องยนต์

19. radiator
หม้อน้ำ / รังผึ้ง

20. battery
แบตเตอรี่

21. jumper cables
สายเคเบิลถ่ายไฟแบตเตอรี่

22. lug wrench
ประแจมือ

23. spare tire
ยางอะไหล่

24. jack
แม่แรง

The Dashboard and Instrument Panel
หน้าปัดรถและแผงอุปกรณ์

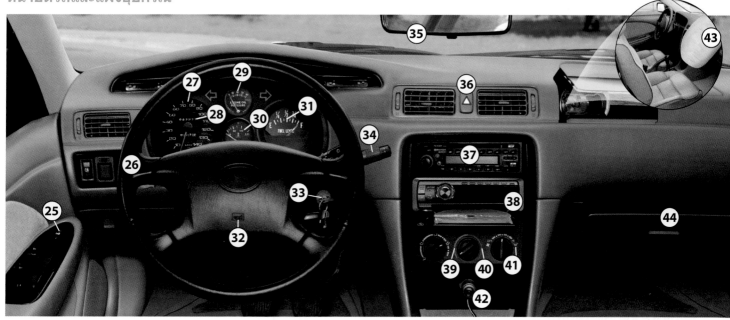

25. **door lock**
ล็อคประตู

26. **steering wheel**
พวงมาลัย

27. **speedometer**
มิเตอร์ความเร็ว

28. **odometer**
มาตรระยะทาง

29. **oil gauge**
มาตรวัดน้ำมันเครื่อง

30. **temperature gauge**
มาตรวัดอุณหภูมิ

31. **gas gauge**
มาตรวัดน้ำมันเชื้อเพลิง

32. **horn**
แตร

33. **ignition**
จุดสตาร์ทเครื่องยนต์

34. **turn signal**
ไฟเลี้ยว

35. **rearview mirror**
กระจกเงามองหลัง

36. **hazard lights**
ไฟสัญญาณอันตราย

37. **radio**
วิทยุ

38. **CD player**
เครื่องเล่นซีดี

39. **air conditioner**
เครื่องปรับอากาศ

40. **heater**
เครื่องทำความอุ่น

41. **defroster**
เครื่องกำจัดละอองน้ำแข็ง

42. **power outlet**
จุดเสียบไฟ

43. **air bag**
ถุงลมนิรภัย

44. **glove compartment**
ลิ้นชักเก็บของ

An Automatic Transmission
เกียร์อัตโนมัติ

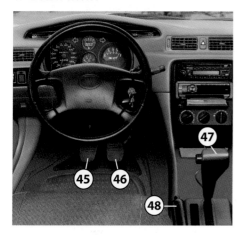

A Manual Transmission
เกียร์มือ / เกียร์ธรรมดา

Inside the Car
ภายในรถ

45. **brake pedal**
คันบังคับเบรค

46. **gas pedal / accelerator**
คันบังคับน้ำมัน
เชื้อเพลิง / คันเร่ง

47. **gear shift**
คันเกียร์

48. **hand brake**
เบรคมือ

49. **clutch**
คลัช

50. **stick shift**
เกียร์กระปุก

51. **front seat**
ที่นั่งด้านหน้า

52. **seat belt**
เข็มขัดนิรภัย

53. **child safety seat**
เก้าอี้นิรภัยของเด็ก

54. **backseat**
ที่นั่งด้านหลัง

In the Airline Terminal ในอาคารสนามบิน

At the Security Checkpoint
ที่จุดตรวจเพื่อความปลอดภัย

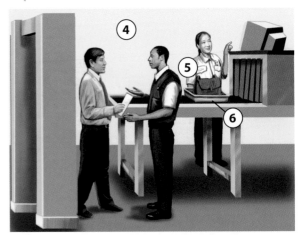

1. skycap
   พนักงานขนสัมภาระที่สนามบิน

2. check-in kiosk
   ตู้เช็คอิน

3. ticket agent
   พนักงานขายตั๋ว

4. screening area
   บริเวณตรวจเพื่อความปลอดภัย

5. TSA* agent / security screener
   เจ้าหน้าดูแลความปลอดภัย /
   ผู้ตรวจเพื่อความปลอดภัย

6. bin
   ถาดใส่ของ

Taking a Flight ไปกับเที่ยวบิน

A. **Check in** electronically.
เช็คอินทางคอมพิวเตอร์

B. **Check** your bags.
เช็คกระเป๋าของคุณ

C. **Show** your boarding pass and ID.
แสดงบัตรขึ้นเครื่องและบัตร
ประจำตัว

D. **Go through** security.
เดินผ่านการตรวจเพื่อความ
ปลอดภัย

E. **Board** the plane.
ขึ้นเครื่องบิน

F. **Find** your seat.
หาที่นั่งของคุณ

G. **Stow** your carry-on bag.
เก็บกระเป๋าที่ถือติดตัวมา

H. **Fasten** your seat belt.
รัดเข็มขัดนิรภัย

I. **Turn off** your cell phone.
ปิดโทรศัพท์มือถือของคุณ

J. **Take off**. / **Leave**.
เครื่องบินขึ้น / ออกเดินทาง

K. **Land**. / **Arrive**.
เครื่องบินลง / มาถึง

L. **Claim** your baggage.
รับกระเป๋าสัมภาระของคุณ

* Transportation Security Administration

At the Gate
ที่ประตูทางเข้าออ

On the Airplane
บนเครื่องบิน

At Customs
ที่ด่านศุลกากร

7. **arrival and departure monitors**
จอแสดงเวลาเครื่องบินมาถึง และเวลาออก

8. **gate**
ประตูทางออกขึ้นเครื่อง

9. **boarding area**
บริเวณทางขึ้นเครื่อง

10. **cockpit**
ห้องเครื่อง / ห้องนักบิน

11. **pilot**
นักบิน

12. **flight attendant**
พนักงานบริการบนเครื่อง

13. **overhead compartment**
ที่เก็บของเหนือศีรษะ

14. **emergency exit**
ทางออกฉุกเฉิน

15. **passenger**
ผู้โดยสาร

16. **declaration form**
แบบฟอร์มสำแดงสิ่งของที่นำมา

17. **customs officer**
เจ้าหน้าที่ศุลกากร

18. **luggage / bag**
กระเป๋าเดินทาง / กระเป๋า

19. **e-ticket**
ตั๋วที่ออกทางคอมพิวเตอร์

20. **boarding pass**
บัตรขึ้นเครื่อง

21. **tray table**
โต๊ะพับหลังพนักเก้าอี้

22. **turbulence**
อากาศปั่นป่วน

23. **baggage carousel**
รางเลื่อนส่งกระเป๋า

24. **oxygen mask**
หน้ากากออกซิเจน

25. **life vest**
เสื้อชูชีพ

26. **emergency card**
บัตรอธิบายเหตุฉุกเฉิน

27. **reclined seat**
ที่นั่งพนักเอนหลัง

28. **upright seat**
ที่นั่งพนักตั้งตรง

29. **on-time**
ตรงตามกำหนดเวลา

30. **delayed flight**
เที่ยวบินมาช้า

More vocabulary

departure time: the time the plane takes off
arrival time: the time the plane lands
direct flight: a trip with no stops

Pair practice. Make new conversations.

A: *Excuse me. Where do I check in?*
B: *At the check-in kiosk.*
A: *Thanks.*

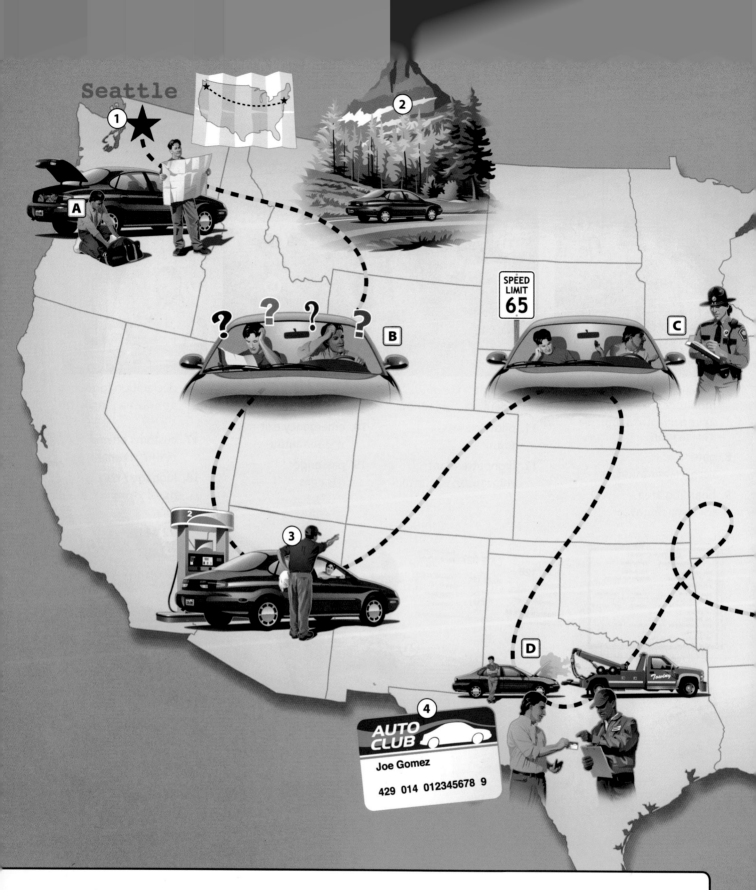

Seattle

SPEED LIMIT 65

AUTO CLUB
Joe Gomez
429 014 012345678 9

1. starting point
จุดเริ่มต้น

2. scenery
ทิวทัศน์

3. gas station attendant
พนักงานปั๊มน้ำมัน

4. auto club card
บัตรสโมสรผู้ใช้ยานยนต์

5. destination
จุดหมายปลายทาง

A. **pack**
เก็บของลงกระเป๋า

B. **get** lost
หลงทาง

C. **get** a speeding ticket
โดนใบสั่งเพราะขับเร็วเกิน
กำหนด

D. **break down**
รถเสีย

E. **run out** of gas
น้ำมันหมด

F. **have** a flat tire
มียางแบน

Look at the pictures.
What do you see?

Answer the questions.

1. What are the young men's starting point and destination?

2. What do they see on their trip?

3. What kinds of problems do they have?

 Read the story.

A Road Trip

On July 7th Joe and Rob <u>packed</u> their bags for a road trip. Their <u>starting point</u> was Seattle. Their <u>destination</u> was New York City.

The young men saw beautiful <u>scenery</u> on their trip. But there were also problems. They <u>got lost</u>. Then, a <u>gas station attendant</u> gave them bad directions. Next, they <u>got a speeding ticket</u>. Joe was very upset. After that, their car <u>broke down</u>. Joe called a tow truck and used his <u>auto club card</u>.

The end of their trip was difficult, too. They <u>ran out of gas</u> and then they had a <u>flat tire</u>.

After 7,000 miles of problems, Joe and Rob arrived in New York City. They were happy, but tired. Next time, they're going to take the train.

Think about it.

1. What is the best way to travel across the U.S.? by car? by plane? by train? Why?

2. Imagine your car breaks down on the road. Who can you call? What can you do?

1. entrance
   ทางเข้า

2. customer
   ลูกค้า

3. office
   สำนักงาน

4. employer /
   boss
   นายจ้าง /
   เจ้านาย

5. receptionist
   พนักงานต้อนรับ

6. safety regulations
   ข้อกำหนดเพื่อความ
   ปลอดภัย

Listen and point. Take turns.

A: Point to the front entrance.

B: Point to the receptionist.

A: Point to the time clock.

Dictate to your partner. Take turns.

A: *Can you spell employer?*

B: *I'm not sure. Is it e-m-p-l-o-y-e-r?*

A: *Yes, that's right.*

7. time clock
นาฬิกาลงเวลา

8. supervisor
หัวหน้างาน

9. employee
ลูกจ้าง / พนักงาน

10. payroll clerk
พนักงานจ่ายค่าจ้าง

11. pay stub
ต้นขั้วใบจ่าย

12. wages
ค่าจ้าง

13. deductions
ส่วนหักลด

14. paycheck
เช็คค่าจ้าง

Fix this first.

OK.

IRINA'S COMPUTER SERVICE
7000 Main Street
Houston, TX 77031

10/17/11 to 10/23/11

Kate Babic
000-23-4567

12	**Salary**		**$ 800.00**
	Deductions		
13	Federal	88.00	
	State	22.40	
	Social Security	51.00	
	Medicare	12.00	
	SDI	7.50	
	Net		**$ 619.10**

IRINA'S COMPUTER SERVICE
7000 Main Street
Houston, TX 77031

Check number:
123456789 999999999 123

14

Pay to the order of _____ Kate Babic _____ $ 619.10

Six hundred nineteen and 10/100 dollars

Town Bank

Irina Jorkov

Ways to talk about wages

I **earn** $250 a week.
He **makes** $7 an hour.
I'm **paid** $1,000 a month.

Role play. Talk to an employer.

A: *Is everything correct on your paycheck?*
B: *No, it isn't. I make $250 a week, not $200.*
A: *Let's talk to the payroll clerk. Where is she?*

1. accountant
พนักงานบัญชี

2. actor
นักแสดง

3. administrative assistant
ผู้ช่วยฝ่ายบริหาร

4. appliance repair person
พนักงานซ่อมแซมเครื่องใช้

5. architect
สถาปนิก

6. artist
ศิลปิน

7. assembler
พนักงานประกอบผลิตภัณฑ์

8. auto mechanic
ช่างเครื่องรถยนต์

9. babysitter
คนดูแลเด็ก

10. baker
คนทำขนมปัง

11. business owner
เจ้าของธุรกิจ

12. businessperson
นักธุรกิจ

13. butcher
คนเชือดเนื้อ / คนขายเนื้อ

14. carpenter
ช่างไม้

15. cashier
พนักงานรับเงิน

16. childcare worker
พนักงานดูแลเด็ก

Ways to ask about someone's job

What's her job?
What does he do?
What kind of work do they do?

Pair practice. Make new conversations.

A: *What kind of work <u>does she</u> do?*
B: *<u>She's an accountant</u>. What <u>do they</u> do?*
A: *<u>They're actors</u>.*

17. commercial fisher
ชาวประมงเชิงพานิชย์

18. computer software engineer
วิศวกรผู้ผลิตซอฟท์แวร์คอมพิวเตอร์

19. computer technician
ช่างเทคนิคด้านคอมพิวเตอร์

We have that shirt in red.

20. customer service representative
พนักงานบริการลูกค้า

21. delivery person
พนักงานส่งมอบสินค้า

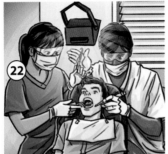

22. dental assistant
ผู้ช่วยทันตแพทย์

23. dockworker
พนักงานท่าเรือ

24. electronics repair person
ช่างซ่อมแซมเครื่องไฟฟ้า

25. engineer
วิศวกร

26. firefighter
พนักงานดับเพลิง

27. florist
คนขายดอกไม้

28. gardener
คนทำสวน

29. garment worker
พนักงานตัดเย็บเสื้อผ้า

30. graphic designer
นักออกแบบกราฟิก

31. hairdresser / hair stylist
ช่างทำผม / ช่างแต่งผม

32. home health care aide
ผู้ช่วยดูแลสุขภาพผู้สูงอายุในบ้าน

Ways to talk about jobs and occupations

Sue's a <u>garment worker</u>. She works **in** a factory.
Tom's <u>an engineer</u>. He works **for** <u>a large company</u>.
Ann's a <u>dental assistant</u>. She works **with** <u>a dentist</u>.

Role play. Talk about a friend's new job.

A: *Does your friend like <u>his</u> new job?*
B: *Yes, <u>he</u> does. <u>He's a graphic designer</u>.*
A: *Does <u>he</u> work <u>in an office</u>?*

167

33. homemaker
แม่บ้าน

34. housekeeper
พนักงานแม่บ้าน

35. interpreter / translator
ล่าม / นักแปล

36. lawyer
นักกฎหมาย

37. machine operator
ช่างเครื่อง /
พนักงานเดินเครื่อง

38. manicurist
ช่างแต่งเล็บ

39. medical records
technician
เจ้าหน้าที่ผู้บันทึกการแพทย์

40. messenger / courier
พนักงานส่งเอกสาร /
คนส่งจดหมาย

41. model
นางแบบ

42. mover
พนักงานขนย้าย

43. musician
นักดนตรี

44. nurse
พยาบาล

45. occupational therapist
พนักงานบำบัดฝึกหัดงาน
อาชีพ

46. (house) painter
ช่างทาสี (บ้าน)

47. physician assistant
ผู้ช่วยแพทย์

48. police officer
เจ้าหน้าที่ตำรวจ

Grammar Point: past tense of be

*I **was** a machine operator for 5 years.*

*She **was** a nurse for a year.*

*They **were** movers from 2003–2007.*

Pair practice. Make new conversations.

A: *What was your first job?*

B: *I was <u>a musician</u>. How about you?*

A: *I was <u>a messenger for a small company</u>.*

49. postal worker
พนักงานไปรษณีย์

50. printer
ช่างพิมพ์

51. receptionist
พนักงานต้อนรับ

52. reporter
นักข่าว

53. retail clerk
พนักงานขายปลีก

54. sanitation worker
พนักงานสุขาภิบาล

55. security guard
เจ้าหน้าที่รักษาความ
ปลอดภัย

56. server
พนักงานเสิร์ฟอาหาร

Here are some programs that will help you.

57. social worker
เจ้าหน้าที่สังคมสงเคราะห์

58. soldier
ทหาร

59. stock clerk
พนักงานดูแลสต็อกสินค้า

Hello. I'm calling with a very special offer.

60. telemarketer
นักการตลาดทางโทรศัพท์

61. truck driver
คนขับรถบรรทุก

62. veterinarian
สัตวแพทย์

63. welder
ช่างเชื่อมโลหะ

Norma's Story

64. writer / author
นักเขียน / นักประพันธ์

Ask your classmates. Share the answers.

1. Which of these jobs could you do now?
2. What is one job you don't want to have?
3. Which jobs do you want to have?

Think about it. Discuss.

1. Which jobs need special training?
2. What kind of person makes a good interpreter?
A good nurse? A good reporter? Why?

A. assemble components
ประกอบชิ้นส่วน

B. assist medical patients
ช่วยเหลือผู้ป่วย

C. cook
ทำอาหาร

D. do manual labor
ทำงานที่ใช้แรงงาน

E. drive a truck
ขับรถ

F. fly a plane
ขับเครื่องบิน

G. make furniture
ทำเฟอร์นิเจอร์

H. operate heavy machinery
เดินเครื่องจักรขนาดใหญ่

I. program computers
ทำโปรแกรมคอมพิวเตอร์

J. repair appliances
ซ่อมแซมเครื่องใช้ต่างๆ

K. sell cars
ขายรถ

L. sew clothes
เย็บเสื้อผ้า

M. solve math problems
ไขโจทย์เลข /
คำนวณหาคำตอบ

N. speak another language
พูดต่างภาษา

O. supervise people
ควบคุมดูแลผู้อื่น

P. take care of children
ดูแลเด็ก

Q. teach
สอน

R. type
พิมพ์

S. use a cash register
ใช้เครื่องรับทอนเงิน

T. wait on customers
บริการลูกค้า

Grammar Point: *can, can't*

I am a chef. **I can** *cook.*
I'm not a pilot. **I can't** *fly a plane.*
I **can't** *speak French, but I* **can** *speak Spanish.*

Role play. Talk to a job counselor.

A: *Tell me about your skills. Can you* <u>*type*</u>*?*
B: <u>*No, I can't*</u>*, but I* <u>*can use a cash register*</u>*.*
A: *OK. What other skills do you have?*

Customers need better service…

Vancouver...

Scan Complete

Let's meet at 2:00.
Sure.

Dear Mr. Smith…

Hello. ABC Company. How may I help you?

Please hold.

Mr. Perez, I'm transferring you.

Hello. This is Sue Jones. Please call me.

Message Pad
Call From: Ana Puerta
Tel: 555-1234
Message:
Please Call

This is Lee Tran. Please call me back.

Office Skills
ทักษะการทำงานใน
สำนักงาน

A. **type** a letter
พิมพ์จดหมาย

B. **enter** data
ใส่ข้อมูล

C. **transcribe** notes
แปลงบันทึกจากเสียง
เป็นอักษร

D. **make** copies
ถ่ายเอกสาร

E. **collate** papers
จัดเอกสารต่างๆเข้าเล่ม

F. **staple**
เย็บเล่ม

G. **fax** a document
ส่งเอกสารทางโทรสาร
(แฟกซ์)

H. **scan** a document
สแกนเอกสาร

I. **print** a document
พิมพ์เอกสาร

J. **schedule** a meeting
ทำหมายกำหนดการ
ประชุม

K. **take** dictation
เขียนตามคำบอก

L. **organize** materials
จัดระเบียบวัสดุต่างๆ

Telephone Skills
ทักษะในการโทรศัพท์

M. **greet** the caller
ทักทายผู้ที่โทรเข้ามา

N. **put** the caller on hold
จัดสายให้ผู้โทรเข้ารออยู่

O. **transfer** the call
โอนสาย

P. **leave** a message
ฝากข้อความทิ้งไว้

Q. **take** a message
รับฝากข้อความ

R. **check** messages
ตรวจฟังข้อความ

171

Career Path เส้นทางอาชีพ

1. entry-level job
งานระดับขั้นเริ่มต้น

2. training
การฝึกอบรม

3. new job
งานใหม่

4. promotion
การเลื่อนขั้น

Types of Job Training ประเภทของการฝึกอบรมงาน

5. vocational training
การฝึกอบรมงานอาชีพ

6. internship
การฝึกงานหลังสำเร็จ
การศึกษา

7. on-the-job training
การฝึกอบรมระหว่าง
การทำงาน

8. online course
วิชาทางออนไลน์

Planning a Career การวางแผนอาชีพ

9. resource center
ศูนย์กลางข้อมูล / แหล่งสนับสนุน

10. career counselor
ผู้ให้คำปรึกษางานอาชีพ

11. interest inventory
รายการงานที่มีเสนอ

12. skill inventory
รายการทักษะต่างๆ

13. job fair
มหกรรมจัดหางาน

14. recruiter
เจ้าหน้าที่ผู้ทำการจัดจ้าง

Ways to talk about job training

I'm looking into <u>an online course</u>.
I'm interested in <u>on-the-job training</u>.
I want to sign up for <u>an internship</u>.

Ask your classmates. Share the answers.

1. What kind of job training are you interested in?
2. Would your rather learn English in an online course or in a classroom?

A. talk to friends / **network**
คุยกับเพื่อน / เครือข่าย

B. look in the classifieds
ค้นหาในหมวดประกาศ

C. look for help wanted signs
มองหาป้ายเรียกจ้างคนงาน

D. check Internet job sites
ตรวจดูงานเสนอในไซท์อินเทอร์เน็ต

E. go to an employment agency
ไปที่หน่วยบริการจัดหางาน

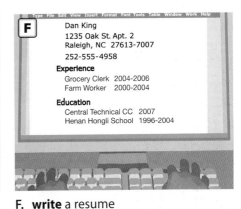

F. write a resume
เขียนประวัติการทำงาน

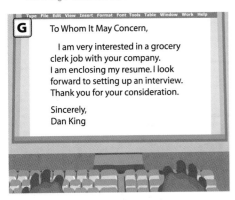

G. write a cover letter
เขียนจดหมายปะหน้า

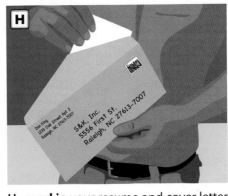

H. send in your resume and cover letter
ส่งประวัติการทำงาน
และจดหมายปะหน้าของคุณ

I. set up an interview
กำหนดเวลาการสัมภาษณ์

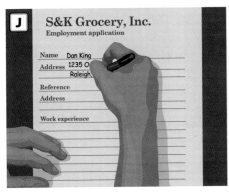

J. fill out an application
กรอกใบสมัคร

K. go on an interview
ไปรับการสัมภาษณ์

L. get hired
ได้รับการว่าจ้าง

A. Prepare for the interview.
เตรียมตัวสำหรับการสัมภาษณ์

B. Dress appropriately.
แต่งตัวให้เหมาะสม

C. Be neat.
ทำให้ดูเรียบร้อย

D. Bring your resume and ID.
นำประวัติการทำงานและบัตรประจำตัวของคุณมา

E. Don't be late.
อย่ามาสาย

F. Be on time.
ต้องตรงเวลา

G. Turn off your cell phone.
ปิดโทรศัพท์มือถือของคุณ

H. Greet the interviewer.
ทักทายผู้สัมภาษณ์

I. Shake hands.
จับมือทักทาย

J. Make eye contact.
มองสบตา

K. Listen carefully.
ฟังอย่างตั้งอกตั้งใจ

L. Talk about your experience.
พูดถึงประสบการณ์ของคุณ

M. Ask questions.
ถามคำถามต่างๆ

N. Thank the interviewer.
ขอบคุณผู้สัมภาษณ์

O. Write a thank-you note.
เขียนคำขอบคุณ

More vocabulary

benefits: health insurance, vacation pay, or other things the employer can offer an employee
inquire about benefits: ask about benefits

Think about it. Discuss.

1. How can you prepare for an interview?
2. Why is it important to make eye contact?
3. What kinds of questions should you ask?

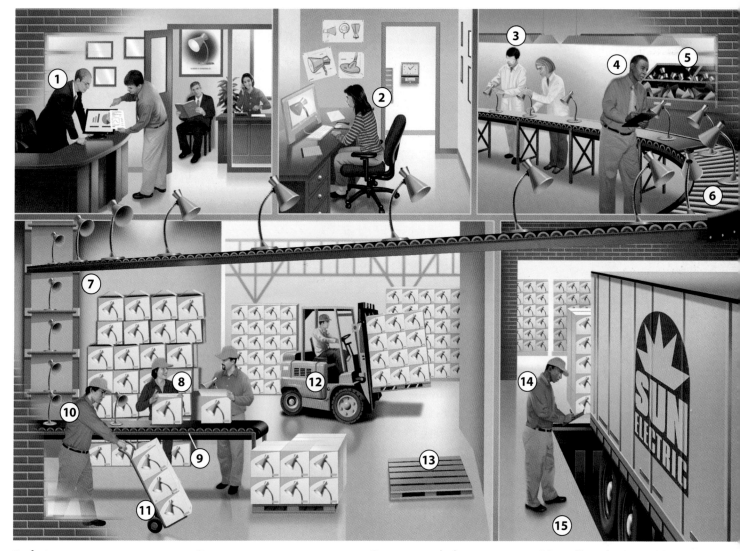

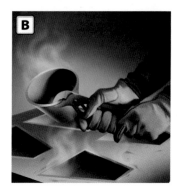

1. factory owner
เจ้าของโรงงาน

2. designer
นักออกแบบ

3. factory worker
คนงานในโรงงาน

4. line supervisor
ผู้ดูแลสายงาน

5. parts
ชิ้นส่วน

6. assembly line
สายงานประกอบชิ้นส่วน

7. warehouse
โกดังสินค้า

8. packer
พนักงานบรรจุ

9. conveyer belt
สายพานส่งของ

10. order puller
พนักงานเข็น

11. hand truck
รถเข็น

12. forklift
รถยกสินค้า

13. pallet
แท่นวางสินค้า

14. shipping clerk
พนักงานจัดส่งสินค้า

15. loading dock
ท่าเทียบขึ้นสินค้า

A. **design**
ออกแบบ

B. **manufacture**
ผลิต

C. **assemble**
ประกอบชิ้นส่วน

D. **ship**
จัดส่ง

1. gardening crew
   กลุ่มคนงานทำสวน
2. leaf blower
   เครื่องเป่าใบไม้
3. wheelbarrow
   ล้อลากเข็น
4. gardening crew leader
   หัวหน้าคนงานทำสวน

5. landscape designer
   นักออกแบบงานจัดสวน
6. lawn mower
   เครื่องตัดหญ้า
7. shovel
   พลั่ว
8. rake
   เหล็กกวาด

9. pruning shears
   กรรไกรตัดแต่ง
10. trowel
    เกรียง
11. hedge clippers
    กรรไกรตัดกิ่ง
12. weed whacker / weed eater
    เครื่องเล็มหญ้า / เครื่องตัดแต่งหญ้า

A. **mow** the lawn
   ตัดหญ้า
B. **trim** the hedges
   เล็มกิ่งรั้วต้นไม้

C. **rake** the leaves
   กวาดใบไม้
D. **fertilize** / **feed** the plants
   ใส่ปุ๋ย / ให้อาหารพืช

E. **plant** a tree
   ปลูกต้นไม้
F. **water** the plants
   ให้น้ำพืช / รดน้ำต้นไม้

G. **weed** the flower beds
   กำจัดวัชพืชในแปลงดอกไม้
H. **install** a sprinkler system
   ติดตั้งระบบฉีดรดน้ำต้นไม้

Use the new words.
Look at page 53. Name what you can do in the yard.

A: *I can <u>mow the lawn</u>.*
B: *I can <u>weed the flower bed</u>.*

Ask your classmates. Share the answers.

1. Do you know someone who does landscaping? Who?
2. Do you enjoy gardening? Why or why not?
3. Which gardening activity is the hardest to do? Why?

Crops ผลผลิตทางเกษตร

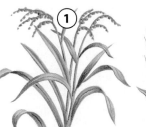

1. rice
ข้าว

2. wheat
ข้าวสาลี

3. soybeans
ถั่วเหลือง

4. corn
ข้าวโพด

5. alfalfa
อัลฟัลฟา

6. cotton
ฝ้าย

7. field
ไร่ / นา

8. farmworker
คนงานในไร่

9. tractor
รถไถ

10. orchard
สวนผลไม้

11. barn
โรงนา

12. farm equipment
อุปกรณ์ทำไร่

13. farmer / grower
ชาวไร่ / ผู้ปลูก

14. vegetable garden
สวนผัก

15. livestock
ปศุสัตว์

16. vineyard
ไร่องุ่น

17. corral
คอกสัตว์

18. hay
หญ้าแห้ง

19. fence
รั้ว

20. hired hand
คนงานรับจ้าง

21. cattle
ฝูงสัตว์เลี้ยงวัวควาย

22. rancher
ผู้ทำงานปศุสัตว์

A. plant
พืช

B. harvest
เก็บเกี่ยวพืชผล

C. milk
รีดนม

D. feed
ให้อาหาร

1. **construction worker**
คนงานก่อสร้าง

2. **ladder**
บันได

3. **I beam/girder**
คาน / ตงเหล็ก

4. **scaffolding**
นั่งร้าน

5. **cherry picker**
รถยกคนงาน

6. **bulldozer**
รถไถกราด

7. **crane**
รถเครน / รถยกอุปกรณ์

8. **backhoe**
รถแบ็คโฮ / รถตัก

9. **jackhammer / pneumatic drill**
เครื่องกระทุ้ง / เครื่องเจาะด้วยแรงลม

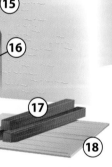

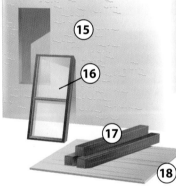

10. **concrete**
คอนกรีต /
ปูนผสมสำเร็จ

11. **tile**
แผ่นกระเบื้อง

12. **bricks**
อิฐ

13. **trowel**
เกรียง

14. **insulation**
แผ่นใยบุกันความ
ร้อนหรือความเย็น

15. **stucco**
ผนังฉาบปูน

16. **window pane**
แผงหน้าต่าง

17. **wood / lumber**
ไม้ / ไม้แปรรูป

18. **plywood**
ไม้อัด

19. **drywall**
วัสดุปิดผนัง

20. **shingles**
แผ่นไม้มุงหลังคา

21. **pickax**
ขวานเจาะ / เหล็กขุด

22. **shovel**
พลั่ว

23. **sledgehammer**
ค้อนทุบ

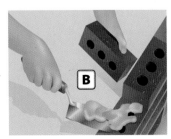

A. **paint**
ทาสี

B. **lay** bricks
ก่ออิฐ

C. **install** tile
ติดวางกระเบื้อง

D. **hammer**
ทุบด้วยค้อน

Safety Hazards and Hazardous Materials ความเสี่ยงอันตรายและวัสดุอันตราย

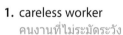

1. careless worker
คนงานที่ไม่ระมัดระวัง

2. careful worker
คนงานที่ระมัดระวัง

3. poisonous fumes
ไอระเหยที่เป็นพิษ

4. broken equipment
อุปกรณ์ที่เสีย

5. frayed cord
สายไฟที่ขาดรุ่ย

6. slippery floor
พื้นที่ลื่น

7. radioactive materials
วัสดุที่แผ่รังสี

8. flammable liquids
ของเหลวที่ติดไฟได้

Safety Equipment อุปกรณ์เพื่อความปลอดภัย

9. hard hat
หมวกแข็งใส่ทำงาน

10. safety glasses
แว่นตาเพื่อความปลอดภัย

11. safety goggles
แว่นบังตาเพื่อความปลอดภัย

12. safety visor
เครื่องบังตาเพื่อความปลอดภัย

13. respirator
เครื่องช่วยหายใจ

14. particle mask
หน้ากากกรองฝุ่น

15. ear plugs
จุกอุดหู

16. earmuffs
ฝาครอบหู

17. work gloves
ถุงมือทำงาน

18. back support belt
เข็มขัดพยุงหลัง

19. knee pads
แผ่นรองเข่า

20. safety boots
รองเท้านิรภัย

21. fire extinguisher
เครื่องดับเพลิง

22. two-way radio
วิทยุรับส่ง (สองทาง)

HAND TOOLS

HARDWARE

POWER TOOLS

1. hammer
ค้อน

2. mallet
ค้อนไม้

3. ax
ขวาน

4. handsaw
เลื่อยมือ

5. hacksaw
เลื่อยโลหะแบบเปลี่ยนใบได้

6. C-clamp
ที่หนีบยึดงานรูปตัวซี

7. pliers
คีมปากนก

8. electric drill
สว่านไฟฟ้า

9. circular saw
เลื่อยวงเดือน

10. jigsaw
เลื่อยฉลุลาย

11. power sander
หินขัดไฟฟ้า

12. router
เครื่องเซาะรู

26. vise
เครื่องหนีบจับ

27. blade
ใบมีด

28. drill bit
หัวเจาะ

29. level
เครื่องวัดระดับ

30. screwdriver
ไขควงแบน

31. Phillips screwdriver
ไขควงแฉก

32. machine screw
สกรูเครื่องจักร

33. wood screw
สกรูไม้

34. nail
ตะปู

35. bolt
สลักเกลียว

36. nut
แป้นเกลียว

37. washer
แหวนราบ

38. toggle bolt
สลักเกลียวอัดยึด

39. hook
ตะขอเกี่ยว

40. eye hook
ห่วงเกี่ยวตะขอ

41. chain
โซ่

Use the new words.
Look at pages 62–63. Name the tools you see.

A: *There's a hammer.*
B: *There's a pipe wrench.*

Ask your classmates. Share the answers.
1. Are you good with tools?
2. Which tools do you have at home?
3. Where can you shop for building supplies?

ELECTRICAL

PLUMBING

LUMBER

PAINT

13. wire
ลวด / สายไฟ

14. extension cord
สายไฟพ่วงต่อ

15. bungee cord
สายยางยืดสำหรับรัดของ

16. yardstick
ไม้วัดความยาวเป็นหลา

17. pipe
ท่อ

18. fittings
ข้อต่อท่อแบบต่างๆ

19. 2 x 4 (two by four)
2 x 4 (ไม้ขนาดหน้า
กว้างสองคูณสี่นิ้ว)

20. particle board
ไม้อัดทำจากเศษไม้

21. spray gun
เครื่องฉีดทาสี

22. paintbrush
แปรงทาสี

23. paint roller
ลูกกลิ้งทาสี

24. wood stain
น้ำยาทาสีไม้

25. paint
สีทาบ้าน

42. wire stripper
กรรไกรปอกสายไฟ

43. electrical tape
เทปสายไฟ

44. work light
ไฟทำงาน

45. tape measure
สายวัด

46. outlet cover
ฝาครอบจุดเสียบปลั๊กไฟ

47. pipe wrench
ประแจมือจับท่อ

48. adjustable wrench
ประแจมือที่ปรับขนาดได้

49. duct tape
เทปติดท่อลม

50. plunger
แกนกระทุ้ง

51. paint pan
จานทาสี

52. scraper
ใบมีดสำหรับขูด

53. masking tape
เทปปิดทับชั่วคราว

54. drop cloth
ผ้าคลุมกันสีหยดเลอะ

55. chisel
สิ่ว

56. sandpaper
กระดาษทราย

57. plane
กบไสไม้

Role play. Find an item in a building supply store.

A: *Where can I find <u>particle board</u>?*
B: *It's <u>on the back wall</u>, in the <u>lumber</u> section.*
A: *Great. And where <u>are the nails</u>?*

Think about it. Discuss.

1. Which tools are the most important to have? Why?
2. Which tools can be dangerous? Why?
3. Do you borrow tools from friends? Why or why not?

1. supply cabinet
ตู้เก็บของใช้ในสำนักงาน
2. clerk
พนักงาน
3. janitor
ภารโรง
4. conference room
ห้องประชุม

5. executive
ผู้บริหาร
6. presentation
การนำเสนอ
7. cubicle
บริเวณที่กั้นสำหรับพนักงาน
แต่ละคน
8. office manager
ผู้จัดการสำนักงาน

9. desk
โต๊ะทำงาน
10. file clerk
พนักงานจัดเก็บเอกสาร
11. file cabinet
ตู้เก็บเอกสาร
12. computer technician
ช่างเทคนิคคอมพิวเตอร์

13. PBX
เครื่องสลับสายโทรศัพท์
14. receptionist
พนักงานต้อนรับ
15. reception area
บริเวณต้อนรับแขก
16. waiting area
บริเวณนั่งรอ

Ways to greet a receptionist

I'm here for a job interview.
I have a 9:00 a.m. appointment with Mr. Lee.
I'd like to leave a message for Mr. Lee.

Role play. Talk to a receptionist.

A: *Hello. How can I help you?*
B: *I'm here for a job interview with Mr. Lee.*
A: *OK. What is your name?*

Office Equipment อุปกรณ์สำนักงาน

17. computer
คอมพิวเตอร์

18. inkjet printer
เครื่องพิมพ์แบบอิงค์เจ็ท

19. laser printer
เครื่องพิมพ์แบบเลเซอร์

20. scanner
เครื่องสแกน

21. fax machine
เครื่องรับส่งโทรสาร

22. paper cutter
ที่ตัดกระดาษ

23. photocopier
เครื่องถ่ายเอกสาร

24. paper shredder
เครื่องย่อยกระดาษ

25. calculator
เครื่องคิดเลข

26. electric pencil sharpener
เครื่องเหลาดินสอไฟฟ้า

27. postal scale
ตาชั่งของส่งไปรษณีย์

Office Supplies วัสดุเครื่องใช้ในสำนักงาน

ORDER
PAPER
CLIPS

R.F. Browne
15 Grand Concourse
Bronx, NY 10451

R. F. Browne
15 Grand Concourse
Bronx, NY 10451
(718) 555-1221

28. stapler
ที่เย็บกระดาษ

29. staples
ลวดเย็บกระดาษ

30. clear tape
เทปใส

31. paper clip
คลิปหนีบกระดาษ

32. packing tape
เทปปิดหีบห่อ

33. glue
กาว

34. rubber band
ยางรัด

35. pushpin
เข็มหมุด

36. correction fluid
น้ำยาลบคำผิด

37. correction tape
เทปลบคำผิด

38. legal pad
สมุดจดขนาดยาว

39. sticky notes
กระดาษโน๊ตมีกาวติด

40. mailer
ซองไปรษณีย์

41. mailing label
ป้ายปะหน้าซองไปรษณีย์

42. letterhead / stationery
หัวจดหมาย /
กระดาษเขียนจดหมาย

43. envelope
ซองจดหมาย

44. rotary card file
แฟ้มใส่การ์ดแบบหมุน

45. ink cartridge
กระเป๋าหมึก

46. ink pad
แผ่นหมึก

47. stamp
ตรายาง

48. appointment book
สมุดนัดหมาย

49. organizer
แฟ้มจัดระเบียบ

50. file folder
แฟ้มใส่เอกสาร

1. **doorman**
   ยามเฝ้าประตู

2. **revolving door**
   ประตูหมุน

3. **parking attendant**
   พนักงานจอดรถ

4. **concierge**
   พนักงานบริการทั่วไป

5. **gift shop**
   ร้านขายของที่ระลึก

6. **bell captain**
   หัวหน้าพนักงานขนกระเป๋า

7. **bellhop**
   พนักงานขนกระเป๋า

8. **luggage cart**
   ล้อเข็นกระเป๋าเสื้อผ้า

9. **elevator**
   ลิฟท์

10. **guest**
    แขก

11. **desk clerk**
    พนักงานรับแขกโรงแรม

12. **front desk**
    ฝ่ายรับแขกส่วนหน้า

13. **guest room**
    ห้องพักในโรงแรม

14. **double bed**
    เตียงคู่

15. **king-size bed**
    เตียงขนาดใหญ่พิเศษ

16. **suite**
    ห้องชุด

17. **room service**
    การบริการส่งอาหารถึงห้องพัก

18. **hallway**
    โถงทางเดิน

19. **housekeeping cart**
    ล้อเข็นของใช้งานแม่บ้านโรงแรม

20. **housekeeper**
    แม่บ้านโรงแรม

21. **pool service**
    การบำรุงรักษาสระว่ายน้ำ

22. **pool**
    สระน้ำ

23. **maintenance**
    การซ่อมบำรุง

24. **gym**
    โรง / ห้องบริหารร่างกาย

25. **meeting room**
    ห้องประชุม

26. **ballroom**
    ห้องโถงงานเต้นรำ

A Restaurant Kitchen ครัวของร้านอาหาร

1. short-order cook
   คนทำอาหารจานด่วน

2. dishwasher
   คนล้างจาน

3. walk-in freezer
   ห้องเย็น (ห้องเก็บของแช่แข็ง)

4. food preparation worker
   พนักงานเตรียมอาหาร

5. storeroom
   ห้องเก็บของ

6. sous chef
   พ่อครัวมือรอง

7. head chef / executive chef
   หัวหน้าพ่อครัว / พ่อครัวมือเอก

Restaurant Dining การรับประทานในร้านอาหาร / ภัตตาคาร

8. server
   พนักงานเสิร์ฟ

9. diner
   ผู้มารับประทานอาหาร

10. buffet
    บุฟเฟต์

11. maitre d'
    พนักงานต้อนรับในร้านอาหาร

12. headwaiter
    หัวหน้าคนเสิร์ฟอาหารชาย

13. bus person
    คนเก็บถ้วยชามใช้แล้ว

14. banquet room
    ห้องจัดเลี้ยง

15. runner
    พนักงานบริการทั่วไป

16. caterer
    พนักงานจัดส่งอาหาร

More vocabulary

line cook: short-order cook

wait staff: servers, headwaiters, and runners

Ask your classmates. Share the answers.

1. Have you ever worked in a hotel? What did you do?
2. What is the hardest job in a hotel?
3. Would you prefer to stay at a hotel in the city or in the country?

185

1. dangerous
อันตราย

2. clinic
คลินิค

3. budget
งบประมาณ

4. floor plan
ผังแสดงพื้นที่อาคาร

5. contractor
ผู้รับเหมา (ก่อสร้าง)

6. electrical hazard
อันตรายจากไฟฟ้า

7. wiring
การเดินสายไฟ

8. bricklayer
คนงานก่ออิฐ

A. **call in** sick
โทรศัพท์ลาป่วย

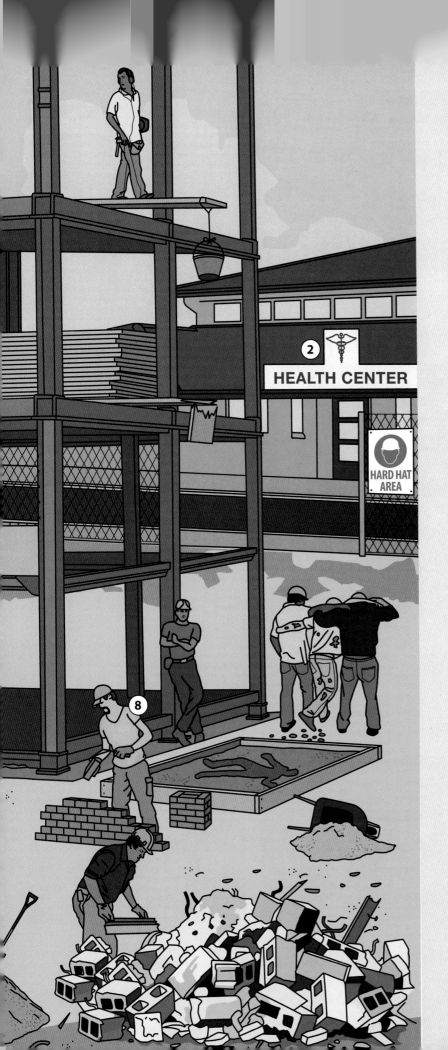

Look at the picture.
What do you see?

Answer the questions.

1. How many workers are there? How many are working?

2. Why did two workers call in sick?

3. What is dangerous at the construction site?

📖 **Read the story.**

A Bad Day at Work

Sam Lopez is the <u>contractor</u> for a new building. He makes the schedule and supervises the <u>budget</u>. He also solves problems. Today there are a lot of problems.

Two <u>bricklayers</u> <u>called in sick</u> this morning. Now Sam has only one bricklayer at work. One hour later, a construction worker fell. Now he has to go to the <u>clinic</u>. Sam always tells his workers to be careful. Construction work is <u>dangerous</u>. Sam's also worried because the new <u>wiring</u> is an <u>electrical hazard</u>.

Right now, the building owner is in Sam's office. Her new <u>floor plan</u> has 25 more offices. Sam has a headache. Maybe he needs to call in sick tomorrow.

Think about it.

1. What do you say when you can't come in to work? to school?

2. Imagine you are Sam. What do you tell the building owner? Why?

1. preschool /
   nursery school
   เด็กก่อนวัยเรียน /
   โรงเรียนอนุบาล

2. elementary school
   โรงเรียนประถม

3. middle school /
   junior high school
   โรงเรียนมัธยมต้น

4. high school
   โรงเรียนมัธยมปลาย

5. vocational school /
   technical school
   โรงเรียนอาชีวศึกษา /
   โรงเรียนเทคนิค

6. community college
   วิทยาลัยชุมชน

7. college / university
   วิทยาลัย / มหาวิทยาลัย

8. adult school
   โรงเรียนผู้ใหญ่

Listen and point. Take turns.

A: *Point to the preschool.*
B: *Point to the high school.*
A: *Point to the adult school.*

Dictate to your partner. Take turns.

A: *Write preschool.*
B: *Is that p-r-e-s-c-h-o-o-l?*
A: *Yes. That's right.*

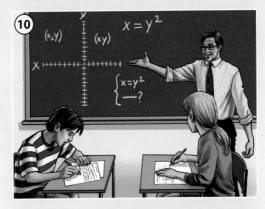

9. language arts
   ศิลปะด้านภาษา

10. math
    คำนวณ

11. science
    วิทยาศาสตร์

12. history
    ประวัติศาสตร์

13. world languages
    ภาษาต่างๆของโลก

14. ESL / ESOL
    การเรียนภาษาอังกฤษ
    เป็นภาษาที่สอง

15. arts
    ศิลปะสาขาต่างๆ

16. music
    ดนตรี

17. physical education
    พลศึกษา

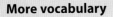

More vocabulary

core course: a subject students have to take. Math is a core course.

elective: a subject students choose to take. Art is an elective.

Pair practice. Make new conversations.

A: *I go to community college.*

B: *What subjects are you taking?*

A: *I'm taking history and science.*

English Composition

การเรียงความภาษาอังกฤษ

① factory

② I worked in a factory.

③ Little by little, work and success came to me. My first job wasn't good. I worked in a small factory. Now, I help manage two factories.

④

1. word
   คำ

2. sentence
   ประโยค

3. paragraph
   ย่อหน้า

4. essay
   เรียงความ

Parts of an Essay
ส่วนต่างๆของ เรียงความ

5. title
   ชื่อเรื่อง

6. introduction
   คำนำ

7. body
   เนื้อความ

8. conclusion
   สรุป

9. quotation
   การยกเอาคำพูด ของผู้อื่นมา

10. footnote
    หมายเหตุท้ายหน้า

Carlos Lopez
Eng. Comp.
10/21/10

⑤ Success in the U.S.

⑥ I came to Los Angeles from Mexico in 2006. I had no job, no friends, and no family here. I was homesick and scared, but I did not go home. I took English classes (always at night) and I studied hard. I believed in my future success!

⑦ More than 400,000 new immigrants come to the U.S every year. Most of us need to find work. During my first year here, my routine was the same: get up; look for work; go to class; go to bed. I had to take jobs with long hours and low pay. Often I had two or three jobs.

Little by little, work and success came to me. My first job wasn't good. I worked in a small factory. Now, I help manage two factories.

⑧ Hard work makes success possible. Henry David Thoreau said, "Men are born to succeed, not fail." **⑨** My story shows that he was right.

⑩ ¹ U.S. Census

Punctuation
เครื่องหมายวรรคตอน

. 11. period
   จุดลงท้ายประโยค

? 12. question mark
   เครื่องหมายคำถาม

! 13. exclamation mark
   เครื่องหมายตกใจ

, 14. comma
   จุลภาค

" " 15. quotation marks
   เครื่องหมายคำพูด

' 16. apostrophe
   เครื่องหมายแสดง
   ความเป็นเจ้าของ

: 17. colon
   เครื่องหมายจุดคู่

; 18. semicolon
   เครื่องหมายอัฒภาค

( ) 19. parentheses
   วงเล็บ

- 20. hyphen
   อติภังค์

Writing Rules กฎในการเขียน

A

Carlos

Mexico

Los Angeles

A. **Capitalize** names.
เขียนชื่อเริ่มด้วยอักษร ตัวใหญ่

B

Hard work makes success possible.

B. **Capitalize** the first letter in a sentence.
เริ่มต้นประโยคด้วยอักษร ตัวใหญ่

C

I was homesick and scared, but I did not go home.

C. **Use** punctuation.
ใช้เครื่องหมายวรรคตอน

D

I came to Los Angeles from Mexico in 2006. I had no job, no friends, and no family here. I was homesick and scared, but I did not go home. I took English classes (always at night) and I studied hard. I believed in my future success!

D. **Indent** the first sentence in a paragraph.
ย่อหน้าเมื่อเริ่มประโยคแรก ของย่อหน้า

Ways to ask for suggestions on your compositions

What do you think of this <u>title</u>?
Is this <u>paragraph</u> OK? Is the <u>punctuation</u> correct?
Do you have any suggestions for the <u>conclusion</u>?

Pair practice. Make new conversations.

A: *What do you think of this <u>title</u>?*
B: *I think you need to <u>revise</u> it.*
A: *Thanks. Do you have any more suggestions?*

190

The Writing Process กระบวนการในการเขียน

PREWRITING

E. Think about the assignment.
คิดเรื่องงานที่ได้รับมอบหมาย

F. Brainstorm ideas.
ระดมแนวคิดต่างๆ

G. Organize your ideas.
จัดระเบียบแนวคิดต่างๆของคุณ

WRITING AND REVISING

H. Write a first draft.
เขียนร่างฉบับแรก

I. Edit. / Proofread.
ตรวจแก้ / อ่านตรวจทาน

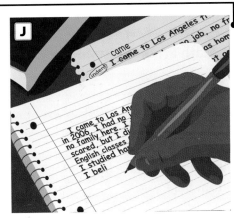

J. Revise. / Rewrite.
แก้ไข / เขียนใหม่

SHARING AND RESPONDING

K. Get feedback.
ขอรับฟังความคิดเห็น

L. Write a final draft.
เขียนร่างฉบับสุดท้าย

M. Turn in your paper.
ส่งงานเขียนของคุณ

Ask your classmates. Share the answers.

1. Do you like to write essays?
2. Which part of the writing process do you like best? least?

Think about it. Discuss.

1. In which jobs are writing skills important?
2. What tools can help you edit your writing?
3. What are some good subjects for essays?

191

Mathematics

Integers ตัวจำนวนเต็ม

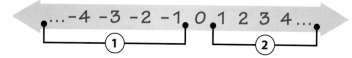

$$\dots -4 \ -3 \ -2 \ -1 \ 0 \ 1 \ 2 \ 3 \ 4 \dots$$

1. negative integers
   ตัวเลขจำนวนเต็มติดลบ
2. positive integers
   ตัวเลขจำนวนเต็มเป็นบวก

Fractions เศษส่วน

$$\frac{3}{8} \quad \frac{3}{8}$$

3. odd numbers
   เลขคี่
   $1, 3, 5, 7, 9, 11\dots$
4. even numbers
   เลขคู่
   $2, 4, 6, 8, 10 \dots$

5. numerator
   เศษ
6. denominator
   ส่วน

Math Operations การคิดเลข

A. **add**
   บวก

B. **subtract**
   ลบ

C. **multiply**
   คูณ

D. **divide**
   หาร

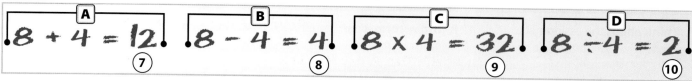

A	B	C	D
$8 + 4 = 12$	$8 - 4 = 4$	$8 \times 4 = 32$	$8 \div 4 = 2$

7. sum
   ผลรวม
8. difference
   ผลต่าง / ส่วนต่าง
9. product
   ผลคูณ
10. quotient
    ผลหาร

A Math Problem โจทย์เลข

11.
Tom is 10 years older than Kim. Next year he will be twice as old as Kim. How old is Tom this year?

12.
$x = $ Kim's age now
$x + 10 = $ Tom's age now
$x + 1 = $ Kim's age next year
$2(x + 1) = $ Tom's age next year

13.
$x + 10 + 1 = 2(x + 1)$
$x + 11 = 2x + 2$
$11 - 2 = 2x - x$

14.
$x = 9$, Kim is 9, Tom is 19

15.
horizontal axis
vertical axis

11. word problem
    โจทย์ปรนัย / โจทย์แบบบรรยาย
12. variable
    โจทย์ตัวแปร
13. equation
    สมการ
14. solution
    ผลเฉลย
15. graph
    กราฟ

Types of Math ประเภทของวิชาคำนวณ

16.

How much are they?
$79 NOW 40% OFF!
x = the sale price
x = 79.00 - .40 (79.00)
x = $47.40

17.

How many do I need?
area of path = 24 square ft.
area of brick = 2 square ft.
24 / 2 = 12 bricks

18.
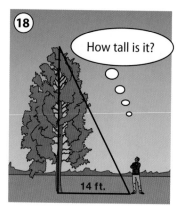
How tall is it?
14 ft.
$\tan 63° = $ height / 14 feet
height = 14 feet $(\tan 63°)$
height $\approx$ 27.48 feet

19.
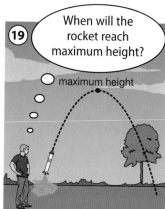
When will the rocket reach maximum height?
maximum height
$s(t) = -\frac{1}{2} gt^2 + V_0 t + h$
$s^{|}(t) = -gt + V_0 = 0$
$t = V_0 / g$

16. algebra
    พีชคณิต
17. geometry
    เรขาคณิต
18. trigonometry
    ตรีโกณมิติ
19. calculus
    วิชาคำนวณขั้นสูง

Lines เส้น

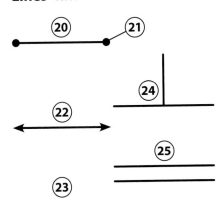

Angles มุม

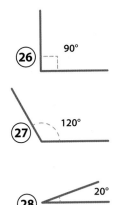

Shapes รูปทรง

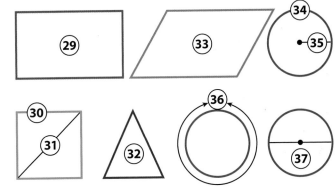

20. **line segment**
ส่วนหนึ่งของเส้น

21. **endpoint**
จุดปลาย

22. **straight line**
เส้นตรง

23. **curved line**
เส้นโค้ง

24. **perpendicular lines**
เส้นตั้งฉาก

25. **parallel lines**
เส้นขนาน

26. **right angle / 90° angle**
มุมฉากขวา / มุม 90 องศา

27. **obtuse angle**
มุมป้าน

28. **acute angle**
มุมแหลม

29. **rectangle**
สี่เหลี่ยมผืนผ้า

30. **square**
สี่เหลี่ยมจัตุรัส

31. **diagonal**
แนวทแยงมุม

32. **triangle**
สามเหลี่ยม

33. **parallelogram**
สี่เหลี่ยมด้านขนาน

34. **circle**
วงกลม

35. **radius**
รัศมีวงกลม

36. **circumference**
เส้นรอบวง

37. **diameter**
เส้นผ่าศูนย์กลาง

Geometric Solids
รูปทรงเรขาคณิต

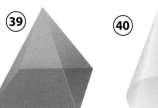

Measuring Area and Volume
การวัดพื้นที่และปริมาตร

$\ell \times w = $ area

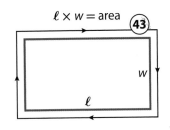

$6 \times f = $ surface area

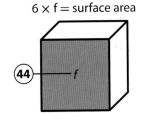

38. **cube**
ลูกบาศก์

39. **pyramid**
ปิรามิด

40. **cone**
กรวย

43. **perimeter**
ความยาวรอบรูป / เส้นรอบรูป

44. **face**
หน้า

$\pi \times r^2 \times h = $ volume

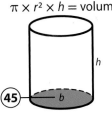

$\frac{4}{3} \times \pi \times r^3 = $ volume

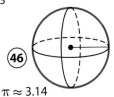

$\pi \approx 3.14$

41. **cylinder**
กระบอก

42. **sphere**
ทรงกลม

45. **base**
ฐาน

46. **pi**
ไพ

Ask your classmates. Share the answers.

1. Are you good at math?
2. Which types of math are easy for you?
3. Which types of math are difficult for you?

Think about it. Discuss.

1. What's the best way to learn mathematics?
2. How can you find the area of your classroom?
3. Which jobs use math? Which don't?

Biology ชีววิทยา

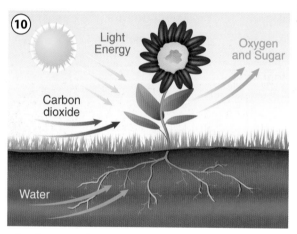

1. **organisms**
พืชและสัตว์ต่างๆ /
สิ่งมีชีวิต

2. **biologist**
นักชีววิทยา

3. **slide**
สไลด์

4. **cell**
เซลล์

5. **cell wall**
ผนังเซลล์

6. **cell membrane**
เยื่อหุ้มเซลล์

7. **nucleus**
นิวเคลียส

8. **chromosome**
โครโมโซม

9. **cytoplasm**
ไซโตพลาซึม

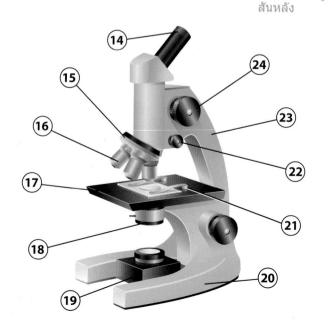

10. **photosynthesis**
การสังเคราะห์แสง

11. **habitat**
ที่อาศัยอยู่

12. **vertebrates**
สัตว์มีกระดูกสันหลัง

13. **invertebrates**
สัตว์ไม่มีกระดูก
สันหลัง

A Microscope กล้องจุลทรรศน์

14. **eyepiece**
ส่วนที่ส่องมอง

15. **revolving nosepiece**
ส่วนหมุนปรับ

16. **objective**
เลนส์วัตถุที่แทนกันได้

17. **stage**
แท่น

18. **diaphragm**
ไดอะแฟรม

19. **light source**
แหล่งให้แสง

20. **base**
ฐาน

21. **stage clips**
คลิปแท่น

22. **fine adjustment knob**
ปุ่มปรับภาพละเอียด

23. **arm**
แขน

24. **coarse adjustment knob**
ปุ่มปรับภาพหยาบ

Chemistry วิชาเคมี

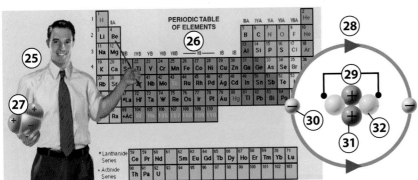

25. chemist
นักเคมี

26. periodic table
ตารางแบ่งธาตุแท้

27. molecule
โมเลกุล

28. atom
อะตอม

29. nucleus
นิวเคลียส

30. electron
อีเล็คตรอน

31. proton
โปรตอน

32. neutron
นิวตรอน

33. physicist
นักฟิสิกส์

Physics ฟิสิกส์

34. formula
สูตร

35. prism
ปริซึม

36. magnet
แม่เหล็ก

A Science Lab ห้องทดลองวิทยาศาสตร์

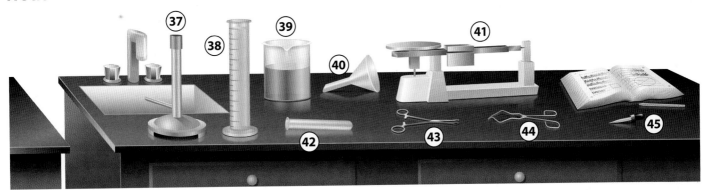

37. Bunsen burner
หัวเผาบันเซน

38. graduated cylinder
กระบอกที่มีขีดวัด

39. beaker
แก้วมีพวย / แก้วปากนก

40. funnel
กรวย

41. balance / scale
ตาชั่ง / เครื่องชั่ง

42. test tube
หลอดทดลอง

43. forceps
ปากคีบ

44. crucible tongs
คีมทนไฟ

45. dropper
ดรอปเปอร์

An Experiment การทดลอง

A. State a hypothesis.
ระบุข้อสมมุติฐาน

B. Do an experiment.
ทำการทดลอง

C. Observe.
สังเกตการณ์

D. Record the results.
บันทึกผลที่ได้รับ

E. Draw a conclusion.
หา / ทำบทสรุป

Desktop Computer คอมพิวเตอร์แบบตั้งโต๊ะ

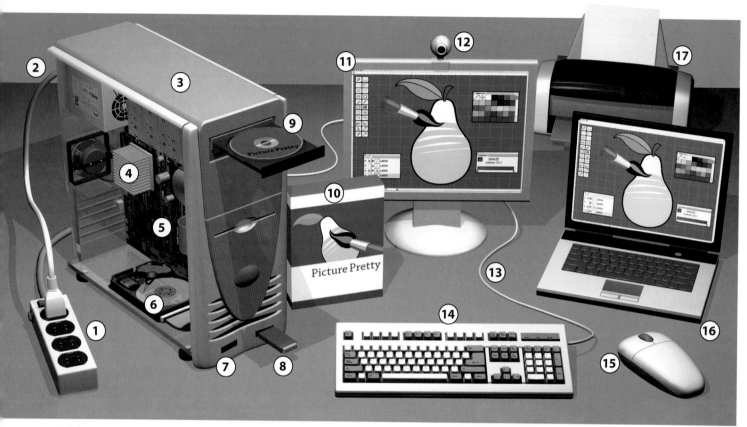

1. surge protector
เครื่องกันไฟกระชาก

2. power cord
สายไฟของเครื่อง

3. tower
ตัวเครื่องแบบตั้ง

4. microprocessor / CPU
ไมโครโปรเซสเซอร์ / ซีพียู

5. motherboard
แผงวงจรหลัก

6. hard drive
ฮาร์ดไดรฟ์

7. USB port
พอร์ตยูเอสบี

8. flash drive
ไดรฟ์หน่วยความจำ

9. DVD and CD-ROM drive
ไดรฟ์สำหรับดีวีดีและซีดีรอม

10. software
ซอฟท์แวร์

11. monitor /screen
จอภาพ / หน้าจอ

12. webcam
กล้องถ่ายรูปติดคอมพิวเตอร์

13. cable
สายเคเบิล

14. keyboard
แป้นคีย์

15. mouse
เม้าส์

16. laptop
คอมพิวเตอร์แบบกระเป๋าหิ้ว

17. printer
เครื่องพรินท์ / เครื่องพิมพ์

Keyboarding การใช้แป้นคีย์

A. **type**
พิมพ์

B. **select**
เลือก

C. **delete**
ลบ

D. **go to** the next line
ไปที่บรรทัดถัดไป

Navigating a Webpage การนำทางไปที่หน้าเว็บ

1. **menu bar**
แถบเมนู

2. **back button**
ปุ่มถอยหลัง

3. **forward button**
ปุ่มต่อไปข้างหน้า

4. **URL / website address**
ที่อยู่ของเว็บไซต์

5. **search box**
กล่องค้นหา

6. **search engine**
เครื่องมือค้นหา

7. **tab**
แท็บ

8. **drop-down menu**
เมนูแบบดึงลง

9. **pop-up ad**
โฆษณาแบบป๊อปอัป

10. **links**
จุดเชื่อมต่อไปเว็บอื่น

11. **video player**
เครื่องเล่นวิดีโอ

12. **pointer**
ศรชี้

13. **text box**
กล่องข้อความ
ตัวอักษร

14. **cursor**
เคอร์เซอร์

15. **scroll bar**
แถบเลื่อน

Logging on and Sending Email การต่อเข้าระบบและการส่งอีเมล

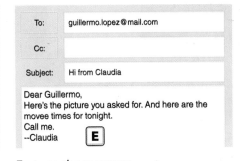

A. **type** your password
พิมพ์รหัสผ่านของคุณ

B. **click** "sign in"
คลิกที่ "ลงชื่อเข้า"

C. **address** the email
ใส่ที่อยู่อีเมล

D. **type** the subject
พิมพ์หัวเรื่อง

E. **type** the message
พิมพ์ข้อความ

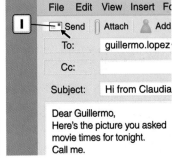

F. **check** your spelling
ตรวจการสะกดคำของคุณ

G. **attach** a picture
แนบภาพ

H. **attach** a file
แนบแฟ้ม

I. **send** the email
ส่งอีเมล

197

Colonial Period ยุคเมืองขึ้น

1. thirteen colonies
เมืองขึ้นสิบสามเมือง

2. colonists
คนที่อาศัยอยู่ใน
เมืองขึ้น

3. Native Americans
ชนพื้นเมืองอเมริกัน

4. slave
ทาส

5. Declaration of Independence
การประกาศอิสรภาพ

6. First Continental Congress
สภาคองเกรสแรกในภาคพื้นทวีป

7. founders
ผู้ก่อตั้ง

8. Revolutionary War
สงครามปฏิวัติ

9. redcoat
ทหารอังกฤษยุคนั้น
(ใส่เสื้อสีแดง)

10. minuteman
ทหารฝ่ายอเมริกายุคนั้น

11. first president
ประธานาธิบดีคนแรก

12. Constitution
รัฐธรรมนูญ

13. Bill of Rights
บทบัญญัติว่า
ด้วยสิทธิต่างๆ

Western Expansion
1803 – 1893

Civil War
1861 – 1865

World War I
1914 – 1918

Jazz Age
1920 – 1929

World War II
1941 – 1945

Civil Rights Movement
1954 – 1972

Information Age
1959 – now

1800   **1850**   **1900**   **1950**   **2000 →**

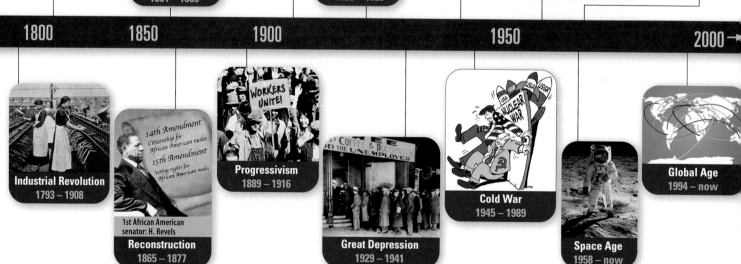

Industrial Revolution
1793 – 1908

14th Amendment
Citizenship for
African American males

15th Amendment
Voting rights for
African American males

1st African American
senator: H. Revels
Reconstruction
1865 – 1877

Progressivism
1889 – 1916

Great Depression
1929 – 1941

Cold War
1945 – 1989

Space Age
1958 – now

Global Age
1994 – now

Civilizations อารยธรรม

Pyramids | Parthenon

Times Square

Caesar

Qin Shi Huang

King Henry VIII

Queen Elizabeth I

Juarez

Mussolini

Churchill

1. ancient
โบราณ

2. modern
สมัยใหม่

3. emperor
จักรพรรดิ

4. monarch
กษัตริย์

5. president
ประธานาธิบดี

6. dictator
ผู้เผด็จการ

7. prime minister
นายกรัฐมนตรี

Historical Terms ศัพท์ทางประวัติศาสตร์

Vikings | Astronauts

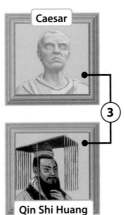

8. exploration
การสำรวจ

9. explorer
นักสำรวจ

10. war
สงคราม

11. army
กองทัพ

12. immigration
การย้ายเข้ามาอาศัยอยู่

13. immigrant
คนเข้าเมือง

Mozart | Duke Ellington

Susan B. Anthony | César Chávez

Edison | Camarena

14. composer
นักประพันธ์เพลง

15. composition
การแต่งเพลงหรือดนตรี

16. political movement
การเคลื่อนไหวทางการเมือง

17. activist
นักเคลื่อนไหว

18. inventor
นักประดิษฐ์

19. invention
การประดิษฐ์

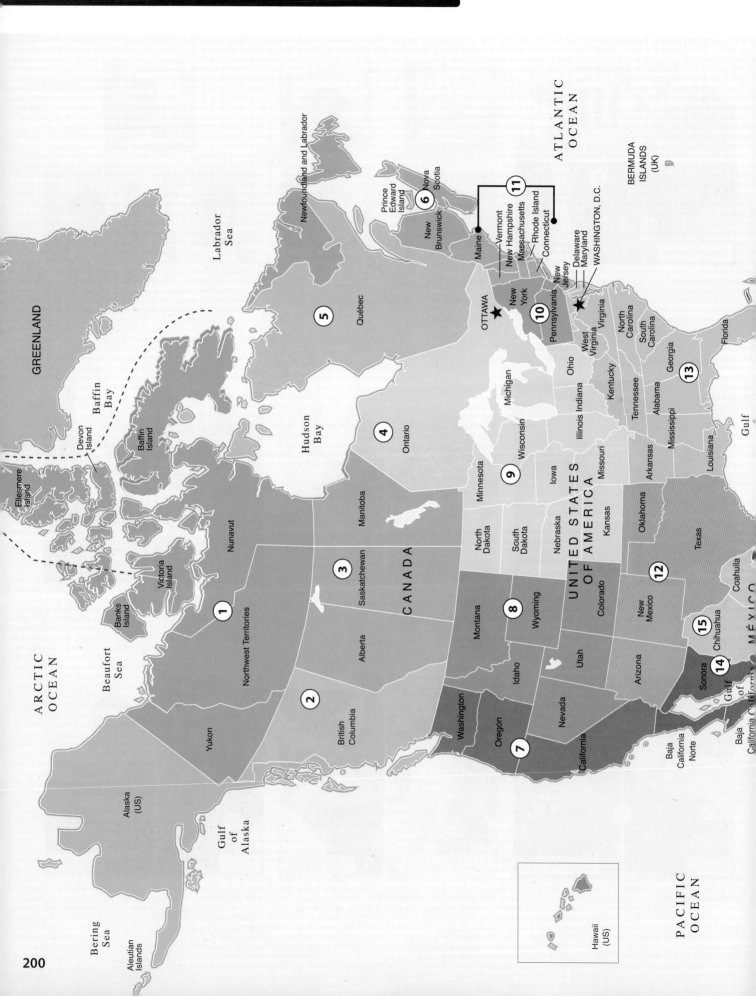

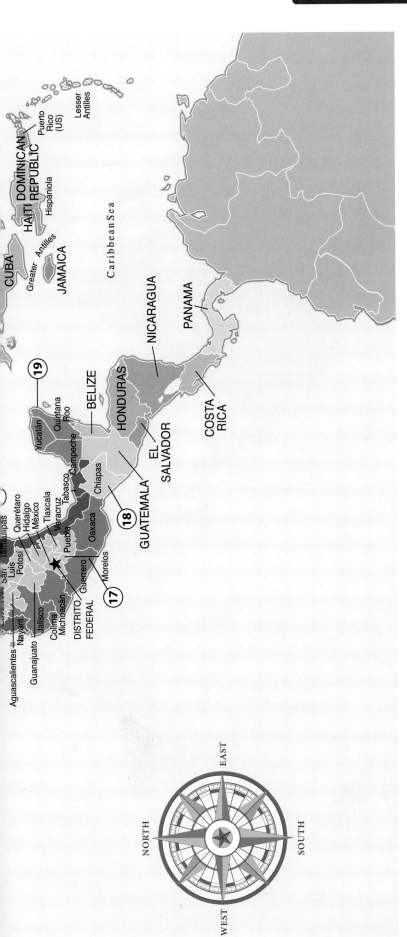

Puerto Rico (US)
Lesser Antilles
DOMINICAN REPUBLIC
HAITI
Hispaniola
CUBA
Greater Antilles
JAMAICA
Caribbean Sea
Caribbean Sea
NICARAGUA
PANAMA
BELIZE
HONDURAS
Quintana Roo
Yucatán
Campeche
Chiapas
EL SALVADOR
COSTA RICA
Tabasco
Tlaxcala
Veracruz
Querétaro
Hidalgo
México
Puebla
Oaxaca
GUATEMALA
Morelos
San Luis Potosí
Tamaulipas
Guerrero
Michoacán
Colima
DISTRITO FEDERAL
Aguascalientes
Nayarit
Jalisco
Guanajuato

⑲ ⑱ ⑰

EAST
NORTH
SOUTH
WEST

Regions of Canada
ภูมิภาคต่างๆ ของแคนาดา

1. Northern Canada
   แคนาดาภาคเหนือ
2. British Columbia
   บริติชโคลัมเบีย
3. The Prairie Provinces
   จังหวัดในแถบทุ่งหญ้าที่พื้นราบ
4. Ontario
   ออนทาริโอ
5. Québec
   ควิเบก
6. The Maritime Provinces
   จังหวัดใต้ในแถบมณฑลชายฝั่งทะเล

Regions of the United States
ภูมิภาคต่างๆ ในสหรัฐอเมริกา

7. The Pacific States / the West Coast
   รัฐในแถบฝั่งแปซิฟิก / ภาคฝั่งตะวันตก
8. The Rocky Mountain States
   รัฐในแถบเทือกเขาร็อกกี
9. The Midwest
   รัฐในแถบตอนกลาง
10. The Mid-Atlantic States
    รัฐในแถบตอนกลางฝั่งแอตแลนติก
11. New England
    นิวอิงแลนด์
12. The Southwest
    ตะวันตกเฉียงใต้
13. The Southeast / the South
    ตะวันออกเฉียงใต้ / ใต้

Regions of Mexico
ภูมิภาคต่างๆ ในเม็กซิโก

14. The Pacific Northwest
    ตะวันตกเฉียงเหนือฝั่งแปซิฟิก
15. The Plateau of Mexico
    แถบที่ราบสูงของเม็กซิโก
16. The Gulf Coastal Plain
    ที่ราบริมฝั่งอ่าว (เม็กซิโก)
17. The Southern Uplands
    ที่สูงภาคใต้
18. The Chiapas Highlands
    พื้นที่สูงเชียปาส
19. The Yucatan Peninsula
    คาบสมุทรยูคาทัน

Continents
ทวีป

1. **North America**
   อเมริกาเหนือ
2. **South America**
   อเมริกาใต้
3. **Europe**
   ยุโรป
4. **Asia**
   เอเชีย
5. **Africa**
   อัฟริกา
6. **Australia**
   ออสเตรเลีย
7. **Antarctica**
   แอนตาร์คติกา

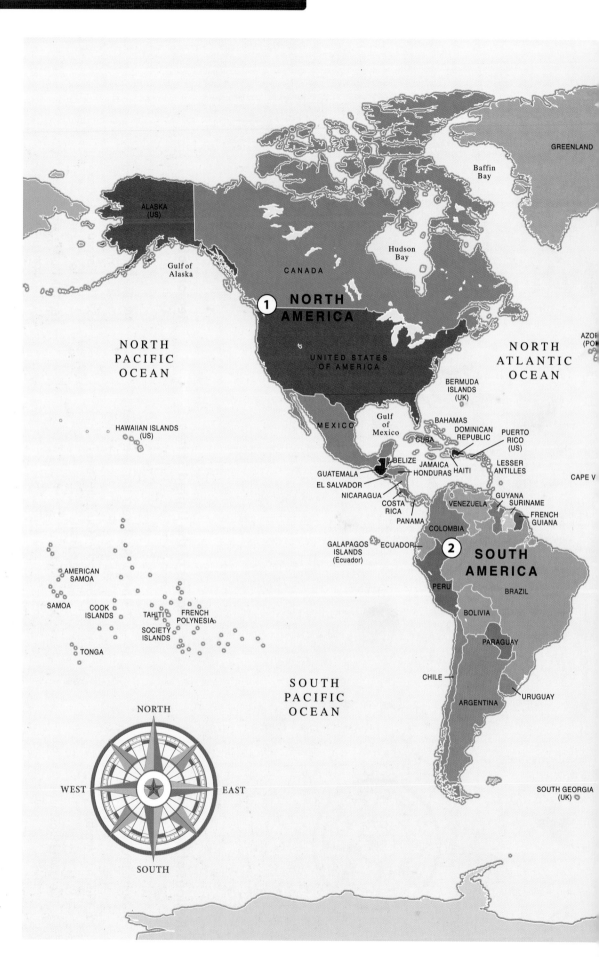

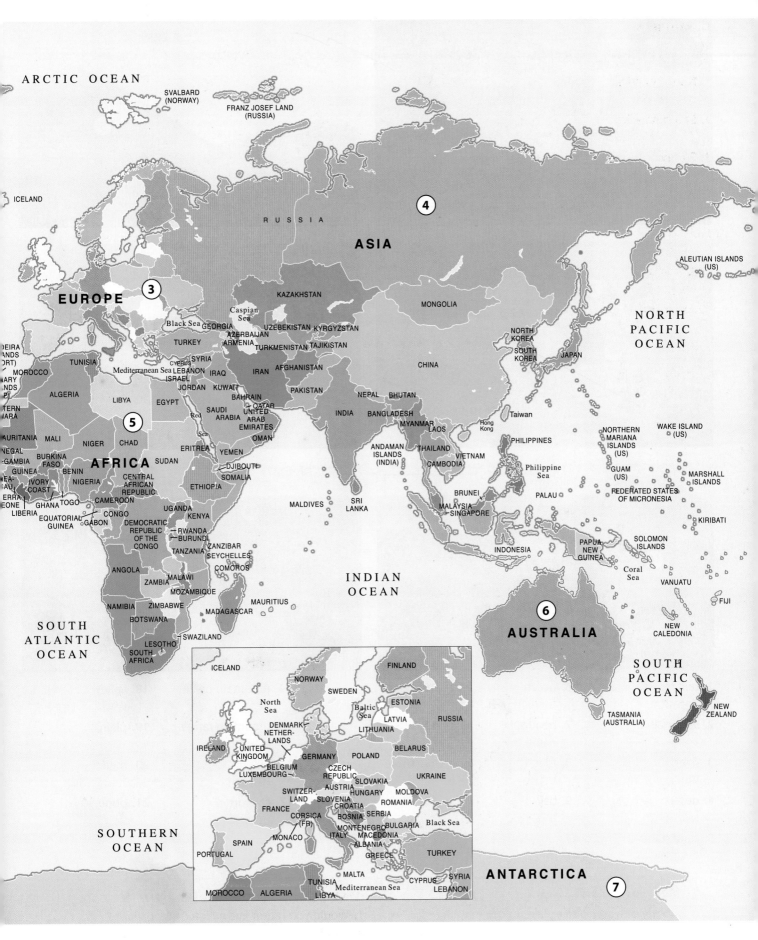

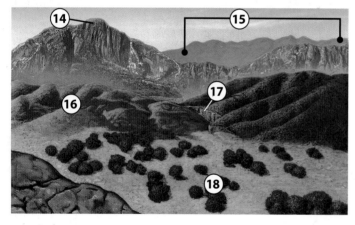

1. **rain forest**
ป่าร้อนชื้น

2. **waterfall**
น้ำตก

3. **river**
แม่น้ำ

4. **desert**
ทะเลทราย

5. **sand dune**
ภูเขาทราย

6. **ocean**
มหาสมุทร

7. **peninsula**
คาบสมุทร

8. **island**
เกาะ

9. **bay**
อ่าว

10. **beach**
ชายหาด

11. **forest**
ป่า

12. **shore**
ฝั่ง

13. **lake**
ทะเลสาบ

14. **mountain peak**
ยอดเขา

15. **mountain range**
เทือกเขา

16. **hills**
เขาเตี้ยๆ

17. **canyon**
หุบเขาลึก

18. **valley**
พื้นที่หว่างเขา

19. **plains**
ที่ราบ

20. **meadow**
ทุ่งหญ้าในป่า

21. **pond**
บึง

More vocabulary

a body of water: a river, lake, or ocean

stream / creek: a very small river

Ask your classmates. Share the answers.

1. Would you rather live near a river or a lake?
2. Would you rather travel through a forest or a desert?
3. How often do you go to the beach or the shore?

8. sun
   ดวงอาทิตย์

9. sky
   ท้องฟ้า

10. mammals
    สัตว์เลี้ยงลูกด้วยนม

11. insects
    แมลง

12. nest
    รัง

13. water
    น้ำ

14. fish
    ปลา

Ways to talk about nature

Look at the sky! Isn't it beautiful?
Did you see the fish / insects?
It's / They're so interesting.

Pair practice. Make new conversations.

A: *Do you know the name of that yellow flower?*
B: *I think it's a sunflower.*
A: *Oh, and what about that blue bird?*

209

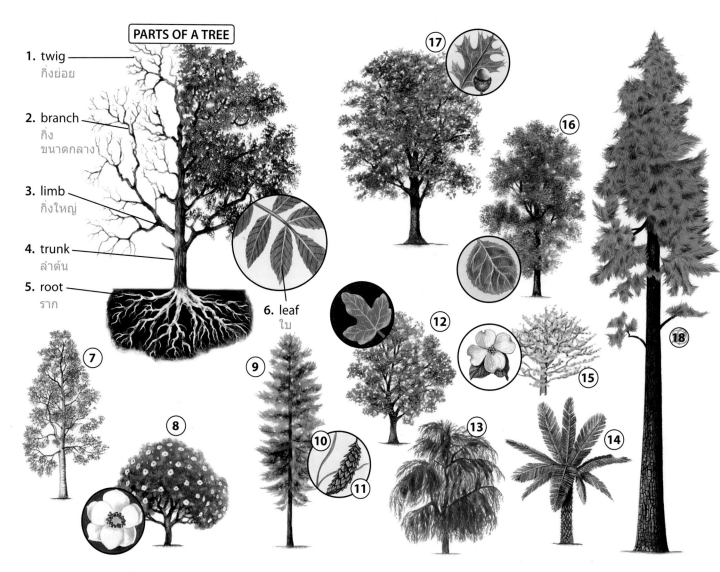

PARTS OF A TREE

1. twig
   กิ่งย่อย

2. branch
   กิ่ง
   ขนาดกลาง

3. limb
   กิ่งใหญ่

4. trunk
   ลำต้น

5. root
   ราก

6. leaf
   ใบ

7. birch ต้นเบิร์ช	**10. needle** ใบสน	**13. willow** หลิว	**16. elm** ต้นเอล์ม
8. magnolia แม็กโนเลีย / ดอกจำพวกมณฑา	**11. pinecone** ดอกสน	**14. palm** ปาล์ม	**17. oak** ต้นโอ๊ค
9. pine สน	**12. maple** เมเปิ้ล	**15. dogwood** ไม้ชนิดหนึ่งดอกสีขาวๆ	**18. redwood** ต้นเรดวูด

Plants พืชพันธุ์

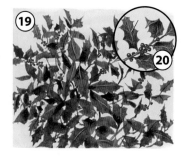

19. holly ไม้ประดับเทศกาลคริสต์มาส	**21. cactus** ตะบองเพชร	**23. poison sumac** ซูแมคมีพิษ	**25. poison ivy** ไอวี่มีพิษ
20. berries ผลเบอร์รี่	**22. vine** เครือเถา	**24. poison oak** โอ๊คมีพิษ	

Parts of a Flower ส่วนต่างๆของดอกไม้

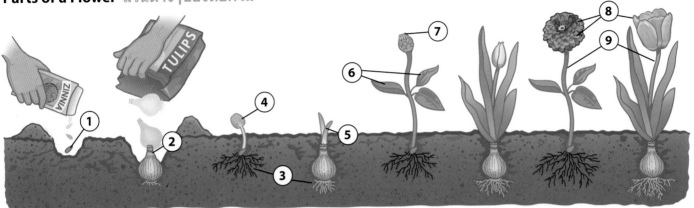

1. **seed**
เมล็ด / เมล็ดพันธุ์

2. **bulb**
หัวพันธุ์

3. **roots**
ราก

4. **seedling**
ต้นอ่อน

5. **shoot**
หน่อ

6. **leaves**
ใบ

7. **bud**
ดอกตูม

8. **petals**
กลีบดอก

9. **stems**
ก้านดอก

10. **sunflower**
ทานตะวัน

11. **tulip**
ทิวลิป

12. **hibiscus**
ชบา

13. **marigold**
ยี่สุ่น / ดาวเรือง

14. **daisy**
เดซี่

15. **rose**
กุหลาบ

16. **iris**
ไอริส

17. **crocus**
ดอกดิน / กันกุมา

18. **gardenia**
พุดจีน / พุทธชาด

19. **orchid**
กล้วยไม้

20. **carnation**
คาร์เนชั่น

21. **chrysanthemum**
เบญจมาศ

22. **jasmine**
มะลิ

23. **violet**
ไวโอเล็ต

24. **poinsettia**
ดอกต้นคริสต์มาส

25. **daffodil**
จุ้ยเซียน

26. **lily**
พลับพลึง

27. **houseplant**
ไม้ประดับภายในบ้าน

28. **bouquet**
ช่อดอกไม้

29. **thorn**
หนาม

Sea Animals สัตว์ทะเล

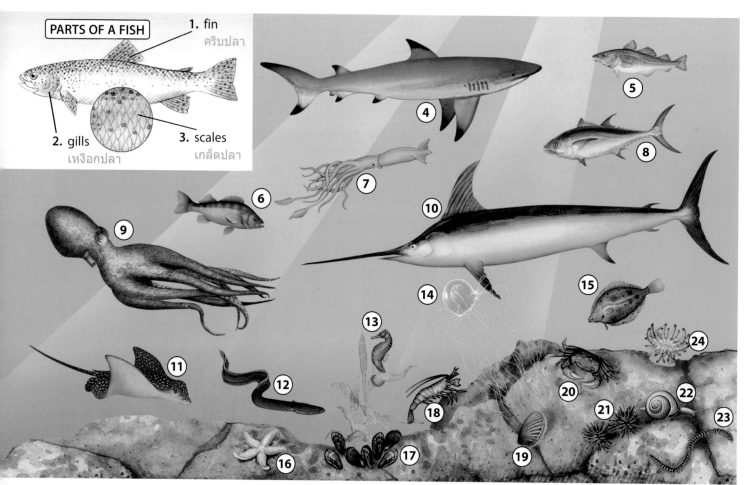

PARTS OF A FISH

1. fin
ครีบปลา

2. gills
เหงือกปลา

3. scales
เกล็ดปลา

4. shark ฉลาม	9. octopus หมึกยักษ์	14. jellyfish แมงกะพรุน	18. shrimp กุ้ง	23. worm หนอน
5. cod ค้อด	10. swordfish ปลาดาบ	15. flounder ปลาทะเลตัวแบน (ปลาตาเดียว ปลาลิ้นหมา)	19. scallop หอยแครง	24. sea anemone สัตว์ทะเลลำตัวเป็น ปล้องมีหนวดปาก
6. bass กะพง	11. ray กะเบน	16. starfish ปลาดาว	20. crab ปู	
7. squid หมึก	12. eel ปลาไหล	17. mussel หอยกาบ หอยแมลงภู่	21. sea urchin สัตว์ทะเลคล้ายหอย	
8. tuna ทูน่า	13. seahorse ม้าน้ำ		22. snail หอยทาก	

Amphibians สัตว์ครึ่งบกครึ่งน้ำ

25. frog กบ	26. newt แลน	27. salamander กิ้งก่าประเภทหนึ่ง	28. toad อึ่งอ่าง

212

Sea Mammals สัตว์ทะเลเลี้ยงลูกด้วยนม

29. whale
ปลาวาฬ

30. porpoise
โลมาประเภทหนึ่ง

31. dolphin
โลมา

32. walrus
สัตว์ถิ่นขั้วโลกเหนือชนิดหนึ่ง

33. sea lion
สิงโตทะเล

34. seal
แมวน้ำ

35. sea otter
นากทะเล

Reptiles สัตว์เลื้อยคลาน

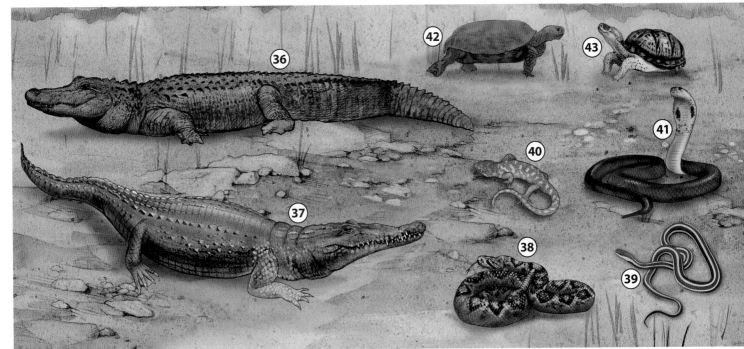

36. alligator
จระเข้ตีนเป็ด

37. crocodile
จระเข้

38. rattlesnake
งูกระดิ่ง

39. garter snake
งูเล็กไม่มีพิษ

40. lizard
กิ้งก่า

41. cobra
งูเห่า

42. tortoise
กระ

43. turtle
เต่า

PARTS OF A BIRD

1. wing
ปีก

2. claw
อุ้งเล็บ

3. beak / bill
ปากนก

4. feather
ขนนก

5. owl
นกเค้าแมว

6. blue jay
นกกะขาบน้ำเงิน

7. sparrow
นกกระจอก

8. woodpecker
นกหัวขวาน

9. eagle
นกอินทรีย์

10. hummingbird
นกเล็กชนิดหนึ่ง

11. penguin
นกเพนกวิน

12. duck
เป็ด

13. goose
ห่าน

14. peacock
นกยูง

15. pigeon
พิราบ

16. robin
นกเล็กชนิดหนึ่ง
แผงอกสีแดงร้องเสียงเพราะ

Insects and Arachnids แมลงและแมง

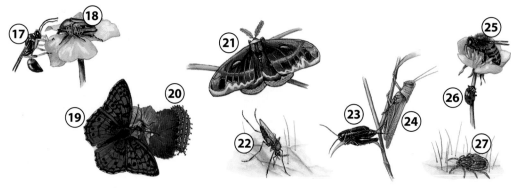
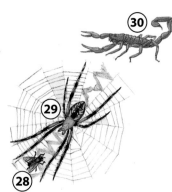

17. wasp
ตัวต่อ

18. beetle
แมลงปีกแข็ง / แมงช้าง

19. butterfly
ผีเสื้อ

20. caterpillar
ดักแด้ / ตัวด้วง

21. moth
ผีเสื้อกลางคืน

22. mosquito
ยุง

23. cricket
จิ้งหรีด

24. grasshopper
ตั๊กแตน

25. honeybee
ผึ้ง

26. ladybug
แมลงทับ

27. tick
หมัด / เห็บ

28. fly
แมลงวัน

29. spider
แมงมุม

30. scorpion
แมงป่อง

Farm Animals สัตว์เลี้ยงในฟาร์ม

1. cow
วัว

2. pig
หมู

3. donkey
ลา

4. horse
ม้า

5. goat
แพะ

6. sheep
แกะ

7. rooster
ไก่ตัวผู้

8. hen
ไก่ตัวเมีย

Pets สัตว์เลี้ยงดูเล่น

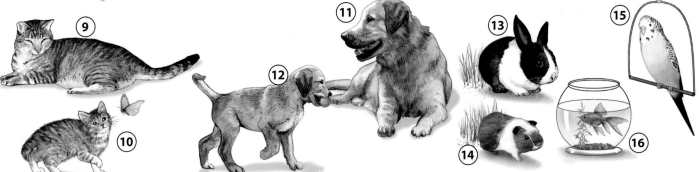

9. cat
แมว

10. kitten
ลูกแมว

11. dog
หมา

12. puppy
ลูกหมา

13. rabbit
กระต่าย

14. guinea pig
หนูตะเพา

15. parakeet
นกแก้ว / นกแขกเต้า

16. goldfish
ปลาเงินปลาทอง

Rodents สัตว์ประเภทหนู

17. rat
หนูตัวใหญ่

18. mouse
หนูตัวเล็ก

19. gopher
สัตว์ชนิดหนึ่งคล้ายกระรอก

20. chipmunk
กระแตชนิดหนึ่ง

21. squirrel
กระรอก

22. prairie dog
หนูทุ่งหญ้า

More vocabulary

domesticated: animals that work for and / or live with people

wild: animals that live away from people

Ask your classmates. Share the answers.

1. Have you worked with farm animals? Which ones?
2. Are you afraid of rodents? Which ones?
3. Do you have a pet? What kind?

1. moose
   สัตว์ชนิดหนึ่งคล้ายลา
   มีเขาเป็นแฉก

2. mountain lion
   สิงโตภูเขา

3. coyote
   หมาป่าชนิดหนึ่ง

4. opossum
   สัตว์ชนิดหนึ่งคล้ายกระรอก

5. wolf
   หมาป่า

6. buffalo / bison
   ควาย / ควายไบสัน

7. bat
   ค้างคาว

8. armadillo
   ตัวนิ่ม / ตัวนางอาย

9. beaver
   นาก

10. porcupine
    เม่น

11. bear
    หมี

12. skunk
    ตัวเหม็น

13. raccoon
    แรคคูน

14. deer
    กวาง

15. fox
    หมาจิ้งจอก

16. antlers
    เขาละมั่ง / เขากวาง

17. hooves
    กีบเท้า

18. whiskers
    หนวดสัตว์

19. coat / fur
    ขนตามตัวสัตว์

20. paw
    อุ้งเท้า

21. horn
    เขา

22. tail
    หาง

23. quill
    ขนเม่น

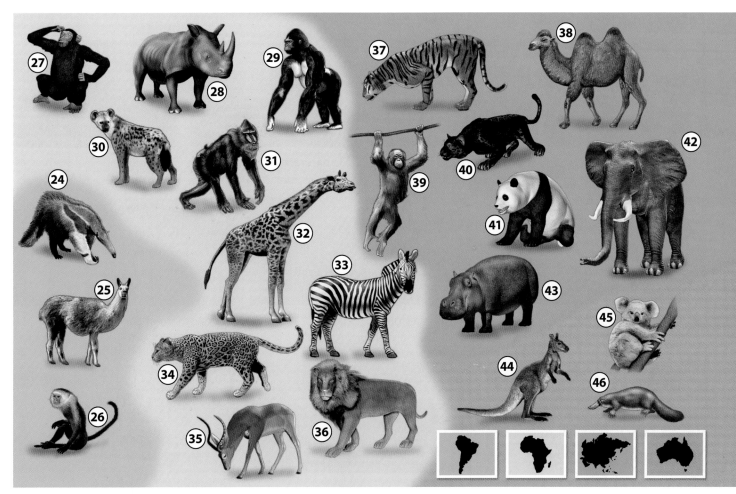

24. anteater
ตัวกินมด

25. llama
ลามา

26. monkey
ลิง

27. chimpanzee
ลิงชิมแปนซี

28. rhinoceros
แรด

29. gorilla
ลิงกอริลลา /
ลิงสุครีพ

30. hyena
หมาป่าชนิดหนึ่ง

31. baboon
ลิงหน้าหมู

32. giraffe
ยีราฟ

33. zebra
ม้าลาย

34. leopard
เสือดาว

35. antelope
กวางแอนตาโลป

36. lion
สิงโต

37. tiger
เสือ

38. camel
อูฐ

39. orangutan
ลิงอุรังอุตัง

40. panther
เสือดำ

41. panda
หมีแพนด้า

42. elephant
ช้าง

43. hippopotamus
ฮิปโป

44. kangaroo
จิงโจ้

45. koala
หมีโคอาล่า

46. platypus
สัตว์ชนิดหนึ่งของ
ออสเตรเลียคล้ายตุ่น

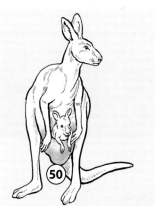

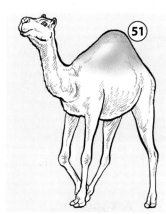

47. trunk
งวง

48. tusk
งา

49. mane
ขนคอ

50. pouch
ถุง

51. hump
โหนกหลัง

Energy Sources แหล่งพลังงาน

1. solar energy
พลังงานแสงอาทิตย์

2. wind power
พลังงานลม

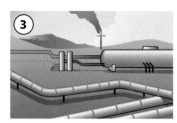

3. natural gas
ก๊าซธรรมชาติ

4. coal
ถ่านหิน

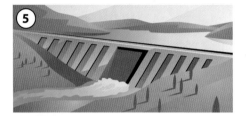

5. hydroelectric power
ไฟฟ้าพลังน้ำ

6. oil / petroleum
น้ำมัน / ปิโตรเลียม

7. geothermal energy
พลังงานอุณหธรณี /
พลังงานความร้อนใต้พิภพ

8. nuclear energy
พลังงานนิวเคลียร์

9. biomass / bioenergy
มวลชีวภาพ / พลังงานจากชีวภาพ

10. fusion
การหลอมรวม /
ปฏิกิริยานิวเคลียร์แบบรวมตัว

Pollution มลภาวะ

11. air pollution / smog
มลภาวะในอากาศ / หมอกควัน

12. hazardous waste
ขยะอันตราย

13. acid rain
ฝนพิษ

14. water pollution
มลภาวะในน้ำ

15. radiation
การแผ่รังสี

16. pesticide poisoning
การใช้ยาฆ่าแมลง

17. oil spill
การหกไหลล้นของน้ำมัน

Ask your classmates. Share the answers.

1. What types of things do you recycle?
2. What types of energy sources are in your area?
3. What types of pollution do you worry about?

Think about it. Discuss.

1. How can you save energy in the summer? winter?
2. What are some other ways that people can conserve energy or prevent pollution?

Ways to Conserve Energy and Resources วิธีต่างๆในการประหยัดพลังงานและแหล่งทรัพยากร

A. reduce trash
ลดขยะ

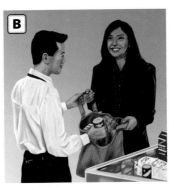

B. reuse shopping bags
ใช้ถุงบรรจุของซ้ำ

C. recycle
นำกลับมาใช้ใหม่

D. buy recycled products
ซื้อสินค้าที่ผลิตจาก
วัสดุใช้แล้ว

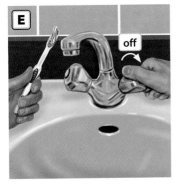

E. save water
ประหยัดน้ำ

F. fix leaky faucets
ซ่อมแซมก๊อกน้ำที่รั่วไหล

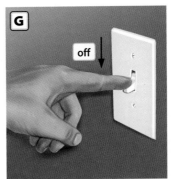

G. turn off lights
ปิดไฟ

H. use energy-efficient bulbs
ใช้หลอดไฟแบบประหยัด

I. carpool
โดยสารรถร่วมกัน

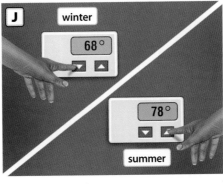

J. adjust the thermostat
ปรับเครื่องควบคุมอุณหภูมิ

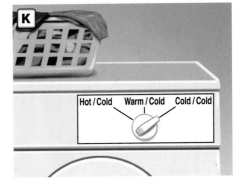

K. wash clothes in cold water
ซักผ้าในน้ำเย็น

L. don't litter
อย่าทิ้งขยะเรี่ยราด

M. compost food scraps
ทำปุ๋ยหมักด้วยเศษอาหาร

N. plant a tree
ปลูกต้นไม้

Yosemite
NATIONAL PARK

Dry Tortugas
NATIONAL PARK

Half Dome

1

Fort Jefferson

2

4

3

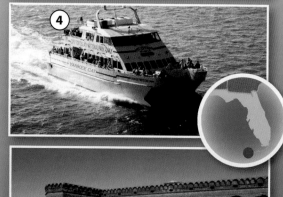

5

1. **landmarks**
จุดที่หมาย /
หลักปันเขตที่ดิน

2. **park ranger**
เจ้าหน้าที่อุทยาน

3. **wildlife**
สัตว์ป่า

4. **ferry**
เรือนำเที่ยว / เรือข้ามฟาก

5. **coral**
ปะการัง

6. **cave**
ถ้ำ

7. **caverns**
โพรงถ้ำ

A. **take** a tour
ไปเที่ยวดู /
ไปเที่ยวเป็นกลุ่ม

CARLSBAD CAVERNS
NATIONAL PARK

6

7

A

Answer the questions.

1. How many U.S. landmarks are in the pictures?

2. What kinds of wildlife do you see?

3. What can you do at Carlsbad Caverns?

 Read the story.

U.S. National Parks

More than 200 million people visit U.S. National Parks every year. These parks protect the <u>wildlife</u> and <u>landmarks</u> of the United States. Each park is different, and each one is beautiful.

At Yosemite, in California, you can take a nature walk with a <u>park ranger</u>. You'll see waterfalls, redwoods, and deer there.

In south Florida, you can take a <u>ferry</u> to Dry Tortugas. It's great to snorkel around the park's <u>coral</u> islands.

There are 113 <u>caves</u> at Carlsbad <u>Caverns</u> in New Mexico. The deepest cave is 830 feet below the desert! You can <u>take a tour</u> of these beautiful caverns.

There are 391 national parks to see. Go online for information about a park near you.

Think about it.

1. Why are national parks important?

2. Imagine you are a park ranger at a national park. Give your classmates a tour of the landmarks and wildlife.

Places to Go   สถานที่น่าไป

1. zoo
   สวนสัตว์
2. movies
   โรงภาพยนตร์
3. botanical garden
   สวนพฤกษชาติ
4. bowling alley
   ลานโบว์ลิ่ง
5. rock concert
   คอนเสิร์ตเพลงร็อค
6. swap meet /
   flea market
   ตลาดนัดขายของเก่า
7. aquarium
   สถานแสดงสัตว์น้ำ

| File | Edit | View | History | Bookmarks | Tools |

Places to Go in Our City

Listen and point. Take turns.

A: *Point to the zoo.*
B: *Point to the flea market.*
A: *Point to the rock concert.*

Dictate to your partner. Take turns.

A: *Write these words: zoo, movies, aquarium.*
B: *Zoo, movies, and what?*
A: *Aquarium.*

Search 🔍

8. play
   ละคร

9. art museum
   พิพิธภัณฑ์งานศิลปะ

10. amusement park
    สวนสนุก

11. opera
    ละครร้องโอเปร่า

12. nightclub
    ไนท์คลับ

13. county fair
    งานออกร้านในชุมชน

14. classical concert
    คอนเสิร์ตแบบคลาสิค

Ways to make plans using *Let's go*

Let's go to <u>the amusement park</u> tomorrow.
Let's go to <u>the opera</u> on Saturday.
Let's go to <u>the movies</u> tonight.

Pair practice. Make new conversations.

A: <u>Let's go to the zoo this afternoon</u>.
B: *OK. And let's go to <u>the movies tonight</u>.*
A: *That sounds like a good plan.*

1. **ball field**
สนามบอล

2. **cyclist**
นักปั่นจักรยาน

3. **bike path**
ทางจักรยาน

4. **jump rope**
กระโดดเชือก

5. **fountain**
น้ำพุ

6. **tennis court**
สนามเทนนิส

7. **skateboard**
สเก็ตบอร์ด

8. **picnic table**
โต๊ะปิคนิค

9. **water fountain**
ก๊อกน้ำดื่ม

10. **bench**
ม้านั่ง

11. **swings**
ชิงช้า

12. **tricycle**
รถสามล้อ

13. **slide**
สไลด์ / รางลื่น

14. **climbing apparatus**
เครื่องเล่นปีนป่าย

15. **sandbox**
ลานทราย

16. **seesaw**
ไม้กระดก

A. pull the wagon
ดึงล้อลาก

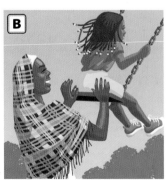

B. push the swing
ผลักชิงช้า

C. climb the bars
ปีนบาร์

D. picnic / have a picnic
ปิคนิค / นำอาหาร
ไปรับประทานที่สวน

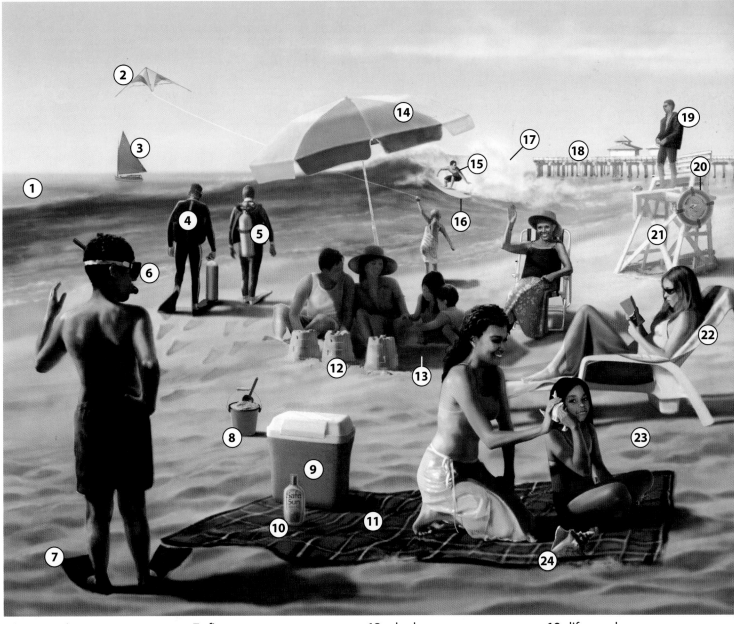

1. ocean / water
มหาสมุทร / น้ำ

2. kite
ว่าว

3. sailboat
เรือใบ

4. wet suit
ชุดนักประดาน้ำ

5. scuba tank
แท้งค์ประดาน้ำ

6. diving mask
หน้ากากดำน้ำ

7. fins
ครีบ

8. pail / bucket
ถัง

9. cooler
คูลเลอร์ / หีบเก็บความเย็น

10. sunscreen / sun block
ครีมกันแดดเผา / ครีมปกป้
องผิวจากแดด

11. blanket
ผ้าห่ม

12. sand castle
ปราสาททราย

13. shade
ในร่ม

14. beach umbrella
ร่มชายหาด

15. surfer
นักโต้คลื่น

16. surfboard
กระดานโต้คลื่น

17. wave
คลื่น

18. pier
ท่า

19. lifeguard
ยามเฝ้าระวังและช่วยชีวิต

20. lifesaving device
อุปกรณ์ช่วยชีวิต

21. lifeguard station
สถานียามเฝ้าระวัง
และช่วยชีวิต

22. beach chair
เก้าอี้ชายหาด

23. sand
ทราย

24. seashell
หอยทะเล

More vocabulary

seaweed: a plant that grows in the ocean
tide: the level of the ocean. The tide goes in and out every 12 hours.

Ask your classmates. Share the answers.

1. Do you like to go to the beach?
2. Are there famous beaches in your native country?
3. Do you prefer to be on the sand or in the water?

225

1. boating
   การเล่นเรือ

2. rafting
   การล่องแพ

3. canoeing
   การเล่นเรือคานู

4. fishing
   การตกปลา

5. camping
   การไปแคมป์ / กางเต๊นท์นอน

6. backpacking
   การแบกสัมภาระ

7. hiking
   การเดินเท้า

8. mountain biking
   การปั่นจักรยานไปตามภูเขา

9. horseback riding
   การขี่ม้า

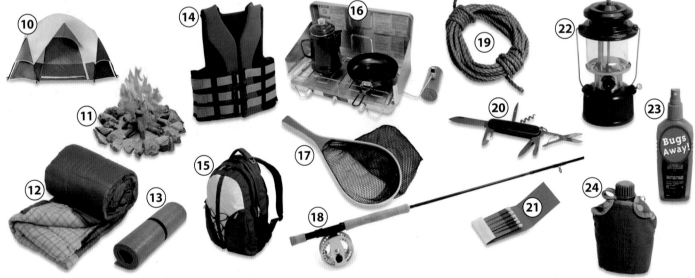

10. tent
    เต๊นท์

11. campfire
    แคมป์ไฟ

12. sleeping bag
    ถุงนอน

13. foam pad
    แผ่นโฟม

14. life vest
    เสื้อกั๊กนิรภัย

15. backpack
    กระเป๋าสะพายหลัง / เป๋แบกหลัง

16. camping stove
    เตาหุงต้มสำหรับแคมป์

17. fishing net
    ตาข่ายช้อนปลา

18. fishing pole
    คันเบ็ด

19. rope
    เชือก

20. multi-use knife
    มีดสารพัดใช้

21. matches
    ไม้ขีดไฟ

22. lantern
    ตะเกียงน้ำมัน

23. insect repellent
    น้ำยาไล่แมลง

24. canteen
    กระติกน้ำ

1. downhill skiing
การเล่นสกีลงเขา

2. snowboarding
การเล่นกระดานลื่นหิมะ

3. cross-country skiing
การเล่นสกีไปตามที่ราบโล่ง

4. ice skating
การเล่นสเก็ตน้ำแข็ง

5. figure skating
การเล่นสเก็ตน้ำแข็งแบบลีลาสวยงาม

6. sledding
การเล่นเลื่อน

7. waterskiing
การเล่นสกีน้ำ

8. sailing
การแล่นเรือใบ

9. surfing
การโต้คลื่น

10. windsurfing
การโต้ลม

11. snorkeling
สนอร์เกิล /
การใส่ท่อหายใจลงดูปลาในน้ำ

12. scuba diving
การดำน้ำด้วยเครื่องประดาน้ำ

More vocabulary

speed skating: racing while ice skating
windsurfing: sailboarding

Ask your classmates. Share the answers.

1. Which of these sports do you like?
2. Which of these sports would you like to learn?
3. Which of these sports is the most fun to watch?

1. archery
ยิงธนู

2. billiards / pool
บิลเลียด

3. bowling
โบว์ลิ่ง

4. boxing
มวย

5. cycling / biking
ปั่นจักรยาน /
ถีบจักรยาน

6. badminton
แบดมินตัน

7. fencing
ฟันดาบ

8. golf
กอล์ฟ

9. gymnastics
ยิมนาสติก

10. inline skating
สเก็ตแบบล้อ
แนวเดียว

11. martial arts
ศิลปะการป้องกันตัว

12. racquetball
แร็คเก็ตบอล

13. skateboarding
สเก็ตบอร์ด

14. table tennis
ปิงปอง

15. tennis
เทนนิส

16. weightlifting
ยกน้ำหนัก

17. wrestling
มวยปล้ำ

18. track and field
ลู่และลาน (กรีฑา)

19. horse racing
แข่งม้า

Pair practice. Make new conversations.

A: *What sports do you like?*
B: *I like <u>bowling</u>. What do you like?*
A: *I like <u>gymnastics</u>.*

Think about it. Discuss.

1. Why do people like to watch sports?
2. Which sports can be dangerous?
3. Why do people do dangerous sports?

1. score
แต้ม

2. coach
ผู้ทำการฝึกซ้อม

3. team
ทีม / กลุ่มที่เล่นร่วมกัน

4. fan
แฟนกีฬา

5. player
ผู้เล่น

6. official / referee
กรรมการตัดสิน

7. basketball court
สนามบาสเก็ตบอล

8. basketball
บาสเก็ตบอล

9. baseball
เบสบอล

10. softball
ซอฟท์บอล

11. football
ฟุตบอล (อเมริกัน) / รักบี้

12. soccer
ฟุตบอล

13. ice hockey
ฮ๊อคกี้บนลานน้ำแข็ง

14. volleyball
วอลเลย์บอล

15. water polo
โปโลน้ำ

More Vocabulary

win: to have the best score
lose: the opposite of win
tie: to have the same score

captain: the team leader
umpire: the name of the referee in baseball
Little League: a baseball and softball program for children

A. **pitch**
ขว้างลูก

B. **hit**
ตี

C. **throw**
โยน / ขว้าง

D. **catch**
จับ / คว้า

E. **kick**
เตะ

F. **tackle**
จับตัวคนเล่นที่พาลูกวิ่ง

G. **pass**
ส่งต่อ

H. **shoot**
ยิงลูก

I. **jump**
กระโดด

J. **dribble**
เลี้ยงลูกบอล

K. **dive**
ดำน้ำ

L. **swim**
ว่ายน้ำ

M. **stretch**
ยืดเส้นสาย

N. **exercise / work out**
บริหารร่างกาย /
ออกกำลังกาย

O. **bend**
โก้งโค้ง

P. **serve**
เสิร์ฟลูก

Q. **swing**
เหวี่ยง

R. **start**
เริ่ม

S. **race**
วิ่งแข่งขัน

T. **finish**
ถึงเส้นชัย

U. **skate**
สเก็ต

V. **ski**
สกี

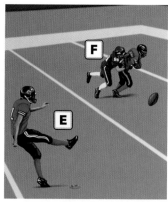

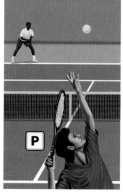

Use the new words.
Look on page 229. Name the actions you see.

A: *He's <u>throwing</u>.*
B: *She's <u>jumping</u>.*

Ways to talk about your sports skills
I can <u>throw</u>, but I can't <u>catch</u>.
I <u>swim</u> well, but I don't <u>dive</u> well.
I'm good at <u>skating</u>, but I'm terrible at <u>skiing</u>.

1. **golf club**
   ไม้กอล์ฟ

2. **tennis racket**
   ไม้เทนนิส

3. **volleyball**
   วอลเลย์บอล

4. **basketball**
   บาสเก็ตบอล

5. **bowling ball**
   บอลโบว์ลิ่ง

6. **bow**
   คันธนู

7. **target**
   เป้า

8. **arrow**
   ศร

9. **ice skates**
   สเก็ตน้ำแข็ง

10. **inline skates**
    สเก็ตแบบล้อแนวเดียว

11. **hockey stick**
    ไม้ตีฮ็อคกี้

12. **soccer ball**
    ลูกบอลสำหรับฟุตบอล

13. **shin guards**
    สนับแข้ง

14. **baseball bat**
    ไม้ตีเบสบอล

15. **catcher's mask**
    หน้ากากคนคว้าบอล

16. **uniform**
    เครื่องแบบ

17. **glove**
    ถุงมือ

18. **baseball**
    ลูกบอลสำหรับเบสบอล

19. **football helmet**
    หมวกนิรภัยสำหรับคนเล่น
    ฟุตบอล (รักบี้)

20. **shoulder pads**
    แผงกันไหล่

21. **football**
    ฟุตบอล (รักบี้)

22. **weights**
    น้ำหนัก

23. **snowboard**
    กระดานหิมะ

24. **skis**
    สกี

25. **ski poles**
    ไม้ถ่อสำหรับเล่นสกี

26. **ski boots**
    บู๊ทสำหรับเล่นสกี

27. **flying disc***
    จานขว้าง

* **Note:** one brand is
   Frisbee®, of Wham-O, Inc.

Use the new words.
Look at pages 228–229. Name the sports equipment you see.

A: *Those are ice skates.*
B: *That's a football.*

Ask your classmates. Share the answers.

1. Do you own any sports equipment? What kind?
2. What do you want to buy at this store?
3. Where is the best place to buy sports equipment?

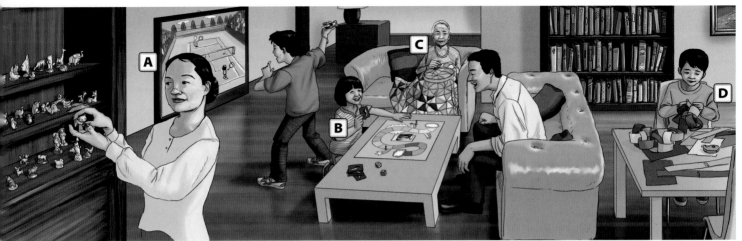

A. collect things
สะสมสิ่งของ

B. play games
เล่นเกม

C. quilt
เย็บผ้าต่อลาย

D. do crafts
ทำการฝีมือ

1. figurine
รูปปั้นหล่อขนาดเล็ก

2. baseball cards
การ์ดเบสบอล

3. video game console
คอนโซลเกมวิดีโอ

4. video game control
ตัวควบคุมเกมวิดีโอ

5. board game
เกมแบบกระดาน

6. dice
ลูกเต๋า

7. checkers
ตา / กระดานหมากรุก

8. chess
หมากรุก

9. model kit
ชุดแบบการต่อ

10. acrylic paint
สีอาครีลิค

11. glue stick
แท่งกาว

12. construction paper
กระดาษงานฝีมือ

13. doll making kit
ชุดการทำตุ๊กตา

14. woodworking kit
ชุดงานไม้

15. quilt block
บล็อคสำหรับทำผ้าตัดต่อ
ลาย

16. rotary cutter
มีดตัดแบบกลิ้ง

Grammar Point: *How often do you play cards?*

*I play **all the time**. (every day)*
*I play **sometimes**. (once a month)*
*I **never** play. (0 times)*

Pair practice. Make new conversations.

A: *How often do you do your hobbies?*
B: *I play games all the time. I love chess.*
A: *Really? I never play chess.*

E. paint
วาดภาพ / ระบายสี

F. knit
ถัก

G. pretend
เล่นแสร้งทำ / ตีต่าง

H. play cards
เล่นไพ่

17. canvas
ผ้าใบสำหรับการวาดภาพ

18. easel
ขาตั้ง

19. oil paint
สีน้ำมัน

20. paintbrush
แปรงระบายสี

21. watercolor
สีน้ำ

22. yarn
ไหมพรม

23. knitting needles
เข็มถัก

24. embroidery
งานปัก

25. crochetting
งานถักโครเชต์

26. action figure
ตุ๊กตานักสู้

27. model trains
รถไฟของเล่น

28. paper dolls
ตุ๊กตากระดาษ

29. diamonds
ไพ่ข้าวหลามตัด

30. spades
ไพ่โพดำ

31. hearts
ไพ่โพแดง

32. clubs
ไพ่ดอกจิก

Ways to talk about hobbies and games

*This <u>board game</u> is **interesting**. It makes me think.*
*That <u>video game</u> is **boring**. Nothing happens.*
*I love to <u>play cards</u>. It's **fun** to play with my friends.*

Ask your classmates. Share the answers.

1. Do you collect anything? What?
2. Which games do you like to play?
3. What hobbies did you have as a child?

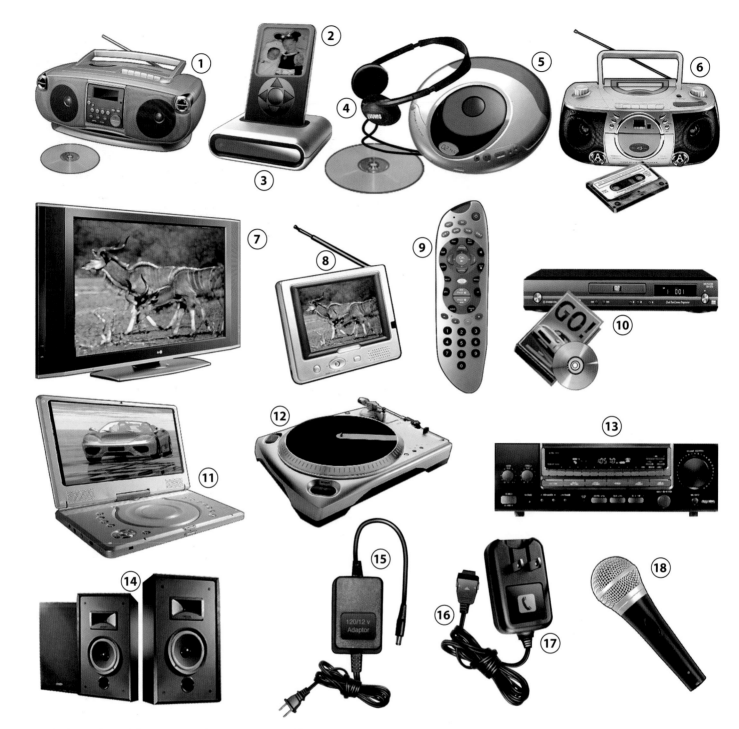

1. CD boombox
   เครื่องเล่นซีดีแบบกระเป๋าหิ้ว

2. MP3 player
   เครื่องเล่นเอ็มพีสาม

3. dock
   ท่า / แท่นเครื่อง

4. headphones
   ชุดหูฟัง

5. personal CD player
   เครื่องเล่นซีดีส่วนตัว

6. portable cassette player
   เครื่องเล่นเทปแบบกระเป๋าหิ้ว

7. flat screen TV / flat panel TV
   ทีวีจอแบน / ทีวีแผงแบน

8. portable TV
   ทีวีกระเป๋าหิ้ว

9. universal remote
   ตัวควบคุมวิถีไกล

10. DVD player
    เครื่องเล่นดีวีดี

11. portable DVD player
    เครื่องเล่นดีวีดีแบบกระเป๋าหิ้ว

12. turntable
    เครื่องเล่นจานเสียง

13. tuner
    เครื่องเทียบปรับเสียง

14. speakers
    ลำโพง

15. adapter
    ตัวปรับต่อ

16. plug
    ปลั๊ก

17. charger
    เครื่องอัดไฟ

18. microphone
    ไมโครโฟน

19. digital camera
กล้องถ่ายรูปแบบดิจิตัล

20. memory card
การ์ดหน่วยความจำ

21. film camera / 35 mm camera
กล้องถ่ายรูปแบบใช้ฟิล์ม /
กล้องถ่ายรูปแบบใช้ฟิล์มขนาด 35 มม

22. film
ฟิล์ม

23. zoom lens
เลนซ์สำหรับซูม

24. camcorder
กล้องถ่ายวิดีโอ

25. tripod
สามขาสำหรับตั้งกล้องถ่าย

26. battery pack
ตลับแบตเตอรี่

27. battery charger
เครื่องอัดไฟแบตเตอรี่

28. camera case
กระเป๋าใส่กล้องถ่ายรูป

29. LCD projector
เครื่องฉายภาพแสง LCD

30. screen
จอ

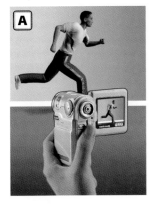

31. photo album
อัลบั้มภาพถ่าย

32. digital photo album
อัลบั้มภาพถ่ายแบบดิจิตัล

33. out of focus
นอกโฟกัส / มัว

34. overexposed
ให้แสงมากเกินไป

35. underexposed
ให้แสงน้อยเกินไป

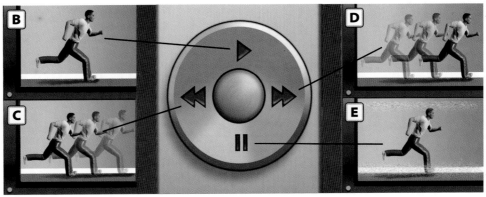

A. record
บันทึก

B. play
เล่น

C. rewind
หมุนกลับ

D. fast forward
ต่อไปข้างหน้าโดยเร็ว

E. pause
หยุดพักชั่วคราว

Types of TV Programs ประเภทของโปรแกรมโทรทัศน์

1. news program
โปรแกรมข่าว

2. sitcom (situation comedy)
รายการตลก

3. cartoon
การ์ตูน

4. talk show
รายการสนทนา

5. soap opera
ละครโทรทัศน์เรื่องยาว

6. reality show
รายการเรื่องจริงนำมาเล่า

7. nature program
รายการเกี่ยวกับธรรมชาติ

8. game show
รายการเกม

9. children's program
รายการเด็ก

10. shopping program
รายการช้อปปิ้ง

11. sports program
รายการกีฬา

12. drama
ละคร

Types of Movies ประเภทของภาพยนตร์

13. comedy
ตลก

14. tragedy
เศร้าสลด

15. western
แบบคาวบอยตะวันตก

16. romance
เรื่องรักใคร่

17. horror story
เรื่องสยองขวัญ

18. science fiction story
เรื่องนวนิยายเชิงวิทยาศาสตร์

19. action story / adventure story
เรื่องตื่นเต้น / ผจญภัย

20. mystery / suspense
เรื่องลึกลับ /
เรื่องเขย่าขวัญที่น่าติดตาม

Types of Music ประเภทของเพลงหรือดนตรี

21. classical
คลาสสิค

22. blues
บลูส์

23. rock
ร็อค

24. jazz
แจ๊ส

25. pop
เพลงยอดนิยม

26. hip hop
ฮิปฮอป

27. country
ลูกทุ่ง

28. R&B / soul
R&B / โซล

29. folk
พื้นเมือง

30. gospel
เพลงร้องในโบสถ์
แบบอเมริกันภาคใต้

31. reggae
เรกเก้

32. world music
ดนตรีของโลก

A. **play** an instrument
เล่นเครื่องดนตรี

B. **sing** a song
ร้องเพลง

C. **conduct** an orchestra
ควบคุมวงดนตรี

D. **be** in a rock band
อยู่ในวงดนตรีร็อค

Woodwinds เครื่องดนตรีแบบเป่า

1. flute
   ขลุ่ย

2. clarinet
   แคลริเน็ท

3. oboe
   โอโบ

4. bassoon
   บาสซูน

5. saxophone
   แซกโซโฟน

Strings เครื่องดนตรีประเภทสาย

6. violin
   ไวโอลิน

7. cello
   เชลโล

8. bass
   เบส

9. guitar
   กีต้าร์

Brass แตรทองเหลือง

10. trombone
    ทรอมโบน

11. trumpet /
    horn
    ทรัมเป็ท / แตร

12. tuba
    ทูบา

13. French horn
    แตรฝรั่งเศส

Percussion เครื่องดนตรีประเภทดีเคาะ

14. piano
    เปียโน

15. xylophone
    ระนาดไฟฟ้า

16. drums
    กลอง

17. tambourine
    ลูกพรวน / แทมบูรีน

Other Instruments เครื่องดนตรีอื่นๆ

18. electric keyboard
    คีบอร์ดไฟฟ้า

19. accordion
    แอคคอร์เดียน

20. organ
    ออร์แกน

21. harmonica
    หีบเพลงปาก

1. parade
   ขบวนแห่ / ขบวนพาเรด

2. float
   ทุ่นแห่ในขบวน

3. confetti
   กระดาษโปรยงานรื่นเริง

4. couple
   คู่รัก

5. card
   การ์ด

6. heart
   หัวใจ

7. fireworks
   พลุไฟ

8. flag
   ธง

9. mask
   หน้ากาก

10. jack-o'-lantern
    ฟักทองคว้านเป็นรูปหน้าผี

11. costume
    เครื่องแต่งกายตัวละคร

12. candy
    ลูกกวาด / ลูกอม

13. feast
    งานเลี้ยงฉลอง

14. turkey
    ไก่งวง

15. ornament
    เครื่องประดับประดา

16. Christmas tree
    ต้นคริสต์มาส

17. candy cane
    แท่งลูกกวาด

18. string lights
    ไฟร้อยติดกันเป็นสาย

*Thanksgiving is on the fourth Thursday in November.

239

1. decorations
สิ่งประดับประดา

2. deck
ระเบียง

3. present / gift
ของขวัญ /
ของกำนัล

A. **videotape**
ถ่ายบันทึกวิดีโอ

B. **make** a wish
ตั้งความปรารถนา /
อธิษฐานขอ

C. **blow out**
เป่าให้ดับ

D. **hide**
ซ่อน

E. **bring**
นำมา / เอามา

F. **wrap**
ห่อ

Happy Birthday!

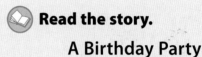

**Look at the picture.
What do you see?**

Answer the questions.

1. What kinds of decorations do you see?

2. What are people doing at this birthday party?

3. What wish did the teenager make?

4. How many presents did people bring?

Read the story.

A Birthday Party

Today is Lou and Gani Bombata's birthday barbecue. There are <u>decorations</u> around the backyard, and food and drinks on the <u>deck</u>. There are also <u>presents</u>. Everyone in the Bombata family likes to <u>bring</u> presents.

Right now, it's time for cake. Gani <u>is blowing out</u> the candles, and Lou <u>is making a wish</u>. Lou's mom wants to <u>videotape</u> everyone, but she can't find Lou's brother, Todd. Todd hates to sing, so he always <u>hides</u> for the birthday song.

Lou's sister, Amaka, has to <u>wrap</u> some <u>gifts</u>. She doesn't want Lou to see. Amaka isn't worried. She knows her family loves to sing. She can put her gifts on the present table before they finish the first song.

Think about it.

1. What wish do you think Gani made?

2. What kinds of presents do you give to relatives? What kinds of presents can you give to friends or co-workers?

Verb Guide

Verbs in English are either regular or irregular in the past tense and past participle forms.

Regular Verbs

The regular verbs below are marked 1, 2, 3, or 4 according to four different spelling patterns.
(See page 244 for the irregular verbs which do not follow any of these patterns.)

Spelling Patterns for the Past and the Past Participle	Example	
1. Add -ed to the end of the verb.	ASK	ASKED
2. Add -d to the end of the verb.	LIVE	LIVED
3. Double the final consonant and add -ed to the end of the verb.	DROP	DROPPED
4. Drop the final y and add -ied to the end of the verb.	CRY	CRIED

The Oxford Picture Dictionary List of Regular Verbs

accept (1)
add (1)
address (1)
adjust (1)
agree (2)
answer (1)
apologize (2)
appear (1)
applaud (1)
apply (4)
arrange (2)
arrest (1)
arrive (2)
ask (1)
assemble (2)
assist (1)
attach (1)
bake (2)
bank (1)
bargain (1)
bathe (2)
board (1)
boil (1)
borrow (1)
bow (1)
brainstorm (1)
breathe (2)
browse (2)
brush (1)
bubble (2)
buckle (2)
burn (1)
bus (1)
calculate (2)
call (1)
capitalize (2)
carpool (1)

carry (4)
cash (1)
celebrate (2)
change (2)
check (1)
chill (1)
choke (2)
chop (3)
circle (2)
claim (1)
clean (1)
clear (1)
click (1)
climb (1)
close (2)
collate (2)
collect (1)
color (1)
comb (1)
comfort (1)
commit (3)
compliment (1)
compost (1)
conceal (1)
conduct (1)
convert (1)
convict (1)
cook (1)
copy (4)
correct (1)
cough (1)
count (1)
cross (1)
cry (4)
dance (2)
debate (2)
decline (2)

delete (2)
deliver (1)
design (1)
dial (1)
dice (2)
dictate (2)
die (2)
disagree (2)
discipline (2)
discuss (1)
dive (2)
divide (2)
dress (1)
dribble (2)
drill (1)
drop (3)
drown (1)
dry (4)
dust (1)
dye (2)
edit (1)
empty (4)
enter (1)
erase (2)
evacuate (2)
examine (2)
exchange (2)
exercise (2)
expire (2)
explain (1)
exterminate (2)
fasten (1)
fast forward (1)
fax (1)
fertilize (2)
fill (1)
finish (1)

fix (1)
floss (1)
fold (1)
follow (1)
garden (1)
gargle (2)
graduate (2)
grate (2)
grease (2)
greet (1)
hail (1)
hammer (1)
hand (1)
harvest (1)
help (1)
hire (2)
hug (3)
immigrate (2)
indent (1)
inquire (2)
insert (1)
inspect (1)
install (1)
introduce (2)
invite (2)
iron (1)
jaywalk (1)
join (1)
jump (1)
kick (1)
kiss (1)
knit (3)
label (1)
land (1)
laugh (1)
learn (1)
lengthen (1)

lift (1)
listen (1)
litter (1)
live (2)
load (1)
lock (1)
look (1)
mail (1)
manufacture (2)
match (1)
measure (2)
microwave (2)
milk (1)
misbehave (2)
miss (1)
mix (1)
mop (3)
move (2)
mow (1)
multiply (4)
negotiate (2)
network (1)
numb (1)
nurse (2)
obey (1)
observe (2)
offer (1)
open (1)
operate (2)
order (1)
organize (2)
overdose (2)
pack (1)
paint (1)
park (1)
participate (2)
pass (1)
pause (2)
peel (1)
perm (1)
pick (1)

pitch (1)
plan (3)
plant (1)
play (1)
polish (1)
pour (1)
praise (2)
preheat (1)
prepare (2)
prescribe (2)
press (1)
pretend (1)
print (1)
program (3)
protect (1)
pull (1)
purchase (2)
push (1)
quilt (1)
race (2)
raise (2)
rake (2)
receive (2)
record (1)
recycle (2)
redecorate (2)
reduce (2)
register (1)
relax (1)
remain (1)
remove (2)
renew (1)
repair (1)
replace (2)
report (1)
request (1)
retire (2)
return (1)
reuse (2)
revise (2)
rinse (2)

rock (1)
sauté (1)
save (2)
scan (3)
schedule (2)
scrub (3)
seat (1)
select (1)
sentence (2)
separate (2)
serve (2)
share (2)
shave (2)
ship (3)
shop (3)
shorten (1)
sign (1)
simmer (1)
skate (2)
ski (1)
slice (2)
smell (1)
smile (2)
smoke (2)
sneeze (2)
solve (2)
sort (1)
spell (1)
spoon (1)
staple (2)
start (1)
state (2)
stay (1)
steam (1)
stir (3)
stop (3)
stow (1)
stretch (1)
study (4)
submit (3)
subtract (1)

supervise (2)
swallow (1)
tackle (2)
talk (1)
taste (2)
thank (1)
tie (2)
touch (1)
transcribe (2)
transfer (3)
translate (2)
travel (1)
trim (3)
try (4)
turn (1)
type (2)
underline (2)
undress (1)
unload (1)
unpack (1)
unscramble (2)
use (2)
vacuum (1)
videotape (2)
volunteer (1)
vomit (1)
vote (2)
wait (1)
walk (1)
wash (1)
watch (1)
water (1)
wave (2)
weed (1)
weigh (1)
wipe (2)
work (1)
wrap (3)

Verb Guide

Irregular Verbs

These verbs have irregular endings in the past and/or the past participle.

The Oxford Picture Dictionary List of Irregular Verbs

simple	past	past participle	simple	past	past participle
be	was	been	make	made	made
beat	beat	beaten	meet	met	met
become	became	become	pay	paid	paid
bend	bent	bent	picnic	picnicked	picnicked
bleed	bled	bled	proofread	proofread	proofread
blow	blew	blown	put	put	put
break	broke	broken	read	read	read
bring	brought	brought	rewind	rewound	rewound
buy	bought	bought	rewrite	rewrote	rewritten
catch	caught	caught	ride	rode	ridden
choose	chose	chosen	run	ran	run
come	came	come	say	said	said
cut	cut	cut	see	saw	seen
do	did	done	seek	sought	sought
draw	drew	drawn	sell	sold	sold
drink	drank	drunk	send	sent	sent
drive	drove	driven	set	set	set
eat	ate	eaten	sew	sewed	sewn
fall	fell	fallen	shake	shook	shaken
feed	fed	fed	shoot	shot	shot
feel	felt	felt	show	showed	shown
find	found	found	sing	sang	sung
fly	flew	flown	sit	sat	sat
get	got	gotten	speak	spoke	spoken
give	gave	given	stand	stood	stood
go	went	gone	steal	stole	stolen
hang	hung	hung	sweep	swept	swept
have	had	had	swim	swam	swum
hear	heard	heard	swing	swung	swung
hide	hid	hidden	take	took	taken
hit	hit	hit	teach	taught	taught
hold	held	held	think	thought	thought
keep	kept	kept	throw	threw	thrown
lay	laid	laid	wake	woke	woken
leave	left	left	withdraw	withdrew	withdrawn
lend	lent	lent	write	wrote	written
let	let	let			

Index

Index Key

Font
bold type = verbs or verb phrases (example: **catch**)
ordinary type = all other parts of speech (example: baseball)
ALL CAPS = unit titles (example: MATHEMATICS)
Initial caps = subunit titles (example: Equivalencies)

Symbols
✦ = word found in exercise band at bottom of page

Numbers/Letters
first number in **bold** type = page on which word appears
second number, or letter, following number in **bold** type = item number on page
(examples: cool [kōol] **13**-5 means that the word *cool* is item number 5 on page 13;
across [ə krös/] **153**–G means that the word *across* is item G on page 153).

Pronunciation Guide

The index includes a pronunciation guide for all the words and phrases illustrated in the book. This guide uses symbols commonly found in dictionaries for native speakers. These symbols, unlike those used in pronunciation systems such as the International Phonetic Alphabet, tend to use English spelling patterns and so should help you to become more aware of the connections between written English and spoken English.

Consonants
[b] as in back [băk]
[ch] as in cheek [chēk]
[d] as in date [dāt]
[dh] as in this [dhĭs]
[f] as in face [fās]
[g] as in gas [găs]
[h] as in half [hăf]
[j] as in jam [jăm]

[k] as in key [kē]
[l] as in leaf [lēf]
[m] as in match [măch]
[n] as in neck [nĕk]
[ng] as in ring [rĭng]
[p] as in park [pärk]
[r] as in rice [rīs]
[s] as in sand [sănd]

[sh] as in shoe [shōō]
[t] as in tape [tāp]
[th] as in three [thrē]
[v] as in vine [vīn]
[w] as in wait [wāt]
[y] as in yams [yămz]
[z] as in zoo [zōō]
[zh] as in measure [mĕzhər]

Vowels
[ā] as in bake [bāk]
[ă] as in back [băk]
[ä] as in car [kär] or box [bäks]
[ē] as in beat [bēt]
[ĕ] as in bed [bĕd]
[ë] as in bear [bër]

[ī] as in line [līn]
[ĭ] as in lip [lĭp]
[ï] as in near [nïr]
[ō] as in cold [kōld]
[ö] as in short [shört] or claw [klö]
[ōō] as in cool [kōōl]

[ōŏ] as in cook [kŏŏk]
[ow] as in cow [kow]
[oy] as in boy [boy]
[ŭ] as in cut [kŭt]
[ü] as in curb [kürb]
[ə] as in above [ə bŭv/]

All the pronunciation symbols used are alphabetical except for the schwa [ə]. The schwa is the most frequent vowel sound in English. If you use the schwa appropriately in unstressed syllables, your pronunciation will sound more natural.

Vowels before [r] are shown with the symbol [¨] to call attention to the special quality that vowels have before [r]. (Note that the symbols [ä] and [ö] are also used for vowels not followed by [r], as in *box* or *claw*.) You should listen carefully to native speakers to discover how these vowels actually sound.

Stress
This index follows the system for marking stress used in many dictionaries for native speakers.
1. Stress is not marked if a word consisting of a single syllable occurs by itself.
2. Where stress is marked, two levels are distinguished:
a bold accent [/] is placed after each syllable with primary (or strong) stress, a light accent [/] is placed after each syllable with secondary (or weaker) stress. In phrases and other combinations of words, stress is indicated for each word as it would be pronounced within the whole phrase.

Syllable Boundaries
Syllable boundaries are indicated by a single space or by a stress mark.

Note: The pronunciations shown in this index are based on patterns of American English. There has been no attempt to represent all of the varieties of American English. Students should listen to native speakers to hear how the language actually sounds in a particular region.

Abbreviations [ə brē/vē ā/shənz] **48**

abdomen [ăb/də mən] **107**–27

about [ə bowt/] **48**–B, **174**–L, **191**–E

above [ə bŭv/] **25**–4

accelerator [ĭk sĕl/ə rā/tər] **159**–46

accept [ĭk sĕpt/] **12**–G, **12**–I, **12** ✦

access number [ăk/sĕs/ nŭm/bər] **14**–16

Accessories [ĭk sĕs/ə rēz] **59, 94**–**95**

accident [ăk/sə dənt] **144**–2

accordion [ə kör/dē ən] **238**–19

account [ə kownt/] **132**–11, **132**–14

    account manager [ə kownt/ măn/ə jər] **132**–9

Account [ə kownt/] **132**

accountant [ə kown/tənt] **166**–1

ache [āk]

    backache [băk/āk/] **110**–5

    earache [ir/āk/] **110**–3

    headache [hĕd/āk/] **110**–1

    stomachache [stŭm/ək/ āk] **110**–4

    toothache [tōōth/āk/] **110**–2

acid rain [ăs/əd rān/] **218**–13

across [ə krös] **153**–G

acrylic paint [ə krīl/ĭk pānt] **232**–10

action [ăk/shən]

    action figure [ăk/shən fĭg/yər] **233**–26

    action story [ăk/shən stör/ē] **237**–19

activist [ăk/tə vĭst] **199**–17

actor [ăk/tər] **166**–2

acupuncture [ăk/yə pŭngk/chər] **122**–2

acute angle [ə kyōōt/ ăng/gəl] **193**–28

ad [ăd] **48**–2, **197**–9

adapter [ə dăp/tər] **234**–15

add [ăd] **77**–N, **101**–B, **192**–A

address [ə drĕs/, ā/drĕs] **4**–5

    mailing address [mā/lĭng ə drĕs/, –ā/drĕs] **134**–22

    return address [rĭ tŭrn/ ə drĕs/, –ā/drĕs] **134**–21

    website address [wĕb/sīt ə drĕs/, –ā/drĕs] **197**–4

address [ə drĕs/] **135**–B, **197**–C

adhesive bandage [əd hē/sĭv băn/dĭj] **117**–5

adjust [ə jŭst/] **219**–J

    adjustable wrench [ə jŭs/tə bəl rĕnch/] **181**–48

    adjustment [ə jŭst/mənt] **194**–23, **194**–24

administrative assistant

    [əd mĭn/ə strā/tĭv ə sĭs/tənt] **166**–3

administrator [əd mĭn/ə strā/tər] **120**–13

Administrators [əd mĭn/ə strā/tərz] **5**

admissions clerk [əd mĭ/shənz klŭrk/] **120**–14

ADULTS AND CHILDREN [ə dŭlts/ en chĭl/ drən] **30**–**31**

adult school [ə dŭlt/ skōōl/, ăd/ŭlt–] **188**–8

adventure story [əd vĕn/chər stör/ē] **237**–19

aerobic exercise [ə rō/bĭk ĕk/sər sīz/] **122**–5

afraid [ə frād/] **43**–23

after [ăf/tər]

    afternoon [ăf/tər nōōn/] **18**–17

    aftershave [ăf/tər shāv/] **109**–30

    five after one [fĭv/ ăf/tər wŭn/] **18**–7

    quarter after one [kwör/tər ăf/tər wŭn/] **18**–9

    ten after one [tĕn/ ăf/tər wŭn/] **18**–8

    twenty after one [twĕn/tē ăf/tər wŭn/] **18**–10

After an Emergency [ăf/tər ən ĭ mŭr/jən sē] **147**

Age [āj] **32**

agency [ā/jən sē] **131**–14

agent [ā/jənt] **160**–3, **160**–5

agree [ə grē/] **12**–K

agreement [ə grē/mənt] **51**–28

aid [ād]

    first aid kit [fürst/ ād/ kĭt/] **117**–1, **146**–18

    first aid manual [fürst/ ād/ măn/yōō əl] **117**–2

    hearing aid [hĭr/ĭng ād/] **115**–10

aide [ād] **167**–32

AIDS (acquired immune deficiency syndrome) [ādz] / [ə kwī/rd ĭ myōōn/ də fĭ/shən sē sĭn/dröm] **111** ✦

air [ĕr]

    air bag [ĕr/ băg/] **159**–43

    air conditioner [ĕr/ kən dĭsh/ə nər] **159**–39

    Air Force [ĕr/ förs/] **138**–16

    airmail [ĕr/māl/] **134**–5

    airplane [ĕr/plān/] **150**–8

    airplane crash [ĕr/plān/ krăsh/] **144**–3

    air pollution [ĕr/ pə lōō/shən] **218**–11

    airport [ĕr/pört/] **151**–10

    air purifier [ĕr/ pyōōr/ə fī ər] **113**–14

Airline Terminal [ĕr/lin/ tür/mə nəl] **160**

Airplane [ĕr/plān/] **161**

AIRPORT [ĕr/pört/] **160**–**161**

Airport Transportation

    [ĕr/ pört/ trăns/pər tā/shən] **152**

aisle [il] **72**–6

alarm clock [ə lärm/ kläk/] **58**–24

Alaska time [ə lăs/kə tīm/] **19**–28

album [ăl/bəm] **235**–31, **235**–32

alfalfa [ăl făl/fə] **177**–5

algebra [al/jə brə] **192**–16

allergic reaction [ə lür/jĭk rē ăk/shən] **116**–E

allergies [ăl/ər jēz] **111**–8

alley [ăl/ē] **51**–24, **222**–4

alligator [ăl/ə gā/tər] **213**–36

alphabet [ăl/fə bĕt/] **7**–13

Alterations [öl/tə rā/shənz] **100**

ALTERATIONS [öl/tə rā/shənz] **100**

Alteration Shop [öl/tə rā/shən shäp/] **100**

aluminum foil [ə lōō/mə nəm foyl/] **72**–23

Alzheimer's disease [älts/hī mərz dī zēz/, älts–] **111** ✦

a.m. [ā/ĕm/] **18**–4

ambulance [ăm/byə ləns] **116**–1, **121**–34

AMERICA [ə mĕr/ə kə] **200**–**201**

American cheese [ə mĕr/ə kən chēz/] **71**–26

Americans [ə mĕr/ə kənz] **198**–3

Amphibians [ăm fĭb/ē ənz] **212**

AMPHIBIANS [ăm fĭb/ē ənz] **212**–**213**

amusement park [ə myōōz/mənt pärk/] **223**–10

ancient [ān/shənt] **199**–1

anemone [ə nĕ/mə nē] **212**–24

anesthesiologist [ă/nəs thē/zē ä/lə jĭst] **121**–35

angle [ăng/gəl] **193**–26, **193**–27, **193**–28

Angles [ăng/gəlz] **193**

angry [ăng/grē] **43**–29

animals [ăn/ə məlz] **59**–15

Animals [ăn/ə məlz] **212, 215**

ANIMALS [ăn/ə məlz] **215**

ankle [ăng/kəl] **106**–23, **110**–18

    ankle socks [ăng/kəl säks/] **91**–7

anklets [ăngk/ləts/] **91**–11

anniversary [ăn/ə vür/sə rē] **22**–3

answer [ăn/sər] **8**–L

answering machine [ăn/sə rĭng mə shēn/] **14**–17

answer sheet [ăn/sər shēt/] **10**–2

antacid [ănt ăs/əd] **113**–28

anteater [ănt/ē/tər] **217**–24

antelope [ăn/tə löp/] **217**–35

antenna [ăn tĕ/nə] **14**–9

antibacterial ointment

    [ăn/tē băk tïr/ē əl oynt/mənt] **117**–10

antihistamine cream [ăn/tī hĭs/tə mēn krēm/] **117**–11

antiperspirant [ăn/tē pürs/pə rənt] **108**–5

antlers [ănt/lərz] **216**–16

ants [ăntz] **63**–23

apartment [ə pärt/mənt] **48**–3, **48**–4

    apartment building [ə pärt/mənt bĭl/dĭng] **50**–1

    apartment number [ə pärt/mənt nŭm/bər] **4**–6

Apartment [ə pärt/mənt] **48**

Apartment Complex [ə pärt/mənt käm/plĕx] **51**

Apartment Entryway [ə pärt/mənt ĕn/trē wā/] **51**

APARTMENTS [ə pärt/məntz] **50**–**51**

APC (automated postal center) [ā/pē/sē/] / [ö/tō mät ĭd pōs/təl–sĕn/tər] **135**–10

apologize [ə päl/sə jīz/] **12**–F

apostrophe [ə päs/trə fē] **190**–16

apparatus [ăp/ə rā/təs] **224**–14

appear [ə pïr/] **141**–C

Appearance [ə pïr/əns] **32**

applaud [ə plöd/] **148**–B

apples [ăp/əlz] **68**–1

    apple juice [ăp/əl jōōs/] **73**–32

appliance repair person

    [ə plī/əns rĭ pĕr/ pür/sən] **166**–4

appliqué [ăp/lə kā/] **99**–31

apply [ə plī/] **109**–P

appointment [ə poynt/mənt] **22**–4, **118**–1

    appointment book [ə poynt/mənt bŏŏk/] **183**–48

apricots [ăp/rə käts/] **68**–12

April [ā/prəl] **21**–28

apron [ā/prən] **92**–11, **93**–30

aquarium [ə kwĕr/ē əm] **222**–7

Arachnids [ə răk/nĭdz/] **214**

ARACHNIDS [ə răk/nĭdz/] **214**

archery [är/chə rē] **228**–1

architect [är/kə tĕkt/] **166**–5

area [ĕr/ē ə]

    area code [ĕr/ē ə köd/] **4**–10, **15**–29

    boarding area [bör/dĭng ĕr/ē ə] **161**–9

    dining area [dī/nĭng ĕr/ē ə] **46**–7

    play area [plā/ ĕr/ē ə] **130**–11

    reception area [rĭ sĕp/shən ĕr/ē ə] **182**–5

    rural area [rŏŏr/əl ĕr/ē ə] **52**–4

    screening area [skrē/nĭng ĕr/ē ə] **160**–4

    testing area [tĕs/tĭng ĕr/ē ə] **136**–2

    urban area [ür/bən ĕr/ē ə] **52**–1

AREA [ĕr/ē ə] **55**

Area and Volume [ĕr/ē ə ən văl/yəm, –yōōm] **193**

arm [ärm] **105**–14, **194**–15

    armchair [ärm/chĕr/] **56**–22

armadillo [är/mə dĭl/ō] **216**–8

Arm, Hand, and Fingers [ärm/ hănd/ ən fĭng/gərz] **106**

Army [är/mē] **138**–14, **199**–11

around [ə rownd/] **153**–H

Around Campus [ə rownd/ kăm/pəs] **5**
arrange [ə rănj/] **49**–Q
arrest [ə rĕst/] **141**–A
arrival [ə rī/vəl] **161**–7, **161** ✦
arrive [ə rīv/] **160**–K
arrow [ăr/ō] **231**–8
arson [är/sən] **142**–7
artery [är/tə rē] **107**–36
arthritis [är thrī/təs] **111**–16
artichokes [är/tə chōks/] **69**–22
artist [är/tĭst] **166**–6
arts [ärts] **189**–9, **189**–15, **228**–11
    art museum [ärt/ myōō zē/əm] **223**–9
ask [ăsk] **2**–B
    ask about [ăsk/ ə bowt/] **48**–B, **157**–B
    ask for [ăsk/ för/] **10**–F
    ask questions [ăsk/ kwĕs/chənz] **8**–K, **174**–M
asparagus [ə spĕr/ə gəs] **69**–26
assault [ə sölt/] **142**–3
assemble [ə sĕm/bəl] **170**–A, **175**–C
assembler [ə sĕm/blər] **166**–7
assembly [ə sĕm/blē] **140**–1
    assembly line [ə sĕm/blē līn/] **175**–6
    assemblyperson [ə sĕm/blē pür/sən] **139**–24
assist [ə sĭst/] **95**–D, **170**–B
assistance [ə sĭs/təns] **14**–22
assistant [ə sĭs/tənt]
    administrative assistant
        [əd mĭn/ ə strā/ tĭv ə sĭs/tənt] **166**–3
    assistant principal [ə sĭs/tənt prĭn/sə pəl] **5**–5
    certified nursing assistant (CNA) [sür/tə fīd/
        nür/sĭng ə sĭs/tənt] / [sē/ĕn/ā/] **120**–12
    dental assistant [dĕn/təl ə sĭs/tənt] **119**–2, **167**–22
    physician assistant [fə zĭ/shən ə sĭs/tənt] **168**–47
Assistant [ə sĭs/tənt] **93**
asthma [ăz/mə] **111**–9
astronaut [ăs/trə nöt/] **205**–17
astronomer [ə strä/nə mər] **205**–22
Astronomy [ə strä/nə mē] **205**
At Customs [ăt/ kŭs/təmz] **161**
athletic [ăth lĕt/ĭk]
    athletic shoes [ăth lĕt/ĭk shōoz/] **86**–7
    athletic supporter [ăth lĕt/ĭk sə pör/tər] **91**–6
Atlantic time [ət lăn/tĭk tīm/] **19**–33
atlas [ăt/ləs] **133**–8
ATM (Automated Teller Machine) [ā/tē/ĕm/] /
    [ö/tə māt ĭd tĕ/lər mə shēn/] **132**
ATM card [ā/tē/ĕm/ kärd/] **132**–15
atom [ăt/əm] **195**–28
attach [ə tăch/] **197**–G, **197**–H
attachments [ə tăch/mənts] **61**–11
attack [ə tăk/] **116**–D
attendant [ə tĕn/dənt] **161**–12, **162**–3, **184**–3
At the Dealer [ăt/ dhə dē/lər] **158**
At the Gate [ăt/ dhə gāt/] **161**
At the Mechanic [ăt/ dhə mə kăn/ĭk] **158**
At the Security Checkpoint
    [ăt/ dhə sə kyōō/ rə tē/ chĕk/ poynt/] **160**
attic [ăt/ĭk] **47**–7
attorney [ə tür/nē] **141**–4, **141**–10
attractive [ə trăk/tĭv] **32**–13
audio book [ö/dē ō bŏŏk/] **133**–17

audiologist [ö dē ä/lə jĭst] **115**–9
auditorium [ö/də tör/ē əm] **5**–18
August [ö/gəst] **21**–32
aunt [ănt] **34**–7
author [ö/thər] **133**–15, **169**–64
auto [ö/tō]
    auto club card [ö/tō klŭb/ kärd/] **162**–4
    auto mechanic [ö/tō mə kăn/ĭk] **166**–8
automated [ö/tə māt ĭd]
    automated phone system
        [ö/tə māt ĭd fōn/ sĭs/təm] **14**–23
    automated postal center (APC)
        [ö/tə māt ĭd pōs/təl sĕn/tər] / [ā/pē/sē/] **135**–10
Automated Teller Machine
    [ö/tə māt ĭd tĕl/ər mə shēn/] **132**
Automatic Transmission
    [ö tə māt/ĭk trănz mĭ/shən] **159**
Automotive Painter [ö tə mōt/ĭv pān/tər] **92**
autumn [ö/təm] **21**–39
avalanche [ăv/ə lănch/] **145**–18
average [ăv/rĭj]
    average height [ăv/rĭj hīt/] **32**–5
    average weight [ăv/rĭj wāt/] **32**–8
avocadoes [ä/və kä/dōz, ăv/ə–] **84**–6
ax [ăks] **180**–3
baboon [bă bōōn/] **217**–31
baby [bā/bē] **31**–7
    baby bag [bā/bē băg/] **37**–16
    baby carrier [bā/bē kă/rē/ər] **37**–17
    baby food [bā/bē fōōd/] **37**–4
    baby lotion [bā/bē lō/shən] **37**–13
    baby monitor [bā/bē män/ə tər] **59**–7
    baby powder [bā/bē pow/dər] **37**–14
    babysitter [bā/bē sĭt/ər] **166**–9
    baby's room [bā/bēz/ rōōm/] **47**–10
back [băk] **104**–5
    backache [băk/āk/] **110**–5
    back button [băk/ bŭt/n] **197**–2
    backhoe [băk/hō/] **178**–8
    backpack [băk/păk/] **94**–18, **226**–15
    backpacking [băk/păk/ĭng] **226**–6
    backseat [băk/sēt/] **159**–54
    back support belt [băk/ sə pört/ bĕlt/] **179**–18
    go back [gō/ băk/] **11**–M
    horseback riding [hörs/băk/ rī/dĭng] **226**–9
    lower back [lō/ər băk/] **107**–29
    pay back [pā/ băk/] **26**–D
Backyard [băk/yärd/] **53**
BACK FROM THE MARKET
    [băk/ frəm dhə mär/kət] **66**–67
bacon [bā/kən] **70**–11, **80**–1
bad [băd] **23**–18
BAD DAY AT WORK [băd/ dā/ ăt würk/] **186**–187
badge [băj] **93**–21
badminton [băd/mĭn tən] **228**–6
bag [băg] **69**–31, **74**–7, **74**–19, **161**–18
    air bag [ĕr/ băg/] **159**–43
    baby bag [bā/bē băg/] **37**–16
    clutch bag [klŭch/ băg/] **89**–19
    grocery bag [grōs/rē băg/] **67**–13
    handbag [hănd/ băg/] **87**–9, **94**–2
    plastic storage bags [plăs/tĭk stör/ĭj băgz/] **72**–25

    shoulder bag [shōl/dər băg/] **94**–17
    sleeping bag [slē/pĭng băg/] **226**–12
    totebag [tōt/ băg/] **94**–19
    trash bags [trăsh/ băgz/] **61**–24
    vacuum cleaner bag
        [văk/yōōm klē/nər băg/] **61**–12
bagels [bā/gəlz] **73**–40
baggage [băg/ĭj]
    baggage carousel [băg/ĭj kăr/ə sĕl/] **161**–23
bagger [băg/ər] **73**–14
baggy [băg/ē] **97**–30
bailiff [bā/lĭf] **141**–13
bake [bāk] **77**–H
Baked Goods [bākt/ gŏŏdz/] **73**
baked potato [bākt/ pə tā/tō] **81**–25
baker [bā/kər] **166**–10
bakery [bā/kə rē] **127**–19
Baking Products [bā/kĭng präd/ŭkts] **73**
balance [băl/əns] **132**–17, **195**–41
balcony [băl/kə nē] **51**–20
bald [böld] **33**–12
ball [böl] **59**–12, **231**–5, **231**–12
    ball field [böl/ fēld/] **224**–1
    ballroom [böl/rōōm/] **184**–26
    baseball [bās/böl/] **231**–18, **231**–14
    basketball [băs/kət böl/] **229**–8, **231**–4
    basketball court [băs/kət böl/ kört/] **229**–7
    football [fŏŏt/böl/] **229**–11, **231**–21
    meatballs [mĕt/bölz/] **81**–27
    racquetball [răk/ət böl/] **228**–12
    softball [söft/böl/] **229**–10
    volleyball [väl/ē böl/] **229**–14, **231**–3
balloons [bə lōōnz/] **44**–4
bananas [bə nän/əz] **68**–2
band [bănd] **183**–34
    headband [hĕd/bănd/] **90**–3
    waistband [wāst/bănd/] **100**–5
bandage [băn/dĭj] **117**–5, **117**–12
bandana [băn dă/nə] **92**–16
bangs [băngz] **33**–8
bank [băngk] **124**–5
    bank statement [băngk/ stāt/mənt] **132**–16
bank online [băngk/ än lin/] **132**–C
BANK [băngk] **132**
banner [băn/ər] **44**–1
banquet room [băng/kwət rōōm/] **185**–14
bar [bär]
    bar code [bär/ kōd/] **27**–4
    candy bar [kăn/dē bär/] **73**–37
    grab bar [grăb/ bär/] **57**–9
    menu bar [mĕn/yōō bär/] **197**–1
    salad bar [săl/əd bär/] **79**–24
    scroll bar [skröl/ bär/] **197**–15
barbecued ribs [bär/bĭ kyōō/d rĭbz/] **76**–2
barbershop [bär/bər shäp/] **129**–19
bargain [bär/gən] **102**–A
barn [bärn] **177**–11
barrette [bə rĕt/] **108**–20
base [bās] **193**–45, **194**–20
baseball [bās/böl/] **229**–9, **231**–18
    baseball bat [bās/böl/ băt/] **231**–14
    baseball cap [bās/böl/ kăp/] **86**–5

Index

baseball cards [bās/böl/ kärds/] **232**–2
baseball game [bās/böl/ gām/] **44**–2
basement [bās/mənt] **47**–13
Basement [bās/mənt] **50**
Basic Colors [bā/sĭk kŭ/lərz] **24**
BASIC TRANSPORTATION
   [bā/sĭk tränz/pər tā/shən] **150**–151
basket [bās/kət] **56**–3
   basketball [bās/kət böl] **229**–8, **231**–4
   basketball court [bās/kət böl kört] **229**–7
   bread basket [brĕd/ bās/kət] **83**–11
   laundry basket [lön/drē bās/kət] **101**–2
   shopping basket [shäp/ĭng bās/kət] **73**–9
   wastebasket [wāst/bās/kət] **57**–26
bass [bās] **212**–6, [bās] **238**–8
bassoon [bə sōōn/] **238**–4
bat [băt] **216**–7, **231**–14
bath [băth]
   bath mat [băth/ măt/] **57**–28
   bath powder [băth/ pow/dər] **108**–4
   bathroom [băth/rōōm/] **46**–4
   bath towel [băth/ tow/əl] **57**–13
   bathtub [băth/tŭb/] **57**–2
   half bath [hăf/ băth/] **57** ✦
bathe [bādh] **36**–F, **108**–B
bathing suit [bā/dhĭng sōōt/] **90**–26
BATHROOM [băth/rōōm/] **57**
battery / batteries [băt/ə rē] / [băt/ə rēz]
   146–15, **158**–20
   battery charger [băt/ə rē chär/jər] **235**–27
   battery pack [băt/ə rē păk/] **235**–26
bay [bā] **204**–9
be [bē]
   be aware [bē ə wër/] **143**–I
   be born [bē börn/] **40**–A
   be 18 or older [bē ā/tēn/ ör ōld/ər] **140**–G
   be hurt [bē hürt/] **116**–C
   be informed [bē ĭn förmd/] **140**–F
   be injured [bē ĭn/jərd] **116**–C
   be in shock [bē ĭn shäk/] **116**–B
   be neat [bē nēt/] **174**–C
   be on time [bē ön tīm/] **174**–F
   be released [bē rĭ lēst/] **141**–H
   be unconscious [bē ŭn kän/shəs] **116**–A
   don't be late [dōnt/ bē lāt/] **174**–D
beach [bēch] **204**–10
   beach chair [bēch/ chër/] **225**–22
   beach umbrella [bēch/ ŭm brĕl/ə] **225**–14
BEACH [bēch] **225**
beads [bēdz] **95**–34, **99**–32
beak [bēk] **214**–3
beaker [bē/kər] **195**–39
beam [bēm] **178**–3
beans [bēnz] **69**–8, **72**–17
   soybeans [soy/bēnz/] **177**–3
bear [bër] **37**–23, **216**–11
beard [bërd] **33**–6
beat [bēt] **77**–S
beater [bē/tər]
   eggbeater [ĕg/bē/tər] **78**–20
beautiful [byōō/tə fəl] **23**–21

beauty shop [byōō/tē shäp/] **130** ✦
beaver [bē/vər] **216**–9
become [bē kŭm/] **40**–G, **41**–N
bed [bĕd] **58**–9
   bedbugs [bĕd/bŭgz/] **63**–24
   bed control [bĕd/ kən trōl/] **121**–27
   bed frame [bĕd/ frām/] **58**–18
   bed pan [bĕd/ păn/] **121**–23
   bedroom [bĕd/rōōm/] **46**–2
   bedspread [bĕd/sprĕd/] **59**–11
   bed table [bĕd/ tā/bəl] **121**–21
   bunk beds [bŭnk/ bĕdz/] **59**–9
   double bed [dŭb/əl bĕd/] **184**–14
   flower bed [flow/ər bĕd/] **53**–20
   hospital bed [häs/pĭ tl bĕd/] **121**–22
   kids' bedroom [kĭdz/ bĕd/rōōm/] **47**–9
   king-size bed [kĭng/sīz/ bĕd/] **184**–15
BEDROOM [bĕd/rōōm/] **58**, **59**
bee [bē]
   honeybee [hŭn/ē bē/] **214**–25
beef [bēf]
   beef ribs [bēf/ rĭbz/] **70**–5
   corned beef [körnd/ bēf/] **71**–22
   ground beef [grownd/ bēf/] **70**–4
   roast beef [rōst/ bēf/] **71**–21
   stewing beef [stōō/ĭng bēf/] **70**–3
   stir-fried beef [stür/frīd/ bēf/] **76**–6
Beef [bēf] **70**
beetle [bēt/l] **214**–18
beets [bēts] **69**–5
Before an Emergency [bĭ för/ ən ĭ mür/ jən sē] **146**
behind [bĭ hīnd/] **25**–8
beige [bāzh] **24**–18
bell [bĕl]
   bell captain [bĕl/ kăp/tən] **184**–6
   bellhop [bĕl/häp/] **184**–7
   bell peppers [bĕl/ pĕp/ərz] **69**–7
   doorbell [dör/bĕl/] **53**–14
below [bĭ lō/] **25**–5
belts [bĕlts] **94**–6
   back support belt [băk/ sə pört/ bĕlt/] **179**–18
   belt buckle [bĕlt/ bŭk/əl] **94**–20
   conveyor belt [kən vā/ər bĕlt/] **175**–9
   garter belt [gär/tər bĕlt/] **91**–16
   seat belt [sēt/ bĕlt/] **159**–52
   tool belt [tōōl/ bĕlt/] **92**–3
bench [bĕnch] **224**–10
bend [bĕnd] **230**–O
benefits [bĕn/ə fĭts] **174** ✦
berries [bĕr/ēz] **210**–20
   blackberries [blăk/bĕr/ēz] **68**–17
   blueberries [blōō/bĕr/ēz] **68**–16
   mixed berries [mĭkst/ bĕr/ēz] **81**–36
   raspberries [răz/bĕr/ēz] **68**–15
   strawberries [strö/bĕr/ēz] **68**–14
between [bĭ twēn/] **25**–12
Beverages [bĕv/rə jəz] **73**, **81**
bib [bĭb] **37**–5
bicycle / bike [bī/sĭ kəl] / [bīk] **129**–22, **151**–15
big [bĭg] **23**–2, **97**–38
   Big Dipper [bĭg/ dĭ/pər] **205** ✦
   big-screen TV [bĭg/skrēn/ tē/vē/] **50**–15

bike / bicycle [bīk] / [bī/sĭ kəl] **129**–22, **151**–15
   bike path [bīk/ păth/] **224**–3
biking [bī/kĭng] **226**–8, **228**–5
bikini panties [bə kē/nē păn/tēz] **91**–13
bill [bĭl] **214**–3
Bill [bĭl] **15**
billiards [bĭl/yərdz] **228**–2
Bill of Rights [bĭl/ əv rīts/] **198**–10
Bills [bĭlz] **26**
bin [bĭn] **51**–23, **61**–2, **160**–6
bioenergy [bī/ō ĕn/ər jē] **218**–9
biography [bī ä/grə fē] **133**–15
biologist [bī ä/lə jĭst] **194**–2
Biology [bī ä/lə jē] **194**
biomass [bī/ō măs/] **218**–9
birch [bürch] **210**–7
bird [bürd] **208**–4
Bird [bürd] **214**
BIRDS, INSECTS, AND ARACHNIDS
   [bürdz/ ĭn/sĕkts ən ə răk/nĭdz] **214**
birth [bürth]
   birth certificate [bürth/ sər tĭf/ə kət] **40**–1
   birthday [bürth/dā/] **22**–1
BIRTHDAY PARTY [bürth/dā/ pär/tē] **240**–241
biscuits [bĭs/kəts] **80**–6
bison [bī/sən] **216**–6
bit [bĭt] **180**–28
bite [bīt] **110**–11
black [blăk] **24**–13
   blackberries [blăk/bĕr/ēz] **68**–17
   black hair [blăk/ hër/] **33**–16
bladder [blăd/ər] **107**–46
blade [blād] **107**–28, **109**–28, **180**–27
blankets [blăng/kəts] **58**–15, **146**–7, **225**–11
   blanket sleeper [blăng/kət slē/pər] **91**–27
blazer [blā/zər] **92**–12
bleach [blēch] **101**–7
bleachers [blē/chərz] **5**–3
bleed [blēd] **116**–M
blender [blĕn/dər] **54**–12
blind [blīnd] **32**–11
blister [blĭs/tər] **110**–15
blizzard [blĭz/ərd] **13**–23, **145**–13
blocks [bläks] **59**–19
   quilt block [kwĭlt/ bläk/] **232**–15
   sunblock [sŭn/bläk/] **108**–8, **225**–10
blond hair [bländ/ hër/] **33**–17
blood [blŭd] **111**–14
   blood pressure gauge [blŭd/ prĕsh/ər gāj/] **118**–9
   blood test [blŭd/ tĕst/] **121**–30
   blood work [blŭd/ würk/] **121**–30
   bloody nose [blŭd/ē nōz/] **110**–17
blouse [blows] **87**–8
blow dryer [blō/ drī/ər] **33**–23, **108**–18
blower [blō/ər] **176**–2
blow out [blō/ owt/] **240**–C
blue [blōō] **24**–3
   blueberries [blōō/bĕr/ēz] **68**–16
   blue jay [blōō/ jā/] **214**–6
   bright blue [brīt/ blōō/] **24**–12
   dark blue [därk/ blōō/] **24**–10
   light blue [līt/ blōō/] **24**–11
   navy blue [nā/vē blōō/] **28**–5

blues [blo͞oz] **237**–22
blush [blŭsh] **109**–37
board [bôrd]
    board game [bôrd/ gām/] **232**–5
    bulletin board [bo͝ol/ə tn bôrd/] **7**–14
    chalkboard [chôk/bôrd/] **6**–1
    cutting board [kŭt/ĭng bôrd/] **54**–27
    emery board [ĕm/ə rē bôrd/, ĕm/rē–] **109**–32
    headboard [hĕd/bôrd/] **58**–10
    ironing board [ī/ər nĭng bôrd/] **101**–14
    motherboard [mŭdh/ər bôrd/] **196**–5
    particle board [pär/tə kəl bôrd/] **181**–20
    skateboard [skāt/bôrd/] **224**–7
    snowboard [snō/bôrd/] **231**–23
    surfboard [sürf/bôrd/] **225**–16
    whiteboard [wīt/bôrd/] **6**–3
board [bôrd] **160**–E
boarding [bôr/dĭng]
    boarding area [bôr/dĭng ër/ē ə] **161**–9
    boarding pass [bôr/dĭng pǎs/] **161**–20
    sailboarding [sāl/bôr/dĭng] **227** ✦
    skateboarding [skāt/bôr/dĭng] **228**–13
    snowboarding [snō/bôr/dĭng] **227**–2
boat [bōt]
    sailboat [sāl/bōt/] **225**–3
boating [bō/tĭng] **226**–1
bobbin [bä/bĭn] **98**–21
bobby pins [bä/bē pĭnz/] **108**–21
body [bäd/ē]
    body lotion [bäd/ē lō/shən] **108**–9
    body of water [bäd/ē əv wô/tər] **204** ✦
    body shaper [bäd/ē/ shā/pər] **91**–15
BODY [bäd/ē] **104–105, 106–107**
boil [boyl] **77**–M
boiled ham [boyld/ hǎm/] **76**–5
boiler [boy/lər] **78**–8
bok choy [bäk/ choy/] **69**–15
bolt [bōlt] **51**–34, **180**–35, **180**–38
    bolt of fabric [bōlt/ əv fǎb/rĭk] **98**–15
bone [bōn] **107**–33, **116**–P
    boneless [bōn/ləs] **70** ✦
book [bo͝ok]
    appointment book [ə poynt/mənt bo͝ok/] **183**–48
    audio book [ô/dē ō bo͝ok/] **133**–17
    bookkeeper [bo͝ok/ kē/pər] **175**–2
    book of stamps [bo͝ok/ əv stǎmps/] **134**–18
    bookcase [bo͝ok/ kās/] **7**–10
    bookstore [bo͝ok/ stôr/] **130**–4
    check book [chĕk/ bo͝ok/] **132**–12
    coloring book [kŭl/ə rĭng bo͝ok/] **59**–13
    DMV handbook [dē/ĕm/vē/ hǎnd/bo͝ok/] **136**–1
    notebook [nōt/bo͝ok/] **7**–27
    passbook [pǎs/bo͝ok/] **132**–10
    picture book [pĭk/chər bo͝ok/] **133**–12
    spiral notebook [spī/rəl nōt/bo͝ok/] **7**–29
    test booklet [tĕst/ bo͝ok/lət] **10**–1
    textbook [tĕkst/bo͝ok/, tĕks/–] **7**–25
    workbook [würk/bo͝ok/] **7**–26
boombox [bo͞om/bäks/] **234**–1
booth [bo͞oth] **82**–4, **122**–3

boots [bo͞ots] **95**–28
    hiking boots [hī/kĭng bo͞ots/] **95**–31
    rain boots [rān/ bo͞ots/] **90**–20
    safety boots [sāf/tē bo͞ots/] **179**–20
    ski boots [skē/ bo͞ots/] **231**–26
    steel toe boots [stēl/ tō/ bo͞ots/] **92**–6
bored [bôrd] **43**–25
borrow [bär/ō, bôr/ō] **26**–B
boss [bäs] **164**–4
botanical garden [bə tǎn/ĭ kəl gär/dn] **222**–3
bottle [bät/l] **37**–1, **74**–1, **74**–13
    bottle return [bät/l rĭ türn/] **73**–16
    hot water bottle [hät/ wô/tər bät/l] **113**–15
bottled water [bät/ld wô/tər] **146**–11
bouquet [bō kā/, bo͞o–] **211**–28
bow [bō] **231**–6
    bow tie [bō/ tī/] **89**–16
bow [bow] **3**–H
bowl [bōl] **55**–2
    mixing bowl [mĭks/ĭng bōl/] **54**–28, **78**–31
    serving bowl [sürv/ĭng bōl/] **55**–21
    soup bowl [so͞op/ bōl/] **83**–21
    sugar bowl [sho͝og/ər bōl/] **55**–14
bowling [bō/lĭng] **228**–3
    bowling alley [bō/lĭng ǎl/ē] **222**–4
    bowling ball [bō/lĭng bôl/] **231**–5
box / boxes [bäks/, bäks/ĭz] **74**–6, **74**–18
    box spring [bäks/ sprĭng/] **58**–19
    CD boombox [sē/dē/ bo͞om/bäks/] **234**–1
    fuse box [fyo͞oz/ bäks/] **62**–13
    mailboxes [māl/bäk/səz] **50**–11, **128**–13
    post office box (PO box)
        [pōst/ ô/fəs bäks/] / [pē/ō bäks/] **135**–9
    safety deposit box [sāf/tē dĭ päz/ət bäks/] **132**–7
    sandbox [sǎnd/bäks/] **224**–15
    search box [sürch/ bäks/] **197**–5
    text box [tĕkst/ bäks/] **197**–13
    to-go box [tə gō/ bäks/] **82**–5
boxer shorts [bäk/sər shôrts/] **91**–4
boxing [bäks/ĭng] **228**–4
boy [boy] **31**–9
bra [brä] **91**–20
bracelets [brās/ləts] **95**–9, **117**–3
braces [brā/səz] **119**–6
brain [brān] **107**–34
brainstorm [brān/stôrm/] **8**–H, **191**–F
brake [brāk] **159**–48
    brake light [brāk/ līt/] **158**–14
    brake pedal [brāk/ pĕd/l] **159**–45
branch [brǎnch] **210**–2
Branch [brǎnch] **138**
Brass [brǎs] **238**
bread [brĕd] **67**–11
    bread-and-butter plate [brĕd/ n bŭt/ər plāt/] **83**–19
    bread basket [brĕd/ bǎs/kət] **83**–11
    garlic bread [gär/lĭk brĕd/] **81**–28
    rye bread [rī/ brĕd/] **71**–20
    wheat bread [wēt/ brĕd/] **71**–19
    white bread [wīt/ brĕd/] **71**–18
break [brāk] **77**–Q, **116**–P
    break down [brāk/ down/] **162**–D

Breakfast Special [brĕk/fəst spĕ/shəl] **80**
breasts [brĕsts] **70**–19, **107**–26
breathe [brēdh] **116**–N
breathing [brē/dhĭng] **117**–16
bricklayer [brĭk/lā/ər] **186**–8
bricks [brĭks] **178**–12, **178**–B
briefcase [brēf/kās/] **88**–13
briefs [brēfs] **91**–5, **91**–14
bright blue [brīt/ blo͞o/] **24**–12
bring [brĭng] **174**–D, **240**–E
broccoli [bräk/ə lē] **69**–13
broiled steak [broyld/ stāk/] **76**–3
broiler [broy/lər] **54**–21
broken [brō/kən] **62**–5, **62**–6, **62**–7, **63**–15, **97**–39
    broken equipment [brō/kən ĭ kwĭp/mənt] **179**–4
broom [bro͞om] **61**–16
brother [brŭdh/ər] **34**–6, **35**–28
    brother-in-law [brŭdh/ər ĭn lô/] **34**–17
    stepbrother [stĕp/brŭdh/ər] **35**–30
brown [brown] **24**–17
    brown hair [brown/ hër/] **33**–18
    hash browns [hǎsh/ brownz/] **80**–3
browse [browz] **102**–B
bruise [bro͞oz] **110**–12
brush [brŭsh] **33**–22, **108**–14
    paintbrush [pānt/brŭsh/] **181**–22, **233**–20
    scrub brush [skrŭb/ brŭsh/] **61**–20
    toilet brush [toy/lət brŭsh/] **57**–18
    toothbrush [to͞oth/brŭsh/] **109**–22
brush [brŭsh] **108**–I, **109**–J
bubble in [bŭ/bəl ĭn/] **10**–K
bucket [bŭk/ət] **61**–7, **225**–8
buckle [bŭk/əl] **94**–20, **99**–28
buckle up [bŭk/əl ŭp/] **36**–L
bud [bŭd] **211**–7
budget [bŭ jĭt/] **186**–3
buffalo [bŭf/ə lō] **216**–6
buffet [bə fā/] **55**–24, **185**–10
bugs [bŭgz]
    bedbugs [bĕd/bŭgz/] **63**–24
building [bĭl/dĭng] **50**–1, **124**–2
BUILDING SUPPLIES [bĭl/dĭng sə plīz/] **180–181**
bulb [bŭlb] **56** ✦, **211**–2
bulldozer [bo͝ol/dō/zər] **178**–6
bulletin board [bo͝ol/ə tn bôrd/] **7**–14
bump cap [bŭmp/ kǎp/] **92**–9
bumper [bŭm/pər] **158**–8
    bumper pad [bŭm/pər pǎd/] **59**–4
bunch [bŭnch] **68**–29
bunk beds [bŭngk/ bĕdz/] **59**–9
Bunsen burner [bŭn/sən bür/nər] **195**–37
bureau [byo͝or/ō] **58**–1
burger [bür/gər]
    cheeseburger [chēz/bür/gər] **79**–3
    hamburger [hǎm/bür/gər] **79**–1
burglary [bür/glə rē] **142**–2
burn [bürn]
    sunburn [sŭn/bürn/] **110**–14
burn [bürn] **116**–H
burner [bür/nər] **54**–19, **195**–37
burrito [bə rē/tō] **79**–9

Index

bus [bŭs] **128**–9, **151**–14
    bus person [bŭs/ pür/sən] **185**–13
    bus route [bŭs/ rōōt/, –rowt/] **152**–1
    bus station [bŭs/ stā/shən] **124**–7
    bus stop [bŭs/ stäp/] **129**–16, **151**–13
    miss the bus [mĭs/ dhə bŭs/] **152** ✦
bus [bŭs] **82**–G
business [bĭz/nəs]
    business owner [bĭz/nəs ō/nər] **166**–11
    businessperson [bĭz/nəs pür/sən] **166**–12
    business suit [bĭz/nəs sōōt/] **88**–11
busser [bŭ/sər] **83**–12
Bus Stop [bŭs/ stäp/] **152**
butcher [bōōch/ər] **166**–13
butter [bŭt/ər] **66**–6, **83**–19
butterfly [bŭt/ər flī/] **214**–19
buttocks [bŭt/əks] **107**–30
button [bŭt/n] **99**–24
    back button [băk/ bŭt/n] **197**–2
    call button [köl/ bŭt/n] **121**–28
    forward button [för/wərd bŭt/n] **197**–3
buy [bī] **27**–G
    buy a home [bī/ ə hōm/] **41**–M
    buy a snack [bī/ ə snăk/] **11**–K
    buy recycled products
        [bī/ rē sī/kəld präd/ŭkts] **219**–D
Buying a House [bī/ĭng ə hows/] **49**
BUYING AND MAINTAINING A CAR
    [bī/ĭng ən mān tā/nĭng ə kär/] **157**
Buying a Used Car [bī/ĭng ə yōōzd/ kär/] **157**
buzzer [bŭz/ər] **51**–31
cab [kăb] **156**–16
cabbage [kăb/ĭj] **69**–2
Cabinet [kăb/ə nət] **138**–10
cabinet [kăb/ə nət] **54**–1
    file cabinet [fīl/ kăb/ə nət] **182**–11
    medicine cabinet [mĕd/ə sən kăb/ə nət] **57**–20
    supply cabinet [sə plī/ kăb/ə nət] **182**–1
cables [kā/bəlz] **158**–21, **196**–13
cactus [kăk/təs] **210**–21
cafeteria [kăf/ə tïr/ē ə] **5**–14
cage [kāj] **107**–48
cake [kāk] **73**–39, **81**–33
    cake pan [kāk/ păn/] **78**–26
    cheesecake [chēz/kāk/] **81**–34
    pancakes [păn/kāks/] **80**–7
Cake [kāk] **77**
calculate [kăl/kyə lāt/] **17**–B
calculator [kăl/kyə lā/tər] **17**–6, **183**–25
calculus [kăl/kyə ləs] **192**–19
CALENDAR [kăl/ən dər] **20**–21
CALENDAR EVENTS [kăl/ən dər ĭ vĕnts/] **22**
calf [kăf] **106**–22
    calf-length [kăf/ lĕnth/] **96**–17
call [köl]
    call button [köl/ bŭt/n] **121**–28
    international call [ĭn/tər năsh/ə nəl köl/] **15**–35
    Internet phone call [ĭn/tər nĕt/ fōn/ köl/] **14**–20
    local call [lō/kəl köl/] **15**–31
    long distance call [löng/ dĭs/təns köl/] **15**–32
call [köl] **48**–A, **147**–L
    call in [köl/ ĭn/] **186**–A

calling card [kö/lĭng kärd/] **14**–15
calm [köm] **42**–8
camcorder [kăm/kör dər] **235**–24
camel [kăm/əl] **217**–38
camera [kăm/rə]
    camera case [kăm/rə kās/] **235**–28
    digital camera [dĭ/jə təl kăm/rə] **235**–19
    film camera [fĭlm/ kăm/rə] **235**–21
    security camera [sĭ kyōōr/ə tē kăm/rə] **50**–19
    35 mm camera
        [thür/tē fīv/ mĭl/ə mē/tər kăm/rə] **235**–21
camisole [kăm/ə sōl/] **91**–21
campaign [kăm pān/] **139**–29
camper [kăm/pər] **156**–9
campfire [kămp/fīr/] **226**–11
camping [kăm/pĭng] **226**–5
    camping stove [kăm/pĭng stōv/] **226**–16
Campus [kăm/pəs] **5**
can [kăn] **74**–3, **74**–15
    can opener [kăn/ ō/pə nər] **78**–1, **146**–8
    electric can opener [ĭ lĕk/trĭk/ kăn/ ō/pə nər] **54**–14
    garbage can [gär/bĭj kăn/] **53**–24
cancer [kăn/sər] **111**–10
candle [kăn/dl] **56**–20
    candle holder [kăn/dl hōl/dər] **56**–21
candy [kăn/dē] **239**–12
    candy bar [kăn/dē bär/] **73**–37
    candy cane [kăn/dē kān/] **239**–17
    candy store [kăn/dē stör/] **131**–17
cane [kān] **113**–16, **239**–17
canned food [kănd/ fōōd/] **146**–9
Canned Foods [kănd/ fōōdz/] **72**
canoeing [kə nōō/ĭng] **226**–3
can't breathe [kănt/ brēdh/] **116**–N
canteen [kăn tēn/] **226**–24
canvas [kăn/vəs] **233**–17
canyon [kăn/yən] **204**–17
cap [kăp] **88**–1, **206**–7
    baseball cap [bās/böl/ kăp/] **86**–5
    bump cap [bŭmp/ kăp/] **92**–9
    shower cap [show/ər kăp/] **108**–1
    surgical cap [sür/jĭ kəl kăp/] **121**–37
    surgical scrub cap [sür/jĭ kəl skrŭb/ kăp/] **93**–35
capital [kă/pət əl] **139**–22
capitalize [kă/pət əl īz/] **190**–A, **190**–B
Capitol [kă/pət əl] **138**–1
capris [kə prēz/] **88**–8
capsule [kăp/səl] **113**–23
car [kär] **150**–1
    car accident [kär/ ăk/sə dənt] **144**–2
    car dealership [kär/ dē/lər shĭp/] **126**–4
    car safety seat [kär/ sāf/tē sēt/] **37**–19
    4-door car [för/dör/ kär/] **156**–1
    sports car [spörts/kär/] **156**–4
    subway car [sŭb/wā/ kär/] **152**–6
    town car [town/ kär/] **152**–20
    2-door car [tōō/dör/ kär/] **156**–2
Car [kär] **157, 159**
CAR [kär] **156, 157, 158**–**159**
card [kärd] **239**–5
    ATM card [ā/tē/ĕm/ kärd/] **132**–15
    auto club card [ö tō/ klŭb/ kärd/] **162**–4

baseball cards [bās/böl/ kärdz/] **232**–2
    card store [kärd/ stör/] **130**–7
    copies of ID and credit cards
        [käp/ēz əv ī/dē/ ən krĕd/ət/ kärdz/] **146**–19
    emergency card [ĭ mür/jən sē/ kärd/] **161**–23
    fare card [fër/ kärd/] **152**–11
    folding card table [fōl/dĭng/ kärd/ tā/bəl] **102**–4
    green card [grēn/ kärd/] **40**–2
    greeting card [grē/tĭng kärd/] **134**–15
    health insurance card
        [hĕlth/ ĭn shōōr/əns kärd/] **118**–3
    memory card [mĕm/ə rē kärd/] **235**–20
    post card [pōst/ kärd/] **134**–16
    Resident Alien card [rĕz/ə dənt ā/lē ən kärd/] **40**–2
    rotary card file [rō/tə rē kärd/ fīl/] **183**–44
    Social Security card
        [sō/shəl sĭ kyōōr/ə tē kärd/] **40**–5
Card [kärd] **135**
cardigan sweater [kär/də gən swĕt/ər] **88**–2
Cardinal Numbers [kärd/nəl nŭm/bərz] **16**
cardiologist [kär/dē äl/ə jĭst] **120**–3
cardiopulmonary resuscitation (CPR)
    [kär/dē ō pōōl mə nër/ē rĭ sŭs/ə tā/shən] /
    [sē/pē/är/] **117**–17
care [kër] **167**–32
    careful worker [kër/fəl wür/kər] **179**–2
    careless worker [kër/ləs wür/kər] **179**–1
    childcare worker [chīld/kër wür/kər] **166**–16
CARE [kër] **114**–**115, 118, 119**
Care of Your Car [kër/ əv yər kär/] **157**
career counselor [kə rër/ kown/slər] **172**–10
Career Path [kə rër/ păth/] **172**
CAREER PLANNING [kə rër/ plăn/ĭng] **172**
cargo van [kär/gō văn/] **156**–13
carnation [kär nā/shən] **211**–20
carousel [kär/ə sĕl/] **161**–23
carpenter [kär/pən tər] **62**–12, **166**–14
carpet [kär/pət] **56**–24
carpool [kär/pōōl/] **219**–I
carriage [kär/ĭj] **37**–20
carrier [kär/ē ər] **37**–17, **134**–20
carrots [kär/əts] **69**–3
carry [kär/ē] **11**–F, **82**–H
CARS AND TRUCKS [kärz/ ən trŭks/] **156**
cart [kärt] **72**–7, **129**–28
    housekeeping cart [hows/kē/pĭng kärt/] **184**–19
    luggage cart [lŭg/ĭj/ kärt/] **184**–8
carton [kär/tn] **74**–4, **74**–16
cartoon [kär/tōōn] **236**–3
cartridge [kär/trĭj] **183**–45
carving knife [kär/vĭng nīf/] **78**–12
case [kās] **94**–5, **235**–28
cash [kăsh]
    cash and coins [kăsh/ ən koynz/] **146**–17
    cash register [kăsh/ rĕj/ə stər] **27**–10, **73**–15
cash [kăsh] **27**–F, **132**–A
cashier [kă shïr/] **73**–13, **166**–15
cashmere [kăzh/mïr/] **98**–4
Casserole [kăs/ə rōl] **77**
    casserole dish [kăs/ə rōl dĭsh/] **78**–10
cassette [kə sĕt/] **234**–6
    videocassette [vĭ/dē ō kə sĕt/] **133**–18

cast [kăst] **113**–20
castle [kă/səl] **225**–12
Casual Clothes [kăzh/ōō əl klōz] **88**
CASUAL, WORK, AND FORMAL CLOTHES
  [kăzh/ōō əl würk/ ən för/məl klōz/] **88**–**89**
cat [kăt] **215**–9
  catfish [kăt/fĭsh] **71**–2
catalog [kăt ə /lög] **133**–11
catch [kăch] **230**–D
catcher's mask [kăch/ərz măsk/] **231**–15
caterer [kā/tər ər] **185**–16
caterpillar [kăt/ə pĭl/ər, kăt/ər–] **214**–20
cattle [kăt/l] **177**–21
cauliflower [kö/lĭ flow/ər, kä/–] **69**–14
cave [kāv] **220**–6
caverns [kă/vərnz] **220**–7
cavity [kăv/ə tē] **119**–7
C-clamp [sē/klămp/] **180**–6
CD [sē/dē/] **196**–9, **234**–5
  CD boombox [sē/dē/ bōōm/băks/] **234**–1
  CD player [sē/dē/ plā/ər] **159**–38
celebrate [sĕl/ə brāt] **206**–C
celery [sĕl/ə rē] **69**–9
cell [sĕl] **194**–4
  cell membrane [sĕl/ mĕm/brān] **194**–6
  cell phone holder [sĕl/ fōn/ hōl/dər] **94**–15
  cell phone kiosk [sĕl/ fōn/ kē/ösk] **131**–22
  cell phone number [sĕl/ fōn/ nŭm/bər] **4**–12
  cell wall [sĕl/ wäl/] **194**–5
cello [chĕl/ō] **238**–7
cellular phone [sĕl/yə lər fōn/] **14**–8
Celsius [sĕl/sē əs] **13**–2
cemetery [sĕ/mə tĕr/ē] **127**–15
cent [sĕnt] **26**–1, **26**–2, **26**–3, **26**–4
center [sĕn/tər]
  automated postal center (APC)
    [ö/tə māt ĭd pōs/təl sĕn/tər] / [ā/pē/sē/] **135**–10
  childcare center [chĭld/kĕr/ sĕn/tər] **129**–30
  convention center [kən vĕn/shən sĕn/tər] **127**–24
  copy center [käp/ē sĕn/tər] **129**–18
  entertainment center
    [ĕn/tər tān/mənt sĕn/tər] **56**–5
  resource center [rē/sörs sĕn/tər] **172**–9
CENTER [sĕn/tər] **208**–**209**
centimeter [cm] [sĕn/tə mē/tər] **17**–14
CENTRAL AMERICA [sĕn/trəl ə mĕr/ə kə] **200**–**201**
Central time [sĕn/trəl tīm/] **19**–31
cereal [sïr/ē əl] **80**–9
ceremony [sĕr/ə mō/nē] **206**–6
certificate [sər tĭf/ə kət] **40**–1, **41**–11
  Certificate of Naturalization
    [sər tĭf/ə kət əv năch/rə lə zā/shən] **40**–6
certified [sür/tə fĭd/]
  Certified Mail® [sür/tə fĭd/ māl] **134**–4
  certified nursing assistant (CNA)
    [sür/tə fĭd/ nür/sĭng ə sĭs/tənt] / [sē/ĕn/ā/]
    120–12
chain [chān] **51**–33, **95**–33, **180**–41
chair [chĕr] **7**–11
  armchair [ärm/chĕr] **56**–22
  beach chair [bēch/ chĕr/] **225**–22
  dining room chair [dī/nĭng rōōm/chĕr/] **55**–8

easy chair [ē/zē/ chĕr] **56**–22
folding chair [fōld/ĭng chĕr/] **102**–5
high chair [hī/ chĕr/] **37**–6, **82**–3
rocking chair [räk/ĭng chĕr/] **37**–21
wheelchair [wēl/chĕr/] **113**–9
chalk [chök] **7**–18
  chalkboard [chök/börd/] **6**–1
challenged [chăl/əngd] **32**–10
change [chānj] **36**–G, **60**–P, **148**–C
change purse [chānj/ pürs/] **94**–14
changing [chān/jĭng]
  changing pad [chān/jĭng păd/] **59**–2
  changing table [chān/jĭng tā/bəl] **59**–1
charger [chär/jər] **14**–10, **234**–17, **235**–27
chart [chärt] **121**–24
cheap [chēp] **23**–20
check [chĕk] **132**–13
  check book [chĕk/ bōōk/] **132**–12
  check-in kiosk [chĕk/ĭn/ kē/ösk] **160**–2
  checkstand [chĕk/stănd/] **73**–12
  paycheck [pā/chĕk/] **165**–14
check [chĕk]
  check blood pressure [chĕk/ blŭd/ prĕsh/ər] **118**–A
  check email [chĕk/ ē/ māl/] **39**–W
  check in [chĕk/ ĭn/] **160**–A
  check Internet job sites
    [chĕk/ ĭn/tər nĕt/ jäb/ sīts/] **173**–D
  check messages [chĕk/ mĕs/ə jĭz] **171**–R
  check out [chĕk/ owt/] **133**–C
  check the correct boxes
    [chĕk/ dhə kə rĕkt/ bäk/səz] **9**–U
  check the oil [chĕk/ dhə oyl/] **157**–H
  check the pronunciation
    [chĕk/ dhe prə nən sē ā/ shən] **8**–D
  check your bags [chĕk/ yər băgz/] **160**–B
  check your spelling [chĕk/ yər spĕl/ĭng] **197**–F
  check your understanding
    [chĕk/ yər ŭn/dər stănd/ĭng] **12**–N
  check your work [chĕk/ yər würk/] **10**–L
checked [chĕkt] **96**–24
checkers [chĕk/ərz] **232**–7
checking account number
  [chĕk/ĭng ə kownt/ nŭm/bər] **132**–14
checkout [chĕk/owt/] **133**–10
Checkpoint [chĕk/poynt/] **160**
cheddar cheese [chĕd/ər chēz/] **71**–28
cheek [chēk] **106**–3
cheese [chēz] **66**–4
  American cheese [ə mĕr/ə kən chēz/] **71**–26
  cheddar cheese [chĕd/ər chēz/] **71**–28
  cheeseburger [chēz/bür/gər] **79**–3
  cheesecake [chēz/kāk/] **81**–34
  grilled cheese sandwich
    [grĭld/ chēz/ săn/wĭch, –sănd–/] **80**–10
  Swiss cheese [swĭs/ chēz/] **71**–27
  Cheesy Tofu Vegetable Casserole
    [chē/zē tō/fōō vĕj/tə bəl kăs/ə rōl] **77**
chef [shĕf] **83**–16
  chef's hat [shĕfs/ hăt/] **93**–28
  chef's jacket [shĕfs/ jăk/ət] **93**–29
  chef's salad [shĕfs/ săl/ əd] **80**–14

executive chef [ĭg zĕk/yə tĭv shĕf/] **185**–7
head chef [hĕd/ shĕf/] **185**–7
sous chef [sōō/ shĕf/] **185**–6
Chef [shĕf] **93**
chemist [kĕm/ĭst] **195**–25
Chemistry [kĕm/ə strē] **195**
cherries [chĕr/ēz] **68**–11
cherry picker [chĕr/ē pĭk/ər] **178**–5
chess [chĕs] **232**–8
chest [chĕst] **59**–16, **104**–4, **107**–25
  chest of drawers [chĕst/ əv drörz/] **59**–6
chicken [chĭk/ən] **66**–3, **70**–16
  chicken pox [chĭk/ən päks/] **111**–6
  chicken sandwich [chĭk/ən săn/wĭch, –sănd–] **79**–5
  fried chicken [frīd/ chĭk/ən] **76**–1
  roast chicken [rōst/ chĭk/ən] **81**–22
Chicken [chĭk/ən] **77**
chief justice [chēf/ jŭs/təs] **138**–13
CHILDCARE AND PARENTING
  [chĭld/kĕr ən pĕr/ən tĭng] **36**–**37**
child / children [chīld] / [chĭl/ drən]
  childcare center [chīld/kĕr sĕn/tər] **129**–30
  childcare worker [chīld/kĕr wür/kər] **166**–16
  children's program [chĭl/drənz prō/grăm] **236**–9
  child safety seat [chīld/ săf/tē sēt/] **159**–53
  grandchild [grăn/chīld/, grănd/–] **34** ✦
  lost child [löst/ chīld/] **144**–1
Childhood Diseases [chīld/hōōd dĭ zē/zəz] **111**
chili peppers [chĭl/ē pĕp/ərz] **69**–29
chill [chĭl] **76**–D
chills [chĭlz] **110**–9
chimney [chĭm/nē] **53**–5
chimpanzee [chĭm/păn zē/] **217**–27
chin [chĭn] **106**–1
chipmunk [chĭp/mŭngk] **215**–20
chips [chĭps] **73**–35
chiropractors [kī/rō prăk/tərz] **120**
chisel [chĭz/əl] **181**–55
choke [chōk] **116**–L
choose [chōōz] **9**–P
chop [chäp] **77**–L
chops [chäps] **70**–10, **70**–15
Christmas [krĭs/məs] **22**–18
  Christmas tree [krĭs/məs trē/] **239**–16
chromosome [krō/mə zōm/] **194**–8
chrysanthemum [krĭ săn/thə məm] **211**–21
church [chürch] **127**–14
chute [shōōt] **51**–26
circle [sür/ kəl] **193**–34
circle [sür/ kəl] **9**–Q
circular saw [sür/kyə lər sö/] **180**–9
circulation desk [sür/kyə lā/shən dĕsk/] **133**–2
circumference [sər kŭm/frəns] **193**–36
citizen [sĭt/ə zən] **30**–5
Citizenship Requirements
  [sĭt/ə zən shĭp/ rĭ kwïr/mənts] **140**
city [sĭt/ē] **4**–7, **52**–1
  city code [sĭt/ē kōd/] **15**–34
  city council [sĭt/ē kown/səl] **139**–27
  city hall [sĭt/ē häl/] **124**–8
City Government [sĭt/ē gŭ/vərn mənt] **139**
CITY STREETS [sĭt/ē strēts/] **126**–**127**

Index

CIVIC RIGHTS AND RESPONSIBILITIES
[sĭ/vĭk rīts n rĭ spän/sə bĭl/ə tēz] **140**
Civilizations [sĭ/və lə zā/shenz] **199**
claim [klām] **160**–L
clamp [klămp] **180**–6
clams [klămz] **71**–15
clarinet [klăr/ə nĕt/] **238**–2
classical [kla/sĭ kəl] **237**–21
classical concert [kla/sĭ kəl kän/sərt] **223**–14
classified ad [klăs/e fĭd] **48**–2
Classmates [klăs/māts/] **8**
classroom [klăs/rōōm/] **5**–7
CLASSROOM [klăs/rōōm/] **6**–**7**
claw [klö] **214**–2
clean [klēn] **101**–16
clean [klēn] **76**–A
clean teeth [klēn/ tēth/] **119**–A
clean the house [klēn/ dhə hows/] **39**–O
clean the lint trap [klēn/ dhə lĭnt/ trăp/] **101**–D
clean the oven [klēn/ dhə ŭv/ən] **60**–C
clean up [klēn/ ŭp/] **147**–M
cleaner [klēn/ər]
dry cleaners [drī/ klēn/ərz] **128**–2
glass cleaner [glăs/ klēn/ər] **61**–14
oven cleaner [ŭv/ən klēn/ər] **61**–3
vacuum cleaner [văk/yōōm klēn/ər] **61**–10
vacuum cleaner attachments
[văk/yōōm klēn/ər ə tăch/mənts] **61**–11
vacuum cleaner bag [văk/yəm klēn/ər băg/] **61**–12
CLEANING SUPPLIES [klē/nĭng sə pliz/] **61**
cleanser [klēn/zər] **61**–18
CLEANUP [klēn/ŭp/] **148**–**149**
clear [klĭr] **13**–9
clear tape [klĭr/tāp/] **183**–30
clear [klĭr] **82**–G
clear off [klĭr/ äf/] **10**–I
clerk [klŭrk] **5**–13, **182**–2
admissions clerk [əd mĭsh/ənz klŭrk/] **120**–14
desk clerk [dĕsk/ klŭrk/] **184**–11
DMV clerk [dē/ĕm/vē/ klŭrk/] **136**–3
file clerk [fīl/ klŭrk/] **182**–10
grocery clerk [grōs/rē klŭrk/, grōsh/–, grō/sə–] **72**–4
library clerk [lī/brër ē klŭrk/] **133**–1
payroll clerk [pā/rōl/ klŭrk/] **165**–10
postal clerk [pō/stəl klŭrk/] **135**–7
retail clerk [rē/tāl/ klŭrk/] **169**–53
salesclerk [sālz/klŭrk/] **94**–3
shipping clerk [shĭp/ĭng klŭrk/] **175**–16
stock clerk [stäk/ klŭrk/] **169**–59
click [klĭk] **197**–B
climb [klīm] **224**–C
climbing apparatus [klīm/ĭng ă/pə ră/təs] **224**–14
clinic [klĭn/ĭk] **186**–2
clip-on earrings [klĭp/än ĭr/ĭngz, –ön–] **95**–37
clipper [klĭp/ər] **109**–31, **176**–11
clips [klĭps] **108**–19, **183**–31, **194**–24
clock [kläk] **7**–9, **58**–24, **165**–7
clock radio [kläk/ rā/dē ō] **102**–6
close [klōz] **6**–H
closet [kläz/ət] **57** ✦, **58**–5
Closures [klō/zhərz] **99**

cloth [klöth] **181**–54
cloth diaper [klöth/ dī/pərz] **37**–8
tablecloth [tā/bəl klöth/] **55**–12
washcloth [wäsh/klöth/] **57**–4
clothes [klōz] **146**–6
clothesline [klōz/līn/] **101**–9
clothespin [klōz/pĭn/] **101**–10
CLOTHES [klōz] **86**–**87**, **88**–**89**, **96**–**97**, **98**–**99**
clothing [klō/dhĭng] **102**–2
CLOTHING [klō/dhĭng] **90**, **92**–**93**
Clothing Problems [klō/dhĭng präb/ləmz] **97**
cloudy [klow/dē] **13**–10
club [klŭb] **162**–4, **223**–12, **231**–1
club sandwich [klŭb săn/wĭch/, –sănd–] **80**–12
clubs [klŭbz] **233**–32
clutch [klŭch] **159**–49
clutch bag [klŭch/ băg/] **89**–19
CNA (certified nursing assistant) [sē/ĕn/ā/] /
[sür/tə tə fĭd/ nür/sĭng ə sĭs/tənt] **120**–12
coach [kōch] **5**–20, **229**–2
coal [kōl] **218**–4
coarse adjustment knob
[körs/ ə jŭst/mənt näb/] **194**–22
Coast Guard [kōst/ gärd/] **138**–18
coat [kōt] **90**–2, **216**–19
lab coat [lăb/ kōt/] **93**–33
raincoat [rān/ kōt/] **90**–18
sports coat [spörts/ kōt/] **89**–14
trench coat [trĕnch/ kōt/] **90**–21
cobra [kō/brə] **213**–41
cockpit [käk/pĭt/] **161**–10
cockroaches [käk/rō/chəz] **63**–26
cocktail dress [käk/tāl/ drĕs/] **89**–20
coconuts [kō/kə nŭts/] **68**–24
cod [käd] **71**–8, **212**–5
code [kōd]
area code [ër/ē ə kōd/] **15**–29
bar code [bär/ kōd/] **27**–4
city code [sĭt/ē kōd/] **15**–34
country code [kŭn/trē kōd/] **15**–33
coffee [kö/fē] **73**–33, **81**–37, **81**–38
coffeemaker [kö/fē mā/kər] **54**–11
coffee mug [kö/fē mŭg/] **55**–7
coffee shop [kö/fē shäp/] **126**–11
coffee table [kö/fē tā/bəl] **56**–19
COFFEE SHOP MENU [kö/fē shäp/ mĕn/yōō] **80**–**81**
coins [koynz] **146**–17
coin purse [koyn/ pürs/] **94**–14
Coins [koynz] **26**
colander [käl/ən dər] **78**–17
cold [kōld] **13**–6, **42**–4, **111**–1
cold tablets [kōld tăb/ləts] **113**–27
cold water [kōld wö/tər] **57**–7
coleslaw [kōl/slö/] **80**–18
collar [käl/ər] **100**–4
collate [kō/lāt/, kə lāt/] **171**–E
collect [kə lĕkt/] **232**–A
college [käl/ĭj] **127**–17, **188**–6, **188**–7
college degree [käl/ĭj də grē/] **41**–7
college dormitory [käl/ĭj dör/mə tör/ē] **52**–8
cologne [kə lōn/] **108**–6
colon [kō/lən] **190**–17

Colonial Period [kə lō/nē əl pïr/ē əd] **198**
colonies [kä/lə nēz] **198**–1
colonists [kä/lə nĭsts] **198**–2
color [kŭl/ər]
watercolor [wö/tər kŭl/ər] **233**–21
color [kŭl/ər] **33**–D
coloring book [kŭl/ə rĭng bŏŏk/] **59**–13
Colors [kŭl/ərs] **24**
COLORS [kŭl/ərs] **24**
Columbus Day [kə lŭm/bəs dā/] **22**–15
column [käl/ŭm] **107**–49
comb [kōm] **33**–21, **108**–13
comb [kōm] **108**–G
come [kŭm] **39**–R
comedy [käm/ə dē] **236**–2, **237**–13
comet [käm/ət] **205**–24
comfort [kŭm/fərt] **36**–I
comma [käm/ə] **190**–14
commercial fisher [kə mür/shəl fĭsh/ər] **167**–17
commit a crime [kə mĭt/ ə krīm/] **142** ✦
Common Illnesses and Childhood Diseases
[käm/ən ĭl/nə səz ən child/hŏŏd–dĭ zē/zəz] **111**
COMMUNITY CLEANUP
[kə myōō/nə tē klēn/ŭp] **148**–**149**
community college
[kə myōō/nə tē käl/ĭj] **127**–17, **188**–6
Comparing Clothing [kəm për/ĭng klō/dhĭng] **97**
compartment [kəm pärt/mənt] **159**–44, **161**–13
complaint [kəm plānt/] **97** ✦
Complex [käm/plĕks/] **51**
compliment [käm/plə mĕnt/] **12** ✦
compliment [käm/plə mĕnt/] **12**–C
composer [kəm pō/zər] **199**–15
composition [käm/pə zĭsh/ən] **199**–14
compost [käm/pōst/] **219**–M
compost pile [käm/pōst pīl/] **53**–25
computer [kəm pyōō/tər] **7**–15, **183**–17
computer lab [kəm pyōō/tər lăb/] **5**–15
computer software engineer
[kəm pyōō/tər söft/wër/ ĕn/jə nïr/] **167**–18
computer technician [kəm pyōō/tər tĕk nĭsh/ən]
167–19, **182**–12
Computer [kəm pyōō/tər] **196**
COMPUTERS [kəm pyōō/tərz] **196**
conceal [kən sēl/] **143**–C
concert [kän/sərt] **222**–5, **223**–14
concierge [kän/sē ërzh/, kön/–] **184**–4
conclusion [kən klōō/zhən] **190**–8
concrete [käng/krēt, kän krēt/] **178**–10
conditioner [kən dĭsh/ə nər] **108**–11, **159**–39
Conditions [kən dĭsh/ənz] **13**, **111**
CONDITIONS [kən dĭsh/ənz] **111**
condominium [kän/də mĭn/ē əm] **52**–5
conduct [kən dŭkt/] **238**–C
conductor [kən dŭk/tər] **152**–13
cone [kōn] **79**–13, **193**–40
pinecone [pīn/kōn] **210**–11
conference room [kän/frəns rōōm/] **182**–4
confetti [kən fĕt/ē] **239**–3
confused [kən fyōōzd/] **43**–26
congestion [kən jĕs/chən] **110**–7
Congress [käng/grəs] **138**–2, **198**–6

congressperson [kän/grəs pür/sən] **138**–4
CONSERVATION [kän/sər vā/shən] **218**–**219**
Conserve Energy and Resources
    [kən sürv/ ĕn/ər jē ən rē/sörs/əz] **219**
console [kän/söl] **232**–3
constellation [kän/stə lā/shən] **205**–14
Constitution [kän/stə tōō/shən] **198**–19
construction [kən strŭk/shən]
    construction paper [kən strŭk/shən pā/pər] **232**–12
    construction site [kən strŭk/shən sīt/] **126**–2
    construction worker
        [kən strŭk/shən wür/kər] **178**–1
CONSTRUCTION [kən strŭk/shən] **178**
Construction Worker [kən strŭk/shən wür/kər] **92**
contact [kän/tăkt] **146**–2
    contact lenses [kän/tăkt lĕn/zəz] **115**–8
container [kən tā/nər] **74**–5, **74**–17, **78**–4
CONTAINERS AND PACKAGING
    [kən tā/nərz ən păk/ĭ jĭng] **74**
continental [kän/tə nĕnt/əl] **198**–6
contractor [kän/trăk tər] **186**–5
control [kən tröl/] **121**–27, **232**–4
convenience store [kən vēn/yəns stör/] **128**–3
convention center [kən vĕn/shən sĕn/tər] **127**–24
convert [kən vürt/] **17**–D, **75**–C
convertible [kən vür/tə bəl] **156**–5
conveyor belt [kən vā/ər bĕlt/] **175**–16
convict [kän/vĭkt] **141**–15
convict [kən vĭkt/] **141**–E
cook [kŏŏk] **185**–1, **185** ✦
cook [kŏŏk] **39**–Q, **76**–C, **170**–C
cooked [kŏŏkt] **70**–25
cookies [kŏŏk/ēz] **73**–38
    cookie sheet [kŏŏk/ē shēt/] **78**–27
cool [kōōl] **13**–5
cooler [kōō/lər] **225**–19
co-op [kō/äp/] **52** ✦
copier [kä/pē ər]
    photocopier [fō/tō kä/pē ər] **183**–23
copies / copy [kä/pēz] / [kä/pē]
    copies of ID and credit cards
        [käp/ēz əv ī/dē ən krĕd/ət kärdz/] **146**–19
    copies of important papers
        [käp/ēz əv ĭm pört/ənt pā/pərz] **146**–20
    copy center [käp/ē sĕn/tər] **129**–18
copy [käp/ē] **8**–E
coral [kör/əl] **220**–5
cord [körd] **14**–2
    bungee cord [bŭn/jē körd/] **181**–15
    cordless phone [körd/ləs fōn/] **15**–24
    extension cord [ĭk stĕn/shən körd/] **181**–14
    frayed cord [frād/ körd/] **179**–5
    power cord [pow/ər körd/] **196**–2
corduroy [kör/də roy/] **99**–11
core course [kör/ körs/] **189** ✦
corn [körn] **69**–12, **177**–4
    corn rows [körn/ rōz/] **33**–14
corned beef [körnd/ bēf/] **71**–22
corner [kör/nər] **128**–7
coronary disease [kör/ə nĕr/ē dĭ zēz/] **111** ✦
corral [kə răl/] **177**–17
correct [kə rĕkt/] **10**–N

correction [kə rĕk/shən]
    correction fluid [kə rĕk/shən flōō/əd] **183**–36
    correction tape [kə rĕk/shən tāp/] **183**–37
cost [köst] **27**–7, **122**–1
costume [käs/tōōm] **239**–11
cotton [kät/n] **98**–1, **177**–6
couch [kowch] **56**–18
cough [köf] **110**–A
cough syrup [köf/ sĭr/əp, –sür/–] **113**–29
council [kown/səl] **139**–27
    councilperson [kown/səl pür/sən] **139**–28
counselor [kown/slər] **5**–6, **172**–10
count [kownt] **84**–A
counter [kown/tər] **54**–22, **113**–18
    counterperson [kown/tər pür/sən] **79**–17
Counterperson [kown/tər pür/sən] **93**
country [kŭn/trē] **52**–4, **227**–3, **237**–27
    country code [kŭn/trē kōd/] **15**–33
county fair [kown/tē fĕr/] **223**–13
coupe [kōōp] **156**–2
couple [kŭ/pəl] **35**–20, **35**–21, **239**–4
coupons [kōō/pönz/] **67**–15
courier [kür/ē ər, kōōr/–] **168**–40
course [körs] **172**–8, **189** ✦
court [kört]
    basketball court [băs/kət böl/ kört/] **229**–7
    courthouse [kört/hows/] **125**–13
    courtroom [kört/rōōm/] **141**–7
    court reporter [kört/ rĭ pör/tər] **141**–12
    courtyard [kört/yärd/] **51**–21
    food court [fōōd/ kört/] **131**–15
    Supreme Court [sə prēm/ kört/] **138**–11
    tennis court [tĕ/nəs kört/] **224**–6
cousin [kŭz/ən] **34**–9
cover [kŭv/ər] **158**–9, **181**–46
    coveralls [kŭv/ər ölz/] **92**–8
    cover-up [kŭv/ər ŭp/] **90**–25
cow [kow] **215**–1
cowboy hat [kow/boy/ hăt/] **92**–18
coyote [kī ō/tē, kī/ōt/] **216**–3
CPR (cardiopulmonary resuscitation) [sē/pē/är/] /
    [kär/dē ō pŏŏl/mə nĕr/ē-rē sŭs/ə tā/shən] **117**–17
CPU [sē/pē/yōō/] **196**–4
crab [krăb] **71**–9, **212**–20
cracked [krăkt] **62**–4
cradle [krād/l] **59**–20
crane [krān] **178**–7
crash [krăsh] **144**–3
crayons [krā/änz] **59**–14
cream [krēm] **24**–16, **81**–41, **113**–25
    antihistamine cream
        [ăn/tĭ hĭs/tə mēn krēm/] **117**–11
    ice-cream [īs/ krēm/] **72**–26
    ice-cream cone [īs/ krēm kōn/] **79**–13
    ice cream shop [īs/ krēm shäp/] **131**–16
    shaving cream [shā/vĭng krēm/] **109**–29
    sour cream [sow/ər krēm/] **72**–21
creamer [krē/mər] **55**–15
credit [krĕd/ət] **146**–19
creek [krēk, krĭk] **204** ✦
crescent moon [krĕs/ənt mōōn/] **205**–10

crew [krōō] **176**–1, **176**–4
    crewneck [krōō/nĕk] **96**–7
    crew socks [krōō/säks/] **91**–8
crib [krĭb] **59**–3
cricket [krĭk/ət] **214**–23
crime [krīm] **142** ✦
CRIME [krīm] **142**
criminal [krĭm/ə nəl] **142** ✦
crochetting [krō shā/ĭng] **233**–25
crocodile [kräk/ə dīl/] **213**–37
crocus [krō/kəs] **211**–17
Crops [kräps] **177**
cross [krös]
    cross-country skiing [krös/kŭn/trē skē/ĭng] **227**–3
    crosswalk [krös/wök/] **128**–15
cross [krös] **128**–A
    cross out [krös/ owt/] **9**–R
crossing [krö/sĭng] **154**–13, **154**–14, **154**–15
crown [krown] **119**–9
crucible tongs [krōō/sə bəl tängz/, –töngz/] **195**–44
crutches [krŭch/əz] **113**–10
cry [krī] **206**–B
cube [kyōōb] **193**–38
cubicle [kyōōb/ə kəl] **182**–7
cucumbers [kyōō/kŭm bərz] **69**–10
cuff [kŭf] **100**–9
cup [kŭp] **75**–2, **75**–10, **83**–24
    1/2 cup [hăf/ kŭp/] **75**–9
    1/4 cup [kwör/tər kŭp/] **75**–8
    teacup [tē/kŭp/] **55**–6
curb [kürb] **129**–21
curling iron [kür/lĭng ī/ərn] **108**–17
curly hair [kür/lē hĕr/] **33**–11
cursor [kür/sər] **197**–14
curtains [kür/tnz] **57**–12, **58**–7
curved line [kürvd/ lin/] **193**–23
cushion [kōō/shən] **56** ✦, **100**–13
customer [kŭs/tə mər] **72**–1, **94**–4, **132**–2, **164**–2
    customer service [kŭs/tə mər sür/vəs] **97** ✦
    customer service representative
        [kŭs/tə mər-sür/vəs rĕ/prə zĕn/tə tĭv] **167**–20
Customs [kŭs/təmz] **161**
customs officer [kŭs/təmz ö/fə sər] **161**–17
cut [kŭt] **91**–10, **110**–13
cut [kŭt] **33**–A, **109**–N
    cut up [kŭt/ ŭp/] **77**–I
cute [kyōōt] **32**–14
cutlets [kŭt/ləts] **70**–6
cutter [kut/ər] **183**–22, **232**–16
cutting board [kŭt/ĭng börd/] **54**–27
cycling [sī/klĭng] **228**–5
cyclist [sī/klĭst] **224**–2
cylinder [sĭl/ən dər] **193**–41, **195**–38
cytoplasm [sī/tə plăzm/] **194**–9
daffodil [dăf/ə dĭl/] **211**–25
daily [dā/lē] **20**–21
DAILY ROUTINES [dā/lē rōō tēnz/] **38**–**39**
Dairy [dĕr/ē] **72**
daisy [dā/zē] **211**–14
dance [dăns] **64**–A
dangerous [dān/jər əs] **186**–1
dark blue [därk/ blōō/] **24**–10

Index

Dashboard and Instrument Panel
[dăsh/bôrd/ ən ĭn/strə mənt păn/əl] **159**
dates [dāts] **20**–1, **68**–28
  date of birth [dāt əv bürth/] **4**–13
  expiration date
    [ĕk/spə rā/shən dāt/] **112**–7, **136**–10
daughter [dö/tər] **34**–14
  daughter-in-law [dö/tər ĭn lö/] **34** ✦
  granddaughters [grăn/dö/tərz] **34** ✦
  stepdaughter [stĕp/dö/tər] **35** ✦
day [dā] **20**–2
  birthday [bürth/dā/] **22**–1
  Columbus Day [kə lŭm/bəs dā] **22**–15
  daylight saving time [dā/līt/ sā/vĭng tīm/] **19**–25
  every day [ĕv/rē dā/] **20**–21
  Independence Day [ĭn/də pĕn/dəns dā/] **22**–13
  Labor Day [lā/bər dā/] **22**–14
  Martin Luther King Jr. Day
    [mär/tən lōō/thər kĭng/ jōōn/yər-dā/] **22**–10
  Memorial Day [mə mör/ē əl dā/] **22**–12
  New Year's Day [nōō/ yïrz/ dā/] **22**–9
  Presidents' Day [prĕz/ə dənts dā/] **22**–11
  Veterans Day [vĕt/ər ənz dā/] **22**–16
Day [dā] **18**
DAY AT SCHOOL [dā/ ăt skōōl/] **11**
DAY AT WORK [dā/ ăt würk/] **186**–**187**
Days of the Week [dāz/ əv dhə wēk/] **20**
dead [dĕd]
  dead-bolt lock [dĕd/bōlt/ läk/] **51**–34
  dead end [dĕd/ĕnd/] **154**–6
deaf [dĕf] **32**–12
Dealer [dē/lər] **158**
dealership [dē/lər shĭp/] **126**–4
death certificate [dĕth/ sər tĭf/ə kət] **41**–11
debate [də bāt/] **139**–B
decaf coffee [dē/kăf/ kö/fē] **81**–38
decay [də kā/] **119**–7
December [dĭ sĕm/bər] **21**–36
decimal point [dĕ/sə məl poynt/] **17**–7
Decimals [dĕ/sə məlz] **17**
deck [dĕk] **240**–2
declaration [dĕk/lə rā/shən]
  declaration form [dĕk/lə rā/shən förm/] **161**–16
  Declaration of Independence
    [dĕk/lə rā/shən əv ĭn/də pĕn/dəns] **198**–5
decline [də klīn/] **12**–J
decorations [dĕk/ə rā/shənz] **240**–1
deductions [də dŭk/shənz] **165**–13
deed [dĕd] **41**–9
deer [dïr] **216**–14
defendant [dĭ fĕn/dənt] **141**–5
defense attorney [dĭ fĕns/ ə tür/nē] **141**–4
defroster [də frös/tər] **159**–41
degrees [də grēz/] **13**–8, **193**–26
delayed flight [də lād/ flīt/] **161**–30
delete [də lĕt/] **196**–C
DELI [dĕl/ē] **71**
deliver [də lĭv/ər] **11**–G, **135**–E
delivery person [də lĭv/ə rē pür/sən] **167**–21
dementia [də mĕn/shə] **111**–18
demonstration [dĕ/mən strā/shən] **122**–6
denim [dĕ/nəm] **99**–7

denominator [də nömə nā/tər] **192**–6
dental [dĕn/təl]
  dental assistant [dĕn/təl ə sĭs/tənt] **119**–2, **167**–22
  dental floss [dĕn/təl flös/, –flăs/] **109**–24
  dental hygienist [dĕn/təl hī jē/nĭst, –jē/nĭst] **119**–3
  dental instruments [dĕn/təl ĭn/strə mənts] **119**–4
DENTAL CARE [dĕn/təl kër/] **119**
Dental Problems [dĕn/təl präb/ləmz] **119**
dentist [dĕn/tĭst] **119**–1
Dentistry [dĕn/təs trē/] **119**
dentures [dĕn/chərz] **119**–10
deodorant [dē ō/dər ənt] **108**–5
department [dĭ pärt/mənt] **95**–7, **95**–8
  Department of Motor Vehicles
    [dĭ pärt/mənt əv mō/tər vē/ĭ kəlz] **124**–4
  department store [dĭ pärt/mənt stör/] **131**–13
DEPARTMENT OF MOTOR VEHICLES (DMV)
  [dĭ pärt/mənt əv mō/tər vē/ĭ kəlz] / [dē/ĕm/vē/]
  136–**137**
departure [dĭ pär/chər] **161**–5, **161**–7
deposit [dĭ päz/ət] **132**–3, **132**–7
  deposit slip [dĭ päz/ət slĭp/] **132**–4
depression [də prĕ/shən] **115**–5
depth [dĕpth] **17**–18
DESCRIBING CLOTHES [dĭ skrī/bĭng klöz/] **96**–**97**
DESCRIBING HAIR [dĭ skrī/bĭng hër/] **33**
DESCRIBING PEOPLE [dĭ skrī/bĭng pē/pəl] **32**
DESCRIBING THINGS [dĭ skrī/bĭng thĭngz/] **23**
desert [dĕz/ərt] **204**–4
design [dĭ zīn/] **175**–A
designated drivers [dĕz/ĭg nā/təd drī/vərz] **143** ✦
designer [dĭ zī/nər] **98** ✦, **167**–30, **175**–2, **176**–5
desk [dĕsk] **6**–7, **182**–9
  circulation desk [sür/kyə lā/shən dĕsk/] **133**–2
  desk clerk [dĕsk klürk/] **184**–11
  front desk [frŭnt/ dĕsk/] **184**–12
Desktop Computer [dĕsk/täp/ kəm pyōō/tər] **196**
Desserts [dĭ zürts/] **81**
dessert tray [dĭ zürt/ trā/] **83**–10
destination [dĕs/tə nā/shən] **161** ✦
detector [dĭ tĕk/tər] **51**–29
detergent [dĭ tür/jənt] **101**–8
device [də vīs/] **225**–20
diabetes [dī/ə bē/tēz, –təs] **111**–12
diagonal [dī ăg/ə nəl, –ăg/nəl] **193**–31
dial [dī/əl] **15**–A, **15**–E
diameter [dī ăm/ə tər] **193**–37
diamonds [dī/məndz] **233**–29
diaper [dī/pər] **37**–8, **37**–10
  diaper pail [dī/pər pāl/] **37**–7
diaphragm [dī/ə frăm] **194**–19
dice [dīs] **232**–6
dice [dīs] **77**–J
dictate [dĭk/tāt] **8**–N
dictator [dĭk/tā/tər] **199**–6
dictionary [dĭk/shə nër/ē] **7**–30, **7**–31
die [dī] **41**–R
dietician [dī/ə tĭsh/ən] **120**–15
difference [dĭf/rəns] **192**–8
different [dĭ/frənt, dĭ/fə rənt] **23**–16
DIFFERENT [dĭ/frənt, dĭ/fə rənt] **28**–**29**

DIFFERENT PLACES TO LIVE
  [dĭ/frənt plā/səz tə lĭv/, dĭ/fə rənt] **52**
difficult [dĭf/ĭ kŭlt/] **23**–24
digital [dĭ/jə təl]
  digital camera [dĭ/jə təl kăm/rə] **235**–19
  digital photo album [dĭ/jə təl fō/tō ăl/bəm] **235**–32
dime [dīm] **26**–3
Dimensions [də mĕn/shənz] **17**
diner [dī/nər] **82**–6, **185**–9
dining [dī/nĭng]
  dining area [dī/nĭng ër/ē ə] **46**–7
  dining room [dī/nĭng rōōm/] **82**–1
  dining room chair [dī/nĭng rōōm/ chër/] **55**–8
  dining room table [dī/nĭng rōōm/tā/bəl] **55**–9
Dining [dī/nĭng] **185**
DINING AREA [dī/nĭng ër/ē ə] **55**
dinner [dĭn/ər] **72**–28
  dinner fork [dĭn/ər förk/] **83**–28
  dinner plate [dĭn/ər plāt/] **83**–18
  dinner salad [dĭn/ər săl/əd] **80**–15
Dinner [dĭn/ər] **81**
diploma [də plō/mə] **40**–3
direct flight [də rĕkt/ flīt/, dī–] **161** ✦
Directions [də rĕk/shənz] **9**, **155**
DIRECTIONS AND MAPS
  [də rĕk/shənz ən măps/, dī–] **155**
directory [də rĕk/tə rē, dī–] **131**–24
  directory assistance
    [də rĕk/tə rē ə sĭs/təns, dī–] **14**–22
dirty [dür/tē] **101**–15
Disabilities [dĭ/sə bĭ/lə tēz] **32**
disagree [dĭ/sə grē/] **12**–L
disappointed [dĭ/sə poyn/təd] **28**–4
DISASTERS [dĭ/zăs tərz] **144**–**145**
disc [dĭsk] **231**–27
discipline [dĭs/ə plən] **36**–K
discuss [dĭ skŭs/] **8**–G
disease [dĭ zēz/] **111**–11, **111** ✦, **119**–11
Diseases [dĭ zē/zəz] **111**
disgusted [dĭ skŭs/təd] **42**–7
dish [dĭsh] **55**–1
  casserole dish [kăs/ə rōl dĭsh/] **78**–10
  dish rack [dĭsh/ răk/] **54**–5
  dish room [dĭsh/ rōōm/] **83**–13
  dish towel [dĭsh/ tow/əl] **61**–22
  dishwasher [dĭsh/wä/shər, –wö/–]
    54–8, **83**–14, **185**–2
  dishwashing liquid [dĭsh/wä/shĭng lĭk/wəd] **61**–21
  satellite dish [să/tə lĭt dĭsh/] **53**–6
  soap dish [sōp/ dĭsh/] **57**–25
disinfectant wipes [dĭs/ən fĕk/tənt wīps/] **61**–23
display case [dĭ splā/ kās/] **94**–5
disposable [dĭ spō/zə bəl]
  disposable diaper [dĭ spō/zə bəl dī/pər] **37**–10
  disposable gloves [dĭ spō/zə bəl glŭvz/] **93**–27
disposal [dĭ spō/zəl] **54**–7, **121**–31
dive [dīv] **230**–K
divide [də vīd/] **17**–A, **192**–D
diving [dī/vĭng] **227**–12
  diving mask [dī/vĭng măsk/] **225**–6
divorced couple [də vörst/ kŭ/pəl] **35**–21
DJ [dē/jā/] **64**–4

DMV [dē/ĕm/vē/]
DMV clerk [dē/ĕm/vē/ klŭrk/] **136**–3
DMV handbook [dē/ĕm/vē/ hănd/bŏŏk/] **136**–1
do [dōō] **39**–T
do an experiment [dōō ən ĭk spĕr/ə mənt] **195**–B
do crafts [dōō krăfts/] **232**–D
do errands [dōō ĕr/əndz] **128** ✦
do manual labor [dōō măn/yōō əl lā/bər] **170**–D
do not drink [dōō nät drĭnk/] **112**–F
do not enter [dōō nät/ ĕn/tər] **154**–2
do not operate [dōō nät/ äp/ə rāt/] **112**–E
do not take [dōō nät/ tāk/] **112**–F
don't be late [dōnt/ bē/ lāt/] **174**–E
don't litter [dōnt/ lĭ/tər] **219**–L
don't smoke [dōnt/ smōk/] **114**–G
dock [däk] **175**–15, **234**–3
dockworker [däk/wür/kər] **167**–23
doctor [däk/tər] **118**–5
DOCUMENTS [dä/kyə mənts] **40**–**41**
dog [dög] **79**–6, **215**–11, **215**–22
dogwood [dög/wŏŏd/] **210**–15
DOING THE LAUNDRY [dō/ĭng dhə lön/drē] **101**
doll [däl] **59**–21, **233**–28
dollhouse [däl/hows/] **59**–16
doll making kit [däl/ mā/kĭng kĭt/] **232**–13
dollar [däl/ər] **26**–7
dollar coin [däl/ər koyn] **26**–6
fifty dollars [fĭf/tē däl/ərz] **26**–11
five dollars [fĭv/ däl/ərz] **26**–8
half dollar [hăf/ däl/ər] **26**–5
one hundred dollars [wŭn/ hŭn/drəd däl/ərz] **26**–12
ten dollars [tĕn/ däl/ərz] **26**–9
twenty dollars [twĕn/tē däl/ərz] **26**–10
dolphin [däl/fən, döl/–] **213**–31
domesticated [də mĕs/tə kā/təd] **215** ✦
DOMESTIC ANIMALS AND RODENTS [də mĕs/tĭk ăn/ə məlz ən rōd/nts] **215**
donkey [däng/kē, dŭng/–, döng/–] **215**–3
donut [dō/nŭt] **79**–15
donut shop [dō/nŭt shäp/] **129**–17
door [dör] **46**–3
doorbell [dör/bĕl/] **53**–14
door chain [dör/ chān/] **51**–33
doorknob [dör/näb/] **53**–12
door lock [dör/ läk] **159**–25
doorman [dör/măn/] **184**–1
4-door car [för/dör kär/] **156**–1
front door [frŭnt/ dör/] **53**–11
garage door [gə räj/ dör/] **53**–7
revolving door [rĭ väl/vĭng dör/] **184**–2
screen door [skrēn/ dör/] **53**–15
sliding glass door [slī/dĭng glăs/dör/] **53**–18
storm door [störm/ dör/] **53**–10
2-door car [tōō/ dör kär/] **156**–2
dorm / dormitory [dörm] / [dör/mə tör/ē] **52**–8
dosage [dō/sĭj] **112**–6
double [dŭb/əl]
double bed [dŭb/əl bĕd/] **184**–14
double boiler [dŭb/əl boy/lər] **78**–8

down [down]
break down [brāk/ down/] **162**–D
downhill skiing [down/hĭl/ skē/ĭng] **227**–1
down jacket [down jăk/ət] **90**–16
down vest [down vĕst/] **90**–14
drop-down menu [dräp/ down/ mĕn/yōō/] **197**–8
put down [pŏŏt/ down/] **6**–J
sit down [sĭt down/] **6**–F
walk down [wäk down/] **153**–D
downstairs [down/stĕrz/] **51** ✦
DOWNTOWN [down/town/] **124**–**125**
drain [drān] **57**–5
drama [drä/mə] **236**–12
drapes [drāps] **56**–16
draw [drö] **8**–F, **118**–F, **195**–E
drawer [drör] **54**–23, **58**–2, **59**–6
dress [drĕs] **86**–3, **88**–5, **89**–20
dressmaker [drĕs/mā/kər] **100**–1
dressmaker's dummy [drĕs/mā/kərz dŭ/mē] **100**–2
dress socks [drĕs/ säks/] **91**–9
dress [drĕs] **36**–H, **174**–B
dressed [drĕst] **38**–D
dresser [drĕs/ər] **58**–1
Dressings [drĕs/ĭngz] **80**
dribble [drĭb/əl] **230**–J
drill [drĭl] **178**–9, **180**–8
drill bit [drĭl bĭt/] **180**–28
drill [drĭl] **119**–D
drink [drĭnk] **11**–J
do not drink alcohol [dōō/ nät drĭnk/ ăl/kə höl/] **112**–F
don't drink and drive [dōnt/ drĭnk ən drīv/] **143**–G
drink fluids [drĭnk flōō/ədz] **114**–C
drip [drĭp] **121**–25
dripping [drĭp/ĭng] **63**–17
drive [drīv] **196**–6, **196**–8, **196**–9
drive-thru window [drīv/thrōō/ wĭn/dō] **128**–11
driveway [drīv/wā/] **53**–8
drive [drīv]
don't drink and **drive** [dōnt/drĭnk ən drīv/] **143**–G
drive a truck [drīv ə trŭk/] **170**–E
drive through [drīv/ thrōō/] **153**–K
drive to work [drīv/ tə würk/] **38**–I
driver [drī/vər] **152**–21, **169**–61
designated drivers [dĕz/ĭg nā/təd drī/vərz] **143** ✦
driver's license [drī/vərz lī/səns] **40**–4, **136**–9
driver's license number [drī/vərz lī/səns nŭm/bər] **136**–11
Phillips screwdriver [fĭl/ĭps skrōō/drī/vər] **180**–31
screwdriver [skrōō/drī/vər] **180**–30
driving [drī/vĭng] **142**–5
drop [dräp]
drop cloth [dräp/ klöth/] **181**–54
drop-down menu [dräp/ down/ mĕn/yōō/] **197**–8
drop off [dräp/ öf/] **38**–G
dropper [dräp/ər] **195**–45
drops [dräps] **113**–31
drought [drowt] **145**–11
drown [drown] **116**–I
drugs [drŭgz] **116**–K, **142**–6
drums [drŭmz] **238**–16
drumsticks [drŭm/stĭks/] **70**–23
drunk driving [drŭngk/ drī/vĭng] **142**–5

dry [drī] **101**–18
dry cleaners [drī/ klē/nərz] **128**–2
dry erase marker [drī/ ĭ rās/ mär/kər] **7**–17
drywall [drī/wöl/] **178**–19
dry [drī] **60**–N, **108**–H
dryer [drī/ər] **50**–13, **101**–4
blow dryer [blō/ drī/ər] **33**–23, **108**–18
dryer sheets [drī/ər shēts/] **101**–5
Dry Measures [drī/ mĕzh/ərz] **75**
duck [dŭk] **70**–18, **214**–12
duct tape [dŭkt/ tāp/] **181**–49
dummy [dŭ/mē] **100**–2
dump truck [dŭmp/ trŭk/] **156**–19
dune [dōōn] **204**–5
duplex [dōō/plĕks] **52** ✦
During an Emergency [dōō/rĭng ən ĭ mür/jən sē] **147**
dust [dŭst]
dustpan [dŭst/păn/] **61**–17
dust ruffle [dŭst/ rŭf/əl] **58**–17
dust storm [dŭst/ störm/] **13**–19
dust [dŭst] **60**–A
duster [dŭs/tər] **61**–1
DVD [dē/vē/dē/] **133**–19, **234**–11
DVD and CD-ROM drive [dē/vē/dē/ ən sē/dē/räm/ drīv/] **196**–9
DVD player [dē/vē/dē/ plā/ ər] **56**–7, **234**–10
dye [dī] **33**–D
eagle [ē/gəl] **214**–9
ear [ĭr] **32**–17, **105**–11
earache [ĭr/āk/] **110**–3
ear infection [ĭr/ ĭn fĕk/shən] **111**–3
earmuffs [ĭr/mŭfs/] **90**–13, **179**–16
ear plugs [ĭr/ plŭgz/] **179**–15
pierced earrings [pĭrst/ ĭr/ĭngz] **95**–36
early [ür/lē] **19**–22
Earth [ürth] **205**–3
earthquake [ürth/kwāk/] **144**–5
easel [ē/zəl] **233**–18
east [ēst] **155**–4
Eastern time [ē/stərn tīm/] **19**–32
easy [ē/zē] **23**–23, **76**–11
easy chair [ē/zē chĕr/] **56**–22
Easy Chicken Soup [ē/zē chĭk/ən sōōp/] **77**
eat [ēt] **11**–1
eat a healthy diet [ēt ə hĕl/thē dī/ət] **114**–F
eat breakfast [ēt brĕk/fəst] **38**–E
eat dinner [ēt dĭn/ər] **39**–S
eat out [ēt/ owt/] **82** ✦
eater [ē/tər] **176**–12
eclipse [ĭ klĭps/] **205**–16, **205** ✦
edit [ĕd/ət] **191**–I
education [ĕ jyōō/ kā/shən] **189**–17
eel [ēl] **212**–12
eggplants [ĕg/plänts/] **69**–23
eggs [ĕgz] **66**–7
eggbeater [ĕg/bē/tər] **78**–20
eggs over easy [ĕgz ō/vər ē/zē] **76**–11
eggs sunny-side up [ĕgz sŭn/ē sīd/ ŭp/] **76**–10
hardboiled eggs [härd/ boyld/ ĕgz/] **76**–8
poached eggs [pōcht/ ĕgz/] **76**–9
scrambled eggs [skräm/bəld ĕgz/] **76**–7
Eggs [ĕgz] **76**

Index

eight [āt] **16**
eighteen [ā/tēn/] **16**
eighteenth [ā/tēnth/] **16**
eighth [ātth, āth] **16**
eightieth [ā/tē/əth] **16**
eighty [ā/tē] **16**
elastic bandage [ĭ lăs/tĭk băn/dĭj] **117**–12
elbow [ĕl/bō] **106**–12
elderly [ĕl/dər lē] **32**–3
elected [ĭ lĕk/təd] **139**–C
    elected official [ĭ lĕk/təd ə fĭ/shəl] **139**–32
Election [ĭ lĕk/shən] **139**
election results [ĭ lĕk/shən rĭ zŭltz/] **139**–31
elective [ĭ lĕk/tĭv] **189** ✦
electric [ĭ lĕk/trĭk] **116**–F
    electric can opener [ĭ lĕk/trĭk kăn/ ō/pə nər] **54**–14
    electric drill [ĭ lĕk/trĭk drĭl/] **180**–8
    electric keyboard [ĭ lĕk/trĭk kē/bôrd/] **238**–18
    electric mixer [ĭ lĕk/trĭk mĭk/sər] **54**–25
    electric pencil sharpener
        [ĭ lĕk/trĭk pĕn/səl shär/pə nər] **183**–26
    electric shaver [ĭ lĕk/trĭk shā/vər] **109**–26
electrical [ĭ lĕk/trĭ kəl]
    electrical hazard [ĭ lĕk/trĭ kəl hăz/ərd] **186**–6
    electrical tape [ĭ lĕk/trĭ kəl tāp/] **181**–43
electrician [ĭ lĕk trĭsh/ən] **62**–9
electron [ĭ lĕk/trän] **195**–30
electronics [ĭ lĕk trän/ĭks]
    electronics repair person
        [ĭ lĕk trän/ĭks rĭ pĕr/ pür/sən] **167**–24
    electronics store [ĭ lĕk trän/ĭks stôr/] **131**–20
ELECTRONICS AND PHOTOGRAPHY
    [ĭ lĕk trän/ĭks ən fə täg/rə fē] **234**–**235**
elementary school [ĕl/ə mĕn/trē skool/] **188**–2
elephant [ĕl/ə fənt] **217**–42
elevator [ĕl/ə vā/tər] **50**–9, **131**–21, **184**–9
eleven [ĭ lĕv/ən] **16**
eleventh [ĭ lĕv/ənth] **16**
elm [ĕlm] **210**–16
Email [ē/māl/] **197**
embarrassed [ĭm băr/əst] **43**–24
embroidery [ĭm broy/də rē] **233**–24
EMERGENCIES [ĭ mür/jən sēz] **116**
EMERGENCIES AND NATURAL DISASTERS
    [ĭ mür/jən sēz ən năch/rəl dĭ zăs/tərz,–năch/ə rəl–]
    144–**145**
emergency [ĭ mür/jən sē] **117**–3
    emergency card [ĭ mür/jən sē kärd/] **161**–26
    emergency exit
        [ĭ mür/jən sē ĕg/zət,–ĕk/sət] **51**–25, **161**–14
    emergency medical technician (EMT) [ĭ mür/jən sē
        mĕd/ĭ kəl tĕk nĭsh/ən] / [ē/ĕm/tē/] **121**–32
Emergency [ĭ mür/jən sē] **146**–**147**
Emergency Call [ĭ mür/jən sē kôl/] **15**
EMERGENCY PROCEDURES
    [ĭ mür/jən sē prə sē/jərz] **146**–**147**
Emergency Room Entrance
    [ĭ mür/jən sē room/ ĕn/trəns] **121**
Emergency Worker [ĭ mür/jən sē wür/kər] **93**
emery board [ĕm/ə rē bôrd/, ĕm/rē–] **109**–32
emperor [ĕm/pər ər] **199**–3
employee [ĕm ploy/ē] **165**–9

employer [ĕm ploy/ər] **164**–4
empty [ĕmp/tē] **23**–10
empty [ĕmp/tē] **60**–L
EMT (emergency medical technician) [ē/ĕm/tē/] /
    [ĭ mür/jən sē mĕd/ĭ kəl tĕk nish/ən] **121**–32
end [ĕnd] **154**–6
    endpoint [ĕnd/poynt/] **193**–21
    end table [ĕnd/ tā/bəl] **56**–14
energy [ĕn/ər jē] **218**–1, **218**–7, **218**–8
    bioenergy [bi/ō ĕn/ər jē] **218**–9
ENERGY AND CONSERVATION
    [ĕn/ər jē ən kän/sər vā/shən] **218**–**219**
Energy and Resources [ĕn/ər jē ən rē/sôr/səz] **219**
Energy Sources [ĕn/ər jē sôr/səz] **218**
engine [ĕn/jən] **158**–18, **197**–6
engineer [ĕn/jə nïr/] **167**–18, **167**–25
ENGLISH COMPOSITION
    [ĭng/glĭsh käm/pə zĭsh/ən] **190**–**191**
English muffin [ĭng/glĭsh mŭf/ən] **80**–5
enter [ĕn/tər]
    do not **enter** [doo/ nät/ ĕn/tər] **154**–2
    enter data [ĕn/tər dā/tə] **171**–B
    enter the room [ĕn/tər dhe room/] **11**–A
    enter your PIN [ĕn/tər yər pĭn/] **132**–E
ENTERTAINMENT [ĕn/tər tān/mənt] **236**–**237**
entertainment center [ĕn/tər tān/mənt sĕn/tər] **56**–5
entrance [ĕn/trəns] **164**–1
Entrance [ĕn/trəns] **50, 121**
entry-level job [ĕn/trē lĕv/əl jäb/] **172**–1
Entryway [ĕn/trē wā/] **51**
envelope [ĕn/və löp/] **134**–14, **183**–43
equation [ĭ kwā/zhən] **192**–13
equipment [ĭ kwĭp/mənt] **177**–12, **179**–4
Equipment [ĭ kwĭp/mənt] **179, 183**
EQUIPMENT [ĭ kwĭp/mənt] **231**
Equivalencies [ĭ kwĭ/və lən sēz/] **17, 75**
erase [ĭ rās/] **10**–M
eraser [ĭ rā/sər] **7**–19, **7**–21
errands [ĕr/əndz] **128** ✦
eruption [ĭ rŭp/shən] **145**–16
escalator [ĕs/kə lā/tər] **131**–23
escape [ĭs kāp/] **50**–2
    escape route [ĭs kāp/ root/, rowt/] **146**–3
ESL [ē/ĕs/ĕl/] **189**–14
ESOL [ē/ĕs/ō/ĕl/] **189**–14
essay [ĕs/ā] **190**–4
Essay [ĕs/ā] **190**
e-ticket [ē/tĭ kət] **161**–19
evacuate [ĭ văk/yoo/ āt] **147**–K
evacuation route [ĭ văk/yoo/ā shən root/, rowt/] **146**–5
evening [ĕv/nĭng] **18**–19
    evening gown [ĕv/nĭng gown/] **89**–18
even numbers [ē/vən nŭm/bərz] **192**–4
EVENTS [ĭ vĕnts/] **22, 40**–**41**
every day [ĕv/rē dā/] **20**–21
EVERYDAY CLOTHES [ĕv/rē dā/ klōz] **86**–**87**
EVERDAY CONVERSATION
    [ĕv/rē dā/ kän/vər sā/shən] **12**
evidence [ĕv/ĭ dəns/] **141**–9
exam [ĭg zăm/] **122**–1, **136**–6
examination table [ĭg zăm/ə nā/shən tā/bəl] **118**–7
examine [ĭg zăm/ən] **118**–D, **118**–E

Examining Room [ĭg zăm/ə nĭng room/] **118**
exchange [ĭks chänj/] **27**–I
excited [ĭk sī/təd] **43**–22
exclamation mark [ĕk/sklə mā/shən märk/] **190**–13
executive [ĭg zĕk/yə tĭv] **182**–5
    executive chef [ĭg zĕk/yə tĭv shĕf/] **185**–7
    Executive Branch [ĭg zĕk/yə tĭv brănch/] **138**
exercise [ĕk/sər sĭz/] **122**–4
exercise [ĕk/sər sĭz/] **39**–P, **230**–N
Exercise Wear [ĕk/sər sĭz/wër] **89**
exhausted [ĭg zô/stəd] **43** ✦
ex-husband [ĕks/ hŭz/bənd] **35** ✦
exit [eg/zət, ĕk/sət] **51**–25, **51** ✦, **161**–14
expensive [ĭk spĕn/sĭv] **23**–19, **97**–44
Experiment [ĭk spër/ə mənt] **195**
expiration date [ĕk/spə rā/shən dāt/] **112**–7, **136**–10
expire [ĕk/spīr/] **136** ✦
explain [ĭk splän/] **12**–M
exploration [ĕk/splə rā/shən] **199**–8
explorer [ĭk splôr/ər] **199**–9
explosion [ĭk splō/zhən] **144**–4
exposed [ĭk spōzd/]
    overexposed [ō/vər ĭk spōzd/] **235**–34
    underexposed [ŭn/dər ĭk spōzd/] **235**–35
Express Mail® [ĭk sprĕs/ māl/] **134**–2
Extended Family [ĭk stĕn/dəd făm/lē, făm/ə lē] **34**
extension cord [ĭk stĕn/shən kôrd/] **181**–14
exterminate [ĭk stür/mə nāt/] **62** ✦
exterminator [ĭk stür/mə nā/tər] **63**–21
extinguisher [ĭk stĭn/gwə shər] **179**–21
extra [ĕk/strə]
    extra large [ĕk/strə lärj/] **96**–5
    extra small [ĕk/strə smôl/] **96**–1
ex-wife [ĕks/ wif/] **35** ✦
eye [ī] **99**–27, **105**–11
    eyebrow [ī/brow/] **106**–9
    eyebrow pencil [ī/brow/ pĕn/səl] **109**–34
    eye drops [ī/dräps/] **113**–31
    eye hook [ī/hook/] **180**–40
    eyelashes [ī/lăsh/əz] **106**–11
    eyelid [ī/lĭd/] **106**–10
    eyeliner [ī/li/nər] **109**–36
    eyepiece [ī/pēs/] **194**–14
    eye shadow [ī/shă/dō] **109**–35
Eye [ī] **106**
fabric [făb/rĭk] **98**–15
    fabric softener [făb/rĭk sö/fə nər] **101**–6
Fabric Store [făb/rĭk stör/] **99**
face [fās] **193**–44
    face mask [fās măsk/] **93**–32
    face powder [fās/ pow/dər] **109**–41
Face [fās] **106**
factory [făk/tə rē, –trē] **126**–3
    factory owner [făk/tə rē ō/nər] **175**–1
    factory worker [făk/tə rē wür/kər] **175**–3
Factory [făk/tə rē] **98**
FACTORY [făk/tə rē] **175**
Fahrenheit [făr/ən hīt/] **13**–1
fair [fër] **172**–13, **223**–13
    fair trial [fër/ trī/əl] **140**–5
FAIR [fër] **122**–**123**
fall [fôl] **21**–39

fall [föl] **40**–H, **116**–O
FAMILIES [făm/lēz, făm/ə lēz] **34**–**35**
Family [făm/lē, făm/ə lē] **34**
FAMILY REUNION
  [făm/lē rē yōōn/yən, făm/ə lē] **44**–**45**
famine [fă/mĭn] **145**–12
fan [făn] **55**–19, **229**–4
fancy [făn/sē] **97**–34
far from [fär/ frŭm/, –frəm/] **25** ✦
fare [fër] **152**–2
  fare card [fër kärd/] **152**–11
farm [färm] **52**–9
  farm equipment [färm ĭ kwĭp/mənt] **177**–12
  farmworker [färm/ wür/kər] **177**–8
Farm Animals [färm/ ăn/ə məlz] **215**
farmer [fär/mər] **177**–13
FARMERS' MARKET [fär/mərz mär/kət] **84**–**85**
FARMING AND RANCHING
  [fär/mĭng ən răn/chĭng] **177**
Farmworker [färm/ wür/kər] **92**
fashion [făsh/ən] **88** ✦
  fashion designer [făsh/ən dĭ zī/nər] **98** ✦
fast [făst] **23**–3
  fast food restaurant [făst/ fōōd/ rĕs/tə rənt, –ränt]
    128–10
fasten [făs/ən] **160**–H
fastener [făs/nər] **99**–29
FAST FOOD RESTAURANT
  [făst/ fōōd/ rĕs/tə rənt, –ränt] **79**
fast forward [făst/ för/wərd] **235**–D
fat [făt] **32**–7
father [fä/dhər] **34**–4, **35**–23
  father-in-law [fä/dhər ĭn lö/] **34**–11
  grandfather [grăn/fä/dhər, grănd/–] **34**–2
  stepfather [stĕp/fädhər] **35**–25
faucet [fö/sət] **57**–6
fax [făks] **171**–G
  fax machine [făks/ mə shēn/] **183**–21
feast [fēst] **239**–13
feather [fĕdh/ər] **214**–4
  feather duster [fĕdh/ər dŭs/tər] **61**–1
February [fĕb/yōō ër/ē, fĕb/rōō–] **21**–26
Federal Government
  [fĕ/də rəl gŭ/vərn mənt, fĕ/drəl] **138**
feed [fēd] **36**–C, **176**–D, **177**–D
feed dog / feed bar [fēd/dög/ / fēd/ bär/] **98**–20
feel [fēl] **110**–C, **110**–D
FEELINGS [fē/lĭngz] **42**
female [fē/māl/] **4**–18
fence [fĕns] **177**–19
fencing [fĕn/sĭng] **228**–7
ferry [fĕr/ē] **220**–4
fertilize [fürt/ əl īz/] **176**–D
fever [fē/vər] **110**–8
fiction [fĭk/shən] **237**–18
field [fēld] **5**–2, **177**–7
  ball field [böl/ fēld/] **224**–1
  track and field [trăk/ ən fēld/] **228**–18
fifteen [fĭf/tēn/] **16**
fifteenth [fĭf/tēnth/] **16**
fifth [fĭfth] **16**
fiftieth [fĭf/tē əth/] **16**

fifty [fĭf/tē] **16**
  fifty dollars [fĭf/tē däl/ərz] **26**–11
  50 percent [fĭf/tē pər sĕnt/] **17**–10
fighter [fī/tər]
  firefighter [fīr/fī/tər] **144**–9, **167**–26
figs [fĭgz] **68**–27
figure [fĭg/yər] **233**–26
  figure skating [fĭg/yər skā/tĭng] **227**–5
figurine [fĭg/yə rēn/] **232**–1
file [fīl] **183**–44
  file cabinet [fīl kăb/ə nət] **182**–11
  file clerk [fīl klürk/] **182**–10
  file folder [fīl föl/dər] **183**–50
fill [fĭl]
  fill a cavity [fĭl/ ə kăv/ə tē] **119**–E
  fill prescriptions [fĭl/ prĭ skrĭp/shənz] **112** ✦
  fill in [fĭl/ ĭn] **9**–O
  fill out [fĭl/ owt/] **173**–J
  fill the tank [fĭl/ dhe tănk/] **157**–G
  fill the tires [fĭl/ dhe tīrz/] **157**–L
filling [fĭl/ĭng] **119**–8
Filling Out a Form [fĭl/ĭng owt ə förm/] **4**
film [fĭlm] **235**–22
  film camera [fĭlm kăm/rə] **235**–21
find [fīnd] **160**–F
FINDING A HOME [fīn/dĭng ə hōm/] **48**–**49**
fine adjustment knob [fīn/ ə jŭst/mənt näb/] **194**–23
fingers [fĭng/gərz] **105**–16, **110**–16
  fingernail [fĭng/gər nāl/] **106**–18
  fingerprint [fĭng/gər prĭnt/] **136**–5
Fingers [fĭng/gərz] **106**
finish [fĭn/ĭsh] **112**–C, **230**–T
fins [fĭnz] **212**–1, **225**–7
fire [fīr] **144**–7, **144**–8
  campfire [kămp/fīr/] **226**–11
  fire escape [fīr ĭ skāp/] **50**–2
  fire exit [fīr/ ĕg/zət, –ĕk/sət] **51** ✦
  fire extinguisher [fīr ĭk stĭng/gwĭ shər] **179**–21
  firefighter [fīr/fī/tər] **144**–9, **167**–26
  fire hydrant [fīr hī/drənt] **129**–27
  fireplace [fīr/plās/] **56**–13
  fire screen [fīr skrēn/] **56**–12
  fire station [fīr stā/shən] **125**–12
  fire truck [fīr trŭk/] **144**–10
  fireworks [fīr/würks/] **239**–7
first [fürst] **16**
  first aid kit [fürst/ ād/ kĭt/] **117**–1, **146**–18
  first aid manual [fürst/ ād/ măn/yōō əl] **117**–2
  First Continental Congress
    [fürst/ kän/tə nĕnt/ əl käng/grəs] **198**–6
  first name [fürst/ nām/] **4**–2
  first president [fürst/ prĕz/ə dənt] **198**–11
First Aid [fürst/ ād/] **117**
FIRST AID [fürst/ ād/] **117**
First Aid Procedures [fürst/ ād/ prə sē/ jərz] **117**
First Floor [fürst/ flör/] **50**
First License [fürst/ lī/səns] **137**
fish [fĭsh] **66**–1, **81**–29, **209**–14
  catfish [kăt/fĭsh/] **71**–2
  goldfish [gōld/fĭsh/] **215**–16
  jellyfish [jĕ/lē fĭsh/] **212**–14
  starfish [stär/fĭsh/] **212**–16
  swordfish [sörd/fĭsh/] **71**–5

Fish [fĭsh] **71**, **212**
fisher [fĭsh/ər] **167**–17
fishing [fĭsh/ĭng] **226**–4
  fishing net [fĭsh/ĭng nĕt/] **226**–17
  fishing pole [fĭsh/ĭng pōl/] **226**–18
fitted sheet [fĭt/əd shēt/] **58**–12
fittings [fĭt/ĭngz] **181**–18
five [fīv] **16**
  five after one [fīv ăf/tər wŭn/] **18**–7
  five dollars [fīv däl/ərz] **26**–8
fix [fĭks] **62** ✦, **219**–F
fixture [fĭks/chər] **55**–18
flag [flăg] **239**–8
flammable liquids [flăm/ə bəl lĭk/wədz] **179**–8
flashlight [flăsh/līt/] **146**–14
flat [flăt]
  flat panel TV [flăt/ păn/əl tē/vē/] **234**–7
  flat screen TV [flăt/ skrēn/ tē/vē/] **234**–7
  flat sheet [flăt/ shēt/] **58**–13
  have a flat tire [hăv/ ə flăt/ tīr/] **162**–F
flats [flăts] **95**–27
fleas [flēz] **63**–25
  flea market [flē/ mär/kət] **222**–6
flight [flīt] **161**–30, **161** ✦
  flight attendant [flīt/ ə tĕn/dənt] **161**–12
Flight [flīt] **160**
float [flōt] **239**–2
flood [flŭd] **145**–19
floor [flör] **46**–6, **58**–21, **179**–6
  floor lamp [flör lămp/] **56**–15
  floor plan [flör plăn/] **186**–4
Floor [flör] **50**
floral [flör/əl] **96**–25
florist [flör/ĭst] **130**–8, **167**–27
floss [flös, fläs] **109**–24
floss [flös, fläs] **109**–K
flounder [flown/dər] **212**–15
flour [flow/ər] **73**–29
Flower [flow/ər] **211**
flowers [flow/ərz] **208**–7
  flower bed [flow/ər bĕd/] **53**–20
FLOWERS [flow/ərz] **211**
flu [flōō] **111**–2
fluid [flōō/əd] **183**–36
  fluid ounce [flōō/əd owns/] **75**–1
flute [flōōt] **238**–1
fly [flī] **214**–28
fly [flī] **170**–F
flyer [flī/ər] **102**–1
flying disc [flī/ĭng dĭsk/] **231**–27
foam pad [fōm/ păd/] **226**–13
focus [fō/kəs] **235**–33
foggy [fö/gē, fäg/ē] **13**–20
foil [foyl] **72**–23
fold [fōld] **101**–F
folder [fōl/dər] **183**–50
folding [fōl/dĭng]
  folding card table [fōl/dĭng kärd/ tā/bəl] **102**–4
  folding chair [fōl/dĭng chër/] **102**–5
folk [fōk] **237**–29
follow [fäl/ō] **114**–J, **147**–F
Following Directions [fäl/ō də rek/shənz, –dĭ–] **9**

Index

food [fōōd]
  baby food [bā/bē fōōd/] **37**–4
  canned food [kănd/ fōōd/] **146**–9
  fast food restaurant [făst/ fōōd/ rĕs/tə ränt] **128**–10
  food court [fōōd/kört] **131**–15
  food preparation worker
    [fōōd/ prĕ/pə rā/shən wür/kər] **185**–4
  food processor [fōōd/ prä/sĕ sər] **54**–26
  packaged food [păk/ĭjd fōōd/] **146**–10
  pet food [pĕt/ fōōd/] **72**–5
FOOD [fōōd] **79**
FOOD PREPARATION AND SAFETY
  [fōōd/ prĕ/pə rā/shən ən săf/tē] **76**–77
Food Processor [fōōd/ prä/sĕ sər] **92**
Foods [fōōdz] **72, 73**
Food Safety [fōōd/ săf/tē] **76**
FOOD SERVICE [fōōd/sür/vəs] **185**
foot [fōōt] **104**–8
  football [fōōt/böl] **229**–11, **231**–21
  football helmet [fōōt/böl/ hĕl/mət] **231**–19
  footnote [fōōt/nōt/] **190**–10
Foot [fōōt] **106**
for [för] **128**–B, **173**–C
forceps [för/səps, –sĕps] **195**–43
forearm [för/ärm/] **106**–13
forehead [för/əd/, –hĕd/, fär/–] **106**–2
forest [för/əst, fär/–] **204**–1, **204**–11
  forest fire [för/əst fir/] **144**–7
fork [förk] **55**–3, **83**–27, **83**–28
  forklift [förk/lift/] **175**–12
Form [förm] **4**
Formal Clothes [förm/əl klōz/] **89**
former husband [för/mər hŭz/bənd] **35** ✦
former wife [för/mər wif/] **35** ✦
forms [förmz] **118**–4, **134**–19, **161**–16
formula [för/myə lə] **37**–3, **195**–34
fortieth [för/tē əth] **16**
forty [för/tē] **16**
forward [för/wərd] **235**–D
  forward button [för/wərd bŭt/n] **197**–3
foundation [fown dā/shən] **109**–40
founders [fown/dərz] **198**–7
fountain [fown/tn] **224**–5, **224**–9
four [för] **16**
  4-door car [för/ dör kär/] **156**–1
  2 x 4 (two by four) [tōō/ bī för/] **181**–19
fourteen [för/tēn/] **16**
fourteenth [för/tēnth/] **16**
fourth [förth] **16**
Fourth Floor [förth flör/] **50**
Fourth of July [förth əv jōō lī/] **22**–13
fox [fäks] **216**–15
Fractions [frăk/shənz] **192**
Fractions and Decimals [frăk/shənz ən dĕ/sə məlz] **17**
frame [frām] **58**–4, **58**–18
frayed cord [frād/ körd/] **179**–5
free [frē] **122**–7
  free speech [frē/ spēch/] **140**–2
freedom [frē/dəm]
  freedom of religion [frē/dəm əv rĭ lĭ/jən] **140**–3
  freedom of the press [frē/dəm əv dhə prĕs/] **140**–4
freezer [frē/zər] **54**–10, **185**–3

freezing [frē/zĭng] **13**–7
French [frĕnch]
  french fries [frĕnch/ friz/] **79**–2
  French horn [frĕnch/ hörn/] **238**–13
Frequency [frē/kwən sē] **20**
fresh [frĕsh] **71**–16
Friday [fri/dā, –dē] **20**–13
fried [frid] **76**–6
  fried chicken [frid/ chĭk/ən] **76**–1
fringe [frĭnj] **99**–34
frog [frög, fräg] **212**–25
front [frŭnt] **25**–7
  front desk [frŭnt/ dĕsk/] **184**–12
  front door [frŭnt/ dör/] **53**–11
  front seat [frŭnt/ sēt/] **159**–51
  front walk [frŭnt/ wök/] **53**–2
Front Porch [frŭnt/ pörch/] **53**
Font Yard and House [frŭnt/ yärd/ en hows/] **53**
frostbite [fräst/bit/] **116**–G
frozen [frō/zən] **63**–16, **71**–17
  frozen dinner [frō/zən dĭn/ər] **72**–28
  frozen vegetables [frō/zən vĕj/tə bəlz] **72**–27
Frozen Foods [frō/zən fōōdz/] **72**
fruit [frōōt] **67**–9
  fruit salad [frōōt săl/əd] **80**–21
FRUIT [frōōt] **68**
frustrated [frŭs/trā/təd] **43**–27
frying pan [fri/ĭng pän/] **78**–5
fuel injection system
  [fyōō/əl ĭn jĕk/shən sĭs/təm] **158**–17
full [fōōl] **23**–9, **42**–6
  full-length mirror [fōōl/lĕnth/ mĭr/ər] **58**–6
  full moon [fōōl/ mōōn/] **205**–12
  full slip [fōōl/ slĭp/] **91**–22
fumes [fyōōmz] **179**–3
funnel [fŭn/əl] **195**–40
funny photo [fŭn/ē fō/tō] **206**–2
fur [für] **216**–19
furious [fyōōr/ē əs] **43** ✦
furnished apartment [für/nĭsht ə pärt/mənt] **48**–3
furniture [für/nĭ chər] **53**–19
  furniture polish [für/nĭ chər päl/ĭsh] **61**–8
  furniture store [für/nĭ chər stör/] **126**–8
Furniture and Accessories
  [für/nĭ chər ən ĭk sĕs/ə rēz] **59**
fuse box [fyōōz/ bäks/] **62**–13
fusion [fyōō/zhən] **218**–10
galaxy [găl/ək sē] **205**–15
gallbladder [göl/blăd/ər] **107**–44
gallon [găl/ən] **75**–5
game [gām]
  baseball game [bās/böl gām/] **44**–2
  board game [börd/ gām/] **232**–5
  game show [gām/ shō/] **236**–8
  video game console [vĭd/ē ō gām/ kän/sōl] **232**–3
  video game control [vĭd/ē ō gām kən trōl/] **232**–4
Games [gāmz] **59**
GAMES [gāmz] **232**–233
gang violence [găng/ vi/ə ləns] **142**–4
garage [gə räzh/, –räj/] **47**–14, **124**–1
  garage door [gə räzh/ dör/] **53**–7
Garage [gə räzh/, –räj/] **50**

GARAGE SALE [gə räzh/ säl/] **102**–103
garbage [gär/bĭj]
  garbage can [gär/bĭj kăn/] **53**–24
  garbage disposal [gär/bĭj dĭ spō/zəl] **54**–7
  garbage truck [gär/bĭj trŭk/] **127**–22
garden [gär/dn]
  botanical garden [bə tăn/ə kəl gär/dn] **222**–3
  roof garden [rōōf/gär/dn] **50**–4
  vegetable garden [vĕj/tə bəl gär/dn] **53**–27, **177**–14
garden [gär/dn] **53**–B
gardener [gär/dn er, gärd/nər] **167**–28
gardenia [gär dēn/yə] **211**–18
gardening [gärd/nĭng]
  gardening crew [gärd/nĭng krōō/] **176**–1
  gardening crew leader
    [gärd/nĭng krōō lēd/ər] **176**–4
GARDENING [gärd/nĭng] **176**
gargle [gär/gəl] **109**–L
garlic [gär/lĭk] **69**–30
  garlic bread [gär/lĭk brĕd/] **81**–28
  garlic press [gär/lĭk prĕs/] **78**–11
Garment Factory [gär/mənt făk/tə rē, făk/trē] **98**
garment worker [gär/mənt wür/kər] **167**–29
garter [gär/tər]
  garter belt [gär/tər bĕlt/] **91**–16
  garter snake [gär/tər snāk/] **213**–39
gas [găs] **218**–3
  gas gauge [găs/gāj/] **159**–31
  gas meter [găs mē/tər] **62**–14
  gas pedal [găs pĕd/l] **159**–46
  gas shut-off valve [găs/ shŭt/öf vălv/] **146**–4
  gas station [găs stā/shən] **125**–10
  gas station attendant
    [găs stā/shən ə tĕn/dənt] **162**–3
  gas tank [găs tăngk/] **158**–10
gate [gāt] **50**–16, **53**–9, **161**–8
Gate [gāt] **161**
gauge [gāj]
  blood pressure gauge [blŭd/ prĕsh/ər gāj/] **118**–9
  gas gauge [găs/gāj/] **159**–31
  oil gauge [oyl/gāj/] **159**–29
  temperature gauge [tĕm/prə chər gāj/] **159**–30
gauze [göz] **117**–8
gear shift [gir/ shĭft/] **159**–47
gel [jĕl] **108**–2, **108**–16
GEOGRAPHY AND HABITATS
  [jē äg/rə fē ən hă/bə tăts/] **204**
Geometric Solids [jē/ə mĕ/trĭk säl/ədz] **193**
geometry [jē äm/ə trē] **192**–17
geothermal energy [jē/ō thür/məl ĕn/ər jē] **218**–7
get [gĕt]
  get a job [gĕt/ ə jäb/] **40**–F
  get a learner's permit
    [gĕt/ ə lürn/ərz pür/mĭt] **137**–F
  get a library card [gĕt/ ə li/brĕr ē kärd/] **133**–A
  get a loan [gĕt/ ə lōn/] **49**–J
  get an electric shock [gĕt/ ən ĭ lĕk/trĭk shäk/] **116**–F
  get a speeding ticket [gĕt/ ə spē/dĭng tĭk/ət] **162**–C
  get bed rest [gĕt/ bĕd/ rĕst/] **114**–B
  get change [gĕt/ chānj/] **26**–A
  get dressed [gĕt/ drĕst/] **38**–D
  get elected [gĕt/ ĭ lĕk/təd] **139**–C

get engaged [gĕt/ ĭn gājd/] **41**–J
get feedback [gĕt/ fēd/băk/] **191**–K
get frostbite [gĕt/ frŏst/bīt/] **116**–G
get good grades [gĕt/ good/ grādz/] **10**–H
get hired [gĕt/ hīrd/] **173**–L
get home [gĕt/ hōm/] **39**–R
get immunized [gĕt/ ĭm/yə nīzd/] **114**–I
get into [gĕt/ ĭn/tōō] **153**–E
get lost [gĕt/ lŏst/] **162**–B
get married [gĕt/ măr/ēd/] **41**–K
get off [gĕt/ öf/] **153**–J
get on [gĕt/ än/, ön/] **153**–I
get out of [gĕt/ owt/ əv] **153**–F
get the title [gĕt/ dhə tīt/l] **157**–E
get up [gĕt/ ŭp/] **38**–B
get your license [gĕt/ yər lī/səns] **137**–I
Getting Your First License
[gĕt/ĭng yər fŭrst/ lī/səns] **137**
Get Well [gĕt/ wĕl/] **114**
gift [gĭft] **94** ✦, **240**–3
gift shop [gĭft/ shäp/] **130** ✦, **184**–5
gills [gĭlz] **212**–2
giraffe [jə răf/] **217**–32
girder [gŭr/dər] **178**–3
girdle [gŭr/dl] **91**–15
girl [gŭrl] **31**–10
give [gĭv] **15**–F, **122**–B, **148**–A,
glad [glăd] **44**–5
glass [glăs] **53**–18, **83**–22, **83**–23
glass cleaner [glăs klē/nər] **61**–14
glasses [glăs/əz] **92**–10, **115**–7, **179**–10
sunglasses [sŭn/glăs/əz] **90**–27
global positioning system (GPS) [glō/bəl
pə zĭ/shə nĭng sĭs/təm] / [jē/pē/ĕs/] **155**–11
gloves [glŭvz] **90**–6, **231**–17
disposable gloves [dĭ spō/ zə bəl glŭvz/] **93**–27
glove compartment [glŭv/ kəm pärt/mənt] **159**–44
latex gloves [lā/tĕks glŭvz/] **93**–34
rubber gloves [rŭb/ər glŭvz/] **61**–4
surgical gloves [sŭr/jĭ kəl glŭvz/] **121**–39
work gloves [wŭrk/ glŭvz/] **92**–17, **179**–17
glue [glōō] **183**–33
glue stick [glōō/ stĭk] **232**–11
go [gō]
go back [gō/ băk/] **11**–M
go for [gō/ fər] **157**–J
go on [gō/ än] **173**–K
go over [gō/ ō/vər] **153**–B
go past [gō/ păst/] **155**–E
go straight [gō/ strāt/] **155**–A
go through [gō/ throo/] **160**–D
go to an employment agency
[gō/ tə ən ĭm ploy/mənt ā/jən sē] **173**–E
go to bed [gō/ tə bĕd/] **39**–Y
go to college [gō/ tə käl/ĭj] **41**–I
go to jail [gō/ tə jāl/] **141**–G
go to prison [gō/ tə prĭz/ən] **141**–G
go to school [gō/ tə skool/] **38**–J
go to sleep [gō/ tə slēp/] **39**–Z

go to the grocery store
[gō/ tə dhə grōs/rē stör/, grōsh/rē] **38**–L
go to the next line [gō/ tə dhə nĕkst/ līn] **196**–D
go to work [gō/ tə wŭrk/] **38**–I
go under [gō/ ŭn/dər] **153**–A
to-go box [tə gō/ bäks/] **82**–5
GO [gō] **222**–**223**
goat [gōt] **215**–5
goggles [gäg/əlz] **179**–11
goldfish [gōld/fĭsh/] **215**–16
golf [gälf, gölf] **228**–8
golf club [gälf/ klŭb/] **231**–1
good [good] **23**–17
Goods [goodz] **73**
goose [goos] **214**–13
gopher [gō/fər] **215**–19
gorilla [gə rĭl/ə] **217**–29
gospel [gäs/pəl] **237**–30
Government [gŭ/ vərn mənt] **138**–**139**
GOVERNMENT AND MILITARY SERVICE
[gŭ/ vərn mənt ən mĭ/ lə tër ē sŭr/vəs] **138**–**139**
governor [gŭ/ vər nər] **139**–20, **139**–21
gown [gown] **206**–8
evening gown [ĕv/nĭng gown/] **89**–18
hospital gown [häs/pĭ tl gown/] **121**–19
nightgown [nīt/gown/] **91**–25
surgical gown [sŭr/jə kəl gown/] **93**–37, **121**–38
GPS (global positioning system) [jē/pē/ĕs/] /
[glō/bəl pə zĭ/shə nĭng sĭs/təm] **155**–11
grab bar [grăb/ bär/] **57**–9
grades [grādz] **10**–4
graduate [grăj/oo āt/] **40**–D
graduated cylinder [grăj/oo ā/təd sĭl/ən dər] **195**–38
GRADUATION [grăj/oo ā/shən] **206**–**207**
graffiti [grə fēt/tē] **148**–1
grandchild [grăn/chīld, grănd/–] **34** ✦
granddaughters [grăn/dö/tərz] **34** ✦
grandfather [grăn/fä/dhər, grănd/–] **34**–2
grandmother [grăn/mŭdh/ər, grănd/–] **34**–1
Grandparents [grăn/për/ənts, grănd/–] **34**
grandson [grăn/sŭn/, grănd/–] **34** ✦
grapefruit [grāp/froot/] **68**–6
grapes [grāps] **68**–3
graph [grăf] **192**–15
graphic designer [grăf/ĭk dĭ zī/nər] **167**–30
grasshopper [grăs/häp/ər] **214**–24
grate [grāt] **77**–G
grater [grā/tər] **78**–2
gray [grā] **24**–15
gray hair [grā hër] **33**–13
grease [grēs] **77**–B
green [grēn] **24**–5
green card [grēn/ kärd/] **40**–2
green onions [grēn/ ŭn/yənz] **69**–20
greet [grēt] **3**–G, **171**–M, **174**–H
GREETING [grē/tĭng] **2**–**3**
greeting card [grē/tĭng kärd/] **134**–15
grill [grĭl] **53**–17
grilled [grĭld/]
grilled cheese sandwich
[grĭld/ chēz/ săn/wĭch, –sănd/–] **80**–10

grilled fish [grĭld/ fĭsh/] **81**–29
grilled ribs [grĭld/ rĭbz/] **76**–2
grocery [grōs/rē, grōsh/rē]
grocery bag [grōs/rē băg/] **67**–13
grocery clerk [grōs/rē klŭrk/] **72**–4
Grocery Products [grōs/rē präd/ŭkts] **72**
GROCERY STORE [grōs/ rē stör/] **72**–**73**
ground [grownd]
ground beef [grownd/ bēf/] **70**–4
ground post [grownd/ pōst/] **134**–6
playground [plā/grownd/] **50**–3
group [grōōp] **115**–15
grower [grō/ər] **177**–13
guard [gärd] **141**–3
Coast Guard [kōst/ gärd/] **138**–18
lifeguard [līf/gärd/] **225**–19
lifeguard station [līf/gärd/ stā/shən] **225**–21
National Guard [nă/shə nəl gärd/] **138**–19
security guard [sĭ kyoor/ə tē gärd/] **132**–5, **169**–55
shin guards [shĭn/ gärdz/] **231**–13
guest [gĕst] **184**–10
guest room [gĕst/ rōōm] **184**–13
guest services [gĕst/ sŭr/vəs əs] **130**–12
guest speaker [gĕst/ spē/kər] **206**–4
guinea pig [gĭn/ē pĭg/] **215**–14
guitar [gĭ tär/] **238**–9
gums [gŭmz] **106**–6
gum disease [gŭm/ dĭ zēz/] **119**–11
gun [gŭn] **142**–13, **181**–21
gurney [gŭr/nē] **121**–33
gutter [gŭt/ər] **53**–4
gym [jĭm] **5**–19, **126**–10, **184**–24
gymnastics [jĭm năs/tĭks] **228**–9
gynecologists [gī/nə käl/ə jĭsts] **120** ✦
habitat [hă/bə tăt/] **194**–12
HABITATS [hă/bə tăts/] **204**
hacksaw [hăk/sö/] **180**–5
hail a taxi [hāl/ ə tăx/ē/] **152** ✦
hailstorm [hāl/störm/] **13**–21
hair [hër] **104**–2
black hair [blăk/ hër/] **33**–16
blond hair [bländ/ hër/] **33**–17
brown hair [brown/ hër/] **33**–18
curly hair [kŭr/lē hër/] **33**–11
gray hair [grā/ hër] **33**–13
hair clip [hër klĭp/] **108**–19
hairdresser [hër/drĕs/ər] **167**–31
hair gel [hër jĕl/] **108**–16
hairnet [hër nĕt/] **93**–25
hair salon [hër sə län/] **131**–18
hair spray [hër sprā/] **108**–12
hair stylist [hër stī/lĭst] **167**–31
long hair [löng/ hër/] **33**–3
red hair [rĕd/ hër/] **33**–15
short hair [shört/hër/] **33**–1
shoulder-length hair [shōl/dər lĕnth/ hër/] **33**–2
straight hair [strāt/ hër/] **33**–9
wavy hair [wā/vē hër/] **33**–10
HAIR [hër] **33**

half [hăf]
  half bath [hăf/ băth/] **57** ✦
  half brother [hăf/ brŭdh/ər] **35**–28
  1/2 cup [hăf/ kŭp/] **75**–9
  half dollar [hăf/ däl/ər] **26**–5
  half past one [hăf/ păst/ wŭn/] **18**–11
  half sister [hăf/ sĭs/tər] **35**–27
  half slip [hăf/ slĭp/] **91**–23
halibut steak [hăl/ə bət stāk/] **71**–6
hall [höl] **124**–8
  hallway [höl/wā/] **5**–10, **184**–18
Hallway [höl/wā/] **51**
ham [hăm] **70**–9, **76**–5
hamburger [hăm/bür/gər] **79**–1
hammer [hăm/ər] **180**–1
  jackhammer [jăk/hăm/ər] **178**–9
  sledgehammer [slĕj/ hăm/ər] **178**–23
hammer [hăm/ər] **178**–D
hammock [hăm/ək] **53**–23
hamper [hăm/pər] **57**–1
hand [hănd] **105**–15, **177**–20
  DMV handbook [dē/ĕm/vē/ hănd/bŏŏk] **136**–1
  handbag [hănd/băg/] **87**–9, **94**–2
  handbrake [hănd/ brāk/] **59**–48
  handcuffs [hănd/kŭfs/] **141**–2
  handsaw [hănd/sö/] **180**–4
  handset [hănd/sĕt] **14**–1
  hand towel [hănd tow/əl] **57**–15
  hand truck [hănd trŭk/] **175**–11
Hand [hănd] **106**
handicapped parking [hăn/dē kăpt pär/kĭng]
  128–6, **154**–12
hand in [hănd/ ĭn/] **10**–O
hanger [hăng/gər] **101**–11
hang up [hăng/ ŭp/] **15**–D, **101**–H
happy [hăp/ē] **28**–6, **43**–31
hard [härd] **23**–5, **23**–24
  hardboiled eggs [härd/boyld/ ĕgz/] **76**–8
  hard drive [härd/ drīv/] **196**–6
  hard hat [härd/ hăt/] **92**–1, **179**–9
hardware store [härd/wër/ stör/] **148**–4
harmonica [här mä/ nĭ kə] **238**–21
harvest [här/vəst] **177**–B
hash browns [hăsh/ brownz/] **80**–3
hats [hăts] **90**–1, **95**–11
  chef's hat [shĕfs/ hăt/] **93**–28
  cowboy hat [kow/boy/ hăt/] **92**–18
  hard hat [härd/ hăt/] **92**–1, **179**–9
  ski hat [skē/ hăt/] **90**–11
  straw hat [strö/ hăt/] **90**–23
have [hăv]
  have a baby [hăv/ ə bā/bē] **41**–L
  have a conversation [hăv/ ə kän/vər sā/shən] **11**–L
  have a heart attack [hăv/ ə härt/ ə tăk/] **116**–D
  have an allergic reaction
    [hăv/ ən ə lür/jĭk rē ăk/shən] **116**–E
  have a picnic [hăv/ ə pĭk/nĭk] **224**–D
  have dinner [hăv/ dĭn/ər] **39**–S
  have regular checkups
    [hăv/ rĕg/yə lər chĕk/ups] **114**–H
Hawaii-Aleutian time [hə wī/ē ə lōō/shən tim/] **19**–27

hay [hā] **177**–18
hazard [hăz/ərd] **186**–6
  hazard lights [hăz/ərd līts/] **159**–36
Hazardous Materials [hăz/ər dəs mə tïr/ē əlz] **179**
hazardous waste [hăz/ər dəs wāst/] **218**–12
Hazards [hăz/ərdz] **179**
head [hĕd] **69**–32, **104**–1
  headache [hĕd/āk/] **110**–1
  headband [hĕd/bănd/] **90**–3
  headboard [hĕd/börd/] **58**–10
  head chef [hĕd/ shĕf/] **185**–7
  headlight [hĕd/līt/] **158**–7
  headline [hĕd/līn] **133**–7
  headphones [hĕd/fōnz/] **6**–8, **234**–4
  headset [hĕd/sĕt] **14**–13
  headwaiter [hĕd/wā/tər] **185**–12
  headwrap [hĕd/răp/] **90**–7
  letterhead [lĕt/ər hĕd] **183**–42
  overhead compartment
    [ō/ vər hĕd/ kəm pärt/mənt] **161**–13
  overhead projector [ō/ vər hĕd/prə jĕk/tər] **7**–16
  wireless headset [wīr/ləs hĕd/sĕt] **14**–14
health [hĕlth] **167**–32
  health history form [hĕlth/ hĭs/tə rē förm/] **118**–4
  health insurance card
    [hĕlth/ ĭn shŏŏr/əns kärd/] **118**–3
HEALTH [hĕlth] **114**–115
HEALTH FAIR [hĕlth/ fër/] **122**–123
Health Problems [hĕlth/ präb/ləmz] **115**
hear [hïr] **106**–B
hearing [hïr/ĭng]
  hearing aid [hïr/ĭng ād/] **115**–10
  hearing impaired [hïr/ĭng ĭm përd/] **32**–12
  hearing loss [hïr/ĭng lös/] **115**–2
heart [härt] **107**–38, **116**–D, **239**–6
  heart disease [härt/ dĭ zēz/] **111**–11
hearts [härts] **233**–31
heater [hē/tər] **159**–40
heating pad [hē/tĭng păd/] **113**–13
heat wave [hēt/ wāv/] **13**–13
heavy [hĕv/ē] **23**–13, **32**–7, **97**–27
hedge clippers [hĕj/ klĭp/ərz] **176**–11
heel [hēl] **94**–22, **106**–24
  high heels [hī/ hēlz/] **89**–21, **95**–25
height [hīt] **17**–16, **32**–5
Height [hīt] **32**
Heimlich maneuver [hīm/lĭk mə nōō/vər] **117**–18
helicopter [hĕl/ə käp/tər] **151**–9
helmet [hĕl/mət] **93**–23, **231**–19
help [hĕlp] **8**–J, **147**–G
Help with Health Problems
  [hĕlp/ wĭth/ hĕlth/ präb/ləmz] **115**
hem [hĕm] **100**–8
hen [hĕn] **215**–8
herbal tea [ür/bəl tē/, hür/bəl–] **81**–40
herbs [ürbz, hürbz] **84**–9
hibiscus [hī bĭs/kəs, hĭ–] **211**–12
hide [hīd] **240**–D
high [hī] **91**–12, **97**–32, **188**–3
  high blood pressure [hī/ blŭd/ prĕsh/ər] **111**–14
  high chair [hī/ chër/] **37**–6, **82**–3
  high heels [hī/ hēlz/] **89**–21, **95**–25

high-rise [hī/ rīz/] **127**–13
high school [hī/ skōōl] **188**–4
highway [hī/wā] **155**–9
  highway marker [hī/wā mär/kər] **154**–17
hiking [hī/kĭng] **226**–7
  hiking boots [hī/kĭng bōōts/] **95**–31
hills [hĭlz] **204**–16
  downhill skiing [down/hĭl/ skē/ĭng] **227**–1
hip hop [hĭp/häp] **237**–26
hippopotamus [hĭp/ə pät/ə məs] **217**–43
hire [hīr] **141**–B
hired hand [hīrd/ hănd/] **177**–20
Historical Terms [hĭs/tör/ə kəl türmz/] **199**
history [hĭs/tə rē] **118**–4, **189**–12
HISTORY [hĭs/tə rē] **198**–199
hit [hĭt] **230**–B
HIV (human immunodeficiency virus)
  [āch/ī/vē/] / [hyōō/mən ĭm/yə nō
  dĭ fĭsh/ən sē vī/rəs] **111**–17
Hi-Visibility safety vest [hī/vĭ/zə bĭl/ə tē vĕst/] **92**–4
HOBBIES AND GAMES [häb/ēz ən gāmz/] **232**–233
hockey [häk/ē] **229**–13
  hockey stick [häk/ē stĭk/] **231**–11
hold [hōld] **36**–A
holder [hōl/dər]
  candle holder [kăn/dl hōl/dər] **56**–21
  cell phone holder [sĕl/ fōn/ hōld/ər] **94**–15
  magazine holder [măg/ə zēn/ hōld/ər] **56**–23
  pot holders [pät/ hōl/dərz] **78**–29
  toothbrush holder [tōōth/brŭsh/ hōld/ər] **57**–22
holiday [hăl/ə dā/] **22**–7, **22**–8
Holidays [hăl/ə dāz/] **22**
HOLIDAYS [hăl/ə dāz/] **239**
holly [hăl/ē] **210**–19
home [hōm] **52**–7, **52**–12
  home health care aide [hōm/ hĕlth/ kër ād] **167**–32
  home improvement store
    [hōm/ ĭm prōōv/mənt stör/] **127**–20
  homemaker [hōm/mā/kər] **168**–33
  homesick [hōm/sĭk/] **43**–20
HOME [hōm] **46**–47, **48**–49
honeybee [hŭn/ē bē/] **214**–25
hood [hŏŏd] **158**–4
Hood [hŏŏd] **158**
hoof / hooves [hŏŏf/] / [hŏŏvz] **216**–17
hook [hŏŏk] **180**–39, **180**–40
  hook and eye [hŏŏk/ ən ī/] **99**–27
  hook and loop fastener
    [hŏŏk/ ən lōōp/ fă/sən ər] **99**–29
horn [hörn] **159**–32, **216**–21, **238**–11
  French horn [frĕnch/ hörn] **238**–13
horror story [hör/ər stör/ē, här/–] **237**–17
horse [hörs] **215**–4
  horseback riding [hörs/băk rī/dĭng] **226**–9
  horse racing [hörs/ rā/sĭng] **228**–19
  seahorse [sē/hörs/] **212**–13
hose [hōz] **53**–21, **91**–18
hospital [häs/pī tl] **125**–9, **154**–18
  hospital bed [häs/pī tl bĕd/] **121**–22
  hospital gown [häs/pī tl gown/] **121**–19
HOSPITAL [häs/pī tl] **120**–121
Hospital Room [häs/pī tl rōōm/] **121**

Hospital Staff [häs/pĭ tl stăf/] **120**
hostess [hō/stəs] **82**–2
hot [hät] **13**–3, **42**–1
   hot cereal [hät sĭr/ē əl] **80**–9
   hot dog [hät/ dög/] **79**–6
   hot water [hät/ wö/tər] **57**–8
   hot water bottle [hät/ wö/tər băt/l] **113**–15
hotel [hō tĕl/] **124**–3
A HOTEL [hō tĕl/] **184**
hour [ow/ər] **18**–1
house [hows]
   courthouse [kört/hows/] **125**–13
   dollhouse [däl/hows/] **59**–18
   housekeeper [hows/kē/pər] **168**–34, **184**–20
   housekeeping cart [hows/kē/pĭng kärt/] **184**–19
   House of Representatives
      [hows/ əv rĕp/rĭ zĕn/tə tĭvz] **138**–3
   house painter [hows/ pān/tər] **168**–46
   houseplant [hows/plănt/] **56**–4, **211**–27
   townhouse [town/hows/] **52**–6
   two-story house [tōō/stör/ē hows/] **52** ✦
   warehouse [wër/hows/] **175**–7
   White House [wīt/ hows/] **138**–7
House [hows] **49, 53**
A HOUSE AND YARD [hows/ən yärd/] **53**
HOUSEHOLD PROBLEMS AND REPAIRS
   [hows/hōld/ präb/ləmz ən rĭ përz/] **62–63**
HOUSEWORK [hows/würk/] **60**
housing [how/zĭng] **52**–11
hubcap [hŭb/kăp/] **158**–9
hug [hŭg] **2**–E
human immunodeficiency virus (HIV)
   [hyōō/mən ĭm/yə nō dĭ fĭsh/ən sē vī/rəs] /
   [āch/ī/vē/] **111**–17
humid [hyōō/məd] **13**–15
humidifier [hyōō mĭd/ə fī/ər] **113**–11
humiliated [hyōō mĭl/ē ā/təd] **43** ✦
hummingbird [hŭm/ĭng bürd/] **214**–10
hump [hŭmp] **217**–51
hungry [hŭng/grē] **42**–5
hurricane [hür/ə kān/] **145**–14
hurt [hürt] **42**–16, **116**–C
husband [hŭz/bənd] **34**–13
   ex-husband [ĕks/ hŭz/bənd] **35** ✦
   former husband [för/mər hŭz/bənd] **35** ✦
hutch [hŭch] **55**–22
hybrid [hy/brĭd] **156**–3
hydrant [hī/drənt] **129**–27
hydroelectric power [hī/drō ĭ lĕk/trĭk pow/ər] **218**–5
hydrogen peroxide [hī/drə jən pə räk/sīd] **117**–9
hyena [hī ē/nə] **217**–30
HYGIENE [hy/jēn] **108–109**
hygienist [hī jē/nĭst, –jĕn/ĭst] **119**–3
hypertension [hī/pər tĕn/shən] **111**–14
hyphen [hy/fən] **190**–20
hypoallergenic [hī/pō ăl/ər jĕn/ĭk] **108** ✦
I beam [ī/ bēm/] **178**–3
ice [īs]
   ice cream [īs/ krēm/] **72**–26
   ice-cream cone [īs/ krēm/ kōn] **79**–13
   ice cream shop [īs/ krēm/ shäp/] **131**–16
   ice hockey [īs/ häk/ē] **229**–13

ice pack [īs/ păk/] **117**–13
ice skates [īs/ skāts/] **231**–9
ice skating [īs/ skā/tĭng] **227**–4
iced tea [īst/ tē/] **79**–12
icy [ī/sē] **13**–22
ID [ī/dē/] **146**–19
identity theft [ī dĕn/tə tē thĕft/] **142**–9
ignition [ĭg nĭsh/ən] **159**–33
illegal drugs [ĭ lē/gəl drŭgz/] **142**–6
Illnesses and Childhood Diseases
   [ĭl/nə səz ən chīld/hōōd dĭ zēz/ əz] **111**
ILLNESSES AND MEDICAL CONDITIONS
   [ĭl/nə səz ən mĕd/ĭ kəl kən dĭsh/ənz] **111**
Immediate Family
   [ĭ mē/ dē ət făm/lē, –fă/məlē] **34**
immigrant [ĭm/ə grənt] **199**–19
immigrate [ĭm/ə grāt/] **40**–C
immigration [ĭm/ə grā/shən] **199**–18
immunization [ĭm/yə nə zā/shən] **114** ✦
immunodeficiency [ĭm/yə nō dĭ fĭsh/ən sē] **111**–17
impaired [ĭm përd/] **32**–11, **32**–12
important [ĭm pört/ənt] **146**–19
improvement [ĭm prōōv/mənt] **127**–20
in [ĭn] **25**–6
   be in shock [bē/ ĭn shäk/] **116**–B
   bubble in [bŭb/l ĭn/] **10**–K
   call in [käl/ ĭn/] **186**–A
   check in [chĕk/ ĭn/] **160**–A
   check-in kiosk [chĕk/ĭn kē/äsk/] **160**–2
   fall in love [fäl/ ĭn lŭv/] **40**–H
   fill in [fĭl/ ĭn/] **9**–O
   hand in [hănd/ĭn/] **10**–O
   in fashion [ĭn făsh/ən] **88** ✦
   in front of [ĭn frŭnt/ əv] **24**–7
   in love [ĭn lŭv/] **42**–18
   in pain [ĭn pān/] **42**–11
   in style [ĭn stīl/] **88** ✦
   in the middle [ĭn dhə mĭd/l] **24**–2
   look in [lōōk/ ĭn/] **173**–B
   move in [mōōv/ ĭn/] **48**–F
   send in [sĕnd/ ĭn/] **173**–H
   take in [tăk/ ĭn/] **100**–D
   turn in [türn/ ĭn/] **191**–M
   walk-in freezer [wäk/ĭn frē/zər] **185**–3
inch [ĭnch] **17**–15
indent [ĭn dĕnt/] **190**–D
independence [ĭn/də pĕn/dəns]
   Declaration of Independence
      [dĕk/lə rā/shən əv ĭn/də pĕn/dəns] **198**–5
   Independence Day [ĭn/də pĕn/dəns dā/] **22**–13
INDIVIDUAL SPORTS [ĭn/də vĭj/ōō əl spörts/] **228**
infant [ĭn/fənt] **31**–6
infection [ĭn fĕk/shən] **111**–3
infectious disease [ĭn fĕk/shəs dĭ zēz/] **111** ✦
influenza [ĭn/flōō ĕn/zə] **111** ✦
INFORMATION [ĭn/fər mā/shən] **4**
inhaler [ĭn hā/lər] **113**–33
injection [ĭn jŏk/shən] **114** ✦, **158**–17
injured [ĭn/ jərd] **116**–C
INJURIES [ĭn/jə rēz] **110**

ink [ĭnk]
   ink cartridge [ĭnk/ kär/trĭj] **183**–45
   inkjet printer [ĭnk/jĕt prĭn/tər] **183**–18
   ink pad [ĭnk/ păd/] **183**–46
inline [ĭn/lĭn/]
   inline skates [ĭn/lĭn/ skāts/] **231**–10
   inline skating [ĭn/lĭn/ skā/tĭng] **228**–10
inquire about benefits
   [ĭn kwīr/ ə bowt/bĕn/ə fĭts] **174** ✦
insects [ĭn/sĕkts] **209**–11
   insect bite [ĭn/sĕkt bīt/] **110**–11
   insect repellent [ĭn/sĕkt rĭ pĕl/ənt] **226**–23
Insects [ĭn/sĕkts] **214**
INSECTS [ĭn/sĕkts] **214**
insert [ĭn sürt/] **132**–D
INSIDE AND OUTSIDE THE BODY
   [ĭn/sīd/ ən owt/sīd/ dhə băd/ē] **106–107**
Inside the Car [ĭn/sīd/ dhə kär/] **159**
Inside the Kit [ĭn/sīd/ dhə kĭt/] **117**
Inside the Trunk [ĭn/sīd/ dhə trŭnk/] **158**
inspect [ĭn spĕkt/] **147**–N
install [ĭn stäl/] **176**–H, **178**–C
instructor [ĭn strŭk/tər] **6**–4
Instrument Panel [ĭn/strə mənt păn/əl] **159**
instruments [ĭn/strə mənts] **119**–4, **238**
insulation [ĭn/sə lā/shən] **178**–14
insurance [ĭn shōōr/əns] **118**–3, **136**–8
integers [ĭn/tə jərz] **192**–1, **192**–2
Integers [ĭn/tə jərz] **192**
intercom [ĭn/tər käm/] **50**–5
interest inventory [ĭn/trəst ĭn/vən tör/ ē] **172**–11
international call [ĭn/tər năsh/ə nəl köl/] **15**–35
Internet [ĭn/tər nĕt/]
   Internet listing [ĭn/tər nĕt/ lĭst/ĭng] **48**–1
   Internet map [ĭn/tər nĕt/ măp/] **155**–12
   Internet phone call [ĭn/tər nĕt/ fōn/ käl/] **14**–20
INTERNET [ĭn/tər nĕt/] **197**
internist [ĭn/tür/nĭst] **120**–1
internship [ĭn/türn shĭp/] **172**–6
interpreter [ĭn tür/prə tər] **168**–35
INTERSECTION [ĭn/tər sĕk/shən] **128–129**
INTERVIEW SKILLS [ĭn/tər vyōō/ skĭlz/] **174**
intestinal parasites [ĭn tĕs/tə nəl păr/ə sīts/] **111**–13
intestines [ĭn tĕs/tənz] **107**–42
In the Airline Terminal [ĭn dhə ër/lĭn tür/mə nəl] **160**
In the Examining Room
   [ĭn dhə ĭg zăm/ə nĭng rōōm/] **118**
In the Waiting Room [ĭn dhə wā/tĭng rōōm/] **118**
into [ĭn/tōō, –tə] **153**–E
intravenous drip (IV)
   [ĭn/trə vē/nəs drĭp/] / [ī/vē/] **121**–25
introduce [ĭn/trə dōōs/] **2**–C, **3**–I
introduction [ĭn/trə dŭk/shən] **190**–6
invention [ĭn vĕn/shən] **199**–12
inventor [ĭn vĕn/tər] **199**–13
inventory [ĭn/vən tör/ ē] **172**–11, **172**–12
invertebrates [ĭn vür/ tə brəts/] **194**–13
invitation [ĭn və tā/shən] **12**–I, **12**–J, **64**–9
invite [ĭn vīt/] **12**–H
iris [ī/rəs] **211**–16
iron [ī/ərn] **101**–13, **108**–17
iron [ī/ərn] **101**–G

Index

ironed [ī/ərnd] **101**–20
ironing board [ī/ər nĭng börd/] **101**–14
irritated [ĭr/ə tā/təd] **64**–6
island [ī/lənd] **204**–8
IV (intravenous drip)
   [ī/vē/] / [ĭn/trə vē/nəs drĭp/] **121**–25
ivory [ī/vər ē] **24**–16
ivy [ī/vē] **210**–25
jack [jăk] **158**–24
jacket [jăk/ət] **90**–8
   chef's jacket [shĕfs/ jăk/ət] **93**–29
   down jacket [down/ jăk/ət] **90**–16
   leather jacket [lĕdh/ər jăk/ət] **90**–4
   sports jacket [spörts/ jăk/ət] **89**–14
jackhammer [jăk/ hăm/ər] **178**–9
jack-o'-lantern [jăk/ə lăn/tərn] **239**–10
janitor [jăn/ĭ tər] **182**–3
January [jăn/yōo ĕr/ē] **21**–25
jar [jär] **74**–2, **74**–14
jasmine [jăz/mən] **211**–22
jaw [jö] **106**–4
jay [jā] **214**–6
jaywalk [jā/wäk] **128**–C
jazz [jăz] **237**–24
jeans [jēnz] **86**–2, **92**–19
jellyfish [jĕl/ē fĭsh] **212**–14
jewelry [jōo/əl rē]
   jewelry department [jōo/əl rē dĭ pärt/mənt] **95**–8
   jewelry store [jōo/əl rē stör/] **130**–2
jigsaw [jĭg/sö/] **180**–10
job [jäb] **172**–1, **172**–3, **172**–7
   job fair [jäb/ fĕr] **172**–13
JOB SAFETY [jäb/ sāf/tē] **179**
JOBS AND OCCUPATIONS
   [jäbz/ ən äk/yə pā/shənz] **166**–169
JOB SEARCH [jäb/ sürch/] **173**
JOB SKILLS [jäb/ skĭlz/] **170**
Job Training [jäb/ trān/ĭng] **172**
jockstrap [jäk/străp/] **91**–6
join [joyn] **143**–L
judge [jŭj] **141**–6
Judicial Branch [jōo dĭ/shəl brănch/] **138**
juice [jōos] **73**–32
July [jōo lī/] **21**–31
jump [jŭmp] **230**–I
jumper cables [jŭm/pər kā/bəlz] **158**–21
jump rope [jŭmp/ rōp/] **224**–4
jumpsuit [jŭmp/sōot/] **93**–24
June [jōon] **21**–30
junior high school [jōon/yər hī/ skōol] **188**–3
junk mail [jŭnk/ māl/] **135** ✦
Jupiter [jōo/pə tər] **205**–5
jury [jür/ē] **141**–8
justices [jŭs/tə səz] **138**–12, **138**–13
kangaroo [kăng/gə rōo/] **217**–44
keep [kēp] **28**–B
ketchup [kĕch/əp, kăch/–] **79**–21
kettle [kĕt/l] **54**–21
key [kē] **51**–30, **155**–9
   key pad [kē/ păd/] **14**–5
   pound key [pownd/ kē/] **14**–7
   star key [stär/ kē/] **14**–6

keyboard [kē/börd/] **196**–14, **238**–18
Keyboarding [kē/börd/ĭng] **196**
kick [kĭk] **230**–E
kidney [kĭd/nē] **107**–43
kids' bedroom [kĭdz/ bĕd/rōom/] **47**–9
KIDS' BEDROOM [kĭdz/ bĕd/rōom/] **59**
king-size bed [kĭng/sīz/ bĕd/] **184**–15
kiosk [kē/äsk/] **131**–22, **160**–2
kiss [kĭs] **3**–K, **36**–P
kit [kĭt]
   doll making kit [däl/ mā/kĭng kĭt/] **232**–13
   first aid kit [fürst/ ād/ kĭt/] **117**–1, **146**–18
   model kit [mäd/l kĭt/] **232**–9
   woodworking kit [wood/wür/kĭng kĭt/] **232**–14
Kit [kĭt] **117**
kitchen [kĭch/ən] **46**–5, **83**–15
   kitchen timer [kĭch/ən tī/mər] **78**–18
A KITCHEN [ə kĭch/ən] **54**
Kitchen [kĭch/ən] **185**
KITCHEN UTENSILS [kĭch/ən yōo tĕn/səlz] **78**
kite [kīt] **225**–2
kitten [kĭt/n] **215**–10
kiwi [kē/wē] **68**–22
knee [nē] **106**–20
   knee highs [nē/hīz/] **91**–12
   knee pads [nē/ pădz/] **179**–19
knife [nīf] **55**–4, **83**–30
   carving knife [kär/vĭng nīf/] **78**–12
   multi-use knife [mŭl/tē yōos/nīf/, mŭl/tī–] **226**–20
   paring knife [për/ĭng nīf/] **78**–16
   steak knife [stāk/ nīf/] **83**–29
knit [nĭt] **233**–F
knitting needles [nĭt/ĭng nēd/lz] **233**–23
knit top [nĭt/ täp/] **88**–7
knob [näb] **194**–22, **194**–23
   doorknob [dör/näb/] **53**–12
knuckle [nŭk/l] **106**–17
koala [kō ä/lə] **217**–45
lab [lăb] **5**–15
   lab coat [lăb/ kōt/] **93**–33
Lab [lăb] **195**
label [lā/bəl]
   mailing label [mā/lĭng lā/bəl] **183**–41
   nutrition label [nōo trĭ/shən lā/bəl] **122**–8
   prescription label [prĭ skrĭp/shən lā/bəl] **112**–4
   warning label [wär/nĭng lā/bəl] **112**–8
label [lā/bəl] **9**–V
Labor Day [lā/bər dā/] **22**–14
lace [lās] **99**–9
   shoelaces [shōo/lā səz] **94**–24
ladder [lăd/ər] **178**–2
ladle [lā/dl] **78**–7
ladybug [lā/dē bŭg/] **214**–26
lake [lāk] **204**–13
lamb [lăm] **70**–14
   lamb chops [lăm/ chäps/] **70**–15
   lamb shanks [lăm/ shăngks/] **70**–13
Lamb [lăm] **70**
lamp [lămp] **56**–15, **58**–25
   lampshade [lămp/shād/] **56** ✦, **58**–26
land [lănd] **160**–K
landlord [lănd/lörd/] **51**–27

landmarks [lănd/märks/] **220**–1
landscape designer [lănd/skāp/ dĭ zī/nər] **176**–5
LANDSCAPING AND GARDENING
   [lănd/skā/pĭng ən gärd/nĭng] **176**
languages [lăng/gwĭ jəz] **189**–13
   language arts [lăng/gwĭj ärts/] **189**–9
lantern [lăn/tərn] **226**–22, **239**–10
laptop [lăp/täp/] **196**–16
large [lärj] **96**–4, **96**–5
laser printer [lā/zər prĭn/tər] **183**–19
lashes [lăsh/əz]
   eyelashes [ī/lăsh/əz] **106**–11
last [lăst]
   last name [lăst/ nām/] **4**–4
   last week [lăst/ wēk/] **20**–18
late [lāt] **19**–24
latex gloves [lā/tĕks glŭvz/] **93**–34
laugh [lăf] **44**–A
laundromat [lön/drə mät/] **128**–1
laundry [lön/drē] **101**–1
   laundry basket [lön/drē băs/kət] **101**–2
   laundry detergent [lön/drē dĭ tür/jənt] **101**–8
LAUNDRY [lön/drē] **101**
Laundry Room [lön/drē rōom/] **50**
lawn [lön] **53**–26
   lawn mower [lön/ mō/ər] **176**–6
lawyer [lö/yər] **168**–36
lay [lā] **178**–B
layer cake [lā/ər kāk/] **81**–33
LCD projector [ĕl/sē/dē/ prə jĕk/tər] **6**–6, **235**–29
leader [lē/dər] **176**–4
leaf / leaves [lēf/ / lēvz] **210**–6, **211**–6
   leaf blower [lēf/ blō/ər] **176**–2
leaking [lē/kĭng] **62**–3
learn [lürn] **40**–E
Learning New Words [lür/nĭng nōo/ würdz/] **8**
lease [lēs] **48** ✦, **51**–28
leather [lĕdh/ər] **98**–6
   leather jacket [lĕdh/ər jăk/ət] **90**–4
leave [lēv] **11**–O, **38**–N, **82**–J, **160**–J, **171**–P
leaves / leaf [lēvz/ / lēf] **210**–6, **211**–6
   leaf blower [lēf/ blō/ər] **176**–2
lecture [lĕk/chər] **122**–9
left [lĕft] **25**–1, **154**–8, **155**–C
legal [lē/gəl]
   legal holiday [lē/gəl häl/ə dā/] **22**–8
   legal pad [lē/gəl păd/] **183**–38
Legal Holidays [lē/gəl häl/ə dāz/] **22**
LEGAL SYSTEM [lē/gəl sĭs/təm] **141**
Leg and Foot [lĕg/ ən fŏot/] **106**
leggings [lĕg/ĭngz] **90**–12
Legislature [lĕ/jəs lā/chər] **139**–23
legs [lĕgz] **70**–21, **105**–9
   leg of lamb [lĕg/ əv lăm/] **70**–14
lemonade [lĕm/ə nād/] **84**–2
lemons [lĕm/ənz] **68**–7
lend [lĕnd] **26**–C
length [lĕngkth] **17**–17, **96**–17
lengthen [lĕngk/thən] **100**–A
lens / lenses [lĕnz] / [lĕnz/əz] **115**–8, **235**–23
leopard [lĕp/ərd] **217**–34
let out [lĕt/ owt/] **100**–C

letter [lĕt/ər] **134**–13
    letter carrier [lĕt/ər kăr/ ē ər] **134**–20
    letterhead [lĕt/ər hĕd/] **183**–42
lettuce [lĕt/əs] **69**–1
level [lĕv/əl] **172**–1, **180**–29
librarian [lī brër/ē ən] **133**–9
library [lī/brër ē] **5**–17, **125**–15
    library clerk [lī/brër ē klürk/] **133**–1
    library patron [lī/brër ē pā/trən] **133**–3
LIBRARY [lī/brër ē] **133**
license [lī/səns]
    driver's license [drī/vərz lī/səns] **40**–4, **136**–9
    driver's license number
      [drī/vərz lī/səns nŭm/bər] **136**–11
    license plate [lī/səns plāt/] **136**–12, **158**–12
    marriage license [măr/ĭj lī/səns] **41**–8
    renew a license [rĭ nōō/ ə lī/səns, –nyōō/–] **136** ✦
    taxi license [tăk/sē lī/səns] **152**–22
License [lī/səns] **137**
licensed practical nurse (LPN)
    [lī/sənst prăk/tə kəl nürs/] / [ĕl/pē/ĕn/] **120**–11
lid [lĭd] **78**–24
lieutenant governor [lōō tĕ/nənt gŭ/ vər nər] **139**–21
life [līf]
    lifeguard [līf/gärd/] **225**–19
    lifeguard station [līf/gärd/ stā/shən] **225**–21
    lifesaving device [līf/sā/vĭng dĭ vīs/] **225**–20
    life vest [līf/ vĕst/] **161**–25, **226**–14
    wildlife [wīld/ līf/] **220**–3
LIFE [līf] **212**–**213**
LIFE EVENTS AND DOCUMENTS
    [līf/ ĭ vĕnts/ ən dä/kyə mənts] **40**–**41**
lift [lĭft] **11**–E
light [līt] **23**–14, **97**–28
    brake light [brāk/ līt/] **158**–14
    daylight saving time [dā/līt/ sā/vĭng tīm/] **19**–25
    flashlight [flăsh/līt/] **146**–14
    hazard lights [hăz/ərd līts/] **159**–36
    headlight [hĕd/ līt/] **158**–7
    light blue [līt/ blōō/] **24**–11
    light bulb [līt/ bŭlb/] **56** ✦
    light fixture [līt/ fĭks/chər] **55**–18
    light source [līt/ sörs/] **194**–21
    light switch [līt/ swĭch/] **58**–27
    night light [nīt/ līt/] **37**–27
    porch light [pörch/ līt/] **53**–13
    streetlight [strēt/līt/] **148**–3
    string lights [strĭng/ līts/] **239**–18
    tail light [tāl/ līt/] **158**–13
    traffic light [trăf/ĭk līt/] **128**–8
    work light [würk/ līt/] **181**–44
lightning [līt/nĭng] **13**–17
lily [lĭl/ē] **211**–26
limbs [lĭmz] **106** ✦, **210**–3
limes [līmz] **68**–8
limit [lĭ/mət] **154**–4
limo / limousine [lĭ/mō] / [lĭ/mə zēn] **156**–11
line [līn] **73**–11
    assembly line [ə sĕm/blē līn] **175**–6
    clothesline [klōz/līn/] **101**–9
    curved line [kürvd/ līn/] **193**–23
    headline [hĕd/līn/] **133**–7

line cook [līn/ kōōk/] **93, 185** ✦
line segment [līn/ sĕg/mənt] **193**–20
line supervisor [līn/ sōō/pər vī zər] **175**–4
    parallel lines [pă/rə lĕl līnz/] **193**–25
    perpendicular lines
      [pür/pən dĭk/yə lər līnz/] **193**–24
    straight line [strāt/ līn/] **193**–22
linen [lĭn/ən] **98**–2
    linen closet [lĭn/ən kläz/ət] **57** ✦
liner [lī/nər]
    eyeliner [ī/lī/nər] **109**–36
Lines [līnz] **193**
lingerie [län/zhə rā/, –jə–] **91** ✦
links [lĭnkz] **197**–10
lion [lī/ən] **213**–33, **216**–2, **217**–36
lip [lĭp] **106**–5
    lipstick [lĭp/stĭk/] **109**–38
Liquid Measures [lĭk/wəd mĕzh/ərz] **75**
liquids [lĭk/wədz] **61**–21, **179**–8
list [lĭst] **67**–14
listen [lĭs/ən] **6**–C, **118**–C, **174**–K
listing [lĭst/ĭng] **48**–1
litter [lĭ/tər] **148**–2
litter [lĭ/tər] **219**–L
little [lĭt/l] **23**–1
Little League [lĭt/l lēg/] **229** ✦
live [lĭv] **140**–H
LIVE [līv] **52**
live music [līv/ myōō/zĭk] **84**–1
liver [lĭv/ər] **70**–7, **107**–40
livestock [līv/stäk/] **177**–15
living room [lĭv/ĭng rōōm/] **47**–12
LIVING ROOM [lĭv/ĭng rōōm/] **56**
lizard [lĭz/ərd] **213**–40
llama [lä/mə] **217**–25
load [lōd] **101**–C
loading dock [lō/dĭng däk/] **175**–15
loaf [lōf] **74**–10, **74**–22
    meatloaf [mēt/lōf/] **81**–31
loafers [lō/fərz] **95**–30
Lobby [läb/ē] **50**
lobster [läb/stər] **71**–10
local call [lō/kəl köl/] **15**–31
lock [läk] **51**–34, **159**–25
    locksmith [läk/smĭth/] **62**–11
lock [läk] **143**–E
locker [lä/kər] **5**–11, **50**–17
locket [läk/ət] **95**–35
Logging on and Sending Email
    [lög/ĭng än/ ən sĕnd/ĭng ē/māl, –ön–] **197**
lonely [lōn/lē] **42**–17
long [löng] **96**–18
    long distance call [löng/ dĭs/təns köl/] **15**–32
    long hair [löng/ hër/] **33**–3
    long-sleeved [löng/slēvd/] **96**–14
    long underwear [löng/ ŭn/dər wër/] **91**–3
look [lōōk]
    look at [lōōk/ ăt/, –ət] **49**–H, **157**–A
    look for [lōōk/ för/] / [lōōk/ fər] **133**–B, **173**–C
    look in [lōōk/ ĭn] **173**–B
    look up [lōōk/ ŭp] **8**–A
loop [lōōp] **99**–29

loose [lōōs] **97**–30
lose [lōōz] **229** ✦
loss [lös] **115**–2
lost child [löst/ chīld/] **144**–1
lotion [lō/shən] **37**–13, **108**–9
loud [lowd] **23**–11
loungewear [lownj/wër/] **91** ✦
love [lŭv] **40**–H, **42**–18
    love seat [lŭv sēt/] **56**–1
low [lō] **97**–31
    low-cost exam [lō/köst ĭg zăm/] **122**–1
    low-cut socks [lō/kŭt/ säks/] **91**–10
    low-fat milk [lō/făt/ mĭlk/] **81**–42
lower back [lō/ər băk/] **107**–29
lozenges [läz/ən jəz] **113**–30
LPN (licensed practical nurse) [ĕl/pē/ĕn/] /
    [lī/sənt prăk/tə kəl nürs/] **120**–11
luggage [lŭg/ĭj] **161**–18
    luggage cart [lŭg/ĭj kärt/] **184**–8
lug wrench [lŭg/ rĕnch/] **158**–22
lumber [lŭm/bər] **178**–17
Lunch [lŭnch] **80**
lung [lŭng] **107**–39
machine [mə shēn/]
    answering machine [ăn/sər ĭng mə shēn/] **14**–17
    ATM (Automated Teller Machine) [ā/tē/ĕm/] /
      [ö/tə mät ĭd tĕ/lər mə shēn/] **132**
    fax machine [făks/ mə shēn/] **183**–21
    machine operator [mə shēn/ äp/ə rā tər] **168**–37
    machine screw [mə shēn/ skrōō/] **180**–32
    sewing machine [sō/ĭng mə shēn/] **98**–13
    sewing machine operator
      [sō/ĭng mə shēn/ äp/ə rā/tər] **98**–14
    stamp machine [stămp/ mə shēn/] **135**–11
    vending machine [vĕnd/ĭng mə shēn/] **152**–9
Machine [mə shēn/] **98, 132**
magazine [măg/ə zēn/, măg/ə zēn/] **133**–5
    magazine holder [măg/ə zēn/ hōl/dər] **56**–23
magnet [măg/nət] **195**–36
magnolia [măg nōl/yə] **210**–8
mail
    airmail [ër/māl/] **134**–5
    Certified Mail® [sür/tə fīd māl/] **134**–4
    Express Mail® [ĭk sprĕs/ māl/] **134**–2
    junk mail [jŭnk/ māl/] **135** ✦
    mailboxes [māl/bäk/səz] **50**–11, **53**–1, **128**–13,
      135–12
    media mail [mē/dē ə māl/] **134**–3
    overnight / next day mail
      [ō/vər nīt/ / nĕkst/ dā/ māl/] **135** ✦
    Priority Mail® [prī/ör ə tē māl/] **134**–1
mail [māl/] **135**–D
mailer [mā/lər] **183**–40
mailing [mā/lĭng]
    mailing address [mā/lĭng ə drĕs/, ă/drĕs] **134**–22
    mailing label [mā/lĭng lā/bəl] **183**–41
main office [mān/ ö/fəs] **5**–12
MAINTAINING A CAR [mān/tā nĭng ə kär/] **157**
maintenance [mān/tn əns] **184**–23
maitre d' [mā/trə dē/] **185**–11
make [māk] **156** ✦

make [māk]
  make a deposit [māk/ ə dĭ päz/ət] **132**–B
  make a disaster kit [māk/ ə dĭz/ās tər kĭt/] **146**–B
  make a mortgage payment
    [māk/ ə mör/gəj pā/mənt] **49**–L
  make an offer [māk/ ən ö/fər] **49**–I
  make a wish [māk/ ə wĭsh/] **240**–B
  make copies [māk/ käp/ēz] **171**–D
  make dinner [māk/ dĭn/ər] **39**–Q
  make eye contact [māk/ ī/ kän/tākt] **174**–J
  make furniture [māk/ für/nĭ chər] **170**–G
  make lunch [māk/ lŭnch/] **38**–F
  make progress [māk/ prä/grəs] **10**–G
  make small talk [māk/ smöl/tök] **12**–B
  make the bed [māk/dhə bĕd/] **60**–F
maker [mā/kər]
  dressmaker [drĕs/mā/kər] **100**–1
  dressmaker's dummy [drĕs/mā/kərz dŭ/mē] **100**–2
  homemaker [hōm/mā/kər] **168**–33
Makeup [māk/ŭp] **109**
makeup remover [māk/ŭp rĭ mōōv/ər] **109**–42
making [mā/kĭng] **232**–13
MAKING ALTERATIONS [māk/ĭng öl/tə rā/shənz] **100**
MAKING CLOTHES [māk/ĭng klōz/] **98**–**99**
Making an Emergency Call
  [mā/kĭng ən ĭ mür/jən sē köl/] **15**
Making a Phone Call [mā/kĭng ə fōn/ köl/] **15**
male [māl] **4**–17
mall [möl] **126**–7
MALL [möl] **130**–**131**
mallet [māl/ət] **180**–2
mammals [măm/əlz] **209**–10
Mammals [măm/əlz] **213**
MAMMALS [măm/əlz] **216**–**217**
manager [măn/ĭ jər] **50**–8, **72**–8
  account manager [ə kownt/ măn/ĭ jər] **132**–9
  office manager [ö/fəs măn/ĭ jər] **182**–8
Manager [măn/ĭ jər] **92**
mane [mān] **217**–49
maneuver [mə nōō/vər] **117**–18
mangoes [măng/gōz] **68**–21
manicurist [măn/nə kyōō/rĭst] **168**–38
man / men [măn] / [mĕn] **30**–1, **30**–4
  doorman [dör/măn/] **184**–1
mantle [măn/təl] **56**–11
manual [măn/yōō əl] **117**–2
Manual Transmission [măn/yōō əl trănz mĭsh/ən] **159**
manufacture [măn/yə fāk/chər] **175**–B
map [măp] **7**–12, **155**–12
Map [măp] **13**
maple [mā/pəl] **210**–12
Maps [măps] **155**
MAPS [măps] **155**
March [märch] **21**–27
margarine [mär/jər ən] **72**–20
marigold [mär/ə gōld] **211**–13
MARINE LIFE, AMPHIBIANS, AND REPTILES
  [mə rēn/ lĭf/ ăm fĭb/ē ənz ən rĕp/tĭlz] **212**–**213**
Marines [mə rēnz/] **138**–17
mark [märk] **190**–12, **190**–13, **190**–15
  postmark [pōst/märk/] **134**–24

markers [mär/kərz] **7**–17, **7**–24, **154**–17
market [mär/kət] **222**–6
  supermarket [sōō/pər mar/kət] **127**–18
MARKET [mär/kət] **66**–**67**
marriage license [mär/ĭj lĭ/səns] **41**–8
married couple [mär/ĕd kŭ/pəl] **35**–20
Mars [märz] **205**–4
martial arts [mär/shəl ärts/] **228**–11
Martin Luther King Jr. Day
  [mär/tən lōō/thər-kĭng/ jōōn/yər dā/] **22**–10
mascara [mă skär/ə] **109**–39
mashed potatoes [măsht/ pə tā/tōz] **81**–23
mask [măsk] **239**–9
  catcher's mask [kăch/ərz măsk/] **231**–15
  diving mask [dī/vĭng măsk/] **225**–6
  face mask [fās/ măsk/] **93**–32
  oxygen mask [äk/sĭ jən măsk/] **161**–24
  particle mask [pär/tĭ kəl măsk/] **179**–14
  ski mask [skē/ măsk/] **90**–15
  surgical mask [sür/jĭ kəl măsk/] **93**–36
  ventilation mask [vĕnt/əl ā/shən măsk/] **92**–7
masking tape [măs/kĭng tāp/] **181**–53
mat [măt] **57**–3, **57**–28
  placemat [plās/măt] **55**–11
match [măch] **9**–T
matches [măch/əz] **146**–16, **226**–21
matching [mă/chĭng] **28**–3
Material [mə tïr/ē əl] **98**
materials [mə tïr/ē əlz] **98** ✦, **179**–7
Materials [mə tïr/ē əlz] **179**
maternity [mə tür/nə tē]
  maternity dress [mə tür/nə tē drĕs/] **88**–5
  maternity store [mə tür/nə tē stör/] **131**–19
math [măth] **189**–10
MATHEMATICS [măth/ə măt/ĭks] **192**–**193**
Math Operations [măth/ äp/ə rā/shənz] **192**
Math Problem [măth/ präb/ləmz] **192**
mattress [mă/trəs] **58**–20
May [mā] **21**–29
mayonnaise [mā/ə nāz/, mā/ə nāz/] **79**–23
mayor [mā/ər] **139**–26
meadow [mĕd/ō] **204**–20
measles [mē/zəlz] **111**–5
measure [mĕzh/ər] **100**–17, **181**–45
measure [mĕzh/ər] **17**–C
Measurement [mĕzh/ər mənt] **17**
MEASUREMENTS [mĕzh/ər mənts] **17**, **75**
Measures [mĕzh/ərz] **75**
Measuring Area and Volume
  [mē/zhər ĭng ĕr/ē ə ən văl/yəm, –yōōm] **193**
meat [mēt] **66**–2
  meatballs [mēt/bölz] **81**–27
  meatloaf [mēt/lōf/] **81**–31
Meat [mēt] **70**, **76**
MEAT AND POULTRY [mēt/ n pōl/trē] **70**
mechanic [mə kăn/ĭk] **166**–8
Mechanic [mə kăn/ĭk] **158**
media mail [mē/dē ə māl/] **134**–3
medical [mĕd/ĭ kəl] **121**–32
  medical chart [mĕd/ĭ kəl chärt/] **121**–24
  medical emergency bracelet
    [mĕd/ĭ kəl ĭ mür/jən sē brās/lət] **117**–3

medical records technician
  [mĕd/ĭ kəl rĕkərdz tĕk nĭsh/ən] **168**–39
medical waste disposal
  [mĕd/ĭ kəl wāst/ dĭ spō/zəl] **121**–31
MEDICAL CARE [mĕd/ĭ kəl kër/] **118**
MEDICAL CONDITIONS [mĕd/ĭ kəl kən dĭsh/ənz] **111**
MEDICAL EMERGENCIES [mĕd/ĭ kəl ĭ mür/jən sēz] **116**
Medical Procedures [mĕd/ĭ kəl prə se/jərz] **118**
Medical Specialists [mĕd/ĭ kəl spĕ/shə lĭsts] **120**
Medical Technician [mĕd/ĭ kəl tĕk nĭsh/ən] **93**
Medical Warnings [mĕd/ĭ kəl wör/nĭngz] **112**
medication [mĕd/ə kā/shən] **112**–3, **112** ✦,
  113–18, **121**–20
Medication [mĕd/ə kā/shən] **113**
medicine cabinet [mĕd/ə sən kăb/ə nət] **57**–20
medium [mē/dē əm] **96**–3
meet [mēt] **222**–6
meet [mēt] **49**–G, **49**–R
meeting [mē/tĭng]
  meeting place [mē/tĭng plās/] **146**–1
  meeting room [mē/tĭng rōōm/] **184**–25
MEETING AND GREETING [mē/tĭng ən grē/tĭng] **2**–**3**
melons [mĕl/ənz] **68**–19
  watermelons [wö/tər mĕl/ənz] **68**–18
membrane [mĕm/brān] **194**–6
Memorial Day [mə mör/ē əl dā/] **22**–12
memory card [mĕm/ə rē kärd/] **235**–20
men / man [mĕn] / [măn] **30**–1, **30**–4
  doorman [dör/măn/] **184**–1
  men's store [mĕnz/ stör/] **130** ✦
Men's Underwear [mĕnz/ un/dər wër/] **91**
menu [mĕn/yōō] **82**–7, **197**–8
  menu bar [mĕn/yōō bär/] **197**–1
MENU [mĕn/yōō] **80**–**81**
Mercury [mür/kyə rē] **205**–1
merge [mürj] **154**–10
mess [mĕs] **64**–8
message [mĕs/ĭj] **14**–18, **14**–19
messenger [mĕs/ən jər] **168**–40
meter [mē/tər] **62**–14, **129**–25, **152**–23
mice / mouse [mīs] / [mows] **63**–28, **196**–15, **215**–18
microphone [mī/krə fōn/] **234**–18
microprocessor [mī/krō prä/sĕ sər] **196**–4
Microscope [mī/krə skōp/] **194**
microwave [mī/krə wāv/] **77**–T
microwave oven [mī/krə wāv/ ŭv/ən] **54**–13
middle [mĭd/l] **25**–2
  middle-aged [mĭd/l ājd/] **32**–2
  middle initial [mĭd/l ĭ nĭsh/əl] **4**–3
  middle school [mĭd/l skōōl/] **188**–3
mid-length [mĭd/lĕnth] **96**–17
midnight [mĭd/nĭt/] **18**–21
Military [mī/lə tër ē] **138**
MILITARY SERVICE [mī/lə tër ē sür/vəs] **138**–**139**
milk [mĭlk] **66**–5, **81**–42
  milkshake [mĭlk shāk/] **79**–14
milk [mĭlk] **177**–C
mini [mĭn/ē] **96**–15
  mini-blinds [mĭn/ē blĭndz/] **58**–8
  minivan [mĭn/ē văn/] **156**–8
minister [mĭ/nə stər] **199**–7

minutes [mĭn/əts] **18**–2
mirror [mĭr/ər] **57**–16
    full-length mirror [fŏŏl/lĕnth mĭr/ər] **58**–6
    rearview mirror [rĭr/vyōō/ mĭr/ər] **159**–35
    sideview mirror [sīd/vyōō/ mĭr/ər] **158**–3
misbehave [mĭs/bĭ hāv/] **44**–B
miss the bus [mĭs dhə bŭs/] **152** ✦
missing [mĭs/ĭng] **97**–40
mittens [mĭt/nz] **90**–10
mix [mĭks] **77**–R
mixed berries [mĭkst/ bĕr/ēz] **81**–36
mixer [mĭk/sər] **54**–25
mixing bowl [mĭk/sĭng bōl/] **54**–28, **78**–31
mobile [mō/bēl] **59**–5
    mobile home [mō/bəl hōm/] **52**–7
model [mäd/l] **156** ✦, **168**–41
    model kit [mäd/l kĭt/] **232**–9
    model trains [mäd/l trānz/] **233**–27
modern [mä/dərn] **199**–2
moist towelettes [moyst/ tow/əl ĕts] **146**–12
moisturizer [moys/chə rī/zər] **108**–9
mole [mōl] **32**–16
molecule [mäl/ĭ kyōōl/] **195**–27
monarch [mä/nərk, mä/närk/] **199**–4
Monday [mŭn/dā, –dē] **20**–9
MONEY [mŭn/ē] **26**
monitor [män/ə tər] **196**–11
    arrival and departure monitors
        [ə rī/vəl ən dĭ pär/chər män/ə tərz] **161**–7
    baby monitor [bā/bē män/ə tər] **59**–7
    vital signs monitor [vī/təl sīnz män/ə tər] **121**–26
monkey [mŭng/kē] **217**–26
month [mŭnth] **20**–3
Months of the Year [mŭnths/ əv dhə yïr/] **21**
moon [mōōn]
    crescent moon [krĕs/ənt mōōn/] **205**–10
    full moon [fŏŏl/ mōōn/] **205**–12
    new moon [nōō/ mōōn/] **205**–9
    quarter moon [kwör/tər mōōn/] **205**–11
Moon [mōōn] **205**
moose [mōōs] **216**–1
mop [mäp] **61**–6
mop [mäp] **60**–D
morning [mör/nĭng] **18**–15
mosque [mäsk] **126**–5
mosquito [mə skē/tō] **214**–22
motel [mō tĕl/] **126**–12
moth [möth] **214**–21
mother [mŭdh/ər] **34**–3, **35**–22
    grandmother [grän/mŭdh/ər, gränd/–] **34**–1
    motherboard [mŭdh/ər börd/] **196**–5
    mother-in-law [mŭdh/ər ĭn lö/] **34**–10
    stepmother [stĕp/mŭdh/ər] **35**–26
MOTION [mō/shən] **153**
motor [mō/tər] **124**–4
motorcycle [mō/tər sī/kəl] **150**–4
mountain [mown/tn]
    mountain biking [mown/tn bī/kĭng] **226**–8
    mountain lion [mown/tn lī/ən] **216**–2
    mountain peak [mown/tn pēk/] **204**–14
    mountain range [mown/tn rānj/] **204**–15
    Mountain time [mown/tn tīm/] **19**–30

mouse / mice [mows] / [mīs] **63**–28, **196**–15, **215**–18
mouth [mowth] **104**–7
    mouthwash [mowth/wäsh/, –wösh/] **109**–25
Mouth [mowth] **106**
move in [mōōv/ ĭn/] **48**–F
move out [mōōv/ owt/] **48** ✦
movement [mōōv/mənt] **199**–16
mover [mōō/vər] **168**–42
movies [mōō/vēz] **222**–2
    movie theater [mōō/vē thē/ə tər] **126**–6
Movies [mōō/vēz] **237**
Moving In [mōō/vĭng ĭn] **49**
moving van [mōō/vĭng văn/] **156**–18
mow [mō] **176**–A
mower [mō/ər] **176**–6
mozzarella cheese [möts/ə rĕ lə chēz/] **71**–29
MP3 player [ĕm/pē/thrē/ plā/ər] **234**–2
mudslide [mŭd/slīd/] **144**–6
muffin [mŭf/ən] **79**–16, **80**–5
muffler [mŭf/lər] **158**–16
muffs [mŭfs] **179**–16
mug [mŭg] **55**–7
mugging [mŭg/ĭng] **142**–11
multiply [mŭl/tə plī] **192**–C
multi-use knife [mŭl/tē yōōs/ nīf/, mŭl/tī–] **226**–20
mumps [mŭmps] **111**–7
murder [mŭr/dər] **142**–12
muscle [mŭs/əl] **107**–32
mushrooms [mŭsh/rōōmz/] **69**–27
music [myōō/zĭk] **64**–3, **189**–15
    live music [lĭv/ myōō/zĭk] **84**–1
    music store [myōō/zĭk stör/] **130**–1
    world music [würld/ myōō/zĭk] **237**–32
Music [myōō/zĭk] **237**
MUSIC [myōō/zĭk] **238**
musician [myōō zĭsh/ən] **168**–43
mussels [mŭs/əlz] **71**–13, **212**–17
mustache [mŭs/tăsh] **33**–5
mustard [mŭs/tərd] **79**–22
mystery [mĭs/tə rē] **237**–20
nachos [nä/chōz] **79**–7
nail [nāl] **180**–34
    fingernail [fĭng/gər nāl/] **106**–18
    nail clipper [nāl klĭp/ər] **109**–31
    nail polish [nāl päl/ĭsh] **109**–33
    nail salon [nāl sə län/] **130**–3
    toenail [tō/nāl/] **106** ✦
name [nām] **4**–1, **4**–2, **4**–4
    name tag [nām/ tăg/] **92**–15
napkin [năp/kĭn] **55**–10, **83**–26
narrow [năr/ō] **97**–35
nasal [nā/zəl]
    nasal congestion [nā/zəl kən jĕs/chən] **110**–7
    nasal spray [nā/zəl sprā/] **113**–32
National Guard [nă/shə nəl gärd/] **138**–19
NATIONAL PARKS [nă/shə nəl pärks/] **220**–221
Native Americans [nā/tĭv ə mĕr/ə kənz] **198**–3
natural [năch/rəl, năch/ər əl]
    natural gas [năch/rəl gäs/] **218**–3
    natural materials [năch/rəl mə tïr/ē əlz] **98** ✦
NATURE CENTER [nā/chər sĕn/tər] **208**–209
nature program [nā/chər prō/grăm] **236**–7

Navigating a Webpage [nă/və gā/tĭng ə wĕb/pāj] **197**
Navy [nā/vē] **138**–15
navy blue [nā/vē blōō/] **28**–5
near [nïr] **25** ✦
neck [nĕk] **96**–8, **96**–10, **104**–3
    crewneck [krōō/nĕk] **96**–7
    necklaces [nĕk/lə sēz] **95**–10
    turtleneck [tür/tl nĕk] **96**–9
needle [nēd/l] **98**–17, **100**–10, **210**–10, **233**–23
needle plate [nēd/l plāt/] **98**–18
negative integers [nĕ/gə tĭv ĭn/tə jərz] **192**–1
negotiate [nĭ gō/shē āt/] **157**–D
neighborhood [nā/bər hŏŏd/] **128** ✦
nephew [nĕf/yōō] **34**–19
Neptune [nĕp/tōōn] **205**–8
nervous [nür/vəs] **42**–10
nest [nĕst] **209**–12
net [nĕt] **226**–17
    hairnet [hĕr/nĕt/] **93**–25
network [nĕt/würk] **173**–A
Neutral Colors [nōō/trəl kŭl/ərz] **24**
neutron [nōō/trän] **195**–32
new [nōō]
    new job [nōō/ jäb/] **172**–3
    new moon [nōō/ mōōn/] **205**–9
    New Year's Day [nōō/ yïrz/ dā/] **22**–9
Newfoundland time [nōō/fən lənd tīm/, –fənd–] **19**–34
news [nōōz]
    newspaper [nōōz/pā/pər] **133**–6
    news program [nōōz prō/grăm] **236**–1
    newsstand [nōōz/stănd/] **128**–12
newt [nōōt] **212**–26
New Words [nōō/ würdz/] **8**
next [nĕkst]
    next day mail [nĕkst/ dā/ māl/] **135** ✦
    next to [nĕkst/ tōō, –tə] **24**–9
    next week [nĕkst/ wēk/] **20**–20
nickel [nĭk/əl] **26**–2
niece [nēs] **34**–18
night [nīt] **18**–20
    nightclub [nīt/klŭb/] **223**–12
    nightgown [nīt/gown/] **91**–25
    night light [nīt/līt/] **37**–27
    nightshirt [nīt/shürt/] **91**–28
    nightstand [nīt/stănd/] **58**–23
    night table [nīt/ tā/bəl] **58**–23
nine [nīn] **16**
nineteen [nīn/tēn/] **16**
nineteenth [nīn/tēnth/] **16**
ninetieth [nīn/tē əth/] **16**
ninety [nīn/tē] **16**
    90º angle [nīn/tē də grē/ ăng/gəl] **193**–26
ninth [nīnth] **16**
nipple [nĭp/əl] **37**–2
no [nō]
    no left turn [nō/ lĕft/ türn] **154**–8
    no outlet [nō/ owt/lĕt, –lət] **154**–6
    no parking [nō/ pär/kĭng] **154**–11
noise [noyz] **64**–5
noisy [noy/zē] **23**–11
noon [nōōn] **18**–16
    afternoon [ăf/tər nōōn/] **18**–17

north [nörth] **155**–1
NORTH AMERICA AND CENTRAL AMERICA
[nörth/ ə mĕr/ə kə ən sĕn/trəl ə mĕr/ə kə] **200**–**201**
nose [nōz] **104**–6, **110**–17
revolving nosepiece [rə väl/vĭng nōz/pēs] **194**–17
not [nät]
can't breathe [kănt/ brēdh/] **116**–N
do not drink [dōō/ nät/ drĭnk] **112**–F
do not enter [dōō/ nät/ ĕn/tər] **154**–2
do not operate [dōō/ nät/ äp/ər ăt/] **112**–E
do not take [dōō nät/ tāk/] **112**–D
don't be late [dōnt/ bē/ lāt/] **174**–E
don't litter [dōnt/ lĭt/ər] **219**–L
don't smoke [dōnt/ smōk/] **114**–G
not working [nät/ wür/kĭng] **62**–1
note [nōt] **183**–39
footnote [fŏŏt/nōt/] **190**–10
notebook [nōt/bŏŏk/] **7**–27
notebook paper [nōt/bŏŏk pāp/ər] **7**–28
spiral notebook [spī/rəl nōt/bŏŏk/] **7**–29
novel [nä/vəl] **133**–16
November [nō vĕm/bər] **21**–35
nuclear energy [nōō/klē ər ĕn/ər jē] **218**–8
nucleus [nōō/klē əs] **194**–7, **195**–29
numb [nŭm] **119**–C
number [nŭm/bər]
access number [ăk/sĕs/ nŭm/bər] **14**–16
apartment number [ə pärt/mənt nŭm/bər] **4**–6
cell phone number [sĕl/ fōn/ nŭm/bər] **4**–12
checking account number
[chĕk/ĭng ə kownt/ nŭm/bər] **132**–14
driver's license number
[drī/vərz lī/səns nŭm/bər] **136**–11
even numbers [ĕv/ən nŭm/bərz] **192**–4
odd numbers [öd/ nŭm/bərz] **192**–3
phone number [fōn/ nŭm/bər] **4**–11, **15**–30
prescription number
[prĭ skrĭp/shən nŭm/bər] **112**–5
savings account number
[sā/vĭngz ə kownt/ nŭm/bər] **132**–11
SKU number [ĕs/kā/yōō/ nŭm/bər] **27**–5
Social Security number
[sō/shəl sĭ kyŏŏr/ə tē nŭm/bər] **4**–15
Numbers [nŭm/bərz] **16**
NUMBERS [nŭm/bərz] **16**
Numerals [nōō/mər əlz] **16**
numerator [nōō/mər ā/ tər] **192**–5
nurse [nürs] **118**–8, **168**–44
licensed practical nurse (LPN) [lī/sənst
prăk/tə kəl nürs/] / [ĕl/pē/ĕn/] **120**–11
nurse midwives [nürs/ mĭd/wīvz] **120** ✦
nurse practitioners [nürs/ prăk tĭ/shən ərz] **120** ✦
registered nurse (RN) [rĕj/ə stərd nürs/] / [är/ĕn/]
120–10
surgical nurse [sür/jĭ kəl nürs/] **120**–9
nurse [nürs] **36**–B
Nurse [nürs] **93**
nursery [nür/sə rē]
nursery rhymes [nür/sə rē rīmz/] **37**–22
nursery school [nür/sə rē skōōl/] **188**–1
nursing [nür/sĭng] **120**–12
nursing home [nür/sĭng hōm/] **52**–12

Nursing Staff [nür/sĭng stăf/] **120**
nutrition label [nōō trĭ/shən lā/bəl] **122**–8
nuts [nŭts] **73**–36, **180**–36
nylon [nī/län] **99**–12
oak [ōk] **210**–17, **210**–24
obey [ō bā/] **140**–C
objective [əb jĕk/tĭv] **194**–18
oboe [ō/bō] **238**–3
observatory [əb zür/və tör/ē] **205**–21
observe [əb zürv/] **195**–C
obstetrician [äb/stə trĭsh/ən] **120**–2
obtuse angle [äb/tōōs ăng/gəl] **193**–27
occupational therapist
[äk/yə pā/shən əl thĕr/ə pĭst]**168**–45
OCCUPATIONS [äk/yə pā/shənz] **166**–**169**
ocean [ō/shən] **204**–6, **225**–1
o'clock [ə kläk/] **18**–6
October [äk tō/bər] **21**–34
octopus [äk/tə pəs] **212**–9
odd numbers [öd/ nŭm/bərz] **192**–3
odometer [ō däm/ə tər] **159**–28
off [öf]
clear off [klĭr/ öf/] **10**–I
drop off [dräp/ öf/] **38**–G
gas shut-off valve [găs/ shŭt/öf vălv/] **146**–4
get off [gĕt/ öf/] **153**–J
take off [tāk/ öf/] **109**–Q
turn off [türn/ öf/] **11**–P, **160**–I, **174**–G, **219**–G
offer [ö/fər] **12**–D
office [ö/fəs] **164**–3
main office [mān/ ö/fəs] **5**–12
office building [ö/fəs bĭld/ĭng] **124**–2
office manager [ö/fəs măn/ĭ jər] **182**–8
office supply store [ö/fəs sə plī/ stör/] **127**–21
post office [pōst/ ö/fəs] **125**–11
post office box (PO box) [pōst/ ö/fəs bäks/] /
[pē/ō bäks/] **135**–9
run for office [rŭn/ fər ö/fəs] **139**–A
Office [ö/fəs] **51**
OFFICE [ö/fəs] **134**–**135**, **182**–**183**
Office Equipment [ö/fəs ĭ kwĭp/mənt] **183**
officer [ö/fə sər] **161**–17, **168**–48
Office Skills [ö/fəs skĭlz/] **171**
OFFICE SKILLS [ö/fəs skĭlz/] **171**
Office Supplies [ö/fəs sə plīz/] **183**
Office Visit [ö/fəs vĭ/zət] **119**
official [ə fĭsh/əl] **139**–32, **229**–6
oil [oyl] **73**–31, **218**–6
oil gauge [oyl/ gāj/] **159**–29
oil paint [oyl/ pānt/] **233**–19
oil spill [oyl/ spĭl/] **218**–17
ointment [oynt/mənt] **113**–24, **117**–10
OK [ō kā/] **154**–5
old [ōld] **31**–9, **31**–10
omelet [äm/lət, ä/mə lət] **76**–12
on [än, ön] **25**–11
get on [gĕt/ än, –ön] **153**–I
go on [gō/ än, –ön] **173**–K
on-the-job training [än dhə jäb/ trā/nĭng, –ön]
172–7
on the left [än dhə lĕft/, –ön] **25**–1
on the right [än dhə rīt/, –ön] **25**–3

on time [än tīm/, –ön] **19**–23, **16**–29
overdose on drugs [ō/vər dōs/ än drŭgz/] **116**–K
put on [pŏŏt/ än/, –ön/] **87**–B, **108**–D, **109**–P
try on [trī/ än/, –ön/] **95**–C
turn on [türn/ än/, –ön/] **11**–B
once a week [wŭns/ə wēk/] **20**–22
oncologist [än/kö lə jĭst/] **120**–5
one [wŭn] **16**
five after one [fīv/ ăf/ tər wŭn/] **18**–7
one billion [wŭn/ bĭl/yən] **16**
one eighth [wŭn/ ătth/, –āth/] **17**–5
one-fifteen [wŭn/fĭf/tēn/] **18**–9
one-forty [wŭn/för/tē] **18**–12
one-forty-five [wŭn/för/tē fīv/] **18**–13
one fourth [wŭn/ förth/] **17**–4
one half [wŭn/ hăf/] **17**–2
one hundred [wŭn/ hŭn/drəd] **16**
one hundred dollars
[wŭn/ hŭn/drəd däl/ərz] **26**–12
one hundred one [wŭn/ hŭn/drəd wŭn/] **16**
100 percent [wŭn/ hŭn/drəd pər sĕnt/] **17**–8
one hundredth [wŭn/ hŭn/drəth] **16**
one hundred thousand
[wŭn/ hŭn/drəd thow/zənd] **16**
one million [wŭn/ mĭl/yən] **16**
one o'clock [wŭn/ ə kläk/] **18**–6
one-oh-five [wŭn/ō fīv/] **18**–7
one-size-fits-all [wŭn/sīz fĭts/äl] **96**–6
one-ten [wŭn/tĕn/] **18**–8
one third [wŭn/ thürd/] **17**–3
one-thirty [wŭn/thür/tē] **18**–11
one thousand [wŭn/ thow/zənd] **16**
one thousandth [wŭn/ thow/zənth] **16**
one-twenty [wŭn/twĕn/tē] **18**–10
one way [wŭn/ wā/] **154**–3
one-way trip [wŭn/wā/ trĭp/] **152**–16
one whole [wŭn/hōl/] **17**–1
quarter after one [kwör/tər ăf/tər wŭn/] **18**–9
ten after one [tĕn/ ăf/tər wŭn/] **18**–8
twenty after one [twĕn/tē ăf/tər wŭn/] **18**–10
onions [ün/yənz] **69**–19, **69**–20
onion rings [ün/yən rĭngz/] **79**–4
online [än/līn, ön–]
online catalog [än/līn/ kă/tə lög, ön–] **133**–11
online course [än/līn/ körs/, ön–] **172**–8
only [ōn/lē] **154**–7
On the Airplane [än/ dhe ĕr/plān/] **161**
open [ō/pən] **6**–G, **143**–F
opener [ō/pən ər] **54**–8, **78**–1, **146**–8
Opening an Account [ō/pə nĭng ən ə kownt/] **132**
opera [äp/rə] **223**–11, **236**–5
operate [äp/ə rāt/] **112**–E, **170**–H
Operating Room [äp/ə rā/tĭng rōōm/] **121**
operating table [äp/ə rā/tĭng tā/bəl] **121**–40
Operations [äp/ə rā/shənz] **192**
operator [äp/ə rā/tər] **14**–21, **98**–14, **168**–37
ophthalmologist
[äf/thəl mäl/ə jĭst, –thə mäl/–, äp/–] **120**–7
opinion [ə pĭn/yən] **44**–3
opossum [ə päs/əm, päs/əm] **216**–4
opponent [ə pō/nənt] **139**–30
optician [äp tĭsh/ən] **130**–9

optometrist [äp täm/ə trĭst] 115–6
orange [ör/ənj, är/–] 24–4
oranges [ör/ən jəz, är/–] 68–5
orangutan [ə răng/ə tăng/, –tän/] 217–39
orchard [ör/chərd] 177–10
orchid [ör/kĭd] 211–19
order [ör/dər] 185–1
    order puller [ör/dər pŏŏl/ər] 175–10
order [ör/dər] 82–D
orderly [ör/dər lē] 120–16
Ordinal Numbers [ör/dn əl nŭm/bərz] 16
organ [ör/gən] 238–20
organic [ör gä/nĭk] 84–2
organisms [ör/gə nĭzmz] 194–1
organize [ör/gə nīz/] 171–L, 191–G
organizer [ör/gə nī/zər] 183–49
ornament [ör/nə mənt] 239–15
Orthodontics [ör/thə dän/tĭks] 119
orthodontist [ör/thə dän/tĭst] 119–5
orthopedists [ör/thə pē/dĭsts] 120 ✦
Other Instruments [ŭdh/ər ĭn/strə mənts] 238
otter [ät/ər] 213–35
ounce [owns] 75–1, 75–11
out [owt] 62–2
    blow out [blō/ owt/] 240–C
    check out [chĕk/ owt/] 133–C
    cross out [krös/ owt/] 9–R
    eat out [ĕt/ owt/] 82 ✦
    fill out [fĭl/ owt/] 173–J
    get out of [gĕt/ owt/ əv] 153–F
    let out [lĕt/ owt/] 100–C
    move out [mŏŏv/ owt/] 48 ✦
    outfit [owt/fĭt] 88 ✦
    out of focus [owt/ əv fō/kəs] 235–33
    out-of-state contact [owt/əv stāt/ kän/tăkt] 146–2
    run out of gas [rŭn/ owt/ əv găs/] 162–E
    take out [tāk/ owt/] 9–Y, 60–Q, 82 ✦
    work out [würk/ owt/] 230–N
OUTDOOR RECREATION [owt/dör rĕk/rē ā/shən] 226
outlet [owt/lĕt, –lət] 58–28, 154–6, 159–42
    outlet cover [owt/lĕt kŭv/ər] 181–46
OUTSIDE THE BODY [owt/sīd/ dhe bä/dē] 106–107
oven [ŭv/ən] 54–15, 54–20
    oven cleaner [ŭv/ən klē/nər] 61–3
over [ō/vər] 76–11, 153–B
    overalls [ō/vər ölz/] 88–6
    overcoat [ō/vər kōt/] 90–2
    overexposed [ō/vər ĭk spōzd/] 235–34
    overflowing [ō/vər flō/ĭng] 63–17
    overhead compartment
        [ō/vər hĕd/ kəm pärt/mənt] 161–13
    overhead projector [ō/vər hĕd/ prə jĕk/tər] 7–16
    overjoyed [ō/vər joyd/] 43 ✦
    overnight mail [ō/vər nīt/ māl/] 135 ✦
    over-the-counter medication
        [ō/vər dhə -kown/tər mĕd/ə kā/shən] 113–18
overdose [ō/vər dōs/, ō/vər dōs/] 116–K
Over-the-Counter Medication
    [ō/vər dhə kown/tər mĕd/ə kā/shən] 113
owl [owl] 214–5
owner [ō/nər] 166–11, 175–1
oxfords [äks/fərdz] 95–29

oxygen mask [äk/sĭ jən măsk/] 161–24
oysters [oy/stərz] 71–14
Pacific time [pə sĭf/ĭk tīm/] 19–29
pacifier [păs/ə fī/ər] 37–24
pack [păk] 74–9, 117–13, 235–26
    backpack [băk/păk/] 94–18, 226–15
pack [păk] 49–M, 162–A
package [păk/ĭj] 74–8, 74–20, 134–17
packaged food [păk/ĭjd fŏŏd/] 146–10
PACKAGING [păk/ə jĭng] 74
packer [păk/ər] 175–18
packing tape [păk/ĭng tāp/] 183–32
pad [păd]
    bumper pad [bŭm/pər păd/] 59–4
    changing pad [chānj/ĭng păd/] 59–2
    foam pad [fōm/ păd/] 226–13
    heating pad [hē/tĭng păd/] 113–13
    ink pad [ĭnk/ păd/] 183–46
    knee pads [nē/ pădz/] 179–19
    legal pad [lē/gəl păd/] 183–38
    shoulder pads [shōl/dər pădz/] 231–20
    steel-wool soap pads [stēl/wŏŏl/sōp/ pădz/] 61–5
    sterile pad [stĕr/əl păd/] 117–6
pail [pāl] 37–7, 61–7, 225–8
pain [pān] 42–11, 115–3
    pain reliever [pān rĭ lē/vər] 113–26
paint [pānt] 181–25, 232–10, 233–19
    paintbrush [pānt/brŭsh/] 181–22, 233–20
    paint pan [pānt/ păn/] 181–51
    paint roller [pānt/ rō/lər] 181–23
paint [pānt] 49–P, 178–A, 233–E
painter [pān/tər] 168–46
Painter [pān/tər] 92
painting [pān/tĭng] 56–9
pair of scissors [për/ əv sĭz/ərz] 100–16
paisley [pāz/lē] 96–26
pajamas [pə jä/məz, –jä/–] 91–24
pallet [pă/lət] 175–13
palm [päm] 106–15, 210–14
pan [păn] 54–24
    bed pan [bĕd/ păn/] 121–28
    cake pan [kāk/ păn/] 78–26
    dustpan [dŭst/ păn/] 61–17
    frying pan [frī/ĭng păn/] 78–5
    paint pan [pānt/ păn/] 181–51
    pancakes [păn/kāks/] 80–7
    pie pan [pī/ păn/] 78–28
    roasting pan [rō/stĭng păn/] 78–13
    saucepan [sös/păn/] 78–25
pancreas [păng/krē əs] 107–45
panda [păn/də] 217–41
pane [pān] 178–16
panel [păn/əl] 234–7
Panel [păn/əl] 159
panther [păn/thər] 217–40
panties [păn/tēz] 91–13
pants [pănts] 87–12
    security pants [sĭ kyŏŏr/ə tē pănts/] 93–22
    training pants [trā/nĭng pănts/] 37–11
    work pants [würk/ pănts/] 92–5
panty hose [păn/tē hōz/] 91–18
papayas [pə pī/əz] 68–20

paper [pā/pər]
    construction paper [kən strŭk/shən pā/pər] 232–12
    copies of important papers
        [kä/pēz əv ĭm pört/ənt pā/pərz] 146–20
    newspaper [nŏŏz/pā/pər] 133–6
    notebook paper [nōt/bŏŏk/ pā/pər] 7–28
    paper clip [pā/pər klĭp/] 183–31
    paper cutter [pā/pər kŭt/ər] 183–22
    paper dolls [pā/pər dälz/] 233–28
    paper shredder [pā/pər shrĕd/ər] 183–24
    paper towels [pā/pər tow/əlz] 54–3
    sandpaper [sănd/ pā/pər] 181–56
    toilet paper [toy/lət pā/pər] 57–17, 146–13
    wallpaper [wäl/ pā/pər] 59–8
parade [pə rād/] 239–1
paragraph [păr/ə grăf/] 190–3
parakeet [păr/ə kēt/] 215–15
parallel lines [păr/ə lĕl/ līnz/] 193–25
parallelogram [păr/ə lĕl/ə grăm/] 193–33
paramedic [păr/ə mĕ/dĭk] 116–2
parasites [păr/ə sīts/] 111–13
parcel post [păr/səl pōst/] 134–6
parentheses [pə rĕn/thə sēz/] 190–19
PARENTING [păr/ən tĭng, për/–] 36–37
Parents [păr/ənts, për/–] 34
parent-teacher conference
    [păr/ənt tē/chər kän/frəns, për/–] 22–5
paring knife [për/ĭng nīf/] 78–16
park [pärk] 223–10
    park ranger [pärk/ rāng/jər] 220–2
park [pärk] 129–E
parka [pär/kə] 90–9
PARK AND PLAYGROUND [pärk/ ən plā/grownd/] 224
parking [pär/kĭng] 128–6, 154–11, 154–12
    parking attendant [pär/kĭng ə tĕn/dənt] 184–3
    parking garage [pär/kĭng gə räzh/, –räj/] 124–1
    parking meter [pär/kĭng mē/tər] 129–25
    parking space [pär/kĭng spās/] 50–18, 128–5
PARKS [pärks] 220–221
parochial school [pə rō/kē əl skŏŏl/] 5 ✦
parsley [pär/slē] 69–28
part [pärt] 33–4
participate [pär tĭ/sə pāt/] 10–B
particle [pär/tĭ kəl]
    particle board [pär/tĭ kəl börd/] 181–20
    particle mask [pär/tĭ kəl măsk/] 179–14
Partner [pärt/nər] 8
parts [pärts] 175–5
Parts of a Bird [pärts/ əv ə bürd/] 214
PARTS OF A CAR [pärts/ əv ə kär/] 158–159
Parts of a Fish [pärts/ əv ə fĭsh/] 212
Parts of a Flower [pärts/ əv ə flow/ər] 211
Parts of an Essay [pärts/ əv ən ĕs/ā] 190
Parts of a Phone [pärts/ əv ə fōn/] 14
Parts of a Sewing Machine
    [pärts/ əv ə sō/ĭng mə shēn/] 98
Parts of a Tree [pärts/ əv ə trē/] 210
party [pär/tē] 64–2
pass [păs] 161–20
    passbook [păs/bŏŏk/] 132–10
    passport [păs/pört/] 41–10
pass [păs] 10–E, 137–H, 230–G

passenger [păs/ən jər] **150–2**, **161–15**

past [păst] **155**–E

pasta [päs/tə] **67–12**

pasta salad [päs/tə săl/əd] **80–20**

paste [pāst]

toothpaste [tooth/pāst/] **109–23**

pastrami [pə strä/mē] **71–23**

path [păth] **208–3**, **224–3**

Path [păth] **172**

patient [pā/shənt] **118–6**, **121–18**

patio [păt/ē ō] **53–16**

patio furniture [păt/ē ō für/nĭ chər] **53–19**

patron [pā/trən] **82–6**, **133–3**

pattern [păt/ərn] **99–22**

PATTERNS [păt/ərnz] **96**

pause [pöz] **235**–E

paw [pö] **216–20**

pay [pā]

paycheck [pā/chĕk/] **165–14**

payroll clerk [pā/rōl klürk/] **165–10**

pay stub [pā/ stŭb/] **165–11**

pay [pā]

pay a late fine [pā/ ə lāt/ fīn/] **133**–E

pay attention [pā/ ə tĕn/shən] **147**–D

pay back [pā/ băk/] **26**–D

pay cash [pā/ kăsh/] **27**–A

pay for [pā/ för/, –fər] **27**–G

pay phone [pā/ fōn/] **15–25**, **129–23**

pay taxes [pā/ tăks/əz] **140**–B

pay the application fee

[pā/ dhe ăp/lə kā/shən fē/] **137**–D

pay the check [pā/ dhe chĕk/] **82**–I

pay the rent [pā/ dhe rĕnt/] **48**–E

Pay [pā] **27**

PBX [pē/ bē/ ĕks/] **182–13**

peaceful assembly [pēs/fəl ə sĕm/blē] **140–1**

peaches [pē/chəz] **68–10**

peacock [pē/käk/] **214–14**

peak [pēk] **204–14**

pearls [pürlz] **95–39**

pears [pĕrz] **68–4**

peas [pēz] **69–21**

pedal [pĕd/əl] **159–45**, **159–46**

pedestrian [pə dĕs/trē ən] **128–14**

pedestrian crossing [pə dĕs/trē ən krö/sĭng] **154–13**

pediatrician [pē/dē ə trĭsh/ən] **120–4**

peel [pēl] **77**–K

peeler [pē/lər] **78–15**

peephole [pēp/hōl/] **51–32**

pelvis [pĕl/vəs] **107–50**

pen [pĕn] **7–22**

pencil [pĕn/səl] **7–20**, **109–34**

pencil eraser [pĕn/səl ĭ rā/sər] **7–21**

pencil sharpener [pĕn/səl shär/pə nər] **7–23**, **183–26**

penguin [pĕng/wĭn] **214–11**

peninsula [pə nĭn/sə lə] **204–7**

penny [pĕn/ē] **26–1**

PEOPLE [pē/pəl] **32**

pepper [pĕp/ər] **55–13**, **69–7**, **69–29**

percent [pər sĕnt/]

50 percent [fĭf/tē pər sĕnt/] **17–10**

100 percent [wŭn/ hŭn/drəd pər sĕnt/] **17–8**

75 percent [sĕv/ən tē fīv/ pər sĕnt/] **17–9**

10 percent [tĕn/ pər sĕnt/] **17–12**

25 percent [twĕn/tē fīv/ pər sĕnt/] **17–11**

Percents [pər sĕnts/] **17**

Percussion [pər kŭsh/ən] **238**

perfume [pür/fyoom/, pər fyoom/] **108–6**

perimeter [pə rĭ/mə tər] **193–43**

period [pïr/ē əd] **190–11**

Period [pïr/ē əd] **198**

periodicals [pïr/ē äd/ĭ kəlz] **133–4**

periodic table [pïr/ē äd/ĭk tā/bəl] **195–26**

perm [pürm] **33**–B

peroxide [pə räk/ sĭd] **117–9**

perpendicular lines [pür/pən dĭk/yə lər līnz/] **193–24**

person [pür/sən]

appliance repair person

[ə plī/əns rĭ për/ pür/sən] **166–4**

assemblyperson [ə sĕm/blē pür/sən] **139–24**

businessperson [bĭz/nəs pür/sən] **166–12**

bus person [bŭs/ pür/sən] **185–13**

congressperson [kän/grəs pür/sən] **138–4**

councilperson [kown/səl pür/sən] **139–28**

counterperson [kown/tər pür/sən] **79–17**

delivery person [də lĭv/ə rē pür/sən] **167–21**

electronics repair person

[ĭ lĕk trän/ĭks rĭ për/ pür/sən] **167–24**

repair person [rĭ për/ pür/sən] **62–10**

personal CD player [pür/sə nəl sē/dē/ plā/ər] **234–5**

PERSONAL HYGIENE [pür/sə nəl hī/jēn] **108–109**

PERSONAL INFORMATION

[pür/sə nəl ĭn/fər mā/shən] **4**

pesticide poisoning [pĕs/tə sīd/ poy/zə nĭng] **218–16**

pests [pĕsts] **62** ✦

pet [pĕt]

pet food [pĕt food/] **72–5**

pet store [pĕt stör/] **130–6**

petals [pĕt/lz] **211–8**

petition [pə tĭ/shən] **148–5**

petroleum [pə trō/lē əm] **218–6**

Pets [pĕts] **215**

pharmacist [fär/mə sĭst] **112–1**

pharmacy [fär/mə sē] **128–4**

PHARMACY [fär/mə sē] **112–113**

Phase of the Moon [fāz/ əf dhə moon/] **205**

Phillips screwdriver [fĭl/ĭps skroo/drī/vər] **180–31**

phlebotomist [flĭ bä/tə mĭst] **121–29**

phone [fōn]

automated phone system

[ö/tə mät ĭd fōn/ sĭs/təm] **14–23**

cell phone holder [sĕl/ fōn/ hōl/dər] **94–15**

cell phone kiosk [sĕl/ fōn/ kē/ösk] **131–22**

cell phone number [sĕl/ fōn/ nŭm/bər] **4–12**

cellular phone [sĕl/yə lər fōn/] **14–8**

cordless phone [körd/ləs fōn/] **15–24**

headphones [hĕd/ fōnz/] **6–8**, **234–4**

Internet phone call [ĭn/tər nĕt/ fōn/ käl/] **14–20**

microphone [mī/krə fōn/] **234–18**

pay phone [pā/ fōn/] **15–25**, **129–23**

phone bill [fōn/ bĭl/] **15–28**

phone jack [fōn/ jăk/] **14–3**

phone line [fōn/ lĭn/] **14–4**

phone number [fōn/ nŭm/bər] **4–11**, **15–30**

smart phone [smärt/ fōn/] **15–27**

Phone [fōn] **14**

Phone Bill [fōn/ bĭl/] **15**

Phone Call [fōn/ köl/] **15**

photo [fō/tō] **58–3**, **136–4**

digital photo album [dĭ/jə təl fō/tō ăl/bəm] **235–32**

funny photo [fŭn/ē fō/tō] **206–2**

photo album [fō/tō ăl/bəm] **235–31**

photocopier [fō/tə käp/ē ər] **183–23**

serious photo [sïr/ē əs fō/tō] **206–3**

photographer [fə täg/rə fər] **206–1**

PHOTOGRAPHY [fə täg/rə fē] **234–235**

photosynthesis [fō/tō sĭn/thə səs] **194–10**

physical [fĭz/ĭ kəl]

physical education [fĭz/ĭ kəl ĕ jə kā/shən] **189–17**

physical therapist [fĭz/ĭ kəl thĕr/ə pĭst] **115–12**

physical therapy [fĭz/ĭ kəl thĕr/ə pē] **115–11**

physically challenged [fĭz/ĭ klē chăl/ənjd] **32–10**

physician assistant [fĭz/ĭ shən ə sĭs/tənt] **168–47**

physicist [fĭz/ĭ sĭst] **195–33**

Physics [fĭz/ĭks] **195**

pi (π) [pī] **193–46**

piano [pē ăn/ō] **238–14**

pick [pĭk] **108–15**

pickax [pĭk/ăks/] **178–21**

picker [pĭ/kər] **178–5**

pickle [pĭk/l] **80–11**

pick up [pĭk/ ŭp/] **6**–I, **11**–E, **38**–M, **112** ✦

pickup truck [pĭk/ŭp trŭk/] **156–12**

picnic [pĭk/nĭk] **224**–D

picnic table [pĭk/nĭk tā/bəl] **224–8**

picture [pĭk/chər]

picture book [pĭk/chər book/] **133–12**

picture dictionary [pĭk/chər dĭk/shə nër ē] **7–31**

picture frame [pĭk/chər frām/] **58–4**

pie [pī] **81–35**

pie pan [pī/ păn/] **78–28**

pier [pïr] **225–18**

pierced [pïrst]

pierced ear [pïrst/ ïr/] **32–17**

pierced earrings [pïrst/ ïr/ĭngz] **95–36**

pig [pĭg] **215–2**, **215–14**

pigeon [pĭj/ən] **214–15**

pile [pīl] **53–25**

pill [pĭl] **113–21**

pillow [pĭl/ō] **56–2**, **58–11**

pillowcase [pĭl/ō kās/] **58–14**

pilot [pī/lət] **161–11**

pin [pĭn] **95–38**

bobby pins [băb/ē pĭnz/] **108–21**

clothespin [klōz/ pĭn/] **101–10**

pin cushion [pĭn/ koosh/ən] **100–13**

pushpin [poosh/pĭn/] **183–35**

rolling pin [rō/lĭng pĭn/] **78–30**

safety pin [sāf/tē pĭn/] **37–9**, **100–14**

straight pin [strāt pĭn/] **100–12**

pine [pīn] **210–9**

pinecone [pīn/kōn/] **210–11**

pineapples [pī/năp/əlz] **68–23**

pink [pĭnk] **24–7**

pint [pīnt] **75–3**

pipe [pīp] **158–15**, **181–17**

pipe wrench [pīp rĕnch/] **181–47**

pitch [pĭch] **230**–A
pizza [pēt′sə] **79**–10
place [plās] **146**–1
  fireplace [fīr′plās′] **56**–13
  placemat [plās′ măt′] **55**–11
  place of birth [plās′ əv bürth′] **4**–14
  place setting [plās′ sĕt′ĭng] **83**–17
PLACES TO GO [plā′səz tə gō′] **222**–**223**
PLACES TO LIVE [plā′səz tə lĭv′] **52**
plaid [plăd] **96**–22
plain [plān] **97**–33
plains [plānz] **204**–19
plan [plăn] **186**–4
plan [plăn] **146**–A
plane [plān] **144**–3, **150**–8, **181**–57
Planets [plăn′əts] **205**
Planning a Career [plă′nĭng ə kə rēr′] **172**
plant [plănt] **176**–E, **177**–A, **219**–N
plants [plănts] **208**–5
  houseplant [hows′plănt′] **56**–4, **211**–27
Plants [plănts] **210**
PLANTS [plănts] **210**
plaque [plăk] **119**–12
plastic [plăs′tĭk]
  plastic storage bags [plăs′tĭk stör′ĭj băgz′] **72**–25
  plastic storage container
    [plăs′tĭk stör′ĭj kən tā′nər] **78**–4
  plastic utensils [plăs′tĭk yōō tĕn′ səlz] **79**–19
  plastic wrap [plăs′tĭk răp′] **72**–24
plate [plāt] **55**–1
  bread-and-butter plate [brĕd′n bŭt′ər plāt′] **83**–19
  dinner plate [dĭn′ər plāt′] **83**–18
  license plate [lī′səns plāt′] **136**–12, **158**–12
  salad plate [săl′əd plāt′] **83**–20
  vanity plate [vă′nə tē plāt′] **136** ✦
platform [plăt′förm′] **152**–7
platter [plăt′ər] **55**–20
platypus [plăt′ĭ pəs, –pŏŏs′] **217**–46
play [plā] **223**–8
  play area [plā′ ĕr′ē ə] **130**–11
  playground [plā′grownd′] **50**–3
play [plā] **235**–B
  play an instrument [plā′ ən ĭn′strə mənt] **238**–A
  play cards [plā′ kärdz′] **233**–H
  play games [plā′ gāmz′] **232**–B
  play with [plā′ wĭth′] **36**–M
player [plā′ər] **229**–5
  CD player [sē′dē plā′ər] **159**–38
  DVD player [dē′vē′dē′ plā′ər] **56**–7, **234**–10
  MP3 player [ĕm′pē′thrē′ plā′ər] **234**–2
  personal CD player [pür′sə nəl sē′dē plā′ər] **234**–5
  portable cassette player
    [pör′tə bəl kə sĕt′ plā′ər] **234**–6
  portable DVD player
    [pör′tə bəl dē′vē′dē′ plā′ər] **234**–11
  video player [vĭd′ē ō plā′ər] **197**–11
PLAYGROUND [plā′grownd′] **224**
pliers [plī′ərz] **180**–7
plugs [plŭgz] **179**–15, **234**–16
plumber [plŭm′ər] **63**–20
plums [plŭmz] **68**–13
plunger [plŭn′jər] **181**–50

plywood [plī′wŏŏd′] **178**–18
p.m. [pē′ĕm′] **18**–5
pneumatic drill [nŏŏ măt′ĭk drĭl′] **178**–9
poached eggs [pōcht′ ĕgz′] **76**–9
PO box (post office box) [pē′ō bäks′] /
  [pōst′ ö′fəs bäks′] **135**–9
pocket [päk′ət] **100**–7
podium [pō′dē əm] **206**–5
poinsettia [poyn sĕt′ē ə, –sĕt′ə] **211**–24
point [poynt] **17**–7,
  endpoint [ĕnd′poynt′] **193**–21
pointer [poyn′tər] **197**–12
poison [poy′zən] **116**–J
  poison ivy [poy′zən ī′vē] **210**–25
  poison oak [poy′zən ōk′] **210**–24
  poison sumac [poy′zən sōō′măk, –shōō′–] **210**–23
poisoning [poy′zən ĭng] **218**–16
poisonous fumes [poy′zən əs fyōōmz′] **179**–3
poles [pōlz] **226**–18, **231**–25
police [pə lēs′]
  police officer [pə lēs′ ö′fə sər] **141**–1, **168**–48
  police station [pə lēs′ stā′shən] **124**–6
polish [päl′ĭsh] **61**–8, **109**–33
polish [päl′ĭsh] **60**–E, **109**–O
political [pə lĭ′tĭ kəl]
  political campaign [pə lĭ′tĭ kəl kăm pān′] **139**–29
  political movement [pə lĭ′tĭ kəl mōōv′mənt] **199**–16
  political party [pə lĭ′tĭ kəl pär′tē] **139** ✦
polka-dotted [pō′kə dät′əd] **96**–21
pollution [pə lōō′shən] **218**–11, **218**–14
Pollution [pə lōō′shən] **218**
polo [pō′lō] **229**–15
  polo shirt [pō′lō shïrt′] **92**–14
poncho [păn′chō] **90**–19
pond [pänd] **204**–21
pool [pōōl] **51**–22, **184**–22, **228**–2
  pool service [pōōl′ sür′vəs] **184**–21
  pool table [pōōl′ tā′bəl] **50**–14
pop [päp] **73**–34, **237**–25
  pop-up ad [päp′ŭp′ ăd′] **197**–9
porch light [pörch′ līt′] **53**–13
porcupine [pör′kyə pīn′] **216**–10
Pork [pörk] **70**
pork chops [pörk′ chäps′] **70**–10
porpoise [pör′pəs] **213**–30
port [pört] **196**–7
  airport [ĕr′pört′] **151**–10
portable [pör′tə bəl]
  portable cassette player
    [pör′tə bəl kə sĕt′ plā′ər] **234**–6
  portable DVD player
    [pör′tə bəl dē′vē′dē′ plā′ər] **234**–11
  portable TV [pör′tə bəl tē′ vē′] **234**–8
positive integers [pö′zə tĭv ĭn′tə jərz] **192**–2
post [pōst] **134**–6
  post card [pōst′kärd′] **134**–16
  postmark [pōst′märk′] **134**–24
  post office [pōst′ ö′fəs] **125**–11
  post office box (PO box) [pōst′ ö′fəs bäks′] /
    [pē′ō bäks′] **135**–9
postage [pō′stĭj] **135** ✦

postal [pō′stəl] **135**–10
  postal clerk [pō′stəl klürk′] **135**–7
  postal forms [pō′stəl förmz′] **134**–19
  postal scale [pō′stəl skāl′] **183**–27
  postal worker [pō′stəl wür′kər] **169**–49
POST OFFICE [pōst′ ö′fəs] **134**–**135**
pot [pät] **54**–16, **78**–6
  pot holders [pät hōl′dərz] **78**–29
  teapot [tē′pät′] **55**–16
potatoes [pə tā′tōz] **69**–17
  baked potato [bākt′ pə tā′tō] **81**–25
  mashed potatoes [măsht′ pə tā′tōz] **81**–23
  potato chips [pə tā′tō chĭps′] **73**–35
  potato salad [pə tā′tō săl′əd] **80**–19
  sweet potatoes [swēt′ pə tā′tōz] **69**–18
potty seat [pät′ē sēt′] **37**–12
pouch [powch] **217**–50
Poultry [pōl′trē] **70, 76**
POULTRY [pōl′trē] **70**
pound [pownd] **75**–12
  pound key [pownd′ kē′] **14**–7
pour [pör] **82**–C
powder [pow′dər] **37**–14, **108**–4, **109**–41
power [pow′ər] **218**–2, **218**–5
  power cord [pow′ər körd′] **196**–2
  power outlet [pow′ər owt′lĕt′] **159**–42
  power sander [pow′ər săn′dər] **180**–11
pox [pöks] **111**–6
practical [präk′tə kəl] **120**–11
prairie dog [prĕr′ē dög′] **215**–22
praise [prāz] **36**–J
pregnant [prĕg′nənt] **32**–15
preheat [prē′hēt′] **77**–A
preparation [prĕ′pə rā′shən] **185**–4
PREPARATION [prĕ′pə rā′shən] **76**–**77**
prepare [prĭ′pĕr′] **174**–A
PREPOSITIONS [prĕp′ə zĭsh′ənz] **25**
PREPOSITIONS OF MOTION
  [prĕp′ə zĭsh′ənz əv mō′shən] **153**
preschool [prē′skōōl′] **188**–1
prescribe medication [prĭ skrīb′mĕd′ə kā′shən] **112** ✦
prescription [prĭ skrĭp′shən] **112**–2
  pick up a prescription
    [pĭk′ ŭp′ə prĭ skrĭp′shən] **112** ✦
  prescription label [prĭ skrĭp′shən lā′bəl] **112**–4
  prescription medication
    [prĭ skrĭp′shən mĕd′ə kā′shən] **112**–3
  prescription number [prĭ skrĭp′shən nŭm′bər]
    112–5
present [prĕz′ənt] **94** ✦, **240**–3
presentation [prĕ′zən tā′shən] **182**–6
president [prĕz′ə dənt] **138**–8, **199**–5
  first president [fürst′ prĕz′ə dənt] **198**–11
  Presidents' Day [prĕz′ə dənts dā′] **22**–11
  vice president [vīs′ prĕz′ə dənt] **138**–9
press [prĕs] **78**–11, **140**–4
press [prĕs] **15**–B, **15**–D
presser foot [prĕs′ər fŏŏt′] **98**–19
pressure [prĕsh′ər] **111**–14, **118**–9
pretend [prĭ tĕnd′] **233**–G
Prewriting [prē′rī′tĭng] **191**

Index

price [prīs] **27**–2, **27**–3, **27**–7
  price tag [prīs tăg/] **27**–1
prime minister [prīm/ mĭn/ə stər] **199**–7
principal [prĭn/sə pəl] **5**–4
print [prĭnt] **96**–23
  fingerprint [fĭng/gər prĭnt/] **136**–5
print [prĭnt] **4**–C, **171**–I
printer [prĭn/tər] **169**–50, **196**–17
  inkjet printer [ĭnk/jĕt prĭn/tər] **183**–18
  laser printer [lā/zər prĭn/tər] **183**–19
Priority Mail® [prī ör/ə tē māl/, –är/–] **134**–1
prism [prĭz/əm] **195**–35
prisoner [prĭz/nər] **141**–15
private school [prī/vət skool/] **5** ✦
Problem [präb/ləm] **192**
problems [präb/ləmz] **115**–1, **192**–11
Problems [präb/ləmz] **115**, **119**
PROBLEMS [präb/ləmz] **62**–63
Procedures [prə sē/jərz] **117**, **118**
PROCEDURES [prə sē/jərz] **146**–147
Process [prä/sĕs] **191**
processor [prä/sĕ sər] **54**–26
Processor [prä/sĕ sər] **92**
produce section [prō/doos sĕk/shən] **72**–2
product [präd/ŭkt] **192**–9
Products [präd/ŭkts] **72**, **73**
program [prō/grăm]
  children's program [chĭl/drənz prō/grăm] **236**–9
  nature program [nā/chər prō/grăm] **236**–7
  news program [nooz/ prō/grăm] **236**–1
  shopping program [shäp/ĭng prō/grăm] **236**–10
  sports program [spörtz/ prō/grăm] **236**–11
program [prō/grăm] **170**–I
Programs [prō/grămz] **236**
projector [prə jĕk/tər] **6**–6, **7**–16, **235**–29
promotion [prə mō/shən] **172**–4
proof of insurance [proof/ əv ĭn shoor/əns] **136**–8
proofread [proof/rĕd/] **191**–I
prosecuting attorney
  [präs/ĭ kyoo/tĭng ə tür/nē] **141**–10
protect [prə tĕkt/] **143**–D
protector [prə tĕk/tər] **196**–1
proton [prō/tön] **195**–31
proud [prowd] **43**–21
prunes [proonz] **68**–26
pruning shears [proo/nĭng shïrz/] **176**–11
psychiatrist [sī kī/ə trĭst, sə–] **120**–8
PUBLIC SAFETY [pŭb/lĭk sāf/tē] **143**
public school [pŭb/lĭk skool/] **5** ✦
PUBLIC TRANSPORTATION
  [pŭb/lĭk trăns/pər tā/shən] **152**
pull [pool] **119**–F, **224**–A
puller [pool/ər] **175**–10
pullover sweater [pool/ō/vər swĕt/ər] **88**–3
pulse [pŭls] **122**–A
pumps [pŭmps] **95**–26
Punctuation [pŭngk/choo ā/shən] **190**
puppy [pŭp/ē] **215**–12
purchase [pür/chəs] **94**–A
purifier [pyoo/rə fī/ ər] **113**–13
purple [pür/pəl] **24**–6
purses [pür/səz] **94**–2, **94**–14

push [poosh] **224**–B
pushpin [poosh/pĭn/] **183**–35
put [poot] **9**–X
put away
  [poot/ə wā/] **9**–Z, **60**–G
  put down [poot/ down/] **6**–J
  put in coolant [poot/ ĭn koo/lənt] **157**–I
  put on [poot/ än/, –ön/] **87**–B, **108**–D, **109**–P, **135**–C
  put on hold [poot/ än hōld/, –ön] **171**–N
  put the utilities in your name
    [poot/ dhe yoo tĭl/ə tēz ĭn yər nām/] **49**–O
puzzle [pŭz/əl] **59**–17
pyramid [pïr/ə mĭd] **193**–39
quad [kwäd] **5**–1
quart [kwört] **75**–4
quarter [kwör/tər] **26**–4
  quarter after one [kwör/tər ăf/tər wŭn/] **18**–9
  1/4 cup [kwör/tər kŭp/] **75**–8
  quarter moon [kwör/tər moon/] **205**–11
  quarter to two [kwör/tər tə too/] **18**–13
  3/4 sleeved [thrē/ kwör/tər slēvd/] **96**–13
question mark [kwĕs/chən märk/] **190**–12
Quick and Easy Cake [kwĭk/ ən ē/zē kāk/] **77**
quiet [kwī/ət] **23**–12
quill [kwĭl] **216**–23
quilt [kwĭlt] **58**–16
  quilt block [kwĭlt/ blăk/] **232**–15
quilt [kwĭlt] **232**–C
quotation [kwōt tā/shən] **190**–9
  quotation marks [kwō tā/shən märks/] **190**–15
quotient [kwō /shənt] **192**–10
rabbit [răb/ət] **215**–13
raccoon [ră koon/] **216**–13
race [rās] **230**–S
racing [rā/sĭng] **228**–19
rack [răk] **98**–16
  dish rack [dĭsh/ răk/] **54**–5
  roasting rack [rō/stĭng răk/] **78**–14
  towel rack [tow/əl răk/] **57**–13
racket [răk/ət] **231**–2
racquetball [răk/ət böl/] **228**–12
radiation [rā/dē ā/shən] **218**–15
radiator [rā/dē ā/tər] **158**–19
radio [rā/dē ō] **102**–6, **159**–37, **179**–22
radioactive materials
  [rā/dē ō ăk/tĭv mə tïr/ē əlz] **179**–7
radiologist [rā/dē äl/ə jĭst] **120**–6
radishes [răd/ĭ shəz] **69**–4
radius [rā/dē əs] **193**–35
rafting [răf/tĭng] **226**–2
rags [răgz] **61**–9
rail [rāl] **59**–10
railroad crossing [rāl/röd krö/sĭng] **154**–14
rain [rān] **218**–13
  rain boots [rān/ boots/] **90**–20
  raincoat [rān/kōt/] **90**–18
  rain forest [rān/ för/əst, fär/–] **204**–1
raining [rā/nĭng] **13**–11
raise [rāz] **6**–A
raisins [rā/zənz] **68**–25
rake [rāk] **176**–8
rake [rāk] **176**–C

ranch [rănch] **52**–10
rancher [răn/chər] **177**–22
Ranch Hand [rănch hănd/] **92**
RANCHING [răn/chĭng] **177**
R&B [är/n bē/] **237**–28
range [rānj] **204**–15
ranger [rān/jər] **220**–2
rash [răsh] **110**–10
raspberries [răz/bĕr/ēz] **68**–15
rats [răts] **63**–27, **215**–17
rattle [răt/l] **37**–26
  rattlesnake [răt/l snāk/] **213**–38
raw [rö] **70**–24
ray [rā] **212**–11
razor [rā/zər] **109**–27
  razorblade [rā/zər blād/] **109**–28
reaction [rē/ăk shən] **116**–E
read [rēd]
  proofread [proof/rĕd/] **191**–I
  read the card [rēd/ dhe kärd/] **135**–G
  read the definition [rēd/ dhe dĕ/fə nĭ/shən] **8**–B
  read the paper [rēd/ dhe pā/pər] **39**–V
  read to [rēd/ too] **36**–N
Reading a Phone Bill [rē/dĭng ə fōn/ bĭl/] **15**
reality show [rē ă lə tē shō/] **236**–6
rearview mirror [rïr/vyoo/ mïr/ər] **159**–35
receipt [rĭ sēt/] **27**–6
receive [rĭ sēv/] **135**–F
receiver [rĭ sē/vər] **14**–1
reception area [rĭ sĕp/shən ër/ē ə] **182**–15
receptionist [rĭ sĕp/shə nĭst] **118**–2, **164**–5,
  169–51, **182**–14
reclined seat [rĭ klīnd/ sēt/] **161**–27
record [rĭ körd/] **195**–D, **235**–A
records [rĕk/ərdz] **168**–39
RECREATION [rĕk/rē ā/shən] **226**
recreational vehicle (RV)
  [rĕk/rē ā/shən əl vē/ə kəl] / [är/vē/] **156**–10
Recreation Room [rĕk/rē ā/shən room/] **50**
recruiter [rə kroo/tər] **172**–14
rectangle [rĕk/tăng/gəl] **193**–29
recycle [rē sī/kəl] **60**–B, **219**–C
recycling bin [rē sī/klĭng bĭn/] **61**–2
red [rĕd] **24**–1
  red hair [rĕd/ hër/] **33**–15
  redwood [rĕd/wood/] **210**–18
redecorate [rē dĕk/ə rāt/] **48** ✦
reduce [rĭ doos/] **219**–A
referee [rĕf/ə rē/] **229**–6
reference librarian [rĕf/rəns lī brër/ē ən] **133**–9
refrigerator [rĭ frĭj/ə rā/tər] **54**–9
refund [rē/fŭnd] **97** ✦
reggae [rĕ gā/] **237**–31
register [rĕj/ə stər] **73**–15
register [rĕj/ə stər] **140**–D, **157**–F
registered nurse (RN)
  [rĕj/ə stərd nürs/] / [är/ĕn/] **120**–10
registration [rĕj/ə strā/shən]
  registration sticker
    [rĕj/ə strā/shən stĭk/ər] **136**–13
  registration tag [rĕj/ə strā/shən tăg/] **136**–13
regular price [rĕg/yə lər prīs/] **27**–2

regulations [rĕ gyə lā/shənz] **164**–6
relatives [rĕ lə tĭvz] **44**–6
relax [rĭ lăks/] **39**–U
relieved [rĭ lēvd/] **42**–15
reliever [rĭ lēv/ər] **113**–26
religious holiday [rĭ lĭj/əs hăl/ə dā/] **22**–7
remain [rē/mān] **147**–E
remarried [rē măr/ēd] **35**–24
remote [rĭ mōt/] **234**–9
remove [rĭ mōōv/] **109**–Q, **132**–G
remover [rĭ mōō/vər] **109**–42
renew a license [rĭ nōō/ ə lī/səns, –nyōō/–] **136** ✦
rental agreement [rĕn/təl ə grē/mənt] **51**–28
Rental Office [rĕn/təl ö/fəs] **51**
Renting an Apartment [rĕn/tĭng ən ə pärt/mənt] **48**
repair [rĭ për/] **166**–4, **167**–24
    repair person [rĭ për/ pür/sən] **62**–10
repair [rĭ për/] **170**–J
REPAIRS [rĭ përz/] **62**–63
repellent [rĭ pĕl/ənt] **226**–23
replace [rĭ plās/] **157**–K
report [rĭ pört/] **143**–J, **143**–K
reporter [rĭ pör/tər] **169**–52
representative [rĕ/prĭ zĕn/tə tĭv] **138**–3, **167**–20
Reptiles [rĕp/tĭlz] **213**
REPTILES [rĕp/tĭlz] **212**–213
request [rĭ kwĕst/] **12** ✦
Requirements [rĭ kwīr/mənts] **140**
rescue [rĕs/kyōō] **145**–20
    rescue breathing [rĕs/kyōō brē/dhĭng] **117**–16
Resident Alien card [rĕz/ə dənt ā/lē ən kärd/] **40**–2
resource center [rē/sörs sĕn/tər] **172**–9
Resources [rē/sörs/səz, rĭ sör/səz] **219**
respirator [rĕs/pə rā/tər] **179**–13
Responding [rĭ spän/dĭng] **191**
Responsibilities [rĭ spän/sə bĭl/ə tēz] **140**
RESPONSIBILITIES [rĭ spän/sə bĭl/ə tēz] **140**
restaurant [rĕs/tə rənt, –ränt/] **125**–14, **128**–10
RESTAURANT [rĕs/tə rənt, –ränt/] **79, 82**–83
Restaurant Dining [rĕs/tə rənt dī/nĭng, –ränt/] **185**
Restaurant Kitchen [rĕs/tə rənt kĭ/chən, –ränt/] **185**
restrooms [rĕst/ rōōmz/] **5**–10
results [rĭ zŭltz/] **139**–31
resuscitation [rĭ sə sə tā/shən] **117**–17
retail clerk [rē/tāl/ klürk/] **169**–53
retire [rĭ tīr/] **41**–O
return [rĭtürn/] **73**–16
    return address [rĭ türn/ ə drĕs/, –ă/drĕs] **134**–21
return [rĭ türn/] **27**–H, **133**–D
REUNION [rē yōōn/yən] **44**–45
reuse [rē yōōz/] **219**–B
revise [rĭ vīz/] **191**–J
Revising [rĭ vī/zĭng] **191**
Revolutionary War [rĕ/və lōō/shə nër ē wör/] **198**–8
revolving [rĭ väl/vĭng]
    revolving door [rĭ väl/vĭng dör/] **184**–2
    revolving nosepiece [rĭ väl/vĭng nöz/pēs] **194**–17
rewind [rē wīnd/] **235**–C
rewrite [rē rīt/] **191**–J
rhinoceros [rĭ näs/ər əs] **217**–28
ribbon [rĭ/bən] **99**–30

ribs [rĭbz] **70**–5, **76**–2
    rib cage [rĭb/ kāj/] **107**–48
rice [rīs] **67**–10, **81**–30, **177**–1
ride [rīd] **129**–D
rider [rī/dər] **152**–3
riding [rī/dĭng] **226**–9
right [rīt] **25**–3, **155**–B, **198**–10
    right angle [rīt/ ăng/gəl] **193**–26
    right turn only [rīt/ türn/ ön/lē] **154**–7
Rights [rīts] **140**
RIGHTS AND RESPONSIBILITIES
    [rīts/ ən rī spän/sə bĭl/ə tēz] **140**
ring [rĭng] **37**–25, **79**–4, **95**–40
    clip-on earrings [klĭp/än ïr/ĭngz, –ön–] **95**–37
    pierced earrings [pïrst/ ïr/ĭngz] **95**–36
rinse [rĭns] **108**–F
ripe [rīp] **68**–30
ripped [rĭpt] **97**–41
ripper [rĭ/pər] **100**–18
rise [rīz] **127**–13
    sunrise [sŭn/rīz/] **18**–14
river [rĭv/ər] **155**–10, **204**–3
RN (registered nurse) [är/ĕn/] / [rĕj/ə stərd nürs/]
    120–10
road work [rōd/ würk/] **154**–16
Road Worker [rōd/ wür/kər] **92**
roast [rōst] **70**–1
    roast beef [rōst bēf/] **71**–21
    roast chicken [rōst chĭk/ən] **81**–22
    roasted turkey [rō/stəd tür/kē] **76**–4
    roasting pan [rō/stĭng păn/] **78**–13
    roasting rack [rō/stĭng răk/] **78**–14
robe [rōb] **91**–29
robin [räb/ən] **214**–16
rock [räk] **36**–D
rock concert [räk/ kän/sərt] **222**–5
rocking chair [räk/ĭng chër/] **37**–21
rocks [räks] **208**–6, **237**–23
Rodents [rōd/nts] **215**
RODENTS [rōd/nts] **215**
rollers [rō/lərz] **33**–19, **181**–23
rolling pin [rō/lĭng pĭn/] **78**–30
rolls [rōlz] **74**–11, **74**–23, **80**–17
romance [rō măns/, rō/măns] **237**–16
Roman Numerals [rō/mən nōō/mər əlz] **16**
roof [rōōf] **46**–1
roof garden [rōōf/ gär/dn] **50**–4
roofer [rōō/fər] **62**–8
room [rōōm]
    baby's room [bā/bēz rōōm/] **47**–10
    ballroom [böl/ rōōm/] **184**–26
    banquet room [băn/kwət rōōm/] **185**–14
    bathroom [băth/rōōm/] **46**–4
    bedroom [bĕd/rōōm/] **46**–2
    conference room [kän/frəns rōōm/] **182**–4
    dining room [dī/nĭng rōōm/] **82**–1
    dining room chair [dī/nĭng rōōm/ chër/] **55**–8
    dining room table [dī/nĭng rōōm/ tā/bəl] **55**–9
    dish room [dĭsh/ rōōm/] **83**–13
    guest room [gĕst/ rōōm/] **184**–13
    kids' bedroom [kĭdz/ bĕd/rōōm/] **47**–9

living room [lĭv/ĭng rōōm/] **47**–12
meeting room [mē/tĭng rōōm/] **184**–25
roommates [rōōm/māts/] **64**–1
room service [rōōm/ sür/vəs] **184**–17
storeroom [stör/rōōm/] **185**–5
Room [rōōm] **50, 118, 121**
ROOM [rōōm] **56**
rooster [rōō/stər] **215**–7
roots [rōōts] **210**–5, **211**–3
rope [rōp] **224**–4, **226**–19
rose [rōz] **211**–15
rotary [rō/tə rē]
    rotary card file [rō/tə rē kärd/ fīl/] **183**–44
    rotary cutter [rō/tə rē kŭt/ər] **232**–16
rotten [rät/n] **68**–32
round trip [rownd/ trĭp/] **152**–17
route [rōōt] / [rowt]
    bus route [bŭs/ rōōt, –rowt] **152**–1
    escape route [ĕs/kāp rōōt, –rowt] **146**–3
    evacuation route
        [ĭ văk/yōō/ā shən rōōt, –rowt] **146**–5
    U.S. route [yōō/ĕs/ rōōt, –rowt] **154**–17
router [row/tər] **180**–12
ROUTINES [rōō tēnz/] **38**–39
rubber [rŭb/ər]
    rubber band [rŭb/ər bănd/] **183**–34
    rubber gloves [rŭb/ər glŭvz/] **61**–4
    rubber mat [rŭb/ər măt/] **57**–3
ruffle [rŭ/fəl] **58**–17
rug [rŭg] **58**–22
ruler [rōō/lər] **17**–13
rules [rōōlz] **64**–8
Rules [rōōlz] **190**
run [rŭn] **11**–D
    run across [rŭn/ə krös/] **153**–G
    run around [rŭn/ə rownd/] **153**–H
    run for office [rŭn/ fər ö/fəs] **139**–A
    run out [rŭn/owt/] **162**–E
runner [rŭ/nər] **185**–15
rural area [rōōr/əl ër/ē ə] **52**–4
RV (recreational vehicle)
    [är/vē/] / [rĕk/rē ā/shən əl vē/ə kəl] **156**–10
rye bread [rī/ brĕd/] **71**–20
sad [săd] **43**–19
safety [sāf/tē] **37**–19, **92**–4, **159**–53
    safety boots [sāf/tē bōōts/] **179**–20
    safety deposit box [sāf/tē dĭ päz/ət bäks/] **132**–7
    safety glasses [sāf/tē glăs/əz] **92**–10, **179**–10
    safety goggles [sāf/tē gäg/əlz] **179**–11
    safety pin [sāf/tē pĭn/] **37**–9, **100**–14
    safety rail [sāf/tē rāl/] **59**–10
    safety regulations [sāf/tē rĕ/gyə lā/shənz] **164**–6
    safety visor [sāf/tē vī/zər] **179**–12
Safety [sāf/tē] **76**
SAFETY [sāf/tē] **76**–77, **143, 179**
Safety Equipment [sāf/tē ĭ kwĭp/mənt] **179**
Safety Hazards and Hazardous Materials
    [sāf/tē hăz/ərdz ən hăz/ər dəs-mə tïr/ē əlz] **179**
sailboat [sāl/bōt/] **225**–3
sailing [sā/lĭng] **227**–8

salad [săl/əd]
   chef's salad [shĕfs/ săl/əd] **80**–14
   dinner salad [dĭn/ər săl/əd] **80**–15
   fruit salad [frōōt/ săl/əd] **80**–21
   pasta salad [päs/tə săl/əd] **80**–20
   potato salad [pə tā/tō săl/əd] **80**–19
   salad bar [săl/əd bär/] **79**–24
   salad fork [săl/əd förk/] **83**–27
   salad plate [săl/əd plāt/] **83**–20
   spinach salad [spĭ/nĭch săl/əd] **80**–13
Salad Dressings [săl/əd drĕ/sĭngz] **80**
Salads [săl/ədz] **80**
salamander [săl/ə măn/dər] **212**–27
salami [sə lä/mē] **71**–24
SALE [sāl] **102**–**103**
sales [sālz]
   sale price [sāl/ prīs/] **27**–3
   salesclerk [sālz/klürk/] **94**–3
   sales tax [sālz/ tăks/] **27**–8
Salesperson [sālz/pür/sən] **92**
salmon [săm/ən] **71**–3
   salmon steak [săm/ən stāk/] **71**–4
salon [sə lön/] **130**–3, **131**–18
salt and pepper shakers
   [sölt/ n pĕp/ər shā/kərz] **55**–13
same [sām] **23**–15
SAME AND DIFFERENT
   [sām/ ən dĭ/frənt, –dĭ fə rənt] **28**–**29**
samples [săm/pəlz] **84**–5
sand [sănd] **225**–23
   sandbox [sănd/bäks/] **224**–15
   sand castle [sănd kăs/əl] **225**–12
   sand dune [sănd dōōn/] **204**–5
   sandpaper [sănd/pā/pər] **181**–56
sandals [săn/dlz] **88**–9
sander [săn/dər] **180**–11
sandwich [săn/wĭch, –sănd/–] **79**–5, **80**–10, **80**–12
sanitation worker [săn/ə tā/shən wür/kər] **169**–54
satellite [săt/əl īt/] **205**–20
   satellite dish [săt/əl līt/ dĭsh/] **53**–6
satisfied [săt/ĭs fīd/] **42**–6
Saturday [săt/ər dā/, –dē] **20**–14
Saturn [săt/ərn] **205**–6
saucepan [sös/păn/] **78**–25
saucer [sö/sər] **83**–25
sausage [sö/sĭj] **70**–12, **80**–2
sauté [sö tā/, sō –] **77**–E
save [sāv] **219**–E
saving [sā/vĭng] **19**–25, **225**–20
savings account number
   [sā/vĭngz ə kownt/ nŭm/bər] **132**–11
saw [sö] **180**–9
   hacksaw [hăk/sö/] **180**–5
   jigsaw [jĭg/sö/] **180**–10
saxophone [săk/sə fōn/] **238**–5
say [sā] **2**–A, **3**–L, **4**–A
scaffolding [skăf/əl dĭng] **178**–4
scales [skālz] **57**–27, **72**–3, **135**–8, **155**–7, **195**–41, **212**–3
   postal scale [pō/stəl skāl/] **183**–27
scallions [skăl/yənz] **69**–20
scallops [skäl/əps, skăl/–] **71**–12, **212**–19

scan [skăn] **171**–H
scanner [skăn/ər] **183**–20
scared [skĕrd] **43**–23
scarf / scarves [skärf] / [skärvz] **95**–12
   winter scarf [wĭn/tər skärf/] **90**–5
scenery [sē/ nə rē] / [sēn/rē] **162**–3
schedule [skĕj/ōōl, –ōō əl] **152**–4
schedule [skĕj/ōōl, –ōō əl] **171**–J
school [skōōl] **126**–9
   adult school [[ə dŭlt/–, ăd/ŭlt skōōl/] **188**–8
   elementary school [ĕl/ə mĕn/trē skōōl/] **188**–2
   high school [hī/ skōōl/] **188**–4
   junior high school [jōōn/yər hī/ skōōl/] **188**–3
   middle school [mĭd/l skōōl/] **188**–3
   nursery school [nür/sə rē skōōl/] **188**–1
   parochial school [pə rō/kē əl skōōl/] **5** ✦
   preschool [prē/skōōl/] **188**–1
   private school [prī/vət skōōl/] **5** ✦
   public school [pŭb/lĭk skōōl/] **5** ✦
   school bus [skōōl/ bŭs/] **156**–21
   school crossing [skōōl/ krö/sĭng] **154**–15
   technical school [tĕk/nĭ kəl skōōl/] **188**–5
   vocational school [vō kā/shə nəl skōōl/] **188**–5
SCHOOL [skōōl] **5, 10, 11**
School Registration Form
   [skōōl/ rĕj/ə strā/shən förm/] **4**
SCHOOLS AND SUBJECTS
   [sklōōz ən sŭb/jĭkts] **188**–**189**
science [sī/əns] **189**–11
SCIENCE [sī/əns] **194**–**195**
Science Lab [sī/əns lăb/] **195**
scissors [sĭz/ərz] **33**–20, **100**–16
scoop neck [skōōp/ nĕk/] **96**–10
score [skör] **10**–3, **229**–1
scorpion [skör/pē ən] **214**–30
scrambled eggs [skrăm/bəld ĕgz/] **76**–7
scraper [skrā/pər] **181**–52
screen [skrēn] **6**–2, **196**–11, **235**–30
   big-screen TV [bĭg/skrĕn/ tē/ vē/] **50**–15
   fire screen [fīr/ skrĕn/] **56**–12
   flat screen TV [flăt/ skrĕn/ tē/vē/] **234**–7
   screen door [skrēn/ dör/] **53**–15
   sunscreen [sŭn/skrĕn/] **108**–7, **225**–10
screener [skrēn/ər] **160**–5
screening area [skrē/nĭng ĕr/ē ə] **160**–4
screw [skrōō] **180**–32, **180**–33
   Phillips screwdriver [fĭl/ĭps skrōō/drī/vər] **180**–31
   screwdriver [skrōō/drī/vər] **180**–30
scroll bar [skrōl/bär/] **197**–15
scrub [skrŭb] **60**–K
scrubs [skrŭbz] **93**–31
   scrub brush [skrŭb/ brŭsh/] **61**–20
   surgical scrub cap [sür/jĭ kəl skrŭb/ kăp/] **93**–35
   surgical scrubs [sür/jĭ kəl skrŭbz/] **93**–38
scuba [skōō/bə]
   scuba diving [skōō/bə dī/vĭng] **227**–12
   scuba tank [skōō/bə tăngk/] **225**–5
sea [sē]
   sea anemone [sē/ ə nĕm/ə nē] **212**–24
   seahorse [sē/ hörs/] **212**–13
   sea lion [sē/ lī/ən] **213**–33
   sea otter [sē/ ät/ər] **213**–35

   seashell [sē/shĕl/] **225**–24
   sea urchin [sē/ ür/chən] **212**–21
   seaweed [sē/ wĕd/] **225** ✦
Sea Animals [sē/ ăn/ə məlz] **212**
SEAFOOD AND DELI [sē/fōōd/ ən dĕ/lī] **71**
seal [sēl] **213**–34
Sea Mammals [sē/ măm/əlz] **213**
seam ripper [sēm/ rĭp/ər] **100**–18
search [sürch]
   search and rescue team
      [sürch/ ən rĕs/kyōō tēm/] **145**–20
   search box [sürch/ bäks/] **197**–5
   search engine [sürch/ ĕn/jən] **197**–6
SEARCH [sürch] **173**
SEASONAL CLOTHING [sē/zə nəl klō/dhĭng] **90**
Seasons [sē/zənz] **21**
seat [sēt]
   backseat [băk/ sēt/] **159**–54
   car safety seat [kär/ sāf/tē sēt/] **37**–19
   child safety seat [chīld/ sāf/tē sēt/] **159**–53
   front seat [frŭnt/ sēt/] **159**–51
   love seat [lŭv/ sēt/] **56**–1
   potty seat [pät/ē sēt/] **37**–12
   reclined seat [rĭ klīnd/ sēt/] **161**–27
   seat belt [sēt/ bĕlt/] **159**–52
   upright seat [ŭp/rīt/ sēt/] **161**–28
seat [sēt] **82**–B
second [sĕk/ənd] **16**
Second Floor [sĕk/ənd flör/] **50**
seconds [sĕk/əndz] **18**–3
section [sĕk/shən] **72**–2
security [sĭ kyōōr/ə tē]
   security camera [sĭ kyōōr/ə tē kăm/rə] **50**–19
   security gate [sĭ kyōōr/ə tē gāt/] **50**–16
   security guard [sĭ kyōōr/ə tē gärd/] **132**–5, **169**–55
   security pants [sĭ kyōōr/ə tē pănts/] **93**–22
   security screener [sĭ kyōōr/ə tē skrē/nər] **160**–5
   security shirt [sĭ kyōōr/ə tē shürt/] **93**–20
Security Checkpoint [sĭ kyōōr/ə tē chĕk/poynt/] **160**
Security Guard [sĭ kyōōr/ə tē gärd/] **93**
sedan [sə dăn/] **156**–1
see [sē] **106**–A
seed [sēd] **211**–1
   seedling [sēd/lĭng] **211**–4
seek [sēk] **114**–A, **147**–H
seesaw [sē/sö/] **224**–16
select [sə lĕkt/] **196**–B
self-checkout [sĕlf/ chĕk/owt/] **73**–10, **133**–10
sell [sĕl] **170**–K
semi [sĕm/ī] **156**–15
semicolon [sĕm/ē kō/lən] **190**–18
Senate [sĕn/ət] **138**–5
senator [sĕn/ə tər] **138**–6
   state senator [stāt/ sĕn/ə tər] **139**–25
send [sĕnd] **197**–I
   send in [sĕnd/ ĭn/] **173**–H
Sending a Card [sĕn/dĭng ə kärd/] **135**
Sending Email [sĕn/dĭng ē/māl/] **197**
senior [sēn/yər]
   senior citizen [sēn/yər sĭt/ə zən] **30**–5
   senior housing [sēn/yər howz/ĭng] **52**–11
Senses [sĕn/səz] **106**

sentence [sĕn/tns] **190**–2
sentence [sĕn/tns] **141**–E
separate [sĕ/pə rāt/] **76**–B
September [sĕp tĕm/bər] **21**–33
sequins [sē/kwĭnz/] **99**–33
Serious Medical Conditions
    [sïr/ē əs mĕd/ĭ kəl kən dĭsh/ənz] **111**
serious photo [sïr/ē əs fō/tō] **206**–3
serve [sürv] **139**–D, **230**–P
    serve on a jury [sürv/ ăn ə jŏŏr/ē, –ŏn–] **140**–E
    serve the meal [sürv/ dhə mēl/] **82**–F
Serve [sürv] **76**
server [sür/vər] **82**–8, **83**–9, **169**–56, **185**–8
service [sür/vəs]
    customer service [kŭs/tə mər sür/vəs] **97** ✦
    customer service representative
        [kŭs/tə mər-sür/vəs rĕ/prə zĕn/tə tĭv] **167**–20
    guest services [gĕst/ sür/vəs əz] **130**–12
    pool service [pōōl/ sür/vəs] **184**–21
    room service [rōōm/ sür/vəs] **184**–17
SERVICE [sür/vəs] **138**–**139**, **185**
serving bowl [sür/vĭng bōl/] **55**–21
set [sĕt] **10**–A, **33**–C, **82**–A
    set up [sĕt/ ŭp/] **173**–I
    sunset [sŭn/sĕt/] **18**–18
setting [sĕ/tĭng] **83**–17
seven [sĕv/ən] **16**
seventeen [sĕv/ən tēn/] **16**
seventeenth [sĕv/ən tēnth/] **16**
seventh [sĕv/ənth] **16**
seventieth [sĕv/ən tē əth] **16**
seventy [sĕv/ən tē] **16**
    75 percent [sĕv/ən tē fīv/ pər sĕnt/] **17**–9
sew [sō] **98**–A, **98**–B, **170**–L
sewing [sō/ĭng]
    sewing machine [sō/ĭng mə shēn/] **98**–13
    sewing machine operator
        [sō/ĭng mə shēn/ äp/ə rā/ tər] **98**–14
Sewing Machine [sō/ĭng mə shēn/] **98**
Sewing Supplies [sō/ĭng sə plīz/] **100**
sex [sĕks] **4**–16
shade [shād] **225**–13
    lampshade [lămp/shād/] **56** ✦, **58**–26
shadow [shă/dō/] **109**–35
shake [shāk]
    milkshake [mĭlk/shāk/] **79**–14
shake [shāk] **3**–J, **174**–I
shakers [shă/kərz] **55**–13
shampoo [shăm pōō/] **108**–10
shanks [shănks] **70**–13
shaper [shā/pər] **91**–15
Shapes [shāps] **193**
share [shĕr] **8**–M
Sharing and Responding
    [shĕr/ĭng ən rĭ spän/dĭng] **191**
shark [shärk] **212**–4
sharpener [shär/pən ər] **183**–26
shave [shāv]
    aftershave [ăf/tər shāv/] **109**–30
shave [shāv] **109**–M
shaver [shā/vər] **109**–26
shaving cream [shā/vĭng krēm/] **109**–29

shears [shïrz] **176**–9
sheep [shēp] **215**–6
sheet [shēt]
    cookie sheet [kŏŏk/ē shēt/] **78**–27
    dryer sheets [drī/ər shēts/] **101**–5
    fitted sheet [fĭt/əd shēt/] **58**–12
    flat sheet [flăt/ shēt/] **58**–13
shelf [shĕlf] **54**–2
shell [shĕl]
    seashell [sē/shĕl/] **225**–24
Shellfish [shĕl/fĭsh/] **71**
shelter [shĕl/tər] **52**–13
shield [shēld]
    windshield [wĭnd/shēld/] **158**–1
    windshield wipers [wĭnd/shēld wī/pərz] **158**–2
shift [shĭft] **159**–49, **159**–50
shin [shĭn] **106**–21
    shin guards [shĭn/ gärdz/] **231**–13
shingles [shĭng/gəlz] **178**–20
ship [shĭp] **175**–D
shipping clerk [shĭp/ĭng klürk/] **175**–14
shirt [shürt] **86**–1
    nightshirt [nīt/shürt/] **91**–28
    polo shirt [pō/lō shürt/] **92**–14
    security shirt [sĭ kyŏŏr/ə tē shürt/] **93**–20
    sports shirt [spörts/ shürt/] **88**–4
    T-shirt [tē/shürt/] **86**–4
    work shirt [würk/ shürt/] **92**–2
shock [shäk] **116**–B, **116**–F
shoes [shōōz] **86**–7, **87**–13, **95**–32
    shoe department [shōō/ dĭ pärt/mənt] **95**–7
    shoelaces [shōō/lās əz] **94**–24
    shoe store [shōō/ stör/] **130**–10
SHOES AND ACCESSORIES
    [shōōz/ ən ĭk sĕs/ə rēz] **94**–**95**
shoot [shōōt] **211**–5
shoot [shōōt] **230**–H
shop [shäp]
    barbershop [bär/bər shäp/] **129**–19
    beauty shop [byōō/tē shäp/] **130** ✦
    coffee shop [kö/fē shäp/] **126**–11
    donut shop [dō/nŭt shäp/] **129**–17
    gift shop [gĭft/ shäp/] **130** ✦, **184**–5
    ice cream shop [īs/ krēm shäp/] **131**–16
shop [shäp] **28**–A, **143**–H
Shop [shäp] **100**
SHOP [shäp] **80**–**81**
shoplifting [shäp/lĭf/tĭng] **142**–8
shopping [shäp/ĭng]
    shopping basket [shäp/ĭng băs/kət] **73**–9
    shopping list [shäp/ĭng lĭst/] **67**–14
    shopping mall [shäp/ĭng mäl/] **126**–7
    shopping program [shäp/ĭng mäl/] **236**–10
SHOPPING [shäp/ĭng] **27**
shore [shör] **204**–12
short [shört] **32**–6, **96**–16
    short hair [shört/ hĕr/] **33**–1
    short-order cook [shört/ör/dər kŏŏk/] **185**–1
    short-sleeved [shört/slēvd/] **96**–12
shorten [shört/ən] **100**–B
shorts [shörts] **89**–25, **91**–4

shoulder [shōl/dər] **105**–13
    shoulder bag [shōl/dər băg/] **94**–17
    shoulder blade [shōl/dər blād/] **107**–28
    shoulder-length hair [shōl/dər lĕngkth/ hĕr/] **33**–2
    shoulder pads [shōl/dər pădz/] **231**–20
shovel [shŭv/əl] **176**–7, **178**–22
show [shō] **236**–4, **236**–6, **236**–8
show [shō] **137**–C, **160**–C
shower [show/ər]
    shower cap [show/ər kăp/] **108**–1
    shower curtain [show/ər kür/tn] **57**–12
    shower gel [show/ər jĕl/] **108**–2
    showerhead [show/ər hĕd/] **57**–11
    stall shower [stöl/ show/ər] **57** ✦
shredder [shrĕ/dər] **183**–24
shrimp [shrĭmp] **71**–11, **212**–18
shut [shŭt] **146**–4
shuttle [shŭt/l] **152**–19, **205**–19
sick [sĭk] **42**–12
    homesick [hōm/sĭk/] **43**–20
side [sīd] **76**–10
    sideburns [sīd/bürnz/] **33**–7
    sideview mirror [sīd/vyōō/ mĭr/ər] **158**–3
Side Salads [sīd/ săl/ədz] **80**
sidewalk [sīd/wök/] **129**–24
sight impaired [sīt/ ĭm përd/] **32**–11
sign [sīn] **4**–D
    street sign [strēt/ sīn/] **129**–26
    vacancy sign [vā/kən sē sīn/] **50**–7
    vital signs monitor [vīt/l sīnz/ män/ə tər] **121**–26
sign [sīn] **48**–D
signal [sĭg/nəl]
    strong signal [ströng/ sĭg/nəl] **14**–11
    turn signal [türn/ sĭg/nəl] **158**–6, **159**–34
    weak signal [wēk/ sĭg/nəl] **14**–12
signature [sĭg/nə chər] **4**–19
SIGNS [sīnz] **154**
silk [sĭlk] **98**–5
simmer [sĭm/ər] **77**–P
sing [sĭng] **36**–O, **238**–B
single [sĭng/gəl]
    single father [sĭng/gəl fä/dhər] **35**–23
    single mother [sĭng/gəl mŭdh/ər] **35**–22
sink [sĭnk] **54**–4, **57**–23
Sirius [sïr/ē əs] **205** ✦
sister [sĭs/tər] **34**–5, **35**–27
    sister-in-law [sĭs/tər ĭn lö/] **34**–16
    stepsister [stĕp/sĭs/tər] **35**–29
sitcom (situation comedy)
    [sĭt/käm/] / [sĭch/ōō ā/shən käm/ə dē] **236**–2
sit down [sĭt/ down/] **6**–F
site [sīt] **126**–2
sitter [sĭt/ər] **166**–9
situation comedy (sitcom)
    [sĭch/ōō ā/shən-käm/ə dē] / [sĭt/käm/] **236**–2
six [sĭks] **16**
    six-pack [sĭks/păk/] **74**–9, **74**–21
    6-year-old boy [sĭks/yïr öld/boy/] **31**–9
sixteen [sĭks/tēn/] **16**
sixteenth [sĭks/tēnth/] **16**
sixth [sĭksth] **16**
sixtieth [sĭks/tē əth] **16**

Index

sixty [sĭks/tē] **16**

Sizes [sī/zəz] **96**

skate [skāt] **230**–U

skates [skāts] **231**–9, **231**–10

    skateboard [skāt/börd/] **224**–7

    skateboarding [skāt/bör/dĭng] **228**–13

skating [skā/tĭng] **227**–4, **227**–5, **227** ✦, **228**–10

ski [skē] **230**–V

skiing [skē/ĭng] **227**–1, **227**–3

    waterskiing [wö/tər skē/ĭng] **227**–7

skill inventory [skĭl/ ĭn/vən tör/ē] **172**–12

Skills [skĭlz] **171**

SKILLS [skĭlz] **170, 171, 174**

skin [skĭn] **107**–31

    skinless [skĭn/ləs] **70** ✦

skirt [skürt] **87**–10

skis [skēz] **231**–24

    ski boots [skē/ bōōts] **231**–26

    ski hat [skē/ hăt/] **90**–11

    ski mask [skē/ măsk/] **90**–15

    ski poles [skē/ pōlz/] **231**–25

skull [skŭl] **107**–47

skunk [skŭngk] **216**–12

SKU number [ĕs/kā/yōō/ nŭm/bər, skyōō/] **27**–5

sky [skī] **209**–9

    skycap [skē/kăp/] **160**–1

    skyscraper [skī/skrā/pər] **127**–13

slacks [slăks] **87**–12

slaves [slāvz] **198**–4

sledding [slĕd/ĭng] **227**–6

sledgehammer [slĕj/hăm/ər] **178**–23

sleeper [slē/pər] **91**–27

sleeping bag [slē/pĭng băg/] **226**–12

Sleepwear [slēp/wër] **91**

SLEEPWEAR [slēp/wër] **91**

sleepy [slē/pē] **42**–3

sleeve [slēv] **100**–6

    long-sleeved [löng/slēvd/] **96**–14

    short-sleeved [shört/slēvd] **96**–12

    sleeveless [slēv/ləs] **96**–11

    3/4 sleeved [thrē/kwör/tər slēvd/] **96**–13

slender [slĕn/dər] **32**–9

slice [slīs] **77**–C

slide [slīd] **194**–3, **224**–13

    mudslide [mŭd/slīd/] **144**–6

sliding glass door [slī/dĭng glăs/ dör/] **53**–18

sling [slĭng] **113**–19

slip [slĭp] **91**–22, **91**–23, **132**–4

slippers [slĭp/ərz] **91**–26

slippery floor [slĭ/pər ē flör/] **179**–6

slow [slō] **23**–4

small [smöl] **96**–1, **96**–2, **97**–37

    small town [smöl/ town/] **52**–3

smart phone [smärt/ fōn/] **15**–27

smell [smĕl] **106**–C

smile [smīl] **2**–D

smock [smök] **93**–26

smog [smäg, smög] **218**–11

smoggy [smä/gē, smö/–] **13**–14

smoke [smōk] **114**–G

smoke detector [smōk/ dĭ tĕk/tər] **51**–29

smoked turkey [smōkt/ tür/kē] **71**–25

Snack Foods [snăk/ fōōdz/] **73**

snail [snāl] **212**–22

snake [snāk] **213**–39

    rattlesnake [ră/təl snāk] **213**–38

snap [snăp] **99**–26

sneeze [snēz] **110**–B

snorkeling [snör/kə lĭng] **227**–11

snow [snō]

    snowboard [snō/börd/] **231**–23

    snowboarding [snō/bör/dĭng] **227**–2

    snowstorm [snō/störm/] **13**–23

snowing [snō/ĭng] **13**–12

soap [sōp] **57**–24, **61**–5, **108**–3

    soap dish [sōp/ dĭsh/] **57**–25

    soap opera [sōp/ äp/rə] **236**–5

sober [sō/ bər] **143** ✦

soccer [säk/ər] **229**–12

    soccer ball [säk/ər böl/] **231**–12

social [sō/shəl]

    Social Security card

        [sō/shəl sĭ kyōōr/ə tē kärd/] **40**–5

    Social Security number

        [sō/shəl sĭ kyōōr/ə tē nŭm/bər] **4**–15

    social worker [sō/shəl wür/kər] **169**–57

socks [säks] **86**–6

    ankle socks [ang/kəl säks/] **91**–7

    crew socks [krōō/ säks/] **91**–8

    dress socks [drĕs/ säks/] **91**–9

    low-cut socks [lō/kŭt säks/] **91**–10

Socks [säks] **91**

soda [sō/də] **73**–34, **79**–11

sofa [sō/fə] **56**–18

    sofa cushions [sō/fə kōō/shənz] **56** ✦

soft [söft] **23**–6

    softball [söft/böl/] **229**–10

softener [sö/fən ər] **101**–6

software [söft/wër/] **167**–18, **196**–10

soil [soyl] **208**–2

solar [sō/lər]

    solar eclipse [sō/lər ĭ klĭps/] **205**–16, **205** ✦

    solar energy [sō/lər ĕn/ər jē] **218**–1

Solar System and the Planets

    [sō/lər sĭs/təm ən dhə plăn/əts] **205**

soldier [sōl/jər] **169**–58

sole [sōl] **94**–21

solid [säl/əd] **96**–19

Solids [säl/ədz] **193**

solution [sə lōō/ shən] **192**–14

solve [sölv] **170**–M

son [sŭn] **34**–15

    grandson [grăn/sŭn/, grănd/–] **34** ✦

    son-in-law [sŭn/ĭn lö/] **34** ✦

sore throat [sör/ thrōt/] **110**–6

sort [sört] **101**–A

soul [sōl] **237**–28

soup [sōōp] **72**–18, **80**–16

    soup bowl [sōōp/ böl/] **83**–21

    soupspoon [sōōp/spōōn/] **83**–32

Soup [sōōp] **77**

sour [söw/ər] **84**–4

    sour cream [sow/ər krēm/] **72**–21

Sources [sör/səz] **218**

sous chef [sōō/ shĕf/] **185**–6

south [sowth] **155**–3

soybeans [soy/bēnz/] **177**–3

space [spās] **50**–18, **128**–5

    space shuttle [spās/ shŭt/əl] **205**–19

    space station [spās/ stā/shən] **205**–18

Space [spās] **205**

Space Exploration [spās/ ĕk/splə rā/shən] **205**

spades [spādz] **233**–30

spaghetti [spə gĕt/ē] **81**–26

spare tire [spër/ tīr/] **158**–23

sparrow [spăr/ō] **214**–7

spatula [spăch/ə lə] **78**–19

speak [spēk] **170**–N

speakers [spē/kərz] **50**–5, **206**–4, **234**–14

Special [spē/shəl] **80**

Specialists [spĕsh/ə lĭsts/] **120**

speech [spēch] **140**–2

speed limit [spēd/ lĭm/ət] **154**–4

speedometer [spĭ däm/ə tər] **159**–27

speed skating [spēd/skā/tĭng] **227** ✦

spell [spĕl] **4**–B

sphere [sfïr] **193**–42

spider [spī/dər] **214**–29

spill [spĭl] **218**–17

spinach [spĭn/ĭch] **69**–11

    spinach salad [spĭn/ĭch săl/əd] **80**–13

spinal column [spī/nəl käl/əm] **107**–49

spiral notebook [spī/rəl nōt/bōōk/] **7**–29

splint [splĭnt] **117**–14

sponge [spŭnj] **61**–19

    sponge mop [spŭnj/ mäp/] **61**–6

spoon [spōōn] **55**–5, **78**–9

    soupspoon [sōōp/spōōn/] **83**–32

    tablespoon [tā/bəl spōōn/] **75**–7

    teaspoon [tē/spōōn/] **75**–6, **83**–31

spoon [spōōn] **77**–F

sports [spörts]

    sports car [spörts/ kär/] **156**–4

    sports coat [spörts/ kōt/] **89**–14

    sports jacket [spörts/ jăk/ət] **89**–14

    sports program [spörts/ prō/grăm] **236**–11

    sports shirt [spörts/ shürt/] **88**–4

    sport-utility vehicle (SUV) [spört/

        yōō tïl/ə tē vē/ï kəl] / [ĕs/yōō/vē/] **156**–7

SPORTS [spörts] **228, 229, 230, 231**

SPORTS EQUIPMENT [spörts/ ï kwïp/mənt] **231**

SPORTS VERBS [spörts/ vürbz/] **230**

sprained ankle [sprānd/ ăng/kəl] **110**–18

spray [sprā] **108**–12, **113**–32

    spray gun [sprā/ gŭn/] **181**–21

    spray starch [sprā/ stärch/] **101**–12

spread [sprĕd]

    bedspread [bĕd/sprĕd] **59**–11

spring [sprĭng] **21**–37, **58**–19

sprinkler [sprĭng/klər] **53**–22

square [skwër] **193**–30

squash [skwäsh, skwösh] **69**–24

squeegee [skwē/jē] **61**–15

squid [skwĭd] **212**–7

squirrel [skwür/əl] **215**–21

stadium [stā/dē əm] **126**–1

staff [stăf] **185** ✦
Staff [stăf] **120**
stage [stāj] **194**–16
  stage clips [stāj/ klĭps/] **194**–24
stain [stān] **181**–24
stained [stānd] **97**–42
stairs [stĕrz] **50**–10
stairway [stĕr/wā/] **50**–10
stall shower [stöl/ show/ər] **57** ✦
stamps [stămps] **134**–18, **134**–23, **183**–47
  stamp machine [stămp/ mə shēn/] **135**–11
stand [stănd] **152**–18
  checkstand [chĕk/stănd/] **73**–12
  newsstand [nōōz/stănd/] **128**–12
  nightstand [nīt/stănd/] **58**–23
stand [stănd] **141**–D
  stand up [stănd/ ŭp/] **6**–D
standard time [stăn/dərd tīm/] **19**–26
staple [stā/pəl] **171**–F
stapler [stā/plər] **183**–28
staples [stā/pəlz] **183**–29
star [stär] **205**–13
  starfish [stär/fĭsh/] **212**–16
  star key [stär/ kē/] **14**–6
starch [stärch] **101**–12
start [stärt] **12**–A, **40**–B, **230**–R
starting point [stär/tĭng poynt/] **162**–1
starving [stär/vĭng] **43** ✦
state [stāt] **4**–8, **146**–2
  state capital [stāt kă/pət əl] **139**–22
  state senator [stāt sĕn/ə tər] **139**–25
state [stāt] **15**–G, **195**–A
State Government [stāt gŭ/ vərn mənt] **139**
statement [stāt/mənt] **132**–16
station [stā/shən]
  bus station [bŭs/ stā/shən] **124**–7
  fire station [fīr/ stā/shən] **125**–12
  gas station [găs/ stā/shən] **125**–10
  gas station attendant
    [găs/ stā/shən ə tĕn/dənt] **162**–3
  lifeguard station [līf/gärd/ stā/shən] **225**–21
  police station [pə lēs/ stā/shən] **124**–6
  space station [spās/ stā/shən] **205**–18
  station wagon [stā/shən wăg/ən] **156**–6
  subway station [sŭb/wā/ stā/shən] **151**–11
Station [stā/shən] **152**
stationery [stā/shə nĕr/ ē] **183**–42
stay [stā]
  stay away [stā ə wā/] **147**–I
  stay fit [stā fĭt/] **114**–E
  stay on the line [stā ön dhə lĭn/] **15**–H
  stay on well-lit streets [stā ön wĕl lĭt/ strēts/] **143**–B
Stay Well [stā wĕl/] **114**
steak [stāk] **70**–2, **81**–24
  broiled steak [broyld/ stāk/] **76**–3
  halibut steak [hăl/ə bŭt stāk/] **71**–6
  salmon steak [săm/ən stāk/] **71**–4
  steak knife [stāk/ nīf/] **83**–29
steal [stēl] **142** ✦
steam [stēm] **77**–D
steamed vegetables [stēmd/ vĕj/tə bəlz] **81**–32
steamer [stē/mər] **78**–3

steel [stēl]
  steel toe boots [stēl/ tō/ bōōts/] **92**–6
  steel-wool soap pads [stēl/wōōl/ sōp/ pădz/] **61**–5
steering wheel [stĭr/ĭng wēl/] **159**–26
stems [stĕmz] **211**–9
step [stĕp]
  stepbrother [stĕp/brŭdh/ər] **35**–30
  stepdaughter [stĕp/dö/tər] **35** ✦
  stepfather [stĕp/fä/dhər] **35**–25
  stepladder [stĕp/lăd/ər] **61**–13
  stepmother [stĕp/mŭdh/ər] **35**–26
  steps [stĕps] **53**–3
  stepsister [stĕp/sĭs/tər] **35**–29
stereo system [stĕr/ē ō sĭs/təm] **56**–8
sterile [stĕr/əl]
  sterile pad [stĕr/əl păd/] **117**–6
  sterile tape [stĕr/əl tāp/] **117**–7
stethoscope [stĕth/ə skōp/] **118**–10
stewing beef [stōō/ĭng bēf/] **70**–3
stick [stĭk] **231**–11, **232**–11
  drumsticks [drŭm/stĭks/] **70**–23
  lipstick [lĭp/stĭk/] **109**–38
  stick shift [stĭk/ shĭft/] **159**–50
  yardstick [yärd/stĭk/] **181**–16
sticker [stĭk/ər] **102**–3, **136**–13
sticky notes [stĭk/ē nōts/] **183**–39
stir [stür] **77**–O
  stir-fried beef [stür/frīd/ bēf/] **76**–6
stitches [stĭch/əz] **117**–15
stock clerk [stäk/ klürk/] **169**–59
stockings [stäk/ĭngz] **91**–17
stomach [stŭm/ək] **107**–41
  stomachache [stŭm/ək āk/] **110**–4
stop [stäp] **129**–16, **151**–13, **154**–1
  stopover [stäp/ō/vər] **161** ✦
stop [stäp] **155**–D
Stop [stäp] **152**
stopped up [stäpt/ ŭp/] **63**–19
storage [stör/ĭj] **72**–25, **78**–4
  storage locker [stör/ĭj läk/ər] **50**–17
store [stör]
  bookstore [bōōk/stör/] **130**–4
  candy store [kăn/dē stör/] **131**–17
  card store [kärd/stör/] **130**–7
  convenience store [kən vēn/yəns stör/] **128**–3
  department store [dĭ pärt/mənt stör/] **131**–13
  electronics store [ē lĕk trän/ĭks stör/] **131**–20
  furniture store [für/nĭ chər stör/] **126**–8
  hardware store [härd/wër/ stör/] **148**–4
  home improvement store
    [hōm/ ĭm prōōv/mənt stör/] **127**–20
  jewelry store [jōō/əl rē stör/] **130**–2
  maternity store [mə tür/nə tē stör/] **131**–19
  men's store [mĕnz/ stör/] **130** ✦
  music store [myōō/zĭk stör/] **130**–1
  office supply store [ö/fəs sə plī/ stör/] **127**–21
  pet store [pĕt/ stör/] **130**–6
  shoe store [shōō/ stör/] **130**–10
  toy store [toy/ stör/] **130**–5
  video store [vĭd/ē ō stör/] **129**–20
Store [stör] **99**
STORE [stör] **72**–**73**

storeroom [stör/rōōm/] **185**–3
storm [störm] **13**–19
  hailstorm [hāl/störm/] **13**–21
  snowstorm [snō/störm/] **13**–23
  storm door [störm/ dör/] **53**–10
  thunderstorm [thŭn/dər störm/] **13**–16
story [stör/ē]
  action story [ăk/shən stör/ē] **237**–19
  adventure story [ăd vĕn/chər stör/ē] **237**–19
  horror story [hör/ər stör/ē, här/–] **237**–17
  science fiction story [sī/əns fĭk/shən stör/ē] **237**–18
  two-story house [tōō/stör/ē hows/] **52** ✦
stove [stōv] **54**–18, **226**–16
stow [stō] **160**–G
straight [strāt] **155**–A
  straight hair [strāt/ hër/] **33**–9
  straight line [strāt/ līn/] **193**–22
  straight pin [strāt/ pĭn/] **100**–12
strainer [strā/nər] **78**–22
straw [strö] **79**–18
  strawberries [strö/bĕr/ēz] **68**–14
  straw hat [strö/ hăt/] **90**–23
stream [strēm] **204** ✦
street [strēt] **150**–5, **155**–8
  streetlight [strēt/līt/] **148**–3
  street sign [strēt/ sīn] **129**–26
  street vender [strēt/ vĕn/dər] **129**–29
STREETS [strēts] **126**–**127**
strep throat [strĕp/ thrōt/] **111**–4
stress [strĕs] **115**–4
stretch [strĕch] **230**–M
stretcher [strĕch/ər] **121**–33
string [strĭng]
  string beans [strĭng/ bēnz/] **69**–8
  string lights [strĭng/ līts/] **239**–18
  string of pearls [strĭng/ əv pürlz/] **95**–39
Strings [strĭngz] **238**
striped [strīpt] **96**–20
stripper [strī/pər] **181**–42
stroller [strō/lər] **37**–18
strong signal [ströng/ sĭg/nəl] **14**–11
stub [stŭb] **165**–11
stucco [stŭk/ō] **178**–15
student [stōōd/nt] **6**–5
study [stŭ/dē] **10**–D, **137**–A
STUDYING [stŭ/dē ĭng] **8**
stuffed animals [stŭft/ ăn/ə məlz] **59**–15
style [stīl/] **88** ✦
Styles [stīlz] **96**
STYLES [stīlz] **96**
stylist [stī/lĭst] **167**–31
SUBJECTS [sŭb/jĭkts/] **188**–**189**
submit [səb mĭt/] **48**–C
substitute [sŭb/stə tōōt/] **79**–20
subtract [səb trăkt/] **192**–B
suburbs [sŭb/ürbz] **52**–2
subway [sŭb/wā/] **151**–12
  subway car [sŭb/wā/ kär/] **152**–6
  subway station [sŭb/wā/ stā/shən] **151**–11
Subway Station [sŭb/wā/ stā/shən] **152**
Succeed [sək sēd/] **10**
SUCCEEDING IN SCHOOL [sək sē/dĭng ən skōōl/] **10**

Index

suede [swād] **99**–8
sugar [shŏŏg/ər] **73**–30
  sugar bowl [shŏŏg/ər bōl/] **55**–14
  sugar-free [shŏŏg/ər frē/] **122**–7
  sugar substitute [shŏŏg/ər sŭb/stə tōōt/] **79**–20
suit [sōōt] **87**–11
  bathing suit [bā/dhǐng sōōt/] **90**–26
  business suit [bǐz/nəs sōōt/] **88**–11
  jumpsuit [jŭmp/sōōt/] **93**–24
  three piece suit [thrē/pēs/ sōōt/] **88** ✦
  wet suit [wĕt/ sōōt/] **225**–4
suite [swēt] **184**–16
sum [sŭm] **192**–7
sumac [sōō/măk] **210**–23
summer [sŭm/ər] **21**–38
sun [sŭn] **209**–8
  sunblock [sŭn/blăk/] **108**–8, **225**–0
  sunburn [sŭn/bŭrn/] **110**–14
  sunflower [sŭn/flow/ər] **211**–10
  sunglasses [sŭn/glăs/əz] **90**–27
  sunrise [sŭn/ rīz] **18**–14
  sunscreen [sŭn/skrēn/] **108**–7, **225**–10
  sunset [sŭn/ sĕt] **18**–19
Sunday [sŭn/dā, –dē] **20**–8
sunny [sŭn/ē] **13**–9, **76**–10
superintendent [sōō/prǐn tĕn/dənt, sōō/pər ǐn–] **50**–8
supermarket [sōō/pər/ mär/kət] **127**–18
supervise [sōō/pər vīz/] **170**–O
supervisor [sōō/pər vī/zər] **165**–8, **175**–4
Supplies [sə plīz/] **100, 183**
SUPPLIES [sə plīz/] **61, 180**–181
supply [sə plī/] **127**–21
  supply cabinet [sə plī/ kăb/ə nət] **182**–1
support [sə pört/] **179**–18
  support group [sə pört/ grōōp/] **115**–15
supporter [sə pör/tər] **91**–6
Supreme Court [sə prēm/ kört/] **138**–11
surfboard [sürf/börd/] **225**–16
surfer [sür/fər] **225**–15
surfing [sür/fǐng] **227**–9, **227**–10, **227** ✦
surgeon [sür/jən] **121**–36
Surgeon [sür/jən] **93**
surge protector [sürj/ prə tĕk/tər] **196**–1
surgical [sür/jǐ kəl]
  surgical cap [sür/jǐ kəl kăp/] **121**–37
  surgical gloves [sür/jǐ kəl glŭvz/] **121**–39
  surgical gown [sür/jǐ kəl gown/] **93**–37, **121**–38
  surgical mask [sür/jǐ kəl măsk/] **93**–36
  surgical nurse [sür/jǐ kəl nürs/] **120**–9
  surgical scrub cap [sür/jǐ kəl skrŭb/ kăp/] **93**–35
  surgical scrubs [sür/jǐ kəl skrŭbz/] **93**–38
Surgical Assistant [sür/jǐ kəl ə sǐs/tənt] **93**
surprised [sər prīzd/, sə–] **43**–30
suspenders [sə spĕn/dərz] **94**–1
suspense [sŭs/pĕns] **237**–20
SUV (sport-utility vehicle) [ĕs/yōō/vē/] /
  [spört/ yōō tǐl/ə tē vē/ǐ kəl] **156**–7
swallow [swäl/ō] **116**–J
swap meet [swäp/ mēt/] **222**–6
sweat [swĕt]
  sweatpants [swĕt/pănts/] **89**–23
  sweatshirt [swĕt/shürt/] **89**–22

sweater [swĕt/ər] **28**–2, **87**–14
  cardigan sweater [kär/də gən swĕt/ər] **88**–2
  pullover sweater [pŏŏl/ō/vər swĕt/ər] **88**–3
sweep [swēp] **60**–J
sweet potatoes [swĕt pə tā/tōz] **69**–18
sweets [swĕts] **84**–9
swim [swǐm] **230**–L
  swimsuit [swǐm/sōōt/] **90**–26
swimming [swǐm/ǐng]
  swimming pool [swǐm/ǐng pōōl/] **51**–22
  swimming trunks [swǐm/ǐng trŭngks/] **90**–22
swing [swǐng] **230**–Q
swings [swǐngz] **224**–11
Swiss cheese [swǐs/ chēz/] **71**–27
switch [swǐch] **58**–27
swollen finger [swō/lən fǐng/gər] **110**–16
swordfish [sörd/fǐsh/] **71**–5, **212**–10
symbol [sǐm/bəl] **155**–8
SYMPTOMS AND INJURIES
  [sǐmp/təmz ən ǐn/jə rēz] **110**
synagogue [sǐn/ə găg/] **127**–16
synthetic materials [sǐn thĕ/tǐk mə tǐr/ē əlz] **98** ✦
syringe [sə rǐnj/] **118**–12
syrup [sǐr/əp, sür/–] **113**–29
system [sǐs/təm]
  fuel injection system
    [fyōō/əl ǐn jĕk/shən sǐs/təm] **158**–17
  stereo system [stĕr/ē ō sǐs/təm] **56**–8
SYSTEM [sǐs/təm] **141**
tab [tăb] **197**–7
table [tā/bəl]
  bed table [bĕd/ tā/bəl] **121**–21
  changing table [chān/jǐng tā/bəl] **59**–1
  coffee table [kö/fē tā/bəl] **56**–19
  dining room table [dī/nǐng rōōm/ tā/bəl] **55**–9
  end table [ĕnd/ tā/bəl] **56**–14
  examination table [ǐg zăm/ə nā/shən tā/bəl] **118**–7
  folding card table [fōl/dǐng kärd/ tā/bəl] **102**–4
  night table [nīt/ tā/bəl] **58**–23
  operating table [äp/ə rā/tǐng tā/bəl] **121**–40
  periodic table [pǐr/ē äd/ǐk tā/bəl] **195**–26
  picnic table [pǐk/nǐk tā/bəl] **224**–8
  pool table [pōōl/ tā/bəl] **50**–15
  tablecloth [tā/bəl klöth/] **55**–12
  tablespoon [tā/bəl spōōn/] **75**–7
  table tennis [tā/bəl tĕn/əs] **228**–14
  tray table [trā/ tā/bəl] **161**–21
  turntable [türn/tā/bəl] **234**–12
tablet [tăb/lət] **113**–22, **113**–27
tackle [tăk/əl] **230**–F
taco [tä/kō] **79**–8
tags [tăgz] **92**–15, **136**–13
tail [tāl] **216**–22
tail light [tāl/ līt/] **158**–13
tail pipe [tāl/ pīp/] **158**–15
tailor [tā/lər] **100**–3
take [tāk]
  do not take with dairy products
    [dōō nät/ tāk/ with dër/ē präd/ŭkts] **112**–A
  take a bath [tāk/ ə băth/] **108**–B
  take a break [tāk/ ə brāk/] **11**–H
  take a citizenship test
    [tāk/ ə sǐt/ə zən shǐp tĕst/] **140**–I

  take a driver education course
    [tāk/ ə drī/vərz ĕj/ə kā/shən körs/] **137**–B
  take a driver's training course
    [tāk/ ə drī/vərz trā/nǐng körs/] **137**–G
  take a message [tāk/ ə mĕs/ǐj] **171**–Q
  take a nap [tāk/ ə năp/] **53**–A
  take a picture [tāk/ ə pǐk/chər] **206**–B
  take a seat [tāk/ ə sēt/] **6**–F
  take a shower [tāk/ ə show/ər] **38**–C, **108**–A
  take a tour [tāk/ ə tōōr/] **220**–A
  take a written test [tāk/ ə rǐt/ən tĕst] **137**–E
  take care of children [tāk/ kër/ əv chǐl/drən] **170**–P
  take cover [tāk/ kŭv/ər] **147**–J
  take dictation [tāk/ dǐk/tā shən] **171**–K
  take in [tāk/ ǐn] **100**–D
  take medicine [tāk/ mĕd/ə sən] **114**–D
  take notes [tāk/ nōts/] **10**–C
  take off [tāk/ öf/] **109**–Q, **160**–J
  take one hour before eating
    [tāk/ wŭn/ ow/ər bǐ för/ ē/tǐng] **112**–B
  take out [tāk/ owt/] **9**–Y, **60**–Q, **82** ✦
  take ownership [tāk/ ō/nər shǐp/] **49**–K
  take temperature [tāk/ tĕm/prə chər] **118**–B
  take the bus to school
    [tāk/ dhə bŭs/ tə skōōl/] **38**–H
  take the car to a mechanic
    [tāk/ dhə kär/ tə dhə mə kăn/ǐk] **157**–C
  take the children to school
    [tāk/ dhə chǐl/drən tə skōōl/] **38**–G
  take the order [tāk/ dhē ör/dər] **82**–E
  take with food [tāk/ with fōōd/] **112**–A
  take x-rays [tāk/ ĕks/rāz/] **119**–B
Taking a Flight [tā/kǐng ə flīt/] **160**
Taking a Test [tā/kǐng ə tĕst/] **10**
TAKING A TRIP [tā/kǐng ə trǐp/] **162**–163
Taking Care of Your Car [tā/kǐng kër/ əv yər kär/] **157**
TAKING CARE OF YOUR HEALTH
  [tā/kǐng kër əv yər hĕlth/] **114**–115
talk [tök]
  talk show [tök/ shō/] **236**–4
  talk therapy [tök/ thĕr/ ə pē] **115**–13
talk [tök]
  talk about [tök ə bowt/] **174**–L
  talk on the phone [tök/ ön dhə fōn/] **15**–C
  talk to friends [tök/ tə frĕndz/] **173**–A
  talk to the teacher [tök/ tə dhə tē/chər] **6**–B
tall [töl] **32**–4
tambourine [tăm/bə rēn/] **238**–17
tan [tăn] **24**–18
tangerines [tăn/jə rēnz/] **68**–9
tank [tăngk] **158**–10, **225**–5
  tank top [tăngk/ täp/] **89**–24
  tank truck [tăngk/ trŭk/] **156**–20
tape [tāp]
  clear tape [klër/ tāp/] **183**–30
  correction tape [kə rĕk/shən tāp/] **183**–37
  duct tape [dŭkt/ tāp/] **181**–49
  electrical tape [ǐ lek/trǐ kəl tāp/] **181**–43
  masking tape [măs/kǐng tāp/] **181**–53
  packing tape [păk/ǐng tāp/] **183**–32
  sterile tape [stĕr/ əl tāp/] **117**–7
  tape measure [tāp mĕzh/ər] **100**–17, **181**–45

target [tär/gət] **231**–7

taste [tāst] **106**–D

tattoo [tă tōo/] **32**–18

tax / taxes [tăks] / [tăks/əz] **27**–8

taxi [tăk/sē] **150**–3

  hail a taxi [hāl/ ə tăk/sē] **152** ✦

  taxi driver [tăk/sē drī/vər] **152**–21

  taxi license [tăk/sē lī/səns] **152**–22

  taxi stand [tăk/sē stănd/] **152**–18

TB (tuberculosis) [tē/bē/] / [tŏo bür/kyə lō/səs] **111**–15

TDD [tē/dē/dē/] **15**–26

tea [tē] **79**–12, **81**–39, **81**–40

  teacup [tē/kŭp] **55**–6

  tea kettle [tē/ kĕt/l] **54**–21

  teapot [tē/pät/] **55**–16

  teaspoon [tē/spōon/] **75**–6, **83**–31

teach [tēch] **170**–Q

teacher [tē/chər] **5**–8, **6**–4, **22**–5

  teacher's aide [tē/chərz ād/] **5**–16

team [tēm] **145**–20, **229**–3

TEAM SPORTS [tēm/ spörts/] **229**

technical school [tĕk/nĭ kəl skōol/] **188**–5

technician [tĕk nĭsh/ən]

  computer technician

    [kəm pyōo/tər tĕk nĭsh/ən] **167**–19, **182**–12

  emergency medical technician (EMT)

    [ĭ mür/jən sē mĕd/ĭ kəl tĕk nish/ən] / [ē/ĕm/tē/]
    121–32

  medical records technician

    [mĕd/ĭ kəl rĕk/ərdz tĕk nish/ən] **168**–39

Technician [tĕk nĭsh/ən] **93**

teddy bear [tĕd/ē bĕr/] **37**–23

teen / teenager [tēn] / [tē/nā/jər] **31**–11

teething ring [tē/dhĭng ring/] **37**–25

teeth / tooth [tēth] / [tōoth] **106**–7

  toothache [tōoth/āk/] **110**–2

  toothbrush [tōoth/brŭsh/] **57**–21, **109**–22

  toothbrush holder [tōoth/brŭsh/ hōl/dər] **57**–22

  toothpaste [tōoth/pāst/] **109**–23

telemarketer [tĕl/ə mär/kə tər] **169**–60

TELEPHONE [tĕl/ə fōn/] **14**–**15**

Telephone Skills [tĕl/ə fōn/ skĭlz/] **171**

telescope [tĕl/ə skōp/] **205**–23

television / TV [tĕl/ə vĭzh/ən] / [tē/vē/] **56**–6

  big-screen TV [bĭg/skrēn/ tē/vē/] **50**–14

  flat panel TV [flăt/ păn/əl tē/vē/] **234**–7

  flat screen TV [flăt/ skrēn/ tē/vē/] **234**–7

  portable TV [pör/tə bəl tē/vē/] **234**–8

teller [tĕl/ər] **132**–1

Teller [tĕl/ər] **132**

Telling Time [tĕl/ĭng tīm/] **18**

temperature [tĕm/prə chər] **110**–8

  temperature gauge [tĕm/prə chər gāj/] **159**–30

Temperature [tĕm/prə chər] **13**

ten [tĕn] **16**

  ten after one [tĕn/ ăf/tər wŭn/] **18**–8

  ten dollars [tĕn/ däl/ərz] **26**–9

  10 percent [tĕn/ pər sĕnt/] **17**–12

  ten thousand [tĕn/ thow/zənd] **16**

  10-year-old girl [tĕn/yïr ōld/ gürl/] **31**–10

tenant [tĕn/ənt] **50**–6

TENANT MEETING [tĕn/ənt mē/tĭng] **64**–**65**

tennis [tĕn/əs] **228**–15

  table tennis [tā/bəl tĕn/əs] **228**–14

  tennis court [tĕn/əs kört/] **224**–6

  tennis racket [tĕn/əs răk/ət] **231**–2

  tennis shoes [tĕn/əs shōoz/] **95**–32

tent [tĕnt] **226**–10

tenth [tĕnth] **16**

Terminal [tür/mə nəl] **160**

termites [tür/mīts] **63**–22

term [türm] **139** ✦

Terms [türmz] **199**

terrified [tĕr/ə fīd/] **43** ✦

test [tĕst] **121**–30

  test booklet [tĕst/ bŏok/lət] **10**–1

  testing area [tĕs/tĭng ër/ē ə] **136**–2

  test tube [tĕst/ tōob/] **195**–42

Test [tĕst] **10**

text [tĕkst]

  textbook [tĕkst/bŏok/, tĕks/-] **7**–25

  text box [tĕkst/ bäks/, tĕks/-] **197**–13

  text message [tĕkst/ mĕs/ĭj, tĕks/-] **14**–19

thank [thăngk] **12**–E, **174**–N

Thanksgiving [thăngks gĭv/ĭng] **22**–17

theater [thē/ə tər] **126**–6, **127**–23

theft [thĕft] **142**–9

therapist [thĕr/ ə pĭst] **115**–12, **115**–14, **168**–45

therapy [thĕr/ ə pē] **115**–11, **115**–13

thermal undershirt [thür/məl ŭn/dər shürt/] **91**–2

thermometer [thər măm/ə tər] **118**–11

thick [thĭk] **23**–7

thighs [thīz] **70**–22, **106**–19

thimble [thĭm/bəl] **100**–15

thin [thĭn] **23**–8, **32**–9

THINGS [thĭngz] **23**

think [thĭnk] **191**–E

third [thürd] **16**

Third Floor [thürd/ flör/] **50**

thirsty [thür/stē] **42**–2

thirteen [thür/tēn/] **16**

  thirteen colonies [thür/tēn/ kä/lə nēz] **198**–1

thirteenth [thür/tēnth/] **16**

thirtieth [thür/tē əth] **16**

thirty [thür/tē] **16**

  35 mm camera

    [thür/tē fīv/ mĭl/ə mē/tər kăm/rə] **235**–21

this week [dhĭs/ wēk/] **20**–19

thorn [thörn] **211**–29

thread [thrĕd] **99**–23, **100**–11

three [thrē] **16**

  three piece suit [thrē/pēs/ sōot/] **88** ✦

  3-ring binder [thrē/ ring/ bīn/dər] **7**–27

  3/4 sleeved [thrē/kwör/tər slēv/] **96**–13

  three times a week [thrē/ tīmz/ ə wēk/] **20**–24

throat [thrōt] **107**–35, **110**–6, **111**–4

  throat lozenges [thrōt/ läz/ən jəz] **113**–30

through [thrōo] **153**–K

throw [thrō] **230**–C

  throw away [thrō/ ə wā/] **11**–N

  throw up [thrō/ ŭp/] **110**–E

throw pillow [thrō/ pĭl/ō] **56**–2

thumb [thŭm] **106**–16

thunderstorm [thŭn/dər störm/] **13**–16

Thursday [thürz/dā, –dē] **20**–12

tick [tĭk] **214**–27

ticket [tĭk/ət] **152**–15, **161**–19

  ticket agent [tĭk/ət ā/jənt] **160**–3

  ticket window [tĭk/ət wĭn/dō/] **152**–12

tidal wave [tīd/l wāv/] **145**–17

tide [tīd] **225** ✦

tie [tī] **88**–12, **89**–16, **92**–13, **229** ✦

tie [tī] **86**–A

tiger [tī/gər] **217**–37

tight [tīt] **97**–29

tights [tīts] **91**–19

tile [tīl] **57**–10, **178**–11, **178**–D

time [tīm]

  Alaska time [ə lăs/kə tīm/] **19**–28

  arrival time [ə rī/vəl tīm/] **161** ✦

  Atlantic time [ət lăn/tĭk tīm/] **19**–33

  Central time [sĕn/trəl tīm/] **19**–31

  daylight saving time [dā/līt/ sā/vĭng tīm/] **19**–25

  departure time [dĭ pär/chər tīm/] **161** ✦

  Eastern time [ē/stərn tīm/] **19**–32

  Hawaii-Aleutian time

    [hə wī/ē ə lōo/shən tīm/] **19**–27

  Mountain time [mown/tn tīm/] **19**–30

  Newfoundland time

    [nōo/fən lənd tīm/, –fənd–] **19**–34

  on time [än/ tīm/, ön/ tīm/] **19**–23, **161**–29

  Pacific time [pə sĭf/ĭk tīm/] **19**–29

  standard time [stăn/dərd tīm/] **19**–26

  three times a week [thrē tīmz/ ə wēk/] **20**–24

  time clock [tīm/ kläk/] **165**–7

Time [tīm] **18**

TIME [tīm] **18**–**19**

timer [tī/mər] **78**–18

Times of Day [tīmz/ əv dā/] **18**

Time Zones [tīm/ zōnz/] **19**

tire [tīr] **158**–5, **158**–23, **162**–F

tired [tīrd] **43**–32

title [tīt/l] **133**–14, **190**–5

toad [tōd] **212**–28

toast [tōst] **80**–4

toaster [tō/stər] **54**–6

  toaster oven [tō/stər ŭv/ən] **54**–15

today [tə dā/] **20**–5

toddler [täd/lər] **31**–8

toe [tō] **92**–6, **94**–23, **105**–10

  toenail [tō/nāl/] **106** ✦

Tofu [tō/fōo/] **77**

toggle bolt [täg/əl bōlt/] **180**–38

to-go box [tə gō/ bäks/] **82**–5

toilet [toy/lət] **57**–19

  toilet brush [toy/lət brŭsh/] **57**–18

  toilet paper [toy/lət pā/pər] **57**–17, **146**–13

token [tō/kən] **152**–10

tomatoes [tə mā/tōz] **69**–6

tomorrow [tə mär/ō, –mör/ō] **20**–6

tongs [tängz, töngz] **78**–23, **195**–44

tongue [tŭng] **106**–8

too [tōo]

  too big [tōo/ bĭg/] **97**–38

  too expensive [tōo/ ĭk spĕn/sĭv] **97**–44

  too small [tōo/ smöl/] **97**–37

Index

tool belt [tŏōl/ bĕlt/] **92**–3
TOOLS AND BUILDING SUPPLIES
   [tŏōlz/ ən bĭl/dĭng sə plĭz/] **180**–**181**
tooth / teeth [tŏōth] / [tĕth] **106**–7
   toothache [tŏōth/āk/] **110**–2
   toothbrush [tŏōth/brŭsh/] **57**–21, **109**–22
   toothbrush holder [tŏōth/brŭsh/ hōl/dər] **57**–22
   toothpaste [tŏōth/pāst/] **109**–23
top [tăp] **88**–7, **89**–24
torn [tŏrn] **97**–41
tornado [tŏr nā/dō] **145**–15
torso [tŏr/sō/] **106** ✦
tortoise [tŏr/təs] **213**–42
total [tōt/l] **27**–9
totebag [tōt/ băg/] **94**–19
touch [tŭch] **106**–E
towel [tow/əl]
   bath towel [băth/ tow/əl] **57**–14
   dish towel [dĭsh/ tow/əl] **61**–22
   hand towel [hănd/ tow/əl] **57**–15
   paper towels [pā/pər tow/əlz] **54**–3
   towel rack [tow/əl răk/] **57**–13
towelettes [tow/əl ĕts] **146**–12
tower [tow/ər] **196**–3
town [town] **52**–3
   town car [town/ kär/] **152**–20
   townhouse [town/hows/] **52**–6
tow truck [tō/ trŭk/] **156**–14
toy [toy]
   toy chest [toy/ chĕst/] **59**–16
   toy store [toy/ stŏr/] **130**–5
Toys and Games [toyz/ ən gāmz/] **59**
track [trăk] **5**–21, **152**–14
   track and field [trăk/ ən fēld/] **228**–18
tractor [trăk/tər] **177**–9
   tractor trailer [trăk/tər trā/lər] **156**–15
traffic light [trăf/ĭk līt/] **128**–8
TRAFFIC SIGNS [trăf/ĭk sīnz/] **154**
tragedy [trăj/ə dē] **237**–14
trailer [trā/lər] **156**–15, **156**–17
train [trān] **150**–7, **233**–27
training [trā/nĭng] **172**–2, **172**–5, **172**–7
   training pants [trā/nĭng pănts/] **37**–11
Training [trā/nĭng] **172**
Train Station [trān/ stā/shən] **152**
transcribe [trăn skrīb/] **171**–C
transfer [trăns für/, trăns/fər] **152**–5
transfer [trăns für/, trăns/fər] **171**–O
translate [trănz/lāt] **8**–C
translator [trănz/lā/tər, trăns/–] **168**–35
Transmission [trănz mĭsh/ən, trăns–] **159**
Transportation [trăns/pər tā/shən] **152**
TRANSPORTATION [trăns/pər tā/shən] **150**–**151**, **152**
trash [trăsh]
   trash bags [trăsh/ băgz/] **61**–24
   trash bin [trăsh/ bĭn/] **51**–23
   trash chute [trăsh/ shōōt/] **51**–26
travel [trăv/əl] **41**–P
travel agency [trăv/əl ā/jən sē] **131**–14
tray [trā] **55**–17, **83**–10
   tray table [trā tā/bəl] **161**–21
Tree [trē] **210**

trees [trēz] **208**–1, **239**–16
TREES AND PLANTS [trēz/ ən plănts/] **210**
trench coat [trĕnch/ kōt/] **90**–21
trial [trī/əl] **140**–5
triangle [trī/ăng/gəl] **193**–32
tricycle [trī/sĭ kəl] **224**–12
trigonometry [trĭg/ə năm/ə trē] **192**–18
trim [trĭm] **176**–B
trip [trĭp] **152**–16, **152**–17
tripe [trīp] **70**–8
tripod [trī/päd] **235**–25
trombone [träm bōn/] **238**–10
trout [trowt] **71**–1
trowel [trow/əl] **176**–10, **178**–13
truck [trŭk] **150**–5
   dump truck [dŭmp/trŭk/] **156**–19
   fire truck [fīr/ trŭk/] **144**–10
   garbage truck [gär/bĭj trŭk/] **127**–22
   hand truck [hănd/ trŭk/] **175**–11
   pickup truck [pĭk/ŭp trŭk/] **156**–12
   tank truck [tăngk/ trŭk/] **156**–20
   tow truck [tō/ trŭk/] **156**–14
   truck driver [trŭk/ drī/vər] **169**–61
TRUCKS [trŭks] **156**
trumpet [trŭm/pət] **238**–11
Trunk [trŭngk] **158**
trunks [trŭngks] **158**–11, **210**–4, **217**–47
   swimming trunks [swĭm/ĭng trŭngks/] **90**–22
try on [trī/ŏn] **95**–C
TSA agent [tē/ĕs/ā/ ā/jənt] **160**–5
T-shirt [tē/shürt/] **86**–4
tsunami [sōō nä/ mē/, tsōō–] **145**–17
tub [tŭb]
   bathtub [băth/tŭb/] **57**–2
tuba [tōō/bə] **238**–12
tube [tōōb] **74**–12, **74**–24, **195**–42
tuberculosis (TB)
   [tōō bür/kyə lō/səs] / [tē/bē/] **111**–15
Tuesday [tōōz/dā, –dē] **20**–10
tulip [tōō/ləp] **211**–11
tuna [tōō/nə] **71**–7, **72**–19, **212**–8
tuner [tōō/nər] **234**–13
turbulence [tür/byə ləns] **161**–22
turkey [tür/kē] **70**–17, **239**–14
   roasted turkey [rōs/təd tür/kē] **76**–4
   smoked turkey [smōkt/ tür/kē] **71**–25
turn [türn] **154**–5, **154**–7, **154**–8
   turn signal [türn/ sĭg/nəl] **158**–6, **159**–34
   turnstile [türn/stīl/] **152**–8
   turntable [türn/tā/bəl] **234**–12
turn [türn]
   turn in [türn/ ĭn/] **191**–M
   turn left [türn/ lĕft/] **155**–C
   turn off [türn/ ŏf/] **11**–P, **160**–I, **174**–G, **219**–G
   turn on [türn/ ŏn/, –än/] **11**–B
   turn right [türn/ rīt/] **155**–B
turnips [tür/nəps] **69**–16
turquoise [tür/koyz, –kwoyz] **24**–9
turtle [tür/tl] **213**–43
   turtleneck [tür/tl nĕk/] **96**–9
tusk [tŭsk] **217**–48
tuxedo [tŭk sē/dō] **89**–17

TV Programs [tē/vē/ prō/grămz] **236**
TV / television [tē/vē/] / [tĕl/ə vĭzh/ən] **56**–6
   big-screen TV [bĭg/skrēn/ tē/vē/] **50**–14
   flat panel TV [flăt/ păn/əl tē/vē/] **234**–7
   flat screen TV [flăt/ skrēn/ tē/ vē/] **234**–7
   portable TV [pŏr/tə bəl tē/vē/] **234**–8
tweezers [twē/zərz] **117**–4
twelfth [twĕlfth] **16**
twelve [twĕlv] **16**
twentieth [twĕn/tē əth] **16**
twenty [twĕn/tē] **16**
   twenty after one [twĕn/tē ăf/tər wŭn/] **18**–10
   twenty dollars [twĕn/tē däl/ərz] **26**–10
   twenty-first [twĕn/tē fürst/] **16**
   twenty-five [twĕn/tē fīv/] **16**
   25 percent [twĕn/fĭv/ pər sĕnt/] **17**–11
   twenty-four [twĕn/tē fŏr] **16**
   twenty-one [twĕn/tē wŭn/] **16**
   twenty-three [twĕn/tē thrē/] **16**
   twenty to two [twĕn/tē tə tōō/] **18**–12
   twenty-two [twĕn/tē tōō/] **16**
twice a week [twīs/ ə wēk/] **20**–23
twig [twĭg] **210**–1
twins [twĭnz] **28**–1
two [tōō] **16**
   2-door car [tōō/dŏr kär/] **156**–2
   two-story house [tōō/stŏr/ē hows/] **52** ✦
   two-way radio [tōō/wā rā/dē ō] **179**–22
   2 x 4 (two by four) [tōō/ bī/ fŏr/] **181**–19
type [tīp] **170**–R, **196**–A
   type a letter [tīp/ə lĕt/ər] **171**–A
   type the message [tīp/ dhə mĕs/ĭj] **197**–E
   type the subject [tīp/ dhə sŭb/jĭkt] **197**–D
   type your password [tīp/ yər păs/würd/] **197**–A
Types of Health Problems
   [tīps/ əv hĕlth/ präb/ləmz] **115**
Types of Job Training [tīps/ əv jäb/ trā/nĭng] **172**
Types of Material [tīps/ əv mə tïr/ē əl] **99**
Types of Math [tīps/ əv măth/] **192**
Types of Medication [tīps/ əv mĕd/ə kā/shən] **113**
Types of Movies [tīps/ əv mōō/vēz] **237**
Types of Music [tīps/ əv myōō/zĭk] **237**
Types of TV Programs [tīps/ əv tē/vē/ prō/grămz] **236**
ugly [ŭg/lē] **23**–22
umbrella [ŭm brĕl/ə] **90**–17, **225**–14
umpire [ŭm/pīr] **229** ✦
uncle [ŭng/kəl] **34**–8
uncomfortable [ŭn kŭmf/tə bəl, –tər–] **42**–9
unconscious [ŭn/kän/shəs] **116**–A
under [ŭn/dər] **25**–10, **153**–A
   long underwear [lŏng/ ŭn/dər wër/] **91**–3
   thermal undershirt [thür/məl ŭn/dər shürt/] **91**–2
   underexposed [ŭn/dər ĭk spōzd/] **235**–35
   underpants [ŭn/dər pănts/] **91**–14
   undershirt [ŭn/dər shürt/] **91**–1
underline [ŭn/dər līn/] **9**–S
Under the Hood [ŭn/dər dhə hōōd/] **158**
Underwear [ŭn/dər wër/] **91**
UNDERWEAR AND SLEEPWEAR
   [ŭn/dər wër/ ən slēp/wër/] **91**
undress [ən drĕs/] **36**–E

278

unfurnished apartment
[ŭn/fŭr nĭsht ə pärt/ mənt] **48**–4
uniform [yōō/nə förm/] **88**–10, **231**–16
Unisex Socks [yōō/nə sĕks/ säks/] **91**
Unisex Underwear [yōō/nə sĕks/ ŭn/dər wër] **91**
universal remote [yōō/nə vŭr/səl rĭ mōt/] **234**–9
UNIVERSE [yōō/nə vŭrs/] **205**
university [yōō/nə vŭr/sə tē] **188**–7
unload [ŭn lōd/] **101**–E
unpack [ŭn păk/] **49**–N
unraveling [ŭn răv/əl ĭng] **97**–43
unripe [ŭn rīp/] **68**–31
unscented [ŭn sĕn/təd] **108** ✦
unscramble [ŭn skrăm/bəl] **9**–W
up [ŭp]
    buckle up [bŭk/əl ŭp/] **36**–L
    clean up [klēn/ ŭp/] **147**–M
    cut up [kŭt/ ŭp/] **77**–I
    eggs sunny-side up [ĕgz/ sŭn/ē sīd/ ŭp/] **76**–10
    get up [gĕt/ ŭp/] **38**–B
    hang up [hăng/ ŭp/] **15**–D, **101**–H
    look up [lōōk/ ŭp/] **8**–A
    pick up [pĭk/ ŭp/] **6**–I, **11**–E, **38**–M
    pop-up ad [päp/ ŭp ăd/] **197**–9
    set up [sĕt/ ŭp/] **173**–I
    stand up [stănd/ ŭp/] **6**–D
    stopped up [stäpt/ ŭp/] **63**–19
    throw up [thrō/ ŭp/] **110**–E
    wake up [wāk/ ŭp/] **38**–A
    walk up [wök/ ŭp/] **153**–C
upright seat [ŭp/rīt/ sēt/] **161**–28
upset [ŭp sĕt/] **43**–28
upstairs [ŭp/stërz/] **51** ✦
Uranus [yŏor/ə nəs, yŏo rā/nəs] **205**–7
urban area [ŭr/bən ër/ē ə] **52**–1
urchin [ŭr/chən] **212**–21
URL [yōō/är/ĕl/] **197**–4
U.S. [yōō/ĕs/]
    U.S. Capitol [yōō/ĕs/ kă/pət əl] **138**–1
    U.S. route [yōō/ĕs/ rōōt/, –rowt/] **154**–17
USB port [yōō/ĕs/ bē/ pört/] **196**–7
use [yōōz]
    use a cash register [yōōz/ə kăsh/ rĕj/ə stər] **170**–S
    use a credit card [yōōz/ə krĕ/dət kärd/] **27**–B
    use a debit card [yōōz/ə dĕ/bət kärd/] **27**–C
    use a gift card [yōōz/ ə gĭft/ kärd/] **27**–E
    use deodorant [yōōz/dē ō/dər ənt] **108**–C
    use energy-efficient bulbs
        [yōōz/ ĕn/ər jē ĭ fĭ/shənt bŭlbz] **219**–H
    use punctuation [yōōz/ pŭngk/chōō ā/shən] **190**–C
Used Car [yōōzd/ kär/] **157**
used clothing [yōōzd/ klō/dhĭng] **102**–2
U.S. HISTORY [yōō/ĕs/ hĭs/tə rē] **198**
U.S. NATIONAL PARKS
    [yōō/ĕs năsh/ə nəl pärks/] **220**–**221**
utensils [yōō tĕn/səlz] **79**–19
utility / utilities [yōō tĭl/ə tē] / [yōō tĭl/ə tēz]
    48–5, **156**–7
U-turn [yōō/tŭrn/] **154**–5
vacancy sign [vā/kən sē sīn/] **50**–7
vacation [vā kā/shən] **22**–6
vaccination [văk/sə nā/shən] **114** ✦

vacuum [văk/yōōm]
    vacuum cleaner [văk/yōōm klē/nər] **61**–10
    vacuum cleaner attachments
        [văk/yōōm klē/nər ə tăch/mənts] **61**–11
    vacuum cleaner bag
        [văk/yōōm klē/nər băg/] **61**–12
    vacuum [văk/yōōm] **60**–H
valley [văl/ē] **204**–17
valuables [văl/yə bəlz, –yə wə–] **132**–8
valve [vălv/] **146**–4
van [văn] **156**–13, **156**–18
vandalism [văn/də lĭz/əm] **142**–1
vanity plate [vă/nə tē plāt/] **136** ✦
variable [vër/ē ə bəl] **192**–12
vase [vās, vāz, văz] **55**–23
vault [völt] **132**–6
VCR [vē/sē/är/] **102**–7
veal cutlets [vēl/ kŭt/ləts] **70**–6
Vegetable [vĕj/tə bəl] **77**
vegetables [vĕj/tə bəlz] **66**–8, **72**–27, **81**–32
    vegetable garden [vĕj/tə bəl gär/dn] **53**–27, **177**–14
    vegetable peeler [vĕj/tə bəl pē/lər] **78**–15
VEGETABLES [vĕj/tə bəlz] **69**
vegetarian [vĕj/ə tër/ē ən] **70** ✦
vehicles [vē/ĭ kəlz] **124**–4, **156**–7, **156**–10
vein [vān] **107**–37
velvet [vĕl/vət] **99**–10
vending machine [vĕn/dĭng mə shēn/] **152**–9
vendors [vĕn/dərz] **84**–7, **129**–29
ventilation mask [vĕnt/əl ā/shən măsk/] **92**–7
Venus [vē/nəs] **205**–2
verdict [vŭr/dĭkt] **141**–14
vertebrates [vŭr/ tə brəts] **194**–13
vest [vĕst] **89**–15
    down vest [down/ vĕst/] **90**–14
    Hi-Visibility safety vest
        [hī/vĭz/ə bĭl/ə tē săf/tē vĕst/] **92**–6
    life vest [līf/ vĕst/] **161**–25, **226**–14
Veterans Day [vĕt/ər ənz dā/] **22**–16
veterinarian [vĕt/ər ə nër/ē ən] **169**–62
vice president [vīs/ prĕz/ə dənt] **138**–9
victim [vĭk/təm] **142**–10
video [vĭd/ē ō]
    videocassette [vĭd/ē ō kə sĕt/] **133**–18
    video game console [vĭd/ē ō găm/ kän/sōl/] **232**–3
    video game control [vĭd/ē ō găm/ kän trōl/] **232**–4
    video player [vĭd/ē ō plā ər] **197**–11
    video store [vĭd/ē ō stör/] **129**–20
    videotape [vĭd/ē ō tāp/] **240**–A
view [vyōō]
    rearview mirror [rîr/vyōō/ mîr/ər] **159**–35
    sideview mirror [sīd/vyōō/ mîr/ər] **158**–3
village [vĭ/lĭj] **52**–3
vine [vīn] **210**–22
vineyard [vĭn/yərd] **177**–16
violence [vī/ləns, vī/ə–] **142**–4
violet [vī/ə lət, vī/lət] **24**–8, **211**–23
violin [vī/ə lĭn/] **238**–6
virus [vī/rəs] **111**–17
vise [vīs] **180**–26
vision [vĭ/zhən]
    vision exam [vĭ/zhən ĭg zăm/] **136**–6
    vision problems [vĭ/zhən präb/ləmz] **115**–1

Visit [vĭ/zət] **119**
visor [vī zər] **179**–12
vital signs monitor [vīt/l sīnz/ män/ə tər] **121**–26
vitamins [vī/tə mənz] **113**–17
v-neck [vē/nĕk/] **96**–8
vocational [vō kā/shə nəl]
    vocational school [vō kā/shə nəl skōōl/] **188**–5
    vocational training [vō kā/shə nəl trā/nĭng] **172**–5
voice message [voys mĕs/ĭj] **14**–18
volcanic eruption [väl kăn/ĭk ĭ rŭp/shən] **145**–16
volleyball [väl/ē böl/] **229**–14, **231**–3
Volume [väl/yəm, –yōōm] **75**, **193**
volunteer [väl/ən tîr/] **121**–17
volunteer [väl/ən tîr/] **41**–Q
vomit [väm/ət] **110**–E
vote [vōt] **140**–A
waffles [wä/fəlz, wö/–] **80**–8
wages [wā/jĭz] **165**–12
wagon [wä/gən] **156**–6
waist [wāst]
    waist apron [wāst/ ā/prən] **93**–30
    waistband [wāst/bănd/] **100**–5
wait [wāt] **94**–B, **128**–B, **170**–T
waiter [wā/tər] **82**–8
    headwaiter [hĕd/wā/tər] **185**–12
Waiting Room [wā/tĭng rōōm/] **118**
waitress [wā/trəs] **83**–9
wait staff [wāt/ stăf/] **185** ✦
wake up [wāk/ ŭp/] **38**–A
walk [wök] **53**–2
    crosswalk [krös/wök/] **128**–15
    walk-in freezer [wök/ĭn frē/zər] **185**–3
walk [wök]
    walk a dog [wök ə dög/] **129**–F
    walk down [wök/ down/] **153**–D
    walk to class [wök/ tə klăs/] **11**–C
    walk up [wök/ ŭp/] **153**–C
    walk with a friend [wök/ wĭth ə frĕnd/] **143**–A
walker [wö/kər] **113**–11
wall [wöl] **56**–10, **194**–5
    drywall [drī/wöl/] **178**–19
    wallpaper [wöl/pā/pər] **59**–8
wallet [wä/lət, wö/–] **94**–13
walrus [wöl/rəs] **213**–32
war [wör] **199**–10
    Revolutionary War [rĕ/və lōō/shə nër/ē wör/] **198**–8
warehouse [wër/hows/] **175**–7
warm [wörm] **13**–4
    warm clothes [wörm/ klōz/] **146**–6
warning label [wör/nĭng lā/bəl] **112**–8
Warnings [wör/nĭngz] **112**
wash [wäsh, wösh]
    mouthwash [mowth/wäsh/, –wösh/–] **109**–25
    washcloth [wäsh/klöth/, wösh/–] **57**–4
wash [wäsh, wösh]
    wash clothes [wäsh/ klōz/, wösh/–] **219**–K
    wash hair [wäsh/ hër/, wösh/–] **108**–E
    wash the dishes [wäsh/ dhə dĭsh/əz, wösh/–] **60**–M
    wash the windows
        [wäsh/ dhə wĭn/dōz, wösh/–] **60**–I
washer [wä/shər, wö/–] **50**–12, **101**–3, **180**–37
    dishwasher [dĭsh/wäsh/ər, –wö–] **54**–8, **185**–2

Index

washing [wä′shǐng, wö′–] **61**–21

wasp [wäsp, wösp] **214**–17

waste [wāst] **121**–31, **218**–12

    wastebasket [wāst′bǎs′kət] **57**–26

watch [wäch, wöch] **94**–16

watch [wäch, wöch] **39**–X, **147**–C

water [wö′tər] **209**–3, **225**–1

    body of water [bäd′ē əv wö′tər] **204** ✦

    bottled water [bät′ld wö′tər] **146**–11

    cold water [kōld′ wö′tər] **57**–7

    hot water [hät′ wö′tər] **57**–8

    hot water bottle [hät′ wö′tər böt′l] **113**–15

    watercolor [wö′tər kŭl′ər] **233**–21

    waterfall [wä′tər föl′] **204**–2

    water fountain [wö′tər fown′tn] **224**–9

    water glass [wö′tər glǎs′] **83**–22

    watermelons [wö′tər mĕl′ənz] **68**–18

    water pollution [wö′tər pə lōō′shən] **218**–14

    water polo [wö′tər pō′lō] **229**–15

    waterskiing [wö′tər skē′ǐng] **227**–7

water [wö′tər] **176**–F

WATER SPORTS [wö′tər spörts′] **227**

wave [wāv] **145**–17, **225**–17

wave [wāv] **2**–F

wavy hair [wā′vē hër′] **33**–10

way [wā]

    hallway [häl′wā′] **184**–18

    one way [wŭn′ wā′] **154**–3

    one-way trip [wŭn′wā′ trǐp′] **152**–16

    two-way radio [tōō′wā′ rā′dē ō] **179**–22

    wrong way [röng′ wā′] **154**–2

Ways to Conserve Energy and Resources

    [wāz′ tə kən sürv′ ĕn′ər jē n rē′sör′səz,

    –rĭ sör′səz] **219**

Ways to Get Well [wāz′ tə gĕt′ wĕl′] **114**

Ways to Pay [wāz′ tə pā′] **27**

Ways to Serve Eggs [wāz′ tə sürv′ ĕgz′] **76**

Ways to Serve Meat and Poultry

    [wāz′ tə sürv′ mēt′ n pōl′trē′] **76**

Ways to Stay Well [wāz′ tə stā′ wĕl′] **114**

Ways to Succeed [wāz′tə sək sēd′] **10**

weak signal [wēk′ sĭg′nəl] **14**–12

WEATHER [wĕdh′ər] **13**

Weather Conditions [wĕdh′ər kən dĭsh′ənz] **13**

Weather Map [wĕdh′ər măp′] **13**

webcam [wĕb′kăm′] **196**–12

Webpage [wĕb′pāg′] **197**

website address [wĕb′sīt ə drĕs′] **197**–4

wedding [wĕ′dĭng] **22**–2

Wednesday [wĕnz′dā, –dē] **20**–11

weed [wēd]

    seaweed [sē′ wēd′] **225** ✦

    weed eater [wēd′ ē′tər] **176**–12

    weed whacker [wēd′ wăk′ər] **176**–12

weed [wēd] **176**–G

week [wēk] **20**–15

    last week [lăst′ wēk′] **20**–18

    next week [nĕkst′ wēk′] **20**–20

    once a week [wŭns′ ə wēk′] **20**–22

    this week [dhĭs′ wēk′] **20**–19

    three times a week [thrē′ tīmz′ ə wēk′] **20**–24

    twice a week [twīs′ ə wēk′] **20**–23

weekdays [wēk′dāz′] **20**–16

weekend [wēk′ĕnd′] **20**–17

Week [wēk] **20**

weigh [wā] **75**–B

weight [wāt] **32**–8

Weight [wāt] **32, 75**

weightlifting [wāt′lĭf′tĭng] **228**–16

weights [wāts] **231**–22

WEIGHTS AND MEASUREMENTS

    [wāts′ ən mĕzh′ər mənts] **75**

welder [wĕl′dər] **169**–63

well [wĕl] **42**–14

Well [wĕl] **114**

west [wĕst] **155**–2

western [wĕs′tərn] **237**–15

wet [wĕt] **101**–17

    wet suit [wĕt′ sōōt′] **225**–4

whacker [wăk′ər] **176**–12

whale [wāl] **213**–29

wheat [wēt] **177**–2

wheat bread [wēt′ brĕd′] **71**–19

wheel [wēl] **159**–26

    wheelbarrow [wēl′băr′ō] **176**–3

    wheelchair [wēl′chër′] **113**–9

    wheel cover [wēl′ kŭv′ər] **158**–9

whisk [wĭsk] **78**–21

whiskers [wĭs′kərz] **216**–18

white [wīt] **24**–14

    whiteboard [wīt′börd′] **6**–3

    white bread [wīt′ brĕd′] **71**–18

    White House [wīt′ hows′] **138**–7

whole salmon [hōl′ săm′ən] **71**–3

wide [wīd] **97**–36

widow [wĭd′ō] **41** ✦

widower [wĭd′ō ər] **41** ✦

width [wĭdth, wĭtth] **17**–19

wife [wīf] **34**–12

    ex-wife [ĕks′ wīf′] **35** ✦

    former wife [för′mər wīf′] **35** ✦

wild [wīld] **215** ✦

wildlife [wīld′līf′] **220**–3

willow [wĭl′ō] **210**–13

win [wĭn] **229** ✦

wind [wĭnd]

    windbreaker [wĭnd′brā′kər] **90**–24

    wind power [wĭnd′ pow′ər] **218**–2

    windshield [wĭnd′ shēld′] **158**–1

    windshield wipers [wĭnd′shēld/wī′pərz] **158**–2

    windsurfing [wĭnd′sür′fĭng] **227**–10, **227** ✦

window [wĭn′dō] **47**–11, **56**–17, **136**–7

    drive-thru window [drīv′thrōō′ wĭn′dō] **128**–11

    ticket window [tĭk′ət wĭn′dō] **152**–12

    window pane [wĭn′dō pān′] **178**–16

windy [wĭn′dē] **13**–18

wine glass [wīn′ glǎs′] **83**–23

wing [wĭng] **70**–20, **214**–1

winter [wĭn′tər] **21**–40

    winter scarf [wĭn′tər/skärf′] **90**–5

WINTER AND WATER SPORTS

    [wĭn′tər ən wö′tər spörts′] **227**

wipe [wīp] **60**–O

wipers [wī′pərz] **158**–2

wipes [wīps] **37**–15, **61**–23

wire [wīr] **181**–13

    wire stripper [wīr′ strĭp′ər] **181**–42

wireless headset [wīr′ləs hĕd′sĕt] **14**–14

wiring [wīr′ĭng] **186**–7

withdraw [wĭdh drö′, wĭth–] **132**–F

witness [wĭt′nəs] **141**–11

wolf [wŏolf] **216**–5

woman [wŏom′ən] **30**–2

women [wĭ′mən] **30**–3

Women's Socks [wĭ′mənz säks′] **91**

Women's Underwear [wĭ′mənz ŭn′dər wër′] **91**

wood [wŏod] **178**–18

    plywood [plī′wŏod] **178**–17

    redwood [rĕd′wŏod] **210**–18

    wood floor [wŏod′ flör′] **58**–21

    woodpecker [wŏod′pĕk′ər] **214**–8

    wood screw [wŏod′ skrōō′] **180**–33

    wood stain [wŏod′ stān′] **181**–24

    woodworking kit [wŏod′wür′kĭng kĭt′] **232**–14

wooden spoon [wŏod′n spōōn′] **78**–9

Woodwinds [wŏod′wĭndz′] **238**

wool [wŏol] **61**–5, **98**–3

word [würd] **190**–1

word problem [würd′ prä′bləm] **192**–11

Words [wördz] **8**

work [würk′] **121**–30, **154**–16

    workbook [würk′bŏok′] **7**–26

    work gloves [würk′ glŭvz′] **92**–17, **179**–17

    work light [würk′ līt′] **181**–44

    work pants [würk′ pănts′] **92**–5

    work shirt [würk′ shürt′] **92**–2

work [würk′] **8**–I, **10**–J, **38**–K

WORK [würk′] **186**–187

Work Clothes [würk′ klōz′] **88**

worker [wür′kər]

    careful worker [kër′fəl wür′kər] **179**–2

    careless worker [kër′ləs wür′kər] **179**–1

    childcare worker [chīld′kër wür′kər] **166**–16

    construction worker

        [kən strŭk′shən wür′kər] **178**–1

    dockworker [däk′wür′kər] **167**–23

    factory worker [făk′tə rē wür′kər, –trē] **175**–3

    farmworker [färm′wür′kər] **177**–8

    food preparation worker

        [fōod′ prĕp ə rā′shən wür′kər] **185**–4

    garment worker [gär′mənt wür′kər] **167**–29

    postal worker [pō′stəl wür′kər] **169**–49

    sanitation worker [săn′ə tā′shən wür′kər] **169**–54

    social worker [sō′shəl wür′kər] **169**–57

Worker [wür′kər] **92, 93**

working [wür′kĭng]

    not working [nät′ wür′kĭng] **62**–1

    woodworking kit [wŏod′wür′kĭng kĭt] **232**–14

Working with a Partner [wür′kĭng wĭth ə pärt′nər] **8**

Working with Your Classmates

    [wür′kĭng wĭth yər klăs′māts′] **8**

work out [würk′ owt′] **230**–N

WORKPLACE [würk′ plās′] **164**–165

WORKPLACE CLOTHING

    [würk′ plās′ klō′dhĭng] **92**–93

world [würld]
    world languages [würld/ läng/gwĭ jəz] **189**–13
    world music [würld/ myoo/zĭk] **237**–32
WORLD MAP [würld/măp/] **202**–**203**
WORLD HISTORY [würld hĭs/tə rē] **199**
worm [würm] **212**–23
worried [wür/ēd] **42**–13
wrap [răp] **72**–24
wrap [răp] **240**–F
wrench [rĕnch] **158**–22, **181**–47, **181**–48
wrestling [rĕs/lĭng] **228**–17
wrinkled [rĭng/kəld] **101**–19
wrist [rĭst] **106**–14
    wristwatch [rĭst/wäch/, –wöch/] **94**–16
write [rīt]
    write a check [rīt/ ə chĕk/] **27**–D
    write a cover letter [rīt/ ə kŭv/ər lĕt/ər] **173**–G
    write a final draft [rīt/ ə fi/nəl drăft/] **191**–L
    write a first draft [rīt/ ə fürst/ drăft/] **191**–H
    write a note [rīt/ ə nōt/] **135**–A
    write a resume [rīt/ ə rĕ/zə mä/] **173**–F
    write a thank-you note
        [rīt/ ə thăngk/ yoo nōt/] **174**–O
    write back [rīt/ băk/] **135**–H
    write on the board [rīt/ ön dhə börd/] **6**–E
writer [rī/tər] **169**–64
Writing and Revising [rī/tĭng ən rĭ vī/ zĭng] **191**
Writing Process [rī/tĭng prä/sĕs] **191**
Writing Rules [rī/tĭng rōolz] **190**
wrong way [röng/ wā/] **154**–2
xylophone [zī/lə fōn/] **238**–15
yard [yärd]
    courtyard [kört/ yärd/] **51**–21
    yardstick [yärd/stĭk/] **181**–16
YARD [yärd] **53**
yarn [yärn] **233**–22
year [yïr] **20**–4, **31**–9, **31**–10
Year [yïr] **21**
yellow [yĕl/ō] **24**–2
yesterday [yĕs/tər dā/, –dē] **20**–7
yield [yēld] **154**–9
yoga [yō/gə] **122**–4
yogurt [yō/gərt] **72**–22
young [yŭng] **32**–1
Your First License [yər fürst/ lī/səns] **137**
YOUR HEALTH [yər hĕlth/] **114**–**115**
zebra [zē/brə] **217**–33
zero [zïr/ō] **16**
ZIP code [zĭp/ kōd/] **4**–9
zipper [zĭp/ər] **99**–25
Zones [zōnz] **19**
zoo [zoo] **222**–1
zoom lens [zoom/ lĕnz/] **235**–23
zucchini [zoo kē/nē] **69**–25

Geographical Index

Continents

Africa [ăf/rĭ kə] **202–5**
Antarctica [ănt ärk/tĭ kə, –är/tĭ–] **202–7**
Asia [ā/zhə] **202–4**
Australia [ö strāl/yə] **202–6**
Europe [yŏor/əp] **202–3**
North America [nörth/ ə mĕr/ə kə] **200–201, 202–1**
South America [sowth/ ə mĕr/ə kə] **202–2**

Countries and other locations

Afghanistan [ăf găn/ə stăn/] **203**
Albania [ăl bā/nē ə] **203**
Aleutian Islands [ə lōō/shən ī/ləndz] **200, 203**
Algeria [ăl jïr/ē ə] **203**
American Samoa [ə mĕr/ə kən sə mō/ə] **202**
Andaman Islands [ăn/də mən ī/ləndz] **203**
Angola [ăng gō/lə] **203**
Argentina [är/jən tē/nə] **202**
Armenia [är mē/nē ə] **203**
Austria [ö/strē ə] **203**
Azerbaijan [ăz/ər bī jän/] **203**
Azores [ā/zörz] **202**
Baffin Island [băf/ən ī/lənd] **200**
Bahamas [bə hä/məz] **200, 202**
Bahrain [bä rān/] **203**
Bangladesh [băng/glə dĕsh/, băng/–] **203**
Banks Island [bănks/ ī/lənd] **200**
Belarus [bē/lə rōōs/, byĕl/ə–] **203**
Belgium [bĕl/jəm] **203**
Belize [bə lēz/] **201, 202**
Benin [bə nĭn/, –nēn/] **203**
Bermuda Islands [bər myōō/də ī/ ləndz] **200, 202**
Bhutan [bōō tän/] **203**
Bolivia [bə lĭv/ē ə] **202**
Bosnia [băz/nē ə] **203**
Botswana [bät swä/nə] **203**
Brazil [brə zĭl/] **202**
Brunei [brōō nī/] **203**
Bulgaria [bŭl gĕr/ē ə] **203**
Burkina Faso [bər kē/nə fä/sō] **203**
Burma [bür/mə] **203**
Burundi [bōō rōōn/dē] **203**
Cambodia [kăm bō/dē ə] **203**
Cameroon [kăm/ə rōōn/] **203**
Canada [kăn/ə də] **200, 202**
Canary Islands [kə nĕr/ē ī/ ləndz] **203**
Cape Verde [kāp/ vürd/] **202**
Central African Republic
    [sĕn/trəl ăf/rĭ kən rĭ pŭb/lĭk] **203**
Chad [chăd] **203**
Chile [chĭl/ē] **202**
China [chī/nə] **203**
Colombia [kə lŭm/bē ə] **202**
Comoros [kăm/ə rōz] **203**
Congo [käng/gō] **203**
Cook Islands [kŏok/ ī/ləndz] **202**
Corsica [kör/sĭ kə] **203**
Costa Rica [kōs/tə rē/kə, käs/–] **201, 202**
Croatia [krō ā/shə] **203**
Cuba [kyōō/bə] **201, 202**
Cyprus [sī/prəs] **203**
Czech Republic [chĕk/ rĭ pŭb/lĭk] **203**

Democratic Republic of the Congo
    [dĕm/ə krăt/ĭk rĭ pŭb/lĭk əv dhə käng/gō] **203**
Denmark [dĕn/märk] **203**
Devon Island [dĕv/ən ī/lənd] **200**
Djibouti [jĭ bōō/tē] **203**
Dominican Republic [də mĭn/ĭ kən rĭ pŭb/lĭk] **201, 202**
Ecuador [ĕk/wə dör/] **202**
Egypt [ē/jĭpt] **203**
Ellesmere Island [ĕl/əs mïr/ ī/lənd] **200**
El Salvador [ĕl săl/və dör/] **201, 202**
Equatorial Guinea [ē/kwə tör/ē əl gĭn/ē, ĕk/wə–] **203**
Eritrea [ĕr/ə trē/ə] **203**
Estonia [ĕ stō/nē ə] **203**
Ethiopia [ē/thē ō/pē ə] **203**
Federated States of Micronesia
    [fĕ/də rā/təd stāts/ əv mī/krə nē/zhə] **203**
Fiji [fē/jē] **203**
Finland [fĭn/lənd] **203**
France [frăns] **203**
Franz Josef Land [fränz/ yō/səf länd/] **203**
French Guiana [frĕnch/ gē ăn/ə, –ä/nə] **202**
French Polynesia [frĕnch/ păl/ə nē/zhə] **202**
Gabon [gă bôn/] **203**
Galápagos Islands [gə lä pə gōs ī/ləndz] **202**
Gambia [găm/bē ə] **203**
Georgia [jör/jə] **203**
Germany [jür/mə nē] **203**
Ghana [gä/nə] **203**
Greater Antilles [grā/tər ăn tĭl/ēz] **201**
Greece [grēs] **203**
Greenland [grēn/lənd, –lănd/] **200, 202**
Guam [gwäm] **203**
Guatemala [gwä/tə mä/lə] **201, 202**
Guinea [gĭn/ē] **203**
Guinea-Bissau [gĭn/ē bĭ sow/] **203**
Guyana [gī ăn/ə] **202**
Haiti [hā/tē] **201, 202**
Hawaiian Islands [hə wī/ən ī/ləndz] **200, 202**
Hispaniola [hĭs/pən yō/lə] **201**
Honduras [hän dŏor/əs] **201, 202**
Hong Kong [häng/ käng/] **203**
Hungary [hŭng/gə rē] **203**
Iceland [īs/lənd] **203**
India [ĭn/dē ə] **203**
Indonesia [ĭn/də nē/zhə] **203**
Iran [ĭ răn/, ī răn/] **203**
Iraq [ĭ räk/, ī räk/] **203**
Ireland [īr/lənd] **203**
Israel [ĭz/rē əl, –rā–] **203**
Italy [ĭt/l ē] **203**
Ivory Coast [īv/rē kōst/] **203**
Jamaica [jə mā/kə] **201, 202**
Japan [jə păn/] **203**
Jordan [jör/dn] **203**
Kazakhstan [kä/zäk stän] **203**
Kenya [kĕn/yə, kēn/–] **203**
Kiribati [kĭr/ə bäs/] **203**
Kuwait [kōō wāt/] **203**
Kyrgyzstan [kir/gĭ stän/, –stän/] **203**
Laos [lows, lä/ōs] **203**
Latvia [lăt/vē ə] **203**
Lebanon [lĕb/ə nən, –nän/] **203**

Lesotho [lə sō/tō, –sōō/tōō] **203**
Lesser Antilles [lĕ/sər ăn tĭl/ēz] **201, 202**
Liberia [lī bïr/ē ə] **203**
Libya [lĭb/ē ə] **203**
Lithuania [lĭth/ōō ā/nē ə] **203**
Luxembourg [lŭk/səm bürg/] **203**
Macedonia [măs/ə dō/nē ə] **203**
Madagascar [măd/ə găs/kər] **203**
Madeira Islands [mə dïr/ə ī/ləndz] **203**
Malawi [mə lä/wē] **203**
Malaysia [mə lā/zhə] **203**
Maldives [mōl/dēvz, mäl/–] **203**
Mali [mä/lē] **203**
Malta [möl/tə] **203**
Marshall Islands [mär/shəl ī/ləndz] **203**
Mauritania [mör/ə tā/nē ə] **203**
Mauritius [mö rĭsh/əs] **203**
Mexico [mĕk/sĭ kō/] **200, 201, 202**
Moldova [mōl dō/və, mäl–] **203**
Monaco [măn/ə kō/] **203**
Mongolia [mäng gō/lē ə] **203**
Montenegro [măn/tə nē/grō, –nĕ/–] **203**
Morocco [mə räk/ō] **203**
Mozambique [mō/zəm bēk/] **203**
Namibia [nə mĭb/ē ə] **203**
Nepal [nə pöl/, –päl/] **203**
Netherlands [nĕdh/ər ləndz] **203**
New Caledonia [nōō/ kăl/ə dō/nē ə] **203**
New Zealand [nōō/ zē/lənd] **203**
Nicaragua [nĭk/ə rä/gwə] **201, 202**
Niger [nī/jər, nē zhër/] **203**
Nigeria [nī jïr/ē ə] **203**
Northern Mariana Islands
    [nördh/ərn mä/rē ä/nə ī/ləndz] **203**
North Korea [nörth/ kə rē/ə] **203**
Norway [nör/wā] **203**
Oman [ō män/] **203**
Pakistan [păk/ə stăn/] **203**
Palau [pə low/] **203**
Panama [păn/ə mä/] **201, 202**
Papua New Guinea [păp/yōō ə nōō/ gĭn/ē] **203**
Paraguay [păr/ə gwī/, –gwä/] **202**
Peru [pə rōō/] **202**
Philippines [fĭl/ə pēnz/, fĭl/ə pēnz/] **203**
Poland [pō/lənd] **203**
Portugal [pör/chə gəl] **203**
Puerto Rico [pwĕr/tə rē/kō, pör/tə–] **201, 202**
Qatar [kä/tär, kə tär/] **203**
Romania [rō mā/nē ə, rōō–] **203**
Russia [rŭsh/ə] **203**
Rwanda [rōō än/də] **203**
Samoa [sə mō/ə] **202**
Saudi Arabia [sow/dē ə rā/bē ə, sö/dē–] **203**
Senegal [sĕn/ə göl/, –gäl/] **203**
Serbia [sür/bē ə] **203**
Seychelles [sā shĕlz/, –shĕl/] **203**
Sierra Leone [sē ĕr/ə lē ōn/, –lē ō/nē] **203**
Singapore [sĭng/ə pör/] **203**
Slovakia [slō vä/kē ə] **203**
Slovenia [slō vē/nē ə] **203**
Society Islands [sə sī/ə tē ī/ləndz] **202**
Solomon Islands [säl/ə mən ī/ləndz] **203**

Somalia [sə mä**/**lē ə] **203**
South Africa [sowth**/** ăf**/**rĭ kə] **203**
South Georgia [sowth**/** jôr**/**jə] **202**
South Korea [sowth**/** kə rē**/**ə] **203**
Spain [spān] **203**
Sri Lanka [srē**/** läng**/**kə, shrē**/**–] **203**
Sudan [sōō dăn**/**] **203**
Suriname [sŏŏr**/**ə nä**/**mə] **202**
Svalbard [sväl**/**bärd] **203**
Swaziland [swä**/**zē länd**/**] **203**
Sweden [swēd**/**n] **203**
Switzerland [swĭt**/**sər lənd] **203**
Syria [sîr**/**ē ə] **203**
Tahiti [tə hē**/**tē] **202**
Taiwan [tī**/**wän**/**] **203**
Tajikistan [tä jĭk**/**ə stän**/**, –stän**/**] **203**
Tanzania [tăn**/**zə nē**/**ə] **203**
Tasmania [tăz mā**/**nē ə] **203**
Thailand [tī**/**lănd**/**, –lənd] **203**
Togo [tō**/**gō] **203**
Tonga [täng**/**gə] **202**
Tunisia [tōō nē**/**zhə] **203**
Turkey [tûr**/**kē] **203**
Turkmenistan [tûrk mĕn**/**ə stän**/**, –stăn**/**] **203**
Uganda [yōō găn**/**də] **203**
Ukraine [yōō**/**krān, yōō krān**/**] **203**
United Arab Emirates [yōō nī**/**təd är**/**əb ĕm**/**ər əts] **203**
United Kingdom [yōō nī**/**təd kĭng**/**dəm] **203**
United States of America
    [yōō nī**/**təd stāts**/** əv ə mĕr**/**ə kə] **200, 202**
Uruguay [yŏŏr**/**ə gwī**/**, –gwā**/**] **202**
Uzbekistan [ŏŏz bĕk**/**ə stän**/**, –stăn**/**] **203**
Vanuatu [vä**/**nōō ä**/**tōō] **203**
Venezuela [vĕn**/**ə zwā**/**lə] **202**
Victoria Island [vĭk**/**tôr ē ə ī**/**lənd] **200**
Vietnam [vē**/**ĕt näm**/**, –năm**/**] **203**
Wake Island [wāk**/** ī**/**lənd] **203**
Western Sahara [wĕs**/**tərn sə här**/**ə] **203**
Yemen [yĕm**/**ən] **203**
Zambia [zăm**/**bē ə] **203**
Zanzibar [zăn**/**zə bär**/**] **203**
Zimbabwe [zĭm bäb**/**wā] **203**

Bodies of water
Arctic Ocean [ärk**/**tĭk ō**/**shən] **200, 203**
Atlantic Ocean [ət lăn**/** tĭk ō**/**shən] **200, 202–203**
Baffin Bay [băf**/**ən bā**/**] **200, 202**
Baltic Sea [bôl**/**tĭk sē**/**] **203**
Beaufort Sea [bō**/**fərt sē**/**] **200**
Bering Sea [bĕr**/**ĭng sē**/**, bîr**/**–] **200**
Black Sea [blăk**/** sē**/**] **203**
Caribbean Sea [kăr**/**ə bē**/**ən sē**/**, kə rĭb**/**ē ən–] **201**
Caspian Sea [kăs**/**pē ən sē**/**] **203**
Coral Sea [kôr**/**əl sē**/**] **203**
Gulf of Alaska [gŭlf**/** əv ə lăs**/**kə] **200, 202**
Gulf of California [gŭlf**/** əv kăl**/**ə fôrn**/**yə] **200**
Gulf of Mexico [gŭlf**/** əv mĕk**/**sĭ kō**/**] **200, 202**
Hudson Bay [hŭd**/**sən bā**/**] **200, 202**
Indian Ocean [ĭn**/**dē ən ō**/**shən] **203**
Labrador Sea [lăb**/**rə dôr**/** sē**/**] **200**
Mediterranean Sea [mĕd**/**ə tə rā**/**nē ən sē**/**] **203**

North Atlantic Ocean [nôrth**/** ət lăn**/**tĭk ō**/**shən] **202**
North Pacific Ocean [nôrth**/** pə sĭf**/**ĭk ō**/**shən] **202, 203**
North Sea [nôrth**/** sē**/**] **203**
Pacific Ocean [pə sĭf**/**ĭk ō**/**shən] **200, 202, 203**
Philippine Sea [fĭl**/**ə pēn**/** sē**/**] **203**
Red Sea [rĕd**/** sē**/**] **203**
South Atlantic Ocean [sowth**/** ət lăn**/**tĭk ō**/**shən] **203**
Southern Ocean [sŭdh**/**ərn ō**/**shən] **203**
South Pacific Ocean [sowth**/** pə sĭf**/**ĭk ō**/**shən] **202, 203**

The United States of America
Capital: Washington, D.C. (District of Columbia)
    [wä**/**shĭng tən dē**/**sē**/**, wō**/**–] **200**

Regions of the United States
Mid–Atlantic States [mĭd**/**ət lăn**/**tĭk stāts**/**] **201–10**
Midwest [mĭd**/**wĕst**/**] **201–9**
New England [nōō**/** ĭng**/**glənd] **201–11**
Pacific States [pə sĭf**/**ĭk stāts**/**] **201–7**
Rocky Mountain States [räk**/**ē mown**/**tn stāts**/**] **201–8**
South [sowth] **201–13**
Southeast [sowth**/**ēst**/**] **201–13**
Southwest [sowth**/**wĕst**/**] **201–12**
West Coast [wĕst**/** kōst**/**] **201–7**

States of the United States
Alabama [ăl**/**ə băm**/**ə] **200**
Alaska [ə lăs**/**kə] **200, 202**
Arizona [ăr**/**ə zō**/**nə] **200**
Arkansas [är**/**kən sô**/**] **200**
California [kăl**/**ə fôrn**/**yə] **200**
Colorado [kăl**/**ə răd**/**ō, –rä**/**dō] **200**
Connecticut [kə nĕt**/**ĭ kət] **200**
Delaware [dĕl**/**ə wâr**/**] **200**
Florida [flôr**/**ə də, flär**/**–] **200**
Georgia [jôr**/**jə] **200**
Hawaii [hə wī**/**ē] **200**
Idaho [ī**/**də hō**/**] **200**
Illinois [ĭl**/**ə noy**/**] **200**
Indiana [ĭn**/**dē ăn**/**ə] **200**
Iowa [ī**/**ə wə] **200**
Kansas [kăn**/**zəs] **200**
Kentucky [kən tŭk**/**ē] **200**
Louisiana [lōō ē**/**zē ăn**/**ə] **200**
Maine [mān] **200**
Maryland [mĕr**/**ə lənd] **200**
Massachusetts [măs**/**ə chōō**/**səts] **200**
Michigan [mĭsh**/**ĭ gən] **200**
Minnesota [mĭn**/**ə sō**/**tə] **200**
Mississippi [mĭs**/**ə sĭp**/**ē] **200**
Missouri [mə zŏŏr**/**ē, –zŏŏr**/**ə] **200**
Montana [măn tăn**/**ə] **200**
Nebraska [nə brăs**/**kə] **200**
Nevada [nə văd**/**ə, –vä**/**də] **200**
New Hampshire [nōō**/** hămp**/**shər] **200**
New Jersey [nōō**/** jûr**/**zē] **200**
New Mexico [nōō**/** mĕk**/**sĭ kō**/**] **200**
New York [nōō**/** yôrk**/**] **200**
North Carolina [nôrth**/** kăr**/**ə lī**/**nə] **200**
North Dakota [nôrth**/** də kō**/**tə] **200**
Ohio [ō hī**/**ō] **200**
Oklahoma [ō**/**klə hō**/**mə] **200**
Oregon [ôr**/**ĭ gən, –găn**/**, är**/**–] **200**

Pennsylvania [pĕn**/**səl vān**/**yə] **200**
Rhode Island [rōd**/** ī**/**lənd] **200**
South Carolina [sowth**/** kăr**/**ə lī**/**nə] **200**
South Dakota [sowth**/** də kō**/**tə] **200**
Tennessee [tĕn**/**ə sē**/**] **200**
Texas [tĕk**/**səs] **200**
Utah [yōō**/**tô, –tä] **200**
Vermont [vər mänt**/**] **200**
Virginia [vər jĭn**/**yə] **200**
Washington [wä**/**shĭng tən, wô**/**–] **200**
West Virginia [wĕst**/** vər jĭn**/**yə] **200**
Wisconsin [wĭs kän**/**sən] **200**
Wyoming [wī ō**/**mĭng] **200**

Canada
Capital: Ottawa [ät**/**ə wə] **201**

Regions of Canada
British Columbia [brĭt**/**ĭsh kə lŭm**/**bē ə] **201–2**
Maritime Provinces [mĕr**/**ə tim präv**/**ən səz] **201–6**
Northern Canada [nôr**/**dhərn kăn**/**ə də] **201–1**
Ontario [än tĕr**/**ē ō**/**] **201–4**
Prairie Provinces [prĕr**/**ē präv**/**ən səz] **201–3**
Québec [kwĭ bĕk**/**] **201–5**

Provinces of Canada
Alberta [ăl bûr**/**tə] **200**
British Columbia [brĭt**/**ĭsh kə lŭm**/**bē ə] **200**
Manitoba [măn**/**ə tō**/**bə] **200**
New Brunswick [nōō**/** brŭnz**/**wĭk] **200**
Newfoundland and Labrador
    [nōō**/**fən lənd ən lă**/**brə dôr**/**] **200**
Northwest Territories [nôrth**/**wĕst**/** tĕr**/**ə tôr**/**ēz] **200**
Nova Scotia [nō**/**və skō**/**shə] **200**
Nunavut [nōō**/**nə vōōt**/**] **200**
Ontario [än tĕr**/**ē ō**/**] **200**
Prince Edward Island [prĭns**/** ĕd**/**wərd ī**/**lənd] **200**
Québec [kwĭ bĕk**/**] **200**
Saskatchewan [sä skăch**/**ə wən, –wän**/**] **200**
Yukon [yōō**/**kän] **200**

Mexico
Capital: Mexico (City) [mĕk**/**sĭ kō**/** (sĭt**/**ē)] **201**

Regions of Mexico
Chiapas Highlands [chē ä**/**pəs hī**/**ləndz] **201–18**
Gulf Coastal Plain [gŭlf**/** kō**/**stəl plān**/**] **201–16**
Pacific Northwest [pə sĭf**/**ĭk nôrth**/**wĕst] **201–14**
Plateau of Mexico [plă tō**/** əv mĕk**/**sĭ kō**/**] **201–15**
Southern Uplands [sŭdh**/**ərn ŭp**/**ləndz] **201–17**
Yucatan Peninsula
    [yōō**/**kə tăn**/** pə nĭn**/**sə lə, yōō**/**kə tän**/**–] **201–19**

States of Mexico
Aguascalientes [ä**/**gwəs kăl yĕn**/**tās] **201**
Baja California Norte [bä**/**hä kăl**/**ə fôrn**/**yə nôr**/**tā] **200**
Baja California Sur [bä**/**hä kăl**/**ə fôrn**/**yə sŏŏr**/**] **200**
Campeche [käm pā**/**chā, käm pē**/**chē] **201**
Chiapas [chē ä**/**pəs] **201**
Chihuahua [chĭ wä**/**wä, –wə] **200**
Coahuila [kō**/**ə wē**/**lə] **200**
Colima Michoacán [kə lē**/**mə mē**/**chō ə kän**/**] **201**
Distrito Federal [dĭ strē**/**tō fĕd**/**ə räl**/**] **201**
Durango [dŏŏ răng**/**gō, –räng**/**–] **201**

Geographical Index

Guanajuato [gwä/nə hwä/tö] **201**
Guerrero [gə rër/ō] **201**
Hidalgo [hĭ däl/gō, ē dhäl/gō] **201**
Jalisco [hə lĭs/kō, –lēs/–] **201**
México [mĕk/sĭ kō/, mĕ/hē kō] **201**
Morelos [mö rĕl/ōs] **201**
Nayarit [nä/yə rēt/] **201**
Nuevo León [nwā/vō lā ōn/] **200**
Oaxaca [wə hä/kə, wä–] **201**
Puebla [pwĕb/lä] **201**
Querétaro [kə rĕt/ə rō/] **201**
Quintana Roo [kēn tä/nə rō/] **201**
San Luis Potosí [sän/ lōō ēs/ pō/tə sē/] **201**
Sinaloa [sē/nə lō/ə] **200**
Sonora [sə nör/ə] **200**
Tabasco [tə bäs/kō] **201**
Tamaulipas [tä/mow lē/pəs] **201**
Tlaxcala [tlä skä/lə] **201**
Veracruz [vĕr/ə krōōz/, –krōōs/] **201**
Yucatán [yōō/kə tän/, –tän/] **201**
Zacatecas [zä/kə tä/kəs, sä/–] **201**

Index ดัชนี

1 แกลลอน **75**
1 ควอท (= สี่ถ้วยตวง) **75**
1 ถ้วยตวง **75**
1 ไพนต์ (= สองถ้วยตวง) **75**
1 ออนซ์ของเหลว **75**
10 เปอร์เซ็นต์ **17**–12
100 เปอร์เซ็นต์ **17**–8
2 x 4 (ไม้ขนาดหน้ากว้างสองคูณสี่นิ้ว) **181**–19
25 เปอร์เซ็นต์ **17**–11
50 เปอร์เซ็นต์ **17**–10
75 เปอร์เซ็นต์ **17**–9
HIV (ไวรัสที่ทำให้ภูมิคุ้มกันบกพร่อง นำไปสู่โรคเอดส์) **111**–17
R&B **237**–28
กฎในการเขียน **190**
กฎระเบียบ **64**–7
กด "จบ" **15**–D
กด "ส่ง" **15**–B
กัน **107**–30
กบ **212**–25
กบไสไม้ **181**–57
กรกฎาคม **21**–31
กรรไกร **33**–20, **100**–16
กรรไกรตัดกิ่ง **176**–11
กรรไกรตัดแต่ง **176**–9
กรรไกรปอกสายไฟ **181**–42
กรรมการตัดสิน **229**–6
กรวย **193**–40, **195**–40
กรอกใบสมัคร **173**–J
กรอบรูป **58**–4
กรอฟัน **119**–D
กระ **213**–42
กระจกเงา **57**–18
กระจกเงาเต็มตัว **58**–6
กระจกเงามองด้านข้าง **158**–3
กระจกเงามองหลัง **159**–35
กระจกหน้าต่างแตก **62**–5
กระจกหน้ารถ **158**–1
กระจับ **91**–6
กระชอน **78**–22
กระชอนล้างผัก **78**–17
กระดาน **6**–1
กระดานขาว **6**–3
กระดานติดประกาศ **7**–14
กระดานโต้คลื่น **225**–16
กระดานหิมะ **231**–23
กระดาษ **7**–28, **37**–15
กระดาษ/ผ้าเช็ดปาก **55**–10
กระดาษเขียนจดหมาย **183**–42
กระดาษงานฝีมือ **232**–12
กระดาษชำระ **57**–19, **146**–13
กระดาษเช็ดมือ **54**–3
กระดาษเช็ดมือหนึ่งม้วน **74**–23
กระดาษทราย **181**–56
กระดาษโน้ตมีกาวติด **183**–39
กระดาษปะแต่งฝาผนัง **59**–8
กระดาษโปรงงานรื่นเริง **239**–3
กระดุม **99**–24

กระดุมแต๊บ **99**–26
กระดุมหลุดหาย **97**–40
กระดูก **107**–33
กระดูกเชิงกราน **107**–50
กระดูกซี่โครง **107**–48
กระดูกสันหลัง **107**–49
กระดูกหัก **116**–P
กระโดด **230**–I
กระโดดเชือก **224**–4
กระไดแบบเป็นขั้น **61**–13
กระต่าย **215**–13
กระติกน้ำ **226**–24
กระแตชนิดหนึ่ง **215**–20
กระโถนเด็ก **37**–12
กระโถนแบบนอน **121**–23
กระทะก้นแบน **54**–24
กระทะก้นลึก **78**–25
กระทะสำหรับทอด **78**–5
กระเทียม **69**–30
กระบวนการทางกฎหมาย **141**
กระบวนการในการเขียน **191**
กระบอก **193**–41
กระบอกที่มีขีดวัด **195**–38
กระเบื้องแตกร้าว **62**–4
กระเบื้องปูผนังหรือพื้น **57**–12
กระป๋อง **74**–3
กระเป๋า **94**–2, **161**–18
กระเป๋า(เสื้อหรือกางเกง) **100**–7
กระเป๋าเดินทาง **161**–18
กระเป๋าถือ **87**–9, **94**–2
กระเป๋าแบบใส่ของ **94**–19
กระเป๋าเศษสตางค์ **94**–14
กระเป๋าสตางค์ **94**–13
กระเป๋าสะพายหลัง **94**–18, **226**–15
กระเป๋าสะพายไหล่ **94**–17
กระเป๋าสัมภาระของทารก **37**–16
กระเป๋าใส่กล้องถ่ายรูป **235**–28
กระเป๋าใส่เหรียญ **94**–14
กระเป๋าหนีบ **89**–19
กระเป๋าเอกสาร **88**–13
กระเปาะหมึก **183**–45
กระโปรง **87**–10
กระโปรงชุดหญิงมีครรภ์ **88**–5
กระโปรงมินิ **96**–15
กระโปรงยาว **96**–18
กระโปรงยาวครึ่งน่อง **96**–17
กระโปรงยาวแค่เข่า **96**–17
กระโปรงรองใน **91**–23
กระโปรงสั้น **96**–16
กระโปรงหน้ารถ **158**–4
กระโปรงหลังรถ **158**–11
กระเพาะ **107**–41
กระเพาะปัสสาวะ **107**–46
กระรอก **215**–21
กระสวยด้าย **98**–21
กราฟ **192**–15
กราม **106**–4
กริ่ง **51**–31
กริ่งที่ประตู **53**–14

กรีนคาร์ด **40**–2
กล้วย **68**–2
กล้วยจำนวนหนึ่ง **68**–29
กล้วยเน่า **68**–32
กล้วยไม้ **211**–19
กล้วยยังไม่สุก **68**–31
กล้วยสุก **68**–30
กลอง **238**–16
กล่อง **74**–4, **74**–6
กล่องข้อความตัวอักษร **197**–13
กล่องค้นหา **197**–5
กล้องจุลทรรศน์ **194**
กล้องดูดาว **205**–23
กล้องถ่ายรูปติดคอมพิวเตอร์ **196**–12
กล้องถ่ายรูปแบบใช้ฟิล์ม **235**–21
กล้องถ่ายรูปแบบใช้ฟิล์มขนาด 35 มม. **235**–21
กล้องถ่ายรูปแบบดิจิตัล **235**–19
กล้องถ่ายรูปเพื่อความปลอดภัย **50**–19
กล้องถ่ายวิดีโอ **235**–24
กล่องใส่อาหารเพื่อนำออก **82**–5
กลับจากตลาด **66**
กลับไปที่ห้องเรียน **11**–M
กลับรถได้ **154**–5
กลัว **43**–23
กลาง **96**–3
กลางคืน **18**–20
กล้ามเนื้อ **107**–32
กล่าวคำปราศรัย **148**–A
กลีบดอก **211**–8
กลืนสิ่งเป็นพิษ **116**–J
กลุ่มคนงานทำสวน **176**–1
กลุ่มดาว **205**–14
กลุ่มที่เล่นร่วมกัน **229**–3
กลุ่มสนับสนุน **115**–15
กลุ่มอันธพาล **142**–4
กวาง **216**–14
กวางแอนตาโลป **217**–35
กวาดใบไม้ **176**–C
กวาดพื้น **60**–J
กษัตริย์ **199**–4
ก๊อกน้ำ **57**–8
ก๊อกน้ำดื่ม **224**–9
ก๊อกน้ำไหลหยดปิดไม่สนิท **63**–17
กองทัพ **199**–11
กองทัพบก **138**–14
กองทัพเรือ **138**–15
กองทัพอากาศ **138**–16
กองปุ๋ยหมัก **53**–25
กองรักษาการณ์แห่งชาติ **138**–19
กอด **2**–E
ก้อน **74**–10
กอล์ฟ **228**–8
ก่อเหตุรุนแรง **142**–4
ก่ออิฐ **178**–B
กะเบน **212**–11
กะพง **212**–6
กะหล่ำดอก **69**–14

กะหล่ำปลี **69**–2
กะโหลกศีรษะ **107**–47
กันกุมา **211**–17
กันชน **158**–8
กันยายน **21**–33
กาเครื่องหมายในกล่องที่ถูกต้อง **9**–U
กางเกงขายาว **87**–12
กางเกงขาสั้น **89**–25
กางเกงขาสั้นแบบนักมวย **91**–4
กางเกงขาสั้นสำหรับว่ายน้ำ **90**–22
กางเกงในตัวเล็ก **91**–5, **91**–14
กางเกงในรัดรูป **91**–15
กางเกงในสตรี (บิกินี) **91**–13
กางเกงพนักงานรักษาความปลอดภัย **93**–22
กางเกงยีนส์ **86**–2, **92**–19
กางเกงยืดขึ้นในแบบเต็มถึงเอว **91**–19
กางเกงยืดแนบเนื้อ **90**–12
กางเกงรองกันเลอะ **37**–11
กางเกงรัดรูป **97**–29
กางเกงรัดหน้าท้อง **91**–15
กางเกงสามส่วน **88**–8
กางเกงใส่ทำงาน **92**–5
กางเกงใส่ออกกำลังกาย **89**–23
กางเกงหลวม **97**–30
กางเต็นท์นอน **226**–5
ก๊าซธรรมชาติ **218**–3
กาต้มน้ำ **54**–17
ก้านดอก **211**–9
กาน้ำชา **55**–16
กาแฟ **73**–33, **81**–37
กาแฟแบบไม่มีคาเฟอีน **81**–38
กายบริหารแบบแอโรบิค **122**–5
กายภาพบำบัด **115**–11
การกรอกแบบฟอร์ม **4**
การก่อสร้าง **178**
การเก็บกวาดในชุมชน **148**
การแก้ไขดัดแปลง **100**
การขนส่งขั้นพื้นฐาน **150**
การขนส่งที่สนามบิน **152**
การขนส่งสาธารณะ **152**
การขโมยของในร้าน **142**–8
การขโมยใช้ข้อมูลส่วนบุคคล **142**–9
การขอใบขับขี่เป็นครั้งแรก **137**
การขับรถขณะมึนเมา **142**–5
การขีดเขียนเลอะเทอะใน ที่สาธารณะ **148**–1
การขี่ม้า **226**–9
การขูดฟันเทียม **119**–10
การคิดเลข **192**
การเคลื่อนไหวทางการเมือง **199**–16
การจัดวางถ้วยชาม **83**–17
การจัดสวนและการทำสวน **176**
การเจ็บป่วยที่เป็นกันโดยทั่วไป และโรคต่างๆในวัยเด็ก **111**
การเจ็บป่วยและสภาวะป่วยไข้ **111**
การช่วยคนสำลักหลอดลมอุดตัน โดยวิธีเฮมลิค **117**–18
การชุมนุมอย่างสันติ **140**–1

การเช่าอพาร์ตเมนต์ **48**
การเชิญชวน **64**–9
การใช้แป้นคีย์ **196**
การใช้ยาฆ่าแมลง **218**–16
การซ่อมบำรุง **184**–23
การซื้อของ **27**
การซื้อบ้าน **49**
การซื้อรถมือสอง **157**
การซื้อและการซ่อมบำรุงรักษารถ **157**
การเปรียบเทียบเสื้อผ้า **97**
การ์ด **239**–5
การ์ดเบสบอล **232**–2
การ์ดหน่วยความจำ **235**–20
การดำน้ำด้วยเครื่องประดาน้ำ **227**–12
การดูแลเด็กและการเป็น
    ผู้ปกครอง **36**–37
การดูแลรถของคุณ **157**
การดูแลรักษา **118**
การดูแลรักษาฟัน **119**
การดูแลสุขภาพของคุณเอง **114**–115
การเดินทาง **162**
การเดินเท้า **226**–7
การเดินสายไฟ **186**–7
การตกปลา **226**–4
การตรวจที่เสียค่าใช้จ่ายน้อย **122**–1
การตรวจสายตา **136**–6
การตวงของเหลว **75**
การตวงวัดของแห้ง **75**
การตวงวัดต่างๆ **17**
การต่อเข้าระบบและการส่งอีเมล **197**
การตัดเย็บเสื้อผ้า **98**–99
การ์ตูน **236**–3
การเตรียมอาหารและ
    ความปลอดภัย **76**–77
การแต่งเพลงหรือดนตรี **199**–15
การโต้คลื่น **227**–9
การโต้ลม **227**–10
การโต้วาที **139**–B
การทดลอง **195**
การทหาร **138**
การทำร้ายแย่งชิงทรัพย์ **142**–11
การทำร้ายร่างกาย **142**–3
การทำไร่และการทำทุ่งเลี้ยงปศุสัตว์ **177**
การทำลายทรัพย์สิน **142**–1
การโทรทางไกล **15**–32
การโทรในท้องถิ่น **15**–31
การโทรระหว่างประเทศ **15**–35
การโทรเร่งด่วนฉุกเฉิน **15**
การโทรศัพท์ **15**
การโทรศัพท์ผ่านระบบ
    อินเทอร์เน็ต **14**–20
การนัดหมาย **22**–4, **118**–1
การนำทางไปที่หน้าเว็บ **197**
การนำเสนอ **182**–6
การบรรยายเกี่ยวกับผู้คน **32**
การบรรยายเกี่ยวกับเสื้อผ้า **97**
การบรรยายลักษณะผม **33**
การบรรยายสิ่งของ **23**
การบรรลุผลสำเร็จในโรงเรียน **10**

การบริการส่งอาหารถึงห้องพัก **184**–17
การบอกเวลา **18**
การบันเทิง **236**–237
การบำบัดปัญหาด้านการพูด **115**–13
การบำรุงรักษาสระว่ายน้ำ **184**–21
การแบกสัมภาระ **226**–6
การปฐมพยาบาล **117**
การประกาศอิสรภาพ **198**–5
การประชุมครู-ผู้ปกครอง **22**–5
การประชุมผู้เช่า **64**
การประดิษฐ์ **199**–19
การปั่นจักรยานไปตามภูเขา **226**–8
การปั๊มช่วยให้หัวใจ
    และปอดฟื้น **117**–17
การเปิดบัญชี **132**
การเปรียบเทียบเสื้อผ้า **97**
การไปแคมป์ **226**–5
การไปพบทันตแพทย์ **119**
การฝรั่งสี **218**–15
การฝังเข็ม **122**–2
การฝึกงานหลังสำเร็จการศึกษา **172**–6
การฝึกอบรม **172**–2
การฝึกอบรมงานอาชีพ **172**–5
การฝึกอบรมระหว่างการทำงาน **172**–7
การพบปะรวมญาติ **44**
การพบปะและการทักทาย **2**
การพิจารณาคดีอย่างเป็นธรรม **140**–5
การยกเอาคำพูดของผู้อื่นมา **190**–9
การย้ายเข้า **49**
การย้ายเข้ามาอาศัยอยู่ **199**–12
การร้องเรียน **148**–5
การรับประทานในร้านอาหาร/
    ภัตตาคาร **185**
การเรียงความภาษาอังกฤษ **190**–191
การเรียน **8**–9
การเรียนภาษาอังกฤษเป็นภาษา
    ที่สอง **189**–14
การเรียนรู้คำใหม่ๆ **8**
การล่องแพ **226**–2
การลอบวางเพลิง **142**–7
การลักขโมย **142**–2
การเล่นกระดานลื่นหิมะ **227**–2
การเล่นเรือ **226**–1
การเล่นเรือคานู **226**–3
การเล่นเลื่อน **227**–6
การเล่นสกีน้ำ **227**–7
การเล่นสกีไปตามที่ราบโล่ง **227**–3
การเล่นสกีลงเขา **227**–1
การเล่นสเก็ตน้ำแข็ง **227**–4
การเล่นสเก็ตน้ำแข็งแบบลีลา
    สวยงาม **227**–5
การเลือกตั้ง **139**
การเลื่อนขั้น **172**–4
การแล่นเรือใบ **227**–8
การวัด **17**
การวัดพื้นที่และปริมาตร **193**
การวางแผนงานอาชีพ **172**
การวางแผนอาชีพ **172**
การส่งการ์ด **135**

การสังเคราะห์แสง **194**–10
การสนทนาการภายนอก **226**
การสาธิต **122**–6
การสำรวจ **199**–8
การสำเร็จการศึกษา **206**
การสูญเสียความสามารถในการ
    ได้ยิน **115**–2
การใส่ท่อหายใจลงดูปลาในน้ำ **227**–11
การหกไหลลงของน้ำมัน **218**–17
การหลอมรวม **218**–10
การหางาน **173**
การหาเสียงสนับสนุนทาง
    การเมือง **139**–29
การให้ยาหรือน้ำเกลือแบบหยด
    เข้าเส้น **121**–25
การอ่านใบเรียกเก็บเงินค่าโทรศัพท์ **15**
การอุดฟัน **119**–8
กาแล็คซี **205**–15
กาว **183**–33
กำจัดวัชพืชในแปลงดอกไม้ **176**–G
กำมะหยี่ **99**–10
กำลังเจ็บปวด **42**–11
กำลังมีความรัก **42**–18
กำไลข้อมือ **95**–9
กำหนดเวลาการสัมภาษณ์ **173**–I
กิ้งก่า **213**–40
กิ้งก่าประเภทหนึ่ง **212**–27
กิ่งขนาดกลาง **210**–2
กิ่งย่อย **210**–1
กิ่งใหญ่ **210**–3
กิจวัตรประจำวัน **38**–39
กิน **11**–I
กินก่อนอาหารหนึ่งชั่วโมง **112**–B
กินพร้อมกับอาหารหรือนม **112**–A
กินยา **114**–D
กินยาเกินขนาด **116**–K
กินอาหารที่มีประโยชน์ **114**–F
กินอาหารเย็น **39**–S
กั๊บผม **108**–21
กั๊บรวบผม **108**–20
ก่อนเกิดเหตุฉุกเฉิน **146**
กีตาร์ **238**–9
กีบเท้า **216**–17
กีวี **68**–22
กีฬาประเภททีม **229**
กีฬาประเภทรายบุคคล **228**
กีฬาฤดูหนาวและกีฬาทางน้ำ **227**
กุ้ง **71**–11, **212**–18
กุ้งก้ามกราม **71**–10
กุญแจ **51**–30
กุญแจมือ **141**–2
กุมภาพันธ์ **21**–26
กุมารแพทย์ **120**–4
กุหลาบ **211**–15
เก็บ **82**–G
เก็บกระเป๋าที่ถือติดตัวมา **160**–G
เก็บกวาดสิ่งปรักหักพัง **147**–M
เก็บเกี่ยวพืชผล **177**–B
เก็บของลงกระเป๋า **162**–A

เก็บของลงหีบห่อ **49**–M
เก็บของเล่นเข้าที่ **60**–G
เก็บของออกไปจากโต๊ะของคุณ
    ให้หมด **10**–I
เก็บไว้ **28**–B
เก็บหนังสือต่างๆของคุณไว้ **9**–Z
เกมต่อภาพ **59**–17
เกมเบสบอล **44**–2
เกมแบบกระดาน **232**–5
เกรียง **176**–10, **178**–13
เกล็ดปลา **212**–3
เกลือหนึ่งช้อนชา **75**–6
เกษียณ **41**–O
เก้า **16**
เก้าสิบ **16**
เก้าอี้ **7**–11
เก้าอี้แข็ง **23**–5
เก้าอี้ชายหาด **225**–22
เก้าอี้นวมแบบนั่งสองคน **56**–1
เก้าอี้นวมยาว **56**–18
เก้าอี้นิรภัยของเด็ก **159**–53
เก้าอี้นุ่ม **23**–6
เก้าอี้ในห้องอาหาร **55**–8
เก้าอี้มีบมีที่วางแขน **56**–22
เก้าอี้พับ **102**–5
เก้าอี้โยก **37**–21
เก้าอี้สูงสำหรับเด็ก **37**–6, **82**–3
เก้าอี้เอนหลัง **56**–22
เกาะ **204**–8
เกิด **40**–A
เกียร์กระปุก **159**–50
เกียร์ธรรมดา **159**
เกียร์มือ **159**
เกียร์อัตโนมัติ **159**
แก้ข้อที่ผิดให้ถูก **10**–N
แก้ไข **191**–J
แกนกระทุ้ง **181**–50
แก้ม **106**–3
แก้วเต็ม **23**–9
แก้วน้ำ **83**–22
แก้วปากกน **195**–39
แก้วเปล่า **23**–10
แก้วมีพวย **195**–39
แก้วไวน์ **83**–23
แกะ **215**–6
โก้งโค้ง **230**–O
โกดังสินค้า **175**–7
โกน **109**–M
โกรธ **43**–29
ไก่ **66**–3, **70**–16
ไก่งวง **70**–17, **239**–14
ไก่งวงอบ **76**–4
ไก่ดิบ **70**–24
ไก่ตัวผู้ **215**–7
ไก่ตัวเมีย **215**–8
ไก่ทอด **76**–1
ไก่สุก **70**–25
ไก่อบ **81**–22
ขนคอ **217**–49

ขนตา **106**–11
ขนตามตัวสัตว์ **216**–19
ขนนก **214**–4
ขนมปัง **67**–11
ขนมปังกระเทียม **81**–28
ขนมปังก้อนเล็ก **80**–17
ขนมปังขาว **71**–18
ขนมปังแบบบิสคิด **80**–6
ขนมปังปิ้ง **80**–4
ขนมปังแป้งข้าวสาลีไม่ขัดสี **71**–19
ขนมปังแป้งไร **71**–20
ขนมปังมัฟฟินแบบอังกฤษ **80**–5
ขนมปังรูปวง **73**–40
ขนมปังหนึ่งก้อน **74**–22
ขนมรังผึ้ง **80**–8
ขนมหวานชนิดแท่ง **73**–37
ขนมหวานต่างๆ **84**–8
ขนเม่น **216**–23
ขนหนังสือ **11**–F
ขนาด **96**
ขนาด แบบ และลวดลาย **96**
ขนาดเดียวใส่ได้ทุกคน **96**–6
ขนาดรับประทาน/ที่ใช้ **112**–6
ขนาดสัดส่วน **17**
ขบวนพาเรด **239**–1
ขบวนรถใต้ดิน **152**–6
ขบวนแห่ **239**–1
ขยะเกลื่อนกลาด **148**–2
ขยะอันตราย **218**–12
ขยันเรียนเองที่บ้าน **10**–D
ขยายขนาดกางเกง **100**–C
ขลุ่ย **238**–1
ขวด **37**–1, **74**–1
ขวดนม **37**–1
ขวดปากกว้าง **74**–2
ขว้าง **230**–C
ขว้างลูก **230**–A
ขวาน **180**–3
ขวานเจาะ **178**–21
ข้อกำหนดของสถานภาพการเป็น
    พลเมือง **140**
ข้อกำหนดเพื่อความปลอดภัย **164**–6
ขอความช่วยเหลือ **10**–F
ข้อความตัวอักษร **14**–19
ข้อความเสียง **14**–18
ของกำนัล **240**–3
ของขวัญ **240**–3
ของใช้ในการทำความสะอาด **61**
ของเล่นแบบแขวนประดับ **59**–5
ของเล่นและเกม **59**
ของเล่นส่งเสียงให้เด็กเพลิน **37**–26
ของเหลวที่ติดไฟได้ **179**–8
ข้อตกลงการเช่า **51**–28
ข้อต่อท่อแบบต่างๆ **181**–18
ข้อเท้า **106**–23
ข้อเท้าเคล็ด **110**–18
ขอโทษ **12**–F
ข้อนิ้วมือ **106**–14
ขอบคุณใครบางคน **12**–E

ขอบคุณผู้สัมภาษณ์ **174**–N
ขอบถนน **129**–21
ขอบเอว **100**–5
ข้อมือ **106**–14
ข้อมูลส่วนตัว 4
ขอรับการตรวจรักษาจากแพทย์ **114**–A
ขอรับฟังความคิดเห็น **191**–K
ข้ออักเสบ **111**–16
ขัด...ฟัน (ด้วยด้ายขัดฟัน) **109**–K
ขัดเงาเครื่องเรือน **60**–E
ขัดอ่าง **60**–K
ขั้นตอนการดูแลรักษา **118**
ขั้นตอนการปฐมพยาบาล **117**
ขั้นตอนปฏิบัติในเหตุฉุกเฉิน **146**–**147**
ขั้นบันได **53**–3
ขับเครื่องบิน **170**–F
ขับผ่านเข้าไปในอุโมงค์ **153**–K
ขับรถ **170**–E
ขับรถไปทำงาน **38**–I
ขา **70**–21, **105**–9
ขาแกะส่วนบน **70**–14
ขาแกะส่วนล่าง **70**–13
ขาด **97**–41
ขาตั้ง **233**–18
ข้ามถนน **128**–A
ขายของใช้แล้ว **102**
ขายรถ **170**–K
ขาและเท้า **106**
ขาว **24**–14
ข้าว **67**–10, **81**–30, **177**–1
ข้าวครีม **24**–16
ขาวงาช้าง **24**–16
ข้าวโพด **69**–12, **177**–4
ข้าวยากหมากแพง **145**–12
ข้าวสาลี **177**–2
ขาส่วนบน **70**–22
ขาหลังหมูส่วนบน **70**–9
ขี่จักรยาน **129**–D
ขีดฆ่าคำ **9**–R
ขีดจำกัดความเร็ว **154**–4
ขีดเส้นใต้คำ **9**–S
ขึ้นเครื่องบิน **160**–E
ขึ้นเงินจากเช็ค **132**–A
ขึ้นทะเบียนรถ **157**–F
ขึ้นทะเบียนไว้กับหน่วยงาน
    คัดเลือก **140**–D
ขึ้นแท็กซี่ **153**–E
ขึ้นไปทางไฮเวย์ **153**–I
ขึ้นรถประจำทางไปโรงเรียน **38**–H
ขูดเนยแข็ง **77**–G
เขตต่างๆของเวลา **19**
เข็ม **98**–17, **100**–10
เข็มกลัด **95**–38
เข็มกลัดเครื่องหมาย **93**–21
เข็มกลัดซ่อนปลาย **37**–9, **100**–14
เข็มขัด **94**–6
เข็มขัดเครื่องมือ **92**–3
เข็มขัดนิรภัย **159**–52
เข็มขัดพยุงหลัง **179**–18

เข็มฉีดยา **118**–12
เข็มถัก **233**–23
เข็มหมุด **100**–12, **183**–35
เข่า **106**–20
เขา **216**–21
เขาละมั่ง / เขากวาง **216**–16
เข้าคุก **141**–G
เข้าคู่กัน **28**–3
เขาเตี้ยๆ **204**–16
เข้าที่กำบัง **147**–J
เข้าปฏิบัติงาน **139**–D
เข้าไปในห้อง **11**–A
เข้าฝึกหัดวิชาการขับขี่ **137**–G
เข้าร่วมกิจกรรมเฝ้าระวังในชุมชน **143**–L
เข้าร่วมงานในชั้นเรียน **10**–B
เข้ารับการพิจารณาคดี **141**–D
เข้าเรียนวิชาการขับขี่ **137**–B
เขียง **54**–27
เขียนข้อความลงในการ์ด **135**–A
เขียนคำขอบคุณ **174**–O
เขียนจดหมายปะหน้า **173**–G
เขียนชื่อของคุณด้วยตัวบรรจง **4**–C
เขียนชื่อเริ่มด้วยอักษรตัวใหญ่ **190**–A
เขียนเช็ค (ส่วนตัว) **27**–D
เขียนตอบกลับ **135**–H
เขียนตามคำบอก **171**–K
เขียนที่อยู่ (จ่าหน้า) ซอง **135**–B
เขียนบนกระดาน **6**–E
เขียนประวัติการทำงาน **173**–F
เขียนร่างฉบับแรก **191**–H
เขียนร่างฉบับสุดท้าย **191**–L
เขียนใหม่ **191**–J
เขียว **24**–5
เขียวไข่กา **24**–9
แขก **184**–10
แข่งม้า **228**–19
แขน **105**–14, **194**–23
แขน มือ นิ้วมือ **106**
แขนส่วนล่าง **106**–13
แขนเสื้อ **100**–6
แขวนเสื้อผ้า **101**–H
ไข่ **110**–8
ไข **66**–7
ไขโจทย์เลข **170**–M
ไขควงแฉก **180**–31
ไขควงแบน **180**–30
ไข่กวนด้วยนมเนย **76**–7
ไข่เจียว **76**–12
ไข่ดาวสุกด้านเดียว **76**–10
ไข่ดาวสุกเล็กน้อยสองด้าน **76**–11
ไข่ต้มแข็ง **76**–8
ไข่หนึ่งกล่อง **74**–16
ไข้หวัดใหญ่ **111**–2
คณะผู้ค้นหาและช่วยชีวิต **145**–20
คณะรัฐมนตรี **138**–10
คณะลูกขุน **141**–8
คณิตศาสตร์ **193**
คน **77**–O
คนกำจัดแมลง **63**–21

คนเก็บถ้วยชามใช้แล้ว **185**–13
คนขับแท็กซี่ **152**–21
คนขับรถขา **23**–4
คนขับรถบรรทุก **169**–61
คนขับรถเร็ว **23**–3
คนขาย **84**–7
คนขายของข้างถนน **129**–29
คนขายดอกไม้ **167**–27
คนขายเนื้อ **166**–13
คนเข้าเมือง **199**–13
คนไข้ **118**–6
คนงานก่อสร้าง **178**–1
คนงานก่ออิฐ **186**–8
คนงานซ่อมแซม **62**–10
คนงานที่ไม่ระมัดระวัง **179**–1
คนงานที่ระมัดระวัง **179**–2
คนงานในโรงงาน **175**–3
คนงานในไร่ **177**–8
คนงานรับจ้าง **177**–20
คนเชือดเนื้อ **166**–13
คนซ่อมระบบน้ำ **63**–20
คนซ่อมล็อคประตู **62**–11
คนดูแลเด็ก **166**–9
คนเดินเท้า **128**–14
คนทำขนมปัง **166**–10
คนทำสวน **167**–28
คนทำอาหารจานด่วน **185**–1
คนที่อาศัยอยู่ในเมืองขึ้น **198**–2
คนเปิดเพลง **64**–4
คนล้างจาน **185**–2
คนส่งจดหมาย **168**–40
ค้นหาคำ **8**–A
ค้นหาในหมวดประกาศ **173**–B
ค้นหาหนังสือ **133**–B
ครอบครัว **34**–**35**
ครอบฟัน **119**–9
ครัว **46**–5, **54**, **83**–15
ครัวของร้านอาหาร **185**
คราบหินปูน **119**–12
ครีบ **225**–7
ครีบปลา **212**–1
ครีม **81**–41, **113**–25
ครีมกันแดดเผา **225**–10
ครีมกันแสงแดด **108**–8
ครีมแก้อาการแพ้ **117**–10
ครีมโกนหนวด **109**–29
ครีมปกป้องผิวจากแดด **225**–10
ครีมเปรี้ยว **72**–21
ครีมรองพื้น **109**–40
ครึ่งดอลลาร์ **26**–5
ครึ่งถ้วยตวง **75**
ครึ่งหนึ่ง **17**–2
ครู **5**–8, **6**–4
คลัช **159**–49
คลาสสิค **237**–21
คลิกที่ "ลงชื่อเข้า" **197**–B
คลินิค **186**–2
คลิปแท่น **194**–21
คลิปหนีบกระดาษ **183**–31

คลุ้มหมอก **13**–20
คลื่น **225**–17
คลื่นความร้อน **13**–13
คลื่นยักษ์ **145**–17
ควบคุมดูแลผู้อื่น **170**–O
ควบคุมวงดนตรี **238**–C
ควํา **230**–D
ความกว้าง **17**–19
ความเจ็บปวด **115**–3
ความช่วยเหลือเกี่ยวกับปัญหาด้าน
    สุขภาพ **115**
ความดันโลหิตสูง **111**–14
ความดันสูง **111**–14
ความถี่ **20**
ความปลอดภัยด้านอาหาร **76**
ความปลอดภัยในการทำงาน **179**
ความปลอดภัยในที่สาธารณะ **143**
ความพิการ **32**
ความยาว **17**–17
ความยาวรอบรูป **193**–43
ความรู้สึก **42**–43
ความลึก **17**–18
ความสูง **17**–16, **32**
ความสูงโดยเฉลี่ย **32**–5
ความสูงปานกลาง **32**–5
ความเสี่ยงอันตรายและวัสดุอันตราย **179**
ความหมาย **8**–B
ความเห็น **44**–3
ควาย **216**–6
ควายไบสัน **216**–6
ควีเบ็ค **201**–5
คอ **104**–3
คอกสัตว์ **177**–17
ค็อด **212**–5
คอด **71**–8
ค้อน **180**–1
คอนกรีต **178**–10
คอนโซลเกมวิดีโอ **232**–3
คอนโด **52**–5
คอนโดมิเนียม **52**–5
ค้อนทุบ **178**–23
คอนแทคเลนส์ **115**–8
ค้อนไม้ **180**–2
คอนเสิร์ตแบบคลาสิค **223**–14
คอนเสิร์ตเพลงร็อค **222**–5
คอฟฟี่ชอป **126**–11
คอมพิวเตอร์ **7**–15, **183**–17, **196**
คอมพิวเตอร์แบบกระเป๋าหิ้ว **196**–16
คอมพิวเตอร์แบบตั้งโต๊ะ **196**
คออักเสบ **111**–4
คะแนน **10**–3
คัดจมูก **110**–7
คัดลอกคำ **8**–E
คันเกียร์ **159**–47
คันธนู **231**–6
คันบังคับน้ำมันเชื้อเพลิง **159**–46
คันบังคับเบรค **159**–45
คันเบ็ด **226**–18
คันเร่ง **159**–46

คับข้องใจ **43**–27
ค่า **27**–7
คาง **106**–1
ค้างคาว **216**–7
คางทูม **111**–7
ค่าจ้าง **165**–12
ค่าโดยสาร **152**–2
คาน **178**–3
คาบสมุทร **204**–7
คาบสมุทรยูคาทัน **201**–19
คาร์เนชั่น **211**–20
ค่า **18**–19, **190**–1
ค่ากริยาด้านกีฬา **230**
คำเชิญ **64**–9
คำตอบ **8**–H
คำตัดสิน **141**–14
คำเตือนทางการแพทย์ **112**
คำนวณ **17**–B, **189**–10
คำนวณหาคำตอบ **170**–M
คำนำ **190**–6
คำบุพบท **25**
คำบุพบทการเคลื่อนไหว **153**
คิดถึงบ้าน **43**–20
คิดเรื่องงานที่ได้รับมอบหมาย **191**–E
คิ้ว **106**–9
คิว **73**–11
คีบอร์ดไฟฟ้า **238**–18
คีมคีบ **78**–23
คีมทนไฟ **195**–44
คีมปากนก **180**–7
คีมเล็ก **117**–4
คีย์เครื่องหมายสี่เหลี่ยม **14**–7
คีย์ดอกจัน **14**–6
คืนของ **27**–H
คืนเงิน **27**–H
คืนหนังสือ **133**–D
คุกกี้ **73**–38
คุกกี้หนึ่งห่อ **74**–20
คุยกับเพื่อน **173**–A
คูณ **192**–C
คู่ที่แต่งงานแล้ว **35**–20
คู่ที่หย่ากันแล้ว **35**–21
คูปอง **67**–15
คูเป้ **156**–2
คู่แฝด **28**–1
คู่มือการปฐมพยาบาล **117**–2
คู่มือดีวีดี **136**–1
คู่รัก **239**–4
คูลเลอร์ **225**–9
เด็ก **73**–39
เค้กชั้น **81**–33
เค้กชีส **81**–34
เค้กแบบง่ายและรวดเร็ว **77**
เครา **33**–6
เครือข่าย **173**–A
เครื่องกรองอากาศ **113**–14
เครื่องกระทุ้ง **178**–9
เครื่องกันไฟกระชาก **196**–1
เครื่องกำจัดละอองน้ำแข็ง **159**–41

เครื่องกีฬา **231**
เครื่องโกนหนวดไฟฟ้า **109**–26
เครื่องขายแสตมป์ **135**–11
เครื่องขายอัตโนมัติ **152**–9
เครื่องคิดเลข **17**–6, **183**–25
เครื่องเจาะด้วยแรงลม **178**–9
เครื่องฉายภาพแสง LCD **235**–29
เครื่องฉายสไลด์ **7**–16
เครื่องฉีดทาสี **181**–21
เครื่องช่วยการได้ยิน **115**–10
เครื่องช่วยหายใจ **179**–13
เครื่องชั่ง **195**–41
เครื่องใช้ในการตัดเย็บ **100**
เครื่องซักผ้า **50**–12, **101**–3
เครื่องเซาะร่อง **180**–12
เครื่องเหลาดินสอ **7**–23
เครื่องดนตรีแบบเป่า **238**
เครื่องดนตรีประเภทเคาะ **238**
เครื่องดนตรีประเภทสาย **238**
เครื่องดนตรีอื่นๆ **238**
เครื่องดับเพลิง **179**–21
เครื่องดาม **117**–14
เครื่องดื่ม **73**
เครื่องดูดฝุ่น **61**–10
เครื่องตรวจจับควันไฟ **51**–29
เครื่องตอบรับโทรศัพท์ **14**–17
เครื่องตัด/หั่น/เตรียมอาหาร **54**–26
เครื่องตัดแต่งหญ้า **176**–12
เครื่องตัดเล็บ **109**–31
เครื่องตัดหญ้า **176**–6
เครื่องแต่งกายตัวละคร **239**–11
เครื่องแต่งหน้า **109**
เครื่องถ่ายเอกสาร **183**–23
เครื่องทำกาแฟ **54**–11
เครื่องทำครัว **78**
เครื่องทำความชื้น **113**–12
เครื่องทำความอุ่น **159**–40
เครื่องทำความอุ่นเสีย **63**–15
เครื่องทำน้ำร้อนไม่ทำงาน **62**–1
เครื่องเทียบปรับเสียง **234**–13
เครื่องในวัว **70**–8
เครื่องบังตาเพื่อความปลอดภัย **179**–12
เครื่องบันทึกจำนวนเงิน **73**–15
เครื่องบิน **150**–8
เครื่องบินขึ้น **160**–J
เครื่องบินตก **144**–3
เครื่องบินลง **160**–K
เครื่องแบบ **88**–10, **231**–16
เครื่องประดับประดา **239**–15
เครื่องปรับอากาศ **159**–39
เครื่องปั่นผสมอาหาร **54**–12
เครื่องปิ้งขนมปัง **54**–6
เครื่องเป่าใบไม้ **176**–2
เครื่องเป่าผมแห้ง **108**–18
เครื่องเป่าแห้ง **33**–23
เครื่องเปิดกระป๋อง **78**–1, **146**–8
เครื่องเปิดกระป๋องแบบไฟฟ้า **54**–14
เครื่องผสมแบบไฟฟ้า **54**–25
เครื่องเฝ้าระวังเด็ก **59**–7

เครื่องเฝ้าระวังสัญญาณสำคัญของ
    ชีวิต **121**–26
เครื่องพรินท์ **196**–17
เครื่องพิมพ์ **196**–17
เครื่องพิมพ์แบบเลเซอร์ **183**–19
เครื่องพิมพ์แบบอิงค์เจ็ท **183**–18
เครื่องไฟฟ้าและการถ่ายภาพ **234**–**235**
เครื่องมือค้นหา **197**–6
เครื่องมือทันตกรรม **119**–4
เครื่องมือและวัสดุก่อสร้าง **180**–**181**
เครื่องยนต์ **158**–18
เครื่องย่อยกระดาษ **183**–24
เครื่องย่อยขยะทิ้ง **54**–7
เครื่องรับทอนเงิน **27**–10
เครื่องรับส่งโทรสาร **183**–21
เครื่องล้างชาม **54**–8, **83**–14
เครื่องเล่นจานเสียง **234**–12
เครื่องเล่นซีดี **159**–38
เครื่องเล่นซีดีแบบกระเป๋าหิ้ว **234**–1
เครื่องเล่นซีดีส่วนตัว **234**–5
เครื่องเล่นดีวีดี **56**–7, **234**–10
เครื่องเล่นดีวีดีแบบกระเป๋าหิ้ว **234**–11
เครื่องเล่นเทปแบบกระเป๋าหิ้ว **234**–6
เครื่องเล่นปีนป่าย **224**–14
เครื่องเล่นวิดีโอ **197**–11
เครื่องเล่นวีซีอาร์ **102**–7
เครื่องเล่นเอ็มพีสาม **234**–2
เครื่องเล็มหญ้า **176**–12
เครื่องเลาะผ้า **100**–18
เครื่องวัดความดันโลหิต **118**–9
เครื่องวัดระดับ **180**–29
เครื่องสแกน **183**–20
เครื่องสลับสายโทรศัพท์ **182**–13
เครื่องหนีบจับ **180**–26
เครื่องหมายคำถาม **190**–12
เครื่องหมายคำพูด **190**–15
เครื่องหมายจราจร **154**
เครื่องหมายจุดคู่ **190**–17
เครื่องหมายตกใจ **190**–13
เครื่องหมายทางหลวง **154**–17
เครื่องหมายวรรคตอน **190**
เครื่องหมายแสดงความ
    เป็นเจ้าของ **190**–16
เครื่องหมายอัฒภาค **190**–18
เครื่องเหลาดินสอไฟฟ้า **183**–26
เครื่องอบผ้า **50**–13, **101**–4
เครื่องอัดไฟ **14**–10, **234**–17
เครื่องอัดไฟแบตเตอรี **235**–27
เครือเถา **210**–22
เคอร์เซอร์ **197**–14
เคาน์เตอร์ **54**–22
เคารพกฎหมาย **140**–C
แคนาดาภาคเหนือ **201**–1
แคปซูล **113**–23
แคมป์ไฟ **226**–11
แครอท **69**–3
แคลริเน็ท **238**–2
โค้งคำนับ **3**–H
โคมโป๊ะไฟ **58**–26

โคมไฟ 55–18
โคมไฟแบบตั้งพื้น 56–15
โครโมโซม 194–8
โคลนถล่ม 144–6
โคโลญ 108–6
ฆาตกรรม 142–12
โฆษณาที่จัดหมวดหมู่ทางสิ่งพิมพ์ 48–2
โฆษณาแบบป๊อบอัป 197–9
งบประมาณ 186–3
งวง 217–47
งวงนอน 42–3
งา 217–48
งานเกี่ยวกับโลหิต 121–30
งานถนน 154–16
งานถักโครเชต์ 233–25
งานบ้าน 60
งานปัก 233–24
งานระดับขั้นเริ่มต้น 172–1
งานเลี้ยงฉลอง 239–13
งานและอาชีพ เรียงตามอักษร A-C 166
งานและอาชีพ เรียงตามอักษร C-H 167
งานและอาชีพ เรียงตามอักษร H-P 168
งานและอาชีพ เรียงตามอักษร P-W 169
งานวันเกิด 240
งานสังสรรค์ 64–2
งานใหม่ 172–3
งานอดิเรกและเกม 232–233
งานออกร้านเกี่ยวกับสุขภาพ 122
งานออกร้านในชุมชน 223–13
งีบหลับ 53–A
งง 43–26
งูกระดิ่ง 213–38
งูเล็กไม่มีพิษ 213–39
งูเห่า 213–41
เงิน 26
เงินสดและเหรียญ 146–17
จดบันทึกต่างๆ 10–C
จดรับรายการที่สั่ง 82–E
จดหมาย 134–13
จมน้ำ 116–I
จมูก 104–6
จระเข้ 213–37
จระเข้ตีนเป็ด 213–36
จอ 235–30
จอฉายภาพเรืองแสง LCD 6–6
จอดรถ 129–E
จอน 33–7
จอภาพ 6–2, 196–11
จอแสดงเวลาเครื่องบินมาถึงและ
    เวลาออก 161–7
จักรพรรดิ 199–3
จักรยาน 129–22, 151–15
จักรเย็บผ้า 98–13
จักรวาล 205
จักษุแพทย์ 120–7
จังหวัดในแถบชายฝั่งทะเล 201–6
จังหวัดในแถบทุ่งหญ้าพื้นที่ราบ 201–3
จัดเครื่องเรือน 49–Q
จัดโต๊ะ 82–A

จัดประโยคเหล่านี้ให้ถูกต้อง 9–X
จัดระเบียบคำเหล่านี้ 9–W
จัดระเบียบแนวคิดต่างๆของคุณ 191–G
จัดระเบียบวัสดุต่างๆ 171–L
จัดส่ง 175–D
จัดให้ลูกค้านั่ง 82–B
จัดเอกสารต่างๆเข้าเล่ม 171–E
จัตุรัส 5–1
จันทร์ข้างขึ้นเจ็ดค่ำ 205–11
จันทร์เต็มดวง 205–12
จันทร์แรม 205–9
จันทร์เสี้ยว 205–10
จับ 230–D
จับกุมผู้ต้องสงสัย 141–A
จับคู่คำ 9–T
จับตัวคนเล่นที่พาลูกวิ่ง 230–F
จับมือ 3–J
จับมือทักทาย 174–I
จาน 55–1
จานขนมปังและเนย 83–19
จานข้าว 231–27
จานดาวเทียม 53–6
จานทาสี 181–51
จานรอง 83–25
จานสลัด 83–20
จานเสิร์ฟอาหาร 55–20
จานใส่สบู่ 57–3
จานอาหารหลัก 83–18
จาม 110–B
จ่ายค่าเช่าของเดือนแรกและเดือน
    สุดท้าย 48–E
จ่ายค่าปรับที่คืนช้า 133–E
จ่ายค่าสมัคร 137–D
จ่ายคืนเงิน 26–D
จ่ายเงินค่าสินค้า 27–G
จ่ายเงินตามใบเรียกเก็บค่าอาหาร 82–I
จ่ายเงินสด 27–A
จ่าหน้าผู้รับ 134–22
จำแนกเสื้อผ้าที่ต้องซัก 101–A
จำเลย 141–5
จิงโจ้ 217–44
จิ้งหรีด 214–23
จิตแพทย์ 120–8
จี้ห้อยคอแบบตลับ 95–35
จุกอุดหู 179–15
จุดจ่ายค่าสินค้าด้วยตนเอง 73–10
จุดเชื่อมต่อไปเว็บอื่น 197–10
จุดทศนิยม 17–7
จุดที่หมาย 220–1
จุดแท็กซี่หยุดรอรับส่ง 152–18
จุดปลาย 193–21
จุดเริ่มต้น 162–1
จุดลงท้ายประโยค 190–11
จุดสตาร์ทเครื่องยนต์ 159–33
จุดเสียบปลั๊กไฟ 58–28
จุดเสียบไฟ 159–42
จุดหมายปลายทาง 162–5
จุ๋ยเซียน 211–25

จุลภาค 190–14
จูบ 3–K
จูบราตรีสวัสดิ์ 36–P
เจ็ด 16
เจ็ดสิบ 16
เจ็บคอ 110–6
เจ็บปวดใจ/กาย 42–16
เจลใส่ผม 108–16
เจ้าของธุรกิจ 166–11
เจ้าของบ้านเช่า 51–27
เจ้าของโรงงาน 175–1
เจ้านาย 164–4
เจ้าหน้าดูแลความปลอดภัย 160–5
เจ้าหน้าที่ 5–13
เจ้าหน้าที่ดีเอ็มวี 136–3
เจ้าหน้าที่ตำรวจ 141–1, 168–48
เจ้าหน้าที่ผู้ทำการจัดจ้าง 172–14
เจ้าหน้าที่ผู้บันทึกการแพทย์ 168–39
เจ้าหน้าที่แผนกรับผู้ป่วย 120–14
เจ้าหน้าที่พยาบาล 120
เจ้าหน้าที่รักษาการณ์ 141–3
เจ้าหน้าที่รักษาความปลอดภัย
    132–5, 169–55
เจ้าหน้าที่โรงพยาบาล 120
เจ้าหน้าที่ศุลกากร 161–17
เจ้าหน้าที่สังคมสงเคราะห์ 169–57
เจ้าหน้าที่ห้องฉุกเฉิน 121–32
เจ้าหน้าที่ห้องสมุด 133–1
เจ้าหน้าที่ออกหมายจับ 141–13
เจ้าหน้าที่อุทยาน 220–2
เจาะเก็บ...เลือด 118–F
เจาะต่างหู 32–17
แจกัน 55–23
แจ็คเก็ต 90–8
แจ็คเก็ตบาง 97–28
แจ็คเก็ตหนา 97–27
แจ็คเสียบสายโทรศัพท์ 14–3
แจ้งเหตุเร่งด่วนฉุกเฉินนั้น 15–G
แจส 237–24
โจทย์ง่าย 23–23
โจทย์ตัวแปร 192–12
โจทย์แบบบรรยาย 192–11
โจทย์ปรนัย 192–11
โจทย์ยาก 23–24
โจทย์เลข 192
ฉลากคำเตือน 112–8
ฉลากแสดงคุณค่าอาหาร 122–8
ฉลาม 212–4
ฉีดยาชาในปาก 119–C
เฉลิมฉลอง 206–C
โฉนด 41–9
ชนบท 52–4
ชนพื้นเมืองอเมริกัน 198–3
ชนิดของผ้า 98–99
ชนิดของยา 113
ชบา 211–12
ชมเชย 36–J
ชมพู 24–7
ช่วยการหายใจ 117–16

ช่วยเหลือผู้ที่มีความพิการ 147–G
ช่วยเหลือผู้ป่วย 170–B
ช่วยเหลือเพื่อนร่วมชั้นเรียน 8–J
ช่วยเหลือลูกค้า 95–D
ช่อง 136–7
ช่องทิ้งขยะ 51–26
ช่องมองดู 51–32
ช่องหมุนผ่าน 152–8
ช่อดอกไม้ 211–28
ช้อน 55–5
ช้อนชา 83–31
ช้อนซุป 83–32
ช้อนไม้ 78–9
ช้อนส้อมมีดพลาสติก 79–19
ชอล์กเขียนกระดาน 7–18
ชั่งน้ำหนักอาหาร 75–B
ชั้น 54–2
ชั้นวางหนังสือ 7–10
ชั้นอบอย่างในเตา 54–21
ชั่วโมง 18–1
ชา 81–39
ช้าง 217–42
ช่างเครื่อง 168–37
ช่างเครื่องรถยนต์ 166–8
ช่างเชื่อมโลหะ 169–63
ช่างซ่อมแซมเครื่องไฟฟ้า 167–24
ช่างตัดเสื้อผู้ชาย 100–3
ช่างแต่งผม 167–31
ช่างแต่งเล็บ 168–38
ช่างทาสี (บ้าน) 168–46
ช่างทำผม 167–31
ช่างทำหลังคา 62–8
ช่างเทคนิคคอมพิวเตอร์ 182–12
ช่างเทคนิคด้านคอมพิวเตอร์ 167–19
ช่างพิมพ์ 169–50
ช่างไฟฟ้า 62–9
ช่างภาพ 206–1
ช่างไม้ 62–12, 166–14
ช่างเย็บผ้า 100–1
ชานชาลา 152–7
ชานเมือง 52–2
ชามแคชเชอโรล 78–11
ชามใหญ่เสิร์ฟอาหาร 55–21
ชามอ่างสำหรับผสม 54–28, 78–31
ชาย 4–17
ชายกระโปรง 100–8
ชายฝั่งตะวันตก 201–7
ชายหาด 204–10, 225
ชาเย็น 79–12
ชาวประมงเชิงพาณิชย์ 167–17
ชาวไร่ 177–13
ชาสมุนไพร 81–40
ชิงช้า 224–11
ชิ้นส่วน 175–5
ชิ้นส่วนอะไหล่รถ 158–159
ชีววิทยา 194
ชีสเบอร์เกอร์ 79–3
ชื้น 13–15
ชื่อ 4–1

ชื่อกลาง 4–3
ชื่อตัว 4–2
ชื่อเรื่อง 133–14, 190–5
ชุดการทำตุ๊กตา 232–13
ชุดคอกเทล 89–20
ชุดงานไม้ 232–14
ชุดชั้นในของผู้ชาย 91
ชุดชั้นในของผู้หญิง 91
ชุดชั้นในแบบใช้ได้ทั้งหญิงชาย 91
ชุดชั้นในและชุดนอน 91
ชุดทักซิโด 89–47
ชุดนอน 91
ชุดนักประดาน้ำ 225–4
ชุดแบบการต่อ 232–9
ชุดปฐมพยาบาล 117–1, 146–18
ชุดรวมหกชิ้น 74–9
ชุดรองในเต็มตัว 91–22
ชุดรองในแบบยาว 91–3
ชุดรับและโทรศัพท์ 14–1
ชุดราตรี 89–18
ชุดว่ายน้ำ 90–26
ชุดสูท 87–11
ชุดสูทนักธุรกิจ 88–11
ชุดเสื้อกระโปรงติดกัน 86–3
ชุดเสื้อกางเกงติดกัน สำหรับทำงาน 93–24
ชุดเสื้อและกางเกงนอน 91–24
ชุดใส่ออกกำลังกาย 89
ชุดหูฟัง 6–8, 14–13, 234–4
ชุดหูฟังแบบไร้สาย 14–14
ชุดอาบน้ำ 90–26
ชุดเอี๊ยม 88–6
เช็ค 132–13
เช็คกระเป๋าของคุณ 160–B
เช็คค่าจ้าง 165–14
เช็คอินทางคอมพิวเตอร์ 160–A
เช็ดถ้วยชามให้แห้ง 60–N
เช็ดถูพื้น 60–D
เช็ดบนเคาน์เตอร์ 60–O
เช็ดล้างหน้าต่าง 60–I
เช็ดออก 109–Q
เชอรี่ 68–11
เช้า 18–15
เชิงเทียน 56–21
เชือก 226–19
เชือกผูกรองเท้า 94–24
เชื้อเชิญใครบางคน 12–H
แชมพูสระผม 108–10
แช่เย็น 76–D
ใช้/ดูหนังสือด้วยกัน 8–M
ใช้เครื่องรับทอนเงิน 170–S
ใช้เครื่องหมายวรรคตอน 190–C
ใช้ถุงบรรจุของซ้ำ 219–B
ใช้บัตรกำนัล 27–E
ใช้บัตรเครดิต 27–B
ใช้บัตรเดบิต [บัตรที่มีเงินไว้ล่วงหน้า] 27–C
ใช้ยาดับกลิ่นตัว 108–C
ใช้ยาจนนั้นให้หมด 112–C

ใช้หลอดไฟแบบประหยัด 219–H
ซองจดหมาย 134–14, 183–43
ซองไปรษณีย์ 183–40
ซองใส่โทรศัพท์มือถือ 94–15
ซ่อน 240–D
ซอฟท์บอล 229–10
ซอฟท์แวร์ 196–10
ซ่อมแซมก๊อกน้ำที่รั่วไหล 219–F
ซ่อมแซมเครื่องใช้ต่างๆ 170–J
ซอสมะเขือเทศ 79–21
ซักผ้าในน้ำเย็น 219–K
ซักเสื้อผ้า 101
ซิป 99–25
ซิปเสีย 97–39
ซีโครงย่าง 76–2
ซีโครงวัว 70–5
ซีพียู 196–4
ซึมเศร้า 115–5
ซื้อ 27–G, 94–A
ซื้อของทางออนไลน์จากเว็บไซท์ที่ ปลอดภัย 143–H
ซื้อของว่าง/ของกินเล่น 11–K
ซื้อบ้าน 41–M
ซื้อสินค้าที่ผลิตจากวัสดุใช้แล้ว 219–D
ซุป 72–18, 80–16
ซุปไก่แบบง่าย 77
ซุ้มขายโทรศัพท์มือถือ 131–22
ซูเปอร์มาร์เก็ต 127–18
ซูแมคมีพิษ 210–23
เซ็ทผม 33–C
เซ็นชื่อของคุณ 4–D
เซนติเมตร [ซม.] 17–14
เซ็นสัญญาข้อตกลงการเช่า 48–D
เซลส์ 194–4
เซลเซียส 13–2
เซลโล 238–7
แซกโซโฟน 238–5
แซนด์วิชกรอบไส้เนยแข็ง 80–10
แซนด์วิชไก่ 79–5
แซนด์วิชบางวางซ้อนเป็นชั้น 80–12
แซลมอนตัดแบบขวางลำตัว 71–4
แซลมอนทั้งตัว 71–3
โซ่ 180–41
โซดา (น้ำหวาน) รวมกัน หกกระป๋อง 74–21
โซดา 73–34
โซ่ประตู 51–33
โซฟา 56–18
โซล 237–28
ไซโตพลาซึม 194–9
ญาติพี่น้อง 44–6
ฐาน 193–45, 194–20
ฐานเตียง 58–18
ดนตรี 64–3, 189–16, 238
ดนตรีของโลก 237–32
ดนตรีแสดงสด 84–1
ดรอปเปอร์ 195–45
ดวงดาว 205–13
ดวงอาทิตย์ 209–8

ดอกจำพวกมณฑา 210–8
ดอกดิน 211–17
ดอกต้นคริสต์มาส 211–24
ดอกตูม 211–7
ดอกไม้ 208–7, 211
ดอกลายสำหรับเย็บติด 99–31
ดอกสน 210–11
ดักแด้ 214–20
ดัชนี 247
ดัดผม 33–B
ด้าย 99–23, 100–11
ด้ายขัดฟัน 109–24
ดาว 205–13
ดาวเกตุ 205–8
ดาวเทียม 205–20
ดาวพระศุกร์ 205–2
ดาวพฤหัสบดี 205–5
ดาวมฤตยู 205–7
ดาวพุธ 205–1
ดาวเรือง 211–13
ดาวเสาร์ 205–6
ดาวหาง 205–24
ดาวอังคาร 205–4
ด่า 24–13
ดำน้ำ 230–K
ดินปลูกต้นไม้ 208–2
ดินสอ 7–20
ดินสอเขียนขอบตา 109–36
ดินสอเขียนคิ้ว 109–34
ดีใจ 44–5
ดีวีดี 133–19
ดึงล้อลาก 224–A
ดื่ม 11–J
ดื่มน้ำ/เครื่องดื่มของเหลว 114–C
ดุลบัญชี 132–17
ดูดฝุ่นตามพรม 60–H
ดูทีวี 39–X
ดูบ้าน 49–H
ดูแลเด็ก 170–P
เด็กก่อนวัยเรียน 188–1
เด็กเงียบ 23–12
เด็กชายวัย 6 ขวบ 31–9
เด็กวัยรุ่น 31–11
เด็กวัยหัดเดิน 31–8
เด็กส่งเสียงดัง 23–11
เด็กส่งเสียงรบกวน 23–11
เด็กหญิงวัย 10 ขวบ 31–10
เด็กหาย 144–1
เด็กอ่อน 31–7
เดซี่ 211–14
เดินกับเพื่อน 143–A
เดินขึ้นบันได 153–C
เดินเครื่องจักรขนาดใหญ่ 170–H
เดินดู 102–B
เดินทาง 41–P
เดินข้ามถนนนอกทาง 128–C
เดินไปที่ห้องเรียน 11–C
เดินฝ่านการตรวจเพื่อความปลอดภัย 160–D

เดินลงบันได 153–D
เดียวดาย 42–17
เดือน 20–3
เดือนต่างๆในหนึ่งปี 21
แดง 24–1
โดนใบสั่งเพราะขับเร็วเกินกำหนด 162–C
โดนัท 79–15
โดยสารรถร่วมกัน 219–I
ได้กลิ่น 106–C
ได้งานทำ 40–F
ได้จับต้อง 106–E
ได้ยิน 106–B
ไดรฟ์สำหรับดีวีดีและซีดีรอม 196–9
ไดรฟ์หน่วยความจำ 196–8
ได้รส 106–D
ได้รับการว่าจ้าง 173–L
ได้รับบาดเจ็บ 116–C
ได้รับเลือกตั้ง 139–C
ได้สัญชาติเป็นพลเมือง 40–G
ไดอะแฟรม 194–18
ตกหลุมรัก 40–H
ตงเหล็ก 178–3
ต้นขั้วใบจ่าย 165–11
ต้นขา 106–19
ต้นขึ้นฉ่าย 69–9
ต้นคริสต์มาส 239–16
ต้นเบิร์ช 210–7
ต้นแบบสำหรับตัด 99–22
ต้นไม้ 208–1
ต้นไม้ประดับภายในบ้าน 56–4
ต้นไม้และพืชพันธุ์ 210
ต้นเรดวูด 210–18
ต้นหอม 69–20
ต้นอ่อน 211–4
ต้นเอล์ม 210–16
ต้นโอ๊ค 210–17
ต้มไก่ 77–M
ต้มไฟอ่อน 77–P
ตรงตามกำหนดเวลา 19–23, 161–29
ตรงไปตามถนนเอล์ม 155–A
ตรวจ...ชีพจร 122–A
ตรวจการสะกดคำของคุณ 197–F
ตรวจแก้ 191–I
ตรวจดู...คอ 118–E
ตรวจดู...ตา 118–D
ตรวจดูการออกเสียง 8–D
ตรวจดูงานของคุณ 10–L
ตรวจดูงานเสนอในไซท์ อินเทอร์เน็ต 173–D
ตรวจดูน้ำมันเครื่อง 157–H
ตรวจดูอีเมล 39–W
ตรวจฟังข้อความ 171–R
ตรวจยืมหนังสือออก 133–C
ตรวจยืมออกด้วยตนเอง 133–10
ตรวจวัด...ความดันโลหิต 118–A
ตรวจสอบความเข้าใจของคุณ 12–N
ตรวจสอบโลหิต 121–30
ตรวจสอบสาธารณูปโภคต่างๆ (เช่น ไฟฟ้า แก๊ส) 147–N

ตรอก **51**–24
ตระหนักถึงสิ่งแวดล้อมของคุณ
เสมอ **143**–I
ตราไปรษณีย์ **134**–24
ตรายาง **183**–47
ตรีโกณมิติ **192**–18
ตลก **237**–13
ตลับแบตเตอรี่ **235**–26
ตลาดเกษตรกร **84**
ตลาดนัดขายของเก่า **222**–6
ตวง **17**–C
ตวงเครื่องปรุง **75**–A
ต่อ 911 แจ้งชื่อของคุณ **15**–E
ตอกไข่ 2 ฟอง
ลงในชามอ่างที่ใส่เตาไมโครเวฟได้ **77**–Q
ต้องตรงเวลา **174**–F
ตอบคำถาม **8**–L
ต่อไปข้างหน้าโดยเร็ว **235**–D
ต่อรองราคา **102**–A, **157**–D
ต่อหมายเลขโทรฯ **15**–A
ตะกร้า **56**–3
ตะกร้าขนมปัง **83**–11
ตะกร้าจับจ่าย **73**–9
ตะกร้าใส่ขยะ **57**–26
ตะกร้าใส่เสื้อผ้าที่ต้องซัก **101**–2
ตะเกียงน้ำมัน **226**–22
ตะแกรงวางถ้วยชาม **54**–5
ตะแกรงสำหรับอบหรือย่าง **78**–14
ตะขอเกียว **180**–39
ตะขอและห่วงเกียว **99**–27
ตะขอและห่วงรัด **99**–29
ตะบองเพชร **210**–21
ตะปู **180**–34
ตะวันตก **155**–2
ตะวันตกเฉียงใต้ **201**–12
ตะวันตกเฉียงเหนือฝั่งแปซิฟิก **201**–14
ตะวันออก **155**–4
ตะวันออกเฉียงใต้ **201**–13
ตักซอสราดหน้า **77**–F
ตั๊กแตน **214**–24
ตั้งความปรารถนา **240**–B
ตั้งแต่เที่ยงคืนถึง 11 นาฬิกา
59 นาที **18**–4
ตั้งแต่เที่ยงวันถึง 23 นาฬิกา
59 นาที **18**–5
ตั้งเป้าหมาย **10**–A
ตั้งอยู่ในความสงบ **147**–E
ตัด...เล็บ **109**–N
ตัดเต้าหู้เป็นแผ่น **77**–C
ตัดเนื้อไก่เป็นชิ้นๆ **77**–I
ตัดผม **33**–A
ตัดสินลงโทษจำเลย **141**–F
ตัดหญ้า **176**–A
ตับ **70**–7, **107**–40
ตับอ่อน **107**–45
ตั๋ว **152**–15
ตัวกินมด **217**–24
ตัวควบคุมเกมวิดีโอ **232**–4
ตัวควบคุมปรับระดับเตียง **121**–27

ตัวควบคุมวิถีไกล **234**–9
ตัวเครื่องแบบตั้ง **196**–3
ตัวจำนวนเต็ม **192**
ตัวด้วง **214**–20
ตัวต่อ **214**–17
ตั๋วที่ออกทางคอมพิวเตอร์ **161**–19
ตัวแทนขายรถยนต์ **126**–4
ตัวแทนบริการท่องเที่ยว **131**–14
ตัวนางอาย **216**–8
ตัวนิ่ม **216**–8
ตัวปรับต่อ **234**–15
ตัวป้อน **98**–20
ตัวร้อนมีไข้ **110**–8
ตัวเล็กเกินไป **97**–37
ตัวเลข **16**
ตัวเลขจำนวนเต็มติดลบ **192**–1
ตัวเลขจำนวนเต็มเป็นบวก **192**–2
ตัวเลขจำนวนนับ **16**
ตัวเหม็น **216**–12
ตัวใหญ่เกินไป **97**–38
ตัวอย่าง **84**–5
ตัวอักษร **7**–13
ตา **34**–2, **105**–11, **106**
ตา/กระดานหมากรุก **232**–7
ตาข่ายซ้อนปลา **226**–17
ต่างหูแบบเจาะ **95**–36
ต่างหูแบบหนีบ **95**–37
ตาชั่ง **72**–3, **135**–8, **195**–41
ตาชั่งของส่งไปรษณีย์ **183**–27
ตาบอด **32**–11
ตาย **41**–R
ตารางแบ่งธาตุแท้ **195**–26
ตารางเวลา **152**–4
ตำรวจศาล **141**–13
ตำรา **7**–25
ติดตั้งระบบฉีดรดน้ำต้นไม้ **176**–H
ติดตามข่าวสภาพอากาศ **147**–C
ติดวางกระเบื้อง **178**–C
ติดแสตมป์ **135**–C
ตี **230**–B
ตี่ต่าง **233**–G
ตีส่วนผสมนั้น **77**–S
ตึกกระฟ้า **127**–13
ตึงเครียด **115**–4
ตื่นเต้น **43**–22
ตื่นนอน **38**–A
ตุ๊กตา **59**–21
ตุ๊กตากระดาษ **233**–28
ตุ๊กตานักสู้ **233**–26
ตุ๊กตาผ้ารูปสัตว์ต่างๆ **59**–15
ตุ๊กตาหมี **37**–23
ตุ่มพอง **110**–15
ตุลาคม **21**–34
ตู้ **54**–1
ตู้เก็บของ **5**–11, **50**–17
ตู้เก็บของใช้ในสำนักงาน **182**–1
ตู้เก็บเครื่องใช้ในห้องอาหาร **55**–24
ตู้เก็บยา **57**–22
ตู้เก็บเอกสาร **182**–11

ตู้จดหมาย **50**–11, **53**–1
ตู้เช็คอิน **160**–2
ตู้แช่แข็ง **54**–10
ตู้โชว์ **94**–5
ตู้เซฟ **132**–6
ตู้แบบมีชั้นภายในและลิ้นชัก **55**–22
ตู้ไปรษณีย์ (ตู้ ปณ.) **135**–9
ตู้ไปรษณีย์ **128**–13
ตู้ฝากนิรภัย **132**–7
ตู้ฟิวส์ไฟฟ้า **62**–13
ตู้มีลิ้นชักใส่เสื้อผ้า **58**–1
ตู้เย็น **54**–9
ตู้รับจดหมาย **128**–13, **135**–12
ตู้รับไปรษณีย์ **135**–12
ตู้ลิ้นชัก **59**–6
ตู้เสื้อผ้า **58**–1
เต็นท์ **226**–10
เต้นรำ **64**–A
เตรียมตัวสำหรับการสัมภาษณ์ **174**–A
เตะ **230**–E
เต่า **213**–43
เตา **54**–18
เต้านม **107**–26
เตาปิ้งย่าง **53**–17
เตาผิง **56**–13
เตาไมโครเวฟ **54**–13
เตารีด **101**–13
เตาหุงต้มสำหรับแคมป์ **226**–16
เตาอบ **54**–20
เตาอบปิ้งขนาดเล็ก **54**–15
เติมน้ำมันรถ **157**–G
เติมในช่องว่าง **9**–O
เติมผงซักฟอก **101**–B
เติมผัก **77**–N
เติมลมรถ **157**–L
เตี้ย **32**–6
เตียง **58**–9
เตียงขนาดใหญ่พิเศษ **184**–15
เตียงคู่ **184**–14
เตียงผู้ป่วย **121**–22
เตียงล้อเลื่อน **121**–33
เตียงสองชั้น **59**–9
แดง **68**–19
แดง...เล็บ **109**–O
แดงกวา **69**–10
แดงกวาดอง **80**–11
แต่งงาน **22**–2, **41**–K
แต่งงานใหม่ **35**–24
แต่งตัวให้เหมาะสม **174**–B
แดงซูคีนี **69**–25
แดงตัว **38**–D
แดงประเภทฟักทอง **69**–24
แดงโม **68**–18
แต้ม **229**–1
แตร **159**–32, **238**–11
แตรทองเหลือง **238**
แตรฝรั่งเศส **238**–13
โต๊ะ/เตียงตรวจ **118**–7
โต๊ะเก้าอี้สนาม **53**–19

โต๊ะเรียน **6**–7
โต๊ะข้างเก้าอี้ **56**–14
โต๊ะข้างเตียง **58**–23, **121**–21
โต๊ะตรวจยืมและคืนหนังสือ **133**–2
โต๊ะทำงาน **6**–7, **182**–9
โต๊ะในห้องอาหาร **55**–9
โต๊ะบิลเลียด **50**–15
โต๊ะปิคนิค **224**–8
โต๊ะผ่าตัด **121**–40
โต๊ะพับหลังพนักเก้าอี้ **161**–21
โต๊ะรับแขก **56**–19
โต๊ะรีดผ้า **101**–14
โต๊ะเล็กแบบพับได้ **102**–4
โต๊ะสลัด **79**–24
โต๊ะสำหรับเปลี่ยนผ้าอ้อม **59**–1
โต๊ะหัวเตียง **58**–23
ใต้ **155**–3, **201**–13
ใต้ถุนอาคาร **50**
ไต **107**–43
ถนน **150**–5, **155**–8
ถนนในเมือง **126**–127
ถ้วย **55**–2
ถ้วยกาแฟ **83**–24
ถ้วยครีม **55**–15
ถ้วยชา **55**–6
ถ้วยชาม **55**–1
ถ้วยซุป **83**–21
ถ้วยน้ำตาล **55**–14
ถอดเสื้อผ้า **36**–E
ถอนเงินสด **132**–F
ถอนฟัน **119**–F
ถัก **233**–F
ถักเป็นแถว **33**–14
ถัง **225**–8
ถังขยะ **51**–23, **53**–24
ถังขยะรีไซเคิล **61**–2
ถังน้ำ **61**–7
ถังน้ำมัน **158**–10
ถังใส่ผ้าอ้อม **37**–7
ถั่ว **72**–17
ถั่วแขก **69**–8
ถั่วลันเตา **69**–21
ถั่วหนึ่งกระป๋อง **74**–15
ถั่วเหลือง **177**–3
ถาด **55**–17
ถาดของหวาน **83**–10
ถาดสำหรับอบหรือย่าง **78**–13
ถาดใส่ของ **160**–6
ถาดอบคุกกี้ **78**–27
ถาดอบเค้ก **78**–26
ถาดอบพาย **78**–28
ถ่านหิน **218**–4
ถามคนขายเกี่ยวกับรถ **157**–B
ถามคำถาม **8**–K
ถามคำถามต่างๆ **174**–M
ถามว่า "สบายดีไหม" **2**–B
ถ่าย...เอ็กซ์เรย์ **119**–B
ถ่ายบันทึกวิดีโอ **240**–A
ถ่ายรูป **206**–A

ถ่ายเอกสาร **171**–D
ถ้ำ **220**–6
ถีบจักรยาน **228**–5
ถึงบ้าน **39**–R
ถึงเส้นชัย **230**–T
ถือ **11**–F, **82**–H
ถือสายรออยู่ **15**–H
ถุง **74**–7, **217**–50
ถุงขยะ **61**–24
ถุงเท้า **86**–6
ถุงเท้าแบบสวยงาม **91**–9
ถุงเท้ายาวถึงข้อเท้า **91**–11
ถุงเท้ายาวแค่ข้อเท้า **91**–7
ถุงเท้ายาวถึงน่อง **91**–8
ถุงเท้าสั้น **91**–10
ถุงเท้าหญิง **91**
ถุงเท้าหญิงชาย **91**
ถุงน่องยาวถึงเข่า **91**–12
ถุงนอน **226**–12
ถุงน้ำแข็ง **117**–13
ถุงน้ำดี **107**–44
ถุงน้ำร้อน **113**–15
ถุงฝุ่นในเครื่องดูดฝุ่น **61**–12
ถุงพลาสติกจัดเก็บอาหาร **72**–25
ถุงมือ **90**–6, **231**–17
ถุงมือทำงาน **92**–17, **179**–17
ถุงมือที่ใช้แล้วทิ้ง **93**–27
ถุงมือแบบไม่มีนิ้ว **90**–10
ถุงมือยาง **61**–4, **93**–34
ถุงมือศัลยกรรม **121**–39
ถุงใบบัวยาวถึงต้นขา **91**–17
ถุงใบบัวยาวถึงเอว **91**–18
ถุงลมนิรภัย **159**–43
ถุงใส่ของชำ **67**–13
ถูกปล่อยตัว **141**–H
ถูกไฟฟ้าดูด **116**–F
ถูกรบกวน **64**–6
แถบคลุมศีรษะ **90**–3
แถบที่ราบสูงของเม็กซิโก **201**–15
แถบโบว์ **99**–30
แถบเมนู **197**–1
แถบรหัส **27**–4
แถบระบาย **99**–34
แถบเลื่อน **197**–15
โถงทางเดิน **5**–10, **51**,
    184–18
โถส้วม **57**–21
ทนายฝ่ายจำเลย **141**–4
ทนายฝ่ายดำเนินคดี **141**–10
ทรงกลม **193**–42
ทรงผม **33**
ทรวงอก **107**–26
ทรอมโบน **238**–10
ทรัมเป็ท **238**–11
ทราย **225**–23
ท่วม **32**–7
ทวีป **202**
ทหาร **169**–58
ทหารฝ่ายอเมริกายุคนั้น **198**–10

ทหารอังกฤษยุคนั้น
    (ใส่เสื้อสีแดง) **198**–9
ท่อ **181**–17
ท่อ **68**–10
ท้องฟ้า **209**–9
ท้องฟ้าโปร่ง **13**–9
ท่อน **74**–10
ท่อเป็นน้ำแข็ง **63**–16
ท่อไอเสีย **158**–15
ทะเบียนสมรส **41**–8
ทะเลทราย **204**–4
ทะเลสาบ **204**–13
ทักทายผู้คน **3**–G
ทักทายผู้ที่โทรเข้ามา **171**–M
ทักทายผู้สัมภาษณ์ **174**–H
ทักษะการทำงาน **170**
ทักษะการทำงานในสำนักงาน **171**
ทักษะในการโทรศัพท์ **171**
ทักษะในการสัมภาษณ์ **174**
ทันตกรรม **119**
ทันตแพทย์ **119**–1
ทันตแพทย์ผู้เชี่ยวชาญการจัดฟัน **119**–5
ทัพพี **78**–7
ทัศนียภาพที่ไม่น่าดู **23**–22
ทัศนียภาพที่สวยงาม **23**–21
ทา **109**–P
ท่า **225**–18, **234**–3
ทาโก **79**–8
ทาครีมกันแดด **108**–D
ทางข้าม **128**–15
ทางข้ามของโรงเรียน **154**–15
ทางข้ามรางรถไฟ **154**–14
ทางข้ามสำหรับคนเดินเท้า **154**–13
ทางเข้า **50**, **164**–1
ทางเข้าห้องฉุกเฉิน **121**
ทางเข้าอพาร์ตเมนต์ **51**
ทางจักรยาน **224**–3
ทางเชื่อม **154**–10
ทางเดิน **208**–3
ทางเดินข้างถนน **129**–24
ทางเดินระหว่างชั้นวางของ **72**–6
ทางเดินหน้าบ้าน **53**–2
ทางตัน **154**–6
ทางบันได **50**–10
ทางแยก **128**–129
ทางรถเข้าออก **53**–8
ทางหนี **146**–3
ทางหนีไฟ **50**–2
ทางหลวง **155**–9
ทางหลวงระหว่างรัฐในสหรัฐฯ **154**–17
ทางออกฉุกเฉิน **51**–25, **161**–14
ท่าเทียบขึ้นสินค้า **175**–15
ทานตะวัน **211**–10
ทานน้ำมันในถาดอบ **77**–B
ทารก **31**–6
ทาวน์เฮ้าส์ **52**–6
ทาส **198**–4
ทาส **49**–P, **178**–A

ทำการจ่ายเงินจำนอง **49**–L
ทำการทดลอง **195**–B
ทำการบ้าน **39**–T
ทำการฝาก **132**–B
ทำการฝีมือ **232**–D
ทำการพูดคุยเรื่องเล็กน้อยทั่วไป **12**–B
ทำข้อทดสอบเพื่อการเป็นพลเมือง **140**–I
ทำข้อสอบ **10**
ทำขากางเกงให้ยาวขึ้น **100**–A
ทำขากางเกงให้สั้นลง **100**–B
ทำความสะอาด...ฟัน **119**–A
ทำความสะอาดตะแกรงกรอง
    ใยผ้า **101**–D
ทำความสะอาดเตาอบ **60**–C
ทำความสะอาดบ้าน **39**–O
ทำงาน **38**–K
ทำงานกับเพื่อนร่วมชั้นเรียน **8**
ทำงานด้วยตนเอง **10**–J
ทำงานที่ใช้แรงงาน **170**–D
ทำงานเป็นกลุ่ม **8**–I
ทำงานเป็นคู่ **8**
ทำชุดบรรเทาทุกข์ **146**–B
ทำตามคำสั่ง **9**
ทำที่นอน **60**–F
ทำเนียบขาว **138**–7
ทำแบบทดสอบ **137**–E
ทำปุ๋ยหมักด้วยเศษอาหาร **219**–M
ทำโปรแกรมคอมพิวเตอร์ **170**–I
ทำเฟอร์นิเจอร์ **170**–G
ทำวงกลมรอบคำตอบ **9**–Q
ทำสีผม **33**–D
ทำสุก **76**–C
ทำหน้าที่ในคณะลูกขุน **140**–E
ทำหมายกำหนดการประชุม **171**–J
ทำให้ดูเรียบร้อย **174**–C
ทำให้ได้คะแนนดี **10**–H
ทำให้มีความคืบหน้า **10**–G
ทำอาหาร **170**–C
ทำอาหารกลางวัน **38**–F
ทำอาหารเย็น **39**–Q
ทิวทัศน์ **162**–2
ทิวลิป **211**–11
ทิศทาง **155**
ทิศทางและแผนที่ **155**
ที่เก็บของหลังรถ **158**–11
ที่เก็บของเหนือศีรษะ **161**–13
ที่เก้า **16**
ที่เก้าสิบ **16**
ที่ขูด **78**–2
ที่ครอบหูกันหนาว **90**–13
ที่จอดรถ **50**–18, **128**–5
ที่จอดรถสำหรับคนพิการ **128**–6
ที่จอดสำหรับผู้พิการ **154**–12
ที่จุดตรวจเพื่อความปลอดภัย **160**
ที่เจ็ด **16**
ที่เจ็ดสิบ **16**
ที่ชั่งน้ำหนัก **57**–27, **72**–3
ที่ด่านศุลกากร **161**
ที่ตัดกระดาษ **183**–22

ที่ตัวแทนจำหน่าย **158**
ที่ตีไข่ **78**–20
ที่ทำงาน **164**
ที่ทิ้งขยะด้านการแพทย์ **121**–31
ที่นอนเด็ก **59**–3
ที่นั่งด้านหน้า **159**–51
ที่นั่งด้านหลัง **159**–54
ที่นั่งนิรภัยในรถสำหรับเด็ก **37**–19
ที่นั่งพนักตั้งตรง **161**–28
ที่นั่งพนักเอนหลัง **161**–27
ที่นั่งล้อขึ้น **113**–9
ที่ประตูทางเข้าออก **161**
ที่ปราศจากน้ำตาล **122**–7
ที่ปัดน้ำฝน **158**–2
ที่ปั้นไข่แบบแส้ **78**–21
ที่แปด **16**
ที่แปดสิบ **16**
ที่ฝนเล็บ **109**–32
ที่พยุงตัวช่วยเดิน **113**–11
ที่พักพิงยามยาก **52**–13
ที่พักแรมที่มีห้องพักพร้อมที่จอดรถ
    126–12
ที่พัน **16**
ทีม **229**–3
ที่ยี่สิบ **16**
ที่ยี่สิบเอ็ด **16**
ที่เย็บกระดาษ **183**–28
ที่ร้อย **16**
ที่ราบ **204**–19
ที่ราบริมฝั่งอ่าว (เม็กซิโก) **201**–16
ที่ลบกระดาน **7**–19
ที่วางของรอคิดเงิน **73**–12
ทีวี (เครื่องรับโทรทัศน์) **56**–6
ทีวีกระเป๋าหิ้ว **234**–8
ทีวีจอแบน **234**–7
ทีวีจอใหญ่ **50**–14
ทีวีแผงแบน **234**–7
ที่สอง **16**
ที่สาม **16**
ที่สามสิบ **16**
ที่สิบ **16**
ที่สิบเก้า **16**
ที่สิบเจ็ด **16**
ที่สิบแปด **16**
ที่สิบสอง **16**
ที่สิบสาม **16**
ที่สิบสี่ **16**
ที่สิบหก **16**
ที่สิบห้า **16**
ที่สิบเอ็ด **16**
ที่สี่ **16**
ที่สี่สิบ **16**
ที่สูงภาคใต้ **201**–17
ที่สุดดม **113**–33
ที่ใส่เกลือและพริกไทย **55**–13
ที่ใส่ทารก **37**–17
ที่ใส่แปรงสีฟัน **57**–24
ที่ใส่เสื้อผ้ารอซัก **57**–1
ที่ใส่หนังสือพิมพ์/นิตยสาร **56**–23

ที่หก **16**
ที่หกสิบ **16**
ที่หนีบยึดงานรูปตัวซี **180**–6
ที่หนึ่ง **16**
ที่หลบภัย **52**–13
ที่ห้า **16**
ที่ห้าสิบ **16**
ที่อยู่ **4**–5
ที่อยู่ของผู้ส่ง **134**–21
ที่อยู่ของเว็บไซต์ **197**–4
ที่อยู่อาศัยคนชราที่มีคนดูแล **52**–12
ที่อยู่อาศัยในที่ต่างๆ **52**
ที่อยู่อาศัยสำหรับคนชรา **52**–11
ที่อาศัยอยู่ **194**–11
ที่อู่รถ **158**
ทุกวัน **20**–21
ทุ่งหญ้าในป่า **204**–20
ทุ่นแห่นในขบวน **239**–2
ทุบด้วยค้อน **178**–D
ทูน่า **71**–7, **212**–8
ทูบา **238**–12
เทขยะทิ้ง **60**–L
เทนนิส **228**–15
เทน่า **82**–C
เทฆ่าเชื้อแล้ว **117**–7
เทติดทอลม **181**–49
เทปปิดทับชั่วคราว **181**–53
เทปปิดหีบห่อ **183**–32
เทปลบคำผิด **183**–37
เทปวีดีโอ **133**–18
เทปสายไฟ **181**–43
เทปใส **183**–30
เท้า **104**–8
เทา **24**–15
เท้าเข็ม **98**–19
เที่ยงคืน **18**–21
เที่ยงวัน **18**–16
เทียน **56**–20
เที่ยวเดียว **152**–16
เที่ยวบินมาข้า **161**–30
เทือกเขา **204**–15
แท็กซี่ **150**–3
แท่งกาว **232**–11
แท่งค์ประดาน้ำ **225**–5
แท่งลูกกวาด **239**–17
แท่น **194**–17
แท่นเครื่อง **234**–3
แท่นปราศรัย **206**–5
แท่นรับเข็ม **98**–18
แท่นวางสินค้า **175**–13
แท่นสปริงรองฟูก **58**–19
แท่นเหนือเตาผิง **56**–11
แท็บ **197**–7
แทมบูริน **238**–17
โทรถึงผู้จัดการ **48**–A
โทรศัพท์ **14**–15
โทรศัพท์ถึงผู้ที่ติดต่อได้ภายนอกรัฐ
    147–L
โทรศัพท์แบบหยอดเหรียญ **129**–23

โทรศัพท์มือถือ **14**–8
โทรศัพท์ไร้สาย **15**–24
โทรศัพท์ลาป่วย **186**–A
โทรศัพท์สาธารณะ
    (หยอดเหรียญหรือใช้บัตร) **15**–25
โทรศัพท์อัจฉริยะ **15**–27
ไทหูกระต่าย **89**–16
ธง **239**–8
ธนบัตร **26**
ธนาคาร **124**–5, **132**
ธนาคารทางออนไลน์ **132**–C
ธัญพืชร้อน **80**–9
ธัญพืชหนึ่งกล่อง **74**–18
ธันวาคม **21**–36
นก **208**–4
นก แมลง และ แมง **214**
นกกระจอก **214**–7
นกแก้ว **215**–15
นกแขกเต้า **215**–15
นกเค้าแมว **214**–5
นกตะขาบน้ำเงิน **214**–6
นกเพนกวิน **214**–11
นกยูง **214**–14
นกเล็กชนิดหนึ่ง **214**–10
นกเล็กชนิดหนึ่ง
    แผงอกสีแดงร้องเสียงเพราะ **214**–16
นกหัวขวาน **214**–8
นกอินทรีย์ **214**–9
นม **66**–5
นมไขมันต่ำ **81**–42
นมปั่น **79**–14
นมผงสำหรับทารก **37**–3
นมหนึ่งควอท (สี่ถ้วยตวง) **75**–4
นมหนึ่งออนซ์ **75**–1
นวนิยาย **133**–16
นอกโฟกัส **235**–33
น่อง **70**–23, **106**–22
นอนพักผ่อน **114**–B
นักกฎหมาย **168**–36
นักการตลาดทางโทรศัพท์ **169**–60
นักข่าว **169**–52
นักเขียน **169**–64
นักเคมี **195**–25
นักเคลื่อนไหว **199**–17
นักชีววิทยา **194**–2
นักดนตรี **168**–43
นักดาราศาสตร์ **205**–22
นักโต้คลื่น **225**–15
นักโทษ **141**–15
นักธุรกิจ **166**–12
นักบิน **161**–11
นักประดิษฐ์ **199**–18
นักประพันธ์ **169**–64
นักประพันธ์เพลง **199**–14
นักปั่นจักรยาน **224**–2
นักแปล **168**–35
นักฟิสิกส์ **195**–33
นักโภชนาการ **120**–15
นักเรียน ผู้สอน **6**–5

นักศึกษา **6**–5
นักสำรวจ **199**–9
นักแสดง **166**–2
นักอวกาศ **205**–17
นักออกแบบ **175**–2
นักออกแบบกราฟิก **167**–30
นักออกแบบงานจัดสวน **176**–5
นังร้าน **178**–4
นังลง **6**–F
นับ **84**–A
นา **177**–7
นาก **216**–9
นากทะเล **213**–35
นางแบบ **168**–41
นาโชส **79**–7
น่าดึงดูดใจ **32**–13
นาที **18**–2
นามสกุล **4**–4
นายกเทศมนตรี **139**–26
นายกรัฐมนตรี **199**–7
นายจ้าง **164**–4
น่ารัก **32**–14
นาวิกโยธิน **138**–17
นาฬิกา **7**–9
นาฬิกา(ข้อมือ) **94**–16
นาฬิกาแบบมีวิทยุ **102**–6
นาฬิกาปลุก **58**–24
นาฬิกาลงเวลา **165**–7
น่าเอ็นดู **32**–14
นาฬิกาตั้งเวลาในครัว **78**–18
น้ำ **209**–13, **225**–1
นำกลับมาใช้ใหม่ **219**–C
น้ำเงิน **24**–3
น้ำเงินเข้ม **24**–10
น้ำดื่มบรรจุขวด **146**–11
น้ำตก **204**–2
น้ำตาล **24**–17, **73**–30
น้ำตาลแดงเศษหนึ่งส่วนสี่ถ้วยตวง **75**–8
น้ำตาลเทียม **79**–20
น้ำตาลหนึ่งช้อนโต๊ะ **75**–7
น้ำตาลอ่อน **24**–18
น้ำเต้า **69**–24
น้ำท่วม **145**–19
นำประวัติการทำงานและบัตรประจำตัว
    ของคุณมา **174**–D
น่าฝาก **132**–3
น้ำพุ **224**–5
น้ำมะนาว **84**–3
น้ำมัน **73**–31, **218**–6
น้ำมันหนึ่งถ้วยตวง **75**–2
น้ำมันหมด **162**–E
น่ามา **240**–E
น้ำยากันแดด **108**–7
น้ำยาขัดเงาเครื่องเรือน **61**–8
น้ำยาเช็ดกระจก **61**–14
น้ำยาทาสีไม้ **181**–24
น้ำยาทาหลังโกน **109**–30
น้ำยาทำความสะอาด **61**–18
น้ำยาทำความสะอาดเตาอบ **61**–3

น้ำยาปรับผ้านุ่ม **101**–6
น้ำยาปรับเส้นผม **108**–11
น้ำยาฟอกสี **101**–7
น้ำยาลบคำผิด **183**–36
น้ำยาล้างเครื่องแต่งหน้าออก **109**–42
น้ำยาล้างจาน **61**–21
น้ำยาล้างปาก **109**–25
น้ำยาล้างแผล **117**–9
น้ำยาไล่แมลง **226**–23
น้ำเย็น **57**–10
นำรถไปตรวจปริมาณไอเสีย **157**–J
นำรถไปให้ช่างดู **157**–C
น้ำร้อน **57**–9
นำส่งการ์ดไปถึง **135**–E
น้ำหนัก **32**, **75**, **231**–22
น้ำหนักโดยเฉลี่ย **32**–8
น้ำหนักปานกลาง **32**–8
น้ำหนักและการตวงวัด **75**
นำหนังสือพิมพ์ไปใช้ทำ
    ประโยชน์ใหม่ **60**–B
น้ำหนึ่งแกลลอน **75**–5
น้ำหนึ่งขวด **74**–13
น้ำหวาน **73**–34
น้ำหอม **108**–6
น้ำไหลล้นอ่าง **63**–18
น้ำอัดลม **79**–11
นำอาหารไปรับประทานที่สวน **224**–D
น้ำแอปเปิ้ล **73**–32
นิตยสาร **133**–5
นิทานกล่อมเด็ก **37**–22
นิ้ว [น.] **17**–15
นิวเคลียส **194**–7, **195**–29
นิวตรอน **195**–32
นิ้วเท้า **94**–23, **105**–10
นิ้วบวม **110**–16
นิ้วมือ **105**–16
นิ้วหัวแม่มือ **106**–16
นิวอิงแลนด์ **201**–11
นึ่งบร๊อคโคลี่ **77**–D
เนคไท **88**–12, **92**–13
เนคไทแบบเส้นกว้าง **97**–36
เนคไทแบบเส้นแคบ **97**–35
เน็ทคลุมผม **93**–25
เนย **66**–6
เนยแข็ง **66**–4
เนยแข็งคอทเทจหนึ่งภาชนะ **74**–17
เนยแข็งเชดดา **71**–28
เนยแข็งโมซซาเรลลา **71**–29
เนยแข็งสวิส **71**–27
เนยแข็งหนึ่งออนซ์ **75**–11
เนยแข็งอเมริกัน **71**–26
เนยเทียม **72**–20
เนื้อ **66**–2
เนื้อแกะ **70**
เนื้อไก่ย่างรมควัน **71**–25
เนื้อความ **190**–7
เนื้อแดงแกะติดมัน **70**–15
เนื้อแดงหมูติดมัน **70**–10
เนื้อบดอบ **81**–31

เนื้อลูกวัว 70–6
เนื้อวัว 70
เนื้อวัวบด 70–4
เนื้อวัวผัด 76–6
เนื้อวัวหมักปรุงรส 71–22
เนื้อวัวหมักรมควัน 71–23
เนื้อวัวอบ 71–21
เนื้อวัวอบหนึ่งปอนด์ 75–12
เนื้อสัตว์ปีก 70
เนื้อสัตว์และเนื้อสัตว์ปีก 70
เนื้อสำหรับตุ๋น 70–3
เนื้อหน้าอก 70–19
แนบแฟ้ม 197–H
แนบภาพ 197–G
แนวทแยงมุม 193–31
แนะนำ ตนเอง 2–C
แนะนำเพื่อน 3–I
ในคอ 107–35
ในเมือง 124
ในร่ม 225–13
ในระหว่างเหตุฉุกเฉิน 147
ในห้องตรวจ 118
ในห้องนั่งรอ 118
ในอาคารสนามบิน 160
ไนท์คลับ 223–12
บทบัญญัติว่าด้วยสิทธิต่างๆ 198–13
บทสนทนาในชีวิตประจำวัน 12
บนเครื่องบิน 161
บรรณารักษ์แผนกหนังสืออ้างอิง 133–9
บร็อคโคลี่ 69–13
บริการด้านอาหาร 185
บริการลูกค้า 170–T
บริติชโคลัมเบีย 201–2
บริเวณจัดเป็นสัดส่วนเฉพาะ 82–4
บริเวณเด็กเล่น 130–11
บริเวณโดยรอบโรงเรียน 5
บริเวณตรวจเพื่อความปลอดภัย 160–4
บริเวณต้อนรับแขก 182–15
บริเวณตัวเมือง 52–1
บริเวณทดสอบ 136–2
บริเวณท้อง 107–27
บริเวณทางขึ้นเครื่อง 161–9
บริเวณที่กั้นสำหรับพนักงานแต่ละคน 182–7
บริเวณรับประทานอาหาร 46–7, 55
บริเวณห้องคนขับ 156–16
บริหารร่างกาย 39–P, 230–N
บล็อกของเล่น 59–19
บล็อคสำหรับทำผ้าตัดต่อลาย 232–15
บลูเบอร์รี่ 68–16
บลูส์ 237–22
บวก 192–A
บ้วนปาก 109–L
บอกชื่อของคุณ 4–A
บอกประโยคให้เขียนตาม 8–N
บอบบาง 32–9
บอล 59–12
บอลโบว์ลิ่ง 231–5
บังตาขนาดเล็ก 58–8

บัตรขึ้นเครื่อง 161–20
บัตรค่าโดยสาร 152–11
บัตรโทรศัพท์ 14–15
บัตรบุคคลต่างด้าวที่อาศัยอยู่ใน สหรัฐฯ 40–2
บัตรประกันสังคม 40–5
บัตรประกันสุขภาพ 118–3
บัตรผ่าน/เปลี่ยนเส้นทาง 152–5
บัตรสโมสรผู้ใช้ยานยนต์ 162–4
บัตรอธิบายเหตุฉุกเฉิน 161–26
บัตรอวยพร 134–15
บัตรเอทีเอ็ม 132–15
บันได 50–10, 178–2
บันไดเลื่อน 131–23
บันไดหัก 62–7
บันทึก 235–A
บันทึกผลที่ได้รับ 195–D
บาด 110–13
บาดเจ็บ 116–C
บ้าน 46
บ้านตุ๊กตา 59–18
บ้านแบบเคลื่อนย้ายได้ 52–7
บ้านและสนาม 53
ป่าย 18–17
บาสเก็ตบอล 229–8, 231–4
บาสซูน 238–4
บิลเลียด 228–2
บึง 204–21
บุฟเฟต์ 185–10
บู๊ทสำหรับเล่นสกี 231–26
เบคอน 80–1
เบญจมาศ 211–21
เบรคมือ 159–48
เบส 238–8
เบสบอล 229–9
เบอริโต 79–9
เบอร์รี่ต่างๆผสมกัน 81–36
เบาหวาน 111–12
เบิกขึ้นเงินเช็คเดินทาง 27–F
เบื่อหน่าย 43–25
แบ่ง 17–A
แบดมินตัน 228–6
แบตเตอรี่ 146–15, 158–20
แบบ 96
แบบคาวบอยตะวันตก 237–15
แบบฟอร์มการลงทะเบียนเข้าโรงเรียน 4
แบบฟอร์มประวัติสุขภาพ 118–4
แบบฟอร์มไปรษณีย์ 134–19
แบบฟอร์มสำแดงสิ่งของที่นำมา 161–16
แบล็คเบอร์รี่ 68–17
โบกมือ 2–F
โบราณ 199–1
โบว์ลิ่ง 228–3
โบสถ์ 127–14
ใบ 210–6, 211–6
ใบเกิด 40–1
ใบขับขี่ 40–4, 136–9
ใบนำฝาก 132–4
ใบมรณะ 41–11

ใบมีด 180–27
ใบมีดโกน 109–28
ใบมีดสำหรับขูด 181–52
ใบรับรองการแปลงสัญชาติ 40–6
ใบรับรองมรณภาพ 41–11
ใบเรียกเก็บเงินค่าโทรศัพท์ 15–28
ใบวุฒิปริญญา 41–7
ใบสน 210–10
ใบสั่งยาจากแพทย์ 112–2
ใบเสร็จรับเงิน 27–6
ใบแสดงดุลบัญชี 132–16
ใบอนุญาตแท็กซี่ 152–22
ปกปิดหมายเลขรหัสประจำตัว ของคุณ 143–C
ปกเสื้อ 100–4
ปฏิกิริยานิวเคลียร์แบบรวมตัว 218–10
ปฏิทิน 20–21
ปฏิบัติตามคำแนะนำของแพทย์ 114–J
ปฏิบัติตามคำสั่ง 147–F
ปฏิเสธการเชิญชวน 12–J
ปรบมือ 148–B
ประกอบชิ้นส่วน 170–A, 175–C
ประแจมือ 158–22
ประแจมือจับท่อ 181–47
ประแจมือที่ปรับขนาดได้ 181–48
ประตู 46–3
ประตูกระจกแบบเลื่อน 53–18
ประตูกันพายุ 53–10
ประตูทางออกขึ้นเครื่อง 161–8
ประตูเพื่อความปลอดภัย 50–16
ประตูมุ้งลวด 53–15
ประตูรั้ว 53–9
ประตูโรงรถ 53–7
ประตูหน้า 53–11
ประตูหมุน 184–2
ประธานาธิบดี 138–8, 199–5
ประธานาธิบดีคนแรก 198–11
ประพฤติไม่เหมาะสม 44–B
ประเภทของการฝึกอบรมงาน 172
ประเภทของปัญหาด้านสุขภาพ 115
ประเภทของโปรแกรมโทรทัศน์ 236
ประเภทของเพลงหรือดนตรี 237
ประเภทของภาพยนตร์ 237
ประเภทของวิชาคำนวณ 192
ประเภทหอยปู 71
ประโยค 190–2
ประวัติบุคคล 133–13
ประวัติศาสตร์ 189–12
ประวัติศาสตร์โลก 199
ประวัติศาสตร์สหรัฐอเมริกา 198
ประสาทสัมผัส 106
ประหม่า 42–10
ประหยัดน้ำ 219–E
ประหลาดใจ 43–30
ปรับเครื่องควบคุมอุณหภูมิ 219–J
ปรากฏตัวในศาล 141–C
ปราสาททราย 225–12
ปริซึม 195–35
ปริญญา 40–3

ปลวก 63–22
ปลอกนิ้ว 100–15
ปลอกหมอน 58–14
ปล่องไฟ 53–5
ปลอบโยน 36–I
ปลั๊ก 234–16
ปลา 66–1, 71, 209–14
ปลาเงินปลาทอง 215–16
ปลาแช่แข็ง 71–17
ปลาดาบ 71–5, 212–10
ปลาดาว 212–16
ปลาดุก 71–2
ปลาทะเลตัวแบน (ปลาตาเดียว ปลาลิ้นหมา) 212–15
ปลาทูน่า 72–19
ปลาเทราต์ 71–1
ปลายเท้า 94–23
ปลาย่าง 81–29
ปลาวาฬ 213–29
ปลาสด 71–16
ปลาไหล 212–12
ปลูกต้นไม้ 176–E, 219–N
ปวดท้อง 110–4
ปวดฟัน 110–2
ปวดศีรษะ 110–1
ปวดหลัง 110–5
ปวดหู 110–3
ป่วย 42–12
ปศุสัตว์ 177–15
ปอกแครอท 77–K
ปอด 107–39
ป้อนอาหาร 36–C
ปะการัง 220–5
ปัญหาเกี่ยวกับฟัน 119
ปัญหาเกี่ยวกับเสื้อผ้า 97
ปัญหาด้านการมองเห็น 115–1
ปัญหาในบ้านและการซ่อมแซม 62–63
ปัดฝุ่นตามเครื่องเรือน 60–A
ปั่นจักรยาน 228–5
ปั๊มน้ำมัน 125–10
ป่า 204–11
ป่า 34–7
ปาก 104–7, 106
ปากกา 7–22
ปากกาสำหรับทำเครื่องหมาย 7–24
ปากกาสำหรับทำเครื่องหมาย แบบลบได้เมื่อแห้ง 7–17
ปากคีบ 195–43
ปากนก 214–3
ป้าย 136–13
ป้ายโฆษณา 102–1
ป้ายจอดรถประจำทาง 129–16, 151–13, 152
ป้ายชื่อ 92–15
ป้ายชื่อถนน 129–26
ป้ายทะเบียน 158–12
ป้ายทะเบียนรถ 136–12
ป้ายใบสั่งยาจากแพทย์ 112–4
ป้ายประกาศห้องว่างให้เช่า 50–7

ป้ายปะหน้าซองไปรษณีย์ **183**–41
ป้ายราคา **27**–1
ปาร้อนชิ้น **204**–1
ปาล์ม **210**–14
ปิคนิค **224**–D
ปิงปอง **228**–14
ปิดโทรศัพท์มือถือของ
    คุณ **160**–I, **174**–G
ปิดไฟ **11**–P, **219**–G
ปิดหนังสือของคุณ **6**–H
ปิโตรเลียม **218**–6
ปิรามิด **193**–39
ปี **20**–4
ปีก **70**–20, **214**–1
ปีนบาร์ **224**–C
ปืน **142**–13
ปุ่มต่อไปข้างหน้า **197**–3
ปุ่มถอยหลัง **197**–2
ปุ่มปรับภาพละเอียด **194**–22
ปุ่มปรับภาพยาบ **194**–24
ปุ่มเรียก **121**–28
ปู **34**–2, **71**–9, **212**–20
ปูนผสมสำเร็จ **178**–10
เป็ด **70**–18, **214**–12
เป็นน้ำแข็งลื่นไถล **13**–22
เป็นปู่ย่า/ตายาย (มีหลาน) **41**–N
เป็นหมอควัน **13**–14
เป็แบกหลัง **94**–18, **226**–15
เปรี้ยว **84**–4
เปล **59**–20
เปลญวน **53**–23
เปลหาม **121**–33
เปลี่ยน **148**–C
เปลี่ยนผ้าปูที่นอน **60**–P
เปลี่ยนผ้าอ้อม **36**–G
เปลี่ยนแผงยางที่ปัดน้ำฝนหน้ารถ **157**–K
เปลือกตา **106**–10
เปอร์เซ็นต์ **17**
เป้า **231**–7
เป่า...ผมให้แห้ง **108**–H
เป่าให้ดับ **240**–C
เปิดเตาอบให้ร้อนก่อน **77**–A
เปิดไฟ **11**–B
เปิดหนังสือของคุณ **6**–G
เปียโน **238**–14
แป้ง **73**–29
แป้งทาตัว **108**–4
แป้งผัดหน้า **109**–41
แป้งสำหรับทารก **37**–14
แป้งหนึ่งถ้วยตวง **75**–10
แป้งหนึ่งถุง **74**–19
แปด **16**
แปดสิบ **16**
แป้นเกลียว **180**–36
แป้นคีย์ **14**–5, **196**–14
แปรง **33**–22, **108**–14
แปรง...ผม **108**–I
แปรง...ฟัน **109**–J
แปรงขัด **61**–20

แปรงขัดโถส้วม **57**–20
แปรงทาสี **181**–22
แปรงฟัน **109**–22
แปรงระบายสี **233**–20
แปรงสีฟัน **57**–23
แปลค่า **8**–C
แปลงค่า **17**–D
แปลงค่ามาตรตวงวัดต่างๆ **75**–C
แปลงดอกไม้ **53**–20
แปลงบันทึกจากเสียงเป็นอักษร **171**–C
โปรแกรมข่าว **236**–1
โปรตอน **195**–31
โปโลน้ำ **229**–15
โป๊ะไฟ **58**–25
ไป / เข้าวิทยาลัย (มหาวิทยาลัย) **41**–I
ไปกลับ **152**–17
ไปกับเที่ยวบิน **160**
ไปเข้าตาราง **141**–G
ไปใต้สะพาน **153**–A
ไปทำงาน **38**–I
ไปที่ชั้นเรียน **38**–J
ไปที่บรรทัดถัดไป **196**–D
ไปที่ร้านขายของชำ **38**–L
ไปที่หน่วยบริการจัดหางาน **173**–E
ไปเที่ยวดู **220**–A
ไปเที่ยวเป็นกลุ่ม **220**–A
ไปนอน **39**–Y
ไปบนสะพาน **153**–B
ไปผ่านเลยถนนเมน **155**–E
ไปรษณีย์ **134**–135
ไปรษณีย์ด่วนพิเศษแบบประกันความ
    รวดเร็ว **134**–2
ไปรษณีย์ด่วนไม่ประกันความ
    รวดเร็ว **134**–1
ไปรษณีย์ทางอากาศ **134**–5
ไปรษณียบัตร **134**–16
ไปรษณีย์ภาคพื้นดิน (ธรรมดา) **134**–6
ไปรษณีย์ลงทะเบียน **134**–4
ไปรษณีย์สำหรับวัสดุสื่อ **134**–3
ไปรับการสัมภาษณ์ **173**–K
ไปรับเด็ก **38**–M
ไปหนึ่งบล็อคถึงถนนเฟิร์ส **155**–F
ไปหลับ **39**–Z
ผง/น้ำยาซักฟอก **101**–8
ผจญภัย **237**–19
ผนังฉาบปูน **178**–15
ผนังเซลล์ **194**–5
ผม **104**–2
ผมตรง **33**–9
ผมเป็นลอน **33**–10
ผมยาว **33**–3
ผมยาวประบ่า **33**–2
ผมสั้น **33**–1
ผมสีดำ **33**–16
ผมสีแดง **33**–15
ผมสีเทา **33**–13
ผมสีน้ำตาล **33**–18
ผมสีบลอนด์ **33**–17
ผมหงอก **33**–13

ผมหยิก **33**–11
ผลการเลือกตั้ง **139**–31
ผลคูณ **192**–9
ผลเฉลย **192**–14
ผลต่าง **192**–8
ผลเบอร์รี่ **210**–20
ผลผลิตทางเกษตร **177**
ผลมะเดื่อ **68**–27
ผลไม้ **67**–9, **68**
ผลรวม **192**–7
ผลหาร **192**–10
ผลักชิงช้า **224**–B
ผลิต **175**–B
ผลิตภัณฑ์ของชำ **72**
ผลิตภัณฑ์ประเภททำขนมปัง **73**
ผสมเครื่องปรุงต่างๆ **77**–R
ผอม **32**–9
ผัก **66**–8, **69**
ผักกาดหอม **69**–1
ผักชีฝรั่ง **69**–28
ผักแช่แข็ง **72**–27
ผักนึ่ง **81**–32
ผักปวยเล้ง **69**–11
ผักไร้สารเคมี **84**–2
ผักสลัดถุงหนึ่ง **69**–31
ผักสลัดหัวหนึ่ง **69**–32
ผักอบกับเต้าหู้เนยแข็ง **77**
ผักฮ่องเต้ **69**–15
ผังแสดงชื่อและที่ตั้งร้าน **131**–24
ผังแสดงพื้นที่อาคาร **186**–4
ผัดเห็ด **77**–E
ผ้า/กระดาษเช็ดปาก **83**–26
ผ้าก๊อสใช้ปิดแผล **117**–8
ผ้ากันเปื้อน **92**–11
ผ้ากันเปื้อนคาดเอว **93**–30
ผ้าขนสัตว์ **98**–3
ผ้าขนสัตว์ชนิดพิเศษ **98**–4
ผ้าขี้ริ้ว **61**–9, **70**–8
ผ้าคลุมกันสิหยดเลอะ **181**–54
ผ้าคลุมเตียง **59**–11
ผ้าคาดศีรษะ **92**–16
ผ้าจีบผ้าบังฝน **58**–17
ผ้าช่วยพยุง **113**–19
ผ้าชิ้นสำหรับเช็ด **37**–15
ผ้าเช็ดจาน **61**–22
ผ้าเช็ดตัว **57**–16
ผ้าเช็ดมือ **57**–17
ผ้าใช้จับของร้อน **78**–29
ผ้าเดนิม (ผ้ายีน) **99**–7
ผ่านการทดสอบการขับขี่ **137**–H
ผ้านวม **58**–16
ผ้าในลอน **99**–12
ผ้าใบสำหรับการวาดภาพ **233**–17
ผ้าปิดตอกกันเปื้อน **37**–5
ผ้าปูโต๊ะ **55**–12
ผ้าปูที่นอนแบบกระชับส่วนล่าง **58**–12
ผ้าปูที่นอนส่วนบน **58**–13
ผ้าผืนเล็กสำหรับอาบน้ำ **57**–6
ผ้าฝ้าย **98**–1

ผ้าพันคอ **95**–12
ผ้าพันคอกันหนาว **90**–5
ผ้าพันแผล **113**–19
ผ้าพันศีรษะ **90**–7
ผ้าม่าน **56**–16, **58**–7
ผ้ายึดพันแผล **117**–12
ผ้าเย็น **146**–12
ผ้าลินิน **98**–2
ผ้าลูกฟูก **99**–11
ผ้าหนังกลับ **99**–8
ผ้าห่ม **58**–15, **146**–7, **225**–11
ผ้าไหม **98**–5
ผ้าอ้อมที่ทำด้วยผ้า **37**–8
ผ้าอ้อมแบบใช้แล้วทิ้ง **37**–10
ผิดทาง **154**–2
ผิดหวัง **28**–4
ผิวหนัง **107**–31
ผีเสื้อ **214**–19
ผีเสื้อกลางคืน **214**–21
ผึ้ง **214**–25
ผืน **110**–10
ผูก **86**–A
ผู้กล่าวคำปราศัย **206**–4
ผู้ก่อตั้ง **198**–7
ผู้จัดการ **50**–8, **72**–8
ผู้จัดการบัญชี **132**–9
ผู้จัดการสำนักงาน **182**–8
ผู้ช่วยครู **5**–16
ผู้ช่วยงานทันตกรรม **119**–2
ผู้ช่วยดูแลสุขภาพผู้สูงอายุ
    ในบ้าน **167**–32
ผู้ช่วยทันตแพทย์ **167**–22
ผู้ช่วยฝ่ายบริหาร **166**–3
ผู้ช่วยพยาบาลที่ได้รับการรับรอง **120**–12
ผู้ช่วยแพทย์ **168**–47
ผู้ช่วยอาจารย์ใหญ่ **5**–5
ผู้ชาย (คนเดียว) **30**–1
ผู้ชาย (หลายคน) **30**–4
ผู้ชำนาญการเจาะหลอดโลหิตดำ
    121–29
ผู้ชำนาญการบำบัด **115**–14
ผู้ชำนาญด้านกายภาพบำบัด **115**–12
ผู้เช่า **50**–6
ผู้เชี่ยวชาญเกี่ยวกับเนื้องอกวิทยา **120**–5
ผู้เชี่ยวชาญเกี่ยวกับรังสีวิทยา **120**–6
ผู้เชี่ยวชาญด้านการได้ยิน **115**–9
ผู้เชี่ยวชาญด้านสายตา **115**–6
ผู้ดูแล **50**–8
ผู้ดูแลสายงาน **175**–4
ผู้เดินเครื่องจักรเย็บผ้า **98**–14
ผู้โดยสาร **150**–2, **161**–15
ผู้โดยสารรถประจำทาง **152**–3
ผู้ได้รับเลือกตั้ง **139**–32
ผู้ตรวจเพื่อความปลอดภัย **160**–5
ผู้แต่ง **133**–15
ผู้ถูกตัดสินว่าผิด **141**–15
ผู้ทำการฝึกซ้อม **229**–2
ผู้ทำความสะอาดฟัน **119**–3
ผู้ทำงานปศุสัตว์ **177**–22

ผู้ทำรายงานศาล **141**–12
ผู้ที่ติดต่อได้ภายนอกรัฐ **146**–2
ผู้บริหาร **5, 120**–13, **182**–5
ผู้ปลูก **177**–13
ผู้ป่วย **121**–18
ผู้เผด็จการ **199**–6
ผู้ฝึกซ้อม **5**–20
ผู้พิพากษา **138**–12, **141**–6
ผู้มารับประทานอาหาร **82**–6, **185**–9
ผู้รับเคราะห์ **142**–10
ผู้รับบริการ **82**–6
ผู้รับเหมา (ก่อสร้าง) **186**–5
ผู้เล่น **229**–5
ผู้ว่าการรัฐ **139**–20
ผู้สอน **6**–4
ผู้สูงอายุ **30**–5
ผู้หญิง (คนเดียว) **30**–2
ผู้หญิง (หลายคน) **30**–3
ผู้ให้คำปรึกษางานอาชีพ **172**–10
ผู้ใหญ่และเด็ก **30**
แผงกันไฟ **56**–12
แผงกันไหล **231**–20
แผงข้อมูลการดูแลรักษา **121**–24
แผงวงจรหลัก **196**–5
แผงหน้าต่าง **178**–16
แผงหัวเตียง **58**–10
แผงไหล **107**–28
แผนกเครื่องประดับกาย **95**–8
แผนกบริการข้อมูลของศูนย์ **130**–12
แผนกผักผลไม้สด **72**–2
แผ่นกรองเท้า **95**–7
แผ่นกระเบื้อง **178**–11
แผ่นกลับคืนขวด **73**–16
แผ่นกันชน **59**–4
แผ่นคำตอบ **10**–2
แผ่นฆ่าเชื้อแล้ว **117**–6
แผ่นเช็ดฆ่าเชื้อโรค **61**–23
แผ่นดินไหว **144**–5
แผ่นทำความอบอุ่น **113**–13
แผนที่ **7**–12, **155**
แผนที่ทางอินเทอร์เน็ต **155**–12
แผนที่โลก **202**–203
แผนที่แสดงสภาพอากาศ **13**
แผ่นปาดเช็ดน้ำจากกระจก **61**–15
แผ่นป้าย **44**–1
แผ่นปิดแผล **117**–5
แผ่นปูรองสำหรับเปลี่ยนผ้าอ้อม **59**–2
แผ่นพลาสติก **72**–24
แผ่นฟอยอะลูมิเนียม **72**–23
แผ่นโฟม **226**–13
แผ่นไม้มุงหลังคา **178**–20
แผ่นยางปูพื้นในอ่าง **57**–5
แผ่นใยบุกันความร้อนหรือ
    ความเย็น **178**–14
แผ่นใยเหล็กสำหรับขัด **61**–5
แผ่นรองเข่า **179**–19
แผ่นรองจาน **55**–11
แผ่นสำหรับใส่ไปกับผ้าเวลาอบ **101**–5
แผ่นหมึก **183**–46

ฝนตก **13**–11
ฝนพิษ **218**–13
ฝัง **204**–12
ฝา **78**–24
ฝากข้อความทิ้งไว้ **171**–P
ฝาครอบจุดเสียบปลั๊กไฟ **181**–46
ฝาครอบล้อรถ **158**–9
ฝาครอบหู **179**–16
ฝาผนัง **56**–10
ฝ่ามือ **106**–15
ฝ้าย **177**–6
ฝ่ายตรงกันข้าม
    (คู่แข่งขัน) **139**–30
ฝ่ายตุลาการ **138**
ฝ่ายนิติบัญญัติ **138**
ฝ่ายนิติบัญญัติ **139**–23
ฝ่ายบริหาร **138**
ฝ่ายรับแขกส่วนหน้า **184**–12
ฝีเย็บ **117**–15
ฝึกฝนวินัย **36**–K
ฝูงสัตว์เลี้ยงวัวควาย **177**–21
เฝือก **113**–20
ไฝ **32**–16
พจนานุกรม **7**–30
พจนานุกรมภาพ **7**–31
พ้นโทษ **141**–H
พนักงาน **5**–13, **165**–9, **182**–2
พนักงานเก็บเงิน **73**–13
พนักงานเก็บถ้วยชามใช้แล้ว **83**–12
พนักงานขนกระเป๋า **184**–7
พนักงานขนย้าย **168**–42
พนักงานขนสัมภาระที่สนามบิน **160**–1
พนักงานขาย **94**–3
พนักงานขายตั๋ว **160**–3
พนักงานขายปลีก **169**–53
พนักงานเข็น **175**–10
พนักงานจอดรถ **184**–3
พนักงานจัดเก็บเอกสาร **182**–10
พนักงานจัดส่งสินค้า **175**–14
พนักงานจัดส่งอาหาร **185**–16
พนักงานจ่ายค่าจ้าง **165**–10
พนักงานซ่อมแซมเครื่องใช้ **166**–4
พนักงานดับเพลิง **144**–9, **167**–26
พนักงานดูแลเด็ก **166**–16
พนักงานดูแลสต็อกสินค้า **169**–59
พนักงานเดินเครื่อง **168**–37
พนักงานเดินตั๋ว **152**–13
พนักงานต้อนรับ
    118–2, **164**–5, **169**–51, **182**–14
พนักงานต้อนรับในร้านอาหาร **185**–11
พนักงานต้อนรับหญิง **82**–2
พนักงานตัดเย็บเสื้อผ้า **167**–29
พนักงานเตรียมอาหาร **185**–4
พนักงานทั่วไปในโรงพยาบาล **120**–16
พนักงานท่าเรือ **167**–23
พนักงานที่เคาน์เตอร์ **79**–17
พนักงานธนาคาร **132**–1
พนักงานในร้าน **72**–4
พนักงานบรรจุ **175**–8

พนักงานบริการข้อมูลทาง
    โทรศัพท์ **14**–22
พนักงานบริการทั่วไป **184**–4, **185**–15
พนักงานบริการบนเครื่อง **161**–12
พนักงานบริการลูกค้า **167**–20
พนักงานบัญชี **166**–1
พนักงานบำบัดฝึกหัดงานอาชีพ **168**–45
พนักงานประกอบผลิตภัณฑ์ **166**–7
พนักงานปั๊มน้ำมัน **162**–3
พนักงานไปรษณีย์ **135**–7, **169**–49
พนักงานแม่บ้าน **168**–34
พนักงานรับแขกโรงแรม **184**–11
พนักงานรับเงิน **166**–15
พนักงานรับโทรศัพท์ **14**–21
พนักงานส่งจดหมาย **134**–20
พนักงานส่งมอบสินค้า **167**–21
พนักงานส่งเอกสาร **168**–40
พนักงานสุขาภิบาล **169**–54
พนักงานเสิร์ฟ **82**–8, **83**–9, **185**–8
พนักงานเสิร์ฟชาย **82**–8
พนักงานเสิร์ฟหญิง **83**–9
พนักงานเสิร์ฟอาหาร **169**–56
พนักงานใส่ของลงถุง **73**–14
พบกับตัวแทนผู้ซื้อขายบ้านและ
    ที่ดิน **49**–G
พบเพื่อนบ้าน **49**–R
พยาธิในลำไส้ **111**–13
พยาน **141**–11
พยาบาล **118**–8, **168**–44
พยาบาลที่มีใบอนุญาตให้ปฏิบัติงาน
    บางส่วน **120**–11
พยาบาลที่มีวุฒิและได้ขึ้นทะเบียน
    แล้ว **120**–10
พยาบาลห้องผ่าตัด **120**–9
พรม **56**–24
พรมเช็ดเท้าในห้องน้ำ **57**–28
พรมผืน **58**–22
พรั่นใจ **42**–10
พริกขี้ฟ้า **69**–29
พริกหยวก **69**–7
พฤศจิกายน **21**–35
พฤษภาคม **21**–29
พลศึกษา **189**–17
พลังงานความร้อนใต้พิภพ **218**–7
พลังงานจากชีวภาพ **218**–9
พลังงานนิวเคลียร์ **218**–8
พลังงานลม **218**–2
พลังงานและการประหยัด
    พลังงาน **218**–219
พลังงานแสงอาทิตย์ **218**–1
พลังงานอุณหธรณี **218**–7
พลับพลึง **211**–26
พลั่ม **68**–13
พลั่ว **176**–7, **178**–22
พลุไฟ **239**–7
พวงมาลัย **159**–26
พ่อ **34**–4
พ่อครัว **83**–16
พ่อครัวมือรอง **185**–6

พ่อครัวมือเอก **185**–7
พอใจ **42**–6
พ่อตา **34**–11
พ่อที่เลี้ยงลูกโดยลำพัง **35**–23
พอร์ตยูเอสบี **196**–7
พ่อเลี้ยง **35**–25
พ่อสามี **34**–11
พักผ่อน **39**–U
พัดลม **55**–19
พับชายกางเกง **100**–9
พับเสื้อผ้า **101**–F
พาดหัวข่าว **133**–7
พาเด็กไปโรงเรียน **38**–G
พาย **81**–35
พายสำหรับตักหรือป้าย **78**–19
พายฝนฟ้าคะนอง **13**–16
พายฝน **13**–19
พายุรุนแรง **145**–14
พายุลูกเห็บ **13**–21
พายุหมุน **145**–15
พายุหิมะ **13**–23, **145**–13
พายุหิมะรุนแรง **13**–23
พาหมาเดิน **129**–F
พิการทางตา **32**–11
พิการทางหู **32**–12
พิชซ่า **79**–10
พิธีการ **206**–6
พิพากษาจำเลย **141**–E
พิพิธภัณฑ์งานศิลปะ **223**–9
พิมพ์ **170**–R, **196**–A
พิมพ์ข้อความ **197**–E
พิมพ์จดหมาย **171**–A
พิมพ์รหัสผ่านของคุณ **197**–A
พิมพ์หัวเรื่อง **197**–D
พิมพ์เอกสาร **171**–I
พิราบ **214**–15
พี่ (น้อง) เขย **34**–17
พี่ (น้อง) ชาย **34**–6
พี่ (น้อง) ชายต่างบิดามารดา **35**–30
พี่ (น้อง) ชายร่วมบิดาหรือมารดา **35**–28
พี่ (น้อง) สะใภ้ **34**–16
พี่ (น้อง) สาว **34**–5
พี่ (น้อง) สาวต่างบิดามารดา **35**–29
พี่ (น้อง) สาวร่วมบิดาหรือมารดา **35**–27
พีชคณิต **192**–16
พืช **177**–A
พืชพันธุ์ **208**–5
พืชพันธุ์ **210**
พืชและสัตว์ต่างๆ **194**–1
พื้น **46**–6
พื้นที่กว้างสำหรับเลี้ยงปศุสัตว์ **52**–10
พื้นที่การก่อสร้าง **126**–2
พื้นที่จัดเฉพาะเพื่อแสดงสินค้า **122**–3
พื้นที่ลื่น **179**–6
พื้นที่โล่งสี่เหลี่ยม **5**–1
พื้นที่สูงชิอาปาส **201**–18
พื้นที่หว่างเขา **204**–18
พื้นเมือง **237**–29
พื้นไม้ **58**–21

พื้นรองเท้า **94**–21
พุดจีน **211**–18
พุทธชาด **211**–18
พูดกับครู **6**–B
พูดต่างภาษา **170**–N
พูดถึงประสบการณ์ของคุณ **174**–L
พูดในโทรศัพท์ **15**–C
พูดว่า "ลาก่อน" **3**–L
พูดว่า "สวัสดี" **2**–A
เพลง **64**–3
เพลงยอดนิยม **237**–25
เพลงร้องในโบสถ์ แบบอเมริกัน
    ภาคใต้ **237**–30
เพศ **4**–16
เพื่อนร่วมห้อง **64**–1
แพทย์/ผู้ช่วยแพทย์ภาคสนาม **116**–2
แพทย์ผู้เชี่ยวชาญเกี่ยวกับอวัยวะ
    ภายใน **120**–1
แพทย์ผู้เชี่ยวชาญเฉพาะทาง **120**
แพทย์ผู้เชี่ยวชาญด้านโรคหัวใจ **120**–3
แพนเค้ก **80**–7
แพะ **215**–5
โพรงถ้ำ **220**–7
ไพ **193**–46
ไพ่ข้าวหลามตัด **233**–29
ไพ่ดอกจิก **233**–32
ไพ่โพดำ **233**–30
ไพ่โพแดง **233**–31
ฟกช้ำ **110**–12
ฟองน้ำ **61**–19
ฟองน้ำถูพื้น **61**–6
ฟักทองคว้านเป็นรูปหน้าผี **239**–10
ฟัง...การเต้นของหัวใจ **118**–C
ฟังซีดี **6**–C
ฟังอย่างตั้งอกตั้งใจ **174**–K
ฟัน **106**–7
ฟันดาบ **228**–7
ฟันเป็นรู **119**–7
ฟันผุ **119**–7
ฟ้าจรัส **24**–12
ฟาร์ม **52**–9
ฟาเรนไฮต์ **13**–1
ฟ้าแลบ **13**–17
ฟ้าอ่อน **24**–11
ฟิล์ม **235**–22
ฟิสิกส์ **195**
ฟุตบอล (อเมริกัน) **229**–11
ฟุตบอล **229**–12
ฟุตบอล(รักบี้) **231**–21
ฟุทบาท **129**–24
ฟุก **58**–20
เฟอร์นิเจอร์และเครื่องใช้ต่างๆ **59**
แฟนกีฬา **229**–4
แฟ้มจัดระเบียบ **183**–49
แฟ้มใส่การ์ดแบบหมุน **183**–44
แฟ้มใส่เอกสาร **183**–50
แฟ้มเอกสาร **7**–27
ไฟฉาย **146**–14
ไฟดับ **62**–2

ไฟถนน **148**–3
ไฟท้ายรถ **158**–13
ไฟทางาน **181**–44
ไฟเบรค **158**–14
ไฟป่า **144**–7
ไฟฟ้าพลังน้ำ **218**–5
ไฟร้อยติดกันเป็นสาย **239**–18
ไฟเลี้ยว **158**–6, **159**–34
ไฟสัญญาณเจราจร **128**–8
ไฟสัญญาณอันตราย **159**–36
ไฟสำหรับเปิดทิ้งไว้ตอนกลางคืน **37**–27
ไฟหน้าบ้าน **53**–13
ไฟหน้ารถ **158**–7
ไฟไหม้ **144**–8
ภรรยา **34**–12
ภัตตาคาร **83**
ภัยแล้ง **145**–11
ภัตตาคาร **82**
ภาชนะใช้นึ่ง **78**–3
ภาชนะบรรจุ **74**–5
ภาชนะบรรจุและบรรจุภัณฑ์ **74**
ภาชนะพลาสติกสำหรับเก็บอาหาร **78**–4
ภาชนะรับฝนผง **61**–17
ภาพขบขัน **206**–2
ภาพถ่าย **58**–3, **136**–4
ภาพเป็นทางการ **206**–3
ภาพวาด **56**–9
ภายใต้กระโปรงหน้ารถ **158**
ภายในกระโปรงหลังรถ **158**
ภายในชุดปฐมพยาบาล **117**
ภายในรถ **159**
ภายในและภายนอกร่างกาย **106**–**107**
ภารโรง **182**–3
ภาษาต่างๆของโลก **189**–13
ภาษีการขาย **27**–8
ภูเขาทราย **204**–5
ภูเขาไฟระเบิด **145**–16
ภูมิใจ **43**–21
ภูมิพ้างต่างๆ **111**–8
ภูมิภาคต่างๆของแคนาดา **201**
ภูมิภาคต่างๆในเม็กซิโก **201**
ภูมิภาคต่างๆในสหรัฐอเมริกา **201**
ภูมิศาสตร์และที่อยู่อาศัย **204**
เภสัชกร **112**–1
มกราคม **21**–25
มด **63**–23
มลภาวะ **218**
มลภาวะในน้ำ **218**–14
มลภาวะในอากาศ **218**–11
ม่วง **24**–6
ม่วงเข้ม **24**–8
ม้วน **74**–11
ม้วนผ้า **98**–15
มวย **228**–4
มวยปล้ำ **228**–17
มวลชีวภาพ **218**–9
มหกรรมจัดหางาน **172**–13
มหาวิทยาลัย **188**–7
มหาสมุทร **204**–6, **225**–1

มองสบตา **174**–J
มองหาป้ายเรียกจ้างคนงาน **173**–C
มองเห็น **106**–A
มะเขือเทศ **69**–6
มะเขือม่วง **69**–23
มะนาว **68**–8
มะนาวเหลือง **68**–7
มะพร้าว **68**–24
มะม่วง **68**–21
มะเร็ง **111**–10
มะละกอ **68**–20
มะลิ **211**–22
มันเทศ **69**–18
มันฝรั่ง **69**–17
มันฝรั่งทอดแผ่นบาง **73**–35
มันฝรั่งบด **81**–23
มันฝรั่งหั่นแท่งทอด **79**–2
มันฝรั่งหั่นฝอยผัด **80**–3
มันฝรั่งอบ **81**–25
มัฟฟิน **79**–16
มัว **235**–33
มัสตาร์ด **79**–22
ม้า **215**–4
มาตรระยะทาง **159**–28
มาตรวัดน้ำมันเครื่อง **159**–29
มาตรวัดน้ำมันเชื้อเพลิง **159**–31
มาตรวัดอุณหภูมิ **159**–30
มาถึง **160**–K
ม่านกันน้ำกระเซ็น **57**–14
ม้านั่ง **224**–10
ม้าน้ำ **212**–13
มาบ้าน **39**–R
มายองเนส **79**–23
ม้าลาย **217**–33
มิเตอร์ **152**–23
มิเตอร์แก๊ส **62**–14
มิเตอร์ความเร็ว **159**–27
มิเตอร์จอดรถ **129**–25
มิถุนายน **21**–30
มีการตรวจร่างกายเป็นประจำ **114**–H
มีการสนทนา **11**–L
มีครรภ์ **32**–15
มีความลำบากทางกาย **32**–10
มีความสุข **28**–6, **43**–31
มีฉีก **97**–41
มีด **55**–4, **83**–30
มีดโกน **109**–27
มีดตัดแบบกลิ้ง **232**–16
มีดตัดสเต็ก **83**–29
มีดปอกผลไม้ **78**–16
มีดสารพัดใช้ **226**–20
มีดสำหรับปอกเปลือก **78**–15
มีดหั่นเนื้อก้อน **78**–12
มีแดด **13**–9
มีเมฆมาก **13**–10
มียางแบน **162**–F
มีรอยเปื้อน **97**–42
มีราคาแพงเกินไป **97**–44

มีลูก **41**–L
มีหลุดรุ่ย **97**–43
มีอาการช็อค แน่นิ่ง **116**–B
มีอาการเนื้อเยื่อตายเนื่องจาก
    ความเย็นจัด **116**–G
มีอาการโรคภูมิแพ้ **116**–E
มีอาการโรคหัวใจ **116**–D
มีอายุไม่ต่ำกว่า 18 ปี **140**–G
มือ **105**–15
มือเล็ก **23**–1
มือใหญ่ **23**–2
มุข **51**–20, **128**–7, **193**
มุม 90 องศา **193**–26
มุมฉากขวา **193**–26
มุมป้าน **193**–27
มุมแหลม **193**–28
เม็ดแบน **113**–22
เม่น **216**–10
เมนู **82**–7
เมนูแบบดึงลง **197**–8
เมเปิ้ล **210**–12
เมล็ด **211**–1
เมล็ดพันธุ์ **211**–1
เมษายน **21**–28
เม้าส์ **196**–15
เมือง **4**–7, **52**–1
เมืองขึ้นสิบสามเมือง **198**–1
เมืองเล็ก **52**–3
เมืองหลวงของรัฐ **139**–22
เมื่อวาน **20**–7
แม่ **34**–3
แม็กโนเลีย **210**–8
แมงกะพรุน **212**–14
แมงช้าง **214**–18
แมงป่อง **214**–30
แมงมุม **214**–29
แม่ที่เลี้ยงลูกโดยลำพัง **35**–22
แม่น้ำ **155**–10, **204**–3
แม่บ้าน **168**–33
แม่บ้านโรงแรม **184**–20
แม่ยาย **34**–10
แม่แรง **158**–24
แมลง **209**–11
แมลงกัดต่อย **110**–11
แมลงทับ **214**–26
แมลงปีกแข็ง **214**–18
แมลงและแมง **214**
แมลงวัน **214**–28
แมลงสาบเล็ก **63**–26
แมลงสาบใหญ่ **63**–26
แม่เลี้ยง **35**–26
แมว **215**–9
แมวน้ำ **213**–34
แม่สามี **34**–10
แม่เหล็ก **195**–36
โมเลกุล **195**–27
ไม้ **178**–17
ไม้กระดก **224**–16
ไม้กลิ้งนวดแป้ง **78**–30

ไม้กวาด **61**–16
ไม้กอล์ฟ **231**–1
ไม้ขนไก่ปัดฝุ่น **61**–1
ไม้ขีดไฟ **146**–16, **226**–21
ไม้แขวน **101**–11
ไม่ค่อยสบาย **42**–9
ไมโครโปรเซสเซอร์ **196**–4
ไมโครโฟน **234**–18
ไม้ชนิดหนึ่งดอกสีขาวๆ **210**–15
ไม้ตีเบสบอล **231**–14
ไม้ตีฮ็อกกี้ **231**–11
ไม้ถ่อสำหรับเล่นสกี **231**–25
ไม้เทนนิส **231**–2
ไม้เท้า **113**–16
ไม้บรรทัด **17**–13
ไม้ประดับเทศกาลคริสต์มาส **210**–19
ไม้ประดับภายในบ้าน **211**–27
ไม้แปรรูป **178**–17
ไม้พยุงตัว **113**–10
ไม้มีทางออก **154**–6
ไม้วัดความยาวเป็นหลา **181**–16
ไม่เห็นด้วย **12**–L
ไม้อัด **178**–18
ไม้อัดทำจากเศษไม้ **181**–20
ยก **11**–E
ยกกลับ ถ้วยชาม **82**–G
ยกถาด **82**–H
ยกน้ำหนัก **228**–16
ยกมือขึ้น **6**–A
ยอดเขา **204**–14
ยอดคงเหลือ **132**–17
ยอดรวม **27**–9
ย้อมผม **33**–D
ยอมรับการขอโทษ **12**–G
ยอมรับการเชิญชวน **12**–I
ย่อหน้า **190**–3
ย่อหน้าเมื่อเริ่มประโยคแรกของย่อหน้า
    190–D
ยา **34**–1, **121**–20
ยากันกลิ่นเหงื่อ **108**–5
ยาแก้ไอชนิดน้ำเชื่อม **113**–29
ยาฆ่าเชื้อแบคทีเรีย **117**–11
ย่างบาร์บีคิว **76**–2
ยางรถ **158**–5
ยางรัด **183**–34
ยางลบ (ดินสอ) **7**–21
ยางอะไหล่ **158**–23
ยาดับกลิ่นตัว **108**–5
ยาตามใบสั่งแพทย์ **112**–3
ยาที่ซื้อได้โดยไม่มี
    ใบสั่งแพทย์ **113**, **113**–18
ยานอวกาศ **205**–19
ยาบรรเทาปวด **113**–26
ยาแบบขี้ผึ้ง (แบบทาถู) **113**–24
ยาผิดกฎหมาย **142**–6
ยาพ่นในจมูก **113**–32
ย่าม **94**–19
ยามฝั่ง **138**–18
ยามเฝ้าประตู **184**–1

ยามเฝ้าระวังและช่วยชีวิต **225**–19
ยาเม็ด **113**–21
ยาเม็ดแก้หวัด **113**–27
ยาย **34**–1
ย้ายเข้า **48**–F
ย้ายถิ่นฐานเข้ามา **40**–C
ยาลดกรดในกระเพาะ **113**–28
ยาสีฟัน **109**–23
ยาสีฟันหนึ่งหลอด **74**–24
ยาเสพติด **142**–6
ยาหยอดตา **113**–31
ยาอมแก้เจ็บคอ **113**–30
ยิงธนู **228**–1
ยิงลูก **230**–H
ยิ้ม **2**–D
ยิมนาสติก **228**–9
ยีราฟ **217**–32
ยี่สิบ **16**
ยี่สิบดอลลาร์ **26**–10
ยี่สิบนาทีหลังหนึ่งนาฬิกา **18**–10
ยี่สิบสอง **16**
ยี่สิบสาม **16**
ยี่สิบสี่ **16**
ยี่สิบห้า **16**
ยี่สิบห้าเซ็นต์ **26**–4
ยี่สิบเอ็ด **16**
ยี่สุ่น **211**–13
ยืดเส้นสาย **230**–M
ยื่นข้อเสนอ **49**–I
ยืนขึ้น **6**–D
ยืนใบสมัคร **48**–C
ยืมเงิน **26**–B
ยุคเมืองขึ้น **198**
ยุง **214**–22
ยุโรป **202**–3
เย็น **13**–5, **18**–19
เย็บด้วยเครื่อง **98**–A
เย็บด้วยมือ **98**–B
เย็บผ้าต่อลาย **232**–C
เย็บเล่ม **171**–F
เย็บเสื้อผ้า **170**–L
เยือกแข็ง **13**–7
เยือกหนาว **110**–9
เยื่อหุ้มเซลล์ **194**–6
แยกต่างหาก **76**–B
แยมหนึ่งขวด **74**–14
โยก **36**–D
โยเกิร์ต **72**–22
โยเกิร์ตหนึ่งไพนต์ (สองถ้วยตวง) **75**–3
โยคะ **122**–4
โยน **230**–C
โยนขยะทิ้ง **11**–N
รกรุงรัง **64**–8
รดน้ำต้นไม้ **176**–F
รถกระบะ **150**–6
รถเก๋ง **156**–1
รถขนย้าย **156**–18
รถขยะ **127**–22
รถเข็น **175**–11

รถเข็นใส่ของ **72**–7
รถเครน **178**–7
รถดับเพลิง **144**–10
รถโดยสาร **128**–9
รถตัก **178**–8
รถตู้ **156**–6
รถตู้ขนของ **156**–13
รถตู้ขนาดเล็ก **156**–8
รถใต้ดิน **151**–12
รถถังบรรจุของเหลว **156**–20
รถไถ **177**–9
รถไถกราด **178**–6
รถเทขยะ **156**–19
รถนอนค้างแรม **156**–9
รถบรรทุก **150**–6
รถบรรทุกลากพ่วง **156**–15
รถบรรทุกเล็ก **156**–12
รถบรรทุกสำหรับลากจูง **156**–14
รถแบ็คโฮ **178**–8
รถประจำทาง **151**–14
รถเปิดประทุน **156**–5
รถพยาบาล **116**–1, **121**–34
รถเพื่อการพักผ่อนหย่อนใจ
    (อาร์วี) **156**–10
รถไฟ **150**–7
รถไฟของเล่น **233**–27
รถมอเตอร์ไซค์ **150**–4
รถยกคนงาน **178**–5
รถยกสินค้า **175**–12
รถยกอุปกรณ์ **178**–7
รถยนต์ **150**–1
รถยนต์ในเมือง **152**–20
รถยนต์แบบใช้งานการกีฬา
    (เอสยูวี) **156**–7
รถยนต์พลังงานน้ำมันและไฟฟ้า **156**–3
รถยนต์และรถบรรทุก **156**
รถยนต์สปอร์ต **156**–4
รถยนต์สองประตู **156**–2
รถยนต์สี่ประตู **156**–2
รถรับแขกพิเศษ **156**–11
รถโรงเรียน **156**–21
รถลิโม **156**–11
รถวิ่งทางเดียว **154**–3
รถวิ่งบริการเฉพาะที่ **152**–19
รถสามล้อ **224**–12
รถเสีย **162**–D
ร่ม **90**–17
ร่มชายหาด **225**–14
รหัสเขตพื้นที่โทรศัพท์ **15**–29
รหัสโทรฯทางไกล **4**–10
รหัสประเทศ **15**–33
รหัสไปรษณีย์ **4**–9
รหัสเมือง **15**–34
ร็อค **237**–23
รองเท้า **87**–13
รองเท้ากีฬา **86**–7
รองเท้ากีฬาแบบธรรมดา **95**–32
รองเท้าแตะ **91**–26
รองเท้าเทนนิส **95**–32

รองเท้านิรภัย **179**–20
รองเท้าบู๊ท **95**–28
รองเท้าบู๊ทกันฝน **90**–20
รองเท้าบู๊ทที่มีเหล็กคลุมปลายเท้า **92**–6
รองเท้าบู๊ทสำหรับเดินเขา **95**–31
รองเท้าพื้นราบมีเชือกผูก **95**–29
รองเท้าพื้นราบไม่มีเชือกผูก **95**–30
รองเท้าและเครื่องประดับ **94**–95
รองเท้าส้นเตี้ย **95**–27
รองเท้าส้นสูง **89**–21, **95**–25
รองเท้าสาน **88**–9
รองเท้าหุ้มส้นเตี้ย **95**–26
รองประธานาธิบดี **138**–9
รองผู้ว่าการรัฐ **139**–21
ร้องเพลง **238**–B
ร้องเพลงกล่อม **36**–O
ร้องไห้ **206**–B
ร้อน **13**–3, **42**–1
รอในคิว **94**–B
ร้อยดอลลาร์ **26**–12
รอสัญญาณไฟ **128**–B
ระดับแนวคิดต่างๆ **191**–F
ระดับพลังสมองทางออก **8**–H
ระดับคะแนน **10**–4
ระนาดไฟฟ้า **238**–15
ระบบการหาตำแหน่งบนพื้นโลก **155**–11
ระบบฉีดจ่ายเชื้อเพลิง **158**–17
ระบบโทรศัพท์สำหรับคนหูหนวก **15**–26
ระบบโทรศัพท์อัตโนมัติ **14**–23
ระบบสเตริโอ **56**–8
ระบบสื่อสารภายในอาคาร **50**–5
ระบบสุริยะและดาวเคราะห์ **205**
ระบายลงในวงที่คำตอบ **10**–K
ระบายสี **233**–E
ระบุข้อสมมุติฐาน **195**–A
ระเบียง **51**–20, **240**–2
ระเบียงหน้าบ้าน **53**
ระเบียงหลังบ้าน **53**–16
ระวังกระเป๋าถือหรือกระเป๋าสตางค์
    ของคุณ **143**–D
รักบี้ **229**–11
รัง **209**–12
รังเกียจ **42**–7
รังผึ้ง **158**–19
รัฐ **4**–8
รัฐธรรมนูญ **198**–12
รัฐในแถบเทือกเขาร็อคกี้ **201**–8
รัฐในแถบตอนกลาง **201**–9
รัฐในแถบตอนกลางฝั่ง
    แอตแลนติก **201**–10
รัฐในแถบฝั่งแปซิฟิก **201**–7
รัฐบาลกลาง **138**
รัฐบาลท้องถิ่น (ระดับเมือง) **139**
รัฐบาลระดับรัฐ **139**
รัฐบาลและราชการทหาร **138**–139
รัดเข็มขัดนิรภัย **160**–H
รับกระเป๋าสัมภาระของคุณ **160**–L
รับการฉีดวัคซีน **114**–I
รับการ์ด **135**–F

รับบัตรห้องสมุด 133–A
รับใบขับขี่ 137–I
รับใบทะเบียนเจ้าของรถจากผู้ขาย 157–E
รับใบอนุญาตสำหรับผู้กำลังหัดขับ 137–F
รับประทานอาหารเช้า 38–E
รับประทานอาหารเย็น 39–S
รับฝากข้อความ 171–Q
รับรู้ข้อมูลข่าวสาร 140–F
รับหมั้น 41–J
รับเอากรรมสิทธิ์ 49–K
รั้ว 177–19
รัศมีวงกลม 193–35
ราก 210–5, 211–3
ราคา 27–7
ราคาปกติ 27–2
ราคาลด 27–3
ราง 152–14
ร่างกาย 104
รางน้ำ 53–4
รางลื่น 224–13
รางเลื่อนส่งกระเป๋า 161–23
ร้านกาแฟ 126–11
ร้านขนมปัง 127–19
ร้านของเล่น 130–5
ร้านขายการ์ด 130–7
ร้านขายของชำ 72–73, 127–18
ร้านขายของที่ระลึก 184–5
ร้านขายของสำหรับหญิงมีครรภ์ 131–19
ร้านขายเครื่องใช้ในสำนักงาน 127–21
ร้านขายเครื่องไฟฟ้า 131–20
ร้านขายเครื่องเรือน 126–8
ร้านขายโดนัท 129–17
ร้านขายผ้า 99
ร้านขายยา 112,113, 128–4
ร้านขายอุปกรณ์ก่อสร้าง 148–4
ร้านขายอุปกรณ์การซ่อมแซมบ้าน 127–20
ร้านเครื่องประดับกาย 130–2
ร้านซักผ้าด้วยเครื่อง 128–1
ร้านซักแห้ง 128–2
ร้านดนตรี/เพลง 130–1
ร้านดอกไม้ 130–8
ร้านตัดผมชาย 129–19
ร้านแต่งเล็บ 130–3
ร้านถ่ายเอกสาร 129–18
ร้านทำผม 131–18
ร้านรองเท้า 130–10
ร้านรับซ่อมแก้ไขดัดแปลงเสื้อผ้า 100
ร้านลูกกวาด 131–17
ร้านวิดีโอ 129–20
ร้านแว่นตา 130–9
ร้านสะดวกซื้อ 128–3
ร้านสัตว์เลี้ยงดูเล่น 130–6
ร้านหนังสือ 130–4
ร้านหนังสือพิมพ์ข้างถนน 128–12
ร้านอาหาร 82–83, 125–14
ร้านอาหารจานด่วน 79, 128–10
ร้านไอศครีม 131–16
รายการกีฬา 236–11

รายการเกม 236–8
รายการเกี่ยวกับธรรมชาติ 236–7
รายการงานต่างๆตามปฏิทิน 22
รายการงานที่มีเสนอ 172–11
รายการจับจ่ายซื้อของ 67–14
รายการช้อปปิ้ง 236–10
รายการเด็ก 236–9
รายการตลก 236–2
รายการทักษะต่างๆ 172–12
รายการเรื่องจริงน่ามาเล่า 236–6
รายการสนทนา 236–4
รายการเสนอขายในอินเทอร์เน็ต 48–1
รายการหนังสือทางออนไลน์ 133–11
รายการอาหาร 82–7
รายการอาหารในร้านกาแฟ 80–81
รายงาน หากพบเห็นหีบห่อน่าสงสัย 143–J
รายงานอาชญากรรมต่างๆต่อเจ้าหน้าที่ตำรวจ 143–K
รายวัน 20–21
ราวกันตก 59–10
ราวแขวน 98–16
ราวจับ 57–11
ราวตากผ้า 101–9
ราวผ้าเช็ดตัว 57–15
ราสเบอร์รี่ 68–15
ริมฝีปาก 106–5
รีดนม 177–C
รีดเสื้อผ้า 101–F
รื้อของออกจากหีบห่อ 49–N
รูปทรง 193
รูปทรงเรขาคณิต 193
รูปปั้นหล่อขนาดเล็ก 232–1
รูปลักษณ์ภายนอก 32
รูระบายน้ำเสีย 57–7
รู้สึกคลื่นเหียน 110–D
รู้สึกวิงเวียน 110–C
เรกเก้ 237–31
เรขาคณิต 192–17
เร็วก่อนกำหนด 19–22
เริ่ม 230–R
เริ่มการสนทนา 12–A
เริ่มต้นประโยคด้วยอักษรตัวใหญ่ 190–B
เริ่มไปโรงเรียน 40–B
เรียงความ 190–4
เรียนจบ 40–D
เรือข้ามฟาก 220–4
เรื่องเขย่าขวัญที่น่าติดตาม 237–20
เรื่องตื่นเต้น 237–19
เรื่องนวนิยายเชิงวิทยาศาสตร์ 237–18
เรื่องรักใคร่ 237–16
เรื่องลึกลับ 237–20
เรื่องสยองขวัญ 237–17
เรือนำเที่ยว 220–4
เรือใบ 225–3
แร็คเก็ตบอล 228–12
แรคคูน 216–13
แรด 217–28
โรคต่างๆและสภาวะป่วยไข้ขั้นรุนแรง 111

โรคสมองเสื่อม 111–18
โรคหัวใจ 111–11
โรคเหงือก 119–11
โรง/ห้องบริหารร่างกาย 184–24
โรงงาน 126–3, 175
โรงงานตัดเย็บเสื้อผ้า 98
โรงนา 177–11
โรงบริหารร่างกาย 126–10
โรงพยาบาล 120–121, 125–9, 154–18
โรงพลศึกษา 5–19
โรงภาพยนตร์ 126–6, 222–2
โรงมหรสพ 127–23
โรงยิม 126–10
โรงรถ 47–14
โรงเรียน 5, 126–9
โรงเรียนเทคนิค 188–5
โรงเรียนประถม 188–2
โรงเรียนผู้ใหญ่ 188–8
โรงเรียนมัธยมต้น 188–3
โรงเรียนมัธยมปลาย 188–4
โรงเรียนและวิชาต่างๆ 188
โรงเรียนอนุบาล 188–1
โรงเรียนอาชีวศึกษา 188–5
โรงแรม 124–3, 184
โรงอาหาร 5–14
โรลไฟฟ้าม้วนผม 108–17
โรลม้วนผม 33–19
ไร่ 52–9, 177–7
ไร่องุ่น 177–16
ฤดูต่างๆ 21
ฤดูใบไม้ผลิ 21–37
ฤดูใบไม้ร่วง 21–39
ฤดูร้อน 21–38
ฤดูหนาว 21–40
ลงคะแนนเสียง 140–A
ลดขนาดกางเกง 100–D
ลดขยะ 219–A
ลบ 192–B, 196–C
ลบข้อที่ผิด 10–M
ลมแรง 13–18
ลวด 181–13
ลวดเย็บกระดาษ 183–29
ลวดลาย 96
ล้อเข็น 129–28
ล้อเข็นกระเป๋าเสื้อผ้า 184–8
ล้อเข็นของใช้งานแม่บ้านโรงแรม 184–19
ล้อเข็นเด็ก 37–18
ล้อเข็นเด็กแบบมีมุ้ง 37–20
ล็อคแบบลั่นกลอน 51–34
ล็อคประตู 159–25
ล็อคประตูของคุณ 143–E
ล็อคประตูเสีย 62–6
ลองสวมรองเท้า 95–C
ล้อลากเข็น 176–3
ละคร 223–8, 236–12
ละครโทรทัศน์เรื่องยาว 236–5
ละครร้องโอเปร่า 223–11

ลา 215–3
ล้าง...(แชมพู) ออกจากผม 108–F
ล้างชาม 60–M
ลานเด็กเล่น 50–3
ลานทราย 224–15
ลานบ้าน 51–21
ลานโบว์ลิ่ง 222–4
ล่าม 168–35
ลามา 217–25
ลายจุด 96–21
ลายดอก 96–25
ลายตาหมากรุก 96–24
ลายแถบตาราง 96–22
ลายทาง 96–20
ลายพิมพ์ 96–23
ลายพิมพ์นิ้วมือ 136–5
ลายเพสลี่ 96–26
ลายมือชื่อ 4–19
ลายสัก 32–18
ลำต้น 210–4
ลำโพง 50–5, 234–14
ลำไส้ 107–42
ลิง 217–26
ลิงกอริลลา 217–29
ลิงชิมแปนซี 217–27
ลิงสุครีพ 217–29
ลิงหน้าหมู 217–31
ลิงอุรังอุตัง 217–39
ลิ้น 106–8
ลิ้นชัก 54–23, 58–2
ลิ้นชักเก็บของ 159–44
ลิปสติก 109–38
ลิฟท์ 50–9, 131–21, 184–9
ลุกขึ้น 38–B
ลุง 34–8
ลูกกลิ้งทาสี 181–23
ลูกกวาด 239–12
ลูกเกด 68–25
ลูกค้า 72–1, 94–4, 132–2, 164–2
ลูกจ้าง 165–9
ลูกชาย 34–15
ลูกชิ้น 81–27
ลูกเต๋า 232–6
ลูกทุ่ง 237–27
ลูกนัทต่างๆ 73–36
ลูกบอลสำหรับเบสบอล 231–18
ลูกบอลสำหรับฟุตบอล 231–12
ลูกบาศก์ 193–38
ลูกบิดประตู 53–12
ลูกปัด 95–34, 99–32
ลูกโป่ง 44–4
ลูกพรวน 238–17
ลูกพรุน 68–26
ลูกพี่ลูกน้อง 34–9
ลูกแมว 215–10
ลูกไม้ 99–9
ลูกสาว 34–14
ลูกหมา 215–12
ลูกอม 239–12

ลู่และลาน (กรีฑา) **228**–18
ลู่วิ่งแข่ง **5**–21
เล็ก **96**–2
เล็กเป็นพิเศษ **96**–1
เลขคี่ **192**–3
เลขคู่ **192**–4
เลขโรมัน **16**
เลขแสดงลำดับที่ **16**
เล่น **235**–B
เล่นเกม **232**–B
เล่นเครื่องดนตรี **238**–A
เลนซ์สำหรับซูม **235**–23
เล่นด้วย **36**–M
เล่นไฟ **233**–H
เล่นสิ่งของที่แทนกันได้ **194**–16
เล่นแสร้งทำ **233**–G
เล็บนิ้วมือ **106**–18
เล็มกิ่งรั้วต้นไม้ **176**–B
เลอะเทอะ **64**–8
เลี้ยงลูกบอล **230**–J
เลี้ยวขวาเข้าถนนไพน์ **155**–B
เลี้ยวขวาเท่านั้น **154**–7
เลี้ยวซ้ายเข้าถนนโอ๊ค **155**–C
เลือก **196**–B
เลือกคำตอบที่ถูกต้อง **9**–P
เลือกก๋าเดาไหล **110**–17
เลือดไหล **116**–M
เลื่อม **99**–33
เลื่อยฉลุลาย **180**–10
เลื่อยมือ **180**–4
เลื่อยโลหะแบบเปลี่ยนใบได้ **180**–5
เลื่อยวงเดือน **180**–9
แลกเงินธนบัตรเป็นเหรียญ **26**–A
แลกเงินปลีก **26**–A
แลกเปลี่ยน **27**–I
แลน **212**–26
โลก **205**–3
โล่งใจ **42**–15
โลชั่นทาตัว **108**–9
โลชั่นเพื่อความชุ่มชื้น **108**–9
โลชั่นสำหรับทารก **37**–13
โล้น **33**–12
โลมา **213**–31
โลมาประเภทหนึ่ง **213**–30
วงกลม **193**–34
วงเล็บ **190**–19
วนอุทยานแห่งชาติในสหรัฐอเมริกา **220**
วอลเลย์บอล **229**–14, **231**–3
วัณโรค (ทีบี) **111**–15
วัด **17**–C
วัด...ไข้ **118**–B
วัน **20**–2
วันเกิด **22**–1
วันขอบคุณพระเจ้า **22**–17
วันขึ้นปีใหม่ **22**–9
วันครบรอบ **22**–3
วันคริสต์มาส **22**–18
วันจันทร์ **20**–9
วันต่างๆในสัปดาห์ **20**

วันทหารผ่านศึก **22**–16
วันทำงาน **20**–16
วันที่ **20**–1
วันที่เกิด (เดือน/วัน/ปี) **4**–13
วันที่สี่ของเดือนกรกฎาคม **22**–13
วันนี้ **20**–5
วันประธานาธิบดี **22**–11
วันพรุ่งนี้ **20**–6
วันพฤหัสบดี **20**–12
วันพุธ **20**–11
วันไม่ดีในที่ทำงาน **186**
วันระลึกโคลัมบัส **22**–15
วันระลึกทหารที่เสียชีวิตในสงคราม
    ต่างๆ **22**–12
วันระลึกมาร์ติน ลูเธอร์ คิง จูเนียร์ **22**–10
วันระลึกเอกราชของสหรัฐฯ **22**–13
วันแรงงาน **22**–14
วันศุกร์ **20**–13
วันเสาร์ **20**–14
วันหนึ่งที่โรงเรียน **11**
วันหมดอายุ **112**–7, **136**–10
วันหยุดตามกฎหมาย **22**–8
วันหยุดตามกฎหมาย **22**
วันหยุดทางศาสนา **22**–7
วันหยุดเทศกาล **239**
วันหยุดพักผ่อน **22**–6
วันหยุดสุดสัปดาห์ **20**–17
วันอังคาร **20**–10
วันอาทิตย์ **20**–8
วัย **32**
วัยกลางคน **32**–2
วัยชรา **32**–3
วัยรุ่น **31**–11
วัยหนุ่มสาว **32**–1
วัว **215**–1
วัสดุเครื่องใช้ในสำนักงาน **183**
วัสดุที่แผ่รังสี **179**–7
วัสดุปิดผนัง **178**–19
วัสดุไปรษณีย์ **134**–6
วางเงินทิปทิ้งไว้ **82**–J
วางดินสอ **6**–J
วางแผนการรับมือกับเหตุฉุกเฉิน **146**–A
วางหู **15**–D
ว่าจ้างทนาย **141**–B
ว่าจ้างนักกฎหมาย **141**–B
วาดภาพ **233**–E
วาดรูป **8**–F
ว่ายน้ำ **230**–L
วารสาร **133**–4
ว่าว **225**–2
วาวปิดแก๊ส **146**–4
ว่าเหว่ **42**–17
วิ่งข้ามถนน **153**–G
วิ่งแข่งขัน **230**–S
วิ่งไปตามหัวมุม **153**–H
วิ่งไปที่ห้องเรียน **11**–D
วิชาคำนวณ **192**
วิชาคำนวณขั้นสูง **192**–19
วิชาเคมี **195**

วิชาทางออนไลน์ **172**–8
วิตกกังวล **42**–13
วิตามิน **113**–17
วิทยาเขต **5**
วิทยาลัย **188**–7
วิทยาลัยชุมชน **127**–17, **188**–6
วิทยาศาสตร์ **189**–11, **194**–195
วิทยุ **159**–37
วิทยุรับส่ง (สองทาง) **179**–22
วิธีการเสิร์ฟอาหารประเภทไข่ **76**
วิธีจ่ายเงิน **27**
วิธีต่างๆในการประหยัดพลังงานและแหล่ง
    ทรัพยากร **219**
วิธีต่างๆในการเสิร์ฟเนื้อและ
    เนื้อสัตว์ปีก **76**
วิธีที่จะบรรลุผลสำเร็จ **10**
วิธีที่จะมีสุขภาพดี ไม่ป่วยไข้ **114**
วิธีที่จะหายป่วย **114**
วินาที **18**–3
วิศวกร **167**–25
วิศวกรผู้ผลิตซอฟท์แวร์
    คอมพิวเตอร์ **167**–18
วิสัญญีแพทย์ **121**–35
วุฒิสภา (สภาสูง) **138**–5
วุฒิสมาชิก **138**–6
วุฒิสมาชิกของรัฐ **139**–25
เวลา **18–19**
เวลาต่างๆในหนึ่งวัน **18**
เวลาที่ต้องปรับตามฤดูกาล **19**–25
เวลาในเขตตอนกลาง **19**–31
เวลาในเขตตะวันออก **19**–32
เวลาในเขตนิวฟาวด์แลนด์ **19**–34
เวลาในเขตฝั่งแปซิฟิก **19**–29
เวลาในเขตฝั่งแอตแลนติก **19**–33
เวลาในเขตภูเขาค่อนทางตะวันตก **19**–30
เวลาในเขตอาลาสกา **19**–28
เวลาในเขตฮาวาย-อลูเชิน **19**–27
เวลาพระอาทิตย์ขึ้น **18**–14
เวลาพระอาทิตย์ตก **18**–18
เวลามาตรฐาน **19**–26
แว่นตา **115**–7
แว่นตากันแดด **90**–27
แว่นตานิรภัย **92**–10
แว่นตาเพื่อความปลอดภัย **179**–10
แว่นบังตาเพื่อความปลอดภัย **179**–11
ไวโอลิน **238**–6
ไวโอเล็ต **211**–23
ศร **231**–8
ศรชี้ **197**–12
ศอก **106**–12
ศัพท์ **8**–A
ศัพท์ทางประวัติศาสตร์ **199**
ศัลยแพทย์ (หมอผ่าตัด) **121**–36
ศาล **125**–13
ศาลสูง **138**–11
ศาลากลาง **124**–8
ศิลปะการป้องกันตัว **228**–11
ศิลปะด้านภาษา **189**–9
ศิลปะสาขาต่างๆ **189**–15

ศิลปิน **166**–6
ศึกษาคู่มือ **137**–A
ศูนย์ **16**
ศูนย์กลางข้อมูล **172**–9
ศูนย์การค้า **126**–7, **130**–**131**
ศูนย์การประชุม **127**–24
ศูนย์ดูแลเด็ก **129**–30
ศูนย์ธรรมชาติ **208**
ศูนย์บริการไปรษณีย์อัตโนมัติ **135**–10
ศูนย์รวมเครื่องบันเทิง **56**–5
ศูนย์อาหาร **131**–15
เศร้า **43**–19
เศร้าสลด **237**–14
เศษ **192**–5
เศษส่วน **192**
เศษส่วนและทศนิยม **17**
เศษหนึ่งส่วนแปด **17**–5
เศษหนึ่งส่วนสาม **17**–3
เศษหนึ่งส่วนสี่ **17**–4
เศษหนึ่งส่วนสี่ถ้วยตวง **75**
สกรูเครื่องจักร **180**–32
สกรูไม้ **180**–33
สกี **230**–V, **231**–24
สเก็ต **230**–U
สเก็ตน้ำแข็ง **231**–9
สเก็ตบอร์ด **224**–7, **228**–13
สเก็ตแบบล้อแนวเดียว
    228–10, **231**–10
สเกล **155**–7
สแกนเอกสาร **171**–H
ส่งการ์ดทางไปรษณีย์ **135**–D
สงคราม **199**–10
สงครามปฏิวัติ **198**–8
ส่งคืนข้อสอบของคุณ **10**–O
ส่งงานเขียนของคุณ **191**–M
ส่งเด็กลงที่โรงเรียน **38**–G
ส่งต่อ **230**–G
สงบ **42**–8
ส่งประวัติการทำงาน
    และจดหมายปะหน้าของคุณ **173**–H
ส่งมอบหนังสือ **11**–G
ส่งอีเมล **197**–I
ส่งเอกสารทางโทรสาร (แฟกซ์) **171**–G
สตรอเบอร์รี่ **68**–14
สติคเกอร์ **102**–3
สติคเกอร์การจดทะเบียน **136**–13
สเต็ก **70**–2, **81**–24
สเต็กย่างในชั้นเตาอบ **76**–3
สถานที่เกิด **4**–14
สถานที่น่าไป **222**
สถานที่ประชุม **146**–1
สถานแสดงสัตว์น้ำ **222**–7
สถานีดับเพลิง **125**–12
สถานีตำรวจ **124**–6
สถานียามเฝ้าระวังและช่วยชีวิต **225**–21
สถานีรถโดยสาร **124**–7
สถานีรถใต้ดิน **151**–11, **152**
สถานีรถไฟ **152**
สถานีอวกาศ **205**–18

สถาปนิก **166**–5
สน **210**–9
สันเตี้ย **97**–31
สันเท้า **106**–24
สันรองเท้า **94**–22
สันสูง **97**–32
สนอร์เกิล **227**–11
สนับแข้ง **231**–13
สนาม **5**–2
สนามเทนนิส **224**–6
สนามบอล **224**–1
สนามบาสเก็ตบอล **229**–7
สนามบิน **151**–10, **160**–**161**
สนามหญ้า **53**–26
สนามหน้าบ้านและบ้าน **53**
สนามหลังบ้าน **53**
สบายดี **42**–14
สบู่ **57**–4, **108**–3
สบู่เหลว **108**–2
สปาเกตตี **81**–26
สเปรย์ผม **108**–12
สเปรย์ลงแป้ง **101**–12
สภาคองเกรส **138**–2
สภาคองเกรสแรกในภาคพื้นทวีป **198**–6
สภาผู้แทนราษฎร **138**–3
สภาผู้บริหาร **139**–27
สภาพอากาศ **13**
สภาวะต่างๆของอากาศ **13**
ส้ม **24**–4, **68**–5
สมการ **192**–13
ส้มเขียวหวาน **68**–9
ส้มสรวง **68**–6
สมอง **107**–34
สมัครรับเลือกเข้าดำรงตำแหน่ง **139**–A
สมัยใหม่ **199**–2
สมาชิกเทศมนตรี **139**–28
สมาชิกรัฐสภา **138**–4
สมาชิกสภาผู้บริหาร **139**–28
สมาชิกสภาแห่งรัฐ **139**–24
สมาชิกห้องสมุด **133**–3
สมุดข้อสอบ **10**–1
สมุดคู่ฝาก **132**–10
สมุดจด แบบเย็บสามห่วง **7**–27
สมุดจดขนาดยาว **183**–38
สมุดจดที่มีสันเป็นเกลียว **7**–29
สมุดเช็ค **132**–12
สมุดนัดหมาย **183**–48
สมุดบันทึก **7**–28
สมุดแผนที่ **133**–8
สมุดสำหรับระบายสี **59**–13
สมุดแสตมป์ **134**–18
สมุนไพร **84**–9
สร้อย **95**–33
สร้อยข้อมือระบุเกี่ยวกับ
    ผู้ป่วยในกรณีฉุกเฉิน **117**–3
สร้อยไข่มุก **95**–39
สร้อยคอ **95**–10
สระ...ผม **108**–E
สระน้ำ **184**–22

สระว่ายน้ำ **51**–22
สรุป **190**–8
สลักเกลียว **180**–35
สลักเกลียวอัดยึด **180**–38
สลัดกะหล่ำปลี **80**–18
สลัดชนิดหนึ่ง **80**–14
สลัดผลไม้ **80**–21
สลัดผัก **80**–15
สลัดผักปวยเล้ง **80**–13
สลัดพาสตา **80**–20
สลัดมันฝรั่ง **80**–19
สไลด์ **194**–3, **224**–13
สวน **192**–6
สวน **53**–B
สวนครัว **53**–27
สวนต่าง **192**–8
สวนต่างๆของดอกไม้ **211**
สวนต่างๆของเรียงความ **190**
สวนที่สองมอง **194**–14
สวนบนหลังคา **50**–4
สวนประกอบของจักรเย็บผ้า **98**
สวนประกอบเพื่อตกแต่ง **99**
สวนประกอบเสื้อผ้าเพื่อกระชับปิด **99**
สวนผลไม้ **177**–10
สวนผัก **177**–14
สวนพฤษชาติ **222**–3
สวนลากพวง **156**–17
สวนสนุก **223**–10
สวนสัตว์ **222**–1
สวนสาธารณะและลานเด็กเล่น **224**
สวนหนึ่งของเส้น **193**–20
สวนหมุนปรับ **194**–15
สวนหักลด **165**–13
สวม **87**–B
ส้วมอุดตัน **63**–19
สว่านไฟฟ้า **180**–8
สวิทช์ไฟ **58**–27
สอง **16**
สอดบัตรเอทีเอ็มของคุณ **132**–D
สอน **170**–Q
สอบถามเกี่ยวกับรายละเอียดต่างๆ **48**–B
สอบผ่าน **10**–E
ส้อม **55**–3
ส้อมสำหรับสลัด **83**–27
ส้อมสำหรับอาหารหลัก **83**–28
สะกดชื่อของคุณ **4**–B
สะสมสิ่งของ **232**–A
สะอาด **76**–A
สะอิดสะเอียน **42**–7
สังเกตการณ์ **195**–C
สั่งจากรายการอาหาร **82**–D
สัญญาเช่า **51**–28
สัญญาณแรงดี **14**–11
สัญญาณอ่อน **14**–12
สัญลักษณ์ **155**–5
สัดส่วนการย่อขนาด **155**–7
สัตว์ครึงบกครึงน้ำ **212**
สัตว์ชนิดหนึ่งของออสเตรเลีย
    คล้ายตุ่น **217**–46

สัตว์ชนิดหนึ่งคล้ายกระรอก
    215–19, **216**–4
สัตว์ชนิดหนึ่งคล้ายลามีเขา
    เป็นแฉก **216**–1
สัตว์ถิ่นขั้วโลกเหนือชนิดหนึ่ง **213**–32
สัตว์ทะเล **212**
สัตว์ทะเลคล้ายหอย **212**–21
สัตว์ทะเลลำตัวเป็นปล้องมี
    หนวดปาก **212**–24
สัตว์ทะเลเลี้ยงลูกด้วยนม **213**
สัตว์ประเภทหนู **215**
สัตว์ป่า **220**–3
สัตวแพทย์ **169**–62
สัตว์มีกระดูกสันหลัง **194**–12
สัตว์ไม่มีกระดูกสันหลัง **194**–13
สัตว์เลี้ยงเล่น **215**
สัตว์เลี้ยงในฟาร์ม **215**
สัตว์เลี้ยงลูกด้วยนม **209**–10, **216**–**217**
สัตว์เลี้ยงและสัตว์ประเภทหนู **215**
สัตว์เลื้อยคลาน **213**
สับปะรด **68**–23
สับสน **43**–26
สับหัวหอม **77**–L
สัปดาห์ **20**–15
สัปดาห์ที่แล้ว **20**–18
สัปดาห์นี้ **20**–19
สัปดาห์ละครั้ง **20**–22
สัปดาห์ละสองครั้ง **20**–23
สัปดาห์ละสามครั้ง **20**–24
สัปดาห์หน้า **20**–20
สัมผัส **106**–E
สาธารณูปโภคต่างๆ
    (เช่น น้ำ ไฟ แก๊ส) **48**–5
สาม **16**
สามขาสำหรับตั้งกล้องถ่าย **235**–25
สามสิบ **16**
สามสิบนาทีหลังหนึ่งนาฬิกา **18**–11
สามเหลี่ยม **193**–32
สามี **34**–13
สาย **19**–24
สายของเครื่องโทรศัพท์ **14**–2
สายเคเบิล **196**–13
สายเคเบิลถ่ายไฟแบตเตอรี่ **158**–21
สายงานประกอบชิ้นส่วน **175**–6
สายโทรศัพท์ **14**–4
สายพานส่งของ **175**–9
สายไฟ **181**–13
สายไฟของเครื่อง **196**–2
สายไฟที่ขาดรุ่ย **179**–5
สายไฟพ่วงต่อ **181**–14
สายยางยืดสำหรับรัดของ **181**–15
สายยางรดน้ำ **53**–21
สายยืดถุงกระบัว **91**–16
สายรั้งกางเกง **94**–1
สายวัด **181**–45
สายวัดตัว **100**–17
สาลี่ **68**–4
สำนักงาน **164**–3, **182**
สำนักงานเช่า **51**

สำนักงานไปรษณีย์ **125**–11
สำนักงานใหญ่ **5**–12
สำเนาเอกสารสำคัญต่างๆ **146**–20
สำเนาเอกสารแสดงตัวบุคคลและ
    บัตรเครดิต **146**–19
สำรอก **110**–E
สำลัก **116**–L
สิ่งของมีค่าต่างๆ **132**–8
สิงโต **217**–36
สิงโตทะเล **213**–33
สิงโตภูเขา **216**–2
สิ่งประดับประดา **240**–1
สิ่งมีชีวิต **194**–1
สิ่งมีชีวิตในทะเล สัตว์ครึ่งบกครึ่งน้ำ
    และสัตว์เลื้อยคลาน **212**–**213**
สิงหาคม **21**–32
สิทธิ **140**
สิทธิและหน้าที่ของพลเมือง **140**
สินค้าประเภทอบ **73**
สิบ **16**
สิบเก้า **16**
สิบเจ็ด **16**
สิบเซ็นต์ **26**–3
สิบดอลลาร์ **26**–9
สิบนาทีหลังหนึ่งนาฬิกา **18**–8
สิบแปด **16**
สิบสอง **16**
สิบสาม **16**
สิบสี่ **16**
สิบหก **16**
สิบห้า **16**
สิบห้านาทีหลังหนึ่งนาฬิกา **18**–9
สิบเอ็ด **16**
ลิ่ว **181**–55
สี **16**
สีกรมท่า **28**–5
สีกลางๆ **24**
สีต่างกัน **23**–16
สีต่างๆ **24**
สีทาแก้ม **109**–37
สีทาบ้าน **181**–25
สีทาเล็บ **109**–33
สีเทียน **59**–14
สีน้ำ **233**–21
สีน้ำมัน **233**–19
สีเนื้อ **24**–18
สีป้ายขนตา **109**–39
สีล้วนไม่มีลาย **96**–19
สีสิบ **16**
สีหลัก **24**
สีเหมือนกัน **23**–15
สี่เหลี่ยมจัตุรัส **193**–30
สี่เหลี่ยมด้านขนาน **193**–33
สี่เหลี่ยมผืนผ้า **193**–29
สีอาคริลิค **232**–10
สุขอนามัยส่วนตัว **108**–**109**
สุนัขนิสัยดี **23**–17
สุนัขนิสัยไม่ดี **23**–18
สึนามิ **145**–17

สุริยคราส **205**–16
สุสาน **127**–15
สุเหร่า **126**–5
สุเหร่ายิว **127**–16
สูง **32**–4
สูตร **195**–34
สูติแพทย์ **120**–2
เส้น **193**
เส้นขนาน **193**–25
เส้นโค้ง **193**–23
เส้นตรง **193**–22
เส้นตั้งฉาก **193**–24
เส้นทางการเดินรถประจำทาง **152**–1
เส้นทางอพยพผู้คนออกไป **146**–5
เส้นทางอาชีพ **172**
เส้นผ่านศูนย์กลาง **193**–37
เส้นรอบรูป **193**–43
เส้นรอบวง **193**–36
เส้นโลหิตดำ **107**–37
เส้นโลหิตแดง **107**–36
เสมียน **5**–13
เสรีภาพทางสื่อสิ่งพิมพ์ **140**–4
เสรีภาพในการนับถือศาสนา **140**–3
เสรีภาพในการพูด **140**–2
เสาอากาศ **14**–9
เสาะหาที่ที่หลบภัย **147**–H
เสิร์ฟลูก **230**–P
เสิร์ฟอาหาร **82**–F
เสียง **64**–5
เสียภาษี **140**–B
เสือ **217**–37
เสื้อกล้าม **89**–24
เสื้อกั๊ก **89**–15
เสื้อกั๊กที่มองเห็นได้แต่ไกล
   เพื่อความปลอดภัย **92**–4
เสื้อกั๊กนวมขนนก **90**–14
เสื้อกั๊กนิรภัย **226**–14
เสื้อกันฝน **90**–18
เสื้อกันลม **90**–24
เสื้อกันหนาว **28**–2, **87**–14, **96**–7
เสื้อกันหนาวคอกว้าง **96**–10
เสื้อกันหนาวคอตั้ง **96**–9
เสื้อกันหนาวคอตัววี **96**–8
เสื้อกันหนาวตัวยาว (คลุมถึงเข่า) **90**–2
เสื้อกันหนาวแบบเปิดด้านหน้า **88**–2
เสื้อกันหนาวแบบสวมทางศีรษะ **88**–3
เสื้อกันหนาวมีหมวกคลุมศีรษะ **90**–9
เสื้อกันหนาวสีขาวอยู่ข้างหน้า
   เสื้อกันหนาวสีดำ **25**–7
เสื้อกันหนาวสีเขียวไข่กาอยู่ใน
   กล่อง **25**–6
เสื้อกันหนาวสีเขียวอยู่ระหว่าง
   เสื้อกันหนาวสีชมพู **25**–12
เสื้อกันหนาวสีดำอยู่ข้างหลังเสื้อกันหนาว
   สีขาว **25**–8
เสื้อกันหนาวสีแดงอยู่บนเสื้อกันหนาว
   สีฟ้า **25**–5
เสื้อกันหนาวสีเทาอยู่ข้างใต้เสื้อกันหนาว
   สีส้ม **25**–10

เสื้อกันหนาวสีน้ำตาลอยู่ทางขวา **25**–3
เสื้อกันหนาวสีฟ้าอยู่ใต้เสื้อกันหนาว
   สีแดง **25**–5
เสื้อกันหนาวสีม่วงเข้มอยู่ถัดจากเสื้อกัน
   หนาวสีเทา **25**–9
เสื้อกันหนาวสีม่วงอยู่ตรงกลาง **25**–2
เสื้อกันหนาวสีส้มอยู่บนเสื้อกันหนาว
   สีเทา **25**–11
เสื้อกันหนาวสีเหลืองอยู่ทางซ้าย **25**–1
เสื้อกีฬา **88**–4
เสื้อกีฬามีส่วนคลุมศีรษะ **89**–22
เสื้อแขนกุด **96**–11
เสื้อแขนยาว **96**–14
เสื้อแขนสามส่วน **96**–13
เสื้อครุย (ปริญญา) **206**–8
เสื้อคลุม **90**–25
เสื้อคลุมทั้งตัวสำหรับทำงาน **92**–8
เสื้อคลุมทำงาน **93**–26
เสื้อคลุมทำงานพยาบาล **93**–31
เสื้อคลุมทำงานศัลยกรรม **93**–38
เสื้อคลุมทำงานห้องแล็บ **93**–33
เสื้อคลุมยาว **91**–29
เสื้อคลุมศัลยกรรม **93**–37, **121**–38
เสื้อโค้ทกันฝน **90**–21
เสื้อแจ็คเก็ตนวมขนนก **90**–16
เสื้อแจ็คเก็ตหนัง **90**–4
เสื้อชูชีพ **161**–25
เสื้อเชิ้ต **86**–1
เสื้อเชิ้ตแขนสั้น **96**–12
เสือดาว **217**–34
เสือดำ **217**–40
เสื้อแต่งหรูหรา **97**–34
เสื้อที่รีดแล้ว **101**–20
เสื้อนอก **92**–12
เสื้อนอนยาวชาย **91**–28
เสื้อนอนยาวหญิง **91**–25
เสื้อนอนอุ่นแบบเต็มตัว **91**–27
เสื้อใน **91**–20
เสื้อแบบผ้าคลุมกันฝน **90**–19
เสื้อแบบเรียบ **97**–33
เสื้อเปียก **101**–17
เสื้อโปโล **92**–14
เสื้อผ้ากันหนาว **146**–6
เสื้อผ้าชุดทำงาน **88**, **92**–93
เสื้อผ้าใช้แล้ว **102**–2
เสื้อผ้าตามฤดูกาล **90**
เสื้อผ้าที่ใช้ในชีวิตประจำวัน **86**
เสื้อผ้าที่ต้องซัก **101**–1
เสื้อผ้าแบบเป็นทางการ **89**
เสื้อผ้าแบบลำลอง **88**
เสื้อผ้าแบบลำลอง แบบทำงาน
   และแบบเป็นทางการ **88**–89
เสื้อผู้ป่วย **121**–19
เสื้อผู้หญิง **87**–8
เสื้อพนักงานรักษาความปลอดภัย **93**–20
เสื้อยับ **101**–19
เสื้อยืด **88**–7
เสื้อยืดคอกลม **86**–4
เสื้อยืดสกปรก **101**–15

เสื้อยืดสะอาด **101**–16
เสื้อรองใน **91**–1, **91**–21
เสื้อรองในแบบอุ่นพิเศษ **91**–2
เสื้อสเวตเตอร์ **87**–14
เสื้อสเวตเตอร์คอกลม **96**–7
เสื้อสูทแบบลำลอง **89**–14
เสื้อใส่ทำงาน **92**–2
เสื้อใส่ออกกำลังกาย **89**–22
เสื้อหัวหน้าคนครัว **93**–29
เสื้อแห้ง **101**–18
แสก **33**–4
แสดงบัตรขึ้นเครื่องและ
   บัตรประจำตัว **160**–C
แสดงเอกสารระบุตัวบุคคล **137**–C
แสตมป์ **134**–23
ใส่ **87**–B, **109**–P
ใส่การใช้บริการสาธารณูปโภคต่างๆ
   ในชื่อของคุณ **49**–O
ใส่ข้อมูล **171**–B
ใส่เข็มขัดนิรภัย **36**–L
ใส่ใจดูหรือฟังคำเตือน **147**–D
ใส่ที่อยู่อีเมล **197**–C
ใส่น้ำยาทำความเย็น **157**–I
ใส่ป้ายระบุภาพ **9**–V
ใส่ปุ๋ย **176**–D
ใส่รหัส (PIN) ของคุณ **132**–E
ใส่เสื้อผ้า **36**–H
ใส่เสื้อผ้าในเครื่องซัก **101**–C
ไส้กรอก **70**–12, **80**–2
ไส้กรอกชนิดหนึ่ง **71**–24
หก **16**
หกล้ม **116**–O
หกสิบ **16**
หญ้าแห้ง **177**–18
หญิง **4**–18
หนวด **33**–5
หนวดสัตว์ **216**–18
หน่วยงานรัฐแผนกยานยนต์
   (DMV) **136**–137
หน่วยงานรัฐแผนกยานยนต์ **124**–4
หน่อ **211**–5
หนอน **212**–23
หน่อไม้ฝรั่ง **69**–26
หนัง **98**–6
หนังสือเดินทาง **41**–10
หนังสือบาง **23**–8
หนังสือแบบฝึกหัด **7**–26
หนังสือแบบฟังเสียง **133**–17
หนังสือพิมพ์ **133**–6
หนังสือภาพ **133**–12
หนังสือหนา **23**–7
หน้า **106**, **193**–44
หน้ากาก **93**–32, **239**–9
หน้ากากกรองฝุ่น **179**–14
หน้ากากคนคว้าบอล **231**–15
หน้ากากดำน้ำ **225**–6
หน้ากากระบายอากาศ **92**–7
หน้ากากเล่นสกี **90**–15
หน้ากากศัลยกรรม **93**–36

หน้ากากออกซิเจน **161**–24
หน้าแข้ง **106**–21
หน้าจอ **196**–11
หน้าต่าง **47**–11, **56**–17, **136**–7
หน้าต่างขายตั๋ว **152**–12
หน้าต่างให้ขับรถผ่านไปสั่งซื้อ
   อาหาร **128**–11
หน้าตาดี **32**–13
หน้าที่ความรับผิดชอบ **140**
หน้าปัดรถและแผงอุปกรณ์ **159**
หน้าผาก **106**–2
หนาม **211**–29
หน้าม้า **33**–8
หนาว **13**–6, **42**–4
หนาวสั่น **110**–9
หน้าอก **104**–4, **107**–25
หนึ่ง **16**
หนึ่งควอเตอร์ **26**–4
หนึ่งจำนวนเต็ม **17**–1
หนึ่งช้อนชา **75**
หนึ่งช้อนโต๊ะ **75**
หนึ่งเซ็นต์ **26**–1
หนึ่งดอลลาร์ **26**–7
หนึ่งไดม์ **26**–3
หนึ่งถ้วยตวง **75**
หนึ่งนาฬิกา **18**–6
หนึ่งนาฬิกายี่สิบนาที **18**–10
หนึ่งนาฬิกาสามสิบนาที **18**–11
หนึ่งนาฬิกาสิบนาที **18**–8
หนึ่งนาฬิกาสิบห้านาที **18**–9
หนึ่งนาฬิกาสี่สิบนาที **18**–12
หนึ่งนาฬิกาสี่สิบห้านาที **18**–13
หนึ่งนาฬิกาห้านาที **18**–7
หนึ่งนิคเกิล **26**–2
หนึ่งพัน **16**
หนึ่งพันล้าน **16**
หนึ่งร้อย **16**
หนึ่งร้อยหนึ่ง **16**
หนึ่งล้าน **16**
หนึ่งแสน **16**
หนึ่งหมื่น **16**
หนูตะเภา **215**–14
หนูตัวเล็ก **215**–18
หนูตัวเล็ก(หลายตัว) **63**–28
หนูตัวใหญ่ **63**–27, **215**–17
หนูทุ่งหญ้า **215**–22
หมดสติ **116**–A
หมวก (ปริญญา) **206**–7
หมวก **90**–1, **95**–11
หมวกกันชน **92**–9
หมวกแก๊ป **86**–5, **88**–1
หมวกแข็งใส่ทำงาน **92**–1, **179**–9
หมวกคาวบอย **92**–18
หมวกนิรภัย **93**–23
หมวกนิรภัยสำหรับคนเล่นฟุตบอล
   (รักบี้) **231**–19
หมวกฟาง **90**–23
หมวกเล่นสกี **90**–11

หมวกศัลยกรรม (ผ่าตัด) **93**–35
หมวกศัลยกรรม **121**–37
หมวกหัวหน้าคนครัว **93**–28
หมวกอาบน้ำ **108**–1
หมอ **118**–5
หม้อ **54**–16, **78**–6, **78**–25
หมอกควัน **218**–11
หม้อตุ๋น **78**–8
หมอน **58**–11
หมอนปักเข็ม **100**–13
หมอนพิง **56**–2
หม้อน้ำ **158**–19
หมัด **214**–27
หมัดที่นอน **63**–24
หมา **215**–11
หมากรุก **232**–8
หมาจิ้งจอก **216**–15
หมาป่า **216**–5
หมาป่าชนิดหนึ่ง **216**–3, **217**–30
หมายเลขการเข้าถึง **14**–16
หมายเลขโทรศัพท์ **4**–11, **15**–30
หมายเลขโทรศัพท์มือถือ **4**–12
หมายเลขบัญชีกระแสรายวัน **132**–14
หมายเลขบัญชีฝากประจำ **132**–11
หมายเลขใบขับขี่ **136**–11
หมายเลขใบสั่งยา **112**–5
หมายเลขประกันสังคม **4**–15
หมายเลขรหัสสินค้าในสต็อค **27**–5
หมายเลขอพาร์ตเม้นต์ **4**–6
หมายสำคัญ **155**–6
หมายเหตุท้ายหน้า **190**–10
หมี **216**–11
หมีโคอาล่า **217**–45
หมีแพนด้า **217**–41
หมึก **212**–7
หมึกยักษ์ **212**–9
หมุนกลับ **235**–C
หมู **70**, **215**–2
หมู่บ้าน **52**–3
หมูเบคอน **70**–11
หมูสามชั้น **70**–11
หยิบดินสอขึ้นมา **6**–I
หยิบยื่นเสนอบางสิ่งบางอย่าง **12**–D
หยิบหนังสือขึ้นมา **11**–E
หยุด **154**–1
หยุดที่หัวมุมถนน **155**–D
หยุดพัก **11**–H
หยุดพักชั่วคราว **235**–E
หลงทาง **162**–B
หลอด **74**–12
หลอดดูด **79**–18
หลอดทดลอง **195**–42
หลักฐาน **141**–9
หลักฐานการประกัน **136**–8
หลักปันเขตที่ดิน **220**–1
หลัง **104**–5
หลังคา **46**–1
หลังคารั่ว **62**–3
หลังส่วนล่าง **107**–29

หลังเหตุฉุกเฉิน **147**
หลานชาย **34**–19
หลานสาว **34**–18
หลายห่อ **74**–8
หลิว **210**–13
ห่วงเกี่ยวตะขอ **180**–40
ห่วงให้เด็กกัดตอนฟันงอก **37**–25
หัวใจ **239**–6
หวัด **111**–1
หวาดกลัว **43**–23
หวี **33**–21, **108**–13
หวีสับ **108**–15
หวี...ผม **108**–G
ห่อ **240**–F
ห้อง/ตู้ในผนังสำหรับเก็บเสื้อผ้า **58**–5
ห้องเก็บของ **185**–5
ห้องของทารก **47**–10
ห้องเครื่อง **161**–10
ห้องจัดเลี้ยง **185**–14
ห้องชุด **50**–51, **184**–16
ห้องใต้ถุน **47**–13
ห้องใต้หลังคา **47**–8
ห้องแถว **52**–6
ห้องโถงงานเต้นรำ **184**–26
ห้องโถงรับแขก **50**
ห้องทดลองวิทยาศาสตร์ **195**
ห้องนอน **46**–2, **58**
ห้องนอนของเด็ก **47**–9, **59**
ห้องนักบิน **161**–10
ห้องนั่งเล่น **47**–12, **56**
ห้องน้ำ **5**–9, **46**–4, **57**
ห้องนิรภัย **132**–6
ห้องในโรงพยาบาล **121**
ห้องปฏิบัติการคอมพิวเตอร์ **5**–15
ห้องประชุม **182**–4, **184**–25
ห้องประชุมใหญ่ **5**–18
ห้องผ่าตัด **121**
ห้องพักในโรงแรม **184**–13
ห้องพิจารณาคดี **141**–7
ห้องเย็น (ห้องเก็บของแช่แข็ง) **185**–3
ห้องรับประทานอาหาร **82**–1
ห้องเรียน **5**–7, **6**–7
ห้องล้างชาม **83**–13
ห้องแล็บ **121**
ห้องสมุด **5**–17, **125**–15, **133**
หอดูดาว **205**–21
หอพัก **52**–8
หอพักวิทยาลัย **52**–8
หอมใหญ่ชุบแป้งทอดเป็นวง **79**–4
หอยกาบ **71**–15
หอยกาบ หอยแมลงภู่ **212**–17
หอยแครง **71**–12, **212**–19
หอยทะเล **225**–24
หอยทาก **212**–22
หอยนางรม **71**–14
หอยแมลงภู่ **71**–13
หัด **111**–5
หัดขับรถ **40**–E
หั่นต้นขึ้นฉ่ายเป็นชิ้นเล็กๆ **77**–J

หัว **104**–1
หัวเข็มขัด **94**–20, **99**–28
หัวจดหมาย **183**–42
หัวเจาะ **180**–28
หัวใจ **107**–38
หัวฉีดดับเพลิง **129**–27
หัวฉีดรดน้ำ **53**–22
หัวเทอร์นิป **69**–16
หัวนม **37**–2
หัวนมหลอก **37**–24
หัวบนดิน **69**–16
หัวบีท **69**–5
หัวผักกาดแดง **69**–4
หัวเผา **54**–19
หัวเผาบันเซน **195**–37
หัวฝักบัว **57**–13
หัวพันธุ์ **211**–2
หัวเราะ **44**–A
หัวหน้าคนงานทำสวน **176**–4
หัวหน้าคนเสิร์ฟอาหารชาย **185**–12
หัวหน้างาน **165**–8
หัวหน้าผู้พิพากษา **138**–13
หัวหน้าพนักงานขนกระเป๋า **184**–6
หัวหน้าพ่อครัว **185**–7
หัวหอม **69**–19
หัวอาติโชก **69**–22
ห้า **16**
หา/ทำบทสรุป **195**–E
หาง **216**–22
ห้างใหญ่ **131**–13
หาซื้อ **28**–A
ห้าเซ็นต์ **26**–2
ห้าดอลลาร์ **26**–8
หาดูโฆษณารถ **157**–A
หาที่นั่งของคุณ **160**–F
หาที่นั่งลง **6**–F
ห่าน **214**–13
ห้านาทีหลังหนึ่งนาฬิกา **18**–7
หาบ้าน **48**–49
ห้ามเข้า **154**–2
ห้ามจอด **154**–11
ห้ามเลี้ยวซ้าย **154**–8
หายใจไม่ได้ **116**–N
หาร **17**–A, **192**–D
ห้าสิบ **16**
ห้าสิบดอลลาร์ **26**–11
หินขัดไฟฟ้า **180**–11
หิมะตก **13**–12
หิมะถล่ม **145**–18
หิวข้าว **42**–5
หิวน้ำ **42**–2
หีบ **74**–6
หีบเก็บความเย็น **225**–9
หีบเบา **23**–14
หีบเพลงปาก **238**–21
หีบใส่ของเล่น **59**–16
หีบหนัก **23**–13
หีบห่อ **134**–17
หีดหอบ **111**–9

หุงหาอาหารเย็น **39**–Q
หุ่นสำหรับช่างเย็บผ้า **100**–2
หุบเขาลึก **204**–17
หู **105**–12
หูโทรศัพท์ **14**–1
หูน้ำหนวก **111**–3
หูหนวก **32**–12
เหงือก **106**–6
เหงือกปลา **212**–2
เห็ด **69**–27
เหตุการณ์ในชีวิตและเอกสาร
ต่างๆ **40**–41
เหตุฉุกเฉินด้านการรักษาพยาบาล **116**
เหตุฉุกเฉินและภัยธรรมชาติ **144**–145
เหตุระเบิด **144**–4
เห็นด้วย **12**–K
เหนือ **155**–1
เหนื่อย **43**–32
เหมือนกันและต่างกัน **28**
เหยือกกาแฟ **55**–7
เหรียญ **26**
เหรียญแทนเงิน **152**–10
เหรียญหนึ่งดอลลาร์ **26**–6
เหล็กกวาด **176**–8
เหล็กขุด **178**–21
เหลือง **24**–2
เหวี่ยง **230**–Q
เหา **63**–25
แหนบหนีบผม **108**–19
แหนบหนีบผ้า **101**–10
แหล่งพลังงาน **218**
แหล่งสนับสนุน **172**–9
แหล่งให้แสง **194**–19
แหวน **95**–40
แหวนราคาถูก **23**–20
แหวนราคาแพง **23**–19
แหวนราบ **180**–37
โหนกหลัง **217**–51
ให้...คำแนะนำ (สั่งสอน) **122**–B
ใหญ่ **96**–4
ใหญ่เป็นพิเศษ **96**–5
ให้ทาง **154**–9
ให้นมแม่ **36**–B
ให้น้ำพืช **176**–F
ให้ยืมเงิน **26**–C
ให้แสงน้อยเกินไป **235**–35
ให้แสงมากเกินไป **235**–34
ให้อาหาร **177**–D
ให้อาหารพืช **176**–D
ไหม้ (ตนเอง) **116**–H
ไหมแดง **110**–14
ไหมพรม **233**–22
ไหล่ **105**–13
องศา **13**–8
องุ่น **68**–3
องุ่นแห้ง **68**–25
องุ่นแห้งครึ่งถ้วยตวง **75**–9
อดิภังค์ **190**–20

อธิบายบางสิ่งบางอย่าง **12**–M
อธิษฐานขอ **240**–B
อบ **70**–1, **77**–H
อบในไมโครเวฟเป็นเวลา 5 นาที **77**–T
อพยพออกไปจากพื้นที่ **147**–K
อพาร์ตเมนต์ **50–51**
อพาร์ตเมนต์ที่มีเครื่องเรือน **48**–3
อพาร์ตเมนต์ที่ไม่มีเครื่องเรือน **48**–4
อภิปรายถึงปัญหา **8**–G
อเมริกาใต้ **202**–2
อเมริกาเหนือ **202**–1
อเมริกาเหนือและอเมริกา
กลาง **200–201**
อย่ากินพร้อมกับอาหารประเภท
นมเนย **112**–D
อย่าขับรถในขณะมึนเมา **143**–G
อย่าขับรถหรือทำงานกับเครื่อง
จักรกล **112**–E
อย่าดื่มเครื่องดื่มมึนเมา **112**–F
อย่าทิ้งขยะเรี่ยราด **219**–L
อย่าเปิดประตูให้คนแปลกหน้า **143**–F
อย่ามาสาย **174**–E
อย่าสูบบุหรี่ **114**–G
อยู่ในวงดนตรีร็อค **238**–D
อยู่บนถนนที่มีแสงไฟสว่างดี **143**–B
อยู่ให้ไกลจากหน้าต่าง **147**–I
อ้วน **32**–7
ออกกำลังกาย **230**–N
ออกกำลังกายเป็นประจำ **114**–E
ออกจากแท็กซี่ **153**–F
ออกจากไฮเวย์ **153**–J
ออกเดินทาง **160**–J
ออกแบบ **175**–A
ออกไปจากที่ทำงาน **38**–N
ออกไปจากห้อง **11**–O
ออนทาริโอ **201**–4
ออร์แกน **238**–20
ออสเตรเลีย **202**–6
อะตอม **195**–28
อะโวคาโด **84**–6
อัฒจันทร์ **5**–3
อันตราย **186**–1
อันตรายจากไฟฟ้า **186**–6
อับอายขายหน้า **43**–24
อัฟริกา **202**–5
อัยการ **141**–10
อัลบั้มภาพถ่าย **235**–31
อัลบั้มภาพถ่ายแบบดิจิตัล **235**–32
อัลฟัลฟา **177**–5
อาการและการบาดเจ็บ **110**
อากาศปั่นป่วน **161**–22
อาคารที่จอดรถ **124**–1
อาคารรัฐสภาสหรัฐฯ **138**–1
อาคารสนามกีฬา **126**–1
อาคารสำนักงาน **124**–2
อาคารสูง **127**–13
อาคารอพาตเม้นต์ **50**–1
อ่าง **57**–25
อ่างน้ำ **54**–4

อ่างอาบน้ำ **57**–2
อาจารย์แนะแนว **5**–6
อาจารย์ใหญ่ **5**–4
อาเจียน **110**–E
อาชญากรรม **142**
อาณาบริเวณโรงเรียน **5**
อ่านการ์ด **135**–G
อ่านค่าจำกัดความ **8**–B
อ่านตรวจทาน **191**–I
อ่านหนังสือพิมพ์ **39**–V
อ่านให้ฟัง **36**–N
อาบน้ำ (จากฝักบัว) **108**–A
อาบน้ำ (ในอ่าง) **108**–B
อาบน้ำ **36**–F
อาบน้ำฝักบัว **38**–C
อายแชโดว์ (สีทาเปลือกตา) **109**–35
อารมณ์เสีย **43**–28
อารยธรรม **199**
อ่าว **204**–9
อาศัยอยู่ในสหรัฐอเมริกาเป็น
เวลา 5 ปี **140**–H
อาสาสมัคร **41**–Q, **121**–17
อาหารกระป๋อง **72**, **146**–9
อาหารแช่แข็ง **72**
อาหารทะเลและอาหารรายการพิเศษ **71**
อาหารทารก **37**–4
อาหารประเภทนมเนย **72**
อาหารประเภทแป้ง **67**–12
อาหารเย็นสำเร็จแช่แข็ง **72**–28
อาหารว่าง **73**
อาหารสัตว์ **72**–5
อาหารสำเร็จ **146**–10
อิฐ **178**–12
อินทผลัม **68**–28
อินเทอร์เน็ต **197**
อิ่ม **42**–6
อีกยี่สิบนาทีจะสองนาฬิกา **18**–12
อีกสิบห้านาทีจะสองนาฬิกา **18**–13
อีเล็คตรอน **195**–30
อีสุกอีใส **111**–6
อึงอ่าง **212**–28
อึดอัด **42**–9
อุ้งเท้า **216**–20
อุ้งเล็บ **214**–2
อุณหภูมิ **13**
อุดฟันที่เป็นรู **119**–E
อุ่น **13**–4
อุบัติเหตุทางรถ **144**–2
อุปกรณ์การดัดฟัน **119**–6
อุปกรณ์ของเครื่องดูดฝุ่น **61**–11
อุปกรณ์ช่วยชีวิต **225**–20
อุปกรณ์ตรวจฟังเสียงหัวใจ **118**–10
อุปกรณ์ทำไร่ **177**–12
อุปกรณ์ที่เสีย **179**–4
อุปกรณ์เพื่อความปลอดภัย **179**
อุปกรณ์วัดไข้ **118**–11
อุปกรณ์สำนักงาน **183**
อุ้ม **36**–A
อูฐ **217**–38

เอเชีย **202**–4
เอทีเอ็ม (ATM -
เครื่องรับจ่ายเงินอัตโนมัติ) **132**
เอ่ยปากชมใครบางคน **12**–C
เอากระดาษออกมาแผ่นหนึ่ง **9**–Y
เอาขยะออกไป **60**–Q
เอาเงินกู้ **49**–J
เอาบัตรของคุณออก **132**–G
เอามา **240**–E
เอาเสื้อผ้าออกจากเครื่องอบผ้า **101**–E
เอาออก **109**–Q
แอคคอร์เดียน **238**–19
แอนตาร์คติกา **202**–7
แอปเปิ้ล **68**–1
แอพริคอท **68**–12
โอ๊คมีพิษ **210**–24
โอนสาย **171**–O
โอโบ **238**–3
ไอ **110**–A
ไอระเหยที่เป็นพิษ **179**–3
ไอริส **211**–16
ไอวี่มีพิษ **210**–25
ไอศครีม **72**–26
ไอศครีมใส่ในโคน **79**–13
ฮ็อคกี้บนลานน้ำแข็ง **229**–13
ฮอทดอก **79**–6
ฮาร์ดไดรฟ์ **196**–6
ฮาลิบัทตัดแบบวางขวางลำตัว **71**–6
ฮิปโป **217**–43
ฮิปฮอป **237**–26
เฮลิคอปเตอร์ **151**–9
แฮมต้มสุก **76**–5
แฮมเบอร์เกอร์ **79**–1
ไฮเวย์ **155**–9

Research Bibliography

The authors and publisher wish to acknowledge the contribution of the following educators for their research on vocabulary development, which has helped inform the principals underlying OPD.

Burt, M., J. K. Peyton, and R. Adams. *Reading and Adult English Language Learners: A Review of the Research*. Washington, D.C.: Center for Applied Linguistics, 2003.

Coady, J. "Research on ESL/EFL Vocabulary Acquisition: Putting it in Context." In *Second Language Reading and Vocabulary Learning*, edited by T. Huckin, M. Haynes, and J. Coady. Norwood, NJ: Ablex, 1993.

de la Fuente, M. J. "Negotiation and Oral Acquisition of L2 Vocabulary: The Roles of Input and Output in the Receptive and Productive Acquisition of Words." *Studies in Second Language Acquisition* 24 (2002): 81–112.

DeCarrico, J. "Vocabulary learning and teaching." In *Teaching English as a Second or Foreign Language,* edited by M. Celcia-Murcia. 3rd ed. Boston: Heinle & Heinle, 2001.

Ellis, R. *The Study of Second Language Acquisition*. Oxford: Oxford University Press, 1994.

Folse, K. *Vocabulary Myths: Applying Second Language Research to Classroom Teaching*. Ann Arbor, MI: University of Michigan Press, 2004.

Gairns, R. and S. Redman. *Working with Words: A Guide to Teaching and Learning Vocabulary*. Cambridge: Cambridge University Press, 1986.

Gass, S. M. and M.J.A. Torres. "Attention When?: An Investigation Of The Ordering Effect Of Input And Interaction." *Studies in Second Language Acquisition* 27 (Mar 2005): 1–31.

Henriksen, Birgit. "Three Dimensions of Vocabulary Development." *Studies in Second Language Acquisition* 21 (1999): 303–317.

Koprowski, Mark. "Investigating the Usefulness of Lexical Phrases in Contemporary Coursebooks." *Oxford ELT Journal* 59(4) (2005): 322–32.

McCrostie, James. "Examining Learner Vocabulary Notebooks." *Oxford ELT Journal* 61 (July 2007): 246–55.

Nation, P. *Learning Vocabulary in Another Language*. Cambridge: Cambridge University Press, 2001.

National Center for ESL Literacy Education Staff. *Adult English Language Instruction in the 21st Century*. Washington, D.C.: Center for Applied Linguistics, 2003.

National Reading Panel. *Teaching Children to Read: An Evidenced-Based Assessment of the Scientific Research Literature on Reading and its Implications on Reading Instruction*. 2000. http://www.nationalreadingpanel.org/Publications/summary.htm/.

Newton, J. "Options for Vocabulary Learning Through Communication Tasks." *Oxford ELT Journal* 55(1) (2001): 30–37.

Prince, P. "Second Language Vocabulary Learning: The Role of Context Versus Translations as a Function of Proficiency." *Modern Language Journal* 80(4) (1996): 478-93.

Savage, K. L., ed. *Teacher Training Through Video - ESL Techniques: Early Production*. White Plains, NY: Longman Publishing Group, 1992.

Schmitt, N. *Vocabulary in Language Teaching*. Cambridge: Cambridge University Press, 2000.

Smith, C. B. *Vocabulary Instruction and Reading Comprehension*. Bloomington, IN: ERIC Clearinghouse on Reading English and Communication, 1997.

Wood, K. and J. Josefina Tinajero. "Using Pictures to Teach Content to Second Language Learners." *Middle School Journal* 33 (2002): 47–51.